Macroeconomics
UGA Edition
ECON 2105 for Dr. Harrison Hartman

Fourth Edition

William A. McEachern / N. Gregory Mankiw /
William J. Baumol / Alan S. Blinder

THOMSON

SOUTH-WESTERN

Australia · Canada · Mexico · Singapore · Spain · United Kingdom · United States

Macroeconomics - UGA Edition
McEachern / Mankiw / Baumol / Blinder

Executive Editors:
Michele Baird, Maureen Staudt &
Michael Stranz

Project Development Manager:
Linda de Stefano

Marketing Coordinators:
Lindsay Annett and Sara Mercurio

**Production/Manufacturing
Supervisor:**
Donna M. Brown

Pre-Media Services Supervisor:
Dan Plofchan

Rights and Permissions Specialists:
Kalina Hintz and Bahman Naraghi

Cover Image
Getty Images*

The Adaptable Courseware Program consists of products and additions to existing Thomson products that are produced from camera-ready copy. Peer review, class testing, and accuracy are primarily the responsibility of the author(s).

Macroeconomics - UGA Edition /
McEachern / Mankiw / Baumol / Blinder
Fourth Edition
ISBN 0-324-38663-X

International Divisions List

Asia (Including India):
Thomson Learning
(a division of Thomson Asia Pte Ltd)
5 Shenton Way #01-01
UIC Building
Singapore 068808
Tel: (65) 6410-1200
Fax: (65) 6410-1208

Australia/New Zealand:
Thomson Learning Australia
102 Dodds Street
Southbank, Victoria 3006
Australia

Latin America:
Thomson Learning
Seneca 53
Colonia Polano
11560 Mexico, D.F., Mexico
Tel (525) 281-2906
Fax (525) 281-2656

Canada:
Thomson Nelson
1120 Birchmount Road
Toronto, Ontario
Canada M1K 5G4
Tel (416) 752-9100
Fax (416) 752-8102

UK/Europe/Middle East/Africa:
Thomson Learning
High Holborn House
50-51 Bedford Row
London, WC1R 4LS
United Kingdom
Tel 44 (020) 7067-2500
Fax 44 (020) 7067-2600

Spain (Includes Portugal):
Thomson Paraninfo
Calle Magallanes 25
28015 Madrid
España
Tel 34 (0)91 446-3350
Fax 34 (0)91 445-6218

Table of Contents

Macroeconomics
A Contemporary Introduction

Seventh Edition

William A. McEachern
Professor of Economics
University of Connecticut

THOMSON

™

SOUTH-WESTERN

Australia · Canada · Mexico · Singapore · Spain · United Kingdom · United States

Aggregate Expenditure Components

© Wendell Metzen/Index Stock Imagery

When driving through a neighborhood new to you, how can you figure out the income of the residents? How would your spending change if you won the lottery? What's the most predictable and useful relationship in macroeconomics? Why are consumer confidence and business confidence in the economy so important? Answers to these and other questions are addressed in this chapter, which focuses on the makeup of aggregate expenditure. Consumption is the most important, accounting for about two-thirds of all spending. But in this short chapter, we also examine investment, government purchases, and net exports. We will discuss how each relates to income in the economy.

Let's see where this leads. In the next chapter, we combine these spending components to derive the aggregate demand curve. After that, we derive the aggregate

supply curve and see how it interacts with the aggregate demand curve to determine the economy's equilibrium levels of price and output. Topics in the current chapter include:

- Consumption and income
- Marginal propensities to consume and to save
- Changes in consumption and in saving

- Investment
- Government purchases
- Net exports
- Composition of spending

Consumption

What if a new college friend invites you home for the weekend? On your first visit, you would get some idea of the family's standard of living. Is their house a mansion, a dump, or in between? Do they drive a new BMW or take the bus? The simple fact is that consumption tends to reflect income. Although some households can temporarily live beyond their means and others still have the first nickel they ever earned, in general consumption depends on income. *The positive and stable relationship between consumption and income, both for the household and for the economy as a whole, is the main point of this chapter.* Got it?

A key decision in the circular-flow model developed two chapters back was how much households spent and how much they saved. Consumption depends primarily on income. Although this relationship seems obvious, the link between consumption and income is fundamental to understanding how the economy works. Let's look at this link in the U.S. economy over time.

A First Look at Consumption and Income

Exhibit 1 shows consumer spending, or consumption, in the United States since 1959 as the red line and *disposable income* as the blue line. Disposable income, remember, is the income actually available for consumption and saving. Data have been adjusted for inflation so that dollars are of constant purchasing power—in this case, 2000 dollars. Notice that consumer spending and disposable income move together over time. Both increased nearly every year, and the relationship between the two appears stable. Specifically, consumer spending has averaged about 90 percent of disposable income. Disposable income minus consumption equals saving. In Exhibit 1, saving is measured by the vertical distance between the two lines. Saving has averaged about 10 percent of disposable income.

Another way to graph the relationship between consumption and income over time is shown in Exhibit 2, where consumption is measured along the vertical axis and disposable income along the horizontal axis. Notice that each axis measures the same units: trillions of 2000 dollars. Each year is depicted by a point that reflects two values: disposable income and consumption. For example, the combination for 1985, identified by the red point, shows that when disposable income (measured along the horizontal axis) was $4.6 trillion, consumption (measured along the vertical axis) was $4.1 trillion.

As you can see, there is a clear and direct relationship between consumption and disposable income, a relationship that should come as no surprise after Exhibit 1. You need little imagination to see that by connecting the dots in Exhibit 2, you could trace a line relating consumption to income. That relationship has special significance in macroeconomics.

Disposable Income, Consumption, and Saving in the United States

There is a clear and direct relationship between consumption, shown by the red line, and disposable income, shown by the blue line. Disposable income minus consumption equals saving, shown by the vertical distance between disposable income and consumption.

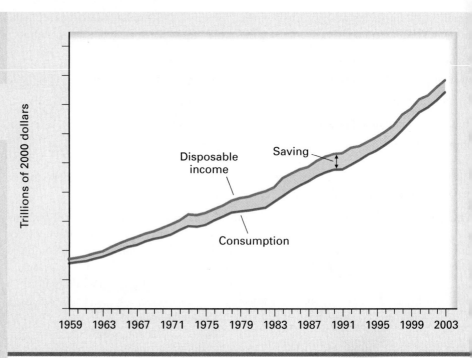

Source: Based on annual estimates from the Bureau of Economic Analysis, U.S. Department of Commerce. For the latest data, go to http://www.bea.doc.gov/bea/pubs.htm.

U.S. Consumption Depends on Disposable Income

Consumption is on the vertical axis and disposable income on the horizontal axis. Notice that each axis measures trillions of 2000 dollars. For example, in 1985, identified by the red point, consumption was $4.1 trillion and disposable income $4.6 trillion. There is a clear and direct relationship over time between disposable income and consumption. As disposable income increases, so does consumption.

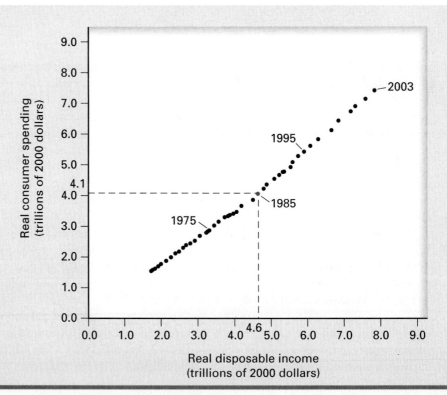

Source: Based on estimates from the Bureau of Economic Analysis, U.S. Department of Commerce. For the latest data, go to http://www.bea.doc.gov/bea/pubs.htm.

The Consumption Function

After examining the link between consumption and income, we found it to be quite stable. Based on their disposable income, households decide how much to consume and how much to save. So consumption depends on disposable income. *Consumption is the dependent variable and disposable income, the independent variable.* Because consumption depends on income, we say that consumption is a *function* of income. Exhibit 3 presents for the economy a hypothetical **consumption function,** which shows that consumption increases with disposable income, assuming other determinants of consumption remain constant. Again, both consumption and disposable income are in real terms, or in inflation-adjusted dollars. Notice that this hypothetical consumption function reflects the historical relationship between consumption and income shown in Exhibit 2.

Marginal Propensities to Consume and to Save

In Chapter 1, you learned that economic analysis focuses on activity at the margin. For example, what happens to consumption if income changes by a certain amount? Suppose U.S. households receive another billion dollars in disposable income. Some of it will be spent on consumption, and the rest will be saved. The fraction of the additional income that is spent is called the marginal propensity to consume. More precisely, the **marginal propensity to consume,** or **MPC,** equals the change in consumption divided by the change in income. Likewise, the fraction of that additional income that is saved is called the marginal propensity to save. More precisely, the **marginal propensity to save,** or **MPS,** equals the change in saving divided by the change in income.

For example, if U.S. income increases from $12.0 trillion to $12.5 trillion, consumption increases by $0.4 trillion and saving by $0.1 trillion. The marginal propensity to consume

HOMEWORK Xpress!
Ask the Instructor Video

CONSUMPTION FUNCTION

The relationship between consumption and income, other things constant

MARGINAL PROPENSITY TO CONSUME (MPC)

The fraction of a change in income that is spent on consumption; the change in consumption divided by the change in income that caused it

MARGINAL PROPENSITY TO SAVE (MPS)

The fraction of a change in income that is saved; the change in saving divided by the change in income that caused it

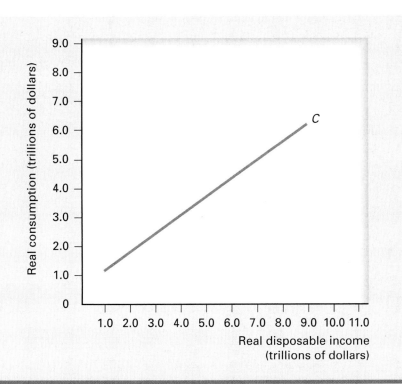

EXHIBIT 3

The Consumption Function

The consumption function, *C,* shows the relationship between disposable income and consumption, other things constant.

equals the change in consumption divided by the change in income. In this case, the change in consumption is $0.4 trillion and the change in income is $0.5 trillion, so the marginal propensity to consume is 0.4/0.5, or 4/5. Income not spent is saved. Saving increases by $0.1 trillion as a result of the $0.5 trillion increase in income, so the marginal propensity to save equals 0.1/0.5, or 1/5. Because disposable income is either spent or saved, the marginal propensity to consume plus the marginal propensity to save must sum to 1. In our example, $4/5 + 1/5 = 1$. We can say more generally that $MPC + MPS = 1$.

MPC, MPS, and the Slope of the Consumption and Saving Functions

You may recall from the appendix to Chapter 1 that the slope of a straight line is the vertical distance between any two points divided by the horizontal distance between those same two points. Consider, for example, the slope between points *a* and *b* on the consumption function in panel (a) of Exhibit 4, where Δ means "change in." The horizontal distance between these points shows the change in disposable income, denoted as ΔDI—in this case $0.5 trillion. The vertical distance shows the change in consumption, denoted as ΔC—in

---

E X H I B I T   4

Marginal Propensities to Consume and to Save

The slope of the consumption function equals the marginal propensity to consume. For the straight-line consumption function in panel (a), the slope is the same at all levels of income and is given by the change in consumption divided by the change in disposable income that causes it. Thus, the marginal propensity to consume equals $\Delta C/\Delta DI$, or 0.4/0.5 = 4/5. The slope of the saving function in panel (b) equals the marginal propensity to save, $\Delta S/\Delta DI$, or 0.1/0.5 = 1/5.

(a) Consumption function

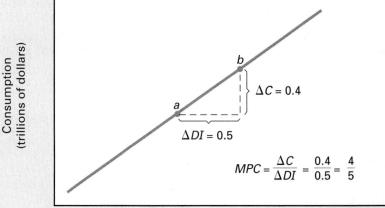

$$MPC = \frac{\Delta C}{\Delta DI} = \frac{0.4}{0.5} = \frac{4}{5}$$

(b) Saving function

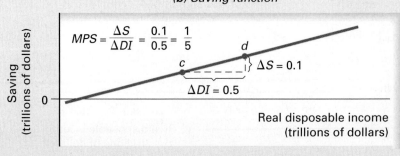

$$MPS = \frac{\Delta S}{\Delta DI} = \frac{0.1}{0.5} = \frac{1}{5}$$

his case, $0.4 trillion. The slope equals the vertical distance divided by the horizontal dis-
ance, or 0.4/0.5, which equals the marginal propensity to consume of 4/5.

Thus, *the marginal propensity to consume is measured graphically by the slope of the consumption
function*. After all, the slope is nothing more than the increase in consumption divided by
he increase in income. *Because the slope of any straight line is constant everywhere along the line,
he MPC for any linear, or straight-line, consumption function is constant at all incomes.* We assume
or convenience that the consumption function is a straight line, though it need not be.

Panel (b) of Exhibit 4 presents the **saving function,** *S,* which relates saving to income.
The slope between any two points on the saving function measures the change in saving divided by the change in income. For example, between points *c* and *d* in panel (b) of Exhibit
4, the change in income is $0.5 trillion and the resulting change in saving is $0.1 trillion.
The slope between these two points therefore equals 0.1/0.5, or 1/5, which by definition
equals the marginal propensity to save. Because the marginal propensity to consume and the
marginal propensity to save are simply different sides of the same coin, from here on we focus more on the marginal propensity to consume.

Nonincome Determinants of Consumption

Along a given consumption function, consumer spending depends on disposable income in
he economy, other things constant. Now let's see what factors are held constant and how
changes in them could cause the entire consumption function to shift.

Net Wealth and Consumption

Given the economy's income, an important influence on consumption is each household's
net wealth—that is, the value of all assets that each household owns minus any liabilities,
or debts. Your family's assets may include a home, furnishings, automobiles, bank accounts,
cash, and the value of stocks, bonds, and pensions. Your family's liabilities, or debts, may
include a mortgage, car loans, student loans, credit card balances, and the like. According to
he Federal Reserve, the net wealth of U.S. households totaled $44.3 trillion at the end of
2003, the highest on record.[1] Net wealth increased in 2003 because of rising house prices
and a recovery in stock market prices. Net wealth is a stock variable. Consumption and
income are flow variables. Net wealth is assumed to be constant along a given consumption
function.

A decrease in net wealth would make consumers less inclined to spend and more inclined to save at each income level. To see why, suppose prices fall sharply on the stock market. Stockholders are poorer than they were, so they spend less. For example, following the
tock market crash of October 1987, consumption declined and saving increased. Household saving as a percentage of disposable income increased from 3.9 percent in the quarter
before the crash to 5.7 percent in the quarter following the crash. Spending on new homes
and cars fell. As another example, stock market declines in 2000, 2001, and 2002 cut into
he purchases of luxury goods. Our original consumption function is depicted as line *C* in
Exhibit 5. If net wealth declines, the consumption function shifts from *C* down to *C'*, because households now spend less and save more at every income level.

Conversely, suppose stock prices increase sharply. This increase in net wealth increases
he desire to spend. For example, stock prices surged in 1999, increasing stockholders' net
wealth. Consumers spent 94 percent of disposable income that year compared with an average of about 90 percent during the first half of the 1990s. Purchases of homes and cars

SAVING FUNCTION

The relationship between saving
and income, other things constant

NET WEALTH

The value of a assets minus
liabilities

---

[1]. James Hagerty and Deborah Lagomarsino, "U.S. Household Wealth Hits Record," *Wall Street Journal*, 5 March
2004.

EXHIBIT 5

Shifts of the Consumption Function

A downward shift of the consumption function, such as from *C* to *C'*, can be caused by a decrease in wealth, an increase in the price level, an unfavorable change in consumer expectations, or an increase in the interest rate. An upward shift, such as from *C* to *C"*, can be caused by an increase in wealth, a decrease in the price level, a favorable change in expectations, or a decrease in the interest rate.

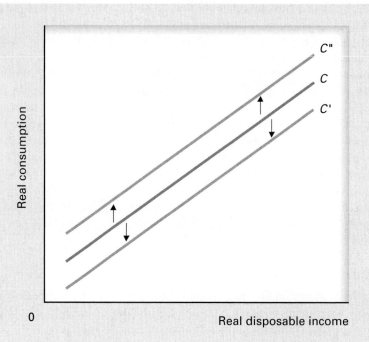

soared. Because of an increase in net wealth, the consumption function shifts from *C* up to *C"*, reflecting households' desire to spend more at each income level. Research by the Federal Reserve indicates that consumer spending eventually rises or falls between three to five cents for every dollar rise or fall in the value of stock market holdings.

Again, *it is a change in net wealth, not a change in disposable income, that shifts the consumption function. A change in disposable income, other things constant, means a movement along a given consumption function, not a shift of that function.* Be mindful of the difference between a movement along the consumption function, which results from a change in income, and a shift of the consumption function, which results from a change in one of the nonincome determinants of consumption, such as net wealth.

The Price Level

Another variable that can affect the consumption function is the price level prevailing in the economy. As we have seen, net wealth is an important determinant of consumption. The greater the net wealth, other things constant, the greater consumption will be at each income level. Some household wealth is held as money, such as cash and bank accounts. When the price level changes, so does the real value of cash and bank accounts.

For example, suppose your wealth consists of a $20,000 bank account. If the economy's price level increases by 5 percent, your bank account will buy about 5 percent less in real terms. You feel poorer because you are poorer. To rebuild the real value of your money holdings to some desired comfort level, you decide to spend less and save more. *An increase in the price level reduces the purchasing power of money holdings, causing households to consume less and save more at each income level.* So the consumption function would shift downward from *C* to *C'*, as shown in Exhibit 5.

Conversely, should the price level ever fall, as it did frequently before World War II and recently in Japan and Hong Kong, the real value money holdings increases. Households would be wealthier, so they decide to consume more and save less at each income level. For example, if the price level declined by 5 percent, your $20,000 bank account would then buy about 5 percent more in real terms. A drop in the price level would shift the consumption function from *C* up to *C"*. *At each income, a change in the price level influences consumption by affecting the real value of money holdings.*

The Interest Rate

Interest is the reward savers earn for deferring consumption and the cost borrowers pay for current spending power. When graphing the consumption function, we assume a given interest rate in the economy. If the interest rate increases, other things constant, savers or lenders are rewarded more, and borrowers are charged more. The higher the interest rate, the less is spent on those items typically purchased on credit, such as cars. Thus, at a higher interest rate, households save more, borrow less, and spend less. Greater saving at each income level means less consumption. Simply put, *a higher interest rate, other things constant, shifts the consumption function downward.* Conversely, *a lower interest rate, other things constant, shifts the consumption function upward.*

Expectations

Expectations influence economic behavior in a variety of ways. For example, suppose as a college senior, you land a good job that starts after graduation. Your consumption will probably jump long before the job actually begins because you expect an increase in your income; you might buy a car, for example. Conversely, a worker who gets a layoff notice to take effect at the end of the year will likely reduce consumption immediately, well before the actual date of the layoff. More generally, if people grow concerned about their job security, they will reduce the amount they consume at each income level.

Changing expectations about price levels and interest rates also affect consumption. For example, a change that leads householders to expect higher car prices or higher interest rates in the future will prompt some to buy new cars now. On the other hand, a change leading householders to expect lower prices or lower interest rates in the future will cause some to defer car purchases. Thus, expectations affect spending at each income, and a change in expectations can shift the consumption function. This is why economic forecasters monitor consumer confidence so closely.

Keep in mind the distinction between *movements along a given consumption function,* which result from a change in income, and *shifts in the consumption function,* which result from a change in one of the factors assumed to remain constant along a given consumption function. We conclude our introduction to consumption with the following case study, which discusses consumption and saving patterns over a lifetime.

The Life-Cycle Hypothesis

Do people with high incomes save a larger fraction of their incomes than those with low income? Both theory and evidence suggest they do. The easier it is to make ends meet, the more income is left over for saving. Does it follow from this that richer economies save more than poorer ones—that economies save a larger fraction of total disposable income as they grow? In his famous book, *The General Theory of Employment, Interest, and Money,* published in 1936, John Maynard Keynes drew that conclusion. But as later economists studied the

© EPA/AKIO SUG/AP Photo

Case **Study**

Bringing
Theory to Life

*e*Activity
Until quite recently, the Japanese government had been trying various changes in government spending and tax policies to encourage more consumer spending. However, the

Japanese public often would just put any extra income into savings. How could they be persuaded to spend more? An innovative policy was to issue purchase vouchers. The Japanese Information Network reports on these at http://web-japan.org/trends98/honbun/ntj981201.html. To whom did the government intend to distribute these coupons? Why? Would receiving 20,000 yen in vouchers ensure that spending would increase by that amount?

LIFE-CYCLE MODEL OF CONSUMPTION AND SAVING

Young people borrow, middle agers pay off debts and save, and older people draw down their savings; on average net savings over a lifetime is small

data—such as that presented in Exhibit 2—it became clear that Keynes was wrong. *The fraction of disposable income saved in an economy seems to stay constant as the economy grows.*

So how can it be that richer people save more than poorer people, yet richer countries do not necessarily save more than poorer ones? Several answers have been proposed. One of the most important is the **life-cycle model of consumption and saving.** According to this model, young people tend to borrow to finance education and home purchases. In middle age, people pay off debts and save more. In old age, they draw down their savings, or dissave. Some still have substantial wealth at death, because they are not sure when death will occur and because some parents want to bequeath wealth to their children. And some people die in debt. But on average net savings over a person's lifetime tend to be small. The life-cycle hypothesis suggests that the saving rate for an economy as a whole depends on, among other things, the relative number of savers and dissavers in the population.

Other factors that influence the saving rate across countries include the tax treatment of interest, the convenience and reliability of saving institutions, national customs, and the relative cost of a household's major purchase—housing. In Japan, for example, about 24,000 post offices nationwide offer convenient savings accounts. Japan's postal savings system holds over $2 trillion in savings deposits, more than one-third of Japan's total. Also, a home buyer in Japan must come up with a substantial down payment, one that represents a large fraction of the home's purchase price, and housing there is more expensive than in the United States. Finally, borrowing is considered by some Japanese to be shameful, so households save to avoid having to borrow. Because saving in Japan is necessary, convenient, and consistent with an aversion to borrowing, the country has one of the highest saving rates in the world. In a recent year, for example, Japanese households saved 13 percent of their disposable income compared with a saving rate of only about 4 percent in the United States.

Sources: "Leviathan Unbound," *The Economist*, 27 May 2003; Martin Browning and Thomas Crossley, "The Life-Cycle Model of Consumption and Saving," *Journal of Economic Perspective* 15 (Summer 2001): 3–22; *OECD Economic Outlook* 75 (June 2004); and "Overview of the Postal Savings Operation" at http://www.yu-cho.japanpost.jp/e_index.htm.

We turn next to the second component of aggregate expenditure—investment. Keep in mind that our initial goal is to understand the relationship between total spending and income.

Investment

The second component of aggregate expenditure is investment, or, more precisely, *gross private domestic investment.* Again, by *investment* we do not mean buying stocks, bonds, or other financial assets. Investment consists of spending on (1) new factories, office buildings, malls, and new equipment, such as computers; (2) new housing; and (3) net increases to inventories. Firms invest now in the expectation of a future return. Because the return is in the future, a would-be investor must estimate how much a particular investment will yield this year, next year, the year after, and in all years during the productive life of the investment. *Firms buy new capital goods only if they expect this investment to yield a higher return than other possible uses of their funds.*

The Demand for Investment

To understand the investment decision, let's consider a simple example. The operators of the Hacker Haven Golf Course are thinking about buying some solar-powered golf carts. The model under consideration, called the Weekend Warrior, sells for $2,000, requires no maintenance or operating expenses, and is expected to last indefinitely. *The expected rate of return* of each cart equals the expected annual earnings divided by the cart's purchase price. The first cart is expected to generate rental income of $400 per year. This income, divided by the cost of the cart, yields an expected rate of return on the investment of $400/$2,000, or 20 percent per year. Additional carts will be used less. A second is expected to generate $300 per year in rental income, yielding a rate of return of $300/$2,000, or 15 percent; a third cart, $200 per year, or 10 percent; and a fourth cart, $100 per year, or 5 percent. They don't expect a fifth cart will get rented at all, so it has a zero expected rate of return.

Should the operators of Hacker Haven invest in golf carts, and if so, how many? Suppose they plan to borrow the money to buy the carts. The number of carts they purchase will depend on the interest rate they must pay for borrowing. If the market interest rate exceeds 20 percent, the cost of borrowing would exceed the expected rate of return for even the first cart, so the club would buy no carts. What if the operators have enough cash on hand to buy the carts? The market interest rate also reflects what club owners could earn on savings. If the interest rate paid on savings exceeded 20 percent, course owners would earn more saving their money than buying golf carts. *The market interest rate is the opportunity cost of investing in capital.*

Suppose the market rate is 8 percent per year. At that rate, the first three carts, all with expected returns exceeding 8 percent, would each yield more than the market rate. A fourth cart would lose money, because its expected rate of return is only 5 percent. Exhibit 6 measures the nominal interest rate along the vertical axis and the amount invested in golf carts along the horizontal axis. The step-like relationship shows the expected rate of return earned on additional dollars invested in golf carts. This relationship also indicates the amount invested in golf carts at each interest rate, so you can view this step-like relationship as Hacker Haven's demand curve for this type of investment. For example, the first cart costs $2,000 and earns a rate of return of 20 percent. A firm should reject any investment with an expected rate of return that falls below the market rate of interest.

The horizontal line at 8 percent indicates the market interest rate, which is Hacker Haven's opportunity cost of investing. The course operators' objective is to choose an investment strategy that maximizes profit. Profit is maximized when $6,000 is invested in the

HOMEWORK
Xpress!
Ask the Instructor
Video

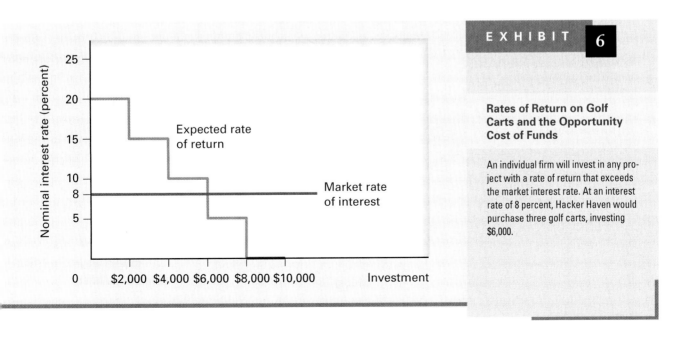

EXHIBIT 6

Rates of Return on Golf Carts and the Opportunity Cost of Funds

An individual firm will invest in any project with a rate of return that exceeds the market interest rate. At an interest rate of 8 percent, Hacker Haven would purchase three golf carts, investing $6,000.

carts—that is, when three carts are purchased. The expected return from a fourth cart is 5 percent, which is below the opportunity cost of funds. Therefore, investing in four or more carts would lower total profit.

From Micro to Macro

So far, we have looked at the investment decision for a single golf course, but there are over 13,000 golf courses in the United States. The industry demand for golf carts shows the relationship between the amount all courses invest and the expected rate of return. Like the step-like relationship in Exhibit 6, the investment demand curve for the golf industry slopes downward.

Let's move beyond golf carts and consider the invest decisions of all industries: publishing, hog farming, fast food, software, and thousands more. Individual industries have downward-sloping demand curves for investment. More is invested when the opportunity cost of borrowing is lower, other things constant. A downward-sloping investment demand curve for the entire economy can be derived, with some qualifications, from a horizontal summation of all industries' downward-sloping investment demand curves. The economy's *investment demand curve* is represented as *D* in Exhibit 7, which shows the inverse relationship between the quantity of investment demanded and the market interest rate, other things—including business expectations—held constant. For example, in Exhibit 7, when the market rate is 8 percent, the quantity of investment demanded is $1.0 trillion. If the interest rate rises to 10 percent, investment declines to $0.9 trillion, and if the rate falls to 6 percent, investment increases to $1.1 trillion. Assumed constant along the investment demand curve are business expectations about the economy. If firms grow more optimistic

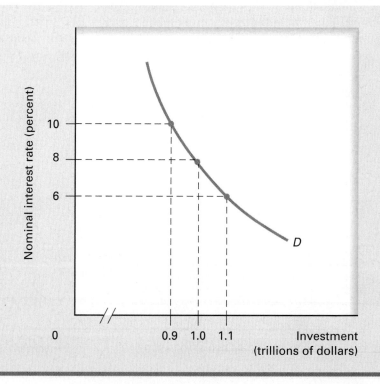

EXHIBIT **7**

Investment Demand Curve for the Economy

The investment demand curve for the economy sums the investment demanded by each firm at each interest rate. At lower interest rates, more investment projects become profitable for individual firms, so total investment in the economy increases.

bout profit prospects, the demand for investment increases, so the investment demand urve shifts to the right.

Planned Investment and the Economy's Income

o integrate the discussion of investment with our earlier analysis of consumption, we need o know if and how investment varies with income in the economy. Whereas we were able o present evidence relating consumption to income over time, the link between investment nd income is weaker. Investment in a particular year shows little relation to income that ear. *Investment depends more on interest rates and on business expectations than on the prevailing income.* One reason investment is less related to income is that some investments, such as a new ower plant, take years to build. And investment, once in place, is expected to last for years, ometimes decades. The investment decision is thus said to be *forward looking,* based more on xpected profit than on current income.

So how does the amount firms plan to invest relate to income? The simplest nvestment function assumes that *planned investment* is unrelated to disposable income. Planned investment is assumed to be **autonomous** with respect to disposable income. For xample, suppose that, given current business expectations and an interest rate of 8 percent, irms plan to invest $1.0 trillion per year, regardless of the economy's income level. Exhibit measures disposable income on the horizontal axis and planned investment on the vertical xis. Planned investment of $1.0 trillion is shown by the flat investment function, *I*. As you an see, along *I*, planned investment does not vary even though real disposable income does.

Nonincome Determinants of Planned Investment

The investment function isolates the relationship between income in the economy and planned investment—the amount firms would like to invest, other things constant. We have lready mentioned two determinants that are assumed constant: the interest rate and business expectations. Now let's look at how changes in these factors affect investment.

N e t B o o k m a r k

For a personal view on Keynes and his work, read "Cairncross on Keynes," an obituary written by one of his students, Sir Alec Cairncross. It originally appeared in the *Economist* and is now available online at a site maintained by Professor Brad DeLong at http://econ161. berkeley.edu/Economists/ cairncrossonkeynes.html.

INVESTMENT FUNCTION

The relationship between the amount businesses plan to invest and the economy's income, other things constant

AUTONOMOUS

A term that means "independent"; for example, autonomous investment is independent of income

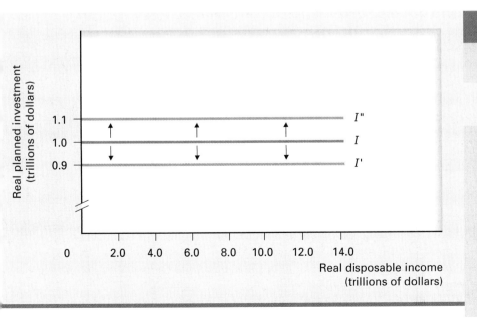

EXHIBIT 8

Planned Investment Function

Planned investment is assumed to be independent of income, as shown by the horizontal lines. Thus, planned investment is assumed to be autonomous. An increase in the interest rate or less favorable business expectations would decrease investment at every level of income, as shown by the downward shift from *I* to *I'*. A decrease in the interest rate or more upbeat business expectations would increase investment at every level of income, as shown by the upward shift from *I* to *I"*.

Market Interest Rate

Exhibit 7 shows that if the interest rate is 8 percent, planned investment is $1.0 trillion. This investment is also shown as *I* in Exhibit 8. If the interest rate increases because of, say, a change in the nation's monetary policy (as happened in 2004), the cost of borrowing increases, which increases the opportunity cost of investment. For example, if the interest rate increases from 8 percent to 10 percent, planned investment drops from $1.0 trillion to $0.9 trillion. This decrease is reflected in Exhibit 8 by a shift of the investment function from down to *I'*. Conversely, if the interest rate decreases because of, say, a change in the nation's monetary policy (as happened in 2001 and 2002), the cost of borrowing decreases, which reduces the opportunity cost of investment. For example, a drop in the rate of interest from 8 percent to 6 percent, other things remaining constant, will reduce the cost of borrowing and increase planned investment from $1.0 trillion to $1.1 trillion, as reflected by the upward shift of the investment function from *I* to *I''*. Notice that the shifts in Exhibit 8 match interest rate movements along the investment demand curve in Exhibit 7.

Business Expectations

Investment depends primarily on business expectations, or on what Keynes called the "animal spirits" of business. Suppose planned investment initially is $1.0 trillion, as depicted by in Exhibit 8. If firms now become more pessimistic about their profit prospects, perhaps expecting the worst, as in 2001 when terrorists leveled the World Trade Center, planned investment will decrease at every income, as reflected in Exhibit 8 by a shift of the investment function from *I* down to *I'*. On the other hand, if profit expectations become rosier, as they did in 2003, firms become more willing to invest, thereby increasing the investment function from *I* up to *I''*. *Examples of factors that could affect business expectations, and thus investment plans, include wars, technological change, tax changes, and destabilizing events such as terrorist attacks.* Changes in business expectations also shift the investment demand curve in Exhibit 7.

Now that we have examined consumption and investment individually, let's take a look at their year-to-year variability in the following case study.

Investment Varies Much More than Consumption

We already know that consumption makes up about two-thirds of GDP and that investment varies from year to year, averaging about one-sixth of GDP over the last decade. Now let's compare their year-to-year variability. Exhibit 9 shows the annual percentage changes in GDP, consumption, and investment, all measured in real terms. Two points are obvious. First, investment fluctuates much more than either consumption or GDP. For example, in the recession year of 1982, GDP declined 1.9 percent but investment crashed 14.0 percent; consumption actually increased 1.4 percent. In 1984, GDP increased 7.2 percent, consumption rose 5.3 percent, but investment soared 29.5 percent. Second, fluctuations in consumption and in GDP appear to be entwined, although consumption varies a bit less than GDP. Consumption varies less than GDP because consumption depends on disposable income, which varies less than GDP.

During years of falling GDP since 1959, the average decline in GDP was 0.6 percent, but investment dropped an average of 11.7 percent. Consumption actually increased 0.6

EXHIBIT	9	**Annual Percentage Change in U.S. Real GDP, Consumption, and Investment**

Investment varies much more year-to-year than consumption does and accounts for nearly all the variability in real GDP. This is why economic forecasters pay special attention to the business outlook and investment plans.

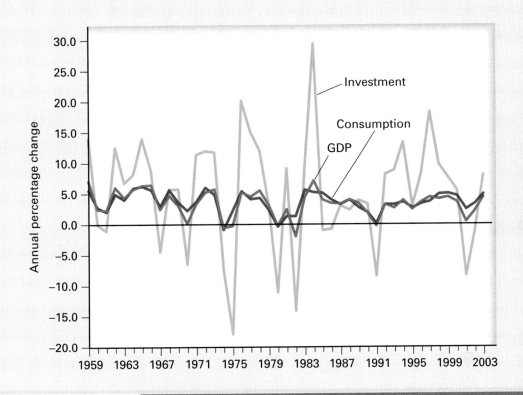

percent. So *while consumption is the largest spending component, investment varies much more than consumption and accounts for nearly all the year-to-year variability in real GDP.* Note that GDP does not always fall during years in which a recession occurs. For example, in the 2001 recession, GDP managed a tiny gain for the year of 0.5 percent and consumption increased 2.5 percent. It was the 8.3 percent fall in investment that caused the recession. This is why economic forecasters pay special attention to business expectations and investment plans.

that the types of consumption and investment spending cited in the text will change and affect real GDP?

Sources: *Economic Report of the President*, February 2004; U.S. Department of Commerce, *Survey of Current Business* 84, various months for 2004; and *OECD Economic Outlook* 75 (June 2004). For data and articles about economic aggregates, go to the Bureau of Economic Analysis site at http://www.bea.doc.gov/.

Government

The third component of aggregate expenditure is government purchases of goods and services. Federal, state, and local governments purchase thousands of goods and services, ranging from weapon systems to road signs. During the last decade, government purchases in the United States accounted for a little less than one-fifth of GDP, most of that by state and local governments.

GOVERNMENT PURCHASE FUNCTION

The relationship between government purchases and the economy's income, other things constant

Government Purchase Function

The **government purchase function** relates government purchases to income in the economy, other things constant. Decisions about government purchases are largely under the control of public officials, such as the decision to build an interstate highway or to boost military spending. These purchases do not depend directly on income in the economy. We therefore assume that *government purchases* are autonomous, or independent of income. Such a function would relate to income as a flat line similar to the investment function shown in Exhibit 8. An increase in government purchases would result in an upward shift of the government purchase function. And a decrease in government purchases would result in a downward shift of the government purchase function.

Net Taxes

As noted earlier, government purchases represent only one of the two components of government outlays; the other is *transfer payments,* such as Social Security, welfare benefits, and unemployment benefits. Transfer payments, which make up about a third of government outlays, are outright grants from governments to households and are thus not considered part of aggregate expenditure. Transfer payments vary inversely with income—as income increases, transfer payments decline.

To fund government outlays, governments impose taxes. Taxes vary directly with income; as income increases, so do taxes. *Net taxes* equal taxes minus transfers. Because taxes tend to increase with income but transfers tend to decrease with income, for simplicity, let's assume that net taxes do not vary with income. Thus, we assume for now that *net taxes* are *autonomous,* or independent of income.

Net taxes affect aggregate spending indirectly by changing disposable income, which in turn changes consumption. We saw from the discussion of circular flow that by subtracting net taxes, we transform real GDP into *disposable income*. Disposable income is take-home pay—the income households can spend or save. We will examine the impact of net taxes in the next few chapters.

Net Exports

The rest of the world affects aggregate expenditure through imports and exports and has a growing influence on the U.S. economy. The United States, with only one-twentieth of the world's population, accounts for about one-sixth of the world's imports and one-ninth of the world's exports.

Net Exports and Income

How do imports and exports relate to the economy's income? When incomes rise, Americans spend more on all normal goods, including imports. Higher incomes lead to more spending on Persian rugs, French wine, Korean DVD players, German cars, Chinese toys, European vacations, African safaris, and thousands of other foreign goods and services.

How do U.S. exports relate to the economy's income? U.S. exports depend on the income of foreigners, not on U.S. income. U.S. disposable income does not affect French purchases of U.S. computers or Saudi Arabian purchases of U.S. military hardware. The **net export function** shows the relationship between net exports and U.S. income, other things constant. Because our exports are insensitive to U.S. income but our imports tend to increase with income, *net exports,* which equal the value of exports minus the value of imports, tend to decline as U.S. incomes increase. Such an inverse relationship is developed

NET EXPORT FUNCTION

The relationship between net exports and the economy's income, other things constant

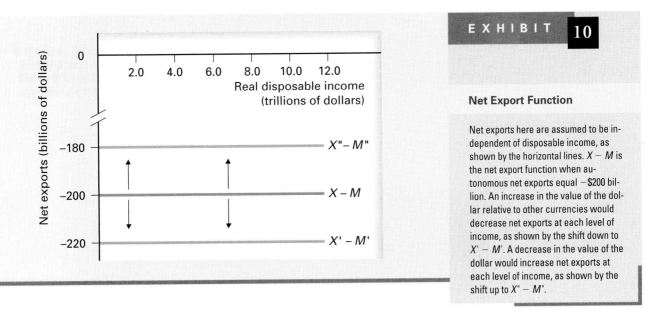

EXHIBIT 10

Net Export Function

Net exports here are assumed to be independent of disposable income, as shown by the horizontal lines. $X - M$ is the net export function when autonomous net exports equal −$200 billion. An increase in the value of the dollar relative to other currencies would decrease net exports at each level of income, as shown by the shift down to $X' - M'$. A decrease in the value of the dollar would increase net exports at each level of income, as shown by the shift up to $X'' - M''$.

graphically in the appendix to this chapter. For now, we assume that net exports are *autonomous*, or independent of income.

If exports exceed imports, net exports are positive; if imports exceed exports, net exports are negative; and if exports equal imports, net exports are zero. U.S. net exports have been negative nearly every year during the past three decades, so let's suppose net exports are autonomous and equal to −$0.2 trillion, or −$200 billion, as shown by the net export function $X - M$ in Exhibit 10.

Nonincome Determinants of Net Exports

Factors assumed constant along the net export function include the U.S. price level, price levels in other countries, interest rates here and abroad, foreign income levels, and the exchange rate between the dollar and foreign currencies. Consider the effects of a change in one of these factors. Suppose the value of the dollar increases relative to foreign currencies such as those of Asia, as happened in 1998. With the dollar worth more on world markets, foreign products become cheaper for Americans, and U.S. products become more costly for foreigners. A rise in the dollar's exchange value will increase imports and decrease exports, thus reducing net exports, shown in Exhibit 10 by a parallel drop in the net export line from $X - M$ down to $X' - M'$, a decline from −$200 billion to −$220 billion.

A decline in the value of the dollar, as occurred in 2003, will have the opposite effect, increasing exports and decreasing imports. An increase in autonomous net exports is shown in our example by a parallel increase in the net export function, from $X - M$ up to $X'' - M''$, reflecting an increase in autonomous net exports from −$200 billion to −$180 billion. A country sometimes tries to devalue its currency in an attempt to increase its net exports and thereby increase employment. The effect of changes in net exports on aggregate spending will be taken up in the next chapter.

Composition of Aggregate Expenditure

Now that we have examined each component of aggregate spending, let's get a better idea of spending over time. Exhibit 11 shows the composition of spending in the United States

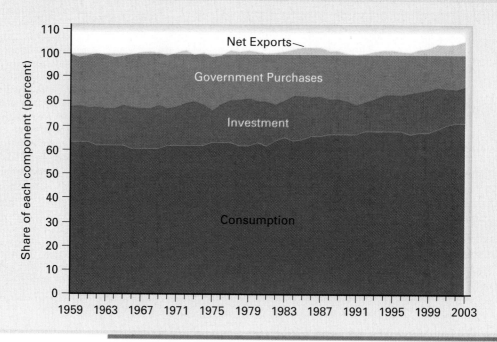

EXHIBIT 11

U.S. Spending Components as Percentages of GDP Since 1959

The composition of U.S. GDP has not changed much since 1959. Consumption's share edged up from an average of 62 percent during the 1960s to 68 percent during the last decade. Investment has fluctuated from year to year but with no clear long-term trend up or down. Government purchases declined slightly from an average of 22 percent of GDP during the 1960s to an average of 18 percent in the last decade. And net exports have become more negative, expressed by that portion exceeding 100 percent of GDP.

Source: Computed from annual estimates in *Survey of Current Business* 84 (February 2004). For the latest data, go to http://www.bea.doc.gov/bea/pubs.htm.

since 1959. As you can see, consumption's share of GDP appears stable from year to year, but the long-term trend shows an increase from an average of 62 percent during the 1960s to 68 percent during the last decade. Investment fluctuates more from year to year but with no long-term trend up or down.

Government purchases declined from an average of 22 percent of GDP during the 1960s to an average of 18 percent during the last decade, due primarily to decreases in defense spending. (But defense spending has picked up lately with the war on terrorism.) Net exports averaged 0.3 percent of GDP in the 1960s but were negative nearly every year since then, averaging a minus 2.5 percent of GDP during the last decade. Negative net exports mean that the sum of spending on consumption, investment, and government purchases exceeds GDP, the amount produced in the U.S. economy. Americans are spending more than they make, and they are covering the difference by borrowing from abroad. U.S. spending exceeds U.S. GDP by the amount shown as negative net exports. Because the spending components must sum to GDP, *negative* net exports are expressed in Exhibit 11 by that portion of spending that exceeds 100 percent of GDP.

In summary: During the last four decades, consumption's share of total spending increased and government purchases decreased. Investment's share bounced around and net exports' share turned negative, meaning that imports exceeded exports.

Conclusion

This chapter has focused on the relationship between spending and income. We considered the four components of aggregate expenditure: consumption, investment, government purchases, and net exports. Consumption increases with income. Investment relates more to interest rates and business expectations than it does to income. Government purchases also tend to be autonomous, or independent of income. And net exports are assumed, for now, to be affected more by such factors as the exchange rate than by U.S. income. The appendix to this chapter develops a more realistic but also more complicated picture by showing how net exports decline as income increases. In the next chapter, we will see how aggregate spending depends on income and how this link helps shape the aggregate demand curve.

SUMMARY

1. The most predictable and most useful relationship in macroeconomics is between consumption and income. The more people have to spend, the more they spend on consumption, other things constant.

2. The consumption function shows the link between consumption and income in the economy. The slope of the consumption function reflects the marginal propensity to consume, which equals the change in consumption divided by the change in income. The slope of the saving function reflects the marginal propensity to save, which equals the change in saving divided by the change in income.

3. Certain factors can cause consumers to change the amount they want to spend at each income level. An increase in net wealth reduces the need to save, thus increasing consumption at every income. A higher price level reduces the value of money holdings, thereby reducing net wealth, which in turn reduces consumption. An increase in the interest rate makes saving more rewarding and borrowing more costly, thus increasing saving and decreasing consumption at each income. Expectations about future incomes, prices, and interest rates also influence consumption.

4. Planned investment depends on the market interest rate and on business expectations. Investment fluctuates from year to year but averaged about one-sixth of GDP during the last decade. We assume for now that investment in the economy is unrelated to income.

5. Government purchases of goods and services averaged a little less than one-fifth of GDP during the last decade. Government purchases are based on the public choices of elected officials and are assumed to be autonomous, or independent of the economy's income level. Net taxes, or taxes minus transfer payments, are also assumed for now to be unrelated to income.

6. Net exports equal the value of exports minus the value of imports. U.S. exports depend on foreign income, not on U.S. income. Imports increase with U.S. income. So net exports decline as income increases. For simplicity, however, we initially assume that net exports are autonomous, or unrelated to domestic income.

QUESTIONS FOR REVIEW

1. *(Consumption Function)* How would an increase in each of the following affect the consumption function? How would it affect the saving function?

   a. Autonomous net taxes

   b. The interest rate

   c. Consumer optimism, or confidence

   d. The price level

   e. Consumers' net wealth

   f. Disposable income

2. *(Consumption Function)* A number of factors can cause the consumption function to shift. What, if anything, happens to the saving function when the consumption function shifts? Explain.

3. (*C a s e* **S t u d y :** The Life-Cycle Hypothesis) According to the life-cycle hypothesis, what is the typical pattern of saving for an individual over his or her lifetime? What impact does this behavior have on an individual's lifetime consumption pattern? What impact does the behavior have on the saving rate in the overall economy?

4. *(Investment)* What are the components of gross private domestic investment? What is the difference between the investment curve shown in Exhibit 6 and the one shown in Exhibit 7?

5. *(Investment)* Why would the following investment expenditures increase as the interest rate declines?

   a. Purchases of a new plant and equipment
   b. Construction of new housing
   c. Accumulation of planned inventories

6. *(Nonincome Determinants of Investment)* What are some factors assumed to be constant along the autonomous planned investment function? What kinds of changes in each factor could cause investment spending to increase a each level of real disposable income?

7. (*C a s e* **S t u d y :** Investment Varies Much More Than Consumption) Why do economic forecasters pay special attention to investment plans? Take a look at the Conference Board's index of leading economic indictors at http://www.conferenceboard.org. Which of those indicators might affect investment?

8. *(Government Spending)* How do changes in disposable income affect government purchases and the government purchase function? How do changes in net taxes affect the consumption function?

9. *(Net Exports)* What factors are assumed constant along the net export function? What would be the impact on net exports of a change in real disposable income?

PROBLEMS AND EXERCISES

10. *(Consumption)* Use the following data to answer the questions below:

Real Disposable Income (billions)	Consumption Expenditures (billions)	Saving (billions)
$100	$150	$_____
200	200	_____
300	250	_____
400	300	_____

   a. Graph the consumption function, with consumption spending on the vertical axis and disposable income on the horizontal axis.
   b. If the consumption function is a straight line, what is its slope?
   c. Fill in the saving column at each level of income. If the saving function is a straight line, what is its slope?

11. *(MPC and MPS)* If consumption increases by $12 billion when disposable income increases by $15 billion, what is the value of the MPC? What is the relationship between the MPC and the MPS? If the MPC increases, what must happen to the MPS? How is the MPC related to the consumption function? How is the MPS related to the saving function?

12. *(Consumption and Saving)* Suppose that consumption equals $500 billion when disposable income is $0 and that each increase of $100 billion in disposable income causes consumption to increase by $70 billion. Draw a graph of the saving function using this information.

13. *(Investment Spending)* Review Exhibit 6 in this chapter. If the operators of the golf course revised their revenue estimates so that each cart is expected to earn $100 less, how many carts would they buy at an interest rate of 8 percent? How many would they buy if the interest rate is 3 percent?

EXPERIENTIAL EXERCISES

4. *(Marginal Propensity to Consume)* Find some recent data on U.S. real disposable income and real consumption spending. (One possible source is the *Economic Report of the President* at http://w3.access.gpo.gov/eop/, but there are many others.) Use the data to compute the marginal propensity to consume for each year, 1991 to 2004. Has the MPC been relatively constant?

5. *(Variability of Consumption and Investment)* Expectations and consumer confidence are important in determining fluctuations in aggregate spending. What is the present status of consumer confidence as measured by the Conference Board's index? You can find the data, with interpretation, at The Conference Board at http://www.conference-board.org/economics/consumerConfidence.cfm.

16. *(Wall Street Journal)* Business investment spending is an important component of aggregate expenditure. Review the "Business Bulletin" column on the front page of Thursday's *Wall Street Journal*. What are some recent trends in investment spending? Are they likely to increase or decrease aggregate expenditure? (Remember that purchases of stocks and bonds are not investment, in the sense described in this chapter!)

HOMEWORK XPRESS! EXERCISES

These exercises require access to McEachern Homework Xpress! If Homework Xpress! did not come with your book, visit **http://homeworkxpress.swlearning.com** *to purchase.*

1. In the diagram for this exercise, plot the consumption function line for the data in the table below. Calculate savings at each level of real disposable income and plot the savings function.

Real Disposable Income (trillions)	Consumption (trillions)
$2.00	$2.50
3.00	3.25
4.00	4.00
5.00	4.75
6.00	5.50
7.00	6.25
8.00	7.00

2. In the diagram draw a linear consumption function. Illustrate the effect on the consumption function of an increase in net wealth. Then illustrate the effect on the consumption function of an increase in the price level.

3. In the diagram sketch an investment demand curve illustrating the relationship between the quantity of investment undertaken and the interest rate.

4. In the diagram sketch an autonomous investment function showing the level of investment as $1 trillion at the current market interest rate. Illustrate the effect on the function of an improvement in business expectations. Then illustrate the effect of an increase in the interest rate.

5. In the diagram, sketch an autonomous net export function showing the U.S. economy with a trade balance of $−50 billion. Illustrate how a decrease in the value of the U.S. dollar could lead to a positive trade balance. Then illustrate the effect of a decrease in the value of the currency of a major trading partner.

Variable Net Exports

In this appendix, we examine the relationship between net exports and U.S. income. We first look at exports and imports separately and then consider exports minus imports, or net exports.

Net Exports and Income

As noted earlier in the chapter, the amount of U.S. output purchased by foreigners depends not on U.S. income but on income in foreign countries. We therefore assume that U.S. exports do not vary with U.S. income. Specifically, suppose the rest of the world spends $0.9 trillion, of $900 billion, per year on U.S. exports of goods and services. The export function, X, is as shown in panel (a) of Exhibit 12. But when income increases, Americans spend more on all goods and services, including imports. Thus, the relationship between imports and income is positive, as expressed by the upward-sloping import function, M, in panel (b) of Exhibit 12. If Americans spend 10 percent of their disposable income on imports, when disposable income is $9.0 trillion, imports are $0.9 trillion.

So far, we have considered imports and exports as separate functions of income. What matters in terms of total spending on U.S. products are exports, X, minus imports, M, or net exports, $X - M$. Because money spent on imports goes to foreign producers, not U.S. producers, imports get subtracted from the circular flow of spending. By subtracting the import function depicted in panel (b) from the export function in panel (a), we derive the *net export function*, depicted as $X - M$ in panel (c) of Exhibit 12.

Because exports in panel (a) equal $0.9 trillion at all levels of income, net exports equal zero when U.S. disposable income is $9.0 trillion. At incomes less than $9.0 trillion, net exports are positive because exports exceed imports. At incomes greater than $9.0 trillion, net exports are negative because imports exceed exports. As a case in point, recessions in 1991 and 2001 reduced the trade deficits those years as imports declined. As the economy recovered, the trade deficit increased, reaching a record to that point in 2004.

Shifts of Net Exports

The net export function, $X - M$, shows the relationship between net exports and disposable income, other things constant. Suppose the value of the dollar increases relative to for-

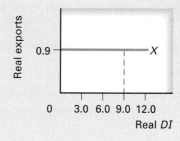

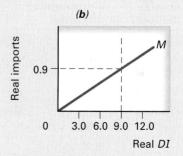

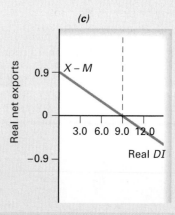

ign currencies, as happened in 1999. With the dollar worth
more, foreign products become cheaper for Americans, and
U.S. products become more expensive for foreigners. The impact of a rising dollar is to decrease exports but increase imports at each income level, thus decreasing net exports. This
relationship is shown in Exhibit 13 by the shift from $X - M$
down to $X' - M'$. A decline in the dollar's value, as occurred
in 2003, has the opposite effect, increasing exports and de-

creasing imports, as reflected in Exhibit 13 by an upward shift
of the net export function from $X - M$ to $X'' - M''$.

In summary, in this appendix we assumed that imports
relate positively to income, whereas exports are independent
of domestic income. Therefore, net exports, which equal exports minus imports, vary inversely with income. The net
export function shifts downward if the value of the dollar
rises and shifts upward if the value of the dollar falls.

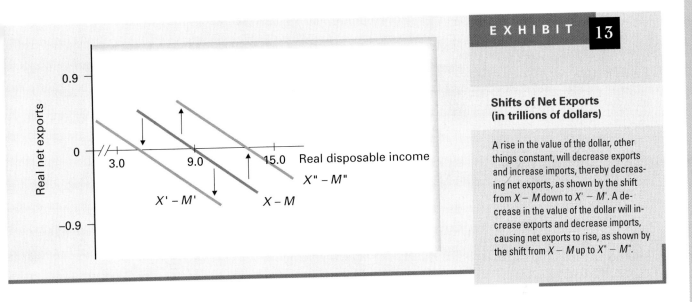

EXHIBIT 13

**Shifts of Net Exports
(in trillions of dollars)**

A rise in the value of the dollar, other
things constant, will decrease exports
and increase imports, thereby decreasing net exports, as shown by the shift
from $X - M$ down to $X' - M'$. A decrease in the value of the dollar will increase exports and decrease imports,
causing net exports to rise, as shown by
the shift from $X - M$ up to $X'' - M''$.

APPENDIX QUESTION

1. *(Rest of the World)* Using a graph of net exports $(X - M)$
   against disposable income, show the effects of the following. Explain each of your answers.

   a. An increase in foreign disposable income
   b. An increase in U.S. disposable income

   c. An increase in the U.S. interest rate
   d. An increase in the value of the dollar against foreign
      currencies

Aggregate Expenditure and Aggregate Demand

N ow that we have considered consumption, investment, government purchases, and net exports, how do we combine them to get aggregate expenditure for the economy? How is aggregate expenditure linked to income? How does a change in spending ripple through the economy, magnifying the impact? For example, how did the fear of flying after the terrorist attacks of September 11 affect the economy as a whole? What happens to spending if the economy's price level changes? Answers to these and other questions are covered in this chapter, which develops the aggregate demand curve.

Your economic success depends in part on the overall performance of the economy. When the economy grows, job opportunities expand, so your chances of finding a good job increase. When the economy contracts, job opportunities shrink, and so do your job prospects. Thus, you have a personal stake in the economy's success.

Use Homework Xpress! for economic application, graphing, videos, and more.

The previous chapter showed how each spending component relates to income in the economy. In this chapter, these components are added to learn how total spending, or aggregate expenditure, relates to income. We then see how a change in the economy's price level affects aggregate expenditure. All this is aimed at getting to the economy's aggregate demand curve. Aggregate supply will be developed in the next chapter. The effects of government spending and taxing will be explored in the chapter after that. Topics discussed include:

- Aggregate expenditure line
- Real GDP demanded
- Changes in aggregate expenditure

- Simple spending multiplier
- Changes in the price level
- Aggregate demand curve

Aggregate Expenditure and Income

In the previous chapter, the big idea was the link between consumption and income, a link that is the most stable in all of macroeconomics. In this section, we build on that connection to uncover the link between total spending in the economy and income. If we try to confront the economy head-on, it soon becomes a bewildering maze, which is why we make progress by beginning with simple models. We continue to assume, as we did in developing the circular-flow model, that there is no capital depreciation and no business saving. Thus, we can say that *each dollar of spending translates directly into a dollar of aggregate income.* Therefore, gross domestic product, or GDP, equals aggregate income. We also continue to assume that investment, government purchases, and net exports are *autonomous,* or independent of the income. Appendix A shows what happens when imports increase with income, and Appendix B develops the algebra behind all this.

The Components of Aggregate Expenditure

Let's begin developing the aggregate demand curve by asking how much aggregate output would be demanded at a given price level. By finding the quantity demanded at a given price level, we'll identify a single point on the aggregate demand curve. We begin by considering the relationship between aggregate spending in the economy and aggregate income. To get us started, suppose the price level in the economy is 130, or 30 percent higher than in the base year. We want to find out how much will be spent at various levels of real income, or real GDP. By *real* GDP, we mean GDP measured in terms of real goods and services produced. Exhibit 1 puts into tabular form relationships introduced in the previous chapter—consumption, saving, planned investment, government purchases, net taxes, and net exports. Although the entries are hypothetical, they bear some relation to levels observed in the U.S. economy. For example, real GDP in the U.S. economy is nearly $12 trillion a year.

Column (1) lists possible real GDP levels in the economy, symbolized by Y. Remember, real GDP also means real income in the economy. Column (2) shows *net taxes,* or *NT,* assumed here to be $1.0 trillion at each real GDP level. Subtracting net taxes from real GDP yields *disposable income,* listed in column (3) as $Y - NT$. Note that at each real GDP level, disposable income equals real GDP minus net taxes of $1.0 trillion. Because net taxes do not vary with income, each time real GDP increases by $0.5 trillion, disposable income also increases by $0.5 trillion.

Households have only two possible uses for disposable income: consumption and saving. Columns (4) and (5) show that the levels of *consumption, C,* and *saving, S,* increase with disposable income. Each time real GDP and disposable income increase by $0.5 trillion, con-

EXHIBIT 1			Real GDP with Net Taxes and Government Purchases (trillions of dollars)						

(1) Real GDP (Y)	(2) Net Taxes (NT)	(3) Disposable Income (Y − NT) (3) =(1) − (2)	(4) Consumption (C)	(5) Saving (S)	(6) Planned Investment (I)	(7) Government Purchases (G)	(8) Net Exports (X − M)	(9) Planned Aggregate Expenditure (AE)	(10) Unplanned Inventory Adjustment (Y − AE) (10) = (1) − (9)
11.0	1.0	10.0	9.4	0.6	1.0	1.0	−0.2	11.2	−0.2
11.5	1.0	10.5	9.8	0.7	1.0	1.0	−0.2	11.6	−0.1
12.0	**1.0**	**11.0**	**10.2**	**0.8**	**1.0**	**1.0**	**−0.2**	**12.0**	**0.0**
12.5	1.0	11.5	10.6	0.9	1.0	1.0	−0.2	12.4	+0.1
13.0	1.0	12.0	11.0	1.0	1.0	1.0	−0.2	12.8	+0.2

sumption increases by $0.4 trillion and saving increases by $0.1 trillion. Thus, as in the previous chapter, the marginal propensity to consume is 4/5, or 0.8, and the marginal propensity to save is 1/5, or 0.2.

Columns (6), (7), and (8) list three now-familiar injections of spending into the circular flow: *planned investment* of $1.0 trillion, *government purchases* of $1.0 trillion, and *net exports* of −$0.2 trillion. In the table, government purchases equal net taxes, so the government budget is balanced. We first want to see how a balanced budget works before we consider the effects of budget deficits or surpluses, which will be discussed in the chapter after next. *The sum of consumption, C, planned investment, I, government purchases, G, and net exports, X − M, is listed in column (9) as planned aggregate expenditure, AE, which shows how much households, firms, governments, and the rest of the world plan to spend on U.S. output at each level of real GDP, or real income.* Note that the only spending component that varies with real GDP is consumption. As real GDP increases, so does disposable income, which increases consumption.

The final column in Exhibit 1 lists any unplanned adjustment to inventories, which equal real GDP minus planned aggregate expenditure, or $Y − AE$. For example, when real GDP is $11.0 trillion, planned aggregate expenditure is $11.2 trillion. Because planned spending exceeds the amount produced by $0.2 trillion, firms must rely on inventories to make up the shortfall in output. So when real GDP is $11.0 trillion, the unplanned inventory adjustment in the final column is −$0.2 trillion. Because firms cannot reduce inventories indefinitely, they respond to shortfalls in output by increasing production, and they continue to do so until they produce the amount people want to buy—that is, until real GDP equals planned aggregate expenditure.

If the amount produced exceeds planned spending, firms get stuck with unsold goods, which become unplanned increases in inventories. For example, if real GDP is $13.0 trillion, planned aggregate expenditure is only $12.8 trillion, so $0.2 trillion in output remains unsold. Thus, inventories increase by $0.2 trillion. Firms respond by reducing output and do so until they produce the amount people want to buy.

Note the distinction here between **planned investment,** the amount firms plan to invest, and **actual investment,** which includes both planned investment and any unplanned

PLANNED INVESTMENT

The amount of investment that firms plan to undertake during a year

ACTUAL INVESTMENT

The amount of investment actually undertaken; equals planned investment plus unplanned changes in inventories

changes in inventories. Unplanned increases in inventories cause firms to smarten up and decrease their production next time around so as not to get stuck with more unsold goods. When the amount people plan to spend equals the amount produced, there are no unplanned inventory adjustments. And when there are no unplanned adjustments in inventories, planned investment equals actual investment. More precisely, *at a given price level, the quantity of real GDP demanded occurs where spending plans match the amount produced*. In Exhibit 1, this occurs where both planned aggregate expenditure and real GDP equal $12.0 trillion.

Real GDP Demanded

Using a table, we have seen how firms adjust output until production just equals desired spending. You may find graphs easier. Graphs are more general than tables and can show relationships between variables without focusing on specific numbers. The tabular relationship between real GDP and planned aggregate expenditure in Exhibit 1 can be expressed as an **aggregate expenditure line** in Exhibit 2. Like the planned aggregate expenditure amounts shown in column (9) of Exhibit 1, the aggregate expenditure line in Exhibit 2 reflects the sum of consumption, planned investment, government purchases, and net exports, or $C + I + G + (X - M)$. Aggregate expenditure is measured on the vertical axis.

Real GDP, measured along the horizontal axis in Exhibit 2, can be viewed in two ways—as the value of *aggregate output* and as the *aggregate income* generated by that output. Because real GDP, or aggregate income, is measured on the horizontal axis and aggregate expenditure is measured on the vertical axis, this graph is often called the **income–expenditure model.** To gain perspective on the relationship between income and expenditure, we use a handy analytical tool: the 45-degree ray from the origin. The special feature of this line is that any point along it is the same distance from each axis. Thus, the 45-degree line

AGGREGATE EXPENDITURE LINE

A relationship showing, for a given price level, planned spending at each income, or real GDP; the total of $C + I + G + (X - M)$ at each income, or real GDP

INCOME-EXPENDITURE MODEL

A relationship between aggregate income and aggregate spending that determines, for a given price level, where the amount people plan to spend equals the amount produced

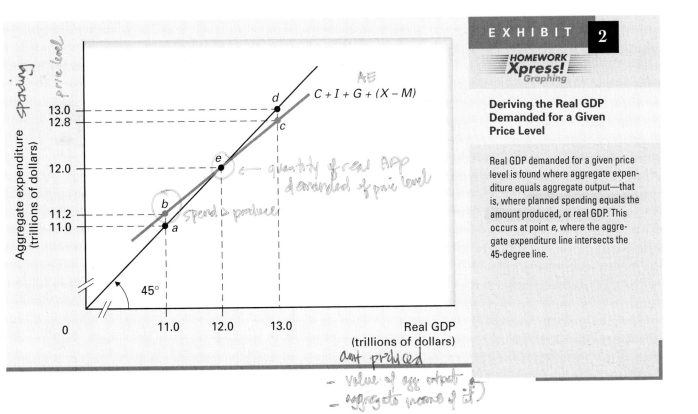

E X H I B I T **2**

HOMEWORK
Xpress!
Graphing

Deriving the Real GDP Demanded for a Given Price Level

Real GDP demanded for a given price level is found where aggregate expenditure equals aggregate output—that is, where planned spending equals the amount produced, or real GDP. This occurs at point *e*, where the aggregate expenditure line intersects the 45-degree line.

identifies all points where planned expenditure equals real GDP. *Aggregate output demanded a▸ a given price level occurs where planned aggregate expenditure, measured along the vertical axis, equals real GDP, measured along the horizontal axis.* In Exhibit 2, this occurs at point *e*, where the aggregate expenditure line intersects the 45-degree line. At point *e*, the amount people plan▸ to spend equals the amount produced. We conclude that, at the given price level of 130, the quantity of real GDP demanded equals \$12.0 trillion.

What If Planned Spending Exceeds Real GDP?

[handwritten: production]

To find the real GDP demanded at the given price level, consider what happens when real GDP is initially less than \$12.0 trillion. As you can see from Exhibit 2, when real GDP is less than \$12.0 trillion, the aggregate expenditure line is above the 45-degree line, indicating that planned spending exceeds the amount produced (give this a little thought). For example, if real GDP is \$11.0 trillion, planned spending is \$11.2 trillion, as indicated by point *b* on the aggregate expenditure line, so planned spending exceeds output by \$0.2 trillion. When the amount people plan to spend exceeds the amount produced, something has to give. Ordinarily what gives is the price, but remember that we are seeking the real GDP demanded for a given price level, so the price level is assumed to remain constant, at least for now. What gives in this model are *inventories*. Unplanned reductions in inventories make up the \$0.2 trillion shortfall in output. Because firms can't draw down inventories indefinitely, *unplanned inventory reductions* prompt firms to produce more. That increases employment and consumer income, leading to more spending. As long as planned spending exceeds output, firms increase production to make up the difference. This process of more output, more income, and more spending will continue until planned spending equals real GDP, an equality achieved at point *e* in Exhibit 2.

When output reaches \$12.0 trillion, planned spending exactly matches output, so no unintended inventory adjustments occur. More importantly, when output reaches \$12.0 trillion, planned spending equals the amount produced and equals the total income generated by that production. Earlier we assumed a price level of 130. Therefore, \$12.0 trillion is the real GDP demanded at that price level.

What If Real GDP Exceeds Planned Spending?

To reinforce the logic of the model, consider what happens when real GDP initially exceeds *[handwritten: Production]* \$12.0 trillion—that is, when the aggregate expenditure line is below the 45-degree line. *[handwritten: Spending]* Notice in Exhibit 2 that, to the right of point *e*, planned spending falls short of production. For example, if the amount produced in the economy is \$13.0 trillion, planned spending, as indicated by point *c* on the aggregate expenditure line, is \$0.2 trillion less than real GDP, indicated by point *d* on the 45-degree line. Because real GDP exceeds the amount people plan to buy, unsold goods accumulate. This swells inventories by \$0.2 trillion more than firms planned. Rather than allow inventories to pile up indefinitely, firms reduce production, which reduces employment and income. As an example of such behavior, a recent news account read, "General Motors will idle two assembly plants in a move to trim inventories in the wake of slowing sales." *Unplanned inventory buildups* cause firms to cut production until the amount they produce equals aggregate spending, which occurs, again, where real GDP is \$12.0 trillion. Given the price level, real GDP demanded is found where the amount people plan to spend equals the amount produced. *For a given price level, there is only one point along the aggregate expenditure line at which planned spending equals real GDP.*

We have now discussed the forces that determine real GDP demanded for a given price level. In the next section, we examine changes that can shift planned spending.

The Simple Spending Multiplier

In the previous section, we used the aggregate expenditure line to find real GDP demanded for a particular price level. In this section, we continue to assume that the price level remains unchanged as we trace the effects of changes in planned spending. Like a stone thrown into a still pond, the effect of any shift of planned spending ripples through the economy, generating changes in aggregate output that exceed the initial change in spending.

An Increase in Planned Spending

We begin at point *e* in Exhibit 3, where planned spending equals real GDP at $12.0 trillion. Now let's consider the effect of an increase in one of the components of spending. Suppose that firms become more optimistic about future profits and decide to increase their investment from $1.0 trillion to $1.1 trillion per year. Exhibit 3 reflects this change by a shift upward of the aggregate expenditure line by $0.1 trillion, from $C + I + G + (X - M)$ to $C + I' + G + (X - M)$.

What happens to real GDP demanded? An instinctive response is to say that real GDP demanded increases by $0.1 trillion. In this case, however, instinct is a poor guide. As you can see, the new spending line intersects the 45-degree line at point *e'*, where real GDP demanded is $12.5 trillion. How can a $0.1 trillion increase in planned spending increase real GDP demanded by $0.5 trillion? What's going on?

The idea of the circular flow is central to an understanding of the adjustment process. As noted earlier, real GDP can be thought of as both the value of production and the income arising from that production. Recall that production yields income, which generates spending. We can think of each trip around the circular flow as a "round" of income and spending.

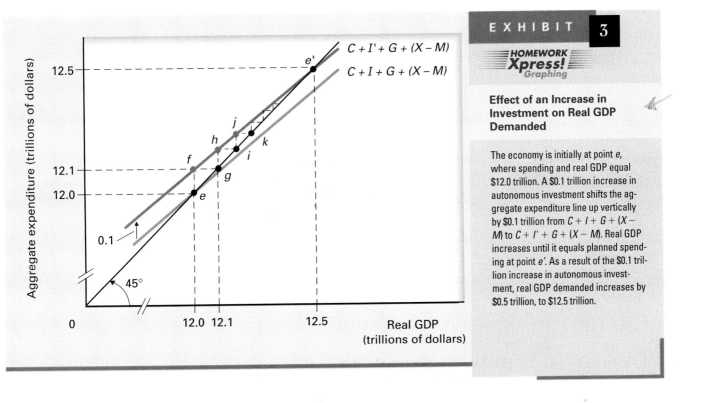

Effect of an Increase in Investment on Real GDP Demanded

The economy is initially at point *e*, where spending and real GDP equal $12.0 trillion. A $0.1 trillion increase in autonomous investment shifts the aggregate expenditure line up vertically by $0.1 trillion from $C + I + G + (X - M)$ to $C + I' + G + (X - M)$. Real GDP increases until it equals planned spending at point *e'*. As a result of the $0.1 trillion increase in autonomous investment, real GDP demanded increases by $0.5 trillion, to $12.5 trillion.

Round One

An upward shift of the aggregate expenditure line means that, at the initial real GDP of $12.0 trillion, planned spending now exceeds output by $0.1 trillion, or $100 billion. This is shown in Exhibit 3 by the distance between point *e* and point *f*. Initially, firms match this increased spending by an unplanned reduction in inventories. But reduced inventories prompt firms to expand production by $100 billion, as shown by the movement from point *f* to point *g*. This generates $100 billion more income. The movement from *e* to *g* shows the first round in the multiplier process. The income-generating process does not stop there, however, because those who earn this additional income spend some of it and save the rest, leading to round two of spending and income.

Round Two

Given a marginal propensity to consume of 0.8, those who earn the additional $100 billion will spend $80 billion on toasters, backpacks, gasoline, restaurant meals, and thousands of other goods and services. They save the other $20 billion. The move from point *g* to point *h* in Exhibit 3 shows this $80 billion spending increase. Firms respond by increasing their output by $80 billion, shown by the movement from point *h* to point *i*. Thus, the initial $100 billion in new income increases real GDP by $80 billion during round two.

Round Three and Beyond

We know that four-fifths of the $80 billion earned during round two will get spent during round three and one-fifth will get saved. Thus, $64 billion is spent during round three on still more goods and services, as reflected by the movement from point *i* to point *j*. The remaining $16 billion gets saved. The added spending causes firms to increase output by $64 billion, as shown by the movement from point *j* to point *k*. Round three's additional production generated $64 billion more income, which sets up subsequent rounds of spending, output, and income. *As long as planned spending exceeds output, production will increase, thereby creating more income, which will generate still more spending.*

Exhibit 4 summarizes the multiplier process, showing the first three rounds, round 10, and the cumulative effect of all rounds. The new spending each round is shown in the second column and the accumulation of new spending appears in the third column. For example, the new spending accumulated as of the third round is $244 billion—the sum of the first three rounds of spending ($100 billion + $80 billion + $64 billion). The new saving

EXHIBIT 4	Round	New Spending This Round	Cumulative New Spending	New Saving This Round	Cumulative New Saving
	1	100	100	—	—
Tracking the Rounds of Spending Following a $100 Billion Increase in Investment (billions of dollars)	2	80	180	20	20
	3	64	244	16	36
	⋮	⋮	⋮	⋮	⋮
	10	13.4	446.3	3.35	86.6
	⋮	⋮	⋮	⋮	⋮
	∞	0	500	0	100

from each round appears in the fourth column, and the accumulation of new saving appears in the final column.

Using the Simple Spending Multiplier

In our model, consumers spend four-fifths of their income each round, with each new round equal to spending from the previous round times the marginal propensity to consume, or the MPC. This goes on round after round, leaving less and less to fuel more spending and income. At some point, the new rounds of income and spending become so small that they disappear and the process stops. The question is, by how much does total spending increase? We can get some idea of the total by working through a limited number of rounds. For example, as shown in Exhibit 4, total new spending after 10 rounds sums to $446.3 billion. But calculating the exact total for all rounds would require us to work through an infinite number of rounds—an impossible task.

Fortunately, we can borrow a shortcut from mathematicians, who have found that the sum of an infinite number of rounds, each of which is MPC times the previous round, equals $1/(1 - MPC)$ times the initial change. Translated, the cumulative spending equals $1/(1 - MPC)$, which, in our example, was $1/0.2$, or 5, times the initial increase in spending, which was $100 billion. In short, the increase in planned investment eventually boosts real GDP demanded by 5 times $100 billion, or $500 billion.

The **simple spending multiplier** is the factor by which real GDP demanded changes for a given initial change in spending.

$$\text{Simple spending multiplier} = \frac{1}{1 - MPC}$$

SIMPLE SPENDING
MULTIPLIER

The ratio of a change in real GDP demanded to the initial change in spending that brought it about; the numerical value of the simple spending multiplier is $1/(1 - MPC)$, called "simple" because only consumption varies with income

The simple spending multiplier provides a shortcut to the total change in real GDP demanded. This multiplier depends on the MPC. The larger the MPC, the larger the simple spending multiplier. That makes sense—the more people spend from each dollar of fresh income, the more total spending will increase. For example, if the MPC was 0.9 instead of 0.8, the denominator of multiplier formula would equal 1.0 minus 0.9, or 0.1, so the multiplier would be 1/0.1, or 10. With an MPC of 0.9, a $0.1 trillion investment increase would boost real GDP demanded by $1.0 trillion. On the other hand, an MPC of 0.75 would yield a denominator of 0.25 and a multiplier of 4. So a $0.1 trillion investment increase would raise real GDP demanded by $0.4 trillion.

Let's return to Exhibit 3. The $0.1 trillion rise in autonomous investment raised real GDP demanded from $12.0 trillion to $12.5 trillion. Note that real GDP demanded would have increased by the same amount if consumers had decided to spend $0.1 trillion more at each income level—that is, if the consumption function, rather than the investment function, had shifted up by $0.1 trillion. Real GDP demanded likewise would have increased if government purchases or net exports increased $0.1 trillion. *The change in aggregate output demanded depends on how much the aggregate expenditure line shifts, not on which spending component causes the shift.*

In our example, planned investment increased by $0.1 trillion in the year in question. *If this greater investment is not sustained the following year, real GDP demanded will fall back.* For example, if planned investment returns to its initial level, other things constant, real GDP demanded would return to $12.0 trillion. Finally, recall from the previous chapter that the MPC and the MPS sum to 1, so 1 minus the MPC equals the MPS. With this information, we can define the simple spending multiplier in terms of the MPS as follows:

$$\text{Simple spending multiplier} = \frac{1}{1 - MPC} = \frac{1}{MPS}$$

We can see that the smaller the MPS, the less leaks from the spending stream as saving. Because less is saved, more gets spent each round, so the spending multiplier is greater. Incidentally, this spending multiplier is called "simple" because consumption is the only spending component that varies with income.

As an example of how a decline in aggregate expenditure can ripple through the economy, consider what happened to air travel in the wake of the September 11 terrorist attacks.

Fear of Flying

When hijacked planes hit the World Trade Center and the Pentagon, America's sense of domestic security changed. The thousands of lives lost and the billions of dollars of property destroyed were chronicled at length in the media. Let's look at the impact of the tragedy on just one industry—air travel—to see how slumping demand there had a multiplier effect on aggregate expenditure.

Once aviation regulators became aware of the hijackings, they grounded all nonmilitary aircraft immediately. This cost the airlines hundreds of millions of dollars a day during the week of the shutdown. During the days following the attack, video of the second plane crashing into the twin towers was shown again and again, freezing this image in people's minds and heightening concerns about airline safety. These worries, coupled with the airport delays from added security (passengers were told to arrive up to three hours before flights), reduced the demand for air travel. Two weeks after the attacks, airlines were operating only 75 percent of their flights, and these flights were only 30 percent full instead of the usual 75 percent full. Airlines requested federal support, saying they would go bankrupt otherwise. Congress quickly approved a $15 billion package of loans and grants.

Despite the promise of federal aid, airlines laid off 85,000 workers, or about 20 percent of their workforce. Flight reductions meant that as many as 900 aircraft would be parked indefinitely, so investment in new planes collapsed. Boeing, the major supplier of new planes, announced layoffs of 30,000 workers. This triggered layoffs among suppliers of airline parts, such as jet engine and electronic components. For example, Rockwell Collins, an electronics supplier, said 15 percent of its workforce would lose jobs. Other suppliers in the airline food chain also cut jobs. Sky Chef, a major airline caterer, laid off 4,800 of its 16,000 employees.

Airports began rethinking their investment plans. Half the major U.S. airports said they were reevaluating their capital improvement plans to see if these investments made sense in this new environment. Honolulu airport, for example, suspended plans to add extra gates and renovate its overseas terminals.

Just within the first three weeks after the attacks, job cuts announced in the industry exceeded 150,000. These were part of only the first round of reduced consumption and investment. In an expanding economy, job losses in one sector can be made up by job expansions in other sectors. But the U.S. economy was already in a recession at the time of the attack. People who lost jobs or who feared for their jobs reduced their demand for housing, clothing, entertainment, restaurant meals, and other goods and services. For example, unemployed flight attendants would be less likely to buy a new car, reducing the income of au-

---

CaseStudy

Public Policy

eActivity

The World Travel and Tourism Council conducts economic research on the impact of the travel industry on GDP in the United States and around the world. Updated reports on the national and global impact of changes in the travel industry are available at http://www.wttc.org/tsa1.htm. Find the latest report for the United States. What is the current contribution of travel and tourism to GDP? What do you think is meant by direct versus indirect impacts? How have these changed following the events of September 11, 2001?

WALL STREET JOURNAL

Reading It **Right**

What's the relevance of the following statement from the Wall Street Journal: *"The U.S. economy is headed for recession in the aftermath of the September 11 terrorist attacks, according to a new* Wall Street Journal *survey of economists."*

coworkers and suppliers. People who lost jobs in this declining auto industry would reduce their demand for goods and services. So the reductions in airline jobs had a multiplier effect.

Airlines are only one part of the travel industry. With fewer people traveling, fewer needed hotels, rental cars, taxi rides, and restaurant meals. Each of those sectors generated a cascade of job losses. The terrorist attacks also shook consumer confidence, which in September 2001 suffered its largest monthly drop since October 1990, on the eve of the first Persian Gulf War. Within 10 days following the attacks, the number of people filing for unemployment benefits jumped to a nine-year high. Again, these early job losses could be viewed as just part of the first round of reduced aggregate expenditure. The second round would occur when people who lost jobs or who feared they would lose their jobs started spending less. The U.S. economy continued to lose jobs for nearly two more years.

Sources: Scott McCartney, "Coast-to-Coast Fares Drop to New Lows," *Wall Street Journal,* 12 May 2004; Susan Carey, "UAL Reports a Narrower Loss, But Profits Remain Elusive," *Wall Street Journal,* 29 April 2004; Will Pinkston, "Airports Reconsider Expansion Plans as Future of Air Travel Gets Murkier," *Wall Street Journal,* 27 September 2001; Luke Timmerman, "Boeing Warns Bad May Get Worse," *Seattle Times,* 21 September 2001; and the Federal Aviation Administration at http://www.faa.gov/.

The Aggregate Demand Curve

In this chapter, we have used the aggregate expenditure line to find real GDP demanded *for a given price level.* But what happens to planned spending if the price level changes? As you will see, for each price level, there is a specific aggregate expenditure line, which yields a unique real GDP demanded. By altering the price level, we can derive the aggregate demand curve.

A Higher Price Level

What is the effect of a higher price level on planned spending and, in turn, on real GDP demanded? Recall that consumers hold many assets that are fixed in dollar terms, such as currency and bank accounts. A higher price level decreases the real value of these money holdings. This cuts consumer wealth, making people less willing to spend at each income level. For reasons that will be explained in a later chapter, a higher price level also tends to increase the market interest rate, and a higher interest rate reduces investment. Finally, a higher U.S. price level means that foreign goods become cheaper for U.S. consumers, and U.S. goods become more expensive abroad. So imports rise and exports fall, decreasing net exports. Therefore, *a higher price level reduces consumption, planned investment, and net exports, which all reduce aggregate spending.* This decrease in planned spending reduces real GDP demanded.

Exhibit 5 represents two different ways of expressing the effects of a change in the price level on real GDP demanded. Panel (a) offers the income–expenditure model, and panel (b) offers the aggregate demand curve, showing the inverse relationship between the price level and real GDP demanded. The idea is to find the real GDP demanded for a given price level in panel (a) and show that price-quantity combination as a point on the aggregate demand curve in panel (b). The two panels measure real GDP on the horizontal axes. At the initial price level of 130 in panel (a), the aggregate expenditure line, now denoted simply as *AE,* intersects the 45-degree line at point *e* to yield real GDP demanded of $12.0 trillion. Panel (b) shows more directly the link between real GDP demanded and the price level. As you can see, when the price level is 130, real GDP demanded is $12.0 trillion. This combination is identified by point *e* on the aggregate demand curve.

What if the price level increases from 130 to, say, 140? As you've just learned, an increase in the price level reduces consumption, planned investment, and net exports. This reduction

The Income-Expenditure Approach and the Aggregate Demand Curve

At the initial price level of 130, the aggregate expenditure line is *AE*, which identifies real GDP demanded of $12.0 trillion. This combination of a price level of 130 and a real GDP demanded of $12.0 trillion determines one combination (point *e*) on the aggregate demand curve in panel (b).

At the higher price level of 140, the aggregate expenditure line shifts down to *AE'*, and real GDP demanded falls to $11.5 trillion. This price-quantity combination is plotted as point *e'* in panel (b).

At the lower price level of 120, the aggregate expenditure line shifts up to *AE"*, which increases real GDP demanded. This combination is plotted as point *e"* in panel (b).

Connecting points *e*, *e'*, and *e"* in panel (b) yields the downward-sloping aggregate demand curve, which shows the inverse relation between price and real GDP demanded.

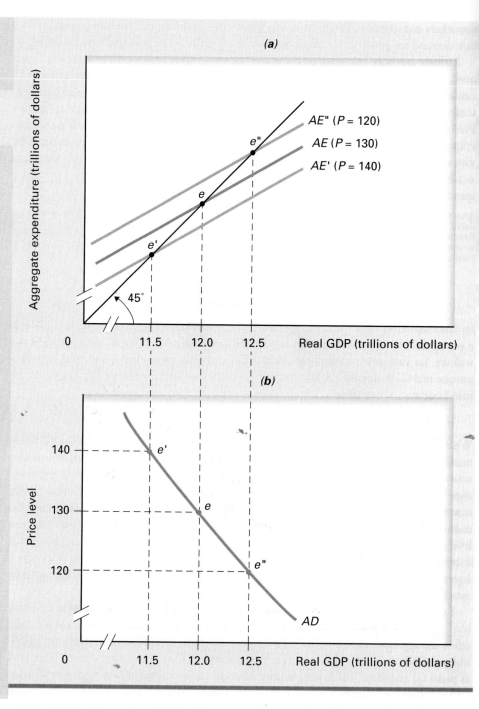

in planned spending is reflected in panel (a) by a downward shift of the aggregate expenditure line from *AE* to *AE'*. As a result, real GDP demanded declines from $12.0 trillion to $11.5 trillion. Panel (b) shows that an increase in the price level from 130 to 140 decreases real GDP demanded from $12.0 trillion to $11.5 trillion, as reflected by the movement from point *e* to point *e'*.

A Lower Price Level

The opposite occurs if the price level falls. At a lower price level, the value of bank accounts, currency, and other money holdings increases. Consumers on average are richer and thus consume more at each real GDP. A lower price level also tends to decrease the market interest rate, which increases investment. Finally, a lower U.S. price level, other things constant, makes U.S. products cheaper abroad and foreign products more expensive here, so exports increase and imports decrease. *Because of a decline in the price level, consumption, investment, and net exports increase at each real GDP.*

Refer again to Exhibit 5 and suppose the price level declines from 130 to, say, 120. This increases planned spending at each income level, as reflected by an upward shift of the spending line from *AE* to *AE"* in panel (a). An increase in planned spending increases real GDP demanded from $12.0 trillion to $12.5 trillion, as indicated by the intersection of the top aggregate expenditure line with the 45-degree line at point *e"*. This same price decrease can be viewed more directly in panel (b). As you can see, when the price level decreases to 120, real GDP demanded increases to $12.5 trillion.

The aggregate expenditure line and the aggregate demand curve present real output from different perspectives. The aggregate expenditure line shows, for a given price level, how planned spending relates to real GDP in the economy. Real GDP demanded is found where planned spending equals real GDP. The aggregate demand curve shows, for various price levels, the quantities of real GDP demanded.

The Multiplier and Shifts in Aggregate Demand

Now that you have some idea how changes in the price level shift the aggregate expenditure line to generate the aggregate demand curve, let's reverse course and return to the situation where the price level is assumed to remain constant. What we want to do now is trace through the effects of a shift of a spending component on aggregate demand, assuming the price level does not change. For example, suppose that a bounce in business confidence spurs a $0.1 trillion increase in planned investment at each real GDP level. Each panel of Exhibit 6 shows a different way of expressing the effects of an increase in planned spending on real GDP demanded, assuming the price level remains unchanged. Panel (a) presents the income-expenditure model and panel (b), the aggregate demand model. Again, the two panels measure real GDP on the horizontal axes. At a price level of 130 in panel (a), the aggregate expenditure line, $C + I + G + (X - M)$, intersects the 45-degree line at point *e* to yield $12.0 trillion in real GDP demanded. Panel (b) shows more directly the link between real GDP demanded and the price level. As you can see, when the price level is 130, real GDP demanded is $12.0 trillion, identified as point *e* on the aggregate demand curve.

Exhibit 6 shows how a shift of the aggregate expenditure line relates to a shift of the aggregate demand curve, given a constant price level. In panel (a), a $0.1 trillion increase in investment shifts the aggregate expenditure line up by $0.1 trillion. Because of the multiplier effect, real GDP demanded climbs from $12.0 trillion to $12.5 trillion. Panel (b) shows the effect of the increase in spending on the aggregate demand curve, which shifts to the right, from *AD* to *AD'*. At the prevailing price level of 130, real GDP demanded increases from $12.0 trillion to $12.5 trillion as a result of the $0.1 trillion increase in planned investment.

Our discussion of the simple spending multiplier exaggerates the actual effect we might expect. For one thing, we have assumed that the price level remains constant. As we shall see in the next chapter, incorporating aggregate supply into the analysis reduces the multiplier because of the resulting price change. Moreover, as income increases there are leakages from the circular flow in addition to saving, such as higher income taxes and greater imports; these

A Shift of the Aggregate Expenditure Line That Shifts the Aggregate Demand Curve

A shift of the aggregate expenditure line at a given price level shifts the aggregate demand curve. In panel (a), an increase in investment of $0.1 trillion, with the price level constant at 130, causes the aggregate expenditure line to increase from $C + I + G + (X - M)$ to $C + I' + G + (X - M)$. As a result, real GDP demanded increases from $12.0 trillion to $12.5 trillion. In panel (b), the aggregate demand curve has shifted from AD out to AD'. At the prevailing price level of 130, real GDP demanded has increased by $0.5 trillion.

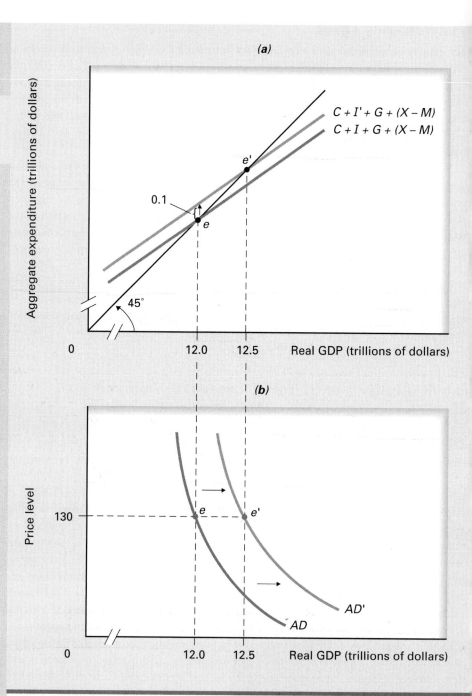

leakages reduce the multiplier. Finally, although we have presented the process in a timeless framework, the spending multiplier takes time to work through rounds—perhaps a year or more.

In summary: For a given price level, the aggregate expenditure line relates spending plans to income, or real GDP. A change in the price level will shift the aggregate expenditure line, changing real GDP demanded. Changes in the price level and consequent changes in real GDP demanded generate points along an aggregate demand curve. But at a given price level, changes in spending plans, such as changes in planned investment, consumption, or government purchases, will shift the aggregate demand curve.

We close with a case study that considers the problem created when Japanese consumers decided to spend less and save more.

Falling Consumption Triggers Japan's Recession

As noted already, consumer spending is the largest component of aggregate expenditure, accounting for about two-thirds of the total. Consumption depends primarily on disposable income. But at any given income level, consumption depends on several other factors, including household wealth, the interest rate, and consumer expectations. Look what happened in Japan, where by 2003 the stock market stood two-thirds below its 1990 level, taking a big bite from household wealth. A collapse in the once-booming real estate market cut household wealth even more.

C a s e **S t u d y**

Bringing
Theory to Life

eActivity
Keep track of what is happening in the Japanese economy through a Web page from NikkeiNet at http://www.nni.nikkei.co.jp sponsored by Nikkei, "the primary source of business information for top executives and decision makers in Japan." What current policies for stimulating consumption can you find among the most current headlines? What are the latest economic indicators reported?

This sharp reduction in household wealth, combined with an erosion of consumer confidence in the economy, prompted Japanese consumers to spend less and save more. Japan's consumption function shifted downward, and their saving function shifted upward. The drop in consumption reduced aggregate expenditure and shifted the aggregate demand curve to the left. The decline in aggregate demand resulted in Japan's longest economic downturn in 50 years, with the unemployment rate doubling between 1990 and 2003. Retail sales declined in 2003 for the seventh consecutive year. Japan, the second largest economy in the world (after the United States), is by far the largest economy in Asia. A weak economy in Japan hurts the already troubled economies across Asia because Japan is a customer for their exports. Thus, the decline in consumption in Japan had global implications. But by 2004 Japan was starting to show signs of life, with a growing real GDP.

Sources: "Japanese Retail Sales Fell Last Year, *Taipei Times*, 29 January 2004; and "Japan Is Flying Again," *The Economist*, 14 February 2004. For a survey of the Japanese economy, go to http://www.oecd.org/home/.

Conclusion

Three ideas central to this chapter are (1) certain forces determine the quantity of real GDP demanded at a given price level, (2) changes in the price level generate the aggregate demand curve, and (3) at a given price level, changes in planned spending shift the aggregate demand curve. The simple multiplier provides a crude but exaggerated idea of how a change in spending plans affects real GDP demanded.

This chapter focused on aggregate spending. A simplifying assumption used throughout was that net exports do not vary with income. Appendix A adds more realism by considering what happens when imports increase with income. Because spending on imports leak from the circular flow, this more realistic approach reduces the spending multiplier.

So far, we have derived real GDP demanded using several approaches, including intuition, tables, and graphs. With the various approaches, we find that for each price level there is a specific quantity of real GDP demanded, other things constant. Appendix B uses algebra to show the same results.

SUMMARY

1. The aggregate expenditure line indicates, for a given price level, planned spending at each income level. At a given price level, real GDP demanded is found where the amount that people plan to spend equals the amount produced.

2. The simple spending multiplier indicates the multiple by which a shift of planned spending changes real GDP demanded. The simple spending multiplier developed in this chapter is $1/(1 - MPC)$. The larger the MPC, the more will be spent and the less will be saved, so the larger the simple multiplier.

3. A higher price level causes a downward shift of the aggregate expenditure line, leading to a lower real GDP de-

manded. A lower price level causes an upward shift of the aggregate expenditure line, increasing real GDP demanded. By tracing the impact of price changes on real GDP demanded, we can derive an aggregate demand curve.

4. The aggregate expenditure line and the aggregate demand curve portray real output from different perspectives. The aggregate expenditure line shows, for a given price level, how much people plan to spend at each income level. Real GDP demanded is found where planned spending equals the amount produced. The aggregate demand curve shows, for various price levels, the quantities of real GDP demanded. At a given price level, a change in spending plans shifts the aggregate demand curve.

QUESTIONS FOR REVIEW

1. *(Aggregate Expenditure)* What are the components of aggregate expenditure? In the model developed in this chapter, which components vary with changes in the level of real GDP? What determines the slope of the aggregate expenditure line?

2. *(Real GDP Demanded)* In your own words, explain the logic of the income-expenditure model. What determines the amount of real GDP demanded?

3. *(Real GDP Demanded)* What equalities hold at the level of real GDP demanded? When determining real GDP demanded, what do we assume about the price level? What do we assume about inventories?

4. *(When Output and Spending Differ)* What role do inventories play in determining real GDP demanded? In answering this question, suppose initially that firms are either producing more than people plan to spend, or producing less than people plan to spend.

5. *(Simple Spending Multiplier)* "A rise in planned investment in an economy will lead to a rise in the amount of planned spending." Use the spending multiplier to verify this statement.

6. (*C a s e* **S t u d y**: Fear of Flying) How do events, such as the World Trade Center and Pentagon attacks described in the case study "Fear of Flying," affect the aggregate expenditure line and the aggregate demand curve? Explain fully.

7. *(The Aggregate Demand Curve)* What is the effect of a lower price level, other things constant, on the aggregate expenditure line and real GDP demanded? How does the multiplier interact with the price change to determine the new real GDP demanded?

8. (*C a s e* **S t u d y**: Falling Consumption Triggers Japan's Recession) What happened to consumption in Japan? Why did this happen? What was the impact on aggregate demand there?

PROBLEMS AND EXERCISES

9. *(Simple Spending Multiplier)* For each of the following values for the MPC, determine the size of the simple spending multiplier and the total change in real GDP demanded following a $10 billion decrease in autonomous spending:

   a. MPC = 0.9
   b. MPC = 0.75
   c. MPC = 0.6

10. *(Simple Spending Multiplier)* Suppose that the MPC is 0.8 and that $12 trillion of real GDP is currently being demanded. The government wants to increase real GDP demanded to $13 trillion at the given price level. By how much would it have to increase government purchases to achieve this goal?

11. *(Simple Spending Multiplier)* Suppose that the MPC is 0.8, while planned investment, government purchases, and net exports sum to $500 billion. Suppose also that the government budget is in balance.

    a. What is the sum of saving and net taxes when desired spending equals real GDP? Explain.
    b. What is the value of the multiplier?
    c. Explain why the multiplier is related to the slope of the consumption function.

12. *(Investment and the Multiplier)* This chapter assumes that investment is autonomous. What would happen to the size of the multiplier if investment increases as real GDP increases? Explain.

13. *(Shifts of Aggregate Demand)* Assume the simple spending multiplier equals 10. Determine the size and direction of any changes of the aggregate expenditure line, real GDP demanded, and the aggregate demand curve for each of the following changes in autonomous spending:

    a. Autonomous spending rises by $8 billion.
    b. Autonomous spending falls by $5 billion.
    c. Autonomous spending rises by $20 billion.

EXPERIENTIAL EXERCISES

14. (*C a s e* **S t u d y**: Falling Consumption Triggers Japan's Recession) Professor Nouriel Roubini of New York University maintains an extensive Web page at http://www.stern.nyu.edu/globalmacro/ devoted to global financial crises. Visit the page and determine what are the latest developments in Japan and around the world.

15. *(Wall Street Journal)* This chapter pointed out that net exports are an important influence on aggregate demand.

Find a story in today's *Wall Street Journal* that describes an event that will affect U.S. imports or exports. A good place to look is the "International" page in the first section of the *Journal*. Analyze the story you have chosen, and illustrate the event using both the aggregate expenditure line and the aggregate demand curve.

HOMEWORK XPRESS! EXERCISES

These exercises require access to McEachern Homework Xpress! If Homework Xpress! did not come with your book, visit **http://homeworkxpress.swlearning.com** *to purchase.*

1. Use the diagram for this exercise to draw a level of aggregate expenditures that would lead to an economy at an equilibrium, *E*, with a real GDP of $8 trillion.

2. Use the diagram for this exercise to draw a level of aggregate expenditures that would lead to an economy at an equilibrium, *E*, with a real GDP of $8 trillion. Illustrate how a change in aggregate expenditures would lead to an increase in the equilibrium level of GDP to $10 trillion.

3. Use the diagram to draw in a level of aggregate expenditures that would lead to an economy at an equilibrium, *E*, with a real GDP of $8 trillion for a price level of *P* = 100. Illustrate the effect of an increase in the price level to *P* = 120. Identify the new equilibrium.

4. In the diagram, draw a level of aggregate expenditures that would lead to an economy at an equilibrium, *E*, with a real GDP of $8 trillion for a price level of *P* = 100. Illustrate the effect of a decrease in the price level to *P* = 80. Identify the new equilibrium.

5. Draw an aggregate demand curve that shows the economy at an equilibrium level of real GDP of $8 trillion when the price level is *P* = 120.

Variable Net Exports Revisited

This chapter has assumed that net exports do not vary with income. A more realistic approach has net exports varying inversely with income. Such a model was developed in the appendix to the previous chapter. The resulting net export function, $X - M$, is presented in panel (a) of Exhibit 7. Recall that the higher the income level in the economy, the more is spent on imports, so the lower the net exports. (If this is not clear, review the appendix to the previous chapter.) Panel (b) of Exhibit 7 shows what happens when vari-

able net exports are added to consumption, government purchases, and investment. We add the variable net export function to $C + I + G$ to get $C + I + G + (X - M)$. Perhaps the easiest way to see how introducing net exports affects planned spending is to begin where real GDP equals $10.0 trillion. Because net exports equal zero when real GDP equals $10.0 trillion, the addition of net exports has no effect on planned spending. So the $C + I + G$ and $C + I + G + (X - M)$ lines intersect where real GDP equals $10.0

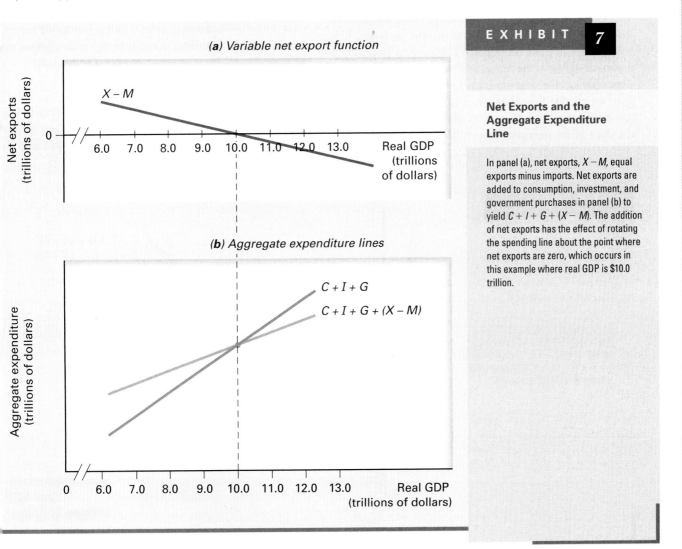

EXHIBIT 7

Net Exports and the Aggregate Expenditure Line

In panel (a), net exports, $X - M$, equal exports minus imports. Net exports are added to consumption, investment, and government purchases in panel (b) to yield $C + I + G + (X - M)$. The addition of net exports has the effect of rotating the spending line about the point where net exports are zero, which occurs in this example where real GDP is $10.0 trillion.

trillion. At real GDP levels less than $10.0 trillion, net exports are positive, so the $C + I + G + (X - M)$ line is above the $C + I + G$ line. At real GDP levels greater than $10.0 trillion, net exports are negative, so the $C + I + G + (X - M)$ line is below the $C + I + G$ line. *Because variable net exports and real GDP are inversely related, the addition of variable net exports has the effect of flattening out, or reducing the slope of, the aggregate expenditure line.*

Net Exports and the Spending Multiplier

The inclusion of variable net exports makes the model more realistic but more complicated, and it requires a reformulation of the spending multiplier. If net exports are autonomous, or independent of income, only the marginal propensity to consume determines how much gets spent and how much gets saved as income changes. The inclusion of variable net exports means that, as income increases, U.S. residents spend more on imports. The *marginal propensity to import,* or *MPM,* is the fraction of each additional dollar of disposable income spent on imported products. Imports leak from the circular flow. Thus, two leakages now increase with income: saving and imports. This additional leakage changes the value of the multiplier from $1/MPS$ to:

$$\text{spending multiplier with variable net exports} = \frac{1}{MPS + MPM}$$

The larger the marginal propensity to import, the greater the leakage during each round of spending and the smaller the resulting spending multiplier. Suppose the MPM equals $1/10$, or 0.1. If the marginal propensity to save is 0.2 and the marginal propensity to import is 0.1, then only $0.70 of each additional dollar of disposable income gets spent on output produced in the United States. We can compute the new multiplier as follows:

$$\text{Spending multiplier with variable net exports}$$
$$= \frac{1}{MPS + MPM} = \frac{1}{0.2 + 0.1} = \frac{1}{0.3} = 3.33$$

Thus, the inclusion of net exports reduces the spending multiplier in our hypothetical example from 5 to 3.33. *Because some of each additional dollar of income goes toward imports, less is spent on U.S. products, so any given shift of the aggregate expenditure line has less of an impact on real GDP demanded.*

A Change in Autonomous Spending

Given the net export function described in the previous section, what is the real GDP demanded, and how does income change when there is a change in autonomous spending? To

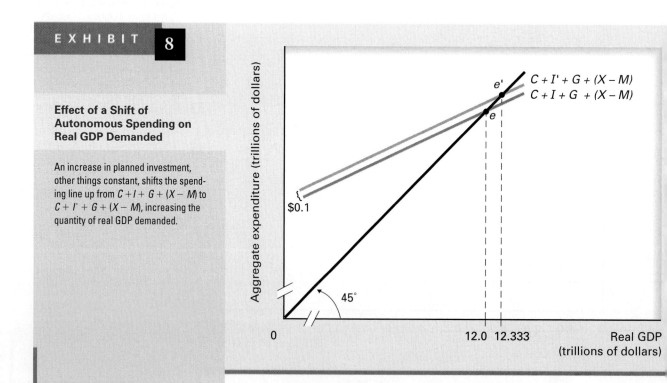

EXHIBIT 8

Effect of a Shift of Autonomous Spending on Real GDP Demanded

An increase in planned investment, other things constant, shifts the spending line up from $C + I + G + (X - M)$ to $C + I' + G + (X - M)$, increasing the quantity of real GDP demanded.

answer these questions, let's begin in Exhibit 8 with an aggregate expenditure line of $C + I + G + (X - M)$, where net exports vary inversely with income. This aggregate expenditure line intersects the 45-degree line at point e, determining real GDP demanded of $12.0 trillion. Suppose now that planned investment increases by $0.1 trillion at every income, with the price level unchanged. This will shift the entire aggregate expenditure line up by $0.1 trillion, from C $+ I + G + (X - M)$ to $C + I' + G + (X - M)$, as shown in Exhibit 8. Output demanded increases from $12.0 trillion to $12.333 trillion, representing an increase of $0.333 trillion, or $333 billion, which is $0.1 trillion times the spending multiplier with variable exports of 3.33. The derivation of the output level and the size of the multiplier are explained in Appendix B.

APPENDIX A QUESTION

1. (*Net Exports and the Spending Multiplier*) Suppose that the marginal propensity to consume (MPC) is 0.8 and the marginal propensity to import (MPM) is 0.05.

   a. What is the value of the spending multiplier?
   b. By how much would the real GDP demanded change if planned investment increased by $100 billion?

   c. Using your answer to part (b), calculate the change in net exports caused by the change in aggregate output.

The Algebra of Income and Expenditure

This appendix explains the algebra behind real GDP demanded. You should see some similarity between this and the circular-flow explanation of national income accounts.

The Aggregate Expenditure Line

We first determine where planned spending equals output and then derive the relevant spending multipliers, assuming a given price level. Initially, let's assume net exports are autonomous. Then we'll incorporate variable net exports into the framework.

Real GDP demanded for a given price level occurs where planned spending equals income, or real GDP. Planned spending is equal to the sum of consumption, C, planned investment, I, government purchases, G, and net exports, $X - M$. Algebraically, we can write the equality as

$$Y = C + I + G + (X - M)$$

where Y equals income, or real GDP. To find where real GDP equals planned spending, we begin with the heart of the income-expenditure model: the consumption function. The consumption function used throughout this chapter is a straight line; the equation for that line can be written as

$$C = 1.4 + 0.8 (Y - 1.0)$$

The marginal propensity to consume is 0.8, Y is income, or real GDP, and 1.0 is autonomous net taxes in trillions of dollars. Thus $(Y - 1.0)$ is real GDP minus net taxes, which equals disposable income. The consumption function can be simplified to

$$C = 0.6 + 0.8Y$$

Consumption at each real GDP, therefore, equals $0.6 trillion (which could be called autonomous consumption—that is, consumption that does not vary with income), plus 0.8 times income, which is the marginal propensity to consume times income.

The second component of spending is investment, I, which we have assumed is autonomous and equal to $1.0 trillion. The third component of spending is autonomous government purchases, G, which we assumed to be $1.0 trillion. Net exports, $X - M$, the final spending component, we assumed to be −$0.2 trillion at all levels of income. Sub-stituting the numerical values for each spending component in planned spending, we get

$$Y = 0.6 + 0.8Y + 1.0 + 1.0 - 0.2$$

Notice there is only one variable in this expression: Y. If we rewrite the expression as

$$Y - 0.8Y = 0.6 + 1.0 + 1.0 - 0.2$$
$$0.2Y = 2.4$$

we can solve for real GDP demanded:

$$Y = \$12.0 \text{ trillion}$$

A More General Form of Income and Expenditure

The advantage of algebra is that it allows us to derive the equilibrium quantity of real GDP demanded in a more general way. Let's begin with a consumption function of the general form

$$C = a + b (Y - NT)$$

where b is the marginal propensity to consume and NT is net taxes. Consumption can be rearranged as

$$C = a - bNT + bY$$

where $a - bNT$ is *autonomous* consumption (the portion of consumption that is independent of income) and bY is *induced* consumption (the portion of consumption generated by higher income in the economy). Real GDP demanded equals the sum of consumption, C, planned investment, I, government purchases, G, and net exports, $X - M$, or

$$\text{Income} = \text{Expenditure}$$
$$Y = a - bNT + bY + I + G + (X - M)$$

Again, by rearranging terms and isolating Y on the left side of the equation, we get

$$Y = \frac{1}{1 - b}(a - bNT + I + G + X - M)$$

The $(a - bNT + I + G + X - M)$ term represents autonomous spending—that is, the amount of spending that is independent of income. And $(1 - b)$ equals 1 minus the MPC. In the chapter, we showed that $1/(1 - MPC)$ equals the simple spending multiplier. One way of viewing what's going on is to keep in mind that autonomous spending is *multiplied* through the economy to arrive at real GDP demanded.

The formula that yields real GDP demanded can be used to derive the spending multiplier. We can increase autonomous spending by, say, $1, to see what happens to real GDP demanded.

$$Y' = \frac{1}{1 - b}(a - bNT + I + G + X - M + \$1)$$

The difference between this expression and the initial one (that is, between Y' and Y) is $\$1/(1 - b)$. Because b equals the MPC, the simple multiplier equals $1/(1 - b)$. Thus, the change in equilibrium income equals the change in autonomous spending times the multiplier.

Varying Net Exports

Here we explore the algebra behind variable net exports, first introduced in the appendix to the previous chapter. We begin with the equality

$$Y = C + I + G + (X - M)$$

Exports are assumed to equal $0.9 trillion at each income level. Imports increase as disposable income increases, with a marginal propensity to import of 0.1. Therefore, net exports equal

$$X - M = 0.9 - 0.1 (Y - 1.0)$$

After incorporating the values for C, I, and G presented earlier, we can express the equality as

$$Y = 0.6 + 0.8Y + 1.0 + 1.0 + 0.9 - 0.1 (Y - 1.0)$$

which reduces to $0.3Y = \$3.6$ trillion, or $Y = \$12.0$ trillion.

Algebra can be used to generalize these results. If m represents the marginal propensity to import, net exports become $X - m(Y - NT)$. Real GDP demanded can be found by solving for Y in the expression

$$Y = a + b(Y - NT) + I + G + X - m(Y - NT)$$

which yields

$$Y = \frac{1}{1 - b + m}(a - bNT + I + G + X + mNT)$$

The expression in parentheses represents autonomous spending. In the denominator, $1 - b$ is the marginal propensity to save and m is the marginal propensity to import. Appendix A demonstrated that $1/(MPS - MPM)$ equals the spending multiplier when variable net exports are included. Thus, real GDP demanded equals the spending multiplier times autonomous spending. And an increase in autonomous spending times the multiplier gives us the resulting increase in real GDP demanded.

APPENDIX B QUESTION

1. Suppose that $C = 100 + 0.75(Y - 100)$, $I = 50$, $G = 30$, and $X - M = -100$, all in billions of dollars. What is the simple spending multiplier? What is real GDP demanded? What would happen to real GDP demanded if government purchases increased to $40 billion?

Principles of
Macroeconomics

Fourth Edition

N. Gregory Mankiw
Harvard University

THOMSON

SOUTH-WESTERN

Australia • Canada • Mexico • Singapore • Spain • United Kingdom • United States

Ten Principles of Economics

The word *economy* comes from the Greek word *oikonomos*, which means "one who manages a household." At first, this origin might seem peculiar. But in fact, households and economies have much in common.

A household faces many decisions. It must decide which members of the household do which tasks and what each member gets in return: Who cooks dinner? Who does the laundry? Who gets the extra dessert at dinner? Who gets to choose what TV show to watch? In short, the household must allocate its scarce resources among its various members, taking into account each member's abilities, efforts, and desires.

Like a household, a society faces many decisions. A society must decide what jobs will be done and who will do them. It needs some people to grow food, other people to make clothing, and still others to design computer software. Once society has allocated people (as well as land, buildings, and machines) to various jobs, it must also allocate the output of goods and services that they produce. It must decide who will eat caviar and who will eat potatoes. It must decide who will drive a Ferrari and who will take the bus.

The management of society's resources is important because resources are scarce. **Scarcity** means that society has limited resources and therefore cannot produce all the goods and services people wish to have. Just as a household cannot give every member everything he or she wants, a society cannot give every individual the highest standard of living to which he or she might aspire.

scarcity
the limited nature of society's resources

economics
the study of how society manages its scarce resources

Economics is the study of how society manages its scarce resources. In most societies, resources are allocated not by an all-powerful dictator but through the combined actions of millions of households and firms. Economists therefore study how people make decisions: how much they work, what they buy, how much they save, and how they invest their savings. Economists also study how people interact with one another. For instance, they examine how the multitude of buyers and sellers of a good together determine the price at which the good is sold and the quantity that is sold. Finally, economists analyze forces and trends that affect the economy as a whole, including the growth in average income, the fraction of the population that cannot find work, and the rate at which prices are rising.

 Although the study of economics has many facets, the field is unified by several central ideas. In this chapter, we look at *Ten Principles of Economics.* Don't worry if you don't understand them all at first or if you don't find them completely convincing. In later chapters, we will explore these ideas more fully. The ten principles are introduced here to give you an overview of what economics is all about. You can think of this chapter as a "preview of coming attractions."

HOW PEOPLE MAKE DECISIONS

There is no mystery to what an economy is. Whether we are talking about the economy of Los Angeles, of the United States, or of the whole world, an economy is just a group of people interacting with one another as they go about their lives. Because the behavior of an economy reflects the behavior of the individuals who make up the economy, we start our study of economics with four principles of individual decision making.

Principle 1: People Face Trade-offs

The first lesson about making decisions is summarized in the adage "There is no such thing as a free lunch." To get one thing that we like, we usually have to give up another thing that we like. Making decisions requires trading off one goal against another.

Consider a student who must decide how to allocate her most valuable resource—her time. She can spend all of her time studying economics; she can spend all of her time studying psychology; or she can divide her time between the two fields. For every hour she studies one subject, she gives up an hour she could have used studying the other. And for every hour she spends studying, she gives up an hour that she could have spent napping, bike riding, watching TV, or working at her part-time job for some extra spending money.

Or consider parents deciding how to spend their family income. They can buy food, clothing, or a family vacation. Or they can save some of the family income for retirement or the children's college education. When they choose to spend an extra dollar on one of these goods, they have one less dollar to spend on some other good.

When people are grouped into societies, they face different kinds of trade-offs. The classic trade-off is between "guns and butter." The more we spend on national defense (guns) to protect our shores from foreign aggressors, the less we can spend on consumer goods (butter) to raise our standard of living at home. Also important in modern society is the trade-off between a clean environment and a high level of income. Laws that require firms to reduce pollution raise the cost of producing goods and services. Because of the higher costs, these firms end up earning smaller profits, paying lower wages, charging higher prices, or some combination of these three. Thus, while pollution regulations give us the benefit of a cleaner environment and the improved health that comes with it, they have the cost of reducing the incomes of the firms' owners, workers, and customers.

Another trade-off society faces is between efficiency and equity. **Efficiency** means that society is getting the maximum benefits from its scarce resources. **Equity** means that those benefits are distributed fairly among society's members. In other words, efficiency refers to the size of the economic pie, and equity refers to how the pie is divided. Often, when government policies are designed, these two goals conflict.

Consider, for instance, policies aimed at achieving a more equal distribution of economic well-being. Some of these policies, such as the welfare system or unemployment insurance, try to help the members of society who are most in need. Others, such as the individual income tax, ask the financially successful to contribute more than others to support the government. Although these policies have the benefit of achieving greater equity, they have a cost in terms of reduced efficiency. When the government redistributes income from the rich to the poor, it reduces the reward for working hard; as a result, people work less and produce fewer goods and services. In other words, when the government tries to cut the economic pie into more equal slices, the pie gets smaller.

Recognizing that people face trade-offs does not by itself tell us what decisions they will or should make. A student should not abandon the study of psychology just because doing so would increase the time available for the study of economics. Society should not stop protecting the environment just because environmental regulations reduce our material standard of living. The poor should not be ignored just because helping them distorts work incentives. Nonetheless, acknowledging life's trade-offs is important because people are likely to make good decisions only if they understand the options that they have available.

Principle 2: The Cost of Something Is What You Give Up to Get It

Because people face trade-offs, making decisions requires comparing the costs and benefits of alternative courses of action. In many cases, however, the cost of some action is not as obvious as it might first appear.

Consider, for example, the decision to go to college. The benefit is intellectual enrichment and a lifetime of better job opportunities. But what is the cost? To answer this question, you might be tempted to add up the money you spend on tuition, books, room, and board. Yet this total does not truly represent what you give up to spend a year in college.

The first problem with this answer is that it includes some things that are not really costs of going to college. Even if you quit school, you need a place to sleep and food to eat. Room and board are costs of going to college only to the extent that they are more expensive at college than elsewhere. Indeed, the cost of room and board at your school might be less than the rent and food expenses that you would pay living on your own. In this case, the savings on room and board are a benefit of going to college.

efficiency
the property of society getting the most it can from its scarce resources

equity
the property of distributing economic prosperity fairly among the members of society

The second problem with this calculation of costs is that it ignores the largest cost of going to college—your time. When you spend a year listening to lectures, reading textbooks, and writing papers, you cannot spend that time working at a job. For most students, the wages given up to attend school are the largest single cost of their education.

opportunity cost
whatever must be given up to obtain some item

The **opportunity cost** of an item is what you give up to get that item. When making any decision, such as whether to attend college, decision makers should be aware of the opportunity costs that accompany each possible action. In fact, they usually are. College athletes who can earn millions if they drop out of school and play professional sports are well aware that their opportunity cost of college is very high. It is not surprising that they often decide that the benefit is not worth the cost.

Principle 3: Rational People Think at the Margin

rational people
people who systematically and purposefully do the best they can to achieve their objectives

Economists normally assume that people are rational. **Rational people** systematically and purposefully do the best they can to achieve their objectives, given the opportunities they have. As you study economics, you will encounter firms that decide how many workers to hire and how much of their product to manufacture and sell to maximize profits. You will encounter consumers who buy a bundle of goods and services to achieve the highest possible level of satisfaction, subject to their incomes and the prices of those goods and services.

marginal changes
small incremental adjustments to a plan of action

Rational people know that decisions in life are rarely black and white but usually involve shades of gray. At dinnertime, the decision you face is not between fasting or eating like a pig but whether to take that extra spoonful of mashed potatoes. When exams roll around, your decision is not between blowing them off or studying 24 hours a day but whether to spend an extra hour reviewing your notes instead of watching TV. Economists use the term **marginal changes** to describe small incremental adjustments to an existing plan of action. Keep in mind that *margin* means "edge," so marginal changes are adjustments around the edges of what you are doing. Rational people often make decisions by comparing *marginal benefits* and *marginal costs*.

For example, consider an airline deciding how much to charge passengers who fly standby. Suppose that flying a 200-seat plane across the United States costs the airline $100,000. In this case, the average cost of each seat is $100,000/200, which is $500. One might be tempted to conclude that the airline should never sell a ticket for less than $500. In fact, however, the airline can raise its profits by thinking at the margin. Imagine that a plane is about to take off with ten empty seats, and a standby passenger waiting at the gate will pay $300 for a seat. Should the airline sell the ticket? Of course it should. If the plane has empty seats, the cost of adding one more passenger is minuscule. Although the *average* cost of flying a passenger is $500, the *marginal* cost is merely the cost of the bag of peanuts and can of soda that the extra passenger will consume. As long as the standby passenger pays more than the marginal cost, selling the ticket is profitable.

Marginal decision making can help explain some otherwise puzzling economic phenomena. Here is a classic question: Why is water so cheap, while diamonds are so expensive? Humans need water to survive, while diamonds are unnecessary; but for some reason, people are willing to pay much more for a diamond than for a cup of water. The reason is that a person's willingness to pay for any good is based on the marginal benefit that an extra unit of the good would yield. The marginal benefit, in turn, depends on how many units a person already has. Although water is essential, the marginal benefit of an extra cup is small because water is plentiful. By contrast, no one needs diamonds to survive, but because diamonds are so rare, people consider the marginal benefit of an extra diamond to be large.

A rational decision maker takes an action if and only if the marginal benefit of the action exceeds the marginal cost. This principle can explain why airlines are willing to sell a ticket below average cost and why people are willing to pay more for diamonds than for water. It can take some time to get used to the logic of marginal thinking, but the study of economics will give you ample opportunity to practice.

Principle 4: People Respond to Incentives

An **incentive** is something (such as the prospect of a punishment or a reward) that induces a person to act. Because rational people make decisions by comparing costs and benefits, they respond to incentives. You will see that incentives play a central role in the study of economics. One economist went so far as to suggest that the entire field could be simply summarized: "People respond to incentives. The rest is commentary."

incentive
something that induces
a person to act

Incentives are crucial to analyzing how markets work. For example, when the price of an apple rises, people decide to eat more pears and fewer apples because the cost of buying an apple is higher. At the same time, apple orchards decide to hire more workers and harvest more apples because the benefit of selling an apple is also higher. As we will see, the effect of a good's price on the behavior of buyers and sellers in a market—in this case, the market for apples—is crucial for understanding how the economy allocates scarce resources.

Public policymakers should never forget about incentives because many policies change the costs or benefits that people face and, therefore, alter their behavior. A tax on gasoline, for instance, encourages people to drive smaller, more fuel-efficient cars. That is one reason people drive smaller cars in Europe, where gasoline taxes are high, than in the United States, where gasoline taxes are low. A gasoline tax also encourages people to take public transportation rather than drive and to live closer to where they work. If the tax were larger, more people would be driving hybrid cars, and if it were large enough, they would switch to electric cars.

When policymakers fail to consider how their policies affect incentives, they often end up with results they did not intend. For example, consider public policy regarding auto safety. Today, all cars have seat belts, but this was not true 50 years ago. In the 1960s, Ralph Nader's book *Unsafe at Any Speed* generated much public concern over auto safety. Congress responded with laws requiring seat belts as standard equipment on new cars.

How does a seat belt law affect auto safety? The direct effect is obvious: When a person wears a seat belt, the probability of surviving a major auto accident rises. But that's not the end of the story because the law also affects behavior by altering incentives. The relevant behavior here is the speed and care with which drivers operate their cars. Driving slowly and carefully is costly because it uses the driver's time and energy. When deciding how safely to drive, rational people compare the marginal benefit from safer driving to the marginal cost. They drive more slowly and carefully when the benefit of increased safety is high. It is no surprise, for instance, that people drive more slowly and carefully when roads are icy than when roads are clear.

Consider how a seat belt law alters a driver's cost–benefit calculation. Seat belts make accidents less costly because they reduce the likelihood of injury or

BASKETBALL STAR LEBRON JAMES UNDERSTANDS OPPORTUNITY COST AND INCENTIVES. HE DECIDED TO SKIP COLLEGE AND GO STRAIGHT TO THE PROS, WHERE HE HAS EARNED MILLIONS OF DOLLARS AS ONE OF THE NBA'S TOP PLAYERS.

death. In other words, seat belts reduce the benefits of slow and careful driving. People respond to seat belts as they would to an improvement in road conditions—by driving faster and less carefully. The end result of a seat belt law, therefore, is a larger number of accidents. The decline in safe driving has a clear, adverse impact on pedestrians, who are more likely to find themselves in an accident but (unlike the drivers) don't have the benefit of added protection.

At first, this discussion of incentives and seat belts might seem like idle speculation. Yet in a classic 1975 study, economist Sam Peltzman showed that auto-safety laws have had many of these effects. According to Peltzman's evidence, these laws produce both fewer deaths per accident and more accidents. He concluded that the net result is little change in the number of driver deaths and an increase in the number of pedestrian deaths.

Peltzman's analysis of auto safety is an offbeat example of the general principle that people respond to incentives. When analyzing any policy, we must consider not only the direct effects but also the indirect and sometimes less obvious effects that work through incentives. If the policy changes incentives, it will cause people to alter their behavior.

Quick Quiz   List and briefly explain the four principles of individual decision making.

HOW PEOPLE INTERACT

The first four principles discussed how individuals make decisions. As we go about our lives, many of our decisions affect not only ourselves but other people as well. The next three principles concern how people interact with one another.

Principle 5: Trade Can Make Everyone Better Off

You have probably heard on the news that the Japanese are our competitors in the world economy. In some ways, this is true because American and Japanese firms produce many of the same goods. Ford and Toyota compete for the same customers in the market for automobiles. Apple and Sony compete for the same customers in the market for digital music players.

Yet it is easy to be misled when thinking about competition among countries. Trade between the United States and Japan is not like a sports contest in which one side wins and the other side loses. In fact, the opposite is true: Trade between two countries can make each country better off.

To see why, consider how trade affects your family. When a member of your family looks for a job, he or she competes against members of other families who are looking for jobs. Families also compete against one another when they go shopping because each family wants to buy the best goods at the lowest prices. So in a sense, each family in the economy is competing with all other families.

Despite this competition, your family would not be better off isolating itself from all other families. If it did, your family would need to grow its own food, make its own clothes, and build its own home. Clearly, your family gains much from its ability to trade with others. Trade allows each person to specialize in the

THE WALL STREET JOURNAL

ENGLEMAN

"FOR $5 A WEEK YOU CAN WATCH BASEBALL WITHOUT BEING NAGGED TO CUT THE GRASS!"

activities he or she does best, whether it is farming, sewing, or home building. By trading with others, people can buy a greater variety of goods and services at lower cost.

Countries as well as families benefit from the ability to trade with one another. Trade allows countries to specialize in what they do best and to enjoy a greater variety of goods and services. The Japanese, as well as the French and the Egyptians and the Brazilians, are as much our partners in the world economy as they are our competitors.

Principle 6: Markets Are Usually a Good Way to Organize Economic Activity

The collapse of communism in the Soviet Union and Eastern Europe in the 1980s may be the most important change in the world during the past half century. Communist countries worked on the premise that government officials were in the best position to determine the allocation of scarce resources in the economy. These central planners decided what goods and services were produced, how much was produced, and who produced and consumed these goods and services. The theory behind central planning was that only the government could organize economic activity in a way that promoted economic well-being for the country as a whole.

Today, most countries that once had centrally planned economies have abandoned this system and are trying to develop market economies. In a **market economy,** the decisions of a central planner are replaced by the decisions of millions of firms and households. Firms decide whom to hire and what to make. Households decide which firms to work for and what to buy with their incomes. These firms and households interact in the marketplace, where prices and self-interest guide their decisions.

market economy
an economy that allocates resources through the decentralized decisions of many firms and households as they interact in markets for goods and services

At first glance, the success of market economies is puzzling. After all, in a market economy, no one is looking out for the economic well-being of society as a whole. Free markets contain many buyers and sellers of numerous goods and services, and all of them are interested primarily in their own well-being. Yet despite decentralized decision making and self-interested decision makers, market economies have proven remarkably successful in organizing economic activity in a way that promotes overall economic well-being.

In his 1776 book *An Inquiry into the Nature and Causes of the Wealth of Nations,* economist Adam Smith made the most famous observation in all of economics: Households and firms interacting in markets act as if they are guided by an "invisible hand" that leads them to desirable market outcomes. One of our goals in this book is to understand how this invisible hand works its magic.

As you study economics, you will learn that prices are the instrument with which the invisible hand directs economic activity. In any market, buyers look at the price when determining how much to demand, and sellers look at the price when deciding how much to supply. As a result of the decisions that buyers and sellers make, market prices reflect both the value of a good to society and the cost to society of making the good. Smith's great insight was that prices adjust to guide these individual buyers and sellers to reach outcomes that, in many cases, maximize the welfare of society as a whole.

There is an important corollary to the skill of the invisible hand in guiding economic activity: When the government prevents prices from adjusting naturally to supply and demand, it impedes the invisible hand's ability to coordinate the millions of households and firms that make up the economy. This corollary explains why taxes adversely affect the allocation of resources: Taxes distort prices and thus the decisions of households and firms. It also explains the even greater harm caused by policies that directly control prices, such as rent control. And it explains the failure of communism. In communist countries, prices were not determined in the marketplace but were dictated by central planners. These planners lacked the information that gets reflected in prices that are free to respond to market forces. Central planners failed because they tried to run the economy with one hand tied behind their backs—the invisible hand of the marketplace.

Principle 7: Governments Can Sometimes Improve Market Outcomes

If the invisible hand of the market is so great, why do we need government? One purpose of studying economics is to refine your view about the proper role and scope of government policy.

One reason we need government is that the invisible hand can work its magic only if the government enforces the rules and maintains the institutions that are

FYI

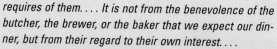

Adam Smith and the Invisible Hand

It may be only a coincidence that Adam Smith's great book *The Wealth of Nations* was published in 1776, the exact year American revolutionaries signed the Declaration of Independence. But the two documents share a point of view that was prevalent at the time: Individuals are usually best left to their own devices, without the heavy hand of government guiding their actions. This political philosophy provides the intellectual basis for the market economy and for free society more generally.

Why do decentralized market economies work so well? Is it because people can be counted on to treat one another with love and kindness? Not at all. Here is Adam Smith's description of how people interact in a market economy:

Man has almost constant occasion for the help of his brethren, and it is vain for him to expect it from their benevolence only. He will be more likely to prevail if he can interest their self-love in his favor, and show them that it is for their own advantage to do for him what he

requires of them.... It is not from the benevolence of the butcher, the brewer, or the baker that we expect our dinner, but from their regard to their own interest....

Every individual ... neither intends to promote the public interest, nor knows how much he is promoting it.... He

Adam Smith

intends only his own gain, and he is in this, as in many other cases, led by an invisible hand to promote an end which was no part of his intention. Nor is it always the worse for the society that it was no part of it. By pursuing his own interest he frequently promotes that of the society more effectually than when he really intends to promote it.

Smith is saying that participants in the economy are motivated by self-interest and that the "invisible hand" of the marketplace guides this self-interest into promoting general economic well-being.

Many of Smith's insights remain at the center of modern economics. Our analysis in the coming chapters will allow us to express Smith's conclusions more precisely and to analyze fully the strengths and weaknesses of the market's invisible hand.

key to a market economy. Most important, markets work only if **property rights** are enforced. A farmer won't grow food if he expects his crop to be stolen; a restaurant won't serve meals unless it is assured that customers will pay before they leave; and a music company won't produce CDs if too many potential customers avoid paying by making illegal copies. We all rely on government-provided police and courts to enforce our rights over the things we produce—and the invisible hand counts on our ability to enforce our rights.

Yet there is another, more profound reason we need government: The invisible hand is powerful, but it is not omnipotent. Although markets are often a good way to organize economic activity, this rule has some important exceptions. There are two broad reasons for a government to intervene in the economy and change the allocation of resources that people would choose on their own: to promote efficiency and to promote equity. That is, most policies aim either to enlarge the economic pie or to change how the pie is divided.

Consider first the goal of efficiency. Although the invisible hand usually leads markets to allocate resources efficiently, this is not always the case. Economists use the term **market failure** to refer to a situation in which the market on its own fails to produce an efficient allocation of resources. One possible cause of market failure is an **externality,** which is the impact of one person's actions on the well-being of a bystander. The classic example of an externality is pollution. Another possible cause of market failure is **market power,** which refers to the ability of a single person (or small group) to unduly influence market prices. For example, if everyone in town needs water but there is only one well, the owner of the well is not subject to the rigorous competition with which the invisible hand normally keeps self-interest in check. In the presence of externalities or market power, well-designed public policy can enhance economic efficiency.

The invisible hand may also fail to ensure that economic prosperity is distributed equitably. A market economy rewards people according to their ability to produce things that other people are willing to pay for. The world's best basketball player earns more than the world's best chess player simply because people are willing to pay more to watch basketball than chess. The invisible hand does not ensure that everyone has sufficient food, decent clothing, and adequate healthcare. Many public policies, such as the income tax and the welfare system, aim to achieve a more equitable distribution of economic well-being.

To say that the government *can* improve on market outcomes at times does not mean that it always *will*. Public policy is made not by angels but by a political process that is far from perfect. Sometimes policies are designed simply to reward the politically powerful. Sometimes they are made by well-intentioned leaders who are not fully informed. As you study economics, you will become a better judge of when a government policy is justifiable because it promotes efficiency or equity and when it is not.

property rights
the ability of an individual to own and exercise control over scarce resources

market failure
a situation in which a market left on its own fails to allocate resources efficiently

externality
the impact of one person's actions on the well-being of a bystander

market power
the ability of a single economic actor (or small group of actors) to have a substantial influence on market prices

Quick Quiz   List and briefly explain the three principles concerning people's economic interactions.

HOW THE ECONOMY AS A WHOLE WORKS

We started by discussing how individuals make decisions and then looked at how people interact with one another. All these decisions and interactions together make up "the economy." The last three principles concern the workings of the economy as a whole.

Principle 8: A Country's Standard of Living Depends on Its Ability to Produce Goods and Services

The differences in living standards around the world are staggering. In 2003, the average American had an income of about $37,500. In the same year, the average Mexican earned $8,950, and the average Nigerian earned $900. Not surprisingly, this large variation in average income is reflected in various measures of the quality of life. Citizens of high-income countries have more TV sets, more cars, better nutrition, better healthcare, and a longer life expectancy than citizens of low-income countries.

Changes in living standards over time are also large. In the United States, incomes have historically grown about 2 percent per year (after adjusting for changes in the cost of living). At this rate, average income doubles every 35 years. Over the past century, average income has risen about eightfold.

productivity
the quantity of goods and services produced from each hour of a worker's time

What explains these large differences in living standards among countries and over time? The answer is surprisingly simple. Almost all variation in living standards is attributable to differences in countries' **productivity**—that is, the amount of goods and services produced from each hour of a worker's time. In nations where workers can produce a large quantity of goods and services per unit of time, most people enjoy a high standard of living; in nations where workers are less productive, most people endure a more meager existence. Similarly, the growth rate of a nation's productivity determines the growth rate of its average income.

The fundamental relationship between productivity and living standards is simple, but its implications are far-reaching. If productivity is the primary determinant of living standards, other explanations must be of secondary importance. For example, it might be tempting to credit labor unions or minimum-wage laws for the rise in living standards of American workers over the past century. Yet the real hero of American workers is their rising productivity. As another example, some commentators have claimed that increased competition from Japan and other countries explained the slow growth in U.S. incomes during the 1970s and 1980s. Yet the real villain was not competition from abroad but flagging productivity growth in the United States.

The relationship between productivity and living standards also has profound implications for public policy. When thinking about how any policy will affect living standards, the key question is how it will affect our ability to produce goods and services. To boost living standards, policymakers need to raise productivity by ensuring that workers are well educated, have the tools needed to produce goods and services, and have access to the best available technology.

Principle 9: Prices Rise When the Government Prints Too Much Money

inflation
an increase in the overall level of prices in the economy

In Germany in January 1921, a daily newspaper cost 0.30 marks. Less than 2 years later, in November 1922, the same newspaper cost 70,000,000 marks. All other prices in the economy rose by similar amounts. This episode is one of history's most spectacular examples of **inflation,** an increase in the overall level of prices in the economy.

Although the United States has never experienced inflation even close to that in Germany in the 1920s, inflation has at times been an economic problem. During the 1970s, for instance, the overall level of prices more than doubled, and President Gerald Ford called inflation "public enemy number one." By contrast, inflation in the 1990s was about 3 percent per year; at this rate, it would take more than 20 years for prices to double. Because high inflation imposes various costs on society, keeping inflation at a low level is a goal of economic policymakers around the world.

What causes inflation? In almost all cases of large or persistent inflation, the culprit is growth in the quantity of money. When a government creates large quantities of the nation's money, the value of the money falls. In Germany in the early 1920s, when prices were on average tripling every month, the quantity of money was also tripling every month. Although less dramatic, the economic history of the United States points to a similar conclusion: The high inflation of the 1970s was associated with rapid growth in the quantity of money, and the low inflation of the 1990s was associated with slow growth in the quantity of money.

"WELL IT MAY HAVE BEEN 68 CENTS WHEN YOU GOT IN LINE, BUT IT'S 74 CENTS NOW!"

Principle 10: Society Faces a Short-Run Trade-off between Inflation and Unemployment

Although a higher level of prices is, in the long run, the primary effect of increasing the quantity of money, the short-run story is more complex and more controversial. Most economists describe the short-run effects of monetary injections as follows:

- Increasing the amount of money in the economy stimulates the overall level of spending and thus the demand for goods and services.
- Higher demand may over time cause firms to raise their prices, but in the meantime, it also encourages them to increase the quantity of goods and services they produce and to hire more workers to produce those goods and services.
- More hiring means lower unemployment.

This line of reasoning leads to one final economywide trade-off: a short-run trade-off between inflation and unemployment.

Although some economists still question these ideas, most accept that society faces a short-run trade-off between inflation and unemployment. This simply means that, over a period of a year or two, many economic policies push inflation and unemployment in opposite directions. Policymakers face this trade-off regardless of whether inflation and unemployment both start out at high levels (as they were in the early 1980s), at low levels (as they were in the late 1990s), or someplace in between. This short-run trade-off plays a key role in the analysis of the **business cycle**—the irregular and largely unpredictable fluctuations in economic activity, as measured by the production of goods and services or the number of people employed.

Policymakers can exploit the short-run trade-off between inflation and unemployment using various policy instruments. By changing the amount that the government spends, the amount it taxes, and the amount of money it prints, policymakers can influence the combination of inflation and unemployment that the economy experiences. Because these instruments of economic policy are potentially so powerful, how policymakers should use these instruments to control the economy, if at all, is a subject of continuing debate.

business cycle
fluctuations in economic activity, such as employment and production

FYI

How to Read This Book

Economics is fun, but it can also be hard to learn. My aim in writing this text is to make it as fun and easy as possible. But you, the student, also have a role to play. Experience shows that if you are actively involved as you study this book, you will enjoy a better outcome both on your exams and in the years that follow. Here are a few tips about how best to read this book.

1. *Summarize, don't highlight.* Running a yellow marker over the text is too passive an activity to keep your mind engaged. Instead, when you come to the end of a section, take a minute and summarize what you just learned in your own words, writing your summary in the wide margins we've provided. When you've finished the chapter, compare your summaries with the one at the end of the chapter. Did you pick up the main points?

2. *Test yourself.* Throughout the book, Quick Quizzes offer instant feedback to find out if you've learned what you are supposed to. Take the opportunity to write down your answer and then check it against the answers provided in the back of the book. The quizzes are meant to test your basic comprehension. If your answer is incorrect, you probably need to review the section.

3. *Practice, practice, practice.* At the end of each chapter, Questions for Review test your understanding, and Problems and Applications ask you to apply and extend the material. Perhaps your instructor will assign some of these exercises as homework. If so, do them. If not, do them anyway. The more you use your new knowledge, the more solid it becomes.

4. *Go online.* The publisher of this book maintains an extensive website to help you in your study of economics. It includes additional examples, applications, and problems, as well as quizzes so you can test yourself. Check it out. The website is http://mankiw.swlearning.com.

5. *Study in groups.* After you've read the book and worked problems on your own, get together with classmates to discuss the material. You will learn from each other—an example of the gains from trade.

6. *Don't forget the real world.* In the midst of all the numbers, graphs, and strange new words, it is easy to lose sight of what economics is all about. The Case Studies and In the News boxes sprinkled throughout this book should help remind you. Don't skip them. They show how the theory is tied to events happening in all of our lives. If your study is successful, you won't be able to read a newspaper again without thinking about supply, demand, and the wonderful world of economics.

Quick Quiz List and briefly explain the three principles that describe how the economy as a whole works.

CONCLUSION

You now have a taste of what economics is all about. In the coming chapters, we will develop many specific insights about people, markets, and economies. Mastering these insights will take some effort, but it is not an overwhelming task. The field of economics is based on a few basic ideas that can be applied in many different situations.

Throughout this book, we will refer back to the *Ten Principles of Economics* highlighted in this chapter and summarized in Table 1. Whenever we do so, an icon will be displayed in the margin, as it is now. But even when that icon is absent, you should keep these building blocks in mind. Even the most sophisticated economic analysis is built using the ten principles introduced here.

TABLE 1

Ten Principles of Economics

How People Make Decisions
1: People Face Trade-offs
2: The Cost of Something Is What You Give Up to Get It
3: Rational People Think at the Margin
4: People Respond to Incentives

How People Interact
5: Trade Can Make Everyone Better Off
6: Markets Are Usually a Good Way to Organize Economic Activity
7: Governments Can Sometimes Improve Market Outcomes

How the Economy as a Whole Works
8: A Country's Standard of Living Depends on Its Ability to Produce Goods and Services
9: Prices Rise When the Government Prints Too Much Money
10: Society Faces a Short-Run Trade-off between Inflation and Unemployment

SUMMARY

- The fundamental lessons about individual decision making are that people face trade-offs among alternative goals, that the cost of any action is measured in terms of forgone opportunities, that rational people make decisions by comparing marginal costs and marginal benefits, and that people change their behavior in response to the incentives they face.

- The fundamental lessons about interactions among people are that trade can be mutually beneficial, that markets are usually a good way of coordi-

nating trade among people, and that the government can potentially improve market outcomes if there is some market failure or if the market outcome is inequitable.

- The fundamental lessons about the economy as a whole are that productivity is the ultimate source of living standards, that money growth is the ultimate source of inflation, and that society faces a short-run trade-off between inflation and unemployment.

KEY CONCEPTS

scarcity, p. 3
economics, p. 4
efficiency, p. 5
equity, p. 5
opportunity cost, p. 6
rational people, p. 6

marginal changes, p. 6
incentive, p. 7
market economy, p. 9
property rights, p. 11
market failure, p. 11
externality, p. 11

market power, p. 11
productivity, p. 12
inflation, p. 12
business cycle, p. 13

QUESTIONS FOR REVIEW

1. Give three examples of important trade-offs that you face in your life.

2. What is the opportunity cost of seeing a movie?

3. Water is necessary for life. Is the marginal benefit of a glass of water large or small?

4. Why should policymakers think about incentives?

5. Why isn't trade among countries like a game with some winners and some losers?

6. What does the "invisible hand" of the marketplace do?

7. Explain the two main causes of market failure and give an example of each.

8. Why is productivity important?

9. What is inflation and what causes it?

10. How are inflation and unemployment related in the short run?

PROBLEMS AND APPLICATIONS

1. Describe some of the trade-offs faced by each of the following:
   a. a family deciding whether to buy a new car
   b. a member of Congress deciding how much to spend on national parks
   c. a company president deciding whether to open a new factory
   d. a professor deciding how much to prepare for class

2. You are trying to decide whether to take a vacation. Most of the costs of the vacation (airfare, hotel, and forgone wages) are measured in dollars, but the benefits of the vacation are psychological. How can you compare the benefits to the costs?

3. You were planning to spend Saturday working at your part-time job, but a friend asks you to go skiing. What is the true cost of going skiing? Now suppose you had been planning to spend the day studying at the library. What is the cost of going skiing in this case? Explain.

4. You win $100 in a basketball pool. You have a choice between spending the money now or putting it away for a year in a bank account that pays 5 percent interest. What is the opportunity cost of spending the $100 now?

5. The company that you manage has invested $5 million in developing a new product, but the development is not quite finished. At a recent meeting, your salespeople report that the introduction of competing products has reduced the expected sales of your new product to $3 million. If it would cost $1 million to finish development and make the product, should you go ahead and do so? What is the most that you should pay to complete development?

6. Three managers of the Magic Potion Company are discussing a possible increase in production. Each suggests a way to make this decision.

   HARRY: We should examine whether our company's productivity—gallons of potion per worker—would rise or fall.

   RON: We should examine whether our average cost—cost per worker—would rise or fall.

   HERMIONE: We should examine whether the extra revenue from selling the additional potion would be greater or smaller than the extra costs.

   Who do you think is right? Why?

7. The Social Security system provides income for people over age 65. If a recipient of Social Security decides to work and earn some income, the amount he or she receives in Social Security benefits is typically reduced.
   a. How does the provision of Social Security affect people's incentive to save while working?
   b. How does the reduction in benefits associated with higher earnings affect people's incentive to work past age 65?

8. A recent bill reforming the government's anti-poverty programs limited many welfare recipients to only 2 years of benefits.
   a. How does this change affect the incentives for working?
   b. How might this change represent a trade-off between equity and efficiency?

9. Your roommate is a better cook than you are, but you can clean more quickly than your roommate can. If your roommate did all of the cooking and you did all of the cleaning, would your chores take you more or less time than if you divided each task evenly? Give a similar example of how specialization and trade can make two countries both better off.

10. Suppose the United States adopted central planning for its economy, and you became the chief planner. Among the millions of decisions that you need to make for next year are how many compact discs to produce, what artists to record, and who should receive the discs.
    a. To make these decisions intelligently, what information would you need about the compact disc industry? What information would you need about each of the people in the United States?
    b. How would your decisions about CDs affect some of your other decisions, such as how many CD players to make or cassette tapes to produce? How might some of your other decisions about the economy change your views about CDs?

11. Nations with corrupt police and court systems typically have lower standards of living than nations with less corruption. Why might that be the case?

12. Explain whether each of the following government activities is motivated by a concern about equity or a concern about efficiency. In the case of efficiency, discuss the type of market failure involved.
    a. regulating cable TV prices

    b. providing some poor people with vouchers that can be used to buy food
    c. prohibiting smoking in public places
    d. breaking up Standard Oil (which once owned 90 percent of all oil refineries) into several smaller companies
    e. imposing higher personal income tax rates on people with higher incomes
    f. instituting laws against driving while intoxicated

13. Discuss each of the following statements from the standpoints of equity and efficiency.
    a. "Everyone in society should be guaranteed the best healthcare possible."
    b. "When workers are laid off, they should be able to collect unemployment benefits until they find a new job."

14. In what ways is your standard of living different from that of your parents or grandparents when they were your age? Why have these changes occurred?

15. Suppose Americans decide to save more of their incomes. If banks lend this extra saving to businesses, which use the funds to build new factories, how might this lead to faster growth in productivity? Who do you suppose benefits from the higher productivity? Is society getting a free lunch?

16. Imagine that you are a policymaker trying to decide whether to reduce the rate of inflation. To make an intelligent decision, what would you need to know about inflation, unemployment, and the trade-off between them?

17. Look at a newspaper or at the website http://www.economist.com to find three stories about the economy that have been in the news lately. For each story, identify one (or more) of the *Ten Principles of Economics* discussed in this chapter that is relevant and explain how it is relevant. Also, for each story, look through this book's Contents and try to find a chapter that might shed light on the news event.

 For further information on topics in this chapter, additional problems, applications, examples, online quizzes, and more, please visit our website at http://mankiw.swlearning.com.

Thinking Like an Economist

Every field of study has its own language and its own way of thinking. Mathematicians talk about axioms, integrals, and vector spaces. Psychologists talk about ego, id, and cognitive dissonance. Lawyers talk about venue, torts, and promissory estoppel.

Economics is no different. Supply, demand, elasticity, comparative advantage, consumer surplus, deadweight loss—these terms are part of the economist's language. In the coming chapters, you will encounter many new terms and some familiar words that economists use in specialized ways. At first, this new language may seem needlessly arcane. But as you will see, its value lies in its ability to provide you with a new and useful way of thinking about the world in which you live.

The single most important purpose of this book is to help you learn the economist's way of thinking. Of course, just as you cannot become a mathematician, psychologist, or lawyer overnight, learning to think like an economist will take some time. Yet with a combination of theory, case studies, and examples of economics in the news, this book will give you ample opportunity to develop and practice this skill.

Before delving into the substance and details of economics, it is helpful to have an overview of how economists approach the world. This chapter discusses the field's methodology. What is distinctive about how economists confront a question? What does it mean to think like an economist?

THE ECONOMIST AS SCIENTIST

"I'M A SOCIAL SCIENTIST, MICHAEL. THAT MEANS I CAN'T EXPLAIN ELECTRICITY OR ANYTHING LIKE THAT, BUT IF YOU EVER WANT TO KNOW ABOUT PEOPLE, I'M YOUR MAN."

Economists try to address their subject with a scientist's objectivity. They approach the study of the economy in much the same way as a physicist approaches the study of matter and a biologist approaches the study of life: They devise theories, collect data, and then analyze these data in an attempt to verify or refute their theories.

To beginners, it can seem odd to claim that economics is a science. After all, economists do not work with test tubes or telescopes. The essence of science, however, is the *scientific method*—the dispassionate development and testing of theories about how the world works. This method of inquiry is as applicable to studying a nation's economy as it is to studying the earth's gravity or a species' evolution. As Albert Einstein once put it, "The whole of science is nothing more than the refinement of everyday thinking."

Although Einstein's comment is as true for social sciences such as economics as it is for natural sciences such as physics, most people are not accustomed to looking at society through the eyes of a scientist. Let's discuss some of the ways in which economists apply the logic of science to examine how an economy works.

The Scientific Method: Observation, Theory, and More Observation

Isaac Newton, the famous 17th-century scientist and mathematician, allegedly became intrigued one day when he saw an apple fall from a tree. This observation motivated Newton to develop a theory of gravity that applies not only to an apple falling to the earth but to any two objects in the universe. Subsequent testing of Newton's theory has shown that it works well in many circumstances (although, as Einstein would later emphasize, not in all circumstances). Because Newton's theory has been so successful at explaining observation, it is still taught today in undergraduate physics courses around the world.

This interplay between theory and observation also occurs in the field of economics. An economist might live in a country experiencing rapid increases in prices and be moved by this observation to develop a theory of inflation. The theory might assert that high inflation arises when the government prints too much money. (As you may recall, this was one of the *Ten Principles of Economics* in Chapter 1.) To test this theory, the economist could collect and analyze data on prices and money from many different countries. If growth in the quantity of money were not at all related to the rate at which prices are rising, the economist would start to doubt the validity of this theory of inflation. If money growth and inflation were strongly correlated in international data, as in fact they are, the economist would become more confident in the theory.

Although economists use theory and observation like other scientists, they do face an obstacle that makes their task especially challenging: Experiments are often difficult in economics. Physicists studying gravity can drop many objects in their laboratories to generate data to test their theories. By contrast, economists studying inflation are not allowed to manipulate a nation's monetary policy simply to generate useful data. Economists, like astronomers and evolutionary biologists, usually have to make do with whatever data the world happens to give them.

To find a substitute for laboratory experiments, economists pay close attention to the natural experiments offered by history. When a war in the Middle East interrupts the flow of crude oil, for instance, oil prices skyrocket around the world. For consumers of oil and oil products, such an event depresses living standards. For economic policymakers, it poses a difficult choice about how best to respond. But for economic scientists, the event provides an opportunity to study the effects of a key natural resource on the world's economies, and this opportunity persists long after the wartime increase in oil prices is over. Throughout this book, therefore, we consider many historical episodes. These episodes are valuable to study because they give us insight into the economy of the past and, more important, because they allow us to illustrate and evaluate economic theories of the present.

The Role of Assumptions

If you ask a physicist how long it would take for a marble to fall from the top of a ten-story building, she will answer the question by assuming that the marble falls in a vacuum. Of course, this assumption is false. In fact, the building is surrounded by air, which exerts friction on the falling marble and slows it down. Yet the physicist will correctly point out that friction on the marble is so small that its effect is negligible. Assuming the marble falls in a vacuum greatly simplifies the problem without substantially affecting the answer.

Economists make assumptions for the same reason: Assumptions can simplify the complex world and make it easier to understand. To study the effects of international trade, for example, we may assume that the world consists of only two countries and that each country produces only two goods. Of course, the real world consists of dozens of countries, each of which produces thousands of different types of goods. But by assuming two countries and two goods, we can focus our thinking on the essence of the problem. Once we understand international trade in an imaginary world with two countries and two goods, we are in a better position to understand international trade in the more complex world in which we live.

The art in scientific thinking—whether in physics, biology, or economics—is deciding which assumptions to make. Suppose, for instance, that we were dropping a beachball rather than a marble from the top of the building. Our physicist would realize that the assumption of no friction is far less accurate in this case: Friction exerts a greater force on a beachball than on a marble because a beachball is much larger. The assumption that gravity works in a vacuum is reasonable for studying a falling marble but not for studying a falling beachball.

Similarly, economists use different assumptions to answer different questions. Suppose that we want to study what happens to the economy when the government changes the number of dollars in circulation. An important piece of this analysis, it turns out, is how prices respond. Many prices in the economy change infrequently; the newsstand prices of magazines, for instance, change only every few years. Knowing this fact may lead us to make different assumptions when studying the effects of the policy change over different time horizons. For studying the short-run effects of the policy, we may assume that prices do not change much. We may even make the extreme and artificial assumption that all prices are completely fixed. For studying the long-run effects of the policy, however, we may assume that all prices are completely flexible. Just as a physicist uses different assumptions when studying falling marbles and falling beachballs, economists use different assumptions when studying the short-run and long-run effects of a change in the quantity of money.

Economic Models

High school biology teachers teach basic anatomy with plastic replicas of the human body. These models have all the major organs: the heart, the liver, the kidneys, and so on. The models allow teachers to show their students in a simple way how the important parts of the body fit together. Of course, no one would mistake these plastic models for a real person. These models are stylized, and they omit many details. Yet despite this lack of realism—indeed, because of this lack of realism—studying these models is useful for learning how the human body works.

Economists also use models to learn about the world, but instead of being made of plastic, they are most often composed of diagrams and equations. Like a biology teacher's plastic model, economic models omit many details to allow us to see what is truly important. Just as the biology teacher's model does not include all of the body's muscles and capillaries, an economist's model does not include every feature of the economy.

As we use models to examine various economic issues throughout this book, you will see that all the models are built with assumptions. Just as a physicist begins the analysis of a falling marble by assuming away the existence of friction, economists assume away many of the details of the economy that are irrelevant for studying the question at hand. All models—in physics, biology, and economics—simplify reality to improve our understanding of it.

Our First Model: The Circular-Flow Diagram

The economy consists of millions of people engaged in many activities—buying, selling, working, hiring, manufacturing, and so on. To understand how the economy works, we must find some way to simplify our thinking about all these activities. In other words, we need a model that explains, in general terms, how the economy is organized and how participants in the economy interact with one another.

circular-flow diagram
a visual model of the economy that shows how dollars flow through markets among households and firms

Figure 1 presents a visual model of the economy called a **circular-flow diagram.** In this model, the economy is simplified to include only two types of decision makers—firms and households. Firms produce goods and services using inputs, such as labor, land, and capital (buildings and machines). These inputs are called the *factors of production*. Households own the factors of production and consume all the goods and services that the firms produce.

Households and firms interact in two types of markets. In the *markets for goods and services*, households are buyers, and firms are sellers. In particular, households buy the output of goods and services that firms produce. In the *markets for the factors of production*, households are sellers, and firms are buyers. In these markets, households provide the inputs that firms use to produce goods and services. The circular-flow diagram offers a simple way of organizing all the economic transactions that occur between households and firms in the economy.

The inner loop of the circular-flow diagram represents the flows of inputs and outputs. The households sell the use of their labor, land, and capital to the firms in the markets for the factors of production. The firms then use these factors to produce goods and services, which in turn are sold to households in the markets for goods and services. Hence, the factors of production flow from households to firms, and goods and services flow from firms to households.

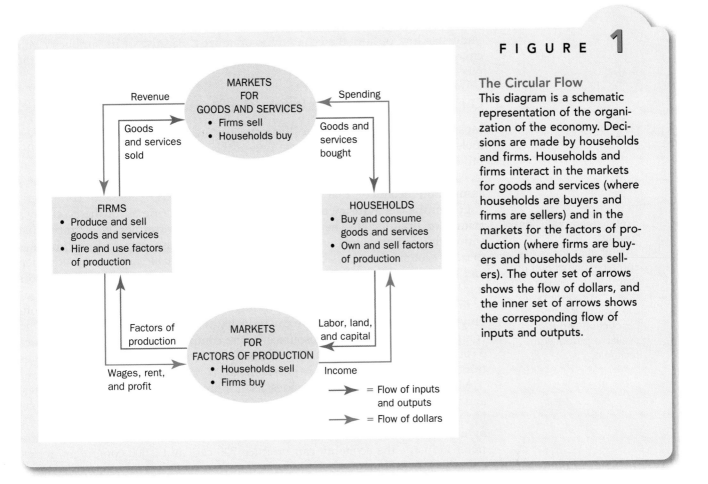

FIGURE 1

The Circular Flow
This diagram is a schematic representation of the organization of the economy. Decisions are made by households and firms. Households and firms interact in the markets for goods and services (where households are buyers and firms are sellers) and in the markets for the factors of production (where firms are buyers and households are sellers). The outer set of arrows shows the flow of dollars, and the inner set of arrows shows the corresponding flow of inputs and outputs.

The outer loop of the circular-flow diagram represents the corresponding flow of dollars. The households spend money to buy goods and services from the firms. The firms use some of the revenue from these sales to pay for the factors of production, such as the wages of their workers. What's left is the profit of the firm owners, who themselves are members of households. Hence, spending on goods and services flows from households to firms, and income in the form of wages, rent, and profit flows from firms to households.

Let's take a tour of the circular flow by following a dollar bill as it makes its way from person to person through the economy. Imagine that the dollar begins at a household, say, in your wallet. If you want to buy a cup of coffee, you take the dollar to one of the economy's markets for goods and services, such as your local Starbucks coffee shop. There you spend it on your favorite drink. When the dollar moves into the Starbucks cash register, it becomes revenue for the firm. The dollar doesn't stay at Starbucks for long, however, because the firm uses it to buy inputs in the markets for the factors of production. For instance, Starbucks might use the dollar to pay rent to its landlord for the space it occupies or to pay the wages of its workers. In either case, the dollar enters the income of some household and, once again, is back in someone's wallet. At that point, the story of the economy's circular flow starts once again.

The circular-flow diagram in Figure 1 is one simple model of the economy. It dispenses with details that, for some purposes, are significant. A more complex and realistic circular-flow model would include, for instance, the roles of government and international trade. Yet these details are not crucial for a basic understanding of how the economy is organized. Because of its simplicity, this circular-flow diagram is useful to keep in mind when thinking about how the pieces of the economy fit together.

Our Second Model: The Production Possibilities Frontier

Most economic models, unlike the circular-flow diagram, are built using the tools of mathematics. Here we use one of the simplest such models, called the production possibilities frontier, to illustrate some basic economic ideas.

Although real economies produce thousands of goods and services, let's assume an economy that produces only two goods—cars and computers. Together, the car industry and the computer industry use all of the economy's factors of production. The **production possibilities frontier** is a graph that shows the various combinations of output—in this case, cars and computers—that the economy can possibly produce given the available factors of production and the available production technology that firms can use to turn these factors into output.

Figure 2 shows this economy's production possibilities frontier. If the economy uses all its resources in the car industry, it can produce 1,000 cars and no computers. If it uses all its resources in the computer industry, it can produce 3,000 computers and no cars. The two endpoints of the production possibilities frontier represent these extreme possibilities.

More likely, the economy divides its resources between the two industries, and this yields other points on the production possibilities frontier. For example, it can produce 600 cars and 2,200 computers, shown in the figure by point A. Or by moving some of the factors of production to the car industry from the computer industry, the economy can produce 700 cars and 2,000 computers, represented by point B.

production possibilities frontier
a graph that shows the combinations of output that the economy can possibly produce given the available factors of production and the available production technology

2 FIGURE

The Production Possibilities Frontier
The production possibilities frontier shows the combinations of output—in this case, cars and computers—that the economy can possibly produce. The economy can produce any combination on or inside the frontier. Points outside the frontier are not feasible given the economy's resources.

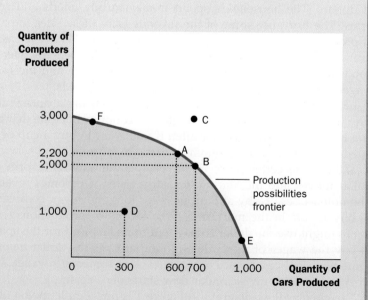

Because resources are scarce, not every conceivable outcome is feasible. For example, no matter how resources are allocated between the two industries, the economy cannot produce the amount of cars and computers represented by point C. Given the technology available for manufacturing cars and computers, the economy simply does not have enough of the factors of production to support that level of output. With the resources it has, the economy can produce at any point on or inside the production possibilities frontier, but it cannot produce at points outside the frontier.

An outcome is said to be *efficient* if the economy is getting all it can from the scarce resources it has available. Points on (rather than inside) the production possibilities frontier represent efficient levels of production. When the economy is producing at such a point, say point A, there is no way to produce more of one good without producing less of the other. Point D represents an *inefficient* outcome. For some reason, perhaps widespread unemployment, the economy is producing less than it could from the resources it has available: It is producing only 300 cars and 1,000 computers. If the source of the inefficiency is eliminated, the economy can increase its production of both goods. For example, if the economy moves from point D to point A, its production of cars increases from 300 to 600, and its production of computers increases from 1,000 to 2,200.

One of the *Ten Principles of Economics* discussed in Chapter 1 is that people face trade-offs. The production possibilities frontier shows one trade-off that society faces. Once we have reached the efficient points on the frontier, the only way of getting more of one good is to get less of the other. When the economy moves from point A to point B, for instance, society produces 100 more cars but at the expense of producing 200 fewer computers.

This trade-off helps us understand another of the *Ten Principles of Economics:* The cost of something is what you give up to get it. This is called the *opportunity cost.* The production possibilities frontier shows the opportunity cost of one good as measured in terms of the other good. When society moves from point A to point B, it gives up 200 computers to get 100 additional cars. That is, at point A, the opportunity cost of 100 cars is 200 computers. Put another way, the opportunity cost of each car is two computers. Notice that the opportunity cost of a car equals the slope of the production possibilities frontier. (If you don't recall what slope is, you can refresh your memory with the graphing appendix to this chapter.)

The opportunity cost of a car in terms of the number of computers is not a constant in this economy but depends on how many cars and computers the economy is producing. This is reflected in the shape of the production possibilities frontier. Because the production possibilities frontier in Figure 2 is bowed outward, the opportunity cost of a car is highest when the economy is producing many cars and fewer computers, such as at point E, where the frontier is steep. When the economy is producing few cars and many computers, such as at point F, the frontier is flatter, and the opportunity cost of a car is lower.

Economists believe that production possibilities frontiers often have this bowed shape. When the economy is using most of its resources to make computers, such as at point F, the resources best suited to car production, such as skilled autoworkers, are being used in the computer industry. Because these workers probably aren't very good at making computers, the economy won't have to lose much computer production to increase car production by one unit. The opportunity cost of a car in terms of computers is small, and the frontier is relatively flat. By contrast, when the economy is using most of its resources to make cars, such as at point E, the resources best suited to making cars are already in the car industry. Producing an additional car means moving some of the best computer technicians out of the computer industry and making them autoworkers. As a result, producing an additional car will mean a substantial loss of computer output. The opportunity cost of a car is high, and the frontier is quite steep.

The production possibilities frontier shows the trade-off between the outputs of different goods at a given time, but the trade-off can change over time. For example, suppose a technological advance in the computer industry raises the number of computers that a worker can produce per week. This advance expands society's set of opportunities. For any given number of cars, the economy can make more computers. If the economy does not produce any computers, it can still produce 1,000 cars, so one endpoint of the frontier stays the same. But the rest of the production possibilities frontier shifts outward, as in Figure 3.

This figure illustrates economic growth. Society can move production from a point on the old frontier to a point on the new frontier. Which point it chooses depends on its preferences for the two goods. In this example, society moves from point A to point G, enjoying more computers (2,300 instead of 2,200) and more cars (650 instead of 600).

The production possibilities frontier simplifies a complex economy to highlight some basic but powerful ideas: scarcity, efficiency, trade-offs, opportunity cost, and economic growth. As you study economics, these ideas will recur in various forms. The production possibilities frontier offers one simple way of thinking about them.

Microeconomics and Macroeconomics

Many subjects are studied on various levels. Consider biology, for example. Molecular biologists study the chemical compounds that make up living things. Cellular biologists study cells, which are made up of many chemical compounds

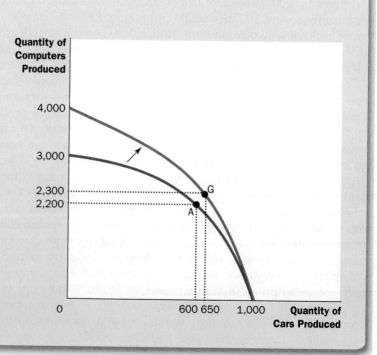

3 FIGURE

A Shift in the Production Possibilities Frontier
A technological advance in the computer industry enables the economy to produce more computers for any given number of cars. As a result, the production possibilities frontier shifts outward. If the economy moves from point A to point G, then the production of both cars and computers increases.

and, at the same time, are themselves the building blocks of living organisms. Evolutionary biologists study the many varieties of animals and plants and how species change gradually over the centuries.

Economics is also studied on various levels. We can study the decisions of individual households and firms. Or we can study the interaction of households and firms in markets for specific goods and services. Or we can study the operation of the economy as a whole, which is the sum of the activities of all these decision makers in all these markets.

The field of economics is traditionally divided into two broad subfields. **Microeconomics** is the study of how households and firms make decisions and how they interact in specific markets. **Macroeconomics** is the study of economy-wide phenomena. A microeconomist might study the effects of rent control on housing in New York City, the impact of foreign competition on the U.S. auto industry, or the effects of compulsory school attendance on workers' earnings. A macroeconomist might study the effects of borrowing by the federal government,

microeconomics
the study of how households and firms make decisions and how they interact in markets

macroeconomics
the study of economy-wide phenomena, including inflation, unemployment, and economic growth

FYI

Who Studies Economics?

As a college student, you might be asking yourself: How many economics classes should I take? How useful will this stuff be to me later in life? Economics can seem abstract at first, but the field is fundamentally very practical, and the study of economics is useful in many different career paths. Here is a small sampling of some well-known people who majored in economics when they were in college.

Meg Witman	Chief Executive Officer, Ebay
Ronald Reagan	Former President of the United States
William F. Buckley	Journalist
Danny Glover	Actor
Barbara Boxer	U.S. Senator
John Elway	NFL Quarterback
Ted Turner	Founder of CNN and Owner of Atlanta Braves
Kofi Annan	Secretary General, United Nations
Lionel Richie	Singer
Michael Kinsley	Journalist
Ben Stein	Political Speechwriter, Actor, and Game Show Host
Cate Blanchett	Actor
Anthony Zinni	General, U.S. Marine Corps

Tiger Woods	Golfer
Steve Ballmer	Chief Executive Officer, Microsoft
Arnold Schwarzenegger	Governor of California
Sandra Day-O'Connor	Former Supreme Court Justice
Mick Jagger	Singer for The Rolling Stones

Having studied at the London School of Economics may not help Mick Jagger hit the high notes, but it has probably given him some insight about how to invest the substantial sums he has earned during his rock-'n'-roll career.

When asked in 2005 why The Rolling Stones were going on tour again, former economics major Mick Jagger replied, "Supply and demand." Keith Richards added, "If the demand's there, we'll supply."

the changes over time in the economy's rate of unemployment, or alternative policies to raise growth in national living standards.

Microeconomics and macroeconomics are closely intertwined. Because changes in the overall economy arise from the decisions of millions of individuals, it is impossible to understand macroeconomic developments without considering the associated microeconomic decisions. For example, a macroeconomist might study the effect of a cut in the federal income tax on the overall production of goods and services. To analyze this issue, he or she must consider how the tax cut affects the decisions of households about how much to spend on goods and services.

Despite the inherent link between microeconomics and macroeconomics, the two fields are distinct. Because they address different questions, each field has its own set of models, which are often taught in separate courses.

Quick Quiz   In what sense is economics like a science?   •   Draw a production possibilities frontier for a society that produces food and clothing. Show an efficient point, an inefficient point, and an infeasible point. Show the effects of a drought.   •   Define microeconomics and macroeconomics.

THE ECONOMIST AS POLICY ADVISER

Often, economists are asked to explain the causes of economic events. Why, for example, is unemployment higher for teenagers than for older workers? Sometimes economists are asked to recommend policies to improve economic outcomes. What, for instance, should the government do to improve the economic well-being of teenagers? When economists are trying to explain the world, they are scientists. When they are trying to help improve it, they are policy advisers.

Positive versus Normative Analysis

To help clarify the two roles that economists play, we begin by examining the use of language. Because scientists and policy advisers have different goals, they use language in different ways.

For example, suppose that two people are discussing minimum-wage laws. Here are two statements you might hear:

POLLY: Minimum-wage laws cause unemployment.

NORMA: The government should raise the minimum wage.

Ignoring for now whether you agree with these statements, notice that Polly and Norma differ in what they are trying to do. Polly is speaking like a scientist: She is making a claim about how the world works. Norma is speaking like a policy adviser: She is making a claim about how she would like to change the world.

In general, statements about the world are of two types. One type, such as Polly's, is positive. **Positive statements** are descriptive. They make a claim about how the world *is*. A second type of statement, such as Norma's, is normative. **Normative statements** are prescriptive. They make a claim about how the world *ought to be*.

A key difference between positive and normative statements is how we judge their validity. We can, in principle, confirm or refute positive statements by examining evidence. An economist might evaluate Polly's statement by analyzing data on changes in minimum wages and changes in unemployment over

positive statements
claims that attempt to describe the world as it is

normative statements
claims that attempt to prescribe how the world should be

time. By contrast, evaluating normative statements involves values as well as facts. Norma's statement cannot be judged using data alone. Deciding what is good or bad policy is not merely a matter of science. It also involves our views on ethics, religion, and political philosophy.

Positive and normative statements are fundamentally different, but they are often closely intertwined in a person's set of beliefs. In particular, positive views about how the world works affect normative views about what policies are desirable. Polly's claim that the minimum wage causes unemployment, if true, might lead her to reject Norma's conclusion that the government should raise the minimum wage. Yet normative conclusions cannot come from positive analysis alone; they involve value judgments as well.

As you study economics, keep in mind the distinction between positive and normative statements because it will help you stay focused on the task at hand. Much of economics is positive: It just tries to explain how the economy works. Yet those who use economics often have goals that are normative: They want to learn how to improve the economy. When you hear economists making normative statements, you know they are speaking not as scientists but as policy advisers.

Economists in Washington

President Harry Truman once said that he wanted to find a one-armed economist. When he asked his economists for advice, they always answered, "On the one hand, . . . On the other hand, . . ."

Truman was right in realizing that economists' advice is not always straight-forward. This tendency is rooted in one of the *Ten Principles of Economics:* People face trade-offs. Economists are aware that trade-offs are involved in most policy decisions. A policy might increase efficiency at the cost of equity. It might help future generations but hurt current generations. An economist who says that all policy decisions are easy is an economist not to be trusted.

Truman was also not alone among presidents in relying on the advice of economists. Since 1946, the president of the United States has received guidance from the Council of Economic Advisers, which consists of three members and a staff of several dozen economists. The council, whose offices are just a few steps from the White House, has no duty other than to advise the president and to write the annual *Economic Report of the President,* which discusses recent developments in the economy and presents the council's analysis of current policy issues.

The president also receives input from economists in many administrative departments. Economists at the Department of the Treasury help design tax policy. Economists at the Department of Labor analyze data on workers and those looking for work to help formulate labor-market policies. Economists at the Department of Justice help enforce the nation's antitrust laws.

Economists are also found outside the administrative branch of government. To obtain independent evaluations of policy proposals, Congress relies on the advice of the Congressional Budget Office, which is staffed by economists. The Federal Reserve, the institution that sets the nation's monetary policy, employs hundreds of economists to analyze economic developments in the United States and throughout the world. Table 1 lists the websites of some of these agencies.

The influence of economists on policy goes beyond their role as advisers: Their research and writings often affect policy indirectly. Economist John Maynard Keynes offered this observation:

The ideas of economists and political philosophers, both when they are right and when they are wrong, are more powerful than is commonly understood.

"LET'S SWITCH. I'LL MAKE THE POLICY, YOU IMPLEMENT IT, AND HE'LL EXPLAIN IT."

In The News

Super Bowl Economics

Economists often offer advice to policymakers. Sometimes those policymakers are football coaches.

Incremental Analysis, with Two Yards to Go
By David Leonhardt

The academic paper that David Romer began writing two years ago did not look like something that could determine the outcome of a Super Bowl. Sure, it was an analysis of whether professional football teams punt more often than is rational, but it seemed intended mainly for the amusement of sports fans who happen to be professors.

Professor Romer, an economist at the University of California at Berkeley, used the phrases "Bellman equation" and "dynamic-programming analysis"—in the paper's title, no less. His footnotes cited work published in *Econometrica*, *Cognitive Science*, and other publications that are not exactly must-reads in N.F.L. locker rooms.

But when his conclusion—teams punt too much—began getting attention last summer, a reporter asked Bill Belichick, the coach of the New England

Patriots, about the paper. "I read it," he said, according to *The Boston Herald*. "I don't know much of the math involved, but I think I understand the conclusions and he has some valid points."

Upon hearing that, Professor Romer's jaw dropped, he said. His paper was available only on his Berkeley Internet site, emlab.berkeley.edu/users/dromer, and the site of a group called the National Bureau of Economic Research.

But the most interesting development was yet to come. Two weeks ago, facing a fourth down in the Patriots' own territory on the very first drive of the game—a sure punting situation in the N.F.L.—Belichick decided to go for a first down and made it. The Patriots soon scored a touchdown and were on their way to today's Super Bowl, against the Carolina Panthers.

Football analysts immediately called the decision an instance of a coach's instinct triumphing over cold analysis. In fact, Professor Romer said last week, Belichick seemed to be "throwing gut

instinct out the window and going on analysis." The information is right there in Figure 5 of the economist's paper: on fourth and 1 on your own 44-yard line, the potential benefit of keeping the drive going outweighs the cost of giving the opponents good field position.

The coach may not have been thinking about Professor Romer's paper at that moment, but he has clearly adopted the methods of a social scientist in a way that few other sports coaches have. Belichick, who majored in economics at Wesleyan University, approaches his job much the way a financial analyst pores over a balance sheet. He seems to view every decision as a chance to perform better cost–benefit analysis than his peers do. Richard Miller, a Wesleyan economist with whom the coach remains in touch, calls the approach "incremental analysis." In plain English, it involves looking for subtle differences in one small area that can affect an entire system, whether that system is a company, a stock market, or a football game.

Source: *The New York Times*, Week in Review, February 1, 2004, page 12.

Indeed, the world is ruled by little else. Practical men, who believe themselves to be quite exempt from intellectual influences, are usually the slaves of some defunct economist. Madmen in authority, who hear voices in the air, are distilling their frenzy from some academic scribbler of a few years back.

Although these words were written in 1935, they remain true today. Indeed, the "academic scribbler" now influencing public policy is often Keynes himself.

TABLE 1

Websites

Here are the websites for a few of the government agencies that are responsible for collecting economic data and making economic policy.

Department of Commerce	http://www.commerce.gov
Bureau of Labor Statistics	http://www.bls.gov
Congressional Budget Office	http://www.cbo.gov
Federal Reserve Board	http://www.federalreserve.gov

CASE STUDY | MR. MANKIW GOES TO WASHINGTON

The author of the textbook you are now reading is, I will readily admit, a typical, nerdy college professor, more comfortable in the world of dusty books than in the world of glad-handing politicians. But from 2003 to 2005, I had the opportunity to leave the ivory tower and become the chairman of Council of Economic Advisers. For two years, I was President Bush's chief economist.

As chair of the CEA, I met with the President about twice a week. Some of these meetings were briefings on the state of the economy; most were discussions of current issues in economic policy. I worked closely with other members of the White House staff to analyze policy options and brief the President on a wide range of topics, such as tax policy, the federal budget, Social Security, and international trade. I also met regularly with economic officials outside the White House, such as Secretary of the Treasury John Snow and Federal Reserve Chairman Alan Greenspan, and with leaders of the business community.

For anyone used to the measured pace and quiet reflection of university life, taking such a job is exhilarating. Sitting in the Oval Office, flying on *Air Force One,* and spending the weekend with the President at Camp David are unforgettable experiences. Testifying as the President's representative before congressional committees, which include members who are usually partisan and sometimes hostile, is also an experience a person does not easily forget—no matter how hard one might try.

During my two years in Washington, I learned a lot about the process by which economic policy is made. It differs in many ways from the idealized policy process assumed in economics textbooks.

Throughout this text, whenever we discuss economic policy, we often focus on one question: What is the best policy for the government to pursue? We act as if policy were set by a benevolent king. Once the king figures out the right policy, he has no trouble putting his ideas into action.

In the real world, figuring out the right policy is only part of a leader's job, sometimes the easiest part. After the President hears from his economic advisers about what policy is best from their perspective, he turns to other advisers for related input. His communications advisers will tell him how best to explain the proposed policy to the public, and they will try to anticipate any misunderstandings that might arise to make the challenge more difficult. His press advisers will tell him how the news media will report on his proposal and what opinions will likely be expressed on the nation's editorial pages. His legislative affairs advisers will tell him how Congress will view the proposal, what amendments members of Congress will suggest, and the likelihood that Congress will pass some version of the President's proposal into law. His political advisers will tell him which groups will organize to support or oppose the proposed policy, how this proposal will affect his standing among different groups in the electorate, and whether it will affect support for any of the President's other policy initiatives. After hearing and weighing all this advice, the President then decides how to proceed.

My two years in Washington were a vivid reminder of an important lesson: Making economic policy in a representative democracy is a messy affair—and there are often good reasons presidents (and other politicians) do not advance the policies that economists advocate. Economists offer crucial input into the policy process, but their advice is only one ingredient of a complex recipe.   •

Quick Quiz Give an example of a positive statement and an example of a normative statement. • Name three parts of government that regularly rely on advice from economists.

WHY ECONOMISTS DISAGREE

"If all economists were laid end to end, they would not reach a conclusion." This quip from George Bernard Shaw is revealing. Economists as a group are often criticized for giving conflicting advice to policymakers. President Ronald Reagan once joked that if the game Trivial Pursuit were designed for economists, it would have 100 questions and 3,000 answers.

Why do economists so often appear to give conflicting advice to policymakers? There are two basic reasons:

- Economists may disagree about the validity of alternative positive theories about how the world works.
- Economists may have different values and therefore different normative views about what policy should try to accomplish.

Let's discuss each of these reasons.

Differences in Scientific Judgments

Several centuries ago, astronomers debated whether the earth or the sun was at the center of the solar system. More recently, meteorologists have debated whether the earth is experiencing global warming and, if so, why. Science is a search for understanding about the world around us. It is not surprising that as the search continues, scientists can disagree about the direction in which truth lies.

Economists often disagree for the same reason. Economics is a young science, and there is still much to be learned. Economists sometimes disagree because they have different hunches about the validity of alternative theories or about the size of important parameters that measure how economic variables are related.

For example, economists disagree about whether the government should tax a household's income or its consumption (spending). Advocates of a switch from the current income tax to a consumption tax believe that the change would encourage households to save more because income that is saved would not be taxed. Higher saving, in turn, would lead to more rapid growth in productivity and living standards. Advocates of the current income tax system believe that household saving would not respond much to a change in the tax laws. These two groups of economists hold different normative views about the tax system because they have different positive views about the responsiveness of saving to tax incentives.

Differences in Values

Suppose that Peter and Paula both take the same amount of water from the town well. To pay for maintaining the well, the town taxes its residents. Peter has income of $50,000 and is taxed $5,000, or 10 percent of his income. Paula has income of $10,000 and is taxed $2,000, or 20 percent of her income.

Is this policy fair? If not, who pays too much and who pays too little? Does it matter whether Paula's low income is due to a medical disability or to her decision to pursue a career in acting? Does it matter whether Peter's high income is due to a large inheritance or to his willingness to work long hours at a dreary job?

These are difficult questions on which people are likely to disagree. If the town hired two experts to study how the town should tax its residents to pay for the well, we would not be surprised if they offered conflicting advice.

This simple example shows why economists sometimes disagree about public policy. As we learned earlier in our discussion of normative and positive analysis, policies cannot be judged on scientific grounds alone. Economists give conflicting advice sometimes because they have different values. Perfecting the science of economics will not tell us whether Peter or Paula pays too much.

Perception versus Reality

Because of differences in scientific judgments and differences in values, some disagreement among economists is inevitable. Yet one should not overstate the amount of disagreement. There are many cases in which economists agree.

Table 2 contains ten propositions about economic policy. In a survey of economists in business, government, and academia, these propositions were endorsed by an overwhelming majority of respondents. Most of these propositions would fail to command a similar consensus among the general public.

The first proposition in the table is about rent control, a policy that sets a legal maximum on the amount landlords can charge for their apartments. Almost all economists believe that rent control adversely affects the availability and quality of housing and is a very costly way of helping the neediest members of society. Nonetheless, many city governments choose to ignore the advice of economists and place ceilings on the rents that landlords may charge their tenants.

The second proposition in the table concerns tariffs and import quotas, two policies that restrict trade among nations. For reasons we will discuss more fully later in this text, almost all economists oppose such barriers to free trade. Nonetheless, over the years, presidents and Congress have chosen to restrict the import of certain goods. In 2002, for example, the Bush administration imposed temporary tariffs on steel to protect domestic steel producers from foreign competition. In this case, economists did offer united advice, but policymakers chose to ignore it.

Why do policies such as rent control and trade barriers persist if the experts are united in their opposition? The reason may be that economists have not yet convinced the general public that these policies are undesirable. One purpose of this book is to help you understand the economist's view of these and other subjects and, perhaps, to persuade you that it is the right one.

2 TABLE

Ten Propositions about Which Most Economists Agree

Proposition (and percentage of economists who agree)

1. A ceiling on rents reduces the quantity and quality of housing available. (93%)
2. Tariffs and import quotas usually reduce general economic welfare. (93%)
3. Flexible and floating exchange rates offer an effective international monetary arrangement. (90%)
4. Fiscal policy (e.g., tax cut and/or government expenditure increase) has a significant stimulative impact on a less than fully employed economy. (90%)
5. If the federal budget is to be balanced, it should be done over the business cycle rather than yearly. (85%)
6. Cash payments increase the welfare of recipients to a greater degree than do transfers-in-kind of equal cash value. (84%)
7. A large federal budget deficit has an adverse effect on the economy. (83%)
8. A minimum wage increases unemployment among young and unskilled workers. (79%)
9. The government should restructure the welfare system along the lines of a "negative income tax." (79%)
10. Effluent taxes and marketable pollution permits represent a better approach to pollution control than imposition of pollution ceilings. (78%)

Source: Richard M. Alston, J. R. Kearl, and Michael B. Vaughn, "Is There Consensus among Economists in the 1990s?" *American Economic Review* (May 1992): 203–209. Reprinted by permission.

Quick Quiz Why might economic advisers to the president disagree about a question of policy?

LET'S GET GOING

The first two chapters of this book have introduced you to the ideas and methods of economics. We are now ready to get to work. In the next chapter, we start learning in more detail the principles of economic behavior and economic policy.

As you proceed through this book, you will be asked to draw on many of your intellectual skills. You might find it helpful to keep in mind some advice from the great economist John Maynard Keynes:

> The study of economics does not seem to require any specialized gifts of an unusually high order. Is it not … a very easy subject compared with the higher branches of philosophy or pure science? An easy subject, at which very few excel! The paradox finds its explanation, perhaps, in that the master-economist must possess a rare *combination* of gifts. He must be mathematician, historian, statesman, philosopher—in some degree. He must understand symbols and speak in words. He must contemplate the particular in terms of the general, and touch abstract and concrete in the same flight of thought. He must study the present in the light of the past for the purposes of the future. No part of man's nature or his institutions must lie entirely outside his regard. He must be purposeful and disinterested in a simultaneous mood; as aloof and incorruptible as an artist, yet sometimes as near the earth as a politician.

It is a tall order. But with practice, you will become more and more accustomed to thinking like an economist.

In The News

Why You Should Study Economics

In this excerpt from a commencement address, the former president of the Federal Reserve Bank of Dallas makes the case for studying economics.

The Dismal Science? Hardly!

By Robert D. McTeer, Jr.

Weeks ago, I had lunch with the smartest woman in the world: Marilyn vos Savant, the "Ask Marilyn" columnist in *Parade* magazine.

According to the folks at the *Guinness Book*, Marilyn has the world's highest recorded I.Q. She is interested in economics education, of all things, and we met at a board meeting of the National Council on Economic Education. I told her I think economics is a good major for smart students, but if they are really, really smart, I'd rather they become doctors so they could do somebody some good. She said, "Yes, but doctors help people one at a time, while an Alan Greenspan can help millions of people at a time." She has a point. Mr. Greenspan is an excellent example of someone making a big difference by applying good economics.

My take on training in economics is that it becomes increasingly valuable as you move up the career ladder. I can't imagine a better major for corporate CEOs, congressmen, or American presidents. . . . Economics training will help you understand fallacies and unintended consequences. In fact, I am inclined to define economics as the study of how to anticipate unintended consequences. . . .

Little in the literature seems more relevant to contemporary economic debates than what usually is called the broken window fallacy. Whenever a government program is justified not on its merits but by the jobs it will create, remember the broken window: Some teenagers, being the little beasts that they are, toss a brick through a bakery window. A crowd gathers and laments, "What a shame." But before you know it, someone suggests a silver lining to the situation: Now the baker will have to spend money to have the window repaired. This will add to the income of the repairman, who will spend his additional income, which will add to another seller's income, and so on. You know the drill. The chain of spending will multiply and generate higher income and employment. If the broken window is large enough, it might produce an economic boom! . . .

Most voters fall for the broken window fallacy, but not economics majors. They will say, "Hey, wait a minute!" If the baker hadn't spent his money on window repair, he would have spent it on the new suit he was saving to buy. Then the tailor would have the new income to spend, and so on. The broken window didn't create net new spending; it just diverted spending from somewhere else. The broken window does not create new activity, just different activity. People see the activity that takes place. They don't see the activity that *would* have taken place.

The broken window fallacy is perpetuated in many forms. Whenever job creation or retention is the primary objective I call it the job-counting fallacy. Economics majors understand the nonintuitive reality that real progress comes from job destruction. It once took 90 percent of our population to grow our food. Now it takes 3 percent. Pardon me, Willie, but are we worse off because of the job losses in agriculture? The would-have-been farmers are now college professors and computer gurus. . . .

So instead of counting jobs, we should make every job count. We will occasionally hit a soft spot when we have a mismatch of supply and demand in the labor market. But that is temporary. Don't become a Luddite and destroy the machinery, or become a protectionist and try to grow bananas in New York City.

Source: *The Wall Street Journal*, June 4, 2003, p. A18. Copyright © 2003 by Robert D. McTeer, Jr.

SUMMARY

- Economists try to address their subject with a scientist's objectivity. Like all scientists, they make appropriate assumptions and build simplified models to understand the world around them. Two simple economic models are the circular-flow diagram and the production possibilities frontier.

- The field of economics is divided into two subfields: microeconomics and macroeconomics. Microeconomists study decision making by households and firms and the interaction among households and firms in the marketplace. Macroeconomists study the forces and trends that affect the economy as a whole.

- A positive statement is an assertion about how the world *is*. A normative statement is an assertion about how the world *ought to be*. When economists make normative statements, they are acting more as policy advisers than scientists.

- Economists who advise policymakers offer conflicting advice either because of differences in scientific judgments or because of differences in values. At other times, economists are united in the advice they offer, but policymakers may choose to ignore it.

KEY CONCEPTS

circular-flow diagram, p. 22
production possibilities frontier, p. 24

microeconomics, p. 27
macroeconomics, p. 27

positive statements, p. 28
normative statements, p. 28

QUESTIONS FOR REVIEW

1. How is economics like a science?
2. Why do economists make assumptions?
3. Should an economic model describe reality exactly?
4. Draw and explain a production possibilities frontier for an economy that produces milk and cookies. What happens to this frontier if disease kills half of the economy's cow population?
5. Use a production possibilities frontier to describe the idea of "efficiency."
6. What are the two subfields into which economics is divided? Explain what each subfield studies.
7. What is the difference between a positive and a normative statement? Give an example of each.
8. What is the Council of Economic Advisers?
9. Why do economists sometimes offer conflicting advice to policymakers?

PROBLEMS AND APPLICATIONS

1. Draw a circular-flow diagram. Identify the parts of the model that correspond to the flow of goods and services and the flow of dollars for each of the following activities.
   a. Selena pays a storekeeper $1 for a quart of milk.
   b. Stuart earns $4.50 per hour working at a fast-food restaurant.
   c. Shanna spends $7 to see a movie.
   d. Sally earns $10,000 from his 10 percent ownership of Acme Industrial.

2. Imagine a society that produces military goods and consumer goods, which we'll call "guns" and "butter."

   a. Draw a production possibilities frontier for guns and butter. Using the concept of opportunity cost, explain why it most likely has a bowed-out shape.

   b. Show a point that is impossible for the economy to achieve. Show a point that is feasible but inefficient.

   c. Imagine that the society has two political parties, called the Hawks (who want a strong military) and the Doves (who want a smaller military). Show a point on your production possibilities frontier that the Hawks might choose and a point the Doves might choose.

   d. Imagine that an aggressive neighboring country reduces the size of its military. As a result, both the Hawks and the Doves reduce their desired production of guns by the same amount. Which party would get the bigger "peace dividend," measured by the increase in butter production? Explain.

3. The first principle of economics discussed in Chapter 1 is that people face trade-offs. Use a production possibilities frontier to illustrate society's trade-off between two "goods"—a clean environment and the quantity of industrial output. What do you suppose determines the shape and position of the frontier? Show what happens to the frontier if engineers develop a new way of producing electricity that emits fewer pollutants.

4. An economy consists of three workers: Larry, Moe, and Curly. Each works 10 hours a day and can produce two services: mowing lawns and washing cars. In an hour, Larry can either mow one lawn or wash one car; Moe can either mow one lawn or wash two cars; and Curly can either mow two lawns or wash one car.

   a. Calculate how much of each service is produced under the following circumstances, which we label A, B, C, and D:

   • all three spend all their time mowing lawns (A)

   • all three spend all their time washing cars (B)

   • all three spend half their time on each activity (C)

   • Larry spends half his time on each activity, while Moe only washes cars and Curly only mows lawns (D)

   b. Graph the production possibilities frontier for this economy. Using your answers to part (a), identify points A, B, C, and D on your graph.

   c. Explain why the production possibilities frontier has the shape it does.

   d. Are any of the allocations calculated in part (a) inefficient? Explain.

5. Classify the following topics as relating to microeconomics or macroeconomics.

   a. a family's decision about how much income to save

   b. the effect of government regulations on auto emissions

   c. the impact of higher national saving on economic growth

   d. a firm's decision about how many workers to hire

   e. the relationship between the inflation rate and changes in the quantity of money

6. Classify each of the following statements as positive or normative. Explain.

   a. Society faces a short-run trade-off between inflation and unemployment.

   b. A reduction in the rate of growth of money will reduce the rate of inflation.

   c. The Federal Reserve should reduce the rate of growth of money.

   d. Society ought to require welfare recipients to look for jobs.

   e. Lower tax rates encourage more work and more saving.

7. Classify each of the statements in Table 2 as positive, normative, or ambiguous. Explain.

8. If you were president, would you be more interested in your economic advisers' positive views or their normative views? Why?

9. Find a recent copy of the *Economic Report of the President* at your library or on the Internet. Read a chapter about an issue that interests you. Summarize the economic problem at hand and describe the council's recommended policy.

10. Look up one of the websites listed in Table 1. What recent economic trends or issues are addressed there?

 For further information on topics in this chapter, additional problems, examples, applications, online quizzes, and more, please visit our website at http://mankiw.swlearning.com.

APPENDIX

GRAPHING: A BRIEF REVIEW

Many of the concepts that economists study can be expressed with numbers—the price of bananas, the quantity of bananas sold, the cost of growing bananas, and so on. Often, these economic variables are related to one another. When the price of bananas rises, people buy fewer bananas. One way of expressing the relationships among variables is with graphs.

Graphs serve two purposes. First, when developing economic theories, graphs offer a way to visually express ideas that might be less clear if described with equations or words. Second, when analyzing economic data, graphs provide a way of finding how variables are in fact related in the world. Whether we are working with theory or with data, graphs provide a lens through which a recognizable forest emerges from a multitude of trees.

Numerical information can be expressed graphically in many ways, just as a thought can be expressed in words in many ways. A good writer chooses words that will make an argument clear, a description pleasing, or a scene dramatic. An effective economist chooses the type of graph that best suits the purpose at hand.

In this appendix, we discuss how economists use graphs to study the mathematical relationships among variables. We also discuss some of the pitfalls that can arise in the use of graphical methods.

Graphs of a Single Variable

Three common graphs are shown in Figure A-1. The *pie chart* in panel (a) shows how total income in the United States is divided among the sources of income, including compensation of employees, corporate profits, and so on. A slice of the pie represents each source's share of the total. The *bar graph* in panel (b) compares

A-1 FIGURE

Types of Graphs

The pie chart in panel (a) shows how U.S. national income is derived from various sources. The bar graph in panel (b) compares the average income in four countries. The time-series graph in panel (c) shows the productivity of labor in U.S. businesses from 1950 to 2000.

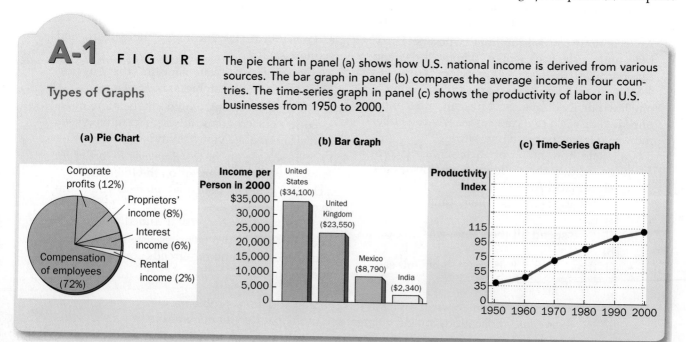

(a) Pie Chart

Corporate profits (12%)
Proprietors' income (8%)
Interest income (6%)
Rental income (2%)
Compensation of employees (72%)

(b) Bar Graph

Income per Person in 2000
United States ($34,100)
United Kingdom ($23,550)
Mexico ($8,790)
India ($2,340)
$35,000
30,000
25,000
20,000
15,000
10,000
5,000
0

(c) Time-Series Graph

Productivity Index
115
95
75
55
35
0
1950 1960 1970 1980 1990 2000

income for four countries. The height of each bar represents the average income in each country. The *time-series graph* in panel (c) traces the rising productivity in the U.S. business sector over time. The height of the line shows output per hour in each year. You have probably seen similar graphs in newspapers and magazines.

Graphs of Two Variables: The Coordinate System

Although the three graphs in Figure A-1 are useful in showing how a variable changes over time or across individuals, such graphs are limited in how much they can tell us. These graphs display information only on a single variable. Economists are often concerned with the relationships between variables. Thus, they need to display two variables on a single graph. The *coordinate system* makes this possible.

Suppose you want to examine the relationship between study time and grade point average. For each student in your class, you could record a pair of numbers: hours per week spent studying and grade point average. These numbers could then be placed in parentheses as an *ordered pair* and appear as a single point on the graph. Albert E., for instance, is represented by the ordered pair (25 hours/week, 3.5 GPA), while his "what-me-worry?" classmate Alfred E. is represented by the ordered pair (5 hours/week, 2.0 GPA).

We can graph these ordered pairs on a two-dimensional grid. The first number in each ordered pair, called the *x-coordinate*, tells us the horizontal location of the point. The second number, called the *y-coordinate*, tells us the vertical location of the point. The point with both an x-coordinate and a y-coordinate of zero is known as the *origin*. The two coordinates in the ordered pair tell us where the point is located in relation to the origin: x units to the right of the origin and y units above it.

Figure A-2 graphs grade point average against study time for Albert E., Alfred E., and their classmates. This type of graph is called a *scatterplot* because it plots scattered points. Looking at this graph, we immediately notice that

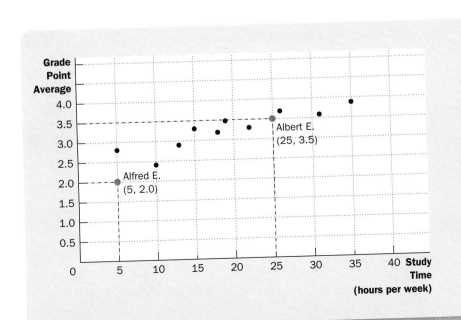

FIGURE **A-2**

Using the Coordinate System
Grade point average is measured on the vertical axis and study time on the horizontal axis. Albert E., Alfred E., and their classmates are represented by various points. We can see from the graph that students who study more tend to get higher grades.

points farther to the right (indicating more study time) also tend to be higher (indicating a better grade point average). Because study time and grade point average typically move in the same direction, we say that these two variables have a *positive correlation*. By contrast, if we were to graph party time and grades, we would likely find that higher party time is associated with lower grades; because these variables typically move in opposite directions, we call this a *negative correlation*. In either case, the coordinate system makes the correlation between the two variables easy to see.

Curves in the Coordinate System

Students who study more do tend to get higher grades, but other factors also influence a student's grade. Previous preparation is an important factor, for instance, as are talent, attention from teachers, even eating a good breakfast. A scatterplot like Figure A-2 does not attempt to isolate the effect that study has on grades from the effects of other variables. Often, however, economists prefer looking at how one variable affects another, holding everything else constant.

To see how this is done, let's consider one of the most important graphs in economics: the *demand curve*. The demand curve traces out the effect of a good's price on the quantity of the good consumers want to buy. Before showing a demand curve, however, consider Table A-1, which shows how the number of novels that Emma buys depends on her income and on the price of novels. When novels are cheap, Emma buys them in large quantities. As they become more expensive, she borrows books from the library instead of buying them or chooses to go to the movies instead of reading. Similarly, at any given price, Emma buys more novels when she has a higher income. That is, when her income increases, she spends part of the additional income on novels and part on other goods.

We now have three variables—the price of novels, income, and the number of novels purchased—which are more than we can represent in two dimensions. To put the information from Table A-1 in graphical form, we need to hold one of the three variables constant and trace out the relationship between the other two. Because the demand curve represents the relationship between price and quantity demanded, we hold Emma's income constant and show how the number of novels she buys varies with the price of novels.

A-1 TABLE

Novels Purchased by Emma
This table shows the number of novels Emma buys at various incomes and prices. For any given level of income, the data on price and quantity demanded can be graphed to produce Emma's demand curve for novels, as shown in Figures A-3 and A-4.

		Income		
Price	$20,000	$30,000	$40,000
$10	2 novels	5 novels	8 novels
9	6	9	12
8	10	13	16
7	14	17	20
6	18	21	24
5	22	25	28
	Demand curve, D_3	Demand curve, D_1	Demand curve, D_2

Suppose that Emma's income is $30,000 per year. If we place the number of novels Emma purchases on the *x*-axis and the price of novels on the *y*-axis, we can graphically represent the middle column of Table A-1. When the points that represent these entries from the table—(5 novels, $10), (9 novels, $9), and so on—are connected, they form a line. This line, pictured in Figure A-3, is known as Emma's demand curve for novels; it tells us how many novels Emma purchases at any given price. The demand curve is downward sloping, indicating that a higher price reduces the quantity of novels demanded. Because the quantity of novels demanded and the price move in opposite directions, we say that the two variables are *negatively related*. (Conversely, when two variables move in the same direction, the curve relating them is upward sloping, and we say the variables are *positively related*.)

Now suppose that Emma's income rises to $40,000 per year. At any given price, Emma will purchase more novels than she did at her previous level of income. Just as earlier we drew Emma's demand curve for novels using the entries from the middle column of Table A-1, we now draw a new demand curve using the entries from the right column of the table. This new demand curve (curve D_2) is pictured alongside the old one (curve D_1) in Figure A-4; the new curve is a similar line drawn farther to the right. We therefore say that Emma's demand curve for novels *shifts* to the right when her income increases. Likewise, if Emma's income were to fall to $20,000 per year, she would buy fewer novels at any given price and her demand curve would shift to the left (to curve D_3).

In economics, it is important to distinguish between *movements along a curve* and *shifts of a curve*. As we can see from Figure A-3, if Emma earns $30,000 per year and novels cost $8 apiece, she will purchase 13 novels per year. If the price

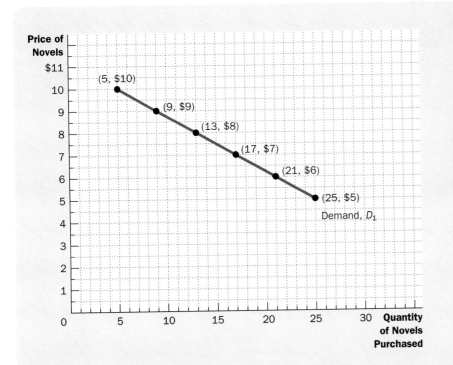

FIGURE **A-3**

Demand Curve
The line D_1 shows how Emma's purchases of novels depend on the price of novels when her income is held constant. Because the price and the quantity demanded are negatively related, the demand curve slopes downward.

of novels falls to $7, Emma will increase her purchases of novels to 17 per year. The demand curve, however, stays fixed in the same place. Emma still buys the same number of novels *at each price,* but as the price falls, she moves along her demand curve from left to right. By contrast, if the price of novels remains fixed at $8 but her income rises to $40,000, Emma increases her purchases of novels from 13 to 16 per year. Because Emma buys more novels *at each price,* her demand curve shifts out, as shown in Figure A-4.

There is a simple way to tell when it is necessary to shift a curve. When a variable that is not named on either axis changes, the curve shifts. Income is on neither the *x*-axis nor the *y*-axis of the graph, so when Emma's income changes, her demand curve must shift. Any change that affects Emma's purchasing habits besides a change in the price of novels will result in a shift in her demand curve. If, for instance, the public library closes and Emma must buy all the books she wants to read, she will demand more novels at each price, and her demand curve will shift to the right. Or if the price of movies falls and Emma spends more time at the movies and less time reading, she will demand fewer novels at each price, and her demand curve will shift to the left. By contrast, when a variable on an axis of the graph changes, the curve does not shift. We read the change as a movement along the curve.

Slope

One question we might want to ask about Emma is how much her purchasing habits respond to price. Look at the demand curve pictured in Figure A-5. If this curve is very steep, Emma purchases nearly the same number of novels regard-

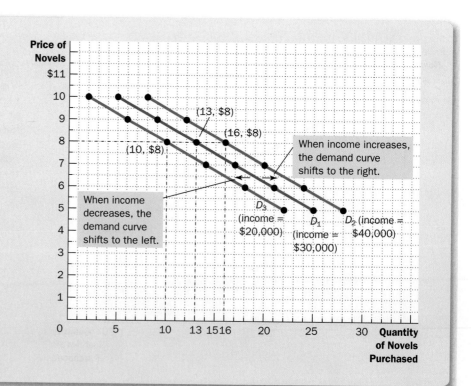

A-4 FIGURE

Shifting Demand Curves
The location of Emma's demand curve for novels depends on how much income she earns. The more she earns, the more novels she will purchase at any given price, and the farther to the right her demand curve will lie. Curve D_1 represents Emma's original demand curve when her income is $30,000 per year. If her income rises to $40,000 per year, her demand curve shifts to D_2. If her income falls to $20,000 per year, her demand curve shifts to D_3.

less of whether they are cheap or expensive. If this curve is much flatter, Emma purchases many fewer novels when the price rises. To answer questions about how much one variable responds to changes in another variable, we can use the concept of *slope*.

The slope of a line is the ratio of the vertical distance covered to the horizontal distance covered as we move along the line. This definition is usually written out in mathematical symbols as follows:

$$\text{slope} = \frac{\Delta y}{\Delta x},$$

where the Greek letter Δ (delta) stands for the change in a variable. In other words, the slope of a line is equal to the "rise" (change in y) divided by the "run" (change in x). The slope will be a small positive number for a fairly flat upward-sloping line, a large positive number for a steep upward-sloping line, and a negative number for a downward-sloping line. A horizontal line has a slope of zero because in this case the y-variable never changes; a vertical line is said to have an infinite slope because the y-variable can take any value without the x-variable changing at all.

What is the slope of Emma's demand curve for novels? First of all, because the curve slopes down, we know the slope will be negative. To calculate a numerical value for the slope, we must choose two points on the line. With Emma's income at $30,000, she will purchase 21 novels at a price of $6 or 13 novels at a price of $8. When we apply the slope formula, we are concerned with the change between these two points; in other words, we are concerned with the difference between

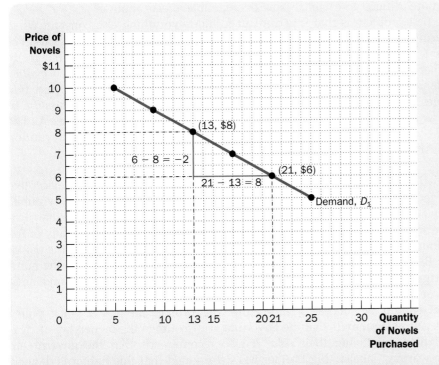

FIGURE **A-5**

Calculating the Slope of a Line
To calculate the slope of the demand curve, we can look at the changes in the x- and y-coordinates as we move from the point (21 novels, $6) to the point (13 novels, $8). The slope of the line is the ratio of the change in the y-coordinate (-2) to the change in the x-coordinate ($+8$), which equals $-1/4$.

them, which lets us know that we will have to subtract one set of values from the other, as follows:

$$\text{slope} = \frac{\Delta y}{\Delta x} = \frac{\text{first } y\text{-coordinate} - \text{second } y\text{-coordinate}}{\text{first } x\text{-coordinate} - \text{second } x\text{-coordinate}} = \frac{6-8}{21-13} = \frac{-2}{8} = \frac{-1}{4}$$

Figure A-5 shows graphically how this calculation works. Try computing the slope of Emma's demand curve using two different points. You should get exactly the same result, $-1/4$. One of the properties of a straight line is that it has the same slope everywhere. This is not true of other types of curves, which are steeper in some places than in others.

The slope of Emma's demand curve tells us something about how responsive her purchases are to changes in the price. A small slope (a number close to zero) means that Emma's demand curve is relatively flat; in this case, she adjusts the number of novels she buys substantially in response to a price change. A larger slope (a number farther from zero) means that Emma's demand curve is relatively steep; in this case, she adjusts the number of novels she buys only slightly in response to a price change.

Cause and Effect

Economists often use graphs to advance an argument about how the economy works. In other words, they use graphs to argue about how one set of events *causes* another set of events. With a graph like the demand curve, there is no doubt about cause and effect. Because we are varying price and holding all other variables constant, we know that changes in the price of novels cause changes in the quantity Emma demands. Remember, however, that our demand curve came from a hypothetical example. When graphing data from the real world, it is often more difficult to establish how one variable affects another.

The first problem is that it is difficult to hold everything else constant when measuring how one variable affects another. If we are not able to hold variables constant, we might decide that one variable on our graph is causing changes in the other variable when actually those changes are caused by a third *omitted variable* not pictured on the graph. Even if we have identified the correct two variables to look at, we might run into a second problem—*reverse causality*. In other words, we might decide that A causes B when in fact B causes A. The omitted-variable and reverse-causality traps require us to proceed with caution when using graphs to draw conclusions about causes and effects.

Omitted Variables   To see how omitting a variable can lead to a deceptive graph, let's consider an example. Imagine that the government, spurred by public concern about the large number of deaths from cancer, commissions an exhaustive study from Big Brother Statistical Services, Inc. Big Brother examines many of the items found in people's homes to see which of them are associated with the risk of cancer. Big Brother reports a strong relationship between two variables: the number of cigarette lighters that a household owns and the probability that someone in the household will develop cancer. Figure A-6 shows this relationship.

What should we make of this result? Big Brother advises a quick policy response. It recommends that the government discourage the ownership of cigarette lighters by taxing their sale. It also recommends that the government require warning labels: "Big Brother has determined that this lighter is dangerous to your health."

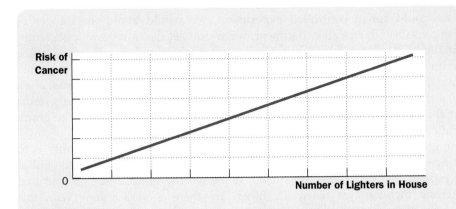

FIGURE A-6

Graph with an Omitted Variable
The upward-sloping curve shows that members of households with more cigarette lighters are more likely to develop cancer. Yet we should not conclude that ownership of lighters causes cancer because the graph does not take into account the number of cigarettes smoked.

In judging the validity of Big Brother's analysis, one question is paramount: Has Big Brother held constant every relevant variable except the one under consideration? If the answer is no, the results are suspect. An easy explanation for Figure A-6 is that people who own more cigarette lighters are more likely to smoke cigarettes and that cigarettes, not lighters, cause cancer. If Figure A-6 does not hold constant the amount of smoking, it does not tell us the true effect of owning a cigarette lighter.

This story illustrates an important principle: When you see a graph used to support an argument about cause and effect, it is important to ask whether the movements of an omitted variable could explain the results you see.

Reverse Causality Economists can also make mistakes about causality by misreading its direction. To see how this is possible, suppose the Association of American Anarchists commissions a study of crime in America and arrives at Figure A-7, which plots the number of violent crimes per thousand people in major cities against the number of police officers per thousand people. The anarchists note the curve's upward slope and argue that because police increase

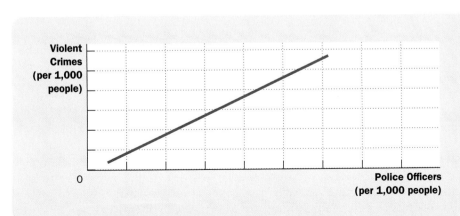

FIGURE A-7

Graph Suggesting Reverse Causality
The upward-sloping curve shows that cities with a higher concentration of police are more dangerous. Yet the graph does not tell us whether police cause crime or crime-plagued cities hire more police.

rather than decrease the amount of urban violence, law enforcement should be abolished.

If we could run a controlled experiment, we would avoid the danger of reverse causality. To run an experiment, we would set the number of police officers in different cities randomly and then examine the correlation between police and crime. Figure A-7, however, is not based on such an experiment. We simply observe that more dangerous cities have more police officers. The explanation for this may be that more dangerous cities hire more police. In other words, rather than police causing crime, crime may cause police. Nothing in the graph itself allows us to establish the direction of causality.

It might seem that an easy way to determine the direction of causality is to examine which variable moves first. If we see crime increase and then the police force expand, we reach one conclusion. If we see the police force expand and then crime increase, we reach the other. Yet there is also a flaw with this approach: Often, people change their behavior not in response to a change in their present conditions but in response to a change in their *expectations* of future conditions. A city that expects a major crime wave in the future, for instance, might hire more police now. This problem is even easier to see in the case of babies and minivans. Couples often buy a minivan in anticipation of the birth of a child. The minivan comes before the baby, but we wouldn't want to conclude that the sale of minivans causes the population to grow!

There is no complete set of rules that says when it is appropriate to draw causal conclusions from graphs. Yet just keeping in mind that cigarette lighters don't cause cancer (omitted variable) and minivans don't cause larger families (reverse causality) will keep you from falling for many faulty economic arguments.

Interdependence and the Gains from Trade

Consider your typical day. You wake up in the morning, and you pour yourself juice from oranges grown in Florida and coffee from beans grown in Brazil. Over breakfast, you watch a news program broadcast from New York on your television made in Japan. You get dressed in clothes made of cotton grown in Georgia and sewn in factories in Thailand. You drive to class in a car made of parts manufactured in more than a dozen countries around the world. Then you open up your economics textbook written by an author living in Massachusetts, published by a company located in Ohio, and printed on paper made from trees grown in Oregon.

Every day, you rely on many people from around the world, most of whom you do not know, to provide you with the goods and services that you enjoy. Such interdependence is possible because people trade with one another. Those people who provide you with goods and services are not acting out of generosity or concern for your welfare. Nor is some government agency directing them to make what you want and give it to you. Instead, people provide you and other consumers with the goods and services they produce because they get something in return.

In subsequent chapters, we will examine how our economy coordinates the activities of millions of people with varying tastes and abilities. As a starting point for this analysis, here we consider the reasons for economic interdependence. One of the *Ten Principles of Economics* highlighted in Chapter 1 is that trade can make everyone better off. This principle explains why people trade with their neighbors and why nations trade with other nations. In this chapter, we examine this principle more closely. What exactly do people gain when they trade with one another? Why do people choose to become interdependent?

A PARABLE FOR THE MODERN ECONOMY

To understand why people choose to depend on others for goods and services and how this choice improves their lives, let's look at a simple economy. Imagine that there are two goods in the world: meat and potatoes. And there are two people in the world—a cattle rancher and a potato farmer—each of whom would like to eat both meat and potatoes.

The gains from trade are most obvious if the rancher can produce only meat and the farmer can produce only potatoes. In one scenario, the rancher and the farmer could choose to have nothing to do with each other. But after several months of eating beef roasted, boiled, broiled, and grilled, the rancher might decide that self-sufficiency is not all it's cracked up to be. The farmer, who has been eating potatoes mashed, fried, baked, and scalloped, would likely agree. It is easy to see that trade would allow them to enjoy greater variety: Each could then have a steak with a baked potato or a burger with fries.

Although this scene illustrates most simply how everyone can benefit from trade, the gains would be similar if the rancher and the farmer were each capable of producing the other good, but only at great cost. Suppose, for example, that the potato farmer is able to raise cattle and produce meat, but that he is not very good at it. Similarly, suppose that the cattle rancher is able to grow potatoes but that her land is not very well suited for it. In this case, it is easy to see that the farmer and the rancher can each benefit by specializing in what he or she does best and then trading with the other.

The gains from trade are less obvious, however, when one person is better at producing *every* good. For example, suppose that the rancher is better at raising cattle *and* better at growing potatoes than the farmer. In this case, should the rancher or farmer choose to remain self-sufficient? Or is there still reason for them to trade with each other? To answer this question, we need to look more closely at the factors that affect such a decision.

Production Possibilities

Suppose that the farmer and the rancher each work 8 hours per day and can devote this time to growing potatoes, raising cattle, or a combination of the two. Table 1 shows the amount of time each person requires to produce 1 ounce of each good. The farmer can produce an ounce of potatoes in 15 minutes and an ounce of meat in 60 minutes. The rancher, who is more productive in both activities, can produce an ounce of potatoes in 10 minutes and an ounce of meat in 20 minutes. The last two columns in the table show the amounts of meat or potatoes the farmer and rancher can produce if they work an 8-hour day producing only that good.

Panel (a) of Figure 1 illustrates the amounts of meat and potatoes that the farmer can produce. If the farmer devotes all 8 hours of his time to potatoes, he produces 32 ounces of potatoes (measured on the horizontal axis) and no meat. If he devotes all his time to meat, he produces 8 ounces of meat (measured on

	Minutes Needed to Make 1 Ounce of:		Amount Produced in 8 Hours		TABLE **1**
	Meat	Potatoes	Meat	Potatoes	The Production Opportunities of the Farmer and the Rancher
Farmer	60 min/oz	15 min/oz	8 oz	32 oz	
Rancher	20 min/oz	10 min/oz	24 oz	48 oz	

FIGURE **1**

Panel (a) shows the combinations of meat and potatoes that the farmer can produce. Panel (b) shows the combinations of meat and potatoes that the rancher can produce. Both production possibilities frontiers are derived from Table 1 and the assumption that the farmer and rancher each work 8 hours per day.

The Production Possibilities Frontier

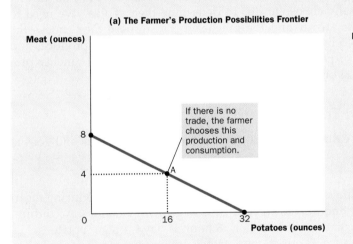

(a) The Farmer's Production Possibilities Frontier

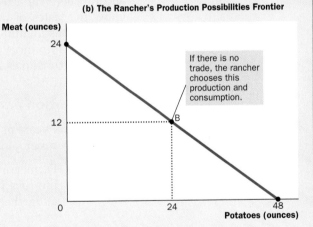

(b) The Rancher's Production Possibilities Frontier

the vertical axis) and no potatoes. If the farmer divides his time equally between the two activities, spending 4 hours on each, he produces 16 ounces of potatoes and 4 ounces of meat. The figure shows these three possible outcomes and all others in between.

This graph is the farmer's production possibilities frontier. As we discussed in Chapter 2, a production possibilities frontier shows the various mixes of output that an economy can produce. It illustrates one of the *Ten Principles of Economics* in Chapter 1: People face trade-offs. Here the farmer faces a trade-off between producing meat and producing potatoes.

You may recall that the production possibilities frontier in Chapter 2 was drawn bowed out. In that case, the rate at which society could trade one good for the other depended on the amounts that were being produced. Here, however, the farmer's technology for producing meat and potatoes (as summarized in Table 1) allows him to switch between the two goods at a constant rate. Whenever the farmer spends 1 hour less producing meat and 1 hour more producing potatoes, he reduces his output of meat by 1 ounce and raises his output of potatoes by 4 ounces—and this is true regardless of how much he is already producing. As a result, the production possibilities frontier is a straight line.

Panel (b) of Figure 1 shows the production possibilities frontier for the rancher. If the rancher devotes all 8 hours of her time to potatoes, she produces 48 ounces of potatoes and no meat. If she devotes all her time to meat, she produces 24 ounces of meat and no potatoes. If the rancher divides her time equally, spending 4 hours on each activity, she produces 24 ounces of potatoes and 12 ounces of meat. Once again, the production possibilities frontier shows all the possible outcomes.

If the farmer and rancher choose to be self-sufficient, rather than trade with each other, then each consumes exactly what he or she produces. In this case, the production possibilities frontier is also the consumption possibilities frontier. That is, without trade, Figure 1 shows the possible combinations of meat and potatoes that the farmer and rancher can each consume.

Although these production possibilities frontiers are useful in showing the trade-offs that the farmer and rancher face, they do not tell us what the farmer and rancher will actually choose to do. To determine their choices, we need to know the tastes of the farmer and the rancher. Let's suppose they choose the combinations identified by points A and B in Figure 1: The farmer produces and consumes 16 ounces of potatoes and 4 ounces of meat, while the rancher produces and consumes 24 ounces of potatoes and 12 ounces of meat.

Specialization and Trade

After several years of eating combination B, the rancher gets an idea and goes to talk to the farmer:

RANCHER: Farmer, my friend, have I got a deal for you! I know how to improve life for both of us. I think you should stop producing meat altogether and devote all your time to growing potatoes. According to my calculations, if you work 8 hours a day growing potatoes, you'll produce 32 ounces of potatoes. If you give me 15 of those 32 ounces, I'll give you 5 ounces of meat in return. In the end, you'll get to eat 17 ounces of potatoes and 5 ounces of meat every day, instead of the 16 ounces of potatoes and 4 ounces of meat you now get. If you go along with my plan, you'll have more of *both* foods. [To illustrate her point, the rancher shows the farmer panel (a) of Figure 2.]

FARMER: (sounding skeptical) That seems like a good deal for me. But I don't understand why you are offering it. If the deal is so good for me, it can't be good for you too.

RANCHER: Oh, but it is! Suppose I spend 6 hours a day raising cattle and 2 hours growing potatoes. Then I can produce 18 ounces of meat and 12 ounces of potatoes. After I give you 5 ounces of my meat in exchange for 15 ounces of your potatoes, I'll end up with 13 ounces of meat and 27 ounces of potatoes, instead of the 12 ounces of meat

The proposed trade between the farmer and the rancher offers each of them a combination of meat and potatoes that would be impossible in the absence of trade. In panel (a), the farmer gets to consume at point A* rather than point A. In panel (b), the rancher gets to consume at point B* rather than point B. Trade allows each to consume more meat and more potatoes.

FIGURE 2

How Trade Expands the Set of Consumption Opportunities

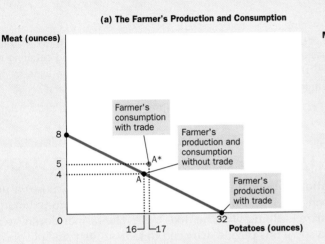

(a) The Farmer's Production and Consumption

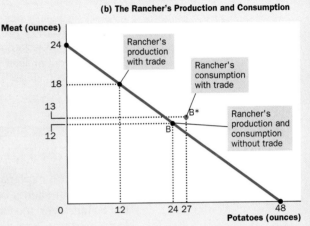

(b) The Rancher's Production and Consumption

(c) The Gains from Trade: A Summary

	Farmer		Rancher	
	Meat	Potatoes	Meat	Potatoes
Without Trade:				
Production and Consumption	4 oz	16 oz	12 oz	24 oz
With Trade:				
Production	0 oz	32 oz	18 oz	12 oz
Trade	Gets 5 oz	Gives 15 oz	Gives 5 oz	Gets 15 oz
Consumption	5 oz	17 oz	13 oz	27 oz
GAINS FROM TRADE:				
Increase in Consumption	+1 oz	+1 oz	+1 oz	+3 oz

and 24 ounces of potatoes that I now get. So I will also consume more of both foods than I do now. [She points out panel (b) of Figure 2.]

FARMER: I don't know. . . . This sounds too good to be true.

RANCHER: It's really not as complicated as it seems at first. Here—I've summarized my proposal for you in a simple table. [The rancher shows the farmer a copy of the table at the bottom of Figure 2.]

FARMER: (after pausing to study the table) These calculations seem correct, but I am puzzled. How can this deal make us both better off?

RANCHER: We can both benefit because trade allows each of us to specialize in doing what we do best. You will spend more time growing potatoes and less time raising cattle. I will spend more time raising cattle and less time growing potatoes. As a result of specialization and trade, each of us can consume more meat and more potatoes without working any more hours.

Quick Quiz

Draw an example of a production possibilities frontier for Robinson Crusoe, a shipwrecked sailor who spends his time gathering coconuts and catching fish. Does this frontier limit Crusoe's consumption of coconuts and fish if he lives by himself? Does he face the same limits if he can trade with natives on the island?

COMPARATIVE ADVANTAGE: THE DRIVING FORCE OF SPECIALIZATION

The rancher's explanation of the gains from trade, though correct, poses a puzzle: If the rancher is better at both raising cattle and growing potatoes, how can the farmer ever specialize in doing what he does best? The farmer doesn't seem to do anything best. To solve this puzzle, we need to look at the principle of *comparative advantage*.

As a first step in developing this principle, consider the following question: In our example, who can produce potatoes at lower cost—the farmer or the rancher? There are two possible answers, and in these two answers lie the solution to our puzzle and the key to understanding the gains from trade.

Absolute Advantage

absolute advantage
the ability to produce a good using fewer inputs than another producer

One way to answer the question about the cost of producing potatoes is to compare the inputs required by the two producers. Economists use the term **absolute advantage** when comparing the productivity of one person, firm, or nation to that of another. The producer that requires a smaller quantity of inputs to produce a good is said to have an absolute advantage in producing that good.

In our example, time is the only input, so we can determine absolute advantage by looking at how much time each type of production takes. The rancher has an absolute advantage both in producing meat and in producing potatoes because she requires less time than the farmer to produce a unit of either good. The rancher needs to input only 20 minutes to produce an ounce of meat, whereas the farmer needs 60 minutes. Similarly, the rancher needs only 10 minutes to produce an ounce of potatoes, whereas the farmer needs 15 minutes. Based on this information, we can conclude that the rancher has the lower cost of producing potatoes, if we measure cost by the quantity of inputs.

Opportunity Cost and Comparative Advantage

There is another way to look at the cost of producing potatoes. Rather than comparing inputs required, we can compare the opportunity costs. Recall from Chapter 1 that the **opportunity cost** of some item is what we give up to get that item. In our example, we assumed that the farmer and the rancher each spend 8 hours a day working. Time spent producing potatoes, therefore, takes away from time available for producing meat. As the rancher and farmer reallocate time between producing the two goods, they move along their production possibility frontiers; they give up units of one good to produce units of the other. The opportunity cost measures the trade-off between the two goods that each producer faces.

Let's first consider the rancher's opportunity cost. According to Table 1, producing 1 ounce of potatoes takes 10 minutes of work. When the rancher spends those 10 minutes producing potatoes, she spends 10 minutes less producing meat. Because the rancher needs 20 minutes to produce 1 ounce of meat, 10 minutes of work would yield $1/2$ ounce of meat. Hence, the rancher's opportunity cost of producing 1 ounce of potatoes is $1/2$ ounce of meat.

Now consider the farmer's opportunity cost. Producing 1 ounce of potatoes takes him 15 minutes. Because he needs 60 minutes to produce 1 ounce of meat, 15 minutes of work would yield $1/4$ ounce of meat. Hence, the farmer's opportunity cost of 1 ounce of potatoes is $1/4$ ounce of meat.

Table 2 shows the opportunity costs of meat and potatoes for the two producers. Notice that the opportunity cost of meat is the inverse of the opportunity cost of potatoes. Because 1 ounce of potatoes costs the rancher $1/2$ ounce of meat, 1 ounce of meat costs the rancher 2 ounces of potatoes. Similarly, because 1 ounce of potatoes costs the farmer $1/4$ ounce of meat, 1 ounce of meat costs the farmer 4 ounces of potatoes.

Economists use the term **comparative advantage** when describing the opportunity cost of two producers. The producer who gives up less of other goods to produce Good X has the smaller opportunity cost of producing Good X and is said to have a comparative advantage in producing it. In our example, the farmer has a lower opportunity cost of producing potatoes than does the rancher: An ounce of potatoes costs the farmer only $1/4$ ounce of meat, but it costs the rancher $1/2$ ounce of meat. Conversely, the rancher has a lower opportunity cost of producing meat than does the farmer: An ounce of meat costs the rancher 2 ounces of potatoes, but it costs the farmer 4 ounces of potatoes. Thus, the farmer has a comparative advantage in growing potatoes, and the rancher has a comparative advantage in producing meat.

Although it is possible for one person to have an absolute advantage in both goods (as the rancher does in our example), it is impossible for one person to have a comparative advantage in both goods. Because the opportunity cost of one good is the inverse of the opportunity cost of the other, if a person's opportunity cost of one good is relatively high, the opportunity cost of the other good must be relatively low. Comparative advantage reflects the relative opportunity cost. Unless two people have exactly the same opportunity cost, one person will

opportunity cost
whatever must be given up to obtain some item

comparative advantage
the ability to produce a good at a lower opportunity cost than another producer

	Opportunity Cost of:		TABLE **2**
	1 Ounce of Meat	1 Ounce of Potatoes	
Farmer	4 oz potatoes	¼ oz meat	The Opportunity Cost of Meat and Potatoes
Rancher	2 oz potatoes	½ oz meat	

have a comparative advantage in one good, and the other person will have a comparative advantage in the other good.

Comparative Advantage and Trade

The gains from specialization and trade are based not on absolute advantage but on comparative advantage. When each person specializes in producing the good for which he or she has a comparative advantage, total production in the economy rises. This increase in the size of the economic pie can be used to make everyone better off.

In our example, the farmer spends more time growing potatoes, and the rancher spends more time producing meat. As a result, the total production of potatoes rises from 40 to 44 ounces, and the total production of meat rises from 16 to 18 ounces. The farmer and rancher share the benefits of this increased production.

There is another way to look at the gains from trade—in terms of the price that each party pays the other. Because the farmer and rancher have different opportunity costs, they can each think they are getting a bargain. That is, each benefits from trade by obtaining a good at a price that is lower than his or her opportunity cost of that good.

Consider the proposed deal from the viewpoint of the farmer. The farmer gets 5 ounces of meat in exchange for 15 ounces of potatoes. In other words, the farmer buys each ounce of meat for a price of 3 ounces of potatoes. This price of meat is lower than his opportunity cost for 1 ounce of meat, which is 4 ounces of potatoes. Thus, the farmer benefits from the deal because he gets to buy meat at a good price.

Now consider the deal from the rancher's viewpoint. The rancher buys 15 ounces of potatoes for a price of 5 ounces of meat. That is, the price of potatoes is $1/3$ ounce of meat. This price of potatoes is lower than her opportunity cost of 1 ounce of potatoes, which is $1/2$ ounce of meat. The rancher benefits because she gets to buy potatoes at a good price.

The principle of comparative advantage establishes that there are gains from specialization and trade, but it leaves open a couple of related questions: What determines the price at which trade takes place? How are the gains from trade shared between the trading parties? The precise answer to these questions is beyond the scope of this chapter, but we can state one general rule: For both parties to gain from trade, the price at which they trade must lie between the two opportunity costs. In our example, the farmer and rancher agreed to trade at a rate of 3 ounces of potatoes for each ounce of meat. This price is between the farmer's opportunity cost (4 ounces of potatoes per ounce of meat) and the rancher's opportunity cost (2 ounces of potatoes per ounce of meat). As long as the trading price lies somewhere in this range, each party will benefit by buying a good at a price that is lower than his or her opportunity cost.

The moral of the story of the farmer and the rancher should now be clear: *Trade can benefit everyone in society because it allows people to specialize in activities in which they have a comparative advantage.*

Quick Quiz Robinson Crusoe can gather 10 coconuts or catch 1 fish per hour. His friend Friday can gather 30 coconuts or catch 2 fish per hour. What is Crusoe's opportunity cost of catching one fish? What is Friday's? Who has an absolute advantage in catching fish? Who has a comparative advantage in catching fish?

FYI

The Legacy of Adam Smith and David Ricardo

Economists have long understood the principle of comparative advantage. Here is how the great economist Adam Smith put the argument:

It is a maxim of every prudent master of a family, never to attempt to make at home what it will cost him more to make than to buy. The tailor does not attempt to make his own shoes, but buys them of the shoemaker. The shoemaker does not attempt to make his own clothes but employs a tailor. The farmer attempts to make neither the one nor the other, but employs those different artificers. All of them find it for their interest to employ their whole industry in a way in which they have some advantage over their neighbors, and to purchase with a part of its produce, or what is the same thing, with the price of part of it, whatever else they have occasion for.

This quotation is from Smith's 1776 book *An Inquiry into the Nature and Causes of the Wealth of Nations*, which was a landmark in the analysis of trade and economic interdependence.

David Ricardo

Smith's book inspired David Ricardo, a millionaire stockbroker, to become an economist. In his 1817 book *Principles of Political Economy and Taxation*, Ricardo developed the principle of comparative advantage as we know it today. His defense of free trade was not a mere academic exercise. Ricardo put his economic beliefs to work as a member of the British Parliament, where he opposed the Corn Laws, which restricted the import of grain.

The conclusions of Adam Smith and David Ricardo on the gains from trade have held up well over time. Although economists often disagree on questions of policy, they are united in their support of free trade. Moreover, the central argument for free trade has not changed much in the past two centuries. Even though the field of economics has broadened its scope and refined its theories since the time of Smith and Ricardo, economists' opposition to trade restrictions is still based largely on the principle of comparative advantage.

APPLICATIONS OF COMPARATIVE ADVANTAGE

The principle of comparative advantage explains interdependence and the gains from trade. Because interdependence is so prevalent in the modern world, the principle of comparative advantage has many applications. Here are two examples, one fanciful and one of great practical importance.

Should Tiger Woods Mow His Own Lawn?

Tiger Woods spends a lot of time walking around on grass. One of the most talented golfers of all time, he can hit a drive and sink a putt in a way that most casual golfers only dream of doing. Most likely, he is talented at other activities too. For example, let's imagine that Woods can mow his lawn faster than anyone else. But just because he *can* mow his lawn fast, does this mean he *should*?

In The News

Evolution and Economics

The theory of comparative advantage may lie at the heart of humanity's evolutionary success.

Homo Economicus?

Since the days of Adam Smith and David Ricardo, advocates of free trade and the division of labor, including this newspaper, have lauded the advantages of those economic principles. Until now, though, no one has suggested that they might be responsible for the very existence of humanity. But that is the thesis propounded by Jason Shogren, of the University of Wyoming, and his colleagues. For Dr Shogren is suggesting that trade and specialization are the reasons *Homo sapiens* displaced previous members of the genus, such as

Homo neanderthalensis (Neanderthal man), and emerged triumphant as the only species of humanity.

Neanderthal man has had a bad cultural rap over the years since the discovery of the first specimen in the Neander valley in Germany, in the mid-19th century. The "caveman" image of a stupid, grunting, hairy, thick-skulled parody of graceful modern humanity has stuck in the public consciousness. But current scholarship suggests Neanderthals were probably about as smart as modern humans, and also capable of speech. If they were hairy, strong and tough—

which they were—that was an appropriate adaptation to the ice-age conditions in which they lived. So why did they become extinct?

Neanderthals existed perfectly successfully for 200,000 years before *Homo sapiens* arrived in their European homeland about 40,000 years ago, after a circuitous journey from Africa via central Asia. But 10,000 years later they were gone, so it seems likely that the arrival of modern man was the cause. The two species certainly occupied more or less the same ecological niche (hunting a wide range of animals, and gathering a

To answer this question, we can use the concepts of opportunity cost and comparative advantage. Let's say that Woods can mow his lawn in 2 hours. In that same 2 hours, he could film a television commercial for Nike and earn $10,000. By contrast, Forrest Gump, the boy next door, can mow Woods's lawn in 4 hours. In that same 4 hours, he could work at McDonald's and earn $20.

In this example, Woods's opportunity cost of mowing the lawn is $10,000 and Forrest's opportunity cost is $20. Woods has an absolute advantage in mowing lawns because he can do the work with a lower input of time. Yet Forrest has a comparative advantage in mowing lawns because he has the lower opportunity cost.

The gains from trade in this example are tremendous. Rather than mowing his own lawn, Woods should make the commercial and hire Forrest to mow the lawn. As long as Woods pays Forrest more than $20 and less than $10,000, both of them are better off.

Should the United States Trade with Other Countries?

Just as individuals can benefit from specialization and trade with one another, as the farmer and rancher did, so can populations of people in different countries.

similarly eclectic range of plant food), and would thus have been competitors.

One theory is that *Homo sapiens* had more sophisticated tools, which gave him an advantage in hunting or warfare. Another is that the modern human capacity for symbolic thinking (manifest at that time in the form of cave paintings and carved animal figurines) provided an edge. Symbolic thinking might have led to more sophisticated language and better co-operation. But according to Dr Shogren's paper in a forthcoming edition of the *Journal of Economic Behavior and Organization*, it was neither cave paintings nor better spear points that led to *Homo sapiens's* dominance. It was a better economic system.

One thing *Homo sapiens* does that *Homo neanderthalensis* shows no sign of having done is trade. The evidence suggests that such trade was going on even 40,000 years ago. Stone tools made of non-local materials, and sea-shell jewelry found far from the coast, are witnesses to long-distance ex-changes. That *Homo sapiens* also prac-ticed division of labor and specialization is suggested not only by the skilled na-ture of his craft work, but also by the fact that his dwellings had spaces ap-parently set aside for different uses.

To see if trade might be enough to account for the dominance of *Homo sapiens,* Dr Shogren and his colleagues created a computer model of population growth that attempts to capture the rel-evant variables for each species. These include fertility, mortality rates, hunting efficiency and the number of skilled and unskilled hunters in each group, as well as levels of skill in making objects such as weapons, and the ability to specialise and trade.

Initially, the researchers assumed that on average Neanderthals and mod-ern humans had the same abilities for most of these attributes. They therefore set the values of those variables equal for both species. Only in the case of the trading and specialization variables did they allow *Homo sapiens* an advantage: specifically, they assumed that the most efficient human hunters specialized in hunting, while bad hunters hung up their spears and made things such as clothes and tools instead. Hunters and craftsmen then traded with one another.

According to the model, this arrangement resulted in everyone get-ting more meat, which drove up fertility and thus increased the population. Since the supply of meat was finite, that left less for Neanderthals, and their popula-tion declined. . . .

Of course, none of this proves ab-solutely that economics led to modern humanity inheriting the Earth. But it does raise the intriguing possibility that the dismal science is responsible for even more than Smith and Ricardo gave it credit.

Many of the goods that Americans enjoy are produced abroad, and many of the goods produced in the United States are sold abroad. Goods produced abroad and sold domestically are called **imports.** Goods produced domestically and sold abroad are called **exports.**

To see how countries can benefit from trade, suppose there are two countries, the United States and Japan, and two goods, food and cars. Imagine that the two countries produce cars equally well: An American worker and a Japanese worker can each produce 1 car per month. By contrast, because the United States has more and better land, it is better at producing food: A U.S. worker can pro-duce 2 tons of food per month, whereas a Japanese worker can produce only 1 ton of food per month.

The principle of comparative advantage states that each good should be pro-duced by the country that has the smaller opportunity cost of producing that good. Because the opportunity cost of a car is 2 tons of food in the United States but only 1 ton of food in Japan, Japan has a comparative advantage in producing cars. Japan should produce more cars than it wants for its own use and export some of them to the United States. Similarly, because the opportunity cost of a ton of food is 1 car in Japan but only 1/2 car in the United States, the United States has a comparative advantage in producing food. The United States should

imports
goods produced abroad and sold domestically

exports
goods produced domes-tically and sold abroad

produce more food than it wants to consume and export some to Japan. Through specialization and trade, both countries can have more food and more cars.

In reality, of course, the issues involved in trade among nations are more complex than this example suggests. Most important among these issues is that each country has many citizens with different interests. International trade can at times make some individuals worse off, even as it makes the country as a whole better off. When the United States exports food and imports cars, the impact on an American farmer is not the same as the impact on an American autoworker. Yet, contrary to the opinions sometimes voiced by politicians and political commentators, international trade is not like war, in which some countries win and others lose. Trade allows all countries to achieve greater prosperity.

Quick Quiz   Suppose that the world's fastest typist happens to be trained in brain surgery. Should he do his own typing or hire a secretary? Explain.

CONCLUSION

The principle of comparative advantage shows that trade can make everyone better off. You should now understand more fully the benefits of living in an interdependent economy. But having seen why interdependence is desirable, you might naturally ask how it is possible. How do free societies coordinate the diverse activities of all the people involved in their economies? What ensures that goods and services will get from those who should be producing them to those who should be consuming them?

In a world with only two people, such as the rancher and the farmer, the answer is simple: These two people can directly bargain and allocate resources between themselves. In the real world with billions of people, the answer is less obvious. We take up this issue in the next chapter, where we see that free societies allocate resources through the market forces of supply and demand.

SUMMARY

- Each person consumes goods and services produced by many other people both in the United States and around the world. Interdependence and trade are desirable because they allow everyone to enjoy a greater quantity and variety of goods and services.

- There are two ways to compare the ability of two people in producing a good. The person who can produce the good with the smaller quantity of inputs is said to have an *absolute advantage* in producing the good. The person who has the smaller

opportunity cost of producing the good is said to have a *comparative advantage*. The gains from trade are based on comparative advantage, not absolute advantage.

- Trade makes everyone better off because it allows people to specialize in those activities in which they have a comparative advantage.

- The principle of comparative advantage applies to countries as well as to people. Economists use the principle of comparative advantage to advocate free trade among countries.

KEY CONCEPTS

absolute advantage, p. 52   comparative advantage, p. 53   exports, p. 57
opportunity cost, p. 53   imports, p. 57

QUESTIONS FOR REVIEW

1. Explain how absolute advantage and comparative advantage differ.
2. Give an example in which one person has an absolute advantage in doing something but another person has a comparative advantage.
3. Is absolute advantage or comparative advantage more important for trade? Explain your reasoning using the example in your answer to Question 2.
4. Will a nation tend to export or import goods for which it has a comparative advantage? Explain.
5. Why do economists oppose policies that restrict trade among nations?

PROBLEMS AND APPLICATIONS

1. Maria can read 20 pages of economics in an hour. She can also read 50 pages of sociology in an hour. She spends 5 hours per day studying.
   a. Draw Maria's production possibilities frontier for reading economics and sociology.
   b. What is Maria's opportunity cost of reading 100 pages of sociology?
2. American and Japanese workers can each produce 4 cars a year. An American worker can produce 10 tons of grain a year, whereas a Japanese worker can produce 5 tons of grain a year. To keep things simple, assume that each country has 100 million workers.
   a. For this situation, construct a table analogous to Table 1.
   b. Graph the production possibilities frontier of the American and Japanese economies.
   c. For the United States, what is the opportunity cost of a car? Of grain? For Japan, what is the opportunity cost of a car? Of grain? Put this information in a table analogous to Table 2.
   d. Which country has an absolute advantage in producing cars? In producing grain?
   e. Which country has a comparative advantage in producing cars? In producing grain?
   f. Without trade, half of each country's workers produce cars and half produce grain. What quantities of cars and grain does each country produce?
   g. Starting from a position without trade, give an example in which trade makes each country better off.
3. Pat and Kris are roommates. They spend most of their time studying (of course), but they leave some time for their favorite activities: making pizza and brewing root beer. Pat takes 4 hours to brew a gallon of root beer and 2 hours to make a pizza. Kris takes 6 hours to brew a gallon of root beer and 4 hours to make a pizza.
   a. What is each roommate's opportunity cost of making a pizza? Who has the absolute advantage in making pizza? Who has the comparative advantage in making pizza?
   b. If Pat and Kris trade foods with each other, who will trade away pizza in exchange for root beer?
   c. The price of pizza can be expressed in terms of gallons of root beer. What is the highest price at which pizza can be traded that would make both roommates better off? What is the lowest price? Explain.
4. Suppose that there are 10 million workers in Canada and that each of these workers can produce either 2 cars or 30 bushels of wheat in a year.

a. What is the opportunity cost of producing a car in Canada? What is the opportunity cost of producing a bushel of wheat in Canada? Explain the relationship between the opportunity costs of the two goods.

b. Draw Canada's production possibilities frontier. If Canada chooses to consume 10 million cars, how much wheat can it consume without trade? Label this point on the production possibilities frontier.

c. Now suppose that the United States offers to buy 10 million cars from Canada in exchange for 20 bushels of wheat per car. If Canada continues to consume 10 million cars, how much wheat does this deal allow Canada to consume? Label this point on your diagram. Should Canada accept the deal?

5. England and Scotland both produce scones and sweaters. Suppose that an English worker can produce 50 scones per hour or 1 sweater per hour. Suppose that a Scottish worker can produce 40 scones per hour or 2 sweaters per hour.

a. Which country has the absolute advantage in the production of each good? Which country has the comparative advantage?

b. If England and Scotland decide to trade, which commodity will Scotland trade to England? Explain.

c. If a Scottish worker could produce only 1 sweater per hour, would Scotland still gain from trade? Would England still gain from trade? Explain.

6. The following table describes the production possibilities of two cities in the country of Baseballia:

	Pairs of Red Socks per Worker per Hour	Pairs of White Socks per Worker per Hour
Boston	3	3
Chicago	2	1

a. Without trade, what is the price of white socks (in terms of red socks) in Boston? What is the price in Chicago?

b. Which city has an absolute advantage in the production of each color sock? Which city has a comparative advantage in the production of each color sock?

c. If the cities trade with each other, which color sock will each export?

d. What is the range of prices at which trade can occur?

7. Suppose that in a year an American worker can produce 100 shirts or 20 computers, while a Chinese worker can produce 100 shirts or 10 computers.

a. Graph the production possibilities curve for the two countries. Suppose that without trade the workers in each country spend half their time producing each good. Identify this point in your graph.

b. If these countries were open to trade, which country would export shirts? Give a specific numerical example and show it on your graph. Which country would benefit from trade? Explain.

c. Explain what price of computers (in terms of shirts) the two countries might trade.

d. Suppose that China catches up with American productivity so that a Chinese worker can produce 100 shirts or 20 computers. What pattern of trade would you predict now? How does this advance in Chinese productivity affect the economic well-being of the citizens of the two countries?

8. Are the following statements true or false? Explain in each case.

a. "Two countries can achieve gains from trade even if one of the countries has an absolute advantage in the production of all goods."

b. "Certain very talented people have a comparative advantage in everything they do."

c. "If a certain trade is good for one person, it can't be good for the other one."

d. "If trade is good for a country, it must be good for everyone in the country."

9. The United States exports corn and aircraft to the rest of the world, and it imports oil and clothing from the rest of the world. Do you think this pattern of trade is consistent with the principle of comparative advantage? Why or why not?

 For further information on topics in this chapter, additional problems, examples, applications, online quizzes, and more, please visit our website at http://mankiw.swlearning.com.

Measuring a Nation's Income

When you finish school and start looking for a full-time job, your experience will, to a large extent, be shaped by prevailing economic conditions. In some years, firms throughout the economy are expanding their production of goods and services, employment is rising, and jobs are easy to find. In other years, firms are cutting back production, employment is declining, and finding a good job takes a long time. Not surprisingly, any college graduate would rather enter the labor force in a year of economic expansion than in a year of economic contraction.

Because the condition of the overall economy profoundly affects all of us, changes in economic conditions are widely reported by the media. Indeed, it is hard to pick up a newspaper without seeing some newly reported statistic about the economy. The statistic might measure the total income of everyone in the economy (GDP), the rate at which average prices are rising (inflation), the percentage of the labor force that is out of work (unemployment), total spending at stores (retail sales), or the imbalance of trade between the United States and the rest of the world (the trade deficit). All these statistics are *macroeconomic*. Rather than telling us about a particular household or firm, they tell us something about the entire economy.

As you may recall from Chapter 2, economics is divided into two branches: microeconomics and macroeconomics. **Microeconomics** is the study of how

microeconomics
the study of how households and firms make decisions and how they interact in markets

macroeconomics
the study of economy-wide phenomena, including inflation, unemployment, and economic growth

individual households and firms make decisions and how they interact with one another in markets. **Macroeconomics** is the study of the economy as a whole. The goal of macroeconomics is to explain the economic changes that affect many households, firms, and markets simultaneously. Macroeconomists address diverse questions: Why is average income high in some countries while it is low in others? Why do prices rise rapidly in some periods of time while they are more stable in other periods? Why do production and employment expand in some years and contract in others? What, if anything, can the government do to promote rapid growth in incomes, low inflation, and stable employment? These questions are all macroeconomic in nature because they concern the workings of the entire economy.

Because the economy as a whole is just a collection of many households and many firms interacting in many markets, microeconomics and macroeconomics are closely linked. The basic tools of supply and demand, for instance, are as central to macroeconomic analysis as they are to microeconomic analysis. Yet studying the economy in its entirety raises some new and intriguing challenges.

In this and the next chapter, we discuss some of the data that economists and policymakers use to monitor the performance of the overall economy. These data reflect the economic changes that macroeconomists try to explain. This chapter considers *gross domestic product*, or simply GDP, which measures the total income of a nation. GDP is the most closely watched economic statistic because it is thought to be the best single measure of a society's economic well-being.

THE ECONOMY'S INCOME AND EXPENDITURE

If you were to judge how a person is doing economically, you might first look at his or her income. A person with a high income can more easily afford life's necessities and luxuries. It is no surprise that people with higher incomes enjoy higher standards of living—better housing, better healthcare, fancier cars, more opulent vacations, and so on.

The same logic applies to a nation's overall economy. When judging whether the economy is doing well or poorly, it is natural to look at the total income that everyone in the economy is earning. That is the task of gross domestic product (GDP).

GDP measures two things at once: the total income of everyone in the economy and the total expenditure on the economy's output of goods and services. The reason that GDP can perform the trick of measuring both total income and total expenditure is that these two things are really the same. *For an economy as a whole, income must equal expenditure.*

Why is this true? An economy's income is the same as its expenditure because every transaction has two parties: a buyer and a seller. Every dollar of spending by some buyer is a dollar of income for some seller. Suppose, for instance, that Karen pays Doug $100 to mow her lawn. In this case, Doug is a seller of a service, and Karen is a buyer. Doug earns $100, and Karen spends $100. Thus, the transaction contributes equally to the economy's income and to its expenditure. GDP, whether measured as total income or total expenditure, rises by $100.

Another way to see the equality of income and expenditure is with the circular-flow diagram in Figure 1. As you may recall from Chapter 2, this diagram describes all the transactions between households and firms in a simple economy. It simplifies matters by assuming that all goods and services are bought by house-

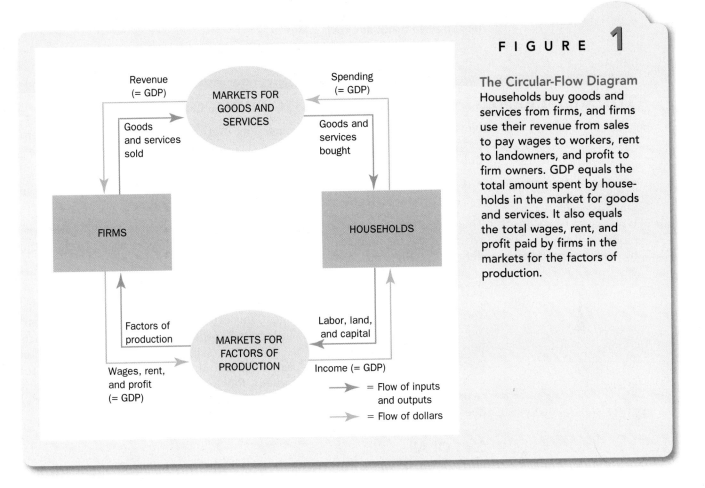

FIGURE **1**

The Circular-Flow Diagram
Households buy goods and services from firms, and firms use their revenue from sales to pay wages to workers, rent to landowners, and profit to firm owners. GDP equals the total amount spent by households in the market for goods and services. It also equals the total wages, rent, and profit paid by firms in the markets for the factors of production.

holds and that households spend all of their income. In this economy, when households buy goods and services from firms, these expenditures flow through the markets for goods and services. When the firms in turn use the money they receive from sales to pay workers' wages, landowners' rent, and firm owners' profit, this income flows through the markets for the factors of production. Money continuously flows from households to firms and then back to households.

GDP measures this flow of money. We can compute it for this economy in one of two ways: by adding up the total expenditure by households or by adding up the total income (wages, rent, and profit) paid by firms. Because all expenditure in the economy ends up as someone's income, GDP is the same regardless of how we compute it.

The actual economy is, of course, more complicated than the one illustrated in Figure 1. Households do not spend all of their income; they pay some of it to the government in taxes, and they save some for use in the future. In addition, households do not buy all goods and services produced in the economy; some goods and services are bought by governments, and some are bought by firms that plan to use them in the future to produce their own output. Yet regardless of whether a household, government, or firm buys a good or service, the transaction has a buyer and seller. Thus, for the economy as a whole, expenditure and income are always the same.

Quick Quiz What two things does gross domestic product measure? How can it measure two things at once?

THE MEASUREMENT OF GROSS DOMESTIC PRODUCT

Now that we have discussed the meaning of gross domestic product in general terms, let's be more precise about how this statistic is measured. Here is a definition of GDP that focuses on GDP as a measure of total expenditure:

gross domestic product (GDP)
the market value of all final goods and services produced within a country in a given period of time

• **Gross domestic product (GDP)** is the market value of all final goods and services produced within a country in a given period of time.

This definition might seem simple enough. But in fact, many subtle issues arise when computing an economy's GDP. Let's therefore consider each phrase in this definition with some care.

"GDP Is the Market Value . . ."

You have probably heard the adage, "You can't compare apples and oranges." Yet GDP does exactly that. GDP adds together many different kinds of products into a single measure of the value of economic activity. To do this, it uses market prices. Because market prices measure the amount people are willing to pay for different goods, they reflect the value of those goods. If the price of an apple is twice the price of an orange, then an apple contributes twice as much to GDP as does an orange.

". . . Of All . . ."

GDP tries to be comprehensive. It includes all items produced in the economy and sold legally in markets. GDP measures the market value of not just apples and oranges but also pears and grapefruit, books and movies, haircuts and healthcare, and on and on.

GDP also includes the market value of the housing services provided by the economy's stock of housing. For rental housing, this value is easy to calculate—the rent equals both the tenant's expenditure and the landlord's income. Yet many people own the place where they live and, therefore, do not pay rent. The government includes this owner-occupied housing in GDP by estimating its rental value. In effect, GDP is based on the assumption that the owner is renting the house to himself. The imputed rent is included both in the homeowner's expenditure and in his income, so it adds to GDP.

There are some products, however, that GDP excludes because measuring them is so difficult. GDP excludes most items produced and sold illicitly, such as illegal drugs. It also excludes most items that are produced and consumed at home and, therefore, never enter the marketplace. Vegetables you buy at the grocery store are part of GDP; vegetables you grow in your garden are not.

These exclusions from GDP can at times lead to paradoxical results. For example, when Karen pays Doug to mow her lawn, that transaction is part of GDP. If Karen were to marry Doug, the situation would change. Even though Doug may continue to mow Karen's lawn, the value of the mowing is now left out of GDP because Doug's service is no longer sold in a market. Thus, when Karen and Doug marry, GDP falls.

"... Final ..."

When International Paper makes paper, which Hallmark then uses to make a greeting card, the paper is called an *intermediate good,* and the card is called a *final good.* GDP includes only the value of final goods. The reason is that the value of intermediate goods is already included in the prices of the final goods. Adding the market value of the paper to the market value of the card would be double counting. That is, it would (incorrectly) count the paper twice.

An important exception to this principle arises when an intermediate good is produced and, rather than being used, is added to a firm's inventory of goods for use or sale at a later date. In this case, the intermediate good is taken to be "final" for the moment, and its value as inventory investment is added to GDP. When the inventory of the intermediate good is later used or sold, the firm's inventory investment is negative, and GDP for the later period is reduced accordingly.

"... Goods and Services ..."

GDP includes both tangible goods (food, clothing, cars) and intangible services (haircuts, housecleaning, doctor visits). When you buy a CD by your favorite band, you are buying a good, and the purchase price is part of GDP. When you pay to hear a concert by the same band, you are buying a service, and the ticket price is also part of GDP.

"... Produced ..."

GDP includes goods and services currently produced. It does not include transactions involving items produced in the past. When General Motors produces and sells a new car, the value of the car is included in GDP. When one person sells a used car to another person, the value of the used car is not included in GDP.

"... Within a Country ..."

GDP measures the value of production within the geographic confines of a country. When a Canadian citizen works temporarily in the United States, his production is part of U.S. GDP. When an American citizen owns a factory in Haiti, the production at his factory is not part of U.S. GDP. (It is part of Haiti's GDP.) Thus, items are included in a nation's GDP if they are produced domestically, regardless of the nationality of the producer.

"... In a Given Period of Time."

GDP measures the value of production that takes place within a specific interval of time. Usually, that interval is a year or a quarter (three months). GDP measures the economy's flow of income and expenditure during that interval.

When the government reports the GDP for a quarter, it usually presents GDP "at an annual rate." This means that the figure reported for quarterly GDP is the amount of income and expenditure during the quarter multiplied by 4. The government uses this convention so that quarterly and annual figures on GDP can be compared more easily.

In addition, when the government reports quarterly GDP, it presents the data after they have been modified by a statistical procedure called *seasonal adjustment.* The unadjusted data show clearly that the economy produces more goods and services during some times of year than during others. (As you might guess,

December's holiday shopping season is a high point.) When monitoring the condition of the economy, economists and policymakers often want to look beyond these regular seasonal changes. Therefore, government statisticians adjust the quarterly data to take out the seasonal cycle. The GDP data reported in the news are always seasonally adjusted.

Now let's repeat the definition of GDP:

- Gross domestic product (GDP) is the market value of all final goods and services produced within a country in a given period of time.

This definition focuses on GDP as total expenditure in the economy. But don't forget that every dollar spent by a buyer of a good or service becomes a dollar of income to the seller of that good or service. Therefore, in addition to applying this definition, the government also adds up total income in the economy. The two ways of calculating GDP give almost exactly the same answer. (Why "almost"? Although the two measures should be precisely the same, data sources are not perfect. The difference between the two calculations of GDP is called the *statistical discrepancy*.)

It should be apparent that GDP is a sophisticated measure of the value of economic activity. In advanced courses in macroeconomics, you will learn more about the subtleties that arise in its calculation. But even now you can see that each phrase in this definition is packed with meaning.

Quick Quiz Which contributes more to GDP—the production of a pound of hamburger or the production of a pound of caviar? Why?

THE COMPONENTS OF GDP

Spending in the economy takes many forms. At any moment, the Smith family may be having lunch at Burger King; General Motors may be building a car factory; the Navy may be procuring a submarine; and British Airways may be buying an airplane from Boeing. GDP includes all of these various forms of spending on domestically produced goods and services.

To understand how the economy is using its scarce resources, economists are often interested in studying the composition of GDP among various types of spending. To do this, GDP (which we denote as Y) is divided into four components: consumption (C), investment (I), government purchases (G), and net exports (NX):

$$Y = C + I + G + NX.$$

This equation is an *identity*—an equation that must be true because of how the variables in the equation are defined. In this case, because each dollar of expenditure included in GDP is placed into one of the four components of GDP, the total of the four components must be equal to GDP. Let's look at each of these four components more closely.

consumption
spending by households on goods and services, with the exception of purchases of new housing

Consumption

Consumption is spending by households on goods and services. Goods include household spending on durable goods, such as automobiles and appliances, and

FYI

Other Measures of Income

When the U.S. Department of Commerce computes the nation's GDP every three months, it also computes various other measures of income to get a more complete picture of what's happening in the economy. These other measures differ from GDP by excluding or including certain categories of income. What follows is a brief description of five of these income measures, ordered from largest to smallest.

- *Gross national product* (GNP) is the total income earned by a nation's permanent residents (called *nationals*). It differs from GDP by including income that our citizens earn abroad and excluding income that foreigners earn here. For example, when a Canadian citizen works temporarily in the United States, his production is part of U.S. GDP, but it is not part of U.S. GNP. (It is part of Canada's GNP.) For most countries, including the United States, domestic residents are responsible for most domestic production, so GDP and GNP are quite close.
- *Net national product* (NNP) is the total income of a nation's residents (GNP) minus losses from depreciation. *Depreciation* is the wear and tear on the economy's stock of equipment and structures, such as trucks rusting and computers becoming obsolete. In the national income accounts prepared by the Department of Commerce, depreciation is called the "consumption of fixed capital."
- *National income* is the total income earned by a nation's residents in the production of goods and services. It differs from net national product by excluding indirect business taxes (such as sales taxes) and including business subsidies. NNP and national income also differ because of the *statistical discrepancy* that arises from problems in data collection.
- *Personal income* is the income that households and noncorporate businesses receive. Unlike national income, it excludes *retained earnings,* which is income that corporations have earned but have not paid out to their owners. It also subtracts corporate income taxes and contributions for social insurance (mostly Social Security taxes). In addition, personal income includes the interest income that households receive from their holdings of government debt and the income that households receive from government transfer programs, such as welfare and Social Security.
- *Disposable personal income* is the income that households and noncorporate businesses have left after satisfying all their obligations to the government. It equals personal income minus personal taxes and certain nontax payments (such as traffic tickets).

Although the various measures of income differ in detail, they almost always tell the same story about economic conditions. When GDP is growing rapidly, these other measures of income are usually growing rapidly. And when GDP is falling, these other measures are usually falling as well. For monitoring fluctuations in the overall economy, it does not matter much which measure of income we use.

nondurable goods, such as food and clothing. Services include such intangible items as haircuts and medical care. Household spending on education is also included in consumption of services (although one might argue that it would fit better in the next component).

Investment

Investment is the purchase of goods that will be used in the future to produce more goods and services. It is the sum of purchases of capital equipment, inventories, and structures. Investment in structures includes expenditure on new housing. By convention, the purchase of a new house is the one form of household spending categorized as investment rather than consumption.

investment
spending on capital equipment, inventories, and structures, including household purchases of new housing

As mentioned earlier in this chapter, the treatment of inventory accumulation is noteworthy. When IBM produces a computer and, instead of selling it, adds it to its inventory, IBM is assumed to have "purchased" the computer for itself. That is, the national income accountants treat the computer as part of IBM's investment spending. (If IBM later sells the computer out of inventory, IBM's inventory investment will then be negative, offsetting the positive expenditure of the buyer.) Inventories are treated this way because one aim of GDP is to measure the value of the economy's production, and goods added to inventory are part of that period's production.

Notice that GDP accounting uses the word *investment* differently from how you might hear the term in everyday conversation. When you hear the word *investment*, you might think of financial investments, such as stocks, bonds, and mutual funds—topics that we study later in this book. By contrast, because GDP measures expenditure on goods and services, here the word *investment* means purchases of investment goods, including capital equipment, inventories, and structures.

Government Purchases

government purchases
spending on goods and services by local, state, and federal governments

Government purchases include spending on goods and services by local, state, and federal governments. It includes the salaries of government workers and spending on public works. Recently, the U.S. national income accounts have switched to the longer label *government consumption expenditure and gross investment*, but in this book, we will use the traditional and shorter term *government purchases*.

The meaning of government purchases requires a bit of clarification. When the government pays the salary of an Army general, that salary is part of government purchases. But what happens when the government pays a Social Security benefit to one of the elderly? Such government spending is called a *transfer payment* because it is not made in exchange for a currently produced good or service. Transfer payments alter household income, but they do not reflect the economy's production. (From a macroeconomic standpoint, transfer payments are like negative taxes.) Because GDP is intended to measure income from, and expenditure on, the production of goods and services, transfer payments are not counted as part of government purchases.

Net Exports

net exports
spending on domestically produced goods by foreigners (exports) minus spending on foreign goods by domestic residents (imports)

Net exports equal the purchases of domestically produced goods by foreigners (exports) minus the domestic purchases of foreign goods (imports). A domestic firm's sale to a buyer in another country, such as the Boeing sale to British Airways, increases net exports.

The *net* in *net exports* refers to the fact that imports are subtracted from exports. This subtraction is made because imports of goods and services are included in other components of GDP. For example, suppose that a household buys a $30,000 car from Volvo, the Swedish carmaker. That transaction increases consumption by $30,000 because car purchases are part of consumer spending. It also reduces net exports by $30,000 because the car is an import. In other words, net exports include goods and services produced abroad (with a minus sign) because these goods and services are included in consumption, investment, and government purchases (with a plus sign). Thus, when a domestic household, firm, or government buys a good or service from abroad, the purchase reduces net exports—but because it also raises consumption, investment, or government purchases, it does not affect GDP.

	Total (in billions of dollars)	Per Person (in dollars)	Percent of Total	TABLE 1
Gross domestic product, Y	$11,728	$39,904	100%	**GDP and Its Components** This table shows total GDP for the U.S. economy in 2004 and the breakdown of GDP among its four components. When reading this table, recall the identity $Y = C + I + G + NX$.
Consumption, C	8,232	28,009	70	
Investment, I	1,922	6,539	16	
Government purchases, G	2,184	7,431	19	
Net exports, NX	−609	−2,072	−5	

Source: U.S. Department of Commerce.

CASE STUDY | THE COMPONENTS OF U.S. GDP

Table 1 shows the composition of U.S. GDP in 2004. In this year, the GDP of the United States was almost $12 trillion. Dividing this number by the 2004 U.S. population of 294 million yields GDP per person (sometimes called GDP per capita). We find that in 2004 the income and expenditure of the average American was $39,904.

Consumption made up 70 percent of GDP, or $28,009 per person. Investment was $6,539 per person. Government purchases were $7,431 per person. Net exports were −$2,072 per person. This number is negative because Americans earned less from selling to foreigners than they spent on foreign goods.

These data come from the Bureau of Economic Analysis, which is the part of the U.S. Department of Commerce that produces the national income accounts. You can find more recent data on GDP at its website http://www.bea.doc.gov. •

Quick Quiz List the four components of expenditure. Which is the largest?

REAL VERSUS NOMINAL GDP

As we have seen, GDP measures the total spending on goods and services in all markets in the economy. If total spending rises from one year to the next, one of two things must be true: (1) the economy is producing a larger output of goods and services, or (2) goods and services are being sold at higher prices. When studying changes in the economy over time, economists want to separate these two effects. In particular, they want a measure of the total quantity of goods and services the economy is producing that is not affected by changes in the prices of those goods and services.

To do this, economists use a measure called *real GDP*. Real GDP answers a hypothetical question: What would be the value of the goods and services produced this year if we valued these goods and services at the prices that prevailed in some specific year in the past? By evaluating current production using prices that are fixed at past levels, real GDP shows how the economy's overall production of goods and services changes over time.

To see more precisely how real GDP is constructed, let's consider an example.

A Numerical Example

Table 2 shows some data for an economy that produces only two goods: hot dogs and hamburgers. The table shows the quantities of the two goods produced and their prices in the years 2005, 2006, and 2007.

To compute total spending in this economy, we would multiply the quantities of hot dogs and hamburgers by their prices. In the year 2005, 100 hot dogs are sold at a price of $1 per hot dog, so expenditure on hot dogs equals $100. In the same year, 50 hamburgers are sold for $2 per hamburger, so expenditure on hamburgers also equals $100. Total expenditure in the economy—the sum of expenditure on hot dogs and expenditure on hamburgers—is $200. This amount, the production of goods and services valued at current prices, is called **nominal GDP.**

nominal GDP

the production of goods and services valued at current prices

The table shows the calculation of nominal GDP for these three years. Total spending rises from $200 in 2005 to $600 in 2006 and then to $1,200 in 2007. Part of this rise is attributable to the increase in the quantities of hot dogs and hamburgers, and part is attributable to the increase in the prices of hot dogs and hamburgers.

To obtain a measure of the amount produced that is not affected by changes in prices, we use **real GDP,** which is the production of goods and services valued at constant prices. We calculate real GDP by first choosing one year as a *base year*. We then use the prices of hot dogs and hamburgers in the base year to compute the value of goods and services in all of the years. In other words, the prices in the base year provide the basis for comparing quantities in different years.

real GDP

the production of goods and services valued at constant prices

2 TABLE

Real and Nominal GDP
This table shows how to calculate real GDP, nominal GDP, and the GDP deflator for a hypothetical economy that produces only hot dogs and hamburgers.

		Prices and Quantities			
Year	Price of Hot dogs	Quantity of Hot dogs	Price of Hamburgers	Quantity of Hamburgers	
2005	$1	100	$2	50	
2006	$2	150	$3	100	
2007	$3	200	$4	150	

Calculating Nominal GDP

2005	($1 per hot dog × 100 hot dogs) + ($2 per hamburger × 50 hamburgers) = $200
2006	($2 per hot dog × 150 hot dogs) + ($3 per hamburger × 100 hamburgers) = $600
2007	($3 per hot dog × 200 hot dogs) + ($4 per hamburger × 150 hamburgers) = $1,200

Calculating Real GDP (base year 2005)

2005	($1 per hot dog × 100 hot dogs) + ($2 per hamburger × 50 hamburgers) = $200
2006	($1 per hot dog × 150 hot dogs) + ($2 per hamburger × 100 hamburgers) = $350
2007	($1 per hot dog × 200 hot dogs) + ($2 per hamburger × 150 hamburgers) = $500

Calculating the GDP Deflator

2005	($200/$200) × 100 = 100
2006	($600/$350) ×100 = 171
2007	($1,200/$500) × 100 = 240

Suppose that we choose 2005 to be the base year in our example. We can then use the prices of hot dogs and hamburgers in 2005 to compute the value of goods and services produced in 2005, 2006, and 2007. Table 2 shows these calculations. To compute real GDP for 2005, we use the prices of hot dogs and hamburgers in 2005 (the base year) and the quantities of hot dogs and hamburgers produced in 2005. (Thus, for the base year, real GDP always equals nominal GDP.) To compute real GDP for 2006, we use the prices of hot dogs and hamburgers in 2005 (the base year) and the quantities of hot dogs and hamburgers produced in 2006. Similarly, to compute real GDP for 2007, we use the prices in 2005 and the quantities in 2007. When we find that real GDP has risen from $200 in 2005 to $350 in 2006 and then to $500 in 2007, we know that the increase is attributable to an increase in the quantities produced because the prices are being held fixed at base-year levels.

To sum up: *Nominal GDP uses current prices to place a value on the economy's production of goods and services. Real GDP uses constant base-year prices to place a value on the economy's production of goods and services.* Because real GDP is not affected by changes in prices, changes in real GDP reflect only changes in the amounts being produced. Thus, real GDP is a measure of the economy's production of goods and services.

Our goal in computing GDP is to gauge how well the overall economy is performing. Because real GDP measures the economy's production of goods and services, it reflects the economy's ability to satisfy people's needs and desires. Thus, real GDP is a better gauge of economic well-being than is nominal GDP. When economists talk about the economy's GDP, they usually mean real GDP rather than nominal GDP. And when they talk about growth in the economy, they measure that growth as the percentage change in real GDP from one period to another.

The GDP Deflator

As we have just seen, nominal GDP reflects both the prices of goods and services and the quantities of goods and services the economy is producing. By contrast, by holding prices constant at base-year levels, real GDP reflects only the quantities produced. From these two statistics, we can compute a third, called the GDP deflator, which reflects the prices of goods and services but not the quantities produced.

The **GDP deflator** is calculated as follows:

$$\text{GDP deflator} = \frac{\text{Nominal GDP}}{\text{Real GDP}} \times 100.$$

GDP deflator
a measure of the price level calculated as the ratio of nominal GDP to real GDP times 100

Because nominal GDP and real GDP must be the same in the base year, the GDP deflator for the base year always equals 100. The GDP deflator for subsequent years measures the change in nominal GDP from the base year that cannot be attributable to a change in real GDP.

The GDP deflator measures the current level of prices relative to the level of prices in the base year. To see why this is true, consider a couple of simple examples. First, imagine that the quantities produced in the economy rise over time but prices remain the same. In this case, both nominal and real GDP rise together, so the GDP deflator is constant. Now suppose, instead, that prices rise over time but the quantities produced stay the same. In this second case, nominal GDP rises but real GDP remains the same, so the GDP deflator rises as well. Notice that, in both cases, the GDP deflator reflects what's happening to prices, not quantities.

Let's now return to our numerical example in Table 2. The GDP deflator is computed at the bottom of the table. For year 2005, nominal GDP is $200, and real GDP is $200, so the GDP deflator is 100. For the year 2006, nominal GDP is $600, and real GDP is $350, so the GDP deflator is 171. Because the GDP deflator rose in year 2006 from 100 to 171, we can say that the price level increased by 71 percent. The percentage increase in the price level is the rate of inflation.

The GDP deflator is one measure that economists use to monitor the average level of prices in the economy and thus the rate of inflation. The GDP deflator gets its name because it can be used to take inflation out of nominal GDP—that is, to "deflate" nominal GDP for the rise that is due to increases in prices. We examine another measure of the economy's price level, called the consumer price index, in the next chapter, where we also describe the differences between the two measures.

CASE STUDY | REAL GDP OVER RECENT HISTORY

Now that we know how real GDP is defined and measured, let's look at what this macroeconomic variable tells us about the recent history of the United States. Figure 2 shows quarterly data on real GDP for the U.S. economy since 1965.

The most obvious feature of these data is that real GDP grows over time. The real GDP of the U.S. economy in 2004 was almost four times its 1965 level. Put differently, the output of goods and services produced in the United States has grown on average 3.2 percent per year. This continued growth in real GDP enables the typical American to enjoy greater economic prosperity than his or her parents and grandparents did.

A second feature of the GDP data is that growth is not steady. The upward climb of real GDP is occasionally interrupted by periods during which GDP declines, called *recessions*. Figure 2 marks recessions with shaded vertical bars. (There is no ironclad rule for when the official business cycle dating committee will declare that a recession has occurred, but an old rule of thumb is two consecutive quarters of falling real GDP.) Recessions are associated not only with

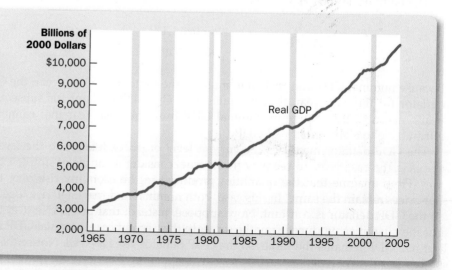

2 FIGURE

Real GDP in the United States
This figure shows quarterly data on real GDP for the U.S. economy since 1965. Recessions—periods of falling real GDP—are marked with the shaded vertical bars.

Source: U.S. Department of Commerce.

In The News

GDP Lightens Up

GDP measures the value of the economy's output of goods and services. What do you think we would learn if, instead, we measured the weight of the economy's output?

From Greenspan, a (Truly) Weighty Idea

By David Wessel

Having weighed the evidence carefully, Federal Reserve Chairman Alan Greenspan wants you to know that the U.S. economy is getting lighter.

Literally.

When he refers to "downsizing" in this instance, Mr. Greenspan means that a dollar's worth of the goods and services produced in the mighty U.S. economy weighs a lot less than it used to, even after adjusting for inflation.

A modern 10-story office building, he says, weighs less than a 10-story building erected in the late 19th century. With synthetic fibers, clothes weigh less. And the electronics revolution has produced televisions so light they can be worn on the wrist.

By conventional measures, the [real] gross domestic product—the value of all goods and services produced in the nation—is five times as great as it was 50 years ago. Yet "the physical weight of our gross domestic product is evidently only modestly higher than it was 50 or 100 years ago," Mr. Greenspan told an audience in Dallas recently.

When you think about it, it's not so surprising that the economy is getting lighter. An ever-growing proportion of the U.S. GDP consists of things that don't weigh anything at all—lawyers' services, psychotherapy, e-mail, online information.

But Mr. Greenspan has a way of making the obvious sound profound. Only "a small fraction" of the nation's economic growth in the past several decades "represents growth in the tonnage of physical materials—oil, coal, ores, wood, raw chemicals," he has observed. "The remainder represents new insights into how to rearrange those physical materials to better serve human needs." . . .

The incredible shrinking GDP helps explain why American workers can produce more for each hour of work than ever before. . . . [It] also helps explain why there is so much international trade these days. "The . . . downsizing of output," Mr. Greenspan said recently, "meant that products were easier and hence less costly to move, and most especially across national borders." . . .

"The world of 1948 was vastly different," Mr. Greenspan observed a few years back. "The quintessential model of industry might in those days was the array of vast, smoke-encased integrated steel mills . . . on the shores of Lake Michigan. Output was things, big physical things."

Today, one exemplar of U.S. economic might is Microsoft Corp., with its almost weightless output. "Virtually unimaginable a half-century ago was the extent to which concepts and ideas would substitute for physical resources and human brawn in the production of goods and services," he has said.

Of course, one thing made in the U.S. is heavier than it used to be: people. The National Institutes of Health says 22.3% of Americans are obese, up from 12.8% in the early 1960s. But Mr. Greenspan doesn't talk about that.

lower incomes but also with other forms of economic distress: rising unemployment, falling profits, increased bankruptcies, and so on.

Much of macroeconomics is aimed at explaining the long-run growth and short-run fluctuations in real GDP. As we will see in the coming chapters, we need different models for these two purposes. Because the short-run fluctuations represent deviations from the long-run trend, we first examine the behavior of key macroeconomic variables, including real GDP, in the long run. Then in later chapters, we build on this analysis to explain short-run fluctuations.   •

In The News

The Underground Economy

The gross domestic product misses many transactions that take place in the underground economy.

Searching for the Hidden Economy

By Doug Campbell

Here is the brief, unremarkable story of how I recently came to participate in the underground economy:

Midafternoon on the iciest day this past winter, a man knocked at my front door. "Shovel your walk?" he asked. "Only $5."

Outside, it was a bone-chilling 15 degrees. "Sold," I said. A half-hour later I handed over a five-dollar bill and thanked him for saving me the trouble.

Officially, this was an unofficial transaction—off the books, with no taxes paid or safety regulations followed. (At least, I assume this hired hand didn't bother to report that income or register with the proper authorities.) As such, it was technically illegal. And,

of course, it's the sort of thing that happens all the time.

International Differences in the Underground Economy

Country	Underground Economy as a Percent of GDP
Bolivia	68 percent
Zimbabwe	63
Peru	61
Thailand	54
Mexico	33
Argentina	29
Sweden	18
Australia	13
United Kingdom	12
Japan	11
Switzerland	9
United States	8

Source: Friedrich Schneider. Figures are for 2002.

The size of the official U.S. economy, as measured by Gross Domestic Product (GDP), was almost $12 trillion in 2004. Measurements of the unofficial economy—not including illegal activities like drug dealing and prostitution—differ substantially. But it's generally agreed to be significant, somewhere between 6 percent and 20 percent of GDP. At the midpoint, this would be about $1.5 trillion a year.

Broadly defined, the underground, gray, informal, or shadow economy involves otherwise legal transactions that go unreported or unrecorded. That's a wide net, capturing everything from babysitting fees, to bartering home repairs with a neighbor, to failing to report pay from moonlighting gigs. The "underground" label tends to make it sound much more sinister than it really is.

Quick Quiz   Define *real GDP* and *nominal GDP*. Which is a better measure of economic well-being? Why?

IS GDP A GOOD MEASURE OF ECONOMIC WELL-BEING?

Earlier in this chapter, GDP was called the best single measure of the economic well-being of a society. Now that we know what GDP is, we can evaluate this claim.

As we have seen, GDP measures both the economy's total income and the economy's total expenditure on goods and services. Thus, GDP per person tells us the income and expenditure of the average person in the economy. Because most people

Criminal activities make up a large portion of what could be termed the total underground economy. Many studies have been done on the economics of drug dealing, prostitution, and gambling. But because money from crime is almost never recovered, many policymakers are more interested in portions of the underground economy that otherwise would be legal if not hidden from authorities. Things like shoveling walks.

Despite its intrigue, the informal economy's importance and consequences remain in debate. The reason: "You're trying to measure a phenomenon whose entire purpose is to hide itself from observation," says Ed Feige, an economist at the University of Wisconsin.

This uncertainty poses problems for policymakers. Without knowing the precise size, scope, and causes of the underground economy, how can they decide what—if anything—to do about it?

Was the man who shoveled my walk engaging in a socially positive or negative activity? Was I? Suffice it to say, some economists have dedicated their entire careers to answering questions about the underground economy—and still there is nothing close to a consensus about its size or description. . . .

Economists generally agree that the shadow economy is worse in developing nations, whose webs of bureaucratic red tape and corruption are notorious. For instance, [economist Friedrich] Schneider in 2003 published "shadow economy" estimates (defined broadly as all market-based, legal production of goods and services deliberately concealed from the authorities) for countries including: Zimbabwe, estimated at a whopping 63.2 percent of GDP, Thailand's at 54.1 percent, and Bolivia's at 68.3 percent. Among former Soviet bloc nations, Georgia led the way with a 68 percent of GDP shadow economy, and together those nations had an average 40.1 percent of GDP underground. This contrasts with an average of 16.7 percent among Western nations. . . .

In his 2003 book, *Reefer Madness: Sex, Drugs and Cheap Labor in the American Black Market,* investigative writer Eric Schlosser invokes Adam Smith's "invisible hand" theory that men pursuing their own self-interest will generate benefits for society as a whole. This invisible hand has produced a fairly sizable underground economy, and we cannot understand our entire economic

A SHADOWY ENTERPRISE?

system without understanding how the hidden underbelly functions, too. "The underground is a good measure of the progress and the health of nations," Schlosser writes. "When much is wrong, much needs to be hidden." Schlosser's implication was that much is wrong in the United States. If he had taken a more global view, he might have decided relatively little is hidden here.

Source: "Region Focus," Federal Reserve Bank of Richmond, Spring 2005.

would prefer to receive higher income and enjoy higher expenditure, GDP per person seems a natural measure of the economic well-being of the average individual.

Yet some people dispute the validity of GDP as a measure of well-being. When Senator Robert Kennedy was running for president in 1968, he gave a moving critique of such economic measures:

> [Gross domestic product] does not allow for the health of our children, the quality of their education, or the joy of their play. It does not include the beauty of our poetry or the strength of our marriages, the intelligence of our public debate or the integrity of our public officials. It measures neither our courage, nor our wisdom, nor our devotion to our country. It measures everything, in short, except that which makes life worthwhile, and it can tell us everything about America except why we are proud that we are Americans.

Much of what Robert Kennedy said is correct. Why, then, do we care about GDP?

GDP REFLECTS THE FACTORY'S PRODUCTION, BUT NOT THE HARM THAT IT INFLICTS ON THE ENVIRONMENT.

© PHOTODISC/GETTY IMAGES

The answer is that a large GDP does in fact help us to lead a good life. GDP does not measure the health of our children, but nations with larger GDP can afford better healthcare for their children. GDP does not measure the quality of their education, but nations with larger GDP can afford better educational systems. GDP does not measure the beauty of our poetry, but nations with larger GDP can afford to teach more of their citizens to read and enjoy poetry. GDP does not take account of our intelligence, integrity, courage, wisdom, or devotion to country, but all of these laudable attributes are easier to foster when people are less concerned about being able to afford the material necessities of life. In short, GDP does not directly measure those things that make life worthwhile, but it does measure our ability to obtain the inputs into a worthwhile life.

GDP is not, however, a perfect measure of well-being. Some things that contribute to a good life are left out of GDP. One is leisure. Suppose, for instance, that everyone in the economy suddenly started working every day of the week, rather than enjoying leisure on weekends. More goods and services would be produced, and GDP would rise. Yet despite the increase in GDP, we should not conclude that everyone would be better off. The loss from reduced leisure would offset the gain from producing and consuming a greater quantity of goods and services.

Because GDP uses market prices to value goods and services, it excludes the value of almost all activity that takes place outside markets. In particular, GDP omits the value of goods and services produced at home. When a chef prepares a delicious meal and sells it at his restaurant, the value of that meal is part of GDP. But if the chef prepares the same meal for his family, the value he has added to the raw ingredients is left out of GDP. Similarly, childcare provided in day-care centers is part of GDP, whereas childcare by parents at home is not. Volunteer work also contributes to the well-being of those in society, but GDP does not reflect these contributions.

Another thing that GDP excludes is the quality of the environment. Imagine that the government eliminated all environmental regulations. Firms could then produce goods and services without considering the pollution they create, and GDP might rise. Yet well-being would most likely fall. The deterioration in the quality of air and water would more than offset the gains from greater production.

GDP also says nothing about the distribution of income. A society in which 100 people have annual incomes of $50,000 has GDP of $5 million and, not surprisingly, GDP per person of $50,000. So does a society in which 10 people earn $500,000 and 90 suffer with nothing at all. Few people would look at those two situations and call them equivalent. GDP per person tells us what happens to the average person, but behind the average lies a large variety of personal experiences.

In the end, we can conclude that GDP is a good measure of economic well-being for most—but not all—purposes. It is important to keep in mind what GDP includes and what it leaves out.

CASE STUDY | INTERNATIONAL DIFFERENCES IN GDP AND THE QUALITY OF LIFE

One way to gauge the usefulness of GDP as a measure of economic well-being is to examine international data. Rich and poor countries have vastly different lev-

Country	Real GDP per Person (2002)	Life Expectancy	Adult Literacy (% of Population)	Internet Usage (% of Population)
United States	$35,750	77 years	99%	55%
Germany	27,100	78	99	41
Japan	26,940	81	99	45
Mexico	8,970	73	91	10
Russia	8,230	67	99	4
Brazil	7,770	68	86	8
China	4,580	71	91	5
Indonesia	3,230	67	88	4
India	2,670	64	61	2
Pakistan	1,940	61	42	1
Bangladesh	1,700	61	41	<0.5
Nigeria	860	52	67	<0.5

TABLE 3

GDP and the Quality of Life
The table shows GDP per person and three other measures of the quality of life for twelve major countries.

Source: *Human Development Report 2004*, United Nations.

els of GDP per person. If a large GDP leads to a higher standard of living, then we should observe GDP to be strongly correlated with various measures of the quality of life. And, in fact, we do.

Table 3 shows twelve of the world's most populous countries ranked in order of GDP per person. The table also shows life expectancy (the expected life span at birth), literacy (the percentage of the adult population who can read), and Internet usage (the percentage of the population that regularly uses the Internet). These data show a clear pattern. In rich countries, such as the United States, Germany, and Japan, people can expect to live into their late seventies, almost all of the population can read, and about half the population uses the Internet. In poor countries, such as Nigeria, Bangladesh, and Pakistan, people typically live only until their fifties or early sixties, only about half of the population is literate, and Internet usage is very rare.

Data on other aspects of the quality of life tell a similar story. Countries with low GDP per person tend to have more infants with low birth weight, higher rates of infant mortality, higher rates of maternal mortality, higher rates of child malnutrition, and less common access to safe drinking water. In countries with low GDP per person, fewer school-age children are actually in school, and those who are in school must learn with fewer teachers per student. These countries also tend to have fewer televisions, fewer telephones, fewer paved roads, and fewer households with electricity. International data leave no doubt that a nation's GDP is closely associated with its citizens' standard of living.   •

CASE STUDY   WHO WINS AT THE OLYMPICS?

Every four years, the nations of the world compete in the Olympic Games. When the games end, commentators use the number of medals a nation takes home as a measure of success. This measure seems very different from the GDP that economists use to measure success. It turns out, however, that this is not so.

Economists Andrew Bernard and Meghan Busse examined the determinants of Olympic success in a study published in the *Review of Economics and Statistics* in 2004. The most obvious explanation is population: Countries with more people will, other things equal, have more star athletes. But this is not the full story. China, India, Indonesia, and Bangladesh together have more than 40 percent of the world's population, but they typically win only 6 percent of the medals. The reason is that these countries are poor: Despite their large populations, they account for only 5 percent of the world's GDP. Their poverty prevents many gifted athletes from reaching their potential.

Bernard and Busse find that the best gauge of a nation's ability to produce world-class athletes is total GDP. A large total GDP means more medals, regardless of whether the total comes from high GDP per person or a large number of people. In other words, if two nations have the same total GDP, they can be expected to win the same number of medals, even if one nation (India) has many people and low GDP per person and the other nation (Netherlands) has few people and high GDP per person.

In addition to GDP, two other factors influence the number of medals won. The host country usually earns extra medals, reflecting the benefit that athletes get from competing on their home turf. In addition, the former communist countries of Eastern Europe (the Soviet Union, Romania, East Germany, and so on) earned more medals than other countries with similar GDP. These centrally planned economies devoted more of the nation's resources to training Olympic athletes than did free-market economies, where people have more control over their own lives. •

Quick Quiz   Why should policymakers care about GDP?

CONCLUSION

This chapter has discussed how economists measure the total income of a nation. Measurement is, of course, only a starting point. Much of macroeconomics is aimed at revealing the long-run and short-run determinants of a nation's gross domestic product. Why, for example, is GDP higher in the United States and Japan than in India and Nigeria? What can the governments of the poorest countries do to promote more rapid growth in GDP? Why does GDP in the United States rise rapidly in some years and fall in others? What can U.S. policymakers do to reduce the severity of these fluctuations in GDP? These are the questions we will take up shortly.

At this point, it is important to acknowledge the significance of just measuring GDP. We all get some sense of how the economy is doing as we go about our lives. But the economists who study changes in the economy and the policymakers who formulate economic policies need more than this vague sense—they need concrete data on which to base their judgments. Quantifying the behavior of the economy with statistics such as GDP is, therefore, the first step to developing a science of macroeconomics.

SUMMARY

- Because every transaction has a buyer and a seller, the total expenditure in the economy must equal the total income in the economy.

- Gross domestic product (GDP) measures an economy's total expenditure on newly produced goods and services and the total income earned from the production of these goods and services. More precisely, GDP is the market value of all final goods and services produced within a country in a given period of time.

- GDP is divided among four components of expenditure: consumption, investment, government purchases, and net exports. Consumption includes spending on goods and services by households, with the exception of purchases of new housing. Investment includes spending on new equipment and structures, including households' purchases of new housing. Government

purchases include spending on goods and services by local, state, and federal governments. Net exports equal the value of goods and services produced domestically and sold abroad (exports) minus the value of goods and services produced abroad and sold domestically (imports).

- Nominal GDP uses current prices to value the economy's production of goods and services. Real GDP uses constant base-year prices to value the economy's production of goods and services. The GDP deflator—calculated from the ratio of nominal to real GDP—measures the level of prices in the economy.

- GDP is a good measure of economic well-being because people prefer higher to lower incomes. But it is not a perfect measure of well-being. For example, GDP excludes the value of leisure and the value of a clean environment.

KEY CONCEPTS

microeconomics, p. 203
macroeconomics, p. 204
gross domestic product (GDP),
   p. 206

consumption, p. 208
investment, p. 209
government purchases, p. 210
net exports, p. 210

nominal GDP, p. 212
real GDP, p. 212
GDP deflator, p. 213

QUESTIONS FOR REVIEW

1. Explain why an economy's income must equal its expenditure.

2. Which contributes more to GDP—the production of an economy car or the production of a luxury car? Why?

3. A farmer sells wheat to a baker for $2. The baker uses the wheat to make bread, which is sold for $3. What is the total contribution of these transactions to GDP?

4. Many years ago, Peggy paid $500 to put together a record collection. Today, she sold her albums at a garage sale for $100. How does this sale affect current GDP?

5. List the four components of GDP. Give an example of each.

6. Why do economists use real GDP rather than nominal GDP to gauge economic well-being?

7. In the year 2005, the economy produces 100 loaves of bread that sell for $2 each. In the year 2006, the economy produces 200 loaves of bread that sell for $3 each. Calculate nominal GDP, real GDP, and the GDP deflator for each year. (Use 2005 as the base year.) By what percentage does each of these three statistics rise from one year to the next?

8. Why is it desirable for a country to have a large GDP? Give an example of something that would raise GDP and yet be undesirable.

PROBLEMS AND APPLICATIONS

1. What components of GDP (if any) would each of the following transactions affect? Explain.
   a. A family buys a new refrigerator.
   b. Aunt Jane buys a new house.
   c. Ford sells a Mustang from its inventory.
   d. You buy a pizza.
   e. California repaves Highway 101.
   f. Your parents buy a bottle of French wine.
   g. Honda expands its factory in Marysville, Ohio.

2. The government purchases component of GDP does not include spending on transfer payments such as Social Security. Thinking about the definition of GDP, explain why transfer payments are excluded.

3. As the chapter states, GDP does not include the value of used goods that are resold. Why would including such transactions make GDP a less informative measure of economic well-being?

4. Below are some data from the land of milk and honey.

Year	Price of Milk	Quantity of Milk (quarts)	Price of Honey	Quantity of Honey (quarts)
2005	$1	100	$2	50
2006	$1	200	$2	100
2007	$2	200	$4	100

   a. Compute nominal GDP, real GDP, and the GDP deflator for each year, using 2005 as the base year.
   b. Compute the percentage change in nominal GDP, real GDP, and the GDP deflator in 2006 and 2007 from the preceding year. For each year, identify the variable that does not change. Explain in words why your answer makes sense.
   c. Did economic well-being rise more in 2006 or 2007? Explain.

5. Consider the following data on U.S. GDP:

Year	Nominal GDP (in billions $)	GDP Deflator (base year 1996)
2000	9,873	118
1999	9,269	113

   a. What was the growth rate of nominal GDP between 1999 and 2000? (Note: The growth rate is the percentage change from one period to the next.)
   b. What was the growth rate of the GDP deflator between 1999 and 2000?
   c. What was real GDP in 1999 measured in 1996 prices?
   d. What was real GDP in 2000 measured in 1996 prices?
   e. What was the growth rate of real GDP between 1999 and 2000?
   f. Was the growth rate of nominal GDP higher or lower than the growth rate of real GDP? Explain.

6. If prices rise, people's income from selling goods increases. The growth of real GDP ignores this gain, however. Why, then, do economists prefer real GDP as a measure of economic well-being?

7. Revised estimates of U.S. GDP are usually released by the government near the end of each month. Find a newspaper article that reports on the most recent release, or read the news release yourself at http://www.bea.doc.gov, the website of the U.S. Bureau of Economic Analysis. Discuss the recent changes in real and nominal GDP and in the components of GDP.

8. One day, Barry the Barber, Inc., collects $400 for haircuts. Over this day, his equipment depreciates in value by $50. Of the remaining $350, Barry sends $30 to the government in sales taxes, takes home $220 in wages, and retains $100 in his business to add new equipment in the future. From the $220 that Barry takes home, he pays $70 in income taxes. Based on this information, compute Barry's contribution to the following measures of income.
   a. gross domestic product
   b. net national product
   c. national income
   d. personal income
   e. disposable personal income

9. A farmer grows wheat, which he sells to a miller for $100. The miller turns the wheat into flour, which he sells to a baker for $150. The baker turns the wheat into bread, which he sells to consumers for $180. Consumers eat the bread.

a. What is GDP in this economy? Explain.

b. *Value added* is defined as the value of a producer's output minus the value of the intermediate goods that the producer buys. Assuming there are no intermediate goods beyond those described above, calculate the value added of each of the three producers.

c. What is total value added of the three producers in this economy? How does it compare to the economy's GDP? Does this example suggest another way of calculating GDP?

10. Goods and services that are not sold in markets, such as food produced and consumed at home, are generally not included in GDP. Can you think of how this might cause the numbers in the second column of Table 3 to be misleading in a comparison of the economic well-being of the United States and India? Explain.

11. Until the early 1990s, the U.S. government emphasized GNP rather than GDP as a measure

of economic well-being. Which measure should the government prefer if it cares about the total income of Americans? Which measure should it prefer if it cares about the total amount of economic activity occurring in the United States?

12. The participation of women in the U.S. labor force has risen dramatically since 1970.

a. How do you think this rise affected GDP?

b. Now imagine a measure of well-being that includes time spent working in the home and taking leisure. How would the change in this measure of well-being compare to the change in GDP?

c. Can you think of other aspects of well-being that are associated with the rise in women's labor-force participation? Would it be practical to construct a measure of well-being that includes these aspects?

For further information on topics in this chapter, additional problems, examples, applications, online quizzes, and more, please visit our website at http://mankiw.swlearning.com.

Measuring the Cost of Living

In 1931, as the U.S. economy was suffering through the Great Depression, the New York Yankees paid famed baseball player Babe Ruth a salary of $80,000. At the time, this pay was extraordinary, even among the stars of baseball. According to one story, a reporter asked Ruth whether he thought it was right that he made more than President Herbert Hoover, who had a salary of only $75,000. Ruth replied, "I had a better year."

In 2005, the median player on the New York Yankees was paid $5.8 million, and shortstop Alex Rodriquez was paid $26 million. At first, this fact might lead you to think that baseball has become vastly more lucrative over the past seven decades. But as everyone knows, the prices of goods and services have also risen. In 1931, a nickel would buy an ice-cream cone, and a quarter would buy a ticket at the local movie theater. Because prices were so much lower in Babe Ruth's day than they are today, it is not clear whether Ruth enjoyed a higher or lower standard of living than today's players.

In the preceding chapter, we looked at how economists use gross domestic product (GDP) to measure the quantity of goods and services that the economy is producing. This chapter examines how economists measure the overall cost of living. To compare Babe Ruth's salary of $80,000 with salaries from today, we need to find some way of turning dollar figures into meaningful measures of purchasing power. That is exactly the job of a statistic called the *consumer price index.* After seeing how the consumer price index is constructed, we discuss how we can use such a price index to compare dollar figures from different points in time.

The consumer price index is used to monitor changes in the cost of living over time. When the consumer price index rises, the typical family has to spend more dollars to maintain the same standard of living. Economists use the term *inflation* to describe a situation in which the economy's overall price level is rising. The *inflation rate* is the percentage change in the price level from the previous period. As we will see in the coming chapters, inflation is a closely watched aspect of macroeconomic performance and is a key variable guiding macroeconomic policy. This chapter provides the background for that analysis by showing how economists measure the inflation rate using the consumer price index.

THE CONSUMER PRICE INDEX

consumer price index (CPI)

a measure of the overall cost of the goods and services bought by a typical consumer

The **consumer price index (CPI)** is a measure of the overall cost of the goods and services bought by a typical consumer. Each month, the Bureau of Labor Statistics (BLS), which is part of the Department of Labor, computes and reports the consumer price index. In this section, we discuss how the consumer price index is calculated and what problems arise in its measurement. We also consider how this index compares to the GDP deflator, another measure of the overall level of prices, which we examined in the preceding chapter.

How the Consumer Price Index Is Calculated

When the Bureau of Labor Statistics calculates the consumer price index and the inflation rate, it uses data on the prices of thousands of goods and services. To see exactly how these statistics are constructed, let's consider a simple economy in which consumers buy only two goods: hot dogs and hamburgers. Table 1 shows the five steps that the BLS follows.

1. *Fix the basket.* Determine which prices are most important to the typical consumer. If the typical consumer buys more hot dogs than hamburgers, then the price of hot dogs is more important than the price of hamburgers and, therefore, should be given greater weight in measuring the cost of living. The Bureau of Labor Statistics sets these weights by surveying consumers and finding the basket of goods and services that the typical consumer buys. In the example in the table, the typical consumer buys a basket of 4 hot dogs and 2 hamburgers.
2. *Find the prices.* Find the prices of each of the goods and services in the basket for each point in time. The table shows the prices of hot dogs and hamburgers for 3 different years.
3. *Compute the basket's cost.* Use the data on prices to calculate the cost of the basket of goods and services at different times. The table shows this calculation for each of the 3 years. Notice that only the prices in this calculation change. By keeping the basket of goods the same (4 hot dogs and 2 hamburgers), we are isolating the effects of price changes from the effect of any quantity changes that might be occurring at the same time.

This table shows how to calculate the consumer price index and the inflation rate for a hypothetical economy in which consumers buy only hot dogs and hamburgers.

TABLE 1

Calculating the Consumer Price Index and the Inflation Rate: An Example

Step 1: Survey Consumers to Determine a Fixed Basket of Goods

Basket = 4 hot dogs, 2 hamburgers

Step 2: Find the Price of Each Good in Each Year

Year	Price of Hot Dogs	Price of Hamburgers
2005	$1	$2
2006	2	3
2007	3	4

Step 3: Compute the Cost of the Basket of Goods in Each Year

2005	($1 per hot dog × 4 hot dogs) + ($2 per hamburger × 2 hamburgers) = $8 per basket
2006	($2 per hot dog × 4 hot dogs) + ($3 per hamburger × 2 hamburgers) = $14 per basket
2007	($3 per hot dog × 4 hot dogs) + ($4 per hamburger × 2 hamburgers) = $20 per basket

Step 4: Choose One Year as a Base Year (2005) and Compute the Consumer Price Index in Each Year

2005	($8/$8) × 100 = 100
2006	($14/$8) × 100 = 175
2007	($20/$8) × 100 = 250

Step 5: Use the Consumer Price Index to Compute the Inflation Rate from Previous Year

2006	(175 − 100)/100 × 100 = 75%
2007	(250 − 175)/175 × 100 = 43%

4. *Choose a base year and compute the index.* Designate one year as the base year, which is the benchmark against which other years are compared. (The choice of base year is arbitrary, as the index is used to measure *changes* in the cost of living.) Once the base year is chosen, the index is calculated as follows:

$$\text{Consumer price index} = \frac{\text{Price of basket of goods and services}}{\text{Price of basket in base year}} \times 100.$$

That is, the price of the basket of goods and services in each year is divided by the price of the basket in the base year, and this ratio is then multiplied by 100. The resulting number is the consumer price index.

In the example in the table, 2005 is the base year. In this year, the basket of hot dogs and hamburgers costs $8. Therefore, the price of the basket in all years is divided by $8 and multiplied by 100. The consumer price index is 100 in 2005. (The index is always 100 in the base year.) The consumer price index is 175 in 2006. This means that the price of the basket in 2006 is 175 percent of its price in the base year. Put differently, a basket of goods that costs $100 in the base year costs $175 in 2006. Similarly, the consumer price index is 250 in 2007, indicating that the price level in 2007 is 250 percent of the price level in the base year.

5. *Compute the inflation rate.* Use the consumer price index to calculate the **inflation rate,** which is the percentage change in the price index from the preceding period. That is, the inflation rate between two consecutive years is computed as follows:

$$\text{Inflation rate in year 2} = \frac{\text{CPI in year 2} - \text{CPI in year 1}}{\text{CPI in year 1}} \times 100.$$

inflation rate
the percentage change in the price index from the preceding period

In our example, the inflation rate is 75 percent in 2006 and 43 percent in 2007.

Although this example simplifies the real world by including only two goods, it shows how the Bureau of Labor Statistics computes the consumer price index and the inflation rate. The BLS collects and processes data on the prices of thousands of goods and services every month and, by following the five foregoing steps, determines how quickly the cost of living for the typical consumer is rising. When the BLS makes its monthly announcement of the consumer price index, you can usually hear the number on the evening television news or see it in the next day's newspaper.

In addition to the consumer price index for the overall economy, the BLS calculates several other price indexes. It reports the index for specific metropolitan areas within the country (such as Boston, New York, and Los Angeles) and for some narrow categories of goods and services (such as food, clothing, and energy). It also calculates the **producer price index** (PPI), which measures the cost of a basket of goods and services bought by firms rather than consumers. Because firms eventually pass on their costs to consumers in the form of higher consumer prices, changes in the producer price index are often thought to be useful in predicting changes in the consumer price index.

producer price index
a measure of the cost of a basket of goods and services bought by firms

Problems in Measuring the Cost of Living

The goal of the consumer price index is to measure changes in the cost of living. In other words, the consumer price index tries to gauge how much incomes must rise to maintain a constant standard of living. The consumer price index, however, is not a perfect measure of the cost of living. Three problems with the index are widely acknowledged but difficult to solve.

The first problem is called *substitution bias.* When prices change from one year to the next, they do not all change proportionately: Some prices rise more than others. Consumers respond to these differing price changes by buying less of the goods whose prices have risen by large amounts and by buying more of the goods whose prices have risen less or perhaps even have fallen. That is, consumers substitute toward goods that have become relatively less expensive. If a price index is computed assuming a fixed basket of goods, it ignores the possibility of consumer substitution and, therefore, overstates the increase in the cost of living from one year to the next.

FYI

What Is in the CPI's Basket?

When construct-
ing the consumer
price index, the
Bureau of Labor Statistics tries to include all the goods and services that the typical consumer buys. Moreover, it tries to weight
these goods and services according to how much consumers
buy of each item.

Figure 1 shows the breakdown of consumer spending into
the major categories of goods and services. By far the largest
category is housing, which makes up 42 percent of the typical
consumer's budget. This category includes the cost of shelter (33
percent), fuel and other utilities (5 percent), and household furnishings and operation (4 percent). The next largest category, at
17 percent, is transportation, which includes spending on cars,
gasoline, buses, subways, and so on. The next category, at 15
percent, is food and beverages; this includes food at home (8
percent), food away from home (6 percent), and alcoholic beverages (1 percent). Next are medical care, recreation, and education and communication, each at about 6 percent. This last category includes, for example, college tuition and personal
computers. Apparel, which includes clothing, footwear, and jewelry, makes up 4 percent of the typical consumer's budget.

Also included in the figure, at 4 percent of spending, is a category for other goods and services. This is a catchall for things
consumers buy that do not naturally fit into the other categories, such as cigarettes, haircuts, and funeral expenses.

F I G U R E   1

The Typical Basket of Goods and Services
This figure shows how the typical consumer divides
spending among various categories of goods and
services. The Bureau of Labor Statistics calls each
percentage the "relative importance" of the
category.

Source: Bureau of Labor Statistics.

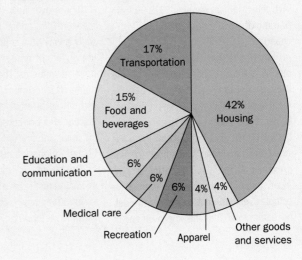

Let's consider a simple example. Imagine that in the base year, apples are
cheaper than pears, and so consumers buy more apples than pears. When the
Bureau of Labor Statistics constructs the basket of goods, it will include more
apples than pears. Suppose that next year pears are cheaper than apples. Consumers will naturally respond to the price changes by buying more pears and
fewer apples. Yet when computing the consumer price index, the BLS uses a
fixed basket, which in essence assumes that consumers continue buying the now
expensive apples in the same quantities as before. For this reason, the index will
measure a much larger increase in the cost of living than consumers actually
experience.

The second problem with the consumer price index is the *introduction of new
goods*. When a new good is introduced, consumers have more variety from which

In The News

Accounting for Quality Change

Behind every macroeconomic statistic are thousands of individual pieces of data, as well as a few key judgment calls.

An Inflation Debate Brews over Intangibles at the Mall
By Timothy Aeppel

To most people, when the price of a 27-inch television set remains $329.99 from one month to the next, the price hasn't changed.

But not to Tim LaFleur. He's a commodity specialist for televisions at the Bureau of Labor Statistics, the government agency that assembles the Consumer Price Index. In this case, which landed on his desk last December, he decided the newer set had important improvements, including a better screen. After running the changes through a complex government computer model, he determined that the improvement in the screen was valued at more than $135. Factoring that in, he concluded the price of the TV had actually fallen 29%.

Mr. LaFleur was applying the principles of hedonics, an arcane statistical technique that's become a flashpoint in a debate over how the U.S. government measures inflation. Hedonics is essentially a way of accounting for the changing quality of products when calculating price movements. That's vital in the dynamic U.S. economy, marked by rapid technological advances. Without hedonics, the effect of consumers getting more for their money wouldn't get fully reflected in inflation numbers.

But even as the Federal Reserve raises interest rates amid a recent uptick in inflation, many critics complain the hedonic method is distorting the picture of what's going on in the economy. They say hedonics is too subjective and fear it helps keep inflation figures artificially low—meaning the Fed may already be lagging in its inflation-fighting mission.

It's critically important for consumers, business, the government and the economy as a whole that the CPI is as accurate as possible. The CPI is used to benchmark how much is paid to Social Security recipients, who last year received outlays of $487 billion. It also plays a role in adjusting lease payments, wages in union contracts, food-stamp benefits, alimony and tax brackets. . . .

Bill Gross, head of the world's largest bond fund, Pimco, caused a stir last fall by proclaiming that the way the CPI is calculated amounts to a "con job" by the government aimed at con-

to choose, and this in turn reduces the cost of maintaining the same level of economic well-being. To see why, consider a hypothetical situation: Suppose you could choose between a $100 gift certificate at a large store that offered a wide array of goods and a $100 gift certificate at a small store with the same prices but a more limited selection. Which would you prefer? Most people would pick the store with greater variety. In essence, the increased set of possible choices makes each dollar more valuable. The same is true with the evolution of economy over time: As new goods are introduced, consumers have more choices, and each dollar is worth more. Yet because the consumer price index is based on a fixed basket of goods and services, it does not reflect the increase in the value of the dollar that arises from the introduction of new goods.

Again, let's consider an example. When VCRs were introduced, consumers were able to watch their favorite movies at home. Although not a perfect substi-

cealing the true rate of inflation. A key culprit, he said, was the CPI's growing reliance on hedonics. . . .

Inflation watchers at the statistics bureau say critics exaggerate the significance of hedonics, noting that it's used in only seven out of 211 product categories in the CPI. In most of those, officials say, hedonics actually magnifies price increases rather than suppressing them.

Take housing, which makes up about 30% of the CPI. . . . The bureau says hedonics actually helps boost the housing component of CPI. In order to take into account the aging of housing, and presumably falling quality that goes with it, the CPI applies a form of hedonics that links the age of a housing unit to rents. If someone is paying the equivalent of $500 a month in rent for several years, the rent has actually gone up as the unit ages and becomes less desirable, according to the government. . . .

The hub of this effort is a warren of beige-walled cubicles at the Bureau of Labor Statistics a few blocks from the Capitol. Here 40 commodity specialists hunch over reports with 85,000 price quotes that flow in from around the country every month. The numbers are gathered by 400 part-time data collectors. They visit stores and note prices on the items that make up the basket of goods in the CPI, ranging from ladies' shoes to skim milk to microwave ovens.

One of the biggest challenges in this process is finding substitutes for products that disappear from store shelves or change so much that they are hard to recognize from one month to the next. With TVs, for instance, data collectors find the models they priced the previous month missing about 19% of the time over the course of a year.

When that happens, the data gatherer goes through a four-page checklist of features such as screen size and the type of remote control to find the nearest comparable model. Once this process identifies a product that appears to be the closest match, the data gatherer notes its price. The commodity specialists back in Washington check over these choices and decide whether to accept them. . . .

Many price adjustments in the CPI are straightforward: When candy bars get smaller, but are sold for the same price, the CPI reflects that as a price increase.

Todd Reese, the commodity specialist for autos, says he doesn't need hedonics to extrapolate the value of quality changes, because auto makers present him with a list of changes to the car and the corresponding prices. Still, Mr. Reese must make some tough calls as he does his job. For instance, he recently considered a 2005 model in which the sticker price went from $17,890 to $18,490. The manufacturer cited an extra cost of $230 to make antilock brakes standard, while it said it saved $5 by dropping the cassette portion of the CD player.

The bureau accepted both those items, so the ostensible price increase shrank by $225. But the car maker also told Mr. Reese it wanted to subtract $30 from the price increase for the cost of putting audio controls on the steering wheel, allowing drivers to change channels without reaching for the radio dial. "We didn't allow that claim," says Mr. Reese. "We didn't judge that to be a functional change."

Source: *The Wall Street Journal*, May 9, 2005, p. A1. Copyright 2005 by DOW JONES & CO INC. Reproduced with permission of DOW JONES & CO INC.

tute for a first-run movie on a large screen, an old movie in the comfort of your family room was a new option that increased consumers' set of opportunities. For any given number of dollars, the introduction of the VCR made people better off; conversely, to achieve the same level of economic well-being required a smaller number of dollars. A perfect cost-of-living index would have reflected the introduction of the VCR with a decrease in the cost of living. The consumer price index, however, did not decrease in response to the introduction of the VCR. Eventually, the Bureau of Labor Statistics did revise the basket of goods to include VCRs, and subsequently, the index reflected changes in VCR prices. But the reduction in the cost of living associated with the initial introduction of the VCR never showed up in the index.

The third problem with the consumer price index is *unmeasured quality change.* If the quality of a good deteriorates from one year to the next, the value of a dollar falls, even if the price of the good stays the same, because you are getting a lesser good for the same amount of money. Similarly, if the quality rises from one year to the next, the value of a dollar rises. The Bureau of Labor Statistics does its best to account for quality change. When the quality of a good in the basket changes—for example, when a car model has more horsepower or gets better gas mileage from one year to the next—the Bureau adjusts the price of the good to account for the quality change. It is, in essence, trying to compute the price of a basket of goods of constant quality. Despite these efforts, changes in quality remain a problem because quality is so hard to measure.

There is still much debate among economists about how severe these measurement problems are and what should be done about them. Several studies written during the 1990s concluded that the consumer price index overstated inflation by about 1 percentage point per year. In response to this criticism, the Bureau of Labor Statistics adopted several technical changes to improve the CPI, and many economists believe the bias is now only about half as large as it once was. The issue is important because many government programs use the consumer price index to adjust for changes in the overall level of prices. Recipients of Social Security, for instance, get annual increases in benefits that are tied to the consumer price index. Some economists have suggested modifying these programs to correct for the measurement problems by, for instance, reducing the magnitude of the automatic benefit increases.

The GDP Deflator versus the Consumer Price Index

In the preceding chapter, we examined another measure of the overall level of prices in the economy—the GDP deflator. The GDP deflator is the ratio of nominal GDP to real GDP. Because nominal GDP is current output valued at current prices and real GDP is current output valued at base-year prices, the GDP deflator reflects the current level of prices relative to the level of prices in the base year.

Economists and policymakers monitor both the GDP deflator and the consumer price index to gauge how quickly prices are rising. Usually, these two statistics tell a similar story. Yet there are two important differences that can cause them to diverge.

The first difference is that the GDP deflator reflects the prices of all goods and services *produced domestically*, whereas the consumer price index reflects the prices of all goods and services *bought by consumers*. For example, suppose that the price of an airplane produced by Boeing and sold to the Air Force rises. Even though the plane is part of GDP, it is not part of the basket of goods and services bought by a typical consumer. Thus, the price increase shows up in the GDP deflator but not in the consumer price index.

As another example, suppose that Volvo raises the price of its cars. Because Volvos are made in Sweden, the car is not part of U.S. GDP. But U.S. consumers buy Volvos, and so the car is part of the typical consumer's basket of goods. Hence, a price increase in an imported consumption good, such as a Volvo, shows up in the consumer price index but not in the GDP deflator.

This first difference between the consumer price index and the GDP deflator is particularly important when the price of oil changes. Although the United States does produce some oil, much of the oil we use is imported from the Mid-

THE WALL STREET JOURNAL

AUDIO-VIDEO

"THE PRICE MAY SEEM A LITTLE HIGH, BUT YOU HAVE TO REMEMBER THAT'S IN TODAY'S DOLLARS."

dle East. As a result, oil and oil products such as gasoline and heating oil are a much larger share of consumer spending than of GDP. When the price of oil rises, the consumer price index rises by much more than does the GDP deflator.

The second and subtler difference between the GDP deflator and the consumer price index concerns how various prices are weighted to yield a single number for the overall level of prices. The consumer price index compares the price of a *fixed* basket of goods and services to the price of the basket in the base year. Only occasionally does the Bureau of Labor Statistics change the basket of goods. By contrast, the GDP deflator compares the price of *currently produced* goods and services to the price of the same goods and services in the base year. Thus, the group of goods and services used to compute the GDP deflator changes automatically over time. This difference is not important when all prices are changing proportionately. But if the prices of different goods and services are changing by varying amounts, the way we weight the various prices matters for the overall inflation rate.

Figure 2 shows the inflation rate as measured by both the GDP deflator and the consumer price index for each year since 1965. You can see that sometimes the two measures diverge. When they do diverge, it is possible to go behind these numbers and explain the divergence with the two differences we have discussed. (For example, in 1979 and 1980, CPI inflation spiked up more than the GDP deflator largely because oil prices more than doubled during these two years.) The figure shows, however, that divergence between these two measures is the exception rather than the rule. In the 1970s, both the GDP deflator and the consumer price index show high rates of inflation. In the late 1980s, 1990s, and early 2000s, both measures show low rates of inflation.

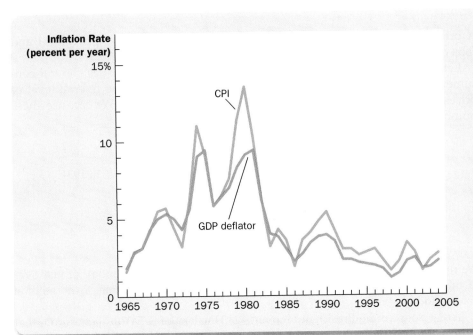

FIGURE **2**

Two Measures of Inflation
This figure shows the inflation rate—the percentage change in the level of prices—as measured by the GDP deflator and the consumer price index using annual data since 1965. Notice that the two measures of inflation generally move together.

Source: U.S. Department of Labor; U.S. Department of Commerce.

Quick Quiz Explain briefly what the consumer price index is trying to measure and how it is constructed.

CORRECTING ECONOMIC VARIABLES FOR THE EFFECTS OF INFLATION

The purpose of measuring the overall level of prices in the economy is to permit comparison between dollar figures from different points in time. Now that we know how price indexes are calculated, let's see how we might use such an index to compare a dollar figure from the past to a dollar figure in the present.

Dollar Figures from Different Times

We first return to the issue of Babe Ruth's salary. Was his salary of $80,000 in 1931 high or low compared to the salaries of today's players?

To answer this question, we need to know the level of prices in 1931 and the level of prices today. Part of the increase in baseball salaries merely compensates players for the higher level of prices today. To compare Ruth's salary to those of today's players, we need to inflate Ruth's salary to turn 1931 dollars into today's dollars.

The formula for turning dollar figures from year T into today's dollars is the following:

$$\text{Amount in today's dollars} = \text{Amount in year } T \text{ dollars} \times \frac{\text{Price level today}}{\text{Price level in year } T}.$$

A price index such as the consumer price index measures the price level and thus determines the size of the inflation correction.

Let's apply this formula to Ruth's salary. Government statistics show a consumer price index of 15.2 for 1931 and 195 for 2005. Thus, the overall level of prices has risen by a factor of 12.8 (which equals 195/15.2). We can use these numbers to measure Ruth's salary in 2005 dollars, as follows:

$$\text{Salary in 2005 dollars} = \text{Salary in 1931 dollars} \times \frac{\text{Price level in 2005}}{\text{Price level in 1931}}$$

$$= \$80,000 \times \frac{195}{15.2}$$

$$= \$1,026,316.$$

We find that Babe Ruth's 1931 salary is equivalent to a salary today of just over $1 million. That is not a bad income, but it is less than a quarter of the median Yankee today.

Let's also examine President Hoover's 1931 salary of $75,000. To translate that figure into 2005 dollars, we again multiply the ratio of the price levels in the two years. We find that Hoover's salary is equivalent to $75,000 \times (195/15.2)$, or $962,171, in 2005 dollars. This is well above President George W. Bush's salary of $400,000. It seems that President Hoover did have a pretty good year after all.

CASE STUDY | MR. INDEX GOES TO HOLLYWOOD

What was the most popular movie of all time? The answer might surprise you.

Movie popularity is usually gauged by box office receipts. By that measure, *Titanic* is the number 1 movie of all time, followed by *Star Wars*, *Shrek II*, and *E.T.* But this ranking ignores an obvious but important fact: Prices, including those of movie tickets, have been rising over time. When we correct box office receipts for the effects of inflation, the story is very different.

Table 2 shows the top ten movies of all time ranked by inflation-adjusted box office receipts. The number 1 movie is *Gone with the Wind*, which was released in 1939 and is well ahead of *Titanic*. In the 1930s, before everyone had televisions in their homes, about 90 million Americans went to the cinema each week, compared to about 25 million today. But the movies from that era rarely show up in popularity rankings because ticket prices were only a quarter. Scarlett and Rhett fare a lot better once we correct for the effects of inflation.   •

© BETTMANN/CORBIS

"FRANKLY, MY DEAR, I DON'T CARE MUCH FOR THE EFFECTS OF INFLATION."

Indexation

As we have just seen, price indexes are used to correct for the effects of inflation when comparing dollar figures from different times. This type of correction shows up in many places in the economy. When some dollar amount is automatically corrected for inflation by law or contract, the amount is said to be *indexed* for inflation.

Film	Year of Release	Total Domestic Gross (in millions of 2004 dollars)
1. *Gone with the Wind*	1939	$1,254
2. *Star Wars*	1977	1,084
3. *The Sound of Music*	1965	870
4. *E.T.: The Extra-Terrestrial*	1982	861
5. *The Ten Commandments*	1956	801
6. *Titanic*	1997	789
7. *Jaws*	1975	783
8. *Doctor Zhivago*	1965	740
9. *The Jungle Book*	1967	662
10. *Snow White and the Seven Dwarfs*	1937	650

TABLE 2

The Most Popular Movies of All Time, Inflation Adjusted

Source: http://www.the-movie-times.com.

indexation
the automatic correction
of a dollar amount for
the effects of inflation by
law or contract

For example, many long-term contracts between firms and unions include partial or complete **indexation** of the wage to the consumer price index. Such a provision is called a *cost-of-living allowance,* or COLA. A COLA automatically raises the wage when the consumer price index rises.

Indexation is also a feature of many laws. Social Security benefits, for example, are adjusted every year to compensate the elderly for increases in prices. The brackets of the federal income tax—the income levels at which the tax rates change—are also indexed for inflation. There are, however, many ways in which the tax system is not indexed for inflation, even when perhaps it should be. We discuss these issues more fully when we discuss the costs of inflation later in this book.

Real and Nominal Interest Rates

Correcting economic variables for the effects of inflation is particularly important, and somewhat tricky, when we look at data on interest rates. The very concept of an interest rate necessarily involves comparing amounts of money at different points in time. When you deposit your savings in a bank account, you give the bank some money now, and the bank returns your deposit with interest in the future. Similarly, when you borrow from a bank, you get some money now, but you will have to repay the loan with interest in the future. In both cases, to fully understand the deal between you and the bank, it is crucial to acknowledge that future dollars may have different value from current dollars. That is, you have to correct for the effects of inflation.

Let's consider an example. Suppose that Sally Saver deposits $1,000 in a bank account that pays an annual interest rate of 10 percent. A year later, after Sally has accumulated $100 in interest, she withdraws her $1,100. Is Sally $100 richer than she was when she made the deposit a year earlier?

The answer depends on what we mean by "richer." Sally does have $100 more than she had before. In other words, the number of dollars in her possession has risen by 10 percent. But Sally does not care about the amount of money itself: She cares about what she can buy with it. If prices have risen while her money was in the bank, each dollar now buys less than it did a year ago. In this case, her purchasing power—the amount of goods and services she can buy—has not risen by 10 percent.

To keep things simple, let's suppose that Sally is a music fan and buys only music CDs. When Sally made her deposit, a CD at her local music store cost $10. Her deposit of $1,000 was equivalent to 100 CDs. A year later, after getting her 10 percent interest, she has $1,100. How many CDs can she buy now? It depends on what has happened to the price of a CD. Here are some examples:

- Zero inflation: If the price of a CD remains at $10, the amount she can buy has risen from 100 to 110 CDs. The 10 percent increase in the number of dollars means a 10 percent increase in her purchasing power.
- Six percent inflation: If the price of a CD rises from $10 to $10.60, then the number of CDs she can buy has risen from 100 to approximately 104. Her purchasing power has increased by about 4 percent.
- Ten percent inflation: If the price of a CD rises from $10 to $11, then even though Sally's dollar wealth has risen from $1,000 to $1,100, she can still buy only 100 CDs. Her purchasing power is the same as it was a year earlier.

- Twelve percent inflation: If the price of a CD increases from $10 to $11.20, then even with her greater number of dollars, the number of CDs she can buy has fallen from 100 to approximately 98. Her purchasing power has decreased by about 2 percent.

And if Sally were living in an economy with deflation—falling prices—another possibility could arise:

- Two percent deflation: If the price of a CD falls from $10 to $9.80, then the number of CDs she can buy rises from 100 to approximately 112. Her purchasing power increases by about 12 percent.

These examples show that the higher the rate of inflation, the smaller the increase in Sally's purchasing power. If the rate of inflation exceeds the rate of interest, her purchasing power actually falls. And if there is deflation (that is, a negative rate of inflation), her purchasing power rises by more than the rate of interest.

To understand how much a person earns in a savings account, we need to consider both the interest rate and the change in the prices. The interest rate that measures the change in dollar amounts is called the **nominal interest rate,** and the interest rate corrected for inflation is called the **real interest rate.** The nominal interest rate, the real interest rate, and inflation are related approximately as follows:

$$\text{Real interest rate} = \text{Nominal interest rate} - \text{Inflation rate}.$$

The real interest rate is the difference between the nominal interest rate and the rate of inflation. The nominal interest rate tells you how fast the number of dollars in your bank account rises over time. The real interest rate tells you how fast the purchasing power of your bank account rises over time.

nominal interest rate
the interest rate as usually reported without a correction for the effects of inflation

real interest rate
the interest rate corrected for the effects of inflation

CASE
STUDY   INTEREST RATES IN THE U.S. ECONOMY

Figure 3 shows real and nominal interest rates in the U.S. economy since 1965. The nominal interest rate in this figure is the rate on 3-month Treasury bills (although data on other interest rates would be similar). The real interest rate is computed by subtracting the rate of inflation from this nominal interest rate. Here the inflation rate is measured as the percentage change in the consumer price index.

One feature of this figure is that the nominal interest rate always exceeds the real interest rate. This reflects the fact that the U.S. economy has experienced rising consumer prices in every year during this period. By contrast, if you looked at the U.S. economy during the late 19th century or at the Japanese economy in some recent years, you will find periods of deflation. During deflation, the real interest rate exceeds the nominal interest rate.

The figure also shows that real and nominal interest rates do not always move together. For example, in the late 1970s, nominal interest rates were high. But because inflation was very high, real interest rates were low. Indeed, during much of the 1970s, real interest rates were negative, for inflation eroded people's

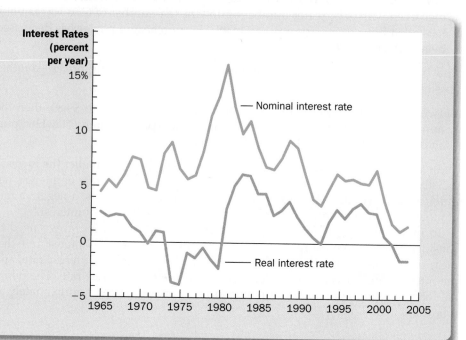

3 FIGURE

Real and Nominal Interest Rates

This figure shows nominal and real interest rates using annual data since 1965. The nominal interest rate is the rate on a 3-month Treasury bill. The real interest rate is the nominal interest rate minus the inflation rate as measured by the consumer price index. Notice that nominal and real interest rates often do not move together.

Source: U.S. Department of Labor; U.S. Department of Treasury.

savings more quickly than nominal interest payments increased them. By contrast, in the late 1990s, nominal interest rates were lower than they had been two decades earlier. But because inflation was much lower, real interest rates were higher. The early 2000s were a period when both real and nominal interest rates were low. In the coming chapters, we will examine the economic forces that determine both real and nominal interest rates. •

Quick Quiz   Henry Ford paid his workers $5 a day in 1914. If the consumer price index was 10 in 1914 and 195 in 2005, how much is the Ford paycheck worth in 2005 dollars?

CONCLUSION

"A nickel ain't worth a dime anymore," baseball player Yogi Berra once observed. Indeed, throughout recent history, the real values behind the nickel, the dime, and the dollar have not been stable. Persistent increases in the overall level of prices have been the norm. Such inflation reduces the purchasing power of each unit of money over time. When comparing dollar figures from different times, it is important to keep in mind that a dollar today is not the same as a dollar 20 years ago or, most likely, 20 years from now.

This chapter has discussed how economists measure the overall level of prices in the economy and how they use price indexes to correct economic variables for the effects of inflation. Price indexes allow us to compare dollar figures from different points in time and, therefore, get a better sense of how the economy is changing.

The discussion of price indexes in this chapter, together with the last chapter's discussion of GDP, is only a first step in the study of macroeconomics. We have not yet examined what determines a nation's GDP or the causes and effects of inflation. To do that, we need to go beyond issues of measurement. Indeed, that is our next task. Having explained how economists measure macroeconomic quantities and prices in the past two chapters, we are now ready to develop the models that explain movements in these variables.

Here is our strategy in the upcoming chapters. First, we look at the long-run determinants of real GDP and related variables, such as saving, investment, real interest rates, and unemployment. Second, we look at the long-run determinants of the price level and related variables, such as the money supply, inflation, and nominal interest rates. Last of all, having seen how these variables are determined in the long run, we examine the more complex question of what causes short-run fluctuations in real GDP and the price level. In all of these chapters, the measurement issues we have just discussed will provide the foundation for the analysis.

SUMMARY

- The consumer price index shows the cost of a basket of goods and services relative to the cost of the same basket in the base year. The index is used to measure the overall level of prices in the economy. The percentage change in the consumer price index measures the inflation rate.

- The consumer price index is an imperfect measure of the cost of living for three reasons. First, it does not take into account consumers' ability to substitute toward goods that become relatively cheaper over time. Second, it does not take into account increases in the purchasing power of the dollar due to the introduction of new goods. Third, it is distorted by unmeasured changes in the quality of goods and services. Because of these measurement problems, the CPI overstates true inflation.

- Like the consumer price index, the GDP deflator measures the overall level of prices in the economy. Although the two price indexes usually move together, there are important differences. The GDP deflator differs from the CPI because it includes goods and services produced rather than goods and services consumed. As a result, imported goods affect the consumer price index

but not the GDP deflator. In addition, while the consumer price index uses a fixed basket of goods, the GDP deflator automatically changes the group of goods and services over time as the composition of GDP changes.

- Dollar figures from different points in time do not represent a valid comparison of purchasing power. To compare a dollar figure from the past to a dollar figure today, the older figure should be inflated using a price index.

- Various laws and private contracts use price indexes to correct for the effects of inflation. The tax laws, however, are only partially indexed for inflation.

- A correction for inflation is especially important when looking at data on interest rates. The nominal interest rate is the interest rate usually reported; it is the rate at which the number of dollars in a savings account increases over time. By contrast, the real interest rate takes into account changes in the value of the dollar over time. The real interest rate equals the nominal interest rate minus the rate of inflation.

KEY CONCEPTS

consumer price index (CPI),
    p. 226
inflation rate, p. 228

producer price index, p. 228
indexation, p. 236

nominal interest rate, p. 237
real interest rate, p. 237

QUESTIONS FOR REVIEW

1. Which do you think has a greater effect on the consumer price index: a 10 percent increase in the price of chicken or a 10 percent increase in the price of caviar? Why?

2. Describe the three problems that make the consumer price index an imperfect measure of the cost of living.

3. If the price of a Navy submarine rises, is the consumer price index or the GDP deflator affected more? Why?

4. Over a long period of time, the price of a candy bar rose from $0.10 to $0.60. Over the same period, the consumer price index rose from 150 to 300. Adjusted for overall inflation, how much did the price of the candy bar change?

5. Explain the meaning of *nominal interest rate* and *real interest rate*. How are they related?

PROBLEMS AND APPLICATIONS

1. Suppose that the residents of Vegopia spend all of their income on cauliflower, broccoli, and carrots. In 2006, they buy 100 heads of cauliflower for $200, 50 bunches of broccoli for $75, and 500 carrots for $50. In 2007, they buy 75 heads of cauliflower for $225, 80 bunches of broccoli for $120, and 500 carrots for $100.
   a. Calculate the price of each vegetable in each year.
   b. Using 2006 as the base year, calculate the CPI for each year.
   c. What is the inflation rate in 2007?

2. Go to the website of the Bureau of Labor Statistics (http://www.bls.gov) and find data on the consumer price index. By how much has the index including all items risen over the past year? For which categories of spending have prices risen the most? The least? Have any categories experienced price declines? Can you explain any of these facts?

3. Suppose that people consume only three goods, as shown in this table:

	Tennis Balls	Golf Balls	Bottle of Gatorade
2006 price	$2	$4	$1
2006 quantity	100	100	200
2007 price	$2	$6	$2
2007 quantity	100	100	200

   a. What is the percentage change in the price of each of the three goods?
   b. Using a method similar to the consumer price index, compute the percentage change in the overall price level.
   c. If you were to learn that a bottle of Gatorade increased in size from 2006 and 2007, should that information affect your calculation of the inflation rate? If so, how?
   d. If you were to learn that Gatorade introduced new flavors in 2007, should that information

affect your calculation of the inflation rate? If so, how?

4. Beginning in 1994, environmental regulations have required that gasoline contain a new additive to reduce air pollution. This requirement raised the cost of gasoline. The Bureau of Labor Statistics decided that this increase in cost represented an improvement in quality.
   a. Given this decision, did the increased cost of gasoline raise the CPI?
   b. What is the argument in favor of the BLS's decision? What is the argument for a different decision?

5. Which of the problems in the construction of the CPI might be illustrated by each of the following situations? Explain.
   a. the invention of the Sony Walkman
   b. the introduction of air bags in cars
   c. increased personal computer purchases in response to a decline in their price
   d. more scoops of raisins in each package of Raisin Bran
   e. greater use of fuel-efficient cars after gasoline prices increase

6. *The New York Times* cost $0.15 in 1970 and $0.75 in 2000. The average wage in manufacturing was $3.23 per hour in 1970 and $14.32 in 2000.
   a. By what percentage did the price of a newspaper rise?
   b. By what percentage did the wage rise?
   c. In each year, how many minutes does a worker have to work to earn enough to buy a newspaper?
   d. Did workers' purchasing power in terms of newspapers rise or fall?

7. The chapter explains that Social Security benefits are increased each year in proportion to the increase in the CPI, even though most economists believe that the CPI overstates actual inflation.
   a. If the elderly consume the same market basket as other people, does Social Security provide the elderly with an improvement in their standard of living each year? Explain.
   b. In fact, the elderly consume more healthcare than younger people, and healthcare costs have risen faster than overall inflation. What would you do to determine whether the elderly are actually better off from year to year?

8. Income tax brackets were not indexed until 1985. When inflation pushed up people's nominal incomes during the 1970s, what do you think happened to real tax revenue? (Hint: This phenomenon was known as "bracket creep.")

9. When deciding how much of their income to save for retirement, should workers consider the real or the nominal interest rate that their savings will earn? Explain.

10. Suppose that a borrower and a lender agree on the nominal interest rate to be paid on a loan. Then inflation turns out to be higher than they both expected.
   a. Is the real interest rate on this loan higher or lower than expected?
   b. Does the lender gain or lose from this unexpectedly high inflation? Does the borrower gain or lose?
   c. Inflation during the 1970s was much higher than most people had expected when the decade began. How did this affect homeowners who obtained fixed-rate mortgages during the 1960s? How did it affect the banks that lent the money?

 For further information on topics in this chapter, additional problems, examples, applications, online quizzes, and more, please visit our website at http://mankiw.swlearning.com.

5

The Real Economy in the Long Run

Production and Growth

W hen you travel around the world, you see tremendous variation in the standard of living. The average income in a rich country, such as the United States, Japan, or Germany, is more than ten times the average income in a poor country, such as India, Indonesia, or Nigeria. These large differences in income are reflected in large differences in the quality of life. People in richer countries have more automobiles, more telephones, more televisions, better nutrition, safer housing, better healthcare, and longer life expectancy.

Even within a country, there are large changes in the standard of living over time. In the United States over the past century, average income as measured by real GDP per person has grown by about 2 percent per year. Although 2 percent might seem small, this rate of growth implies that average income doubles every 35 years. Because of this growth, average income today is about eight times as high as average income a century ago. As a result, the typical American enjoys much greater economic prosperity than did his or her parents, grandparents, and great-grandparents.

Growth rates vary substantially from country to country. In some East Asian countries, such as Singapore, South Korea, and Taiwan, average income has risen about 7 percent per year in recent decades. At this rate, average income doubles every 10 years. These countries have, in the length of one generation, gone from being among the poorest in the world to being among the richest. By contrast, in some African countries, such as Chad, Ethiopia, and Nigeria, average income has been stagnant for many years.

What explains these diverse experiences? How can the rich countries be sure to maintain their high standard of living? What policies should the poor countries pursue to promote more rapid growth and join the developed world? These are among the most important questions in macroeconomics. As economist Robert Lucas put it, "The consequences for human welfare in questions like these are simply staggering: Once one starts to think about them, it is hard to think about anything else."

In the previous two chapters, we discussed how economists measure macroeconomic quantities and prices. In this chapter, we start studying the forces that determine these variables. As we have seen, an economy's gross domestic product (GDP) measures both the total income earned in the economy and the total expenditure on the economy's output of goods and services. The level of real GDP is a good gauge of economic prosperity, and the growth of real GDP is a good gauge of economic progress. Here we focus on the long-run determinants of the level and growth of real GDP. Later in this book, we study the short-run fluctuations of real GDP around its long-run trend.

We proceed here in three steps. First, we examine international data on real GDP per person. These data will give you some sense of how much the level and growth of living standards vary around the world. Second, we examine the role of *productivity*—the amount of goods and services produced for each hour of a worker's time. In particular, we see that a nation's standard of living is determined by the productivity of its workers, and we consider the factors that determine a nation's productivity. Third, we consider the link between productivity and the economic policies that a nation pursues.

ECONOMIC GROWTH AROUND THE WORLD

As a starting point for our study of long-run growth, let's look at the experiences of some of the world's economies. Table 1 shows data on real GDP per person for thirteen countries. For each country, the data cover more than a century of history. The first and second columns of the table present the countries and time periods. (The time periods differ somewhat from country to country because of differences in data availability.) The third and fourth columns show estimates of real GDP per person about a century ago and for a recent year.

The data on real GDP per person show that living standards vary widely from country to country. Income per person in the United States, for instance, is about 7 times that in China and about 13 times that in India. The poorest countries have average levels of income that have not been seen in the developed world for many decades. The typical citizen of India in 2003 had less real income as the typical resident of England in 1870. The typical person in Bangladesh in 2003 had about one-half the real income of a typical American a century ago.

The last column of the table shows each country's growth rate. The growth rate measures how rapidly real GDP per person grew in the typical year. In the United States, for example, real GDP per person was $3,412 in 1870 and $37,500 in 2003. The growth rate was 1.82 percent per year. This means that if real GDP per person, beginning at $3,412, were to increase by 1.82 percent for each of 133 years, it would end up at $37,500. Of course, real GDP per person did not actually rise exactly 1.82 percent every year: Some years it rose by more and other years by less. The growth rate of 1.82 percent per year ignores short-run fluctua-

Country	Period	Real GDP per Person at Beginning of Period[a]	Real GDP per Person at End of Period[a]	Growth Rate (per year)
Japan	1890–2003	$1,280	$28,620	2.79%
Brazil	1900–2003	663	7,480	2.38
Mexico	1900–2003	987	8,950	2.16
China	1900–2003	610	4,990	2.06
Germany	1870–2003	1,859	27,460	2.05
Canada	1870–2003	2,022	29,740	2.04
United States	1870–2003	3,412	37,500	1.82
Argentina	1900–2003	1,952	10,920	1.69
India	1900–2003	575	2,880	1.58
United Kingdom	1870–2003	4,094	27,650	1.45
Indonesia	1900–2003	759	3,210	1.41
Pakistan	1900–2003	628	2,060	1.16
Bangladesh	1900–2003	531	1,870	1.16

[a]Real GDP is measured in 2003 dollars.

TABLE 1

The Variety of Growth Experiences

Source: Robert J. Barro and Xavier Sala-i-Martin, *Economic Growth* (New York: McGraw-Hill, 1995), tables 10.2 and 10.3; *World Development Report 2005*, Table 1; and author's calculations.

tions around the long-run trend and represents an average rate of growth for real GDP per person over many years.

The countries in Table 1 are ordered by their growth rate from the most to the least rapid. Japan tops the list, with a growth rate of 2.79 percent per year. A hundred years ago, Japan was not a rich country. Japan's average income was only somewhat higher than Mexico's, and it was well behind Argentina's. The standard of living in Japan in 1890 was lower than in India today. But because of its spectacular growth, Japan is now an economic superpower, with average income more than twice that of Mexico and Argentina and similar to Germany, Canada, and the United Kingdom. At the bottom of the list of countries are Bangladesh and Pakistan, which have experienced growth of only 1.16 percent per year over the past century. As a result, the typical resident of these countries continues to live in abject poverty.

Because of differences in growth rates, the ranking of countries by income changes substantially over time. As we have seen, Japan is a country that has risen relative to others. One country that has fallen behind is the United Kingdom. In 1870, the United Kingdom was the richest country in the world, with average income about 20 percent higher than that of the United States and about twice that of Canada. Today, average income in the United Kingdom is below the average income in its two former colonies.

These data show that the world's richest countries have no guarantee they will stay the richest and that the world's poorest countries are not doomed forever to remain in poverty. But what explains these changes over time? Why do some countries zoom ahead while others lag behind? These are precisely the questions that we take up next.

Quick Quiz What is the approximate growth rate of real GDP per person in the United States? Name a country that has had faster growth and a country that has had slower growth.

FYI

A Picture Is Worth a Thousand Statistics

George Bernard Shaw once said, "The sign of a truly educated man is to be deeply moved by statistics." Most of us, however, have trouble being deeply moved by data on GDP—until we see what these statistics represent.

The three photos on these pages show a typical family from each of three countries—the United Kingdom, Mexico, and Mali. Each family was photographed outside their home, together with all of their material possessions.

These nations have very different standards of living, as judged by these photos, GDP, or other statistics.

- The United Kingdom is an advanced economy. In 2003, its GDP per person was $27,650. A negligible share of the population lives in extreme poverty, defined here as less than $2 a day. Educational attainment is high: Among children of high-school age, 95 percent are in school. Residents of the United Kingdom can expect to enjoy a long life: The probability of a person surviving to age 65 is 83 percent for men and 89 percent for women.
- Mexico is a middle-income country. In 2003, its GDP per person was $8,950. About a quarter of the population lives on less than $2 a day. Among children of high-school age, 60 percent are in school. The probability of a person surviving to age 65 is 71 percent for men and 82 percent for women.
- Mali is a poor country. In 2003, its GDP per person was only $960. Extreme poverty is the norm: More than half of the population lives on less than $2 per day. Educational attainment in Mali is low: Among children of high-school age, less than 10 percent are in school. And life is often cut short: The probability of a person surviving to age 65 is only 37 percent for men and 41 percent for women.

Economists who study economic growth try to understand what causes such large differences in the standard of living.

© DAVID REED

A Typical Family in the United Kingdom

A Typical Family in Mexico

A Typical Family in Mali

FYI

Are You Richer Than the Richest American?

The magazine *American Heritage* once published a list of the richest Americans of all time. The number 1 spot went to John D. Rockefeller, the oil entrepreneur who lived from 1839 to 1937. According to the magazine's calculations, his wealth would today be the equivalent of $200 billion, more than twice that of Bill Gates, the software entrepreneur who is today's richest American.

Despite his great wealth, Rockefeller did not enjoy many of the conveniences that we now take for granted. He couldn't watch television, play video games, surf the Internet, or send an e-mail. During the heat of summer, he couldn't cool his home with air conditioning. For much of his life, he couldn't travel by car or plane, and he couldn't use a telephone to call friends or family. If he became ill, he couldn't take advantage of many medicines, such as antibiotics, that doctors today routinely use to prolong and enhance life.

John D. Rockefeller

Now consider: How much money would someone have to pay you to give up for the rest of your life all the modern conveniences that Rockefeller lived without? Would you do it for $200 billion? Perhaps not. And if you wouldn't, is it fair to say that you are better off than John D. Rockefeller, allegedly the richest American ever?

The preceding chapter discussed how standard price indexes, which are used to compare sums of money from different points in time, fail to fully reflect the introduction of new goods in the economy. As a result, the rate of inflation is overestimated. The flip side of this observation is that the rate of real economic growth is underestimated. Pondering Rockefeller's life shows how significant this problem might be. Because of tremendous technological advances, the average American today is arguably "richer" than the richest American a century ago, even if that fact is lost in standard economic statistics.

PRODUCTIVITY: ITS ROLE AND DETERMINANTS

Explaining the large variation in living standards around the world is, in one sense, very easy. As we will see, the explanation can be summarized in a single word—*productivity*. But in another sense, the international variation is deeply puzzling. To explain why incomes are so much higher in some countries than in others, we must look at the many factors that determine a nation's productivity.

Why Productivity Is So Important

Let's begin our study of productivity and economic growth by developing a simple model based loosely on Daniel Defoe's famous novel *Robinson Crusoe*. Robinson Crusoe, as you may recall, is a sailor stranded on a desert island. Because Crusoe lives alone, he catches his own fish, grows his own vegetables, and makes his own clothes. We can think of Crusoe's activities—his production and consumption of fish, vegetables, and clothing—as a simple economy. By examining Crusoe's economy, we can learn some lessons that also apply to more complex and realistic economies.

What determines Crusoe's standard of living? In a word, **productivity,** the quantity of goods and services produced from each unit of labor input. If Crusoe

productivity
the quantity of goods and services produced from each unit of labor input

is good at catching fish, growing vegetables, and making clothes, he lives well. If he is bad at doing these things, he lives poorly. Because Crusoe gets to consume only what he produces, his living standard is tied to his productivity.

In the case of Crusoe's economy, it is easy to see that productivity is the key determinant of living standards and that growth in productivity is the key determinant of growth in living standards. The more fish Crusoe can catch per hour, the more he eats at dinner. If Crusoe finds a better place to catch fish, his productivity rises. This increase in productivity makes Crusoe better off: He can eat the extra fish, or he can spend less time fishing and devote more time to making other goods he enjoys.

Productivity's key role in determining living standards is as true for nations as it is for stranded sailors. Recall that an economy's gross domestic product (GDP) measures two things at once: the total income earned by everyone in the economy and the total expenditure on the economy's output of goods and services. The reason GDP can measure these two things simultaneously is that, for the economy as a whole, they must be equal. Put simply, an economy's income is the economy's output.

Like Crusoe, a nation can enjoy a high standard of living only if it can produce a large quantity of goods and services. Americans live better than Nigerians because American workers are more productive than Nigerian workers. The Japanese have enjoyed more rapid growth in living standards than Argentineans because Japanese workers have experienced more rapidly growing productivity. Indeed, one of the *Ten Principles of Economics* in Chapter 1 is that a country's standard of living depends on its ability to produce goods and services.

Hence, to understand the large differences in living standards we observe across countries or over time, we must focus on the production of goods and services. But seeing the link between living standards and productivity is only the first step. It leads naturally to the next question: Why are some economies so much better at producing goods and services than others?

How Productivity Is Determined

Although productivity is uniquely important in determining Robinson Crusoe's standard of living, many factors determine Crusoe's productivity. Crusoe will be better at catching fish, for instance, if he has more fishing poles, if he has been trained in the best fishing techniques, if his island has a plentiful fish supply, and if he invents a better fishing lure. Each of these determinants of Crusoe's productivity—which we can call *physical capital, human capital, natural resources, and technological knowledge*—has a counterpart in more complex and realistic economies. Let's consider each of these factors in turn.

Physical Capital per Worker Workers are more productive if they have tools with which to work. The stock of equipment and structures that are used to produce goods and services is called **physical capital,** or just *capital.* For example, when woodworkers make furniture, they use saws, lathes, and drill presses. More tools allow the woodworkers to produce their output more quickly and more accurately: A worker with only basic hand tools can make less furniture each week than a worker with sophisticated and specialized woodworking equipment.

As you may recall, the inputs used to produce goods and services—labor, capital, and so on—are called the *factors of production.* An important feature of capital is that it is a *produced* factor of production. That is, capital is an input into

physical capital
the stock of equipment and structures that are used to produce goods and services

the production process that in the past was an output from the production process. The woodworker uses a lathe to make the leg of a table. Earlier, the lathe itself was the output of a firm that manufactures lathes. The lathe manufacturer in turn used other equipment to make its product. Thus, capital is a factor of production used to produce all kinds of goods and services, including more capital.

human capital
the knowledge and skills that workers acquire through education, training, and experience

Human Capital per Worker   A second determinant of productivity is human capital. **Human capital** is the economist's term for the knowledge and skills that workers acquire through education, training, and experience. Human capital includes the skills accumulated in early childhood programs, grade school, high school, college, and on-the-job training for adults in the labor force.

Although education, training, and experience are less tangible than lathes, bulldozers, and buildings, human capital is like physical capital in many ways. Like physical capital, human capital raises a nation's ability to produce goods and services. Also like physical capital, human capital is a produced factor of production. Producing human capital requires inputs in the form of teachers, libraries, and student time. Indeed, students can be viewed as "workers" who have the important job of producing the human capital that will be used in future production.

natural resources
the inputs into the production of goods and services that are provided by nature, such as land, rivers, and mineral deposits

Natural Resources per Worker   A third determinant of productivity is **natural resources.** Natural resources are inputs into production that are provided by nature, such as land, rivers, and mineral deposits. Natural resources take two forms: renewable and nonrenewable. A forest is an example of a renewable resource. When one tree is cut down, a seedling can be planted in its place to be harvested in the future. Oil is an example of a nonrenewable resource. Because oil is produced by nature over many thousands of years, there is only a limited supply. Once the supply of oil is depleted, it is impossible to create more.

Differences in natural resources are responsible for some of the differences in standards of living around the world. The historical success of the United States was driven in part by the large supply of land well suited for agriculture. Today, some countries in the Middle East, such as Kuwait and Saudi Arabia, are rich simply because they happen to be on top of some of the largest pools of oil in the world.

Although natural resources can be important, they are not necessary for an economy to be highly productive in producing goods and services. Japan, for instance, is one of the richest countries in the world, despite having few natural resources. International trade makes Japan's success possible. Japan imports many of the natural resources it needs, such as oil, and exports its manufactured goods to economies rich in natural resources.

technological knowledge
society's understanding of the best ways to produce goods and services

Technological Knowledge   A fourth determinant of productivity is **technological knowledge**—the understanding of the best ways to produce goods and services. A hundred years ago, most Americans worked on farms because farm technology required a high input of labor to feed the entire population. Today, thanks to advances in the technology of farming, a small fraction of the population can produce enough food to feed the entire country. This technological change made labor available to produce other goods and services.

Technological knowledge takes many forms. Some technology is common knowledge—after one person uses it, everyone becomes aware of it. For example, once Henry Ford successfully introduced production in assembly lines, other carmakers quickly followed suit. Other technology is proprietary—it is known only by the company that discovers it. Only the Coca-Cola Company, for

FYI

The Production Function

Economists often use a *production function* to describe the relationship between the quantity of inputs used in production and the quantity of output from production. For example, suppose Y denotes the quantity of output, L the quantity of labor, K the quantity of physical capital, H the quantity of human capital, and N the quantity of natural resources. Then we might write

$$Y = A \, F(L, K, H, N),$$

where $F(\ )$ is a function that shows how the inputs are combined to produce output. A is a variable that reflects the available production technology. As technology improves, A rises, so the economy produces more output from any given combination of inputs.

Many production functions have a property called *constant returns to scale*. If a production function has constant returns to scale, then doubling all inputs causes the amount of output to double as well. Mathematically, we write that a production function has constant returns to scale if, for any positive number x,

$$xY = A \, F(xL, xK, xH, xN).$$

A doubling of all inputs would be represented in this equation by $x = 2$. The right side shows the inputs doubling, and the left side shows output doubling.

Production functions with constant returns to scale have an interesting implication. To see what it is, it will prove instructive to set $x = 1/L$. Then the preceding equation becomes

$$Y/L = A \, F(1, K/L, H/L, N/L).$$

Notice that Y/L is output per worker, which is a measure of productivity. This equation says that labor productivity depends on physical capital per worker (K/L), human capital per worker (H/L), and natural resources per worker (N/L). Productivity also depends on the state of technology, as reflected by the variable A. Thus, this equation provides a mathematical summary of the four determinants of productivity we have just discussed.

---

instance, knows the secret recipe for making its famous soft drink. Still other technology is proprietary for a short time. When a pharmaceutical company discovers a new drug, the patent system gives that company a temporary right to be its exclusive manufacturer. When the patent expires, however, other companies are allowed to make the drug. All these forms of technological knowledge are important for the economy's production of goods and services.

It is worthwhile to distinguish between technological knowledge and human capital. Although they are closely related, there is an important difference. Technological knowledge refers to society's understanding about how the world works. Human capital refers to the resources expended transmitting this understanding to the labor force. To use a relevant metaphor, knowledge is the quality of society's textbooks, whereas human capital is the amount of time that the population has devoted to reading them. Workers' productivity depends on both.

CASE STUDY | ARE NATURAL RESOURCES A LIMIT TO GROWTH?

Today, the world's population is over 6 trillion, about four times what it was a century ago. At the same time, many people are enjoying a much higher standard of living than did their great-grandparents. A perennial debate concerns whether this growth in population and living standards can continue in the future.

Many commentators have argued that natural resources will eventually limit how much the world's economies can grow. At first, this argument might seem hard to ignore. If the world has only a fixed supply of nonrenewable natural resources, how can population, production, and living standards continue to grow over time? Eventually, won't supplies of oil and minerals start to run out? When these shortages start to occur, won't they stop economic growth and, perhaps, even force living standards to fall?

Despite the apparent appeal of such arguments, most economists are less concerned about such limits to growth than one might guess. They argue that technological progress often yields ways to avoid these limits. If we compare the economy today to the economy of the past, we see various ways in which the use of natural resources has improved. Modern cars have better gas mileage. New houses have better insulation and require less energy to heat and cool them. More efficient oil rigs waste less oil in the process of extraction. Recycling allows some nonrenewable resources to be reused. The development of alternative fuels, such as ethanol instead of gasoline, allows us to substitute renewable for nonrenewable resources.

Fifty years ago, some conservationists were concerned about the excessive use of tin and copper. At the time, these were crucial commodities: Tin was used to make many food containers, and copper was used to make telephone wire. Some people advocated mandatory recycling and rationing of tin and copper so that supplies would be available for future generations. Today, however, plastic has replaced tin as a material for making many food containers, and phone calls often travel over fiberoptic cables, which are made from sand. Technological progress has made once crucial natural resources less necessary.

But are all these efforts enough to permit continued economic growth? One way to answer this question is to look at the prices of natural resources. In a market economy, scarcity is reflected in market prices. If the world were running out of natural resources, then the prices of those resources would be rising over time. But in fact, the opposite is more nearly true. The prices of most natural resources (adjusted for overall inflation) are stable or falling. It appears that our ability to conserve these resources is growing more rapidly than their supplies are dwindling. Market prices give no reason to believe that natural resources are a limit to economic growth.   •

Quick Quiz   List and describe four determinants of a country's productivity.

ECONOMIC GROWTH AND PUBLIC POLICY

So far, we have determined that a society's standard of living depends on its ability to produce goods and services and that its productivity depends on physical capital per worker, human capital per worker, natural resources per worker, and technological knowledge. Let's now turn to the question faced by policymakers around the world: What can government policy do to raise productivity and living standards?

Saving and Investment

Because capital is a produced factor of production, a society can change the amount of capital it has. If today the economy produces a large quantity of new capital goods, then tomorrow it will have a larger stock of capital and be able to produce more of all types of goods and services. Thus, one way to raise future productivity is to invest more current resources in the production of capital.

One of the *Ten Principles of Economics* presented in Chapter 1 is that people face trade-offs. This principle is especially important when considering the accumulation of capital. Because resources are scarce, devoting more resources to producing capital requires devoting fewer resources to producing goods and services for current consumption. That is, for society to invest more in capital, it must consume less and save more of its current income. The growth that arises from capital accumulation is not a free lunch: It requires that society sacrifice consumption of goods and services in the present to enjoy higher consumption in the future.

The next chapter examines in more detail how the economy's financial markets coordinate saving and investment. It also examines how government policies influence the amount of saving and investment that takes place. At this point, it is important to note that encouraging saving and investment is one way that a government can encourage growth and, in the long run, raise the economy's standard of living.

Diminishing Returns and the Catch-Up Effect

Suppose that a government pursues policies that raise the nation's saving rate—the percentage of GDP devoted to saving rather than consumption. What happens? With the nation saving more, fewer resources are needed to make consumption goods, and more resources are available to make capital goods. As a result, the capital stock increases, leading to rising productivity and more rapid growth in GDP. But how long does this higher rate of growth last? Assuming that the saving rate remains at its new higher level, does the growth rate of GDP stay high indefinitely or only for a period of time?

The traditional view of the production process is that capital is subject to **diminishing returns:** As the stock of capital rises, the extra output produced from an additional unit of capital falls. In other words, when workers already have a large quantity of capital to use in producing goods and services, giving them an additional unit of capital increases their productivity only slightly. This is illustrated in Figure 1, which shows how the amount of capital per worker determines the amount of output per worker, holding constant all the other determinants of output.

diminishing returns
the property whereby the benefit from an extra unit of an input declines as the quantity of the input increases

Because of diminishing returns, an increase in the saving rate leads to higher growth only for a while. As the higher saving rate allows more capital to be accumulated, the benefits from additional capital become smaller over time, and so growth slows down. *In the long run, the higher saving rate leads to a higher level of productivity and income but not to higher growth in these variables.* Reaching this long run, however, can take quite a while. According to studies of international data on economic growth, increasing the saving rate can lead to substantially higher growth for a period of several decades.

The diminishing returns to capital has another important implication: Other things equal, it is easier for a country to grow fast if it starts out relatively poor.

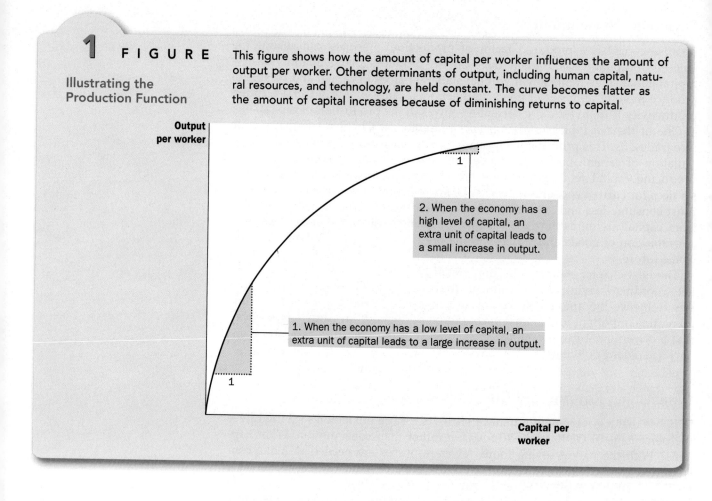

FIGURE 1

Illustrating the Production Function

This figure shows how the amount of capital per worker influences the amount of output per worker. Other determinants of output, including human capital, natural resources, and technology, are held constant. The curve becomes flatter as the amount of capital increases because of diminishing returns to capital.

Output per worker

2. When the economy has a high level of capital, an extra unit of capital leads to a small increase in output.

1. When the economy has a low level of capital, an extra unit of capital leads to a large increase in output.

Capital per worker

catch-up effect
the property whereby countries that start off poor tend to grow more rapidly than countries that start off rich

This effect of initial conditions on subsequent growth is sometimes called the **catch-up effect.** In poor countries, workers lack even the most rudimentary tools and, as a result, have low productivity. Small amounts of capital investment would substantially raise these workers' productivity. By contrast, workers in rich countries have large amounts of capital with which to work, and this partly explains their high productivity. Yet with the amount of capital per worker already so high, additional capital investment has a relatively small effect on productivity. Studies of international data on economic growth confirm this catch-up effect: Controlling for other variables, such as the percentage of GDP devoted to investment, poor countries do tend to grow at a faster rate than rich countries.

This catch-up effect can help explain some of otherwise puzzling facts. Here's an example: From 1960 to 1990, the United States and South Korea devoted a similar share of GDP to investment. Yet over this time, the United States experienced only mediocre growth of about 2 percent, while Korea experienced spectacular growth of more than 6 percent. The explanation is the catch-up effect. In 1960, Korea had GDP per person less than one-tenth the U.S. level, in part because previous investment had been so low. With a small initial capital stock, the benefits to capital accumulation were much greater in Korea, and this gave Korea a higher subsequent growth rate.

This catch-up effect shows up in other aspects of life. When a school gives an end-of-year award to the "Most Improved" student, that student is usually one who began the year with relatively poor performance. Students who began the year not studying find improvement easier than students who always worked hard. Note that it is good to be "Most Improved," given the starting point, but it is even better to be "Best Student." Similarly, economic growth over the last several decades has been much more rapid in South Korea than in the United States, but GDP per person is still higher in the United States.

Investment from Abroad

So far, we have discussed how policies aimed at increasing a country's saving rate can increase investment and, thereby, long-term economic growth. Yet saving by domestic residents is not the only way for a country to invest in new capital. The other way is investment by foreigners.

Investment from abroad takes several forms. Ford Motor Company might build a car factory in Mexico. A capital investment that is owned and operated by a foreign entity is called *foreign direct investment*. Alternatively, an American might buy stock in a Mexican corporation (that is, buy a share in the ownership of the corporation); the Mexican corporation can use the proceeds from the stock sale to build a new factory. An investment that is financed with foreign money but operated by domestic residents is called *foreign portfolio investment*. In both cases, Americans provide the resources necessary to increase the stock of capital in Mexico. That is, American saving is being used to finance Mexican investment.

When foreigners invest in a country, they do so because they expect to earn a return on their investment. Ford's car factory increases the Mexican capital stock and, therefore, increases Mexican productivity and Mexican GDP. Yet Ford takes some of this additional income back to the United States in the form of profit. Similarly, when an American investor buys Mexican stock, the investor has a right to a portion of the profit that the Mexican corporation earns.

Investment from abroad, therefore, does not have the same effect on all measures of economic prosperity. Recall that gross domestic product (GDP) is the income earned within a country by both residents and nonresidents, whereas gross national product (GNP) is the income earned by residents of a country both at home and abroad. When Ford opens its car factory in Mexico, some of the income the factory generates accrues to people who do not live in Mexico. As a result, foreign investment in Mexico raises the income of Mexicans (measured by GNP) by less than it raises the production in Mexico (measured by GDP).

Nonetheless, investment from abroad is one way for a country to grow. Even though some of the benefits from this investment flow back to the foreign owners, this investment does increase the economy's stock of capital, leading to higher productivity and higher wages. Moreover, investment from abroad is one way for poor countries to learn the state-of-the-art technologies developed and used in richer countries. For these reasons, many economists who advise governments in less developed economies advocate policies that encourage investment from abroad. Often, this means removing restrictions that governments have imposed on foreign ownership of domestic capital.

An organization that tries to encourage the flow of capital to poor countries is the World Bank. This international organization obtains funds from the world's advanced countries, such as the United States, and uses these resources to make loans to less developed countries so that they can invest in roads, sewer systems, schools, and other types of capital. It also offers the countries advice about how the funds might best be used. The World Bank, together with its sister organization, the International Monetary Fund, was set up after World War II. One lesson from the war was that economic distress often leads to political turmoil, international tensions, and military conflict. Thus, every country has an interest in promoting economic prosperity around the world. The World Bank and the International Monetary Fund were established to achieve that common goal.

Education

Education—investment in human capital—is at least as important as investment in physical capital for a country's long-run economic success. In the United States, each year of schooling has historically raised a person's wage on average by about 10 percent. In less developed countries, where human capital is especially scarce, the gap between the wages of educated and uneducated workers is even larger. Thus, one way government policy can enhance the standard of living is to provide good schools and to encourage the population to take advantage of them.

Investment in human capital, like investment in physical capital, has an opportunity cost. When students are in school, they forgo the wages they could have earned. In less developed countries, children often drop out of school at an early age, even though the benefit of additional schooling is very high, simply because their labor is needed to help support the family.

Some economists have argued that human capital is particularly important for economic growth because human capital conveys positive externalities. An *externality* is the effect of one person's actions on the well-being of a bystander. An educated person, for instance, might generate new ideas about how best to produce goods and services. If these ideas enter society's pool of knowledge so everyone can use them, then the ideas are an external benefit of education. In this case, the return to schooling for society is even greater than the return for the individual. This argument would justify the large subsidies to human-capital investment that we observe in the form of public education.

One problem facing some poor countries is the *brain drain*—the emigration of many of the most highly educated workers to rich countries, where these workers can enjoy a higher standard of living. If human capital does have positive externalities, then this brain drain makes those people left behind poorer than they otherwise would be. This problem offers policymakers a dilemma. On the one hand, the United States and other rich countries have the best systems of higher education, and it would seem natural for poor countries to send their best students abroad to earn higher degrees. On the other hand, those students who have spent time abroad may choose not to return home, and this brain drain will reduce the poor nation's stock of human capital even further.

Health and Nutrition

Although the term *human capital* usually refers to education, it can also be used to describe another type of investment in people: expenditures that lead to a healthier population. Other things equal, healthier workers are more productive. Making the right investments in the health of the population is one way for a nation to increase productivity and raise living standards.

Economic historian Robert Fogel has suggested that a significant factor in long-run economic growth is improved health from better nutrition. He estimates that in Great Britain in 1780, about one in five people were so malnour-

In The News

Promoting Human Capital

Human capital is a key to economic growth. With this in mind, some developing countries now give parents an immediate financial incentive to keep their children in school.

Brazil Pays Parents to Help Poor Be Pupils, Not Wage Earners

By Celia W. Dugger

ORTALEZA, Brazil—Vandelson Andrade, 13, often used to skip school to work 12-hour days on the small, graceful fishing boats that sail from the picturesque harbor here. His meager earnings helped pay for rice and beans for his desperately poor family.

But this year he qualified for a small monthly cash payment from the government that his mother receives on the condition that he shows up in the classroom.

"I can't skip school anymore," said Vandelson, whose hand-me-down pants were so big that the crotch ended at his knees and the legs bunched up around his ankles. "If I miss one more day, my mother won't get the money."

This year, Vandelson will finally pass the fourth grade on his third try—a small victory in a new breed of social program that is spreading swiftly across Latin America. It is a developing-country version of American welfare reform: to break the cycle of poverty, the government gives the poor small cash payments in exchange for keeping their children in school and taking them for regular medical checkups.

"I think these programs are as close as you can come to a magic bullet in development," said Nancy Birdsall, president of the Center for Global Development, a nonprofit research group in Washington. "They're creating an incentive for families to invest in their own children's futures. Every decade or so, we see something that can really make a difference, and this is one of those things." . . .

Antônio Souza, 48, and Maria Torres, 37, are raising seven children in a mud hut a couple of hills away from Ms. Andrade. Every member of the family is sinewy and lean. The parents cannot remember the last time the family ate meat or vegetables. But their grant of $27 a month makes it possible to buy rice, sugar, pasta and oil.

Mr. Souza and Ms. Torres, illiterate believers in the power of education,

VANDELSON ANDRADE, STUDENT

have always sent their children to school. "If they don't study, they'll turn into dummies like me," said their father, whose weathered, deeply creased face broke into a wide smile as he surveyed his bright-eyed daughters, Ana Paula, 11, and Daniele, 8, among them. "All I can do is work in the fields."

His wife said proudly: "There are fathers who don't want their children to go to school. But this man here has done everything he could to send his children to school."

Source: *The New York Times,* January 3, 2004.

ished that they were incapable of manual labor. Among those who could work, insufficient caloric intake substantially reduced the work effort they could put forth. As nutrition improved, so did workers' productivity.

Fogel studies these historical trends in part by looking at the height of the population. Short height can be an indicator of malnutrition, especially during pregnancy and the early years of life. Fogel finds that as nations develop economically, people eat more, and the population gets taller. From 1775 to 1975, the average caloric intake in Great Britain rose by 26 percent, and the height of the average man rose by 3.6 inches. Similarly, during the spectacular economic growth in South Korea from 1962 to 1995, caloric consumption rose by 44 percent, and average male height rose by 2 inches. Of course, a person's height is determined by a combination of genetic predisposition and environment. But because the genetic makeup of a population is slow to change, such increases in average height are most likely due to changes in the environment—nutrition being the obvious explanation.

Moreover, studies have found that height is an indicator of productivity. Looking at data on a large number of workers at a point in time, researchers have found that taller workers tend to earn more. Because wages reflect a worker's productivity, this finding suggests that taller workers tend to be more productive. The effect of height on wages is especially pronounced in poorer countries, where malnutrition is a bigger risk.

Fogel won the Nobel prize in economics in 1993 for his work in economic history, which includes not only his studies of nutrition but also his studies of American slavery and the role of railroads in the development of the American economy. In the lecture he gave when he was awarded the prize, he surveyed the evidence on health and economic growth. He concluded that "improved gross nutrition accounts for roughly 30 percent of the growth of per capita income in Britain between 1790 and 1980."

Today, malnutrition is fortunately rare in developed nations such as Great Britain and the United States. (Obesity is a more widespread problem.) But for people in developing nations, poor health and inadequate nutrition remain obstacles to higher productivity and improved living standards. The United Nations has recently estimated that almost a third of the population in sub-Saharan Africa is undernourished.

The causal link between health and wealth runs in both directions. Poor countries are poor in part because their populations are not healthy, and their populations are not healthy in part because they are poor and cannot afford adequate healthcare and nutrition. It is a vicious circle. But this fact opens the possibility of a virtuous circle: Policies that lead to more rapid economic growth would naturally improve health outcomes, which in turn would further promote economic growth.

Property Rights and Political Stability

Another way policymakers can foster economic growth is by protecting property rights and promoting political stability. This issue goes to the very heart of how market economies work.

Production in market economies arises from the interactions of millions of individuals and firms. When you buy a car, for instance, you are buying the output of a car dealer, a car manufacturer, a steel company, an iron ore mining company, and so on. This division of production among many firms allows the economy's factors of production to be used as effectively as possible. To achieve this outcome, the economy has to coordinate transactions among these firms, as well as between firms and consumers. Market economies achieve this coordination through market prices. That is, market prices are the instrument with which the invisible hand of the marketplace brings supply and demand into balance in each of the many thousands of markets that make up the economy.

An important prerequisite for the price system to work is an economy-wide respect for *property rights*. Property rights refer to the ability of people to exercise authority over the resources they own. A mining company will not make the effort to mine iron ore if it expects the ore to be stolen. The company mines the ore only if it is confident that it will benefit from the ore's subsequent sale. For this reason, courts serve an important role in a market economy: They enforce property rights. Through the criminal justice system, the courts discourage direct theft. In addition, through the civil justice system, the courts ensure that buyers and sellers live up to their contracts.

Although those of us in developed countries tend to take property rights for granted, those living in less developed countries understand that lack of property rights can be a major problem. In many countries, the system of justice does not work well. Contracts are hard to enforce, and fraud often goes unpunished. In more extreme cases, the government not only fails to enforce property rights but actually infringes upon them. To do business in some countries, firms are expected to bribe powerful government officials. Such corruption impedes the coordinating power of markets. It also discourages domestic saving and investment from abroad.

One threat to property rights is political instability. When revolutions and coups are common, there is doubt about whether property rights will be respected in the future. If a revolutionary government might confiscate the capital of some businesses, as was often true after communist revolutions, domestic residents have less incentive to save, invest, and start new businesses. At the same time, foreigners have less incentive to invest in the country. Even the threat of revolution can act to depress a nation's standard of living.

Thus, economic prosperity depends in part on political prosperity. A country with an efficient court system, honest government officials, and a stable constitution will enjoy a higher economic standard of living than a country with a poor court system, corrupt officials, and frequent revolutions and coups.

Free Trade

Some of the world's poorest countries have tried to achieve more rapid economic growth by pursuing *inward-oriented policies*. These policies attempt to increase productivity and living standards within the country by avoiding interaction with the rest of the world. Domestic firms, claiming they need protection from foreign competition to thrive and grow, often support this infant-industry argument. Together with a general distrust of foreigners, it has at times led policymakers in less developed countries to impose tariffs and other trade restrictions.

Most economists today believe that poor countries are better off pursuing *outward-oriented policies* that integrate these countries into the world economy. When we studied international trade earlier in this book, we showed how trade can improve the economic well-being of a country's citizens. Trade is, in some ways, a type of technology. When a country exports wheat and imports steel, the country benefits as if it had invented a technology for turning wheat into steel. A country that eliminates trade restrictions will, therefore, experience the same kind of economic growth that would occur after a major technological advance.

The adverse impact of inward orientation becomes clear when one considers the small size of many less developed economies. The total GDP of Argentina, for instance, is about that of Philadelphia. Imagine what would happen if the Philadelphia city council were to prohibit city residents from trading with people living outside the city limits. Without being able to take advantage of the gains from trade, Philadelphia would need to produce all the goods it consumes. It would also have to produce all its own capital goods, rather than importing state-of-the-art equipment from other cities. Living standards in Philadelphia would fall immediately, and the problem would likely only get worse over time. This is precisely what happened when Argentina pursued inward-oriented policies throughout much of the 20th century. By contrast, countries that pursued outward-oriented policies, such as South Korea, Singapore, and Taiwan, enjoyed high rates of economic growth.

The amount that a nation trades with others is determined not only by government policy but also by geography. Countries with good natural seaports find trade easier than countries without this resource. It is not a coincidence that many of the world's major cities, such as New York, San Francisco, and Hong Kong, are located next to oceans. Similarly, because landlocked countries find international trade more difficult, they tend to have lower levels of income than countries with easy access to the world's waterways. Many African countries, for example, are landlocked, and some economists point to this fact as one reason the continent is so poor.

Research and Development

The primary reason that living standards are higher today than they were a century ago is that technological knowledge has advanced. The telephone, the transistor, the computer, and the internal combustion engine are among the thousands of innovations that have improved the ability to produce goods and services.

Although most technological advance comes from private research by firms and individual inventors, there is also a public interest in promoting these efforts. To a large extent, knowledge is a *public good:* Once one person discovers an idea, the idea enters society's pool of knowledge, and other people can freely use it. Just as government has a role in providing a public good such as national defense, it also has a role in encouraging the research and development of new technologies.

The U.S. government has long played a role in the creation and dissemination of technological knowledge. A century ago, the government sponsored research about farming methods and advised farmers how best to use their land. More recently, the U.S. government has, through the Air Force and NASA, supported aerospace research; as a result, the United States is a leading maker of rockets and planes. The government continues to encourage advances in knowledge with research grants from the National Science Foundation and the National Institutes of Health and with tax breaks for firms engaging in research and development.

Yet another way in which government policy encourages research is through the patent system. When a person or firm invents a new product, such as a new drug, the inventor can apply for a patent. If the product is deemed truly original, the government awards the patent, which gives the inventor the exclusive right to make the product for a specified number of years. In essence, the patent gives the inventor a property right over his invention, turning his new idea from a public good into a private good. By allowing inventors to profit from their inventions—even if only temporarily—the patent system enhances the incentive for individuals and firms to engage in research.

Population Growth

Economists and other social scientists have long debated how population growth affects a society. The most direct effect is on the size of the labor force: A large population means more workers to produce goods and services. At the

In The News

Rich Farmers versus the World's Poor

According to the presidents of Mali and Burkina Faso, if the United States and other developed countries more consistently followed the tenets of free trade, the world's poor would benefit.

Your Farm Subsidies Are Strangling Us

By Amadou Toumani Toure and Blaise Compaore

After too many years of Africa's being pushed to the global background, it's heartening to see the world's attention being focused on our continent. International support—both financial and otherwise—is certainly needed to help combat the severe poverty and disease gripping our nations. But first and foremost, Africa needs to be allowed to take its destiny into its own hands. Only self-reliance and economic growth and development will allow Africa to become a full member of the world community.

With the creation of the New Economic Partnership for African Development in 2001, African leaders have committed themselves to following the principles of good governance and a market economy. Nothing is more central to this goal than participating in world trade. As the presidents of two of Africa's least developed nations—Mali and Burkina Faso—we are eager to participate in the multilateral trading system and to take on its rights and obligations.

Cotton is our ticket into the world market. Its production is crucial to economic development in West and Central Africa, as well as to the livelihood of millions of people there. Cotton accounts for up to 40 percent of export revenues and 10 percent of gross domestic product in our two countries, as well as in Benin and Chad. . . .

This vital economic sector in our countries is seriously threatened by agricultural subsidies granted by rich countries to their cotton producers. According to the International Cotton Advisory Committee, cotton subsidies amount to about $5.8 billion in the production year of 2001 to 2002, nearly equal the amount of cotton trade for the same period. Such subsidies lead to worldwide overproduction and distort cotton prices, depriving poor African countries of their only comparative advantage in world trade. . . .

America's 25,000 cotton farmers received more in subsidies—some $3 billion—than the entire economic output of Burkina Faso, where two million people depend on cotton. Further, United States subsidies are concentrated on just 10 percent of its cotton farmers. Thus, the payments to about 2,500 relatively well-off farmers have the unintended but nevertheless very real effect of impoverishing some 10 million rural poor people in West and Central Africa. . . .

Our demand is simple: apply free trade rules not only to those products that are of interest to the rich and powerful, but also to those products where poor countries have a proven comparative advantage. We know that the world will not ignore our plea for a fair playing field. The World Trade Organization has said it is committed to addressing the problems of developing countries. The United States has convinced us that a free market economy provides the best opportunities for all members of the world community. Let us translate these principles into deeds.

Source: *The New York Times*, July 11, 2003.

same time, it means more people to consume those goods and services. Beyond these obvious effects, population growth interacts with the other factors of production in ways that are less obvious and more open to debate.

Stretching Natural Resources   Thomas Robert Malthus (1766–1834), an English minister and early economic thinker, is famous for his book called *An Essay on the Principle of Population as It Affects the Future Improvement of Society*. In

In The News

Foreign Aid

Improving the lives of the world's poor is not an easy task.

World Bank Challenged: Are the Poor Really Helped?

By Celia Dugger

Wealthy nations and international organizations, including the World Bank, spend more than $55 billion annually to better the lot of the world's 2.7 billion poor people. Yet they have scant evidence that the myriad projects they finance have made any real difference, many economists say.

That important fact has left some critics of the World Bank, the largest financier of antipoverty programs in de-

veloping countries, dissatisfied, and they have begun throwing down an essential challenge. It is not enough, they say, just to measure how many miles of roads are built, schools constructed or microcredit loans provided. You must also measure whether those investments actually help poor people live longer, more prosperous lives.

It is a common-sense approach that is harder than it sounds, just like the question it seeks to answer: Does aid really work?

A small band of development economists, who a year ago founded the Poverty Action Lab at the Massachusetts

Institute of Technology, have become influential advocates for randomized evaluations as the best way to answer that question. Such trials, generally regarded as the gold standard in social policy research, involve randomly assigning people eligible for an antipoverty program to get the help or not, then comparing outcomes to see whether those who got the help fared better than those who did not.

It is the same approach that has helped drug companies figure out what medicines are effective and Americans decide how best to reform welfare. Advocates for rigorous evaluations hope to

it, he offered what may be history's most chilling forecast. Malthus argued that an ever-increasing population would continually strain society's ability to provide for itself. As a result, mankind was doomed to forever live in poverty.

Malthus's logic was simple. He began by noting that "food is necessary to the existence of man" and that "the passion between the sexes is necessary and will remain nearly in its present state." He concluded that "the power of population is infinitely greater than the power in the earth to produce subsistence for man." According to Malthus, the only check on population growth was "misery and vice." Attempts by charities or governments to alleviate poverty were counterproductive, he argued, because they merely allowed the poor to have more children, placing even greater strains on society's productive capabilities.

Fortunately, Malthus's dire forecast was far off the mark. Although the world population has increased about sixfold over the past two centuries, living standards around the world are on average much higher. As a result of economic growth, chronic hunger and malnutrition are less common now than they were in Malthus's day. Famines occur from time to time, but they are more often the result of an unequal income distribution or political instability than inadequate food production.

Where did Malthus go wrong? As we discussed in a case study earlier in this chapter, growth in human ingenuity has offset the effects of a larger population.

THOMAS ROBERT MALTHUS

© BETTMANN/CORBIS

make aid more effective, not by directing money to particular countries, but by spending it on programs proven to work.

The Poverty Action Lab scholars have made startling discoveries in their own randomized evaluations.

Adding an extra teacher to classrooms in rural India did not improve children's test scores. But hiring high-school graduates who were paid only $10 to $15 a month to give remedial tutoring to groups of lagging students in a Bombay slum markedly improved reading and math skills.

A series of education experiments in Kenya found that providing poor students with free uniforms or a simple porridge breakfast substantially increased attendance. But giving them drugs to treat the intestinal worms that infect more than a quarter of the world's population was more cost effective, with a price tag of only $3.50 for each extra year of schooling achieved.

Healthier children are more likely to go to school. "You can't answer the general question: Does aid work?" said Esther Duflo, an economist and co-founder of the Poverty Action Lab. "You have to go project by project and accumulate the evidence."

The World Bank, a lumbering giant that employs more than 1,200 Ph.D.'s, is beginning to listen to critics like her. This summer, it is organizing large-scale impact evaluations, including randomized trials, of programs to upgrade slums, improve the performance of schools and keep children healthy and in class. The programs will be tested in dozens of countries.

François Bourguignon, the bank's chief economist, said he hoped this new effort would help the bank, other donors and developing countries "learn what does and does not work."

Rigorous impact evaluations should become part of the bank's culture, he said.

That will require deep change. A recent in-house review of bank projects during the past four to five years found that only 2 percent had been properly evaluated for whether they made a difference, according to Mr. Bourguignon. . . .

"The World Bank spent more than a billion dollars without knowing why they were doing what they were doing—that's the tragedy," said Abhijit Banerjee, an M.I.T. economics professor and co-founder of the Poverty Action Lab. . . .

Mr. Pritchett, a veteran bank economist, tried to explain why rigorous evaluations were such a rarity in the culture of the bank. Its highly trained, well-meaning professionals too often think they know the solutions. "They have too little doubt," he said.

Source: *The New York Times*, July 28, 2004.

Pesticides, fertilizers, mechanized farm equipment, new crop varieties, and other technological advances that Malthus never imagined have allowed each farmer to feed ever greater numbers of people. Even with more mouths to feed, few farmers are necessary because each farmer is so productive.

Diluting the Capital Stock   Whereas Malthus worried about the effects of population on the use of natural resources, some modern theories of economic growth emphasize its effects on capital accumulation. According to these theories, high population growth reduces GDP per worker because rapid growth in the number of workers forces the capital stock to be spread more thinly. In other words, when population growth is rapid, each worker is equipped with less capital. A smaller quantity of capital per worker leads to lower productivity and lower GDP per worker.

This problem is most apparent in the case of human capital. Countries with high population growth have large numbers of school-age children. This places a larger burden on the educational system. It is not surprising, therefore, that educational attainment tends to be low in countries with high population growth.

The differences in population growth around the world are large. In developed countries, such as the United States and those in Western Europe, the population has risen only about 1 percent per year in recent decades and is expected to rise even more slowly in the future. By contrast, in many poor African countries, population grows at about 3 percent per year. At this rate, the population doubles every 23 years. This rapid population growth makes it harder to provide workers with the tools and skills they need to achieve high levels of productivity.

Although rapid population growth is not the main reason that less developed countries are poor, some analysts believe that reducing the rate of population growth would help these countries raise their standards of living. In some countries, this goal is accomplished directly with laws that regulate the number of children families may have. China, for instance, allows only one child per family; couples who violate this rule are subject to substantial fines. In countries with greater freedom, the goal of reduced population growth is accomplished less directly by increasing awareness of birth control techniques.

 Another way in which a country can influence population growth is to apply one of the *Ten Principles of Economics:* People respond to incentives. Bearing a child, like any decision, has an opportunity cost. When the opportunity cost rises, people will choose to have smaller families. In particular, women with the opportunity to receive good education and desirable employment tend to want fewer children than those with fewer opportunities outside the home. Hence, policies that foster equal treatment of women are one way for less developed economies to reduce the rate of population growth and, perhaps, raise their standards of living.

Promoting Technological Progress Although rapid population growth may depress economic prosperity by reducing the amount of capital each worker has, it may also have some benefits. Some economists have suggested that world population growth has been an engine of technological progress and economic prosperity. The mechanism is simple: If there are more people, then there are more scientists, inventors, and engineers to contribute to technological advance, which benefits everyone.

Economist Michael Kremer has provided some support for this hypothesis in an article titled "Population Growth and Technological Change: One Million B.C. to 1990," which was published in the *Quarterly Journal of Economics* in 1993. Kremer begins by noting that over the broad span of human history, world growth rates have increased as world population has. For example, world growth was more rapid when the world population was 1 billion (which occurred around the year 1800) than when the population was only 100 million (around 500 B.C.). This fact is consistent with the hypothesis that having more people induces more technological progress.

Kremer's second piece of evidence comes from comparing regions of the world. The melting of the polar icecaps at the end of the Ice Age around 10,000 B.C. flooded the land bridges and separated the world into several distinct regions that could not communicate with one another for thousands of years. If technological progress is more rapid when there are more people to discover things, then larger regions should have experienced more rapid growth.

According to Kremer, that is exactly what happened. The most successful region of the world in 1500 (when Columbus reestablished technological contact) comprised the "Old World" civilizations of the large Eurasia-Africa region. Next in technological development were the Aztec and Mayan civilizations in the Americas, followed by the hunter-gatherers of Australia, and then the primitive people of Tasmania, who lacked even fire-making and most stone and bone tools.

The smallest isolated region was Flinders Island, a tiny island between Tasmania and Australia. With the smallest population, Flinders Island had the fewest opportunities for technological advance and, indeed, seemed to regress.

Around 3000 B.C., human society on Flinders Island died out completely. A large population, Kremer concludes, is a prerequisite for technological advance.

Quick Quiz   Describe three ways a government policymaker can try to raise the growth in living standards in a society. Are there any drawbacks to these policies?

CONCLUSION: THE IMPORTANCE OF LONG-RUN GROWTH

In this chapter, we have discussed what determines the standard of living in a nation and how policymakers can endeavor to raise the standard of living through policies that promote economic growth. Most of this chapter is summarized in one of the *Ten Principles of Economics:* A country's standard of living depends on its ability to produce goods and services. Policymakers who want to encourage growth in standards of living must aim to increase their nation's productive ability by encouraging rapid accumulation of the factors of production and ensuring that these factors are employed as effectively as possible.

Economists differ in their views of the role of government in promoting economic growth. At the very least, government can lend support to the invisible hand by maintaining property rights and political stability. More controversial is whether government should target and subsidize specific industries that might be especially important for technological progress. There is no doubt that these issues are among the most important in economics. The success of one generation's policymakers in learning and heeding the fundamental lessons about economic growth determines what kind of world the next generation will inherit.

SUMMARY

- Economic prosperity, as measured by GDP per person, varies substantially around the world. The average income in the world's richest countries is more than ten times that in the world's poorest countries. Because growth rates of real GDP also vary substantially, the relative positions of countries can change dramatically over time.

- The standard of living in an economy depends on the economy's ability to produce goods and services. Productivity, in turn, depends on the amounts of physical capital, human capital, natural resources, and technological knowledge available to workers.

- Government policies can try to influence the economy's growth rate in many ways: by encouraging saving and investment, encouraging invest-

ment from abroad, fostering education, promoting good health, maintaining property rights and political stability, allowing free trade, promoting the research and development of new technologies, and controlling population growth.

- The accumulation of capital is subject to diminishing returns: The more capital an economy has, the less additional output the economy gets from an extra unit of capital. Because of diminishing returns, higher saving leads to higher growth for a period of time, but growth eventually slows down as the economy approaches a higher level of capital, productivity, and income. Also because of diminishing returns, the return to capital is especially high in poor countries. Other things equal, these countries can grow faster because of the catch-up effect.

• Population growth has a variety of effects on economic growth. On the one hand, more rapid population growth may lower productivity by stretching the supply of natural resources and by reducing the amount of capital available for each worker. On the other hand, a larger population may enhance the rate of technological progress because there are more scientists and engineers.

KEY CONCEPTS

productivity, p. 250
physical capital, p. 251
human capital, p. 252

natural resources, p. 252
technological knowledge, p. 252

diminishing returns, p. 255
catch-up effect, p. 256

QUESTIONS FOR REVIEW

1. What does the level of a nation's GDP measure? What does the growth rate of GDP measure? Would you rather live in a nation with a high level of GDP and a low growth rate or in a nation with a low level of GDP and a high growth rate?

2. List and describe four determinants of productivity.

3. In what way is a college degree a form of capital?

4. Explain how higher saving leads to a higher standard of living. What might deter a policymaker from trying to raise the rate of saving?

5. Does a higher rate of saving lead to higher growth temporarily or indefinitely?

6. Why would removing a trade restriction, such as a tariff, lead to more rapid economic growth?

7. How does the rate of population growth influence the level of GDP per person?

8. Describe two ways the U.S. government tries to encourage advances in technological knowledge.

PROBLEMS AND APPLICATIONS

1. Most countries, including the United States, import substantial amounts of goods and services from other countries. Yet the chapter says that a nation can enjoy a high standard of living only if it can produce a large quantity of goods and services itself. Can you reconcile these two facts?

2. Suppose that society decided to reduce consumption and increase investment.
   a. How would this change affect economic growth?
   b. What groups in society would benefit from this change? What groups might be hurt?

3. Societies choose what share of their resources to devote to consumption and what share to devote to investment. Some of these decisions involve private spending; others involve government spending.
   a. Describe some forms of private spending that represent consumption and some forms that represent investment. The national income accounts include tuition as a part of consumer spending. In your opinion, are the resources you devote to your education a form of consumption or a form of investment?
   b. Describe some forms of government spending that represent consumption and some forms that represent investment. In your opinion, should we view government spend-

ing on health programs as a form of consumption or investment? Would you distinguish between health programs for the young and health programs for the elderly?

4. What is the opportunity cost of investing in capital? Do you think a country can "overinvest" in capital? What is the opportunity cost of investing in human capital? Do you think a country can "overinvest" in human capital? Explain.

5. Suppose that an auto company owned entirely by German citizens opens a new factory in South Carolina.
   a. What sort of foreign investment would this represent?
   b. What would be the effect of this investment on U.S. GDP? Would the effect on U.S. GNP be larger or smaller?

6. In the 1980s, Japanese investors made significant direct and portfolio investments in the United States. At the time, many Americans were unhappy that this investment was occurring.
   a. In what way was it better for the United States to receive this Japanese investment than not to receive it?
   b. In what way would it have been better still for Americans to have made this investment?

7. In the countries of South Asia in 1992, only 56 young women were enrolled in secondary school for every 100 young men. Describe several ways in which greater educational opportu-

nities for young women could lead to faster economic growth in these countries.

8. International data show a positive correlation between income per person and the health of the population.
   a. Explain how higher income might cause better health outcomes.
   b. Explain how better health outcomes might cause higher income.
   c. How might the relative importance of your two hypotheses be relevant for public policy?

9. International data show a positive correlation between political stability and economic growth.
   a. Through what mechanism could political stability lead to strong economic growth?
   b. Through what mechanism could strong economic growth lead to political stability?

10. From 1950 to 2000, manufacturing employment as a percentage of total employment in the U.S. economy fell from 28 percent to 13 percent. At the same time, manufacturing output experienced slightly more rapid growth than the overall economy.
   a. What do these facts say about growth in labor productivity (defined as output per worker) in manufacturing?
   b. In your opinion, should policymakers be concerned about the decline in the share of manufacturing employment? Explain.

For further information on topics in this chapter, additional problems, examples, applications, online quizzes, and more, please visit our website at http://mankiw.swlearning.com.

The Market Forces of Supply and Demand

When a cold snap hits Florida, the price of orange juice rises in supermarkets throughout the country. When the weather turns warm in New England every summer, the price of hotel rooms in the Caribbean plummets. When a war breaks out in the Middle East, the price of gasoline in the United States rises, and the price of a used Cadillac falls. What do these events have in common? They all show the workings of supply and demand.

Supply and *demand* are the two words economists use most often—and for good reason. Supply and demand are the forces that make market economies work. They determine the quantity of each good produced and the price at which it is sold. If you want to know how any event or policy will affect the economy, you must think first about how it will affect supply and demand.

This chapter introduces the theory of supply and demand. It considers how buyers and sellers behave and how they interact with one another. It shows how supply and demand determine prices in a market economy and how prices, in turn, allocate the economy's scarce resources.

MARKETS AND COMPETITION

The terms *supply* and *demand* refer to the behavior of people as they interact with one another in competitive markets. Before discussing how buyers and sellers behave, let's first consider more fully what we mean by the terms *market* and *competition*.

What Is a Market?

market
a group of buyers and sellers of a particular good or service

A **market** is a group of buyers and sellers of a particular good or service. The buyers as a group determine the demand for the product, and the sellers as a group determine the supply of the product.

Markets take many forms. Sometimes markets are highly organized, such as the markets for many agricultural commodities. In these markets, buyers and sellers meet at a specific time and place, where an auctioneer helps set prices and arrange sales.

More often, markets are less organized. For example, consider the market for ice cream in a particular town. Buyers of ice cream do not meet together at any one time. The sellers of ice cream are in different locations and offer somewhat different products. There is no auctioneer calling out the price of ice cream. Each seller posts a price for an ice-cream cone, and each buyer decides how much ice cream to buy at each store. Nonetheless, these consumers and producers of ice cream are closely connected. The ice-cream buyers are choosing from the various ice-cream sellers to satisfy their hunger, and the ice-cream sellers are all trying to appeal to the same ice-cream buyers to make their businesses successful. Even though it is not organized, the group of ice-cream buyers and ice-cream sellers forms a market.

What Is Competition?

The market for ice cream, like most markets in the economy, is highly competitive. Each buyer knows that there are several sellers from which to choose, and each seller is aware that his product is similar to that offered by other sellers. As a result, the price of ice cream and the quantity of ice cream sold are not determined by any single buyer or seller. Rather, price and quantity are determined by all buyers and sellers as they interact in the marketplace.

competitive market
a market in which there are many buyers and many sellers so that each has a negligible impact on the market price

Economists use the term **competitive market** to describe a market in which there are so many buyers and so many sellers that each has a negligible impact on the market price. Each seller of ice cream has limited control over the price because other sellers are offering similar products. A seller has little reason to charge less than the going price, and if he charges more, buyers will make their purchases elsewhere. Similarly, no single buyer of ice cream can influence the price of ice cream because each buyer purchases only a small amount.

In this chapter, we assume that markets are *perfectly competitive*. To reach this highest form of competition, a market must have two characteristics: (1) the goods offered for sale are all exactly the same, and (2) the buyers and sellers are so numerous that no single buyer or seller has any influence over the market price. Because buyers and sellers in perfectly competitive markets must accept the price the market determines, they are said to be *price takers*. At the market price, buyers can buy all they want, and sellers can sell all they want.

There are some markets in which the assumption of perfect competition applies perfectly. In the wheat market, for example, there are thousands of farmers who sell wheat and millions of consumers who use wheat and wheat products. Because no single buyer or seller can influence the price of wheat, each takes the price as given.

Not all goods and services, however, are sold in perfectly competitive markets. Some markets have only one seller, and this seller sets the price. Such a seller is called a *monopoly*. Your local cable television company, for instance, may be a monopoly. Residents of your town probably have only one cable company from which to buy this service. Some markets (covered in the study of microeconomics) fall between the extremes of perfect competition and monopoly.

Despite the diversity of market types we find in the world, assuming perfect competition is a useful simplification and, therefore, a natural place to start. Perfectly competitive markets are the easiest to analyze because everyone participating in the market takes the price as given by market conditions. Moreover, because some degree of competition is present in most markets, many of the lessons that we learn by studying supply and demand under perfect competition apply in more complicated markets as well.

Quick Quiz   What is a market?   •   What are the characteristics of a competitive market?

DEMAND

We begin our study of markets by examining the behavior of buyers. To focus our thinking, let's keep in mind a particular good—ice cream.

The Demand Curve: The Relationship between Price and Quantity Demanded

The **quantity demanded** of any good is the amount of the good that buyers are willing and able to purchase. As we will see, many things determine the quantity demanded of any good, but when analyzing how markets work, one determinant plays a central role—the price of the good. If the price of ice cream rose to $20 per scoop, you would buy less ice cream. You might buy frozen yogurt instead. If the price of ice cream fell to $0.20 per scoop, you would buy more. Because the quantity demanded falls as the price rises and rises as the price falls, we say that the quantity demanded is *negatively related* to the price. This relationship between price and quantity demanded is true for most goods in the economy and, in fact, is so pervasive that economists call it the **law of demand:** Other things equal, when the price of a good rises, the quantity demanded of the good falls, and when the price falls, the quantity demanded rises.

The table in Figure 1 shows how many ice-cream cones Catherine buys each month at different prices of ice cream. If ice cream is free, Catherine eats 12 cones per month. At $0.50 per cone, Catherine buys 10 cones each month. As the price rises further, she buys fewer and fewer cones. When the price reaches $3.00, Catherine doesn't buy any ice cream at all. This table is a **demand schedule,** a table that shows the relationship between the price of a good and the quantity demanded, holding constant everything else that influences how much consumers of the good want to buy.

The graph in Figure 1 uses the numbers from the table to illustrate the law of demand. By convention, the price of ice cream is on the vertical axis, and the

quantity demanded
the amount of a good that buyers are willing and able to purchase

law of demand
the claim that, other things equal, the quantity demanded of a good falls when the price of the good rises

demand schedule
a table that shows the relationship between the price of a good and the quantity demanded

1 FIGURE

Catherine's Demand Schedule and Demand Curve

The demand schedule shows the quantity demanded at each price. The demand curve, which graphs the demand schedule, shows how the quantity demanded of the good changes as its price varies. Because a lower price increases the quantity demanded, the demand curve slopes downward.

Price of Ice-Cream Cone	Quantity of Cones Demanded
$0.00	12 cones
0.50	10
1.00	8
1.50	6
2.00	4
2.50	2
3.00	0

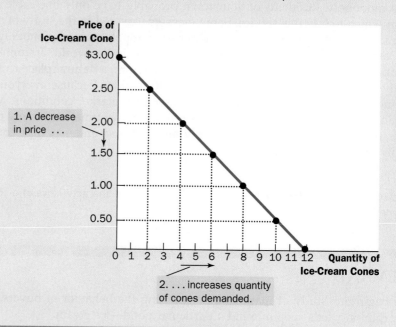

1. A decrease in price ...

2. ... increases quantity of cones demanded.

demand curve
a graph of the relationship between the price of a good and the quantity demanded

quantity of ice cream demanded is on the horizontal axis. The downward-sloping line relating price and quantity demanded is called the **demand curve**.

Market Demand versus Individual Demand

The demand curve in Figure 1 shows an individual's demand for a product. To analyze how markets work, we need to determine the *market demand,* the sum of all the individual demands for a particular good or service.

The table in Figure 2 shows the demand schedules for ice cream of two individuals—Catherine and Nicholas. At any price, Catherine's demand schedule tells us how much ice cream she buys, and Nicholas's demand schedule tells us how much ice cream he buys. The market demand at each price is the sum of the two individual demands.

The graph in Figure 2 shows the demand curves that correspond to these demand schedules. Notice that we sum the individual demand curves horizontally to obtain the market demand curve. That is, to find the total quantity demanded at any price, we add the individual quantities found on the horizontal axis of the individual demand curves. Because we are interested in analyzing how markets work, we will work most often with the market demand curve. The market demand curve shows how the total quantity demanded of a good varies as the price of the good varies, while all the other factors that affect how much consumers want to buy are held constant.

The quantity demanded in a market is the sum of the quantities demanded by all the buyers at each price. Thus, the market demand curve is found by adding horizontally the individual demand curves. At a price of $2.00, Catherine demands 4 ice-cream cones, and Nicholas demands 3 ice-cream cones. The quantity demanded in the market at this price is 7 cones.

FIGURE 2

Market Demand as the Sum of Individual Demands

Price of Ice-Cream Cone	Catherine		Nicholas		Market
$0.00	12	+	7	=	19 cones
0.50	10		6		16
1.00	8		5		13
1.50	6		4		10
2.00	4		3		7
2.50	2		2		4
3.00	0		1		1

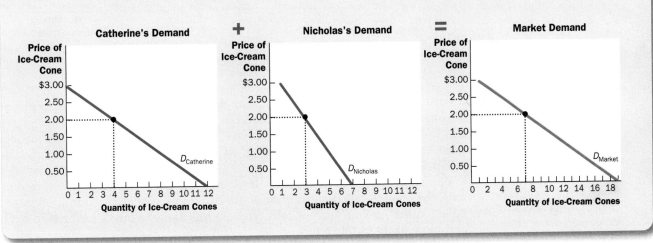

Shifts in the Demand Curve

The demand curve for ice cream shows how much ice cream people buy at any given price, holding constant the many other factors beyond price that influence consumers' buying decisions. As a result, this demand curve need not be stable over time. If something happens to alter the quantity demanded at any given price, the demand curve shifts. For example, suppose the American Medical Association discovered that people who regularly eat ice cream live longer, healthier lives. The discovery would raise the demand for ice cream. At any given price, buyers would now want to purchase a larger quantity of ice cream, and the demand curve for ice cream would shift.

Figure 3 illustrates shifts in demand. Any change that increases the quantity demanded at every price, such as our imaginary discovery by the American Medical Association, shifts the demand curve to the right and is called an *increase in demand*. Any change that reduces the quantity demanded at every price shifts the demand curve to the left and is called a *decrease in demand*.

There are many variables that can shift the demand curve. Here are the most important.

[handwritten margin notes:] price change causes shift... a movement.

change in demand (not b/c price of the item) will cause shift in line.

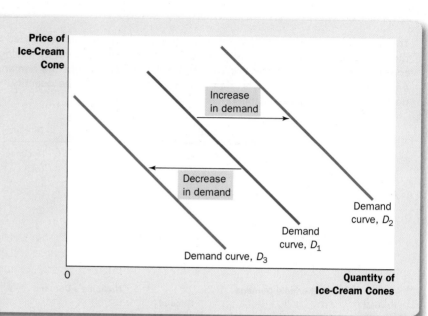

3 FIGURE

Shifts in the Demand Curve
Any change that raises the quantity that buyers wish to purchase at a given price shifts the demand curve to the right. Any change that lowers the quantity that buyers wish to purchase at a given price shifts the demand curve to the left.

① Income   What would happen to your demand for ice cream if you lost your job one summer? Most likely, it would fall. A lower income means that you have less to spend in total, so you would have to spend less on some—and probably most—goods. If the demand for a good falls when income falls, the good is called a **normal good.**

Not all goods are normal goods. If the demand for a good rises when income falls, the good is called an **inferior good.** An example of an inferior good might be bus rides. As your income falls, you are less likely to buy a car or take a cab and more likely to ride a bus.

② Prices of Related Goods   Suppose that the price of frozen yogurt falls. The law of demand says that you will buy more frozen yogurt. At the same time, you will probably buy less ice cream. Because ice cream and frozen yogurt are both cold, sweet, creamy desserts, they satisfy similar desires. When a fall in the price of one good reduces the demand for another good, the two goods are called **substitutes.** Substitutes are often pairs of goods that are used in place of each other, such as hot dogs and hamburgers, sweaters and sweatshirts, and movie tickets and video rentals.

Now suppose that the price of hot fudge falls. According to the law of demand, you will buy more hot fudge. Yet in this case, you will buy more ice cream as well because ice cream and hot fudge are often used together. When a fall in the price of one good raises the demand for another good, the two goods are called **complements.** Complements are often pairs of goods that are used together, such as gasoline and automobiles, computers and software, and peanut butter and jelly.

③ Tastes   The most obvious determinant of your demand is your tastes. If you like ice cream, you buy more of it. Economists normally do not try to explain people's tastes because tastes are based on historical and psychological forces that are beyond the realm of economics. Economists do, however, examine what happens when tastes change.

normal good
a good for which, other things equal, an increase in income leads to an increase in demand

inferior good
a good for which, other things equal, an increase in income leads to a decrease in demand

substitutes
two goods for which an increase in the price of one leads to an increase in the demand for the other

complements
two goods for which an increase in the price of one leads to a decrease in the demand for the other

Variable	A Change in This Variable...
Price	Represents a movement along the demand curve
Income	Shifts the demand curve
Prices of related goods	Shifts the demand curve
Tastes	Shifts the demand curve
Expectations	Shifts the demand curve
Number of buyers	Shifts the demand curve

TABLE 1

Variables That Influence Buyers
This table lists the variables that affect how much consumers choose to buy of any good. Notice the special role that the price of the good plays: A change in the good's price represents a movement along the demand curve, whereas a change in one of the other variables shifts the demand curve.

4. Expectations Your expectations about the future may affect your demand for a good or service today. For example, if you expect to earn a higher income next month, you may choose to save less now and spend more of your current income buying ice cream. As another example, if you expect the price of ice cream to fall tomorrow, you may be less willing to buy an ice-cream cone at today's price.

5. Number of Buyers Because market demand is derived from individual demands, it depends on all those factors that determine the demand of individual buyers, including buyers' incomes, tastes, expectations, and the prices of related goods. In addition, it depends on the number of buyers. If Peter, another consumer of ice cream, were to join Catherine and Nicholas, the quantity demanded in the market would be higher at every price, and the demand curve would shift to the right.

Summary The demand curve shows what happens to the quantity demanded of a good when its price varies, holding constant all the other variables that influence buyers. When one of these other variables changes, the demand curve shifts. Table 1 lists the variables that influence how much consumers choose to buy of a good.

If you have trouble remembering whether you need to shift or move along the demand curve, it helps to recall a lesson from the appendix to Chapter 2. A curve shifts when there is a change in a relevant variable that is not measured on either axis. Because the price is on the vertical axis, a change in price represents a movement along the demand curve. By contrast, income, the prices of related goods, tastes, expectations, and the number of buyers are not measured on either axis, so a change in one of these variables shifts the demand curve.

CASE STUDY   TWO WAYS TO REDUCE THE QUANTITY OF SMOKING DEMANDED

Public policymakers often want to reduce the amount that people smoke. There are two ways that policy can attempt to achieve this goal.

One way to reduce smoking is to shift the demand curve for cigarettes and other tobacco products. Public service announcements, mandatory health warnings on cigarette packages, and the prohibition of cigarette advertising on television are all policies aimed at reducing the quantity of cigarettes demanded at

© ROYALTY-FREE/CORBIS

WHAT IS THE BEST WAY TO STOP THIS?

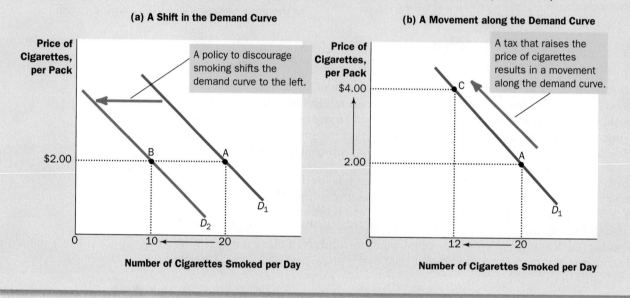

4 FIGURE

Shifts in the Demand Curve versus Movements along the Demand Curve

If warnings on cigarette packages convince smokers to smoke less, the demand curve for cigarettes shifts to the left. In panel (a), the demand curve shifts from D_1 to D_2. At a price of $2.00 per pack, the quantity demanded falls from 20 to 10 cigarettes per day, as reflected by the shift from point A to point B. By contrast, if a tax raises the price of cigarettes, the demand curve does not shift. Instead, we observe a movement to a different point on the demand curve. In panel (b), when the price rises from $2.00 to $4.00, the quantity demanded falls from 20 to 12 cigarettes per day, as reflected by the movement from point A to point C.

(a) A Shift in the Demand Curve

Price of Cigarettes, per Pack

A policy to discourage smoking shifts the demand curve to the left.

$2.00

B   A

D_1

D_2

0   10 ← 20

Number of Cigarettes Smoked per Day

(b) A Movement along the Demand Curve

Price of Cigarettes, per Pack

A tax that raises the price of cigarettes results in a movement along the demand curve.

$4.00

C

2.00   A

D_1

0   12 ← 20

Number of Cigarettes Smoked per Day

any given price. If successful, these policies shift the demand curve for cigarettes to the left, as in panel (a) of Figure 4.

Alternatively, policymakers can try to raise the price of cigarettes. If the government taxes the manufacture of cigarettes, for example, cigarette companies pass much of this tax on to consumers in the form of higher prices. A higher price encourages smokers to reduce the numbers of cigarettes they smoke. In this case, the reduced amount of smoking does not represent a shift in the demand curve. Instead, it represents a movement along the same demand curve to a point with a higher price and lower quantity, as in panel (b) of Figure 4.

How much does the amount of smoking respond to changes in the price of cigarettes? Economists have attempted to answer this question by studying what happens when the tax on cigarettes changes. They have found that a 10 percent increase in the price causes a 4 percent reduction in the quantity demanded. Teenagers are found to be especially sensitive to the price of cigarettes: A 10 percent increase in the price causes a 12 percent drop in teenage smoking.

A related question is how the price of cigarettes affects the demand for illicit drugs, such as marijuana. Opponents of cigarette taxes often argue that tobacco and marijuana are substitutes so that high cigarette prices encourage marijuana use. By contrast, many experts on substance abuse view tobacco as a "gateway drug" leading the young to experiment with other harmful substances. Most studies of the data are consistent with this view: They find that lower cigarette prices are associated with greater use of marijuana. In other words, tobacco and marijuana appear to be complements rather than substitutes.

Quick Quiz Make up an example of a demand schedule for pizza and graph the implied demand curve. • Give an example of something that would shift this demand curve. • Would a change in the price of pizza shift this demand curve?

SUPPLY

We now turn to the other side of the market and examine the behavior of sellers. Once again, to focus our thinking, let's consider the market for ice cream.

The Supply Curve: The Relationship between Price and Quantity Supplied

The **quantity supplied** of any good or service is the amount that sellers are willing and able to sell. There are many determinants of quantity supplied, but once again, price plays a special role in our analysis. When the price of ice cream is high, selling ice cream is profitable, and so the quantity supplied is large. Sellers of ice cream work long hours, buy many ice-cream machines, and hire many workers. By contrast, when the price of ice cream is low, the business is less profitable, and so sellers produce less ice cream. At a low price, some sellers may even choose to shut down, and their quantity supplied falls to zero. Because the quantity supplied rises as the price rises and falls as the price falls, we say that the quantity supplied is *positively related* to the price of the good. This relationship between price and quantity supplied is called the **law of supply:** Other things equal, when the price of a good rises, the quantity supplied of the good also rises, and when the price falls, the quantity supplied falls as well.

The table in Figure 5 shows the quantity of ice-cream cones supplied each month by Ben, an ice-cream seller, at various prices of ice cream. At a price below $1.00, Ben does not supply any ice cream at all. As the price rises, he supplies a greater and greater quantity. This is the **supply schedule,** a table that shows the relationship between the price of a good and the quantity supplied, holding constant everything else that influences how much producers of the good want to sell.

The graph in Figure 5 uses the numbers from the table to illustrate the law of supply. The curve relating price and quantity supplied is called the **supply curve.** The supply curve slopes upward because, other things equal, a higher price means a greater quantity supplied.

Market Supply versus Individual Supply

Just as market demand is the sum of the demands of all buyers, market supply is the sum of the supplies of all sellers. The table in Figure 6 shows the supply schedules for two ice-cream producers—Ben and Jerry. At any price, Ben's supply schedule tells us the quantity of ice cream Ben supplies, and Jerry's supply schedule tells us the quantity of ice cream Jerry supplies. The market supply is the sum of the two individual supplies.

quantity supplied
the amount of a good that sellers are willing and able to sell

law of supply
the claim that, other things equal, the quantity supplied of a good rises when the price of the good rises

supply schedule
a table that shows the relationship between the price of a good and the quantity supplied

supply curve
a graph of the relationship between the price of a good and the quantity supplied

5 FIGURE

Ben's Supply Schedule and Supply Curve

The supply schedule shows the quantity supplied at each price. This supply curve, which graphs the supply schedule, shows how the quantity supplied of the good changes as its price varies. Because a higher price increases the quantity supplied, the supply curve slopes upward.

Price of Ice-Cream Cone	Quantity of Cones Supplied
$0.00	0 cones
0.50	0
1.00	1
1.50	2
2.00	3
2.50	4
3.00	5

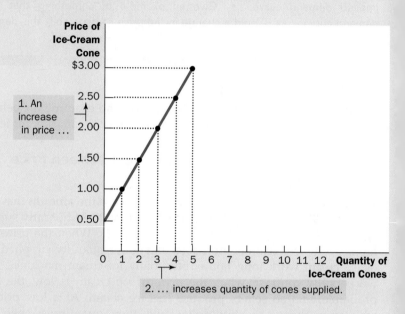

1. An increase in price …

2. … increases quantity of cones supplied.

The graph in Figure 6 shows the supply curves that correspond to the supply schedules. As with demand curves, we sum the individual supply curves *horizontally* to obtain the market supply curve. That is, to find the total quantity supplied at any price, we add the individual quantities found on the horizontal axis of the individual supply curves. The market supply curve shows how the total quantity supplied varies as the price of the good varies.

Shifts in the Supply Curve

The supply curve for ice cream shows how much ice cream producers offer for sale at any given price, holding constant all the other factors beyond price that influence producers' decisions about how much to sell. This relationship can change over time, which is represented by a shift in the supply curve. For example, suppose the price of sugar falls. Because sugar is an input into producing ice cream, the fall in the price of sugar makes selling ice cream more profitable. This raises the supply of ice cream: At any given price, sellers are now willing to produce a larger quantity. Thus, the supply curve for ice cream shifts to the right.

Figure 7 illustrates shifts in supply. Any change that raises quantity supplied at every price, such as a fall in the price of sugar, shifts the supply curve to the right and is called an *increase in supply*. Similarly, any change that reduces the quantity supplied at every price shifts the supply curve to the left and is called a *decrease in supply*.

FIGURE 6

Market Supply as the Sum of Individual Supplies

The quantity supplied in a market is the sum of the quantities supplied by all the sellers at each price. Thus, the market supply curve is found by adding horizontally the individual supply curves. At a price of $2.00, Ben supplies 3 ice-cream cones, and Jerry supplies 4 ice-cream cones. The quantity supplied in the market at this price is 7 cones.

Price of Ice-Cream Cone	Ben		Jerry		Market
$0.00	0	+	0	=	0 cones
0.50	0		0		0
1.00	1		0		1
1.50	2		2		4
2.00	3		4		7
2.50	4		6		10
3.00	5		8		13

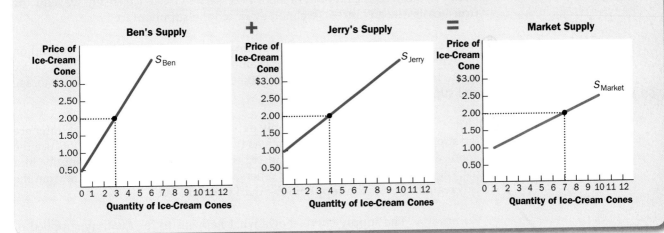

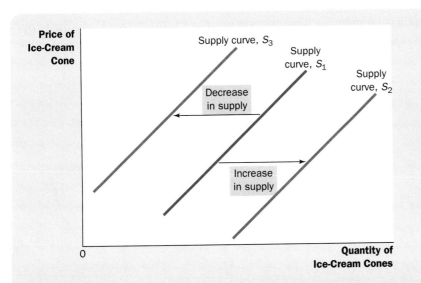

FIGURE 7

Shifts in the Supply Curve

Any change that raises the quantity that sellers wish to produce at a given price shifts the supply curve to the right. Any change that lowers the quantity that sellers wish to produce at a given price shifts the supply curve to the left.

There are many variables that can shift the supply curve. Here are some of the most important.

① **Input Prices**   To produce its output of ice cream, sellers use various inputs: cream, sugar, flavoring, ice-cream machines, the buildings in which the ice cream is made, and the labor of workers to mix the ingredients and operate the machines. When the price of one or more of these inputs rises, producing ice cream is less profitable, and firms supply less ice cream. If input prices rise substantially, a firm might shut down and supply no ice cream at all. Thus, the supply of a good is negatively related to the price of the inputs used to make the good.

② **Technology**   The technology for turning inputs into ice cream is another determinant of supply. The invention of the mechanized ice-cream machine, for example, reduced the amount of labor necessary to make ice cream. By reducing firms' costs, the advance in technology raised the supply of ice cream.

③ **Expectations**   The amount of ice cream a firm supplies today may depend on its expectations of the future. For example, if a firm expects the price of ice cream to rise in the future, it will put some of its current production into storage and supply less to the market today.

④ **Number of Sellers**   Market supply depends on all those factors that influence the supply of individual sellers, such as the prices of inputs used to produce the good, the available technology, and expectations. In addition, the supply in a market depends on the number of sellers. If Ben or Jerry were to retire from the ice-cream business, the supply in the market would fall.

Summary   The supply curve shows what happens to the quantity supplied of a good when its price varies, holding constant all the other variables that influence sellers. When one of these other variables changes, the supply curve shifts. Table 2 lists the variables that influence how much producers choose to sell of a good.

Once again, to remember whether you need to shift or move along the supply curve, keep in mind that a curve shifts only when there is a change in a relevant

2 **TABLE**

Variables That Influence Sellers
This table lists the variables that affect how much producers choose to sell of any good. Notice the special role that the price of the good plays: A change in the good's price represents a movement along the supply curve, whereas a change in one of the other variables shifts the supply curve.

Variable	A Change in This Variable...
Price	Represents a movement along the supply curve
Input prices	Shifts the supply curve
Technology	Shifts the supply curve
Expectations	Shifts the supply curve
Number of sellers	Shifts the supply curve

variable that is not named on either axis. The price is on the vertical axis, so a change in price represents a movement along the supply curve. By contrast, because input prices, technology, expectations, and the number of sellers are not measured on either axis, a change in one of these variables shifts the supply curve.

Quick Quiz Make up an example of a supply schedule for pizza and graph the implied supply curve. • Give an example of something that would shift this supply curve. • Would a change in the price of pizza shift this supply curve?

SUPPLY AND DEMAND TOGETHER

Having analyzed supply and demand separately, we now combine them to see how they determine the quantity of a good sold in a market and its price.

Equilibrium

Figure 8 shows the market supply curve and market demand curve together. Notice that there is one point at which the supply and demand curves intersect. This point is called the market's **equilibrium.** The price at this intersection is called the **equilibrium price,** and the quantity is called the **equilibrium quantity.** Here the equilibrium price is $2.00 per cone, and the equilibrium quantity is 7 ice-cream cones.

The dictionary defines the word *equilibrium* as a situation in which various forces are in balance—and this also describes a market's equilibrium. *At the equilibrium price, the quantity of the good that buyers are willing and able to buy exactly balances the quantity that sellers are willing and able to sell.* The equilibrium price is sometimes called the *market-clearing price* because, at this price, everyone in the

equilibrium
a situation in which the market price has reached the level at which quantity supplied equals quantity demanded

equilibrium price
the price that balances quantity supplied and quantity demanded

equilibrium quantity
the quantity supplied and the quantity demanded at the equilibrium price

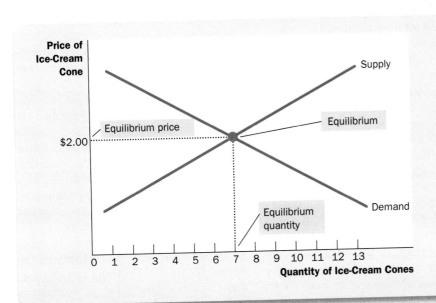

FIGURE 8

The Equilibrium of Supply and Demand
The equilibrium is found where the supply and demand curves intersect. At the equilibrium price, the quantity supplied equals the quantity demanded. Here the equilibrium price is $2.00: At this price, 7 ice-cream cones are supplied, and 7 ice-cream cones are demanded.

9 FIGURE

Markets Not in Equilibrium

In panel (a), there is a surplus. Because the market price of $2.50 is above the equilibrium price, the quantity supplied (10 cones) exceeds the quantity demanded (4 cones). Suppliers try to increase sales by cutting the price of a cone, and this moves the price toward its equilibrium level. In panel (b), there is a shortage. Because the market price of $1.50 is below the equilibrium price, the quantity demanded (10 cones) exceeds the quantity supplied (4 cones). With too many buyers chasing too few goods, suppliers can take advantage of the shortage by raising the price. Hence, in both cases, the price adjustment moves the market toward the equilibrium of supply and demand.

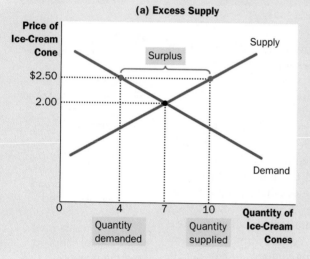

(a) Excess Supply

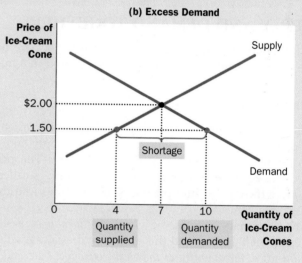

(b) Excess Demand

market has been satisfied: Buyers have bought all they want to buy, and sellers have sold all they want to sell.

The actions of buyers and sellers naturally move markets toward the equilibrium of supply and demand. To see why, consider what happens when the market price is not equal to the equilibrium price.

Suppose first that the market price is above the equilibrium price, as in panel (a) of Figure 9. At a price of $2.50 per cone, the quantity of the good supplied (10 cones) exceeds the quantity demanded (4 cones). There is a **surplus** of the good: Suppliers are unable to sell all they want at the going price. A surplus is sometimes called a situation of *excess supply*. When there is a surplus in the ice-cream market, sellers of ice cream find their freezers increasingly full of ice cream they would like to sell but cannot. They respond to the surplus by cutting their prices. Falling prices, in turn, increase the quantity demanded and decrease the quantity supplied. Prices continue to fall until the market reaches the equilibrium.

Suppose now that the market price is below the equilibrium price, as in panel (b) of Figure 9. In this case, the price is $1.50 per cone, and the quantity of the good demanded exceeds the quantity supplied. There is a **shortage** of the good: Demanders are unable to buy all they want at the going price. A shortage is sometimes called a situation of *excess demand*. When a shortage occurs in the ice-

surplus
a situation in which quantity supplied is greater than quantity demanded

shortage
a situation in which quantity demanded is greater than quantity supplied

cream market, buyers have to wait in long lines for a chance to buy one of the few cones available. With too many buyers chasing too few goods, sellers can respond to the shortage by raising their prices without losing sales. As the price rises, the quantity demanded falls, the quantity supplied rises, and the market once again moves toward the equilibrium.

Thus, the activities of the many buyers and sellers automatically push the market price toward the equilibrium price. Once the market reaches its equilibrium, all buyers and sellers are satisfied, and there is no upward or downward pressure on the price. How quickly equilibrium is reached varies from market to market depending on how quickly prices adjust. In most free markets, surpluses and shortages are only temporary because prices eventually move toward their equilibrium levels. Indeed, this phenomenon is so pervasive that it is called the **law of supply and demand:** The price of any good adjusts to bring the quantity supplied and quantity demanded for that good into balance.

law of supply and demand
the claim that the price of any good adjusts to bring the quantity supplied and the quantity demanded for that good into balance

Three Steps to Analyzing Changes in Equilibrium

So far, we have seen how supply and demand together determine a market's equilibrium, which in turn determines the price of the good and the amount of the good that buyers purchase and sellers produce. Of course, the equilibrium price and quantity depend on the position of the supply and demand curves. When some event shifts one of these curves, the equilibrium in the market changes, resulting in a new price and a new quantity exchanged between buyers and sellers.

When analyzing how some event affects the equilibrium in a market, we proceed in three steps. First, we decide whether the event shifts the supply curve, the demand curve, or in some cases, both curves. Second, we decide whether the curve shifts to the right or to the left. Third, we use the supply-and-demand diagram to compare the initial and the new equilibrium, which shows how the shift affects the equilibrium price and quantity. Table 3 summarizes these three steps. To see how this recipe is used, let's consider various events that might affect the market for ice cream.

Example: A Change in Demand   Suppose that one summer the weather is very hot. How does this event affect the market for ice cream? To answer this question, let's follow our three steps.

1. The hot weather affects the demand curve by changing people's taste for ice cream. That is, the weather changes the amount of ice cream that people want to buy at any given price. The supply curve is unchanged because the weather does not directly affect the firms that sell ice cream.

2. Because hot weather makes people want to eat more ice cream, the demand curve shifts to the right. Figure 10 shows this increase in demand as the shift in the demand curve from D_1 to D_2. This shift indicates that the quantity of ice cream demanded is higher at every price.

3. As Figure 10 shows, the increase in demand raises the equilibrium price from $2.00 to $2.50 and the equilibrium quantity from 7 to 10 cones. In other

10 **FIGURE**

How an Increase in Demand Affects the Equilibrium
An event that raises quantity demanded at any given price shifts the demand curve to the right. The equilibrium price and the equilibrium quantity both rise. Here an abnormally hot summer causes buyers to demand more ice cream. The demand curve shifts from D_1 to D_2, which causes the equilibrium price to rise from $2.00 to $2.50 and the equilibrium quantity to rise from 7 to 10 cones.

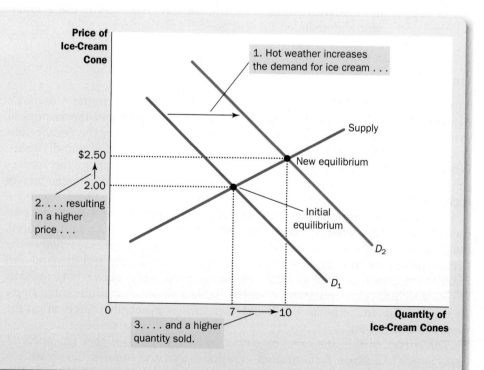

words, the hot weather increases the price of ice cream and the quantity of ice cream sold.

Shifts in Curves versus Movements along Curves   Notice that when hot weather drives up the price of ice cream, the quantity of ice cream that firms supply rises, even though the supply curve remains the same. In this case, economists say there has been an increase in "quantity supplied" but no change in "supply."

Supply refers to the position of the supply curve, whereas the *quantity supplied* refers to the amount suppliers wish to sell. In this example, supply does not change because the weather does not alter firms' desire to sell at any given price. Instead, the hot weather alters consumers' desire to buy at any given price and thereby shifts the demand curve. The increase in demand causes the equilibrium price to rise. When the price rises, the quantity supplied rises. This increase in quantity supplied is represented by the movement along the supply curve.

To summarize, a shift *in* the supply curve is called a "change in supply," and a shift *in* the demand curve is called a "change in demand." A movement *along* a fixed supply curve is called a "change in the quantity supplied," and a movement *along* a fixed demand curve is called a "change in the quantity demanded."

Example: A Change in Supply   Suppose that during another summer, a hurricane destroys part of the sugarcane crop and drives up the price of sugar. How does this event affect the market for ice cream? Once again, to answer this question, we follow our three steps.

1. The change in the price of sugar, an input into making ice cream, affects the supply curve. By raising the costs of production, it reduces the amount of ice cream that firms produce and sell at any given price. The demand curve does not change because the higher cost of inputs does not directly affect the amount of ice cream households wish to buy.
2. The supply curve shifts to the left because, at every price, the total amount that firms are willing and able to sell is reduced. Figure 11 illustrates this decrease in supply as a shift in the supply curve from S_1 to S_2.
3. As Figure 11 shows, the shift in the supply curve raises the equilibrium price from $2.00 to $2.50 and lowers the equilibrium quantity from 7 to 4 cones. As a result of the sugar price increase, the price of ice cream rises, and the quantity of ice cream sold falls.

Example: A Change in Both Supply and Demand   Now suppose that a heat wave and a hurricane occur during the same summer. To analyze this combination of events, we again follow our three steps.

1. We determine that both curves must shift. The hot weather affects the demand curve because it alters the amount of ice cream that households want to buy at any given price. At the same time, when the hurricane drives up sugar prices, it alters the supply curve for ice cream because it changes the amount of ice cream that firms want to sell at any given price.
2. The curves shift in the same directions as they did in our previous analysis: The demand curve shifts to the right, and the supply curve shifts to the left. Figure 12 illustrates these shifts.

11 FIGURE

How a Decrease in Supply Affects the Equilibrium

An event that reduces quantity supplied at any given price shifts the supply curve to the left. The equilibrium price rises, and the equilibrium quantity falls. Here an increase in the price of sugar (an input) causes sellers to supply less ice cream. The supply curve shifts from S_1 to S_2, which causes the equilibrium price of ice cream to rise from $2.00 to $2.50 and the equilibrium quantity to fall from 7 to 4 cones.

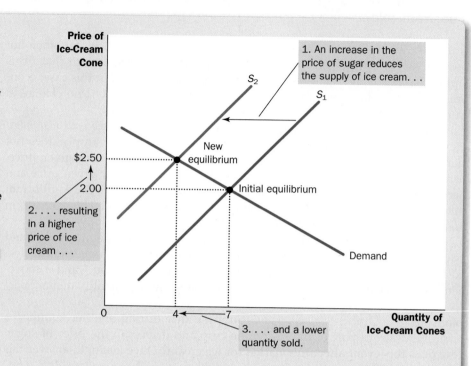

1. An increase in the price of sugar reduces the supply of ice cream. . .

New equilibrium

Initial equilibrium

Demand

2. . . . resulting in a higher price of ice cream . . .

3. . . . and a lower quantity sold.

Quantity of Ice-Cream Cones

12 FIGURE

A Shift in Both Supply and Demand

Here we observe a simultaneous increase in demand and decrease in supply. Two outcomes are possible. In panel (a), the equilibrium price rises from P_1 to P_2, and the equilibrium quantity rises from Q_1 to Q_2. In panel (b), the equilibrium price again rises from P_1 to P_2, but the equilibrium quantity falls from Q_1 to Q_2.

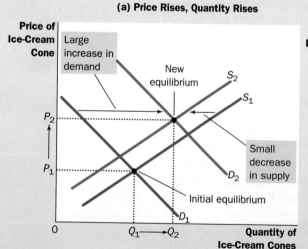

(a) Price Rises, Quantity Rises

Large increase in demand

New equilibrium

Small decrease in supply

Initial equilibrium

Quantity of Ice-Cream Cones

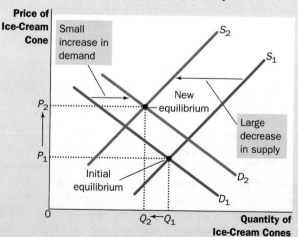

(b) Price Rises, Quantity Falls

Small increase in demand

New equilibrium

Large decrease in supply

Initial equilibrium

Quantity of Ice-Cream Cones

In The News

Political Unrest Shifts the Supply Curve

According to our analysis, a natural disaster that reduces supply reduces the quantity sold and raises the price. Sometimes the same is true with disasters caused by humans.

Chocolate Lovers Fret over Ivory Cocoa Woes

By Jennifer Heldt Powell

Political unrest overseas threatens to disrupt the supply of America's sweetest temptations.

Fighting on the Ivory Coast, which supplies 45 percent of the world's cocoa, has sent cocoa prices soaring just as the harvest season begins. And unless peace-keepers can bring order, chocolate prices could soar as well.

"There is hope that international pressure will quell the fighting," said Ann Prendergast, an analyst with Refco, a commodities trading company in New York. "If it doesn't, it's going to be just horrible and there won't be much cocoa coming out of the Ivory Coast."

The most recent troubles began last week when Ivory Coast government forces attacked the rebel-held towns in the northern part of the country. That was followed by air strikes on a French camp that killed nine soldiers and an American civilian.

Cocoa prices rose 9.7 percent, the steepest increase in five years. . . .

The surge could affect high end chocolate makers who rely on the prime cocoa butter produced by the Ivory Coast, said Prendergast. How much of an effect depends on peace efforts and the farmers.

"As the price goes up, farmers have motivation to do anything they can to get their product to the market," said Prendergast.

Source: *The Boston Herald*, November 9, 2004, p. 3. Reprinted with permission by *The Boston Herald*.

3. As Figure 12 shows, two possible outcomes might result depending on the relative size of the demand and supply shifts. In both cases, the equilibrium price rises. In panel (a), where demand increases substantially while supply falls just a little, the equilibrium quantity also rises. By contrast, in panel (b), where supply falls substantially while demand rises just a little, the equilibrium quantity falls. Thus, these events certainly raise the price of ice cream, but their impact on the amount of ice cream sold is ambiguous (that is, it could go either way).

Summary   We have just seen three examples of how to use supply and demand curves to analyze a change in equilibrium. Whenever an event shifts the supply curve, the demand curve, or perhaps both curves, you can use these tools to predict how the event will alter the amount sold in equilibrium and the price

4 TABLE

What Happens to Price and Quantity When Supply or Demand Shifts?
As a quick quiz, make sure you can explain each of the entries in this table using a supply-and-demand diagram.

	No Change in Supply	An Increase in Supply	A Decrease in Supply
No Change in Demand	P same Q same	P down Q up	P up Q down
An Increase in Demand	P up Q up	P ambiguous Q up	P up Q ambiguous
A Decrease in Demand	P down Q down	P down Q ambiguous	P ambiguous Q down

at which the good is sold. Table 4 shows the predicted outcome for any combination of shifts in the two curves. To make sure you understand how to use the tools of supply and demand, pick a few entries in this table and make sure you can explain to yourself why the table contains the prediction it does.

Quick Quiz   Analyze what happens to the market for pizza if the price of tomatoes rises.   •   Analyze what happens to the market for pizza if the price of hamburgers falls.

CONCLUSION: HOW PRICES ALLOCATE RESOURCES

This chapter has analyzed supply and demand in a single market. Although our discussion has centered around the market for ice cream, the lessons learned here apply in most other markets as well. Whenever you go to a store to buy something, you are contributing to the demand for that item. Whenever you look for a job, you are contributing to the supply of labor services. Because supply and demand are such pervasive economic phenomena, the model of supply and demand is a powerful tool for analysis. We will be using this model repeatedly in the following chapters.

    One of the *Ten Principles of Economics* discussed in Chapter 1 is that markets are usually a good way to organize economic activity. Although it is still too early to judge whether market outcomes are good or bad, in this chapter we have begun to see how markets work. In any economic system, scarce resources have to be allocated among competing uses. Market economies harness the forces of supply and demand to serve that end. Supply and demand together determine the prices of the economy's many different goods and services; prices in turn are the signals that guide the allocation of resources.

For example, consider the allocation of beachfront land. Because the amount of this land is limited, not everyone can enjoy the luxury of living by the beach. Who gets this resource? The answer is whoever is willing and able to pay the price. The price of beachfront land adjusts until the quantity of land demanded exactly balances the quantity supplied. Thus, in market economies, prices are the mechanism for rationing scarce resources.

Similarly, prices determine who produces each good and how much is produced. For instance, consider farming. Because we need food to survive, it is crucial that some people work on farms. What determines who is a farmer and who is not? In a free society, there is no government planning agency making this decision and ensuring an adequate supply of food. Instead, the allocation of workers to farms is based on the job decisions of millions of workers. This decentralized system works well because these decisions depend on prices. The prices of food and the wages of farmworkers (the price of their labor) adjust to ensure that enough people choose to be farmers.

If a person had never seen a market economy in action, the whole idea might seem preposterous. Economies are large groups of people engaged in many interdependent activities. What prevents decentralized decision making from degenerating into chaos? What coordinates the actions of the millions of people with their varying abilities and desires? What ensures that what needs to get done does in fact get done? The answer, in a word, is *prices*. If market economies are guided by an invisible hand, as Adam Smith famously suggested, then the price system is the baton that the invisible hand uses to conduct the economic orchestra.

"Two dollars"

"—and seventy-five cents."

SUMMARY

- Economists use the model of supply and demand to analyze competitive markets. In a competitive market, there are many buyers and sellers, each of whom has little or no influence on the market price.

- The demand curve shows how the quantity of a good demanded depends on the price. According to the law of demand, as the price of a good falls, the quantity demanded rises. Therefore, the demand curve slopes downward.

- In addition to price, other determinants of how much consumers want to buy include income, the prices of substitutes and complements, tastes, expectations, and the number of buyers. If one of these factors changes, the demand curve shifts.

- The supply curve shows how the quantity of a good supplied depends on the price. According to the law of supply, as the price of a good rises, the quantity supplied rises. Therefore, the supply curve slopes upward.

- In addition to price, other determinants of how much producers want to sell include input prices, technology, expectations, and the number of sellers. If one of these factors changes, the supply curve shifts.

- The intersection of the supply and demand curves determines the market equilibrium. At the equilibrium price, the quantity demanded equals the quantity supplied.

- The behavior of buyers and sellers naturally drives markets toward their equilibrium. When the market price is above the equilibrium price, there is a surplus of the good, which causes the market price to fall. When the market price is below the equilibrium price, there is a shortage, which causes the market price to rise.

- To analyze how any event influences a market, we use the supply-and-demand diagram to examine how the event affects the equilibrium price and quantity. To do this, we follow three steps. First, we decide whether the event shifts the supply curve or the demand curve (or both). Second, we decide which direction the curve shifts. Third, we compare the new equilibrium with the initial equilibrium.

- In market economies, prices are the signals that guide economic decisions and thereby allocate scarce resources. For every good in the economy, the price ensures that supply and demand are in balance. The equilibrium price then determines how much of the good buyers choose to purchase and how much sellers choose to produce.

KEY CONCEPTS

market, p. 64
competitive market, p. 64
quantity demanded, p. 65
law of demand, p. 65
demand schedule, p. 65
demand curve, p. 66
normal good, p. 68

inferior good, p. 68
substitutes, p. 68
complements, p. 68
quantity supplied, p. 71
law of supply, p. 71
supply schedule, p. 71
supply curve, p. 71

equilibrium, p. 75
equilibrium price, p. 75
equilibrium quantity, p. 75
surplus, p. 76
shortage, p. 76
law of supply and demand, p. 77

QUESTIONS FOR REVIEW

1. What is a competitive market? Briefly describe a type of market that is not perfectly competitive.
2. What determines the quantity of a good that buyers demand?
3. What are the demand schedule and the demand curve and how are they related? Why does the demand curve slope downward?
4. Does a change in consumers' tastes lead to a movement along the demand curve or a shift in the demand curve? Does a change in price lead to a movement along the demand curve or a shift in the demand curve?
5. Popeye's income declines, and as a result, he buys more spinach. Is spinach an inferior or a normal good? What happens to Popeye's demand curve for spinach?
6. What determines the quantity of a good that sellers supply?

7. What are the supply schedule and the supply curve and how are they related? Why does the supply curve slope upward?
8. Does a change in producers' technology lead to a movement along the supply curve or a shift in the supply curve? Does a change in price lead to a movement along the supply curve or a shift in the supply curve?
9. Define the equilibrium of a market. Describe the forces that move a market toward its equilibrium.
10. Beer and pizza are complements because they are often enjoyed together. When the price of beer rises, what happens to the supply, demand, quantity supplied, quantity demanded, and the price in the market for pizza?
11. Describe the role of prices in market economies.

PROBLEMS AND APPLICATIONS

1. Explain each of the following statements using supply-and-demand diagrams.
   a. "When a cold snap hits Florida, the price of orange juice rises in supermarkets throughout the country."
   b. "When the weather turns warm in New England every summer, the price of hotel rooms in Caribbean resorts plummets."
   c. "When a war breaks out in the Middle East, the price of gasoline rises, and the price of a used Cadillac falls."
2. "An increase in the demand for notebooks raises the quantity of notebooks demanded but not the quantity supplied." Is this statement true or false? Explain.

3. Consider the market for minivans. For each of the events listed here, identify which of the determinants of demand or supply are affected. Also indicate whether demand or supply increases or decreases. Then draw a diagram to show the effect on the price and quantity of minivans.
   a. People decide to have more children.
   b. A strike by steelworkers raises steel prices.
   c. Engineers develop new automated machinery for the production of minivans.
   d. The price of sports utility vehicles rises.
   e. A stock-market crash lowers people's wealth.

4. Consider the markets for DVD movies, TV screens, and tickets at movie theaters.
   a. For each pair, identify whether they are complements or substitutes:
      • DVDs and TV screens
      • DVDs and movie tickets
      • TV screens and movie tickets
   b. Suppose a technological advance reduces the cost of manufacturing TV screens. Draw a diagram to show what happens in the market for TV screens.
   c. Draw two more diagrams to show how the change in the market for TV screens affects the markets for DVDs and movie tickets.

5. Over the past 20 years, technological advances have reduced the cost of computer chips. How do you think this affected the market for computers? For computer software? For typewriters?

6. Consider these two statements from the In The News box:
   a. "Political unrest overseas threatens to disrupt the supply of America's sweetest temptations."
   b. "As the price goes up, farmers have motivation to do anything they can to get their product to the market."

   Which of these statements refers to a movement along the supply curve? Which refers to a shift in the supply curve? Explain.

7. Using supply-and-demand diagrams, show the effect of the following events on the market for sweatshirts.
   a. A hurricane in South Carolina damages the cotton crop.
   b. The price of leather jackets falls.
   c. All colleges require morning exercise in appropriate attire.
   d. New knitting machines are invented.

8. Suppose that in the year 2010 the number of births is temporarily high. How does this baby boom affect the price of baby-sitting services in 2015 and 2025? (Hint: 5-year-olds need baby-sitters, whereas 15-year-olds can be baby-sitters.)

9. Ketchup is a complement (as well as a condiment) for hot dogs. If the price of hot dogs rises, what happens to the market for ketchup? For tomatoes? For tomato juice? For orange juice?

10. The market for pizza has the following demand and supply schedules:

Price	Quantity Demanded	Quantity Supplied
$4	135 pizzas	26 pizzas
5	104	53
6	81	81
7	68	98
8	53	110
9	39	121

Graph the demand and supply curves. What is the equilibrium price and quantity in this market? If the actual price in this market were *above* the equilibrium price, what would drive the market toward the equilibrium? If the actual price in this market were *below* the equilibrium price, what would drive the market toward the equilibrium?

11. Because bagels and cream cheese are often eaten together, they are complements.
    a. We observe that both the equilibrium price of cream cheese and the equilibrium quantity of bagels have risen. What could be responsible for this pattern—a fall in the price of flour or a fall in the price of milk? Illustrate and explain your answer.
    b. Suppose instead that the equilibrium price of cream cheese has risen but the equilibrium quantity of bagels has fallen. What could be responsible for this pattern—a rise in the price of flour or a rise in the price of milk? Illustrate and explain your answer.

12. Suppose that the price of basketball tickets at your college is determined by market forces. Currently, the demand and supply schedules are as follows:

Price	Quantity Demanded	Quantity Supplied
$4	10,000 tickets	8,000 tickets
8	8,000	8,000
12	6,000	8,000
16	4,000	8,000
20	2,000	8,000

a. Draw the demand and supply curves. What is unusual about this supply curve? Why might this be true?

b. What are the equilibrium price and quantity of tickets?

c. Your college plans to increase total enrollment next year by 5,000 students. The additional students will have the following demand schedule:

Price	Quantity Demanded
$4	4,000 tickets
8	3,000
12	2,000
16	1,000
20	0

Now add the old demand schedule and the demand schedule for the new students to calculate the new demand schedule for the entire college. What will be the new equilibrium price and quantity?

13. Market research has revealed the following information about the market for chocolate bars: The demand schedule can be represented by the equation $Q^D = 1{,}600 - 300P$, where Q^D is the quantity demanded and P is the price. The supply schedule can be represented by the equation $Q^S = 1{,}400 + 700P$, where Q^S is the quantity supplied. Calculate the equilibrium price and quantity in the market for chocolate bars.

 For further information on topics in this chapter, additional problems, examples, applications, online quizzes, and more, please visit our website at http://mankiw.swlearning.com.

Aggregate Demand and Aggregate Supply

Economic activity fluctuates from year to year. In most years, the production of goods and services rises. Because of increases in the labor force, increases in the capital stock, and advances in technological knowledge, the economy can produce more and more over time. This growth allows everyone to enjoy a higher standard of living. On average over the past 50 years, the production of the U.S. economy as measured by real GDP has grown by about 3 percent per year.

In some years, however, this normal growth does not occur. Firms find themselves unable to sell all of the goods and services they have to offer, so they cut back on production. Workers are laid off, unemployment rises, and factories are left idle. With the economy producing fewer goods and services, real GDP and other measures of income fall. Such a period of falling incomes and rising unemployment is called a **recession** if it is relatively mild and a **depression** if it is more severe.

What causes short-run fluctuations in economic activity? What, if anything, can public policy do to prevent periods of falling incomes and rising unemployment? When recessions and depressions occur, how can policymakers reduce their length and severity? These are the questions that we take up now.

The variables that we study are largely those we have already seen in previous chapters. They include GDP, unemployment, interest rates, and the price

recession
a period of declining
real incomes and rising
unemployment

depression
a severe recession

level. Also familiar are the policy instruments of government spending, taxes, and the money supply. What differs from our earlier analysis is the time horizon. So far, our focus has been on the behavior of the economy in the long run. Our focus now is on the economy's short-run fluctuations around its long-run trend.

Although there remains some debate among economists about how to analyze short-run fluctuations, most economists use the *model of aggregate demand and aggregate supply*. Learning how to use this model for analyzing the short-run effects of various events and policies is the primary task ahead. This chapter introduces the model's two pieces: the aggregate-demand curve and the aggregate-supply curve. But before turning to the model, let's look at some of the key facts that describe the ups and downs in the economy.

THREE KEY FACTS ABOUT ECONOMIC FLUCTUATIONS

Short-run fluctuations in economic activity occur in all countries and have occurred throughout history. As a starting point for understanding these year-to-year fluctuations, let's discuss some of their most important properties.

Fact 1: Economic Fluctuations Are Irregular and Unpredictable

Fluctuations in the economy are often called *the business cycle*. As this term suggests, economic fluctuations correspond to changes in business conditions. When real GDP grows rapidly, business is good. During such periods of economic expansion, most firms find that customers are plentiful and that profits are growing. When real GDP falls during recessions, businesses have trouble. During such periods of economic contraction, most firms experience declining sales and dwindling profits.

The term *business cycle* is somewhat misleading because it suggests that economic fluctuations follow a regular, predictable pattern. In fact, economic fluctuations are not at all regular, and they are almost impossible to predict with much accuracy. Panel (a) of Figure 1 shows the real GDP of the U.S. economy since 1965. The shaded areas represent times of recession. As the figure shows, recessions do not come at regular intervals. Sometimes recessions are close together, such as the recessions of 1980 and 1982. Sometimes the economy goes many years without a recession. The longest period in U.S. history without a recession was the economic expansion from 1991 to 2001.

Fact 2: Most Macroeconomic Quantities Fluctuate Together

Real GDP is the variable that is most commonly used to monitor short-run changes in the economy because it is the most comprehensive measure of economic activity. Real GDP measures the value of all final goods and services produced within a given period of time. It also measures the total income (adjusted for inflation) of everyone in the economy.

It turns out, however, that for monitoring short-run fluctuations, it does not really matter which measure of economic activity one looks at. Most macroeconomic variables that measure some type of income, spending, or production fluctuate closely together. When real GDP falls in a recession, so do personal income, corporate profits, consumer spending, investment spending, industrial

"YOU'RE FIRED. PASS IT ON."

FIGURE 1

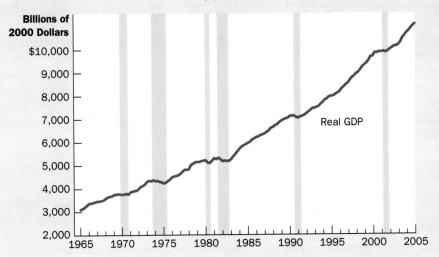

(a) Real GDP

A Look at Short-Run Economic Fluctuations
This figure shows real GDP in panel (a), investment spending in panel (b), and unemployment in panel (c) for the U.S. economy using quarterly data since 1965. Recessions are shown as the shaded areas. Notice that real GDP and investment spending decline during recessions, while unemployment rises.

Source: U.S. Department of Commerce; U.S. Department of Labor.

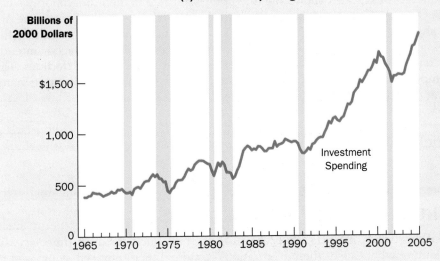

(b) Investment Spending

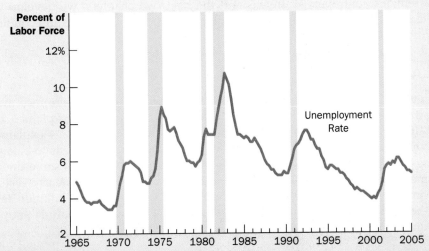

(c) Unemployment Rate

production, retail sales, home sales, auto sales, and so on. Because recessions are economy-wide phenomena, they show up in many sources of macroeconomic data.

Although many macroeconomic variables fluctuate together, they fluctuate by different amounts. In particular, as panel (b) of Figure 1 shows, investment spending varies greatly over the business cycle. Even though investment averages about one-seventh of GDP, declines in investment account for about two-thirds of the declines in GDP during recessions. In other words, when economic conditions deteriorate, much of the decline is attributable to reductions in spending on new factories, housing, and inventories.

Fact 3: As Output Falls, Unemployment Rises

Changes in the economy's output of goods and services are strongly correlated with changes in the economy's utilization of its labor force. In other words, when real GDP declines, the rate of unemployment rises. This fact is hardly surprising: When firms choose to produce a smaller quantity of goods and services, they lay off workers, expanding the pool of unemployed.

Panel (c) of Figure 1 shows the unemployment rate in the U.S. economy since 1965. Once again, recessions are shown as the shaded areas in the figure. The figure shows clearly the impact of recessions on unemployment. In each of the recessions, the unemployment rate rises substantially. When the recession ends and real GDP starts to expand, the unemployment rate gradually declines. The unemployment rate never approaches zero; instead, it fluctuates around its natural rate of about 5 or 6 percent.

Quick Quiz   List and discuss three key facts about economic fluctuations.

EXPLAINING SHORT-RUN ECONOMIC FLUCTUATIONS

Describing what happens to economies as they fluctuate over time is easy. Explaining what causes these fluctuations is more difficult. Indeed, compared to the topics we have studied in previous chapters, the theory of economic fluctuations remains controversial. In this and the next two chapters, we develop the model that most economists use to explain short-run fluctuations in economic activity.

The Assumptions of Classical Economics

In previous chapters, we developed theories to explain what determines most important macroeconomic variables in the long run. Chapter 12 explained the level and growth of productivity and real GDP. Chapters 13 and 14 explained how the financial system works and how the real interest rate adjusts to balance saving and investment. Chapter 15 explained why there is always some unemployment in the economy. Chapters 16 and 17 explained the monetary system and how changes in the money supply affect the price level, the inflation rate, and the nominal interest rate. Chapters 18 and 19 extended this analysis to open economies to explain the trade balance and the exchange rate.

In The News

Offbeat Indicators

When the economy goes into a recession, many economic variables are affected. This article, written during the recession of 2001, gives some examples.

Economic Numbers Befuddle Even the Best

By George Hager

Economists pore over scores of numbers every week, trying to sense when the recession is over. But quirky indicators and gut instinct might be almost as helpful—maybe even more so.

Is your dentist busy? Dentists say people put off appointments when times turn tough, then reschedule when the economy improves.

How far away do you have to park when you go to the mall? Fewer shoppers equal more parking spaces.

If you drive to work, has your commute time gotten shorter or longer?

Economist Michael Evans says a colleague with a pipeline into the garbage business swears by his own homegrown Chicago Trash index. Collections plunged after the Sept. 11 terror attacks, rebounded in October but then fell off again in mid-November. "Trash is a pretty good indicator of what people are buying," says Evans, an economist with Evans Carrol & Associates. "They've got to throw out the wrappings." . . .

What's actually happening is often clear only in hindsight. That's one reason the National Bureau of Economic Research waited until November to declare that a recession began last March—and why it took them until December 1992 to declare that the last recession had ended more than a year earlier, in March 1991.

"The data can fail you," says Allen Sinai, chief economist for Decision Economics. Sinai cautions that if numbers appear to be going up (or down), it's best to wait to see what happens over two or three months before drawing a conclusion—something hair-trigger financial markets routinely don't do.

"We have lots of false predictions of recoveries by (stock) markets that don't happen," he says.

Like a lot of economists, Sinai leavens the numbers with informal observations. These days, he's paying particular attention to what business executives say at meetings and cocktail parties because their mood—and their plans for investing and hiring—are key to a comeback.

Even the Federal Reserve, whose more than 200 economists monitor about every piece of the economy that can be measured, make room for anecdotes. Two weeks before every policy meeting, the Fed publishes its "beige book," a survey based on off-the-record conversations between officials at the Fed's 12 regional banks and local businesses.

The reports are peppered with quotes from unnamed business people ("Everybody's decided to go shopping again," someone told the Richmond Fed Bank last month) and the occasional odd detail that reveals just how far down the Fed inquisitors sometimes drill. Last March, the Dallas Fed Bank reported "healthy sales of singing gorillas" for Valentine's Day.

Source: *USA Today*, December 26, 2001. Reprinted with permission.

All of this previous analysis was based on two related ideas: the classical dichotomy and monetary neutrality. Recall that the classical dichotomy is the separation of variables into real variables (those that measure quantities or relative prices) and nominal variables (those measured in terms of money). According to classical macroeconomic theory, changes in the money supply affect nominal variables but not real variables. As a result of this monetary neutrality, Chapters 12 through 15 were able to examine the determinants of real variables (real GDP, the real interest rate, and unemployment) without introducing nominal variables (the money supply and the price level).

In a sense, money does not matter in a classical world. If the quantity of money in the economy were to double, everything would cost twice as much, and everyone's income would be twice as high. But so what? The change would be *nominal* (by the standard meaning of "nearly insignificant"). The things that people *really* care about—whether they have a job, how many goods and services they can afford, and so on—would be exactly the same.

This classical view is sometimes described by the saying, "Money is a veil." That is, nominal variables may be the first things we see when we observe an economy because economic variables are often expressed in units of money. But what's important are the real variables and the economic forces that determine them. According to classical theory, to understand these real variables, we need to look beneath the veil.

The Reality of Short-Run Fluctuations

Do these assumptions of classical macroeconomic theory apply to the world in which we live? The answer to this question is of central importance to understanding how the economy works. *Most economists believe that classical theory describes the world in the long run but not in the short run.*

Consider again the impact of money on the economy. Most economists believe that, beyond a period of several years, changes in the money supply affect prices and other nominal variables but do not affect real GDP, unemployment, or other real variables—just as classical theory says. When studying year-to-year changes in the economy, however, the assumption of monetary neutrality is no longer appropriate. In the short run, real and nominal variables are highly intertwined, and changes in the money supply can temporarily push real GDP away from its long-run trend.

Even the classical economists themselves, such as David Hume, realized that classical economic theory did not hold in the short run. From his vantage point in 18th-century England, Hume observed that when the money supply expanded after gold discoveries, it took some time for prices to rise, and in the meantime, the economy enjoyed higher employment and production.

To understand how the economy works in the short run, we need a new model. This new model can be built using many of the tools we developed in previous chapters, but it must abandon the classical dichotomy and the neutrality of money. We can no longer separate our analysis of real variables such as output and employment from our analysis of nominal variable such as money and the price level. Our new model focuses on how real and nominal variables interact.

The Model of Aggregate Demand and Aggregate Supply

Our model of short-run economic fluctuations focuses on the behavior of two variables. The first variable is the economy's output of goods and services, as measured by real GDP. The second is the average level of prices, as measured by the CPI or the GDP deflator. Notice that output is a real variable, whereas the price level is a nominal variable. By focusing on the relationship between these two variables, we are departing from the classical assumption that real and nominal variables can be studied separately.

We analyze fluctuations in the economy as a whole with the **model of aggregate demand and aggregate supply,** which is illustrated in Figure 2. On the vertical axis is the overall price level in the economy. On the horizontal axis is the overall quantity of goods and services produced in the economy. The **aggregate-demand curve** shows the quantity of goods and services that households, firms, the government, and customers abroad want to buy at each price level. The **aggregate-supply curve** shows the quantity of goods and services that firms produce and sell at each price level. According to this model, the price level and the quantity of output adjust to bring aggregate demand and aggregate supply into balance.

It is tempting to view the model of aggregate demand and aggregate supply as nothing more than a large version of the model of market demand and market supply introduced in Chapter 4. In fact, this model is quite different. When we consider demand and supply in a particular market—ice cream, for instance—the behavior of buyers and sellers depends on the ability of resources to move from one market to another. When the price of ice cream rises, the quantity demanded falls because buyers will use their incomes to buy products other than ice cream. Similarly, a higher price of ice cream raises the quantity supplied because firms that produce ice cream can increase production by hiring workers away from other parts of the economy. This *microeconomic* substitution from one market to another is impossible for the economy as a whole. After all, the quantity that our model is trying to explain—real GDP—measures the *total* quantity of goods and services produced in *all* markets. To understand why the aggregate-demand curve is downward sloping and why the aggregate-supply curve is upward sloping, we need a *macroeconomic* theory that explains the total quantity of goods and services demanded and the total quantity of goods and services supplied. Developing such a theory is our next task.

model of aggregate demand and aggregate supply
the model that most economists use to explain short-run fluctuations in economic activity around its long-run trend

aggregate-demand curve
a curve that shows the quantity of goods and services that households, firms, the government, and customers abroad want to buy at each price level

aggregate-supply curve
a curve that shows the quantity of goods and services that firms choose to produce and sell at each price level

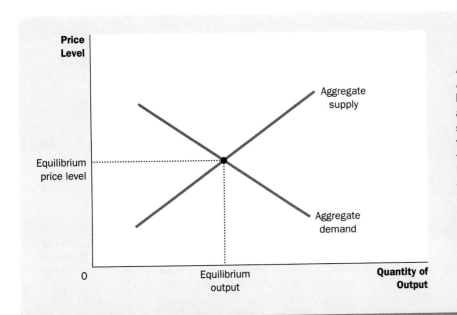

FIGURE 2

Aggregate Demand and Aggregate Supply
Economists use the model of aggregate demand and aggregate supply to analyze economic fluctuations. On the vertical axis is the overall level of prices. On the horizontal axis is the economy's total output of goods and services. Output and the price level adjust to the point at which the aggregate-supply and aggregate-demand curves intersect.

Quick Quiz How does the economy's behavior in the short run differ from its behavior in the long run?   •   Draw the model of aggregate demand and aggregate supply. What variables are on the two axes?

THE AGGREGATE-DEMAND CURVE

The aggregate-demand curve tells us the quantity of all goods and services demanded in the economy at any given price level. As Figure 3 illustrates, the aggregate-demand curve is downward sloping. This means that, other things equal, a decrease in the economy's overall level of prices (from, say, P_1 to P_2) raises the quantity of goods and services demanded (from Y_1 to Y_2). Conversely, an increase in the price level reduces the quantity of goods and services demanded.

Why the Aggregate-Demand Curve Slopes Downward

Why does a change in the price level move the quantity of goods and services demanded in the opposite direction? To answer this question, it is useful to recall that an economy's GDP (which we denote as Y) is the sum of its consumption (C), investment (I), government purchases (G), and net exports (NX):

$$Y = C + I + G + NX.$$

Each of these four components contributes to the aggregate demand for goods and services. For now, we assume that government spending is fixed by policy.

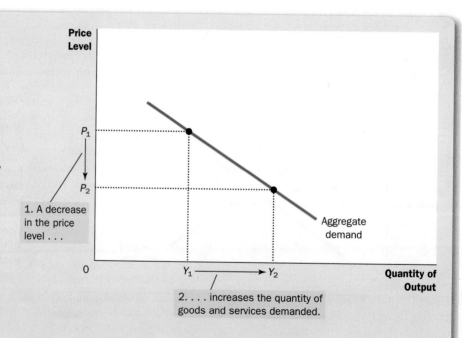

3 FIGURE

The Aggregate-Demand Curve
A fall in the price level from P_1 to P_2 increases the quantity of goods and services demanded from Y_1 to Y_2. There are three reasons for this negative relationship. As the price level falls, real wealth rises, interest rates fall, and the exchange rate depreciates. These effects stimulate spending on consumption, investment, and net exports. Increased spending on any or all of these components of output means a larger quantity of goods and services demanded.

1. A decrease in the price level . . .

2. . . . increases the quantity of goods and services demanded.

Aggregate demand

The other three components of spending—consumption, investment, and net exports—depend on economic conditions and, in particular, on the price level. To understand the downward slope of the aggregate-demand curve, therefore, we must examine how the price level affects the quantity of goods and services demanded for consumption, investment, and net exports.

The Price Level and Consumption: The Wealth Effect   Consider the money that you hold in your wallet and your bank account. The nominal value of this money is fixed: One dollar is always worth one dollar. Yet the *real* value of a dollar is not fixed. If a candy bar costs 1 dollar, then a dollar is worth one candy bar. If the price of a candy bar falls to 50 cents, then 1 dollar is worth two candy bars. Thus, when the price level falls, the dollars you are holding rise in value, which increases your real wealth and your ability to buy goods and services.

price level falls, $ rise in value.

This logic gives us the first reason the aggregate demand curve is downward sloping. *A decrease in the price level raises the real value of money and makes consumers wealthier, which in turn encourages them to spend more. The increase in consumer spending means a larger quantity of goods and services demanded. Conversely, an increase in the price level reduces the real value of money, in turn reducing wealth, consumer spending, and the quantity of goods and services demanded.*

The Price Level and Investment: The Interest-Rate Effect   The price level is one determinant of the quantity of money demanded. The lower the price level, the less money households need to hold to buy the goods and services they want. Therefore, when the price level falls, households try to reduce their holdings of money by lending some of it out. For instance, a household might use its excess money to buy interest-bearing bonds. Or it might deposit its excess money in an interest-bearing savings account, and the bank would use these funds to make more loans. In either case, as households try to convert some of their money into interest-bearing assets, they drive down interest rates. (The next chapter analyzes this in more detail.)

more $ to loan, less interest rate

Interest rates, in turn, affect spending on goods and services. Because a lower interest rate makes borrowing less expensive, it encourages firms to borrow more to invest in new plants and equipment, and it encourages households to borrow more to invest in new housing. (A lower interest rate might also stimulate consumer spending, especially large durable purchases such as cars, which are often bought on credit.) Thus, a lower interest rate increases the quantity of goods and services demanded.

This gives us a second reason the aggregate demand curve is downward sloping. *A lower price level reduces the interest rate, encourages greater spending on investment goods, and thereby increases the quantity of goods and services demanded. Conversely, a higher price level raises the interest rate, reducing investment spending and the quantity of goods and services demanded.*

The Price Level and Net Exports: The Exchange-Rate Effect   As we have just discussed, a lower price level in the United States lowers the U.S. interest rate. In response to the lower interest rate, some U.S. investors will seek higher returns by investing abroad. For instance, as the interest rate on U.S. government bonds falls, a mutual fund might sell U.S. government bonds to buy German government bonds. As the mutual fund tries to convert its dollars into euros to buy the German bonds, it increases the supply of dollars in the market for foreign-currency exchange.

The increased supply of dollars to be turned into euros causes the dollar to depreciate relative to the euro. This leads to a change in the real exchange rate—the relative price of domestic and foreign goods. Because each dollar buys fewer units of foreign currencies, foreign goods become more expensive relative to domestic goods.

The change in relative prices affects spending, both at home and abroad. Because foreign goods are now more expensive, Americans buy less from other countries, causing U.S. imports of goods and services to decrease. At the same time, because U.S. goods are now cheaper, foreigners buy more from the United States, so U.S. exports increase. Net exports equal exports minus imports, so both of these changes cause U.S. net exports to increase. Thus, the fall in the real exchange value of the dollar leads to an increase in the quantity of goods and services demanded.

This gives us a third reason the aggregate demand curve is downward sloping. *When a fall in the U.S. price level causes U.S. interest rates to fall, the real value of the dollar declines in foreign exchange markets, and this depreciation stimulates U.S. net exports and thereby increases the quantity of goods and services demanded. Conversely, when the U.S. price level rises and causes U.S interest rates to rise, the real value of the dollar increases, and this appreciation reduces U.S. net exports and the quantity of goods and services demanded.*

Summary   There are three distinct but related reasons a fall in the price level increases the quantity of goods and services demanded:

1. Consumers are wealthier, which stimulates the demand for consumption goods.
2. Interest rates fall, which stimulates the demand for investment goods.
3. The currency depreciates, which stimulates the demand for net exports.

The same three effects work in reverse: When the price level rises, decreased wealth depresses consumer spending, higher interest rates depress investment spending, and a currency appreciation depresses net exports.

Here is a thought experiment to hone your intuition about these effects. Imagine that one day you wake up and notice that, for some mysterious reason, the prices of all goods and services have fallen by half, so the dollars you are holding are worth twice as much. In real terms, you now have twice as much money as you had when you went to bed the night before. What would you do with the extra money? You could spend it at your favorite restaurant, increasing consumer spending. You could lend it out (by buying a bond or depositing it in your bank), reducing interest rates and increasing investment spending. Or you could invest it overseas (by buying shares in an international mutual fund), reducing the real exchange value of the dollar and increasing net exports. Whichever of these three responses you choose, the fall in the price level leads to an increase in the quantity of goods and services demanded. This is what the downward slope of the aggregate-demand curve represents.

It is important to keep in mind that the aggregate-demand curve (like all demand curves) is drawn holding "other things equal." In particular, our three explanations of the downward-sloping aggregate-demand curve assume that the money supply is fixed. That is, we have been considering how a change in the price level affects the demand for goods and services, holding the amount of money in the economy constant. As we will see, a change in the quantity of money shifts the aggregate-demand curve. At this point, just keep in mind that the aggregate-demand curve is drawn for a given quantity of money.

Why the Aggregate-Demand Curve Might Shift

The downward slope of the aggregate-demand curve shows that a fall in the price level raises the overall quantity of goods and services demanded. Many other factors, however, affect the quantity of goods and services demanded at a given price level. When one of these other factors changes, the aggregate-demand curve shifts.

Let's consider some examples of events that shift aggregate demand. We can categorize them according to which component of spending is most directly affected.

Shifts Arising from Changes in Consumption   Suppose Americans suddenly become more concerned about saving for retirement and, as a result, reduce their current consumption. Because the quantity of goods and services demanded at any price level is lower, the aggregate-demand curve shifts to the left. Conversely, imagine that a stock-market boom makes people wealthier and less concerned about saving. The resulting increase in consumer spending means a greater quantity of goods and services demanded at any given price level, so the aggregate-demand curve shifts to the right.

Thus, any event that changes how much people want to consume at a given price level shifts the aggregate-demand curve. One policy variable that has this effect is the level of taxation. When the government cuts taxes, it encourages people to spend more, so the aggregate-demand curve shifts to the right. When the government raises taxes, people cut back on their spending, and the aggregate-demand curve shifts to the left.

Shifts Arising from Changes in Investment   Any event that changes how much firms want to invest at a given price level also shifts the aggregate-demand curve. For instance, imagine that the computer industry introduces a faster line of computers, and many firms decide to invest in new computer systems. Because the quantity of goods and services demanded at any price level is higher, the aggregate-demand curve shifts to the right. Conversely, if firms become pessimistic about future business conditions, they may cut back on investment spending, shifting the aggregate-demand curve to the left.

Tax policy can also influence aggregate demand through investment. As we saw in Chapter 13, an investment tax credit (a tax rebate tied to a firm's investment spending) increases the quantity of investment goods that firms demand at any given interest rate. It therefore shifts the aggregate-demand curve to the right. The repeal of an investment tax credit reduces investment and shifts the aggregate-demand curve to the left.

Another policy variable that can influence investment and aggregate demand is the money supply. As we discuss more fully in the next chapter, an increase in the money supply lowers the interest rate in the short run. This makes borrowing less costly, which stimulates investment spending and thereby shifts the aggregate-demand curve to the right. Conversely, a decrease in the money supply raises the interest rate, discourages investment spending, and thereby shifts the aggregate-demand curve to the left. Many economists believe that throughout U.S. history, changes in monetary policy have been an important source of shifts in aggregate demand.

Shifts Arising from Changes in Government Purchases   The most direct way that policymakers shift the aggregate-demand curve is through government purchases. For example, suppose Congress decides to reduce purchases of new weapons systems. Because the quantity of goods and services demanded at any price level is lower, the aggregate-demand curve shifts to the left. Conversely, if state governments start building more highways, the result is a greater quantity of goods and services demanded at any price level, so the aggregate-demand curve shifts to the right.

Shifts Arising from Changes in Net Exports   Any event that changes net exports for a given price level also shifts aggregate demand. For instance, when Europe experiences a recession, it buys fewer goods from the United States. This reduces U.S. net exports at every price level and shifts the aggregate-demand curve for the U.S. economy to the left. When Europe recovers from its recession, it starts buying U.S. goods again, and the aggregate-demand curve shifts to the right.

Net exports sometimes change because international speculators cause movements in the exchange rate. Suppose, for instance, that these speculators lose confidence in foreign economies and want to move some of their wealth into the U.S. economy. In doing so, they bid up the value of the U.S. dollar in the foreign exchange market. This appreciation of the dollar makes U.S. goods more expensive compared to foreign goods, which depresses net exports and shifts the aggregate-demand curve to the left. Conversely, speculation that causes a depreciation of the dollar stimulates net exports and shifts the aggregate-demand curve to the right.

Summary   In the next chapter, we analyze the aggregate-demand curve in more detail. There we examine more precisely how the tools of monetary and fiscal policy can shift aggregate demand and whether policymakers should use these tools for that purpose. At this point, however, you should have some idea about why the aggregate-demand curve slopes downward and what kinds of events and policies can shift this curve. Table 1 summarizes what we have learned so far.

Quick Quiz   Explain the three reasons the aggregate-demand curve slopes downward.   •   Give an example of an event that would shift the aggregate-demand curve. Which way would this event shift the curve?

THE AGGREGATE-SUPPLY CURVE

The aggregate-supply curve tells us the total quantity of goods and services that firms produce and sell at any given price level. Unlike the aggregate-demand curve, which is always downward sloping, the aggregate-supply curve shows a relationship that depends crucially on the time horizon examined. *In the long run, the aggregate-supply curve is vertical, whereas in the short run, the aggregate-supply*

T A B L E   **1**

The Aggregate-
Demand Curve:
Summary

Why Does the Aggregate-Demand Curve Slope Downward?

1. *The Wealth Effect:* A lower price level increases real wealth, which encourages spending on consumption.
2. *The Interest-Rate Effect:* A lower price level reduces the interest rate, which encourages spending on investment.
3. *The Exchange-Rate Effect:* A lower price level causes the real exchange rate to depreciate, which encourages spending on net exports.

Why Might the Aggregate-Demand Curve Shift?

1. *Shifts Arising from Consumption:* An event that makes consumers spend more at a given price level (a tax cut, a stock-market boom) shifts the aggregate-demand curve to the right. An event that makes consumers spend less at a given price level (a tax hike, a stock-market decline) shifts the aggregate-demand curve to the left.
2. *Shifts Arising from Investment:* An event that makes firms invest more at a given price level (optimism about the future, a fall in interest rates due to an increase in the money supply) shifts the aggregate-demand curve to the right. An event that makes firms invest less at a given price level (pessimism about the future, a rise in interest rates due to a decrease in the money supply) shifts the aggregate-demand curve to the left.
3. *Shifts Arising from Government Purchases:* An increase in government purchases of goods and services (greater spending on defense or highway construction) shifts the aggregate-demand curve to the right. A decrease in government purchases on goods and services (a cutback in defense or highway spending) shifts the aggregate-demand curve to the left.
4. *Shifts Arising from Net Exports:* An event that raises spending on net exports at a given price level (a boom overseas, speculation that causes an exchange-rate depreciation) shifts the aggregate-demand curve to the right. An event that reduces spending on net exports at a given price level (a recession overseas, speculation that causes an exchange-rate appreciation) shifts the aggregate-demand curve to the left.

curve is upward sloping. To understand short-run economic fluctuations, and how the short-run behavior of the economy deviates from its long-run behavior, we need to examine both the long-run aggregate-supply curve and the short-run aggregate-supply curve.

Why the Aggregate-Supply Curve Is Vertical in the Long Run ~b/c of factor of production~

What determines the quantity of goods and services supplied in the long run? We implicitly answered this question earlier in the book when we analyzed the process of economic growth. *In the long run, an economy's production of goods and services (its real GDP) depends on its supplies of labor, capital, and natural resources and on the available technology used to turn these factors of production into goods and services.*

When we analyzed these forces that govern long-run growth, we did not need to make any reference to the overall level of prices. We examined the price level in a separate chapter, where we saw that it was determined by the quantity of money. We learned that if two economies were identical except that one had twice as much money in circulation as the other, the price level would be twice as high in the economy with more money, but the output of goods and services would be the same.

Because the price level does not affect the long-run determinants of real GDP, the long-run aggregate-supply curve is vertical, as in Figure 4. In other words, in the long run, the economy's labor, capital, natural resources, and technology determine the total quantity of goods and services supplied, and this quantity supplied is the same regardless of what the price level happens to be.

The vertical long-run aggregate-supply curve is a graphical representation of the classical dichotomy and monetary neutrality. As we have already discussed, classical macroeconomic theory is based on the assumption that real variables do not depend on nominal variables. The long-run aggregate-supply curve is consistent with this idea because it implies that the quantity of output (a real variable) does not depend on the level of prices (a nominal variable). As noted earlier, most economists believe that this principle works well when studying the economy over a period of many years but not when studying year-to-year changes. Thus, the aggregate-supply curve is vertical only in the long run.

Why the Long-Run Aggregate-Supply Curve Might Shift

Because classical macroeconomic theory predicts the quantity of goods and services produced by an economy in the long run, it also explains the position of the long-run aggregate-supply curve. The long-run level of production is sometimes called *potential output* or *full-employment output*. To be more precise, we call it the **natural rate of output** because it shows what the economy produces when unemployment is at its natural, or normal, rate. The natural rate of output is the level of production toward which the economy gravitates in the long run.

Any change in the economy that alters the natural rate of output shifts the long-run aggregate-supply curve. Because output in the classical model depends on labor, capital, natural resources, and technological knowledge, we can categorize shifts in the long-run aggregate-supply curve as arising from these four sources.

Shifts Arising from Changes in Labor Imagine that an economy experiences an increase in immigration. Because there would be a greater number of

natural rate of output
the production of goods and services that an economy achieves in the long run when unemployment is at its normal rate

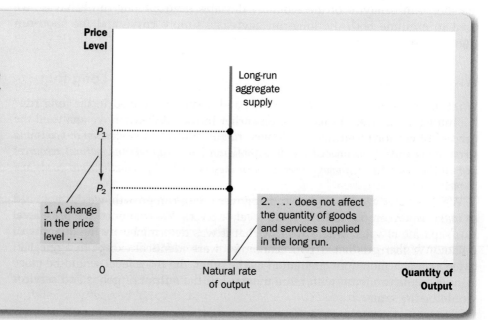

4 FIGURE

The Long-Run Aggregate-Supply Curve
In the long run, the quantity of output supplied depends on the economy's quantities of labor, capital, and natural resources and on the technology for turning these inputs into output. Because the quantity supplied does not depend on the overall price level, the long-run aggregate-supply curve is vertical at the natural rate of output.

workers, the quantity of goods and services supplied would increase. As a result, the long-run aggregate-supply curve would shift to the right. Conversely, if many workers left the economy to go abroad, the long-run aggregate-supply curve would shift to the left.

The position of the long-run aggregate-supply curve also depends on the natural rate of unemployment, so any change in the natural rate of unemployment shifts the long-run aggregate-supply curve. For example, if Congress were to raise the minimum wage substantially, the natural rate of unemployment would rise, and the economy would produce a smaller quantity of goods and services. As a result, the long-run aggregate-supply curve would shift to the left. Conversely, if a reform of the unemployment insurance system were to encourage unemployed workers to search harder for new jobs, the natural rate of unemployment would fall, and the long-run aggregate-supply curve would shift to the right.

Shifts Arising from Changes in Capital   An increase in the economy's capital stock increases productivity and, thereby, the quantity of goods and services supplied. As a result, the long-run aggregate-supply curve shifts to the right. Conversely, a decrease in the economy's capital stock decreases productivity and the quantity of goods and services supplied, shifting the long-run aggregate-supply curve to the left.

Notice that the same logic applies regardless of whether we are discussing physical capital such as machines and factories or human capital such as college degrees. An increase in either type of capital will raise the economy's ability to produce goods and services and, thus, shift the long-run aggregate-supply curve to the right.

Shifts Arising from Changes in Natural Resources   An economy's production depends on its natural resources, including its land, minerals, and weather. A discovery of a new mineral deposit shifts the long-run aggregate-supply curve to the right. A change in weather patterns that makes farming more difficult shifts the long-run aggregate-supply curve to the left.

In many countries, important natural resources are imported. A change in the availability of these resources can also shift the aggregate-supply curve. As we discuss later in this chapter, events occurring in the world oil market have historically been an important source of shifts in aggregate supply for the United States and other oil-importing nations.

Shifts Arising from Changes in Technological Knowledge   Perhaps the most important reason that the economy today produces more than it did a generation ago is that our technological knowledge has advanced. The invention of the computer, for instance, has allowed us to produce more goods and services from any given amounts of labor, capital, and natural resources. As computer use has spread throughout the economy, it has shifted the long-run aggregate-supply curve to the right.

Although not literally technological, there are many other events that act like changes in technology. For instance, opening up international trade has effects similar to inventing new production processes because it allows a country to specialize in higher-productivity industries, so it also shifts the long-run aggregate-supply curve to the right. Conversely, if the government passed new regulations preventing firms from using some production methods, perhaps to address worker safety or environmental concerns, the result would be a leftward shift in the long-run aggregate-supply curve.

Summary Because the long-run aggregate-supply curve reflects the classical model of the economy we developed in previous chapters, it provides a new way to describe our earlier analysis. Any policy or event that raised real GDP in previous chapters can now be described as increasing the quantity of goods and services supplied and shifting the long-run aggregate-supply curve to the right. Any policy or event that lowered real GDP in previous chapters can now be described as decreasing the quantity of goods and services supplied and shifting the long-run aggregate-supply curve to the left.

Using Aggregate Demand and Aggregate Supply to Depict Long-Run Growth and Inflation

Having introduced the economy's aggregate-demand curve and the long-run aggregate-supply curve, we now have a new way to describe the economy's long-run trends. Figure 5 illustrates the changes that occur in an economy from

5 FIGURE

Long-Run Growth and Inflation in the Model of Aggregate Demand and Aggregate Supply

As the economy becomes better able to produce goods and services over time, primarily because of technological progress, the long-run aggregate-supply curve shifts to the right. At the same time, as the Fed increases the money supply, the aggregate-demand curve also shifts to the right. In this figure, output grows from Y_{1980} to Y_{1990} and then to Y_{2000}, and the price level rises from P_{1980} to P_{1990} and then to P_{2000}. Thus, the model of aggregate demand and aggregate supply offers a new way to describe the classical analysis of growth and inflation.

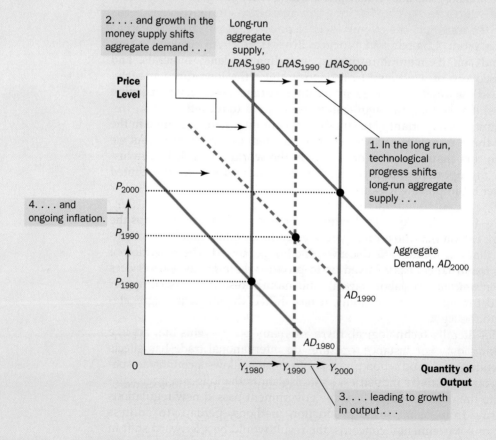

decade to decade. Notice that both curves are shifting. Although there are many forces that govern the economy in the long run and can in theory cause such shifts, the two most important in the real world are technology and monetary policy. Technological progress enhances an economy's ability to produce goods and services, and this increase in output is reflected in the continual shifts of the long-run aggregate-supply curve to the right. At the same time, because the Fed increases the money supply over time, the aggregate-demand curve also shifts to the right. As the figure illustrates, the result is trend growth in output (as shown by increasing Y) and continuing inflation (as shown by increasing P). This is just another way of representing the classical analysis of growth and inflation we conducted in earlier chapters.

The purpose of developing the model of aggregate demand and aggregate supply, however, is not to dress our previous long-run conclusions in new clothing. Instead, it is to provide a framework for short-run analysis, as we will see in a moment. As we develop the short-run model, we keep the analysis simple by not showing the continuing growth and inflation depicted by the shifts in Figure 5. But always remember that long-run trends provide the background for short-run fluctuations. *Short-run fluctuations in output and the price level should be viewed as deviations from the continuing long-run trends of output growth and inflation.*

Why the Aggregate-Supply Curve Slopes Upward in the Short Run

The key difference between the economy in the short run and in the long run is the behavior of aggregate supply. The long-run aggregate-supply curve is vertical because, in the long run, the overall level of prices does not affect the economy's ability to produce goods and services. By contrast, in the short run, the price level *does* affect the economy's output. That is, over a period of a year or two, an increase in the overall level of prices in the economy tends to raise the quantity of goods and services supplied, and a decrease in the level of prices tends to reduce the quantity of goods and services supplied. As a result, the short-run aggregate-supply curve is upward sloping, as shown in Figure 6.

Why do changes in the price level affect output in the short run? Macroeconomists have proposed three theories for the upward slope of the short-run aggregate-supply curve. In each theory, a specific market imperfection causes the supply side of the economy to behave differently in the short run than it does in the long run. Although the following theories differ in their details, they share a common theme: *The quantity of output supplied deviates from its long-run, or "natural," level when the actual price level in the economy deviates from the price level that people expected to prevail.* When the price level rises above the level that people expected, output rises above its natural rate, and when the price level falls below the expected level, output falls below its natural rate.

The Sticky-Wage Theory   The first explanation of the upward slope of the short-run aggregate-supply curve is the sticky-wage theory. Because this theory is the simplest of the three approaches to aggregate supply, it is the one we emphasize in this book.

According to this theory, the short-run aggregate-supply curve slopes upward because nominal wages are slow to adjust to changing economic conditions. In other words, wages are "sticky" in the short run. To some extent, the slow adjustment of nominal wages is attributable to long-term contracts between workers and firms that fix nominal wages, sometimes for as long as three years.

6 FIGURE

The Short-Run Aggregate-Supply Curve
In the short run, a fall in the price level from P_1 to P_2 reduces the quantity of output supplied from Y_1 to Y_2. This positive relationship could be due to sticky wages, sticky prices, or misperceptions. Over time, wages, prices, and perceptions adjust, so this positive relationship is only temporary.

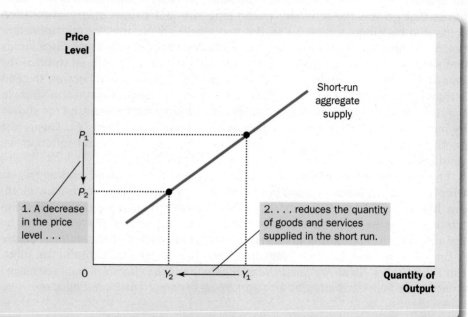

1. A decrease in the price level . . .

2. . . . reduces the quantity of goods and services supplied in the short run.

In addition, this slow adjustment may be attributable to social norms and notions of fairness that influence wage setting and that change only slowly over time.

An example helps explain how sticky nominal wages can result in a short-run aggregate-supply curve that slopes upward. Imagine that a year ago a firm expected the price level to be 100, and based on this expectation, it signed a contract with its workers agreeing to pay them, say, $20 an hour. In fact, the price level, P, turns out to be only 95. Because prices have fallen below expectations, the firm gets 5 percent less than expected for each unit of its product that it sells. The cost of labor used to make the output, however, is stuck at $20 per hour. Production is now less profitable, so the firm hires fewer workers and reduces the quantity of output supplied. Over time, the labor contract will expire, and the firm can renegotiate with its workers for a lower wage (which they may accept because prices are lower), but in the meantime, employment and production will remain below their long-run levels.

The same logic works in reverse. Suppose the price level turns out to be 105, and the wage remains stuck at $20. The firm sees that the amount it is paid for each unit sold is up by 5 percent, while its labor costs are not. In response, it hires more workers and increases the quantity supplied. Eventually, the workers will demand higher nominal wages to compensate for the higher price level, but for a while, the firm can take advantage of the profit opportunity by increasing employment and the quantity of output supplied above their long-run levels.

In short, according to the sticky-wage theory, the short-run aggregate-supply curve is upward sloping because nominal wages are based on the expected prices and do not respond immediately when the actual price level turns out to be different from what was expected. This stickiness of wages gives firms an incentive to produce less than the natural rate of output when the price level turns out lower than expected and to produce more when the price level turns out higher than expected.

The Sticky-Price Theory Some economists have advocated another approach to explaining the upward slope of the short-run aggregate-supply curve, called the sticky-price theory. As we just discussed, the sticky-wage theory emphasizes that nominal wages adjust slowly over time. The sticky-price theory emphasizes that the prices of some goods and services also adjust sluggishly in response to changing economic conditions. This slow adjustment of prices occurs in part because there are costs to adjusting prices, called *menu costs*. These menu costs include the cost of printing and distributing catalogs and the time required to change price tags. As a result of these costs, prices as well as wages may be sticky in the short run.

To see how sticky prices explain the aggregate-supply curve's upward slope, suppose that each firm in the economy announces its prices in advance based on the economic conditions it expects to prevail over the coming year. Suppose further that after prices are announced, the economy experiences an unexpected contraction in the money supply, which (as we have learned) will reduce the overall price level in the long run. Although some firms can reduce their prices immediately in response to an unexpected change in economic conditions, other firms may not want to incur additional menu costs. As a result, they may temporarily lag behind in reducing their prices. Because these lagging firms have prices that are too high, their sales decline. Declining sales, in turn, cause these firms to cut back on production and employment. In other words, because not all prices adjust instantly to changing economic conditions, an unexpected fall in the price level leaves some firms with higher-than-desired prices, and these higher-than-desired prices depress sales and induce firms to reduce the quantity of goods and services they produce.

The same reasoning applies when the money supply and price level turn out to be above what firms expected when they originally set their prices. While some firms raise their prices immediately in response to the new economic environment, other firms lag behind, keeping their prices at the lower-than-desired levels. These low prices attract customers, which induces these firms to increase employment and production. Thus, during the time these lagging firms are operating with outdated prices, there is a positive association between the overall price level and the quantity of output. This positive association is represented by the upward slope of the short-run aggregate-supply curve.

The Misperceptions Theory A third approach to explaining the upward slope of the short-run aggregate-supply curve is the misperceptions theory. According to this theory, changes in the overall price level can temporarily mislead suppliers about what is happening in the individual markets in which they sell their output. As a result of these short-run misperceptions, suppliers respond to changes in the level of prices, and this response leads to an upward-sloping aggregate-supply curve.

To see how this might work, suppose the overall price level falls below the level that suppliers expected. When suppliers see the prices of their products fall, they may mistakenly believe that their *relative* prices have fallen; that is, they may believe that their prices have fallen compared to other prices in the economy. For example, wheat farmers may notice a fall in the price of wheat before they notice a fall in the prices of the many items they buy as consumers. They may infer from this observation that the reward to producing wheat is temporarily low, and they may respond by reducing the quantity of wheat they supply. Similarly, workers may notice a fall in their nominal wages before they notice that the prices of the goods they buy are also falling. They may infer that the reward for working is temporarily low and respond by reducing the quantity of labor they supply. In both cases, a lower price level causes misperceptions about relative prices, and these misperceptions induce suppliers to respond to the lower price level by decreasing the quantity of goods and services supplied.

Similar misperceptions arise when the price level is above what was expected. Suppliers of goods and services may notice the price of their output rising and infer, mistakenly, that their relative prices are rising. They would conclude that it is a good time to produce. Until their misperceptions are corrected, they respond to the higher price level by increasing the quantity of goods and services supplied. This behavior results in a short-run aggregate-supply curve that slopes upward.

Summary   There are three alternative explanations for the upward slope of the short-run aggregate-supply curve: (1) sticky wages, (2) sticky prices, and (3) misperceptions about relative prices. Economists debate which of these theories is correct, and it is very possible each contains an element of truth. For our purposes in this book, the similarities of the theories are more important than the differences. All three theories suggest that output deviates in the short run from its long-run level (the natural rate) when the actual price level deviates from the price level that people had expected to prevail. We can express this mathematically as follows:

$$
\begin{pmatrix} \text{Quantity} \\ \text{of output} \\ \text{supplied} \end{pmatrix} = \begin{pmatrix} \text{Natural} \\ \text{rate of} \\ \text{output} \end{pmatrix} + a \begin{pmatrix} \text{Actual} \\ \text{price} \\ \text{level} \end{pmatrix} - \begin{pmatrix} \text{Expected} \\ \text{price} \\ \text{level} \end{pmatrix}
$$

where a is a number that determines how much output responds to unexpected changes in the price level.

Notice that each of the three theories of short-run aggregate supply emphasizes a problem that is likely to be temporary. Whether the upward slope of the aggregate-supply curve is attributable to sticky wages, sticky prices, or misperceptions, these conditions will not persist forever. Over time, nominal wages will become unstuck, prices will become unstuck, and misperceptions about relative prices will be corrected. In the long run, it is reasonable to assume that wages and prices are flexible rather than sticky and that people are not confused about relative prices. Thus, while we have several good theories to explain why the short-run aggregate-supply curve is upward sloping, they are all consistent with a long-run aggregate-supply curve that is vertical.

Why the Short-Run Aggregate-Supply Curve Might Shift

The short-run aggregate-supply curve tells us the quantity of goods and services supplied in the short run for any given level of prices. This curve is similar to the long-run aggregate-supply curve, but it is upward sloping rather than vertical because of sticky wages, sticky prices, and misperceptions. Thus, when thinking about what shifts the short-run aggregate-supply curve, we have to consider all those variables that shift the long-run aggregate-supply curve plus a new variable—the expected price level—that influences the wages that are stuck, the prices that are stuck, and the perceptions about relative prices.

Let's start with what we know about the long-run aggregate-supply curve. As we discussed earlier, shifts in the long-run aggregate-supply curve normally arise from changes in labor, capital, natural resources, or technological knowledge. These same variables shift the short-run aggregate-supply curve. For example, when an increase in the economy's capital stock increases productivity, the economy is able to produce more output, so both the long-run and short-run aggregate-supply curves shift to the right. When an increase in the minimum wage raises the natural rate of unemployment, the economy has fewer employed workers and thus produces less output, so both the long-run and short-run aggregate-supply curves shift to the left.

The important new variable that affects the position of the short-run aggregate-supply curve is the price level that people expected to prevail. As we have discussed, the quantity of goods and services supplied depends, in the short run, on sticky wages, sticky prices, and misperceptions. Yet wages, prices, and perceptions are set on the basis of the expected price level. So when people change their expectations of the price level, the short-run aggregate-supply curve shifts.

To make this idea more concrete, let's consider a specific theory of aggregate supply—the sticky-wage theory. According to this theory, when workers and firms expect the price level to be high, they are more likely to reach a bargain with a high level of nominal wages. High wages raise firms' costs, and for any given actual price level, higher costs reduce the quantity of goods and services that firms supply. Thus, when the expected price level rises, wages are higher, costs increase, and firms supply a smaller quantity of goods and services at any given actual price level. Thus, the short-run aggregate-supply curve shifts to the left. Conversely, when the expected price level falls, wages are lower, costs decline, firms increase output at any given price level, and the short-run aggregate-supply curve shifts to the right.

A similar logic applies in each theory of aggregate supply. The general lesson is the following: *An increase in the expected price level reduces the quantity of goods and services supplied and shifts the short-run aggregate-supply curve to the left. A decrease in the expected price level raises the quantity of goods and services supplied and shifts the short-run aggregate-supply curve to the right.* As we will see in the next section, this influence of expectations on the position of the short-run aggregate-supply curve plays a key role in explaining how the economy makes the transition from the short run to the long run. In the short run, expectations are fixed, and the economy finds itself at the intersection of the aggregate-demand curve and the short-run aggregate-supply curve. In the long run, if people observe that the price level is different from what they expected, their expectations adjust, and the short-run aggregate-supply curve shifts. This shift ensures that the economy eventually finds itself at the intersection of the aggregate-demand curve and the long-run aggregate-supply curve.

You should now have some understanding about why the short-run aggregate-supply curve slopes upward and what events and policies can cause this curve to shift. Table 2 summarizes our discussion.

Quick Quiz Explain why the long-run aggregate-supply curve is vertical. • Explain three theories for why the short-run aggregate-supply curve is upward sloping. • What variables shift both the long-run and short-run aggregate-supply curves? • What variable shifts the short-run aggregate-supply curve but not the long-run aggregate-supply curve?

2 TABLE

The Short-Run
Aggregate-Supply
Curve: Summary

Why Does the Short-Run Aggregate-Supply Curve Slope Upward?
1. *The Sticky-Wage Theory:* An unexpectedly low price level raises the real wage, which causes firms to hire fewer workers and produce a smaller quantity of goods and services.
2. *The Sticky-Price Theory:* An unexpectedly low price level leaves some firms with higher-than-desired prices, which depresses their sales and leads them to cut back production.
3. *The Misperceptions Theory:* An unexpectedly low price level leads some suppliers to think their relative prices have fallen, which induces a fall in production.

Why Might the Short-Run Aggregate-Supply Curve Shift?
1. *Shifts Arising from Labor:* An increase in the quantity of labor available (perhaps due to a fall in the natural rate of unemployment) shifts the aggregate-supply curve to the right. A decrease in the quantity of labor available (perhaps due to a rise in the natural rate of unemployment) shifts the aggregate-supply curve to the left.
2. *Shifts Arising from Capital:* An increase in physical or human capital shifts the aggregate-supply curve to the right. A decrease in physical or human capital shifts the aggregate-supply curve to the left.
3. *Shifts Arising from Natural Resources:* An increase in the availability of natural resources shifts the aggregate-supply curve to the right. A decrease in the availability of natural resources shifts the aggregate-supply curve to the left.
4. *Shifts Arising from Technology:* An advance in technological knowledge shifts the aggregate-supply curve to the right. A decrease in the available technology (perhaps due to government regulation) shifts the aggregate-supply curve to the left.
5. *Shifts Arising from the Expected Price Level:* A decrease in the expected price level shifts the short-run aggregate-supply curve to the right. An increase in the expected price level shifts the short-run aggregate-supply curve to the left.

TWO CAUSES OF ECONOMIC FLUCTUATIONS

Now that we have introduced the model of aggregate demand and aggregate supply, we have the basic tools we need to analyze fluctuations in economic activity. In particular, we can use what we have learned about aggregate demand and aggregate supply to examine the two basic causes of short-run fluctuations: shifts in aggregate demand and shifts in aggregate supply.

To keep things simple, we assume the economy begins in long-run equilibrium, as shown in Figure 7. Output and the price level are determined in the long run by the intersection of the aggregate-demand curve and the long-run aggregate-supply curve, shown as point A in the figure. At this point, output is at its natural rate. Because the economy is always in a short-run equilibrium, the short-run aggregate-supply curve passes through this point as well, indicating that the expected price level has adjusted to this long-run equilibrium. That is, when an economy is in its long-run equilibrium, the expected price level must equal the actual price level so that the intersection of aggregate demand with short-run aggregate supply is the same as the intersection of aggregate demand with long-run aggregate supply.

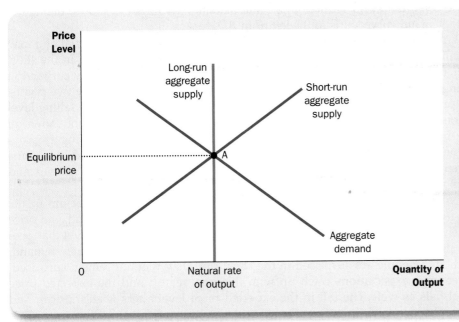

FIGURE 7

The Long-Run Equilibrium
The long-run equilibrium of the economy is found where the aggregate-demand curve crosses the long-run aggregate-supply curve (point A). When the economy reaches this long-run equilibrium, the expected price level will have adjusted to equal the actual price level. As a result, the short-run aggregate-supply curve crosses this point as well.

The Effects of a Shift in Aggregate Demand

Suppose that a wave of pessimism suddenly overtakes the economy. The cause might be a scandal in the White House, a crash in the stock market, or the outbreak of war overseas. Because of this event, many people lose confidence in the future and alter their plans. Households cut back on their spending and delay major purchases, and firms put off buying new equipment.

What is the macroeconomic impact of such a wave of pessimism? In answering this question, we can follow the three steps we used in Chapter 4 when analyzing supply and demand in specific markets. First, we determine whether the event affects aggregate demand or aggregate supply. Second, we decide which direction the curve shifts. Third, we use the diagram of aggregate demand and aggregate supply to compare the initial and the new equilibrium. The new wrinkle is that we need to add a fourth step: We have to keep track of a new short-run equilibrium, a new long-run equilibrium, and the transition between them. Table 3 summarizes the four steps to analyzing economic fluctuations.

The first two steps are easy. First, because the wave of pessimism affects spending plans, it affects the aggregate-demand curve. Second, because households and

TABLE 3

1. Decide whether the event shifts the aggregate demand curve or the aggregate supply curve (or perhaps both).
2. Decide in which direction the curve shifts.
3. Use the diagram of aggregate demand and aggregate supply to see how the shift changes output and the price level in the short run.
4. Use the diagram of aggregate demand and aggregate supply to analyze how the economy moves from its new short-run equilibrium to its long-run equilibrium.

Four Steps for Analyzing Macroeconomic Fluctuations

firms now want to buy a smaller quantity of goods and services for any given price level, the event reduces aggregate demand. As Figure 8 shows, the aggregate-demand curve shifts to the left from AD_1 to AD_2.

With this figure, we can perform step three: By comparing the initial and new equilibrium, we can see the effects of the fall in aggregate demand. In the short run, the economy moves along the initial short-run aggregate-supply curve, AS_1, going from point A to point B. As the economy moves between these two points, output falls from Y_1 to Y_2, and the price level falls from P_1 to P_2. The falling level of output indicates that the economy is in a recession. Although not shown in the figure, firms respond to lower sales and production by reducing employment. Thus, the pessimism that caused the shift in aggregate demand is, to some extent, self-fulfilling: Pessimism about the future leads to falling incomes and rising unemployment.

Now comes step four—the transition from the short-run equilibrium to the long-run equilibrium. Because of the reduction in aggregate demand, the price level initially falls from P_1 to P_2. The price level is thus below the level that people had come to expect (P_1) before the sudden fall in aggregate demand. Although people are surprised in the short run, they will not remain surprised. Over time, expectations catch up with this new reality, and the expected price level falls as well. The fall in the expected price level alters wages, prices, and perceptions, which in turn influences the position of the short-run aggregate-supply curve. For example, according to the sticky-wage theory, once workers and firms come to expect a lower level of prices, they start to strike bargains for lower nominal wages; the reduction in labor costs encourages firms to hire more workers and expands production at any given level of prices. Thus, the fall in the expected price level shifts the short-run aggregate-supply curve to the right

8   FIGURE

A Contraction in Aggregate Demand

A fall in aggregate demand is represented with a leftward shift in the aggregate-demand curve from AD_1 to AD_2. In the short run, the economy moves from point A to point B. Output falls from Y_1 to Y_2, and the price level falls from P_1 to P_2. Over time, as the expected price level adjusts, the short-run aggregate-supply curve shifts to the right from AS_1 to AS_2, and the economy reaches point C, where the new aggregate-demand curve crosses the long-run aggregate-supply curve. In the long run, the price level falls to P_3, and output returns to its natural rate, Y_1.

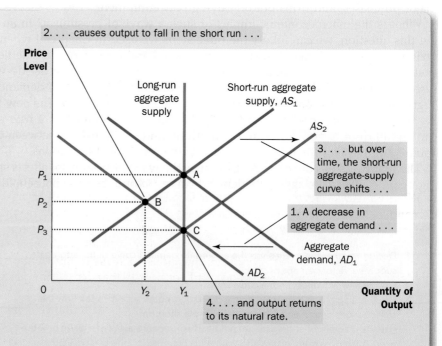

FYI

Monetary Neutrality Revisited

According to classical economic theory, money is neutral. That is, changes in the quantity of money affect nominal variables such as the price level but not real variables such as output. Earlier in this chapter, we noted that most economists accept this conclusion as a description of how the economy works in the long run but not in the short run. With the model of aggregate demand and aggregate supply, we can illustrate this conclusion and explain it more fully.

Suppose that the Federal Reserve reduces the quantity of money in the economy. What effect does this change have? As we discussed, the money supply is one determinant of aggregate demand. The reduction in the money supply shifts the aggregate-demand curve to the left.

The analysis looks just like Figure 8. Even though the cause of the shift in aggregate demand is different, we would observe the same effects on output and the price level. In the short run, both output and the price level fall. The economy experiences a recession. But over time, the expected price level falls as well. Firms and workers respond to their new expectations by, for instance, agreeing to lower nominal wages. As they do so, the short-run aggregate-supply curve shifts to the right. Eventually, the economy finds itself back on the long-run aggregate-supply curve.

Figure 8 shows when money matters for real variables and when it does not. In the long run, money is neutral, as represented by the movement of the economy from point A to point C. But in the short run, a change in the money supply has real effects, as represented by the movement of the economy from point A to point B. An old saying summarizes the analysis: "Money is a veil, but when the veil flutters, real output sputters."

from AS_1 to AS_2 in Figure 8. This shift allows the economy to approach point C, where the new aggregate-demand curve (AD_2) crosses the long-run aggregate-supply curve.

In the new long-run equilibrium, point C, output is back to its natural rate. The economy has corrected itself: The decline in output is reversed in the long run, even without action by policymakers. Although the wave of pessimism has reduced aggregate demand, the price level has fallen sufficiently (to P_3) to offset the shift in the aggregate-demand curve, and people have come to expect this new lower price level as well. Thus, in the long run, the shift in aggregate demand is reflected fully in the price level and not at all in the level of output. In other words, the long-run effect of a shift in aggregate demand is a nominal change (the price level is lower) but not a real change (output is the same).

What should policymakers do when faced with a sudden fall in aggregate demand? In this analysis, we assumed they did nothing. Another possibility is that, as soon as the economy heads into recession (moving from point A to point B), policymakers could take action to increase aggregate demand. As we noted earlier, an increase in government spending or an increase in the money supply would increase the quantity of goods and services demanded at any price and, therefore, would shift the aggregate-demand curve to the right. If policymakers act with sufficient speed and precision, they can offset the initial shift in aggregate demand, return the aggregate-demand curve back to AD_1, and bring the economy back to point A. If the policy is successful, the painful period of depressed output and employment can be reduced in length and severity. The next chapter discusses in more detail the ways in which monetary and fiscal policy influence aggregate demand, as well as some of the practical difficulties in using these policy instruments.

To sum up, this story about shifts in aggregate demand has three important lessons:

- In the short run, shifts in aggregate demand cause fluctuations in the economy's output of goods and services.
- In the long run, shifts in aggregate demand affect the overall price level but do not affect output.
- Policymakers who influence aggregate demand can potentially mitigate the severity of economic fluctuations.

CASE STUDY | TWO BIG SHIFTS IN AGGREGATE DEMAND: THE GREAT DEPRESSION AND WORLD WAR II

At the beginning of this chapter, we established three key facts about economic fluctuations by looking at data since 1965. Let's now take a longer look at U.S. economic history. Figure 9 shows data since 1900 on the percentage change in real GDP over the previous 3 years. In an average 3-year period, real GDP grows about 10 percent—a bit more than 3 percent per year. The business cycle, however, causes fluctuations around this average. Two episodes jump out as being particularly significant: the large drop in real GDP in the early 1930s and the large increase in real GDP in the early 1940s. Both of these events are attributable to shifts in aggregate demand.

9 **FIGURE**

U.S. Real GDP Growth since 1900

Source: U.S. Department of Commerce.

Over the course of U.S. economic history, two fluctuations stand out as especially large. During the early 1930s, the economy went through the Great Depression, when the production of goods and services plummeted. During the early 1940s, the United States entered World War II, and the economy experienced rapidly rising production. Both of these events are usually explained by large shifts in aggregate demand.

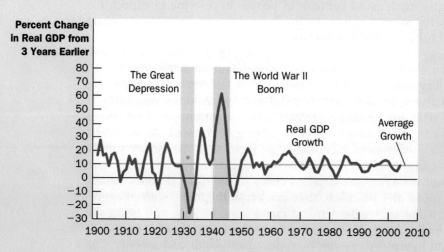

The economic calamity of the early 1930s is called the *Great Depression,* and it is by far the largest economic downturn in U.S. history. Real GDP fell by 27 percent from 1929 to 1933, and unemployment rose from 3 percent to 25 percent. At the same time, the price level fell by 22 percent over these 4 years. Many other countries experienced similar declines in output and prices during this period.

Economic historians continue to debate the causes of the Great Depression, but most explanations center on a large decline in aggregate demand. What caused aggregate demand to contract? Here is where the disagreement arises.

Many economists place primary blame on the decline in the money supply: From 1929 to 1933, the money supply fell by 28 percent. As you may recall from our discussion of the monetary system, this decline in the money supply was due to problems in the banking system. As households withdrew their money from financially shaky banks and bankers became more cautious and started holding greater reserves, the process of money creation under fractional-reserve banking went into reverse. The Fed, meanwhile, failed to offset this fall in the money multiplier with expansionary open-market operations. As a result, the money supply declined. Many economists blame the Fed's failure to act for the Great Depression's severity.

THE OUTCOME OF A MASSIVE DECREASE IN AGGREGATE DEMAND

Other economists have suggested alternative reasons for the collapse in aggregate demand. For example, stock prices fell about 90 percent during this period, depressing household wealth and thereby consumer spending. In addition, the banking problems may have prevented some firms from obtaining the financing they wanted for investment projects, and this would have depressed investment spending. Of course, all of these forces may have acted together to contract aggregate demand during the Great Depression.

The second significant episode in Figure 9—the economic boom of the early 1940s—is easier to explain. The obvious cause of this event was World War II. As the United States entered the war overseas, the federal government had to devote more resources to the military. Government purchases of goods and services increased almost fivefold from 1939 to 1944. This huge expansion in aggregate demand almost doubled the economy's production of goods and services and led to a 20 percent increase in the price level (although widespread government price controls limited the rise in prices). Unemployment fell from 17 percent in 1939 to about 1 percent in 1944—the lowest level in U.S. history.   •

CASE STUDY | THE RECESSION OF 2001

After the longest economic expansion in history, the U.S. economy experienced a recession in 2001. The unemployment rate rose from 3.9 percent in December 2000 to 4.9 percent in August 2001 and to 6.3 percent in June 2003. The unemployment rate then began to decline. By January 2005, unemployment had fallen back to 5.2 percent.

What caused the recession, and what ended it? The answer to both questions is shifts in aggregate demand.

The recession began with the end of the dot-com bubble in the stock market. During the 1990s, many stock-market investors became optimistic about information technology, and they bid up stock prices, particularly of high-tech companies. With hindsight, it is fair to say that this optimism was excessive. Eventually, the optimism faded, and stock prices fell by about 25 percent from August 2000 to August 2001. The fall in the stock market reduced household wealth,

FYI

The Origins of Aggregate Demand and Aggregate Supply

Now that we have a preliminary understanding of the model of aggregate demand and aggregate supply, it is worthwhile to step back from it and consider its history. How did this model of short-run fluctuations develop? The answer is that this model, to a large extent, is a by-product of the Great Depression of the 1930s. Economists and policymakers at the time were puzzled about what had caused this calamity and were uncertain about how to deal with it.

In 1936, economist John Maynard Keynes published a book titled *The General Theory of Employment, Interest, and Money*, which attempted to explain short-run economic fluctuations in general and the Great Depression in particular. Keynes's primary message was that recessions and depressions can occur because of inadequate aggregate demand for goods and services.

Keynes had long been a critic of classical economic theory—the theory we examined earlier in the book—because it could explain only the long-run effects of policies. A few years before offering *The General Theory*, Keynes had written the following about classical economics:

John Maynard Keynes

The long run is a misleading guide to current affairs. In the long run we are all dead. Economists set themselves too easy, too useless a task if in tempestuous seasons they can only tell us when the storm is long past, the ocean will be flat.

Keynes's message was aimed at policymakers as well as economists. As the world's economies suffered with high unemployment, Keynes advocated policies to increase aggregate demand, including government spending on public works.

In the next chapter, we examine in detail how policymakers can use the tools of monetary and fiscal policy to influence aggregate demand. The analysis in the next chapter, as well as in this one, owes much to the legacy of John Maynard Keynes.

---

which in turn reduced consumer spending. In addition, when the new technologies started to appear less profitable than they had originally seemed, investment spending fell. The aggregate-demand curve shifted to the left.

The second shock to the economy was the terrorist attacks on New York and Washington on September 11, 2001. In the week after the attacks, the stock market fell another 12 percent, its biggest weekly loss since the Great Depression of the 1930s. Moreover, the attacks increased uncertainty about what the future would hold. Uncertainty can reduce spending, as households and firms postpone plans, waiting for the uncertainty to be resolved. Thus, the terrorist attacks also shifted the aggregate-demand curve further to the left.

The third event that put downward pressure on aggregate demand was a series of corporate accounting scandals. During 2001 and 2002, several major corporations, including Enron and WorldCom, were found to have misled the public about their profitability. When the truth became known, the value of their stock plummeted. Even honest companies experienced stock declines, as stock-market investors became less trustful of all accounting data. This fall in the stock market further depressed aggregate demand.

Policymakers were quick to respond to these events. As soon as the economic slowdown became apparent, the Federal Reserve pursued expansionary monetary policy. Money growth accelerated, and interest rates fell. The federal funds rate (the interest rate on loans between banks that the Fed uses as its short-term policy target) fell from 6.5 percent in December 2000 to 1.0 percent in June 2003. Lower interest rates stimulated spending by reducing the cost of borrowing. At the same time, with the president's urging, Congress passed a tax cut in 2001, including an immediate tax rebate, and another tax cut in 2003. One goal of these tax cuts was to stimulate consumer and investment spending. Interest-rate cuts and tax cuts both shifted the aggregate-demand curve to the right, offsetting the three contractionary shocks the economy had experienced.

The recession of 2001 is a reminder of the many kinds of events that can influence aggregate demand and, thus, the direction of the economy.   •

The Effects of a Shift in Aggregate Supply

Imagine once again an economy in its long-run equilibrium. Now suppose that suddenly some firms experience an increase in their costs of production. For example, bad weather in farm states might destroy some crops, driving up the cost of producing food products. Or a war in the Middle East might interrupt the shipping of crude oil, driving up the cost of producing oil products.

To analyze the macroeconomic impact of such an increase in production costs, we follow the same four steps. First, which curve is affected? Because production costs affect the firms that supply goods and services, changes in production costs alter the position of the aggregate-supply curve. Second, which direction does the curve shift? Because higher production costs make selling goods and services less profitable, firms now supply a smaller quantity of output for any given price level. Thus, as Figure 10 shows, the short-run aggregate-supply curve shifts to the left from AS_1 to AS_2. (Depending on the event, the long-run aggregate-supply curve might also shift. To keep things simple, however, we will assume that it does not.)

The figure allows us to perform step three of comparing the initial and new equilibrium. In the short run, the economy goes from point A to point B, moving along the existing aggregate-demand curve. The output of the economy falls from Y_1 to Y_2, and the price level rises from P_1 to P_2. Because the economy is experiencing both *stagnation* (falling output) and *inflation* (rising prices), such an event is sometimes called **stagflation.**

Now consider step four—the transition from the short-run equilibrium to the long-run equilibrium. According to the sticky-wage theory, the key issue is how stagflation affects nominal wages. Firms and workers may at first respond to the higher level of prices by raising their expectations of the price level and setting higher nominal wages. In this case, firms' costs will rise yet again, and the short-run aggregate-supply curve will shift further to the left, making the problem of stagflation even worse. This phenomenon of higher prices leading to higher wages, in turn leading to even higher prices, is sometimes called a *wage-price spiral.*

At some point, this spiral of ever-rising wages and prices will slow. The low level of output and employment will put downward pressure on workers' wages because workers have less bargaining power when unemployment is high. As nominal wages fall, producing goods and services becomes more profitable, and

stagflation
a period of falling output and rising prices

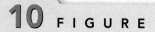

10 FIGURE

An Adverse Shift in Aggregate Supply
When some event increases firms' costs, the short-run aggregate-supply curve shifts to the left from AS_1 to AS_2. The economy moves from point A to point B. The result is stagflation: Output falls from Y_1 to Y_2, and the price level rises from P_1 to P_2.

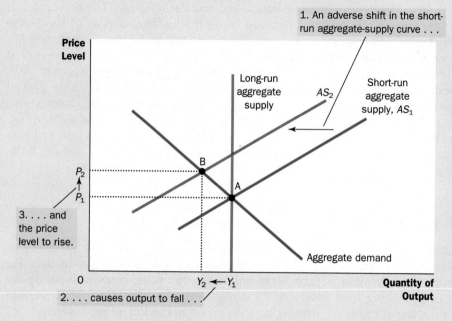

the short-run aggregate-supply curve shifts to the right. As it shifts back toward AS_1, the price level falls, and the quantity of output approaches its natural rate. In the long run, the economy returns to point A, where the aggregate-demand curve crosses the long-run aggregate-supply curve.

This transition back to the initial equilibrium assumes, however, that aggregate demand is held constant throughout the process. In the real world, that may not be the case. Policymakers who control monetary and fiscal policy might attempt to offset some of the effects of the shift in the short-run aggregate-supply curve by shifting the aggregate-demand curve. This possibility is shown in Figure 11. In this case, changes in policy shift the aggregate-demand curve to the right from AD_1 to AD_2—exactly enough to prevent the shift in aggregate supply from affecting output. The economy moves directly from point A to point C. Output remains at its natural rate, and the price level rises from P_1 to P_3. In this case, policymakers are said to *accommodate* the shift in aggregate supply. An accommodative policy accepts a permanently higher level of prices to maintain a higher level of output and employment.

To sum up, this story about shifts in aggregate supply has two important lessons:

- Shifts in aggregate supply can cause stagflation—a combination of recession (falling output) and inflation (rising prices).
- Policymakers who can influence aggregate demand can potentially mitigate the adverse impact on output but only at the cost of exacerbating the problem of inflation.

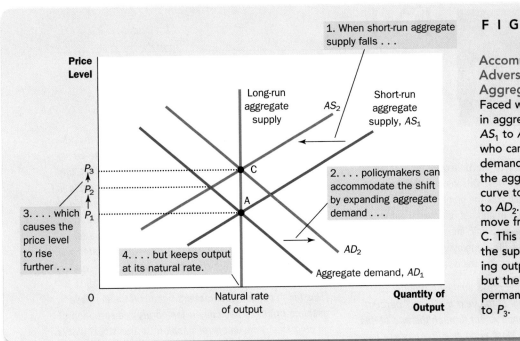

1. When short-run aggregate supply falls . . .

2. . . . policymakers can accommodate the shift by expanding aggregate demand . . .

3. . . . which causes the price level to rise further . . .

4. . . . but keeps output at its natural rate.

FIGURE 11

Accommodating an Adverse Shift in Aggregate Supply
Faced with an adverse shift in aggregate supply from AS_1 to AS_2, policymakers who can influence aggregate demand might try to shift the aggregate-demand curve to the right from AD_1 to AD_2. The economy would move from point A to point C. This policy would prevent the supply shift from reducing output in the short run, but the price level would permanently rise from P_1 to P_3.

CASE STUDY | OIL AND THE ECONOMY

Some of the largest economic fluctuations in the U.S. economy since 1970 have originated in the oil fields of the Middle East. Crude oil is a key input into the production of many goods and services, and much of the world's oil comes from Saudi Arabia, Kuwait, and other Middle Eastern countries. When some event (usually political in origin) reduces the supply of crude oil flowing from this region, the price of oil rises around the world. U.S. firms that make gasoline, tires, and many other products experience rising costs, and they find it less profitable to supply their output of goods and services at any given price level. The result is a leftward shift in the aggregate-supply curve, which in turn leads to stagflation.

The first episode of this sort occurred in the mid-1970s. The countries with large oil reserves got together as members of OPEC, the Organization of Petroleum Exporting Countries. OPEC is a *cartel*—a group of sellers that attempts to thwart competition and reduce production to raise prices. And indeed, oil prices rose substantially. From 1973 to 1975, oil approximately doubled in price. Oil-importing countries around the world experienced simultaneous inflation and recession. The U.S. inflation rate as measured by the CPI exceeded 10 percent for the first time in decades. Unemployment rose from 4.9 percent in 1973 to 8.5 percent in 1975.

Almost the same thing happened a few years later. In the late 1970s, the OPEC countries again restricted the supply of oil to raise the price. From 1978 to 1981, the price of oil more than doubled. Once again, the result was stagflation.

FYI

The Macroeconomic Impact of Hurricane Katrina

In August 2005, as this book was going to press, the Gulf Coast of the United States was hit by Hurricane Katrina, devastating New Orleans and the surrounding area. While the human toll was the primary focus of policymakers' attentions, economists in and out of government immediately started analyzing the economic impact. Here are some excerpts from the analysis of the Congressional Budget Office (CBO), prepared just a few days after the disaster:

Katrina could dampen real gross domestic product (GDP) growth in the second half of the year by 1/2 to 1 percentage point and reduce employment through the end of this year by about 400,000. Most economic forecasters had expected 3 percent to 4 percent growth during the second half, and employment growth of 150,000 to 200,000 per month. Economic growth and employment are likely to rebound during the first half of 2006 as rebuilding accelerates. . . .

Katrina's macroeconomic effects will be greater than those of previous major hurricanes such as Andrew and Hugo, which caused a great deal of devastation but which had a small effect on the macroeconomy. Katrina's effects will be greater because of the greater devastation, the long-term flooding of New Orleans (which will preclude immediate rebuilding), and the destruction of energy and port infrastructure. . . .

The gross state product of Louisiana is about 1.2 percent of U.S. GDP, and that for Mississippi is about 0.7 percent. If half of that product were lost for three months (September to November), the level of real GDP would be lowered by about 1 percent from what it otherwise would be. . . . It is unlikely that production would be hurt that much for that long, however. Presumably some people in New Orleans and other parts of the coast will be able to return to work in one or two months, and construction employment will be picking up during the fourth quarter. . . .

Economic activity in the rest of the United States will be adversely affected through higher energy prices, which will temporarily reduce other consumption. . . . [This fall in consumption occurs because] the increase in gasoline prices is basically a temporary redistribution of income from consumers of gasoline to the stockholders of refiners. . . . If sustained, that would reduce annualized GDP growth for the third quarter by 0.4 percent and for the fourth quarter by 0.9 percent. That effect is temporary: as gasoline prices return to pre-Katrina levels, consumption would bounce back, meaning higher GDP growth.

In other words, the hurricane was expected to reduce aggregate supply by making unavailable some of the productive capacity of the Gulf area. In addition, it was expected to reduce aggregate demand because consumers might respond to higher gasoline prices by cutting back their overall level of spending. The predicted decline in GDP growth from these two shifts was significant, but according to CBO, it was not large enough to push the economy into recession.

As you read this book, you should know if this analysis proved correct.

Inflation, which had subsided somewhat after the first OPEC event, again rose above 10 percent per year. But because the Fed was not willing to accommodate such a large rise in inflation, a recession was soon to follow. Unemployment rose from about 6 percent in 1978 and 1979 to about 10 percent a few years later.

The world market for oil can also be a source of favorable shifts in aggregate supply. In 1986, squabbling broke out among members of OPEC. Member countries reneged on their agreements to restrict oil production. In the world market for crude oil, prices fell by about half. This fall in oil prices reduced costs to U.S. firms, which now found it more profitable to supply goods and services at any given price level. As a result, the aggregate-supply curve shifted to the right. The U.S. economy experienced the opposite of stagflation: Output grew rapidly, unemployment fell, and the inflation rate reached its lowest level in many years.

In recent years, the world market for oil has not been as important a source of economic fluctuations. Part of the reason is that OPEC has been less effective as a cartel: Adjusted for inflation, the price of oil has never again reached the record levels set in the early 1980s. In addition, conservation efforts and changes in technology have reduced the economy's dependence on oil. The amount of oil used to produce a unit of real GDP has declined about 40 percent since the OPEC shocks of the 1970s. As a result, the economic impact of any change in oil prices is smaller today than it was in the past.

Nonetheless, it would be premature to conclude that the United States no longer needs to worry about oil prices. Political troubles in the Middle East or greater cooperation among the members of OPEC could always send oil prices higher. And indeed, during the Iraq war, the price of crude oil did rise significantly. If the rise in oil prices were ever large enough, the macroeconomic result would most likely resemble the stagflation of the 1970s. •

© LANGEVIN JACQUES/CORBIS SYGMA

Quick Quiz Suppose that the election of a popular presidential candidate suddenly increases people's confidence in the future. Use the model of aggregate demand and aggregate supply to analyze the effect on the economy.

CHANGES IN MIDDLE EAST OIL PRODUCTION ARE ONE SOURCE OF U.S. ECONOMIC FLUCTUATIONS.

CONCLUSION

This chapter has achieved two goals. First, we have discussed some of the important facts about short-run fluctuations in economic activity. Second, we have introduced a basic model to explain those fluctuations, called the model of aggregate demand and aggregate supply. We continue our study of this model in the next chapter to understand more fully what causes fluctuations in the economy and how policymakers might respond to these fluctuations.

SUMMARY

- All societies experience short-run economic fluctuations around long-run trends. These fluctuations are irregular and largely unpredictable. When recessions do occur, real GDP and other measures of income, spending, and production fall, and unemployment rises.

- Classical economic theory is based on the assumption that nominal variables such as the money supply and the price level do not influence real variables such as output and employment. Most economists believe that this assump-

tion is accurate in the long run but not in the short run. Economists analyze short-run economic fluctuations using the model of aggregate demand and aggregate supply. According to this model, the output of goods and services and the overall level of prices adjust to balance aggregate demand and aggregate supply.

- The aggregate-demand curve slopes downward for three reasons. The first is the wealth effect: A lower price level raises the real value of households' money holdings, which stimulates consumer spending. The second is the interest-rate effect: A lower price level reduces the quantity of money households demand; as households try to convert money into interest-bearing assets, interest rates fall, which stimulates investment spending. The third is the exchange-rate effect: As a lower price level reduces interest rates, the dollar depreciates in the market for foreign-currency exchange, which stimulates net exports.

- Any event or policy that raises consumption, investment, government purchases, or net exports at a given price level increases aggregate demand. Any event or policy that reduces consumption, investment, government purchases, or net exports at a given price level decreases aggregate demand.

- The long-run aggregate-supply curve is vertical. In the long run, the quantity of goods and services supplied depends on the economy's labor, capital, natural resources, and technology but not on the overall level of prices.

- Three theories have been proposed to explain the upward slope of the short-run aggregate-supply curve. According to the sticky-wage theory, an unexpected fall in the price level temporarily raises real wages, which induces firms to reduce employment and production. According to the sticky-price theory, an unexpected fall in the price level leaves some firms with prices that are temporarily too high, which reduces their sales and causes them to cut back production. According to

the misperceptions theory, an unexpected fall in the price level leads suppliers to mistakenly believe that their relative prices have fallen, which induces them to reduce production. All three theories imply that output deviates from its natural rate when the actual price level deviates from the price level that people expected.

- Events that alter the economy's ability to produce output, such as changes in labor, capital, natural resources, or technology, shift the short-run aggregate-supply curve (and may shift the long-run aggregate-supply curve as well). In addition, the position of the short-run aggregate-supply curve depends on the expected price level.

- One possible cause of economic fluctuations is a shift in aggregate demand. When the aggregate-demand curve shifts to the left, for instance, output and prices fall in the short run. Over time, as a change in the expected price level causes wages, prices, and perceptions to adjust, the short-run aggregate-supply curve shifts to the right, and the economy returns to its natural rate of output at a new, lower price level.

- A second possible cause of economic fluctuations is a shift in aggregate supply. When the aggregate-supply curve shifts to the left, the short-run effect is falling output and rising prices—a combination called stagflation. Over time, as wages, prices, and perceptions adjust, the price level falls back to its original level, and output recovers.

KEY CONCEPTS

recession, p. 435
depression, p. 435
model of aggregate demand and aggregate supply, p. 441

aggregate-demand curve, p. 441
aggregate-supply curve, p. 441

natural rate of output, p. 448
stagflation, p. 463

QUESTIONS FOR REVIEW

1. Name two macroeconomic variables that decline when the economy goes into a recession. Name one macroeconomic variable that rises during a recession.

2. Draw a diagram with aggregate demand, short-run aggregate supply, and long-run aggregate supply. Be careful to label the axes correctly.

3. List and explain the three reasons the aggregate-demand curve is downward sloping.

4. Explain why the long-run aggregate-supply curve is vertical.

5. List and explain the three theories for why the short-run aggregate-supply curve is upward sloping.

6. What might shift the aggregate-demand curve to the left? Use the model of aggregate demand and aggregate supply to trace through the short-run and long-run effects of such a shift on output and the price level.

7. What might shift the aggregate-supply curve to the left? Use the model of aggregate demand and aggregate supply to trace through the short-run and long-run effects of such a shift on output and the price level.

PROBLEMS AND APPLICATIONS

1. Suppose that the economy is in a long-run equilibrium.
   a. Draw a diagram to illustrate the state of the economy. Be sure to show aggregate demand, short-run aggregate supply, and long-run aggregate supply.
   b. Now suppose that a stock-market crash causes aggregate demand to fall. Use your diagram to show what happens to output and the price level in the short run. What happens to the unemployment rate?
   c. Use the sticky-wage theory of aggregate supply to explain what will happen to output and the price level in the long run (assuming there is no change in policy). What role does the expected price level play in this adjustment? Be sure to illustrate your analysis in a graph.

2. Explain whether each of the following events will increase, decrease, or have no effect on long-run aggregate supply.
   a. The United States experiences a wave of immigration.
   b. Congress raises the minimum wage to $10 per hour.
   c. Intel invents a new and more powerful computer chip.
   d. A severe hurricane damages factories along the East Coast.

3. Suppose an economy is in long-run equilibrium.
   a. Use the model of aggregate demand and aggregate supply to illustrate the initial equilibrium (call it point A). Be sure to include both short-run and long-run aggregate supply.
   b. The central bank raises the money supply by 5 percent. Use your diagram to show what happens to output and the price level as the economy moves from the initial to the new short-run equilibrium (call it point B).
   c. Now show the new long-run equilibrium (call it point C). What causes the economy to move from point B to point C?
   d. According to the sticky-wage theory of aggregate supply, how do nominal wages at point A compare to nominal wages at point B? How do nominal wages at point A compare to nominal wages at point C?
   e. According to the sticky-wage theory of aggregate supply, how do real wages at point A compare to real wages at point B? How do real wages at point A compare to real wages at point C?
   f. Judging by the impact of the money supply on nominal and real wages, is this analysis consistent with the proposition that money has real effects in the short run but is neutral in the long run?

4. In 1939, with the U.S. economy not yet fully recovered from the Great Depression, President Roosevelt proclaimed that Thanksgiving would fall a week earlier than usual so that the shopping period before Christmas would be longer. Explain what President Roosevelt might have been trying to achieve, using the model of aggregate demand and aggregate supply.

5. Explain why the following statements are false.
   a. "The aggregate-demand curve slopes downward because it is the horizontal sum of the demand curves for individual goods."

b. "The long-run aggregate-supply curve is vertical because economic forces do not affect long-run aggregate supply."

c. "If firms adjusted their prices every day, then the short-run aggregate-supply curve would be horizontal."

d. "Whenever the economy enters a recession, its long-run aggregate-supply curve shifts to the left."

6. For each of the three theories for the upward slope of the short-run aggregate-supply curve, carefully explain the following:

a. How the economy recovers from a recession and returns to its long-run equilibrium without any policy intervention.

b. What determines the speed of that recovery.

7. Suppose the Fed expands the money supply, but because the public expects this Fed action, it simultaneously raises its expectation of the price level. What will happen to output and the price level in the short run? Compare this result to the outcome if the Fed expanded the money supply but the public didn't change its expectation of the price level.

8. Suppose that the economy is currently in a recession. If policymakers take no action, how will the economy change over time? Explain in words and using an aggregate-demand/aggregate-supply diagram.

9. The economy begins in long-run equilibrium. Then one day, the president appoints a new chairman of the Federal Reserve. This new chairman is well-known for his view that inflation is not a major problem for an economy.

a. How would this news affect the price level that people would expect to prevail?

b. How would this change in the expected price level affect the nominal wage that workers and firms agree to in their new labor contracts?

c. How would this change in the nominal wage affect the profitability of producing goods and services at any given price level?

d. How does this change in profitability affect the short-run aggregate-supply curve?

e. If aggregate demand is held constant, how does this shift in the aggregate-supply curve affect the price level and the quantity of output produced?

f. Do you think this Fed chairman was a good appointment?

10. Explain whether each of the following events shifts the short-run aggregate-supply curve, the aggregate-demand curve, both, or neither. For each event that does shift a curve, draw a diagram to illustrate the effect on the economy.

a. Households decide to save a larger share of their income.

b. Florida orange groves suffer a prolonged period of below-freezing temperatures.

c. Increased job opportunities overseas cause many people to leave the country.

11. For each of the following events, explain the short-run and long-run effects on output and the price level, assuming policymakers take no action.

a. The stock market declines sharply, reducing consumers' wealth.

b. The federal government increases spending on national defense.

c. A technological improvement raises productivity.

d. A recession overseas causes foreigners to buy fewer U.S. goods.

12. Suppose that firms become very optimistic about future business conditions and invest heavily in new capital equipment.

a. Draw an aggregate-demand/aggregate-supply diagram to show the short-run effect of this optimism on the economy. Label the new levels of prices and real output. Explain in words why the aggregate quantity of output *supplied* changes.

b. Now use the diagram from part (a) to show the new long-run equilibrium of the economy. (For now, assume there is no change in the long-run aggregate-supply curve.) Explain in words why the aggregate quantity of output *demanded* changes between the short run and the long run.

c. How might the investment boom affect the long-run aggregate-supply curve? Explain.

13. In economy A, all workers agree in advance on the nominal wages that their employers will pay them. In economy B, half of all workers have these nominal wage contracts, while the other half have indexed employment contracts, so their wages rise and fall automatically with the

price level. According to the sticky-wage theory of aggregate supply, which economy has a more steeply sloped short-run aggregate-supply curve? In which economy would a 5 percent increase in the money supply have a larger impact on output? In which economy would it have a larger impact on the price level? Explain.

14. The National Bureau of Economic Research is a nonprofit economic research group that sets the official dates for the beginning and end of recessions in the United States. Go to its website, http://www.nber.org, and find information about business cycle dating. Notice that the

NBER often uses the term *contraction* for a recession and the term *expansion* for the period of growth between recessions.

a. What was the U.S. economy's most recent turning point? Is the U.S economy now in an expansion or a contraction?

b. When was the most recent completed contraction? How long was it? By historical standards, was this contraction short or long?

c. When was the most recent completed expansion? How long was it? By historical standards, was this expansion short or long?

For further information on topics in this chapter, additional problems, examples, applications, online quizzes, and more, please visit our website at http://mankiw.swlearning.com.

The Monetary System

W hen you walk into a restaurant to buy a meal, you get something of value—a full stomach. To pay for this service, you might hand the restaurateur several worn-out pieces of greenish paper decorated with strange symbols, government buildings, and the portraits of famous dead Americans. Or you might hand him a single piece of paper with the name of a bank and your signature. Whether you pay by cash or check, the restaurateur is happy to work hard to satisfy your gastronomical desires in exchange for these pieces of paper which, in and of themselves, are worthless.

To anyone who has lived in a modern economy, this social custom is not at all odd. Even though paper money has no intrinsic value, the restaurateur is confident that, in the future, some third person will accept it in exchange for something that the restaurateur does value. And that third person is confident that some fourth person will accept the money, with the knowledge that yet a fifth person will accept the money . . . and so on. To the restaurateur and to other people in our society, your cash or check represents a claim to goods and services in the future.

The social custom of using money for transactions is extraordinarily useful in a large, complex society. Imagine, for a moment, that there was no item in the economy widely accepted in exchange for goods and services. People would have to rely on *barter*—the exchange of one good or service for another—to obtain the things they need. To get your restaurant meal, for instance, you would have to offer the restaurateur something of immediate value. You could offer to wash some dishes, clean his car, or give him your family's secret recipe for meat loaf. An economy that relies on barter will have trouble allocating its scarce resources efficiently. In such an economy, trade is said to require the *double coincidence of wants*—the unlikely occurrence that two people each have a good or service that the other wants.

The existence of money makes trade easier. The restaurateur does not care whether you can produce a valuable good or service for him. He is happy to accept your money, knowing that other people will do the same for him. Such a convention allows trade to be roundabout. The restaurateur accepts your money and uses it to pay his chef; the chef uses her paycheck to send her child to day care; the day care center uses this tuition to pay a teacher; and the teacher hires you to mow his lawn. As money flows from person to person in the economy, it facilitates production and trade, thereby allowing each person to specialize in what he or she does best and raising everyone's standard of living.

In this chapter, we begin to examine the role of money in the economy. We discuss what money is, the various forms that money takes, how the banking system helps create money, and how the government controls the quantity of money in circulation. Because money is so important in the economy, we devote much effort in the rest of this book to learning how changes in the quantity of money affect various economic variables, including inflation, interest rates, production, and employment. Consistent with our long-run focus in the previous three chapters, in the next chapter we will examine the long-run effects of changes in the quantity of money. The short-run effects of monetary changes are a more complex topic, which we will take up later in the book. This chapter provides the background for all of this further analysis.

THE MEANING OF MONEY

What is money? This might seem like an odd question. When you read that billionaire Bill Gates has a lot of money, you know what that means: He is so rich that he can buy almost anything he wants. In this sense, the term *money* is used to mean *wealth*.

money
the set of assets in an economy that people regularly use to buy goods and services from other people

Economists, however, use the word in a more specific sense: **Money** is the set of assets in the economy that people regularly use to buy goods and services from other people. The cash in your wallet is money because you can use it to buy a meal at a restaurant or a shirt at a clothing store. By contrast, if you happened to own most of Microsoft Corporation, as Bill Gates does, you would be wealthy, but this asset is not considered a form of money. You could not buy a meal or a shirt with this wealth without first obtaining some cash. According to the economist's definition, money includes only those few types of wealth that are regularly accepted by sellers in exchange for goods and services.

The Functions of Money

Money has three functions in the economy: It is a *medium of exchange*, a *unit of account*, and a *store of value*. These three functions together distinguish money from other assets in the economy, such as stocks, bonds, real estate, art, and even baseball cards. Let's examine each of these functions of money in turn.

A **medium of exchange** is an item that buyers give to sellers when they purchase goods and services. When you buy a shirt at a clothing store, the store gives you the shirt, and you give the store your money. This transfer of money from buyer to seller allows the transaction to take place. When you walk into a store, you are confident that the store will accept your money for the items it is selling because money is the commonly accepted medium of exchange.

A **unit of account** is the yardstick people use to post prices and record debts. When you go shopping, you might observe that a shirt costs $20 and a hamburger costs $2. Even though it would be accurate to say that the price of a shirt is 10 hamburgers and the price of a hamburger is $1/10$ of a shirt, prices are never quoted in this way. Similarly, if you take out a loan from a bank, the size of your future loan repayments will be measured in dollars, not in a quantity of goods and services. When we want to measure and record economic value, we use money as the unit of account.

A **store of value** is an item that people can use to transfer purchasing power from the present to the future. When a seller accepts money today in exchange for a good or service, that seller can hold the money and become a buyer of another good or service at another time. Of course, money is not the only store of value in the economy, for a person can also transfer purchasing power from the present to the future by holding other assets. The term *wealth* is used to refer to the total of all stores of value, including both money and nonmonetary assets.

Economists use the term **liquidity** to describe the ease with which an asset can be converted into the economy's medium of exchange. Because money is the economy's medium of exchange, it is the most liquid asset available. Other assets vary widely in their liquidity. Most stocks and bonds can be sold easily with small cost, so they are relatively liquid assets. By contrast, selling a house, a Rembrandt painting, or a 1948 Joe DiMaggio baseball card requires more time and effort, so these assets are less liquid.

When people decide in what form to hold their wealth, they have to balance the liquidity of each possible asset against the asset's usefulness as a store of value. Money is the most liquid asset, but it is far from perfect as a store of value. When prices rise, the value of money falls. In other words, when goods and services become more expensive, each dollar in your wallet can buy less. This link between the price level and the value of money will turn out to be important for understanding how money affects the economy.

The Kinds of Money

When money takes the form of a commodity with intrinsic value, it is called **commodity money.** The term *intrinsic value* means that the item would have value even if it were not used as money. One example of commodity money is gold. Gold has intrinsic value because it is used in industry and in the making of jewelry. Although today we no longer use gold as money, historically gold has been a common form of money because it is relatively easy to carry, measure, and verify for impurities. When an economy uses gold as money (or uses paper money that is convertible into gold on demand), it is said to be operating under a *gold standard.*

Another example of commodity money is cigarettes. In prisoner-of-war camps during World War II, prisoners traded goods and services with one another using cigarettes as the store of value, unit of account, and medium of

---

medium of exchange
an item that buyers give to sellers when they want to purchase goods and services

unit of account
the yardstick people use to post prices and record debts

store of value
an item that people can use to transfer purchasing power from the present to the future

liquidity
the ease with which an asset can be converted into the economy's medium of exchange

commodity money
money that takes the form of a commodity with intrinsic value

In The News

The History of Money

The social custom of money evolved along with human society.

At This Museum, Money Talks

By Cleo Paskal

Let us think about money as an abstract concept. One place that encourages this concept is the Bank of Canada's Currency Museum in Ottawa. . . . The Currency Museum is the only place you can see a 2-ton chunk of rock that was used as money on the island of Yap. This alone should help us understand money as an abstract, because you know they didn't drag the boulder from store to store.

We used to think there were many things that made humans human. That is, we use tools, we laugh, we have language. But so, it seems, do various other animals. Pretty much the only fundamental we have that these other species do not have is money.

Money is one of those convenient theories, like standardized time, that provides a skeleton for modern society. It is so much a part of our daily lives that we take it for granted (presuming we have money). But, if you think about it, why should I give you a perfectly good cheeseburger in exchange for a small piece of paper?

The museum begins with a bit of history. At first, we humans lived in small family units, and we just shared.

MONEY ON THE ISLAND OF YAP: NOT EXACTLY POCKET CHANGE.

exchange. Similarly, as the Soviet Union was breaking up in the late 1980s, cigarettes started replacing the ruble as the preferred currency in Moscow. In both cases, even nonsmokers were happy to accept cigarettes in an exchange, knowing that they could use the cigarettes to buy other goods and services.

Money without intrinsic value is called **fiat money**. A *fiat* is simply an order or decree, and fiat money is established as money by government decree. For example, compare the paper dollars in your wallet (printed by the U.S. government) and the paper dollars from a game of Monopoly (printed by the Parker Brothers game company). Why can you use the first to pay your bill at a restaurant but not the second? The answer is that the U.S. government has decreed its dollars to be valid money. Each paper dollar in your wallet reads: "This note is legal tender for all debts, public and private."

Although the government is central to establishing and regulating a system of fiat money (by prosecuting counterfeiters, for example), other factors are also required for the success of such a monetary system. To a large extent, the acceptance of fiat money depends as much on expectations and social convention as on government decree. The Soviet government in the 1980s never abandoned the

As societies grew bigger, we bartered. Then we used basic goods (tea bricks in Mongolia, salt blocks in the Madura Islands, cocoa beans in South America).

Livestock was often the "gold" standard. In both Latin and Anglo-Saxon, the word for cattle and money is the same. But it became too unwieldy to lug around cows every time you wanted to buy a canoe, so representative objects were introduced.

Eventually, the objects became purely abstract: elephant hair bracelets (central Africa), glass trade beads (Africa), stone disks (Togo). But, usually, the objects were made out of metal. This gave them intrinsic value, durability, portability and perhaps also divisibility.

This separation between value and specific goods made all sorts of societal changes possible, including specialized craftsmen. It was such a good idea that, by the seventh century B.C., the government (in this case Lydia, which is in western Asia Minor) got involved by creating coins.

Lydia mined huge quantities of gold, and you may have heard of one of the kings of Lydia, referred to in the phrase "as rich as Croesus."

By the third century B.C., the Romans had perfected a coin-based monetary system and used it to expand their empire. Their silver denarii dominated Europe for about 500 years.

The coins were also used for propaganda. Usually the emperor had an image of his head put on one side, and a pro-empire message on the other. Julius Caesar minted coins to finance his conquest of Gaul that featured a fine depiction of Caesar's elephant trampling Gaul's dragon. . . .

It was the Chinese that made that quantum financial leap forward, the acceptance of paper money. About a thousand years ago, carrying around all those coins was impractical if you wanted to run a complex empire over a large territory.

But how do you get a no-nonsense farmer to accept an inedible piece of mulberry tree bark in exchange for several sacks of grain?

It helps if you print on the mulberry bark that not only is it redeemable for "hard" currency but also that forgers will be decapitated. The Chinese were particularly clear when it came to money. For instance, mint-operators who diluted their coins with metals of lesser value had their faces tattooed.

It took longer for paper money to catch on in Europe. In the 16th century, an oversized coin was minted using silver from the mine in Joachimsthal, Bohemia. The coin became known as thalers. The Dutch changed that to daalder, and by the time the coins were used in England, they were being called dollars.

Source: *St. Petersburg Times* (Florida), March 14, 2004. Copyright St. Petersburg Times 2004.

ruble as the official currency. Yet the people of Moscow preferred to accept cigarettes (or even American dollars) in exchange for goods and services because they were more confident that these alternative monies would be accepted by others in the future.

Money in the U.S. Economy

As we will see, the quantity of money circulating in the economy, called the *money stock,* has a powerful influence on many economic variables. But before we consider why that is true, we need to ask a preliminary question: What is the quantity of money? In particular, suppose you were given the task of measuring how much money there is in the U.S. economy. What would you include in your measure?

The most obvious asset to include is **currency**—the paper bills and coins in the hands of the public. Currency is clearly the most widely accepted medium of exchange in our economy. There is no doubt that it is part of the money stock.

currency
the paper bills and coins in the hands of the public

demand deposits
balances in bank accounts that depositors can access on demand by writing a check

Yet currency is not the only asset that you can use to buy goods and services. Many stores also accept personal checks. Wealth held in your checking account is almost as convenient for buying things as wealth held in your wallet. To measure the money stock, therefore, you might want to include **demand deposits**—balances in bank accounts that depositors can access on demand simply by writing a check.

Once you start to consider balances in checking accounts as part of the money stock, you are led to consider the large variety of other accounts that people hold at banks and other financial institutions. Bank depositors usually cannot write checks against the balances in their savings accounts, but they can easily transfer funds from savings into checking accounts. In addition, depositors in money market mutual funds can often write checks against their balances. Thus, these other accounts should plausibly be part of the U.S. money stock.

In a complex economy such as ours, it is not easy to draw a line between assets that can be called "money" and assets that cannot. The coins in your pocket are clearly part of the money stock, and the Empire State Building clearly is not, but there are many assets in between these extremes for which the choice is less clear. Because different analysts can reasonably disagree about where to draw the dividing line between monetary and nonmonetary assets, various measures of the money stock are available for the U.S. economy. Figure 1 shows the two most commonly used, designated M1 and M2. M2 includes more assets in its measure of money than does M1.

For our purposes in this book, we need not dwell on the differences between the various measures of money. None of our discussion will hinge on the distinction between M1 and M2. The important point is that the money stock for the U.S.

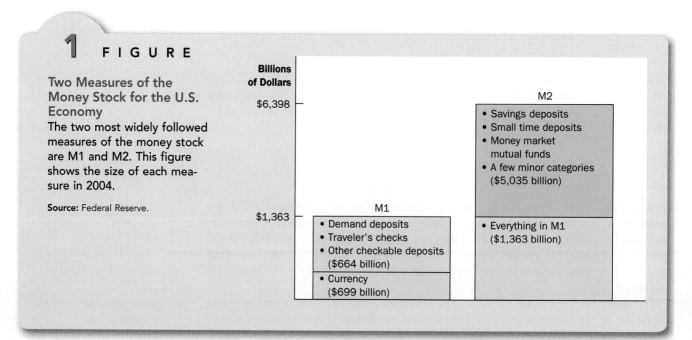

1   FIGURE

Two Measures of the Money Stock for the U.S. Economy
The two most widely followed measures of the money stock are M1 and M2. This figure shows the size of each measure in 2004.

Source: Federal Reserve.

Billions of Dollars

$6,398

$1,363

M2
• Savings deposits
• Small time deposits
• Money market mutual funds
• A few minor categories ($5,035 billion)

M1
• Demand deposits
• Traveler's checks
• Other checkable deposits ($664 billion)
• Currency ($699 billion)

• Everything in M1 ($1,363 billion)

FYI

Credit Cards, Debit Cards, and Money

It might seem natural to include credit cards as part of the economy's stock of money. After all, people use credit cards to make many of their purchases. Aren't credit cards, therefore, a medium of exchange?

Although at first this argument may seem persuasive, credit cards are excluded from all measures of the quantity of money. The reason is that credit cards are not really a method of payment but a method of *deferring* payment. When you buy a meal with a credit card, the bank that issued the card pays the restaurant what it is due. At a later date, you will have to repay the bank (perhaps with interest). When the time comes to pay your credit card bill, you will probably do so by writing a check against your checking account. The balance in this checking account is part of the economy's stock of money.

Notice that credit cards are very different from debit cards, which automatically withdraw funds from a bank account to pay for items bought. Rather than allowing the user to postpone payment for a purchase, a debit card allows the user immediate access to deposits in a bank account. In this sense, a debit card is more similar to a check than to a credit card. The account balances that lie behind debit cards are included in measures of the quantity of money.

Even though credit cards are not considered a form of money, they are nonetheless important for analyzing the monetary system. People who have credit cards can pay many of their bills all at once at the end of the month, rather than sporadically as they make purchases. As a result, people who have credit cards probably hold less money on average than people who do not have credit cards. Thus, the introduction and increased popularity of credit cards may reduce the amount of money that people choose to hold.

economy includes not just currency but also deposits in banks and other financial institutions that can be readily accessed and used to buy goods and services.

CASE STUDY | WHERE IS ALL THE CURRENCY?

One puzzle about the money stock of the U.S. economy concerns the amount of currency. In 2004, there was $699 billion of currency outstanding. To put this number in perspective, we can divide it by 223 million, the number of adults (age 16 and older) in the United States. This calculation implies that the average adult holds about $3,134 of currency. Most people are surprised to learn that our economy has so much currency because they carry far less than this in their wallets.

Who is holding all this currency? No one knows for sure, but there are two plausible explanations.

The first explanation is that much of the currency is held abroad. In foreign countries without a stable monetary system, people often prefer U.S. dollars to domestic assets. It is, in fact, not unusual to see U.S. dollars used overseas as the medium of exchange, unit of account, and store of value.

The second explanation is that much of the currency is held by drug dealers, tax evaders, and other criminals. For most people in the U.S. economy, currency is not a particularly good way to hold wealth. Not only can currency be lost or stolen, but it also does not earn interest, whereas a bank deposit does. Thus, most people hold only small amounts of currency. By contrast, criminals may avoid putting their wealth in banks because a bank deposit gives police a paper trail with which to trace their illegal activities. For criminals, currency may be the best store of value available.   •

Quick Quiz   List and describe the three functions of money.

THE FEDERAL RESERVE SYSTEM

Federal Reserve (Fed)
the central bank of the United States

central bank
an institution designed to oversee the banking system and regulate the quantity of money in the economy

Whenever an economy relies on a system of fiat money, as the U.S. economy does, some agency must be responsible for regulating the system. In the United States, that agency is the **Federal Reserve,** often simply called the **Fed.** If you look at the top of a dollar bill, you will see that it is called a "Federal Reserve Note." The Fed is an example of a **central bank**—an institution designed to oversee the banking system and regulate the quantity of money in the economy. Other major central banks around the world include the Bank of England, the Bank of Japan, and the European Central Bank.

The Fed's Organization

The Federal Reserve was created in 1913 after a series of bank failures in 1907 convinced Congress that the United States needed a central bank to ensure the health of the nation's banking system. Today, the Fed is run by its board of governors, which has seven members appointed by the president and confirmed by the Senate. The governors have 14-year terms. Just as federal judges are given lifetime appointments to insulate them from politics, Fed governors are given long terms to give them independence from short-term political pressures when they formulate monetary policy.

Among the seven members of the board of governors, the most important is the chairman. The chairman directs the Fed staff, presides over board meetings, and testifies regularly about Fed policy in front of congressional committees. The president appoints the chairman to a four-year term. As this book was going to press, the chairman of the Fed was Alan Greenspan, who was originally appointed in 1987 by President Reagan and was later reappointed by Presidents Bush, Clinton, and Bush.

The Federal Reserve System is made up of the Federal Reserve Board in Washington, D.C., and twelve regional Federal Reserve Banks located in major cities around the country. The presidents of the regional banks are chosen by each bank's board of directors, whose members are typically drawn from the region's banking and business community.

The Fed has two related jobs. The first is to regulate banks and ensure the health of the banking system. This task is largely the responsibility of the regional Federal Reserve Banks. In particular, the Fed monitors each bank's financial condition and facilitates bank transactions by clearing checks. It also acts as a bank's bank. That is, the Fed makes loans to banks when banks themselves want to borrow. When financially troubled banks find themselves short of cash, the Fed acts as a *lender of last resort*—a lender to those who cannot borrow anywhere else—to maintain stability in the overall banking system.

The Fed's second and more important job is to control the quantity of money that is made available in the economy, called the **money supply.** Decisions by policymakers concerning the money supply constitute **monetary policy.** At the Federal Reserve, monetary policy is made by the Federal Open Market Committee (FOMC). The FOMC meets about every six weeks in Washington, D.C., to discuss the condition of the economy and consider changes in monetary policy.

money supply
the quantity of money available in the economy

monetary policy
the setting of the money supply by policymakers in the central bank

The Federal Open Market Committee

The Federal Open Market Committee is made up of the seven members of the board of governors and five of the twelve regional bank presidents. All twelve regional presidents attend each FOMC meeting, but only five get to vote. The five with voting rights rotate among the twelve regional presidents over time. The president of the New York Fed always gets a vote, however, because New York is the traditional financial center of the U.S. economy and because all Fed purchases and sales of government bonds are conducted at the New York Fed's trading desk.

Through the decisions of the FOMC, the Fed has the power to increase or decrease the number of dollars in the economy. In simple metaphorical terms, you can imagine the Fed printing dollar bills and dropping them around the country by helicopter. Similarly, you can imagine the Fed using a giant vacuum cleaner to suck dollar bills out of people's wallets. Although in practice the Fed's methods for changing the money supply are more complex and subtle than this, the helicopter-vacuum metaphor is a good first step to understanding the meaning of monetary policy.

Later in this chapter, we discuss how the Fed actually changes the money supply, but it is worth noting here that the Fed's primary tool is the *open-market operation*—the purchase and sale of U.S. government bonds. (Recall that a U.S. government bond is a certificate of indebtedness of the federal government.) If the FOMC decides to increase the money supply, the Fed creates dollars and uses them to buy government bonds from the public in the nation's bond markets. After the purchase, these dollars are in the hands of the public. Thus, an open-market purchase of bonds by the Fed increases the money supply. Conversely, if the FOMC decides to decrease the money supply, the Fed sells government bonds from its portfolio to the public in the nation's bond markets. After the sale, the dollars it receives for the bonds are out of the hands of the public. Thus, an open-market sale of bonds by the Fed decreases the money supply.

Central banks are important institutions because changes in the money supply can profoundly affect the economy. One of the *Ten Principles of Economics* in Chapter 1 is that prices rise when the government prints too much money. Another of the *Ten Principles of Economics* is that society faces a short-run trade-off between inflation and unemployment. The power of the Fed rests on these principles. For reasons we discuss more fully in the coming chapters, the Fed's policy decisions have an important influence on the economy's rate of inflation in the long run and the economy's employment and production in the short run. Indeed, the chairman of the Federal Reserve has been called the second most powerful person in the United States.

Quick Quiz   What are the primary responsibilities of the Federal Reserve? If the Fed wants to increase the supply of money, how does it usually do so?

BANKS AND THE MONEY SUPPLY

So far, we have introduced the concept of "money" and discussed how the Federal Reserve controls the supply of money by buying and selling government bonds in open-market operations. Although this explanation of the money supply is correct, it is not complete. In particular, it omits the central role that banks play in the monetary system.

Recall that the amount of money you hold includes both currency (the bills in your wallet and coins in your pocket) and demand deposits (the balance in your checking account). Because demand deposits are held in banks, the behavior of banks can influence the quantity of demand deposits in the economy and, therefore, the money supply. This section examines how banks affect the money supply and how they complicate the Fed's job of controlling the money supply.

The Simple Case of 100-Percent-Reserve Banking

To see how banks influence the money supply, it is useful to imagine first a world without any banks at all. In this simple world, currency is the only form of money. To be concrete, let's suppose that the total quantity of currency is $100. The supply of money is, therefore, $100.

Now suppose that someone opens a bank, appropriately called First National Bank. First National Bank is only a depository institution—that is, it accepts deposits but does not make loans. The purpose of the bank is to give depositors a safe place to keep their money. Whenever a person deposits some money, the bank keeps the money in its vault until the depositor comes to withdraw it or writes a check against his or her balance. Deposits that banks have received but have not loaned out are called **reserves.** In this imaginary economy, all deposits are held as reserves, so this system is called *100-percent-reserve banking*.

We can express the financial position of First National Bank with a *T-account*, which is a simplified accounting statement that shows changes in a bank's assets and liabilities. Here is the T-account for First National Bank if the economy's entire $100 of money is deposited in the bank:

reserves
deposits that banks have received but have not loaned out

FIRST NATIONAL BANK

Assets		Liabilities	
Reserves	$100.00	Deposits	$100.00

On the left side of the T-account are the bank's assets of $100 (the reserves it holds in its vaults). On the right side are the bank's liabilities of $100 (the amount it owes to its depositors). Notice that the assets and liabilities of First National Bank exactly balance.

Now consider the money supply in this imaginary economy. Before First National Bank opens, the money supply is the $100 of currency that people are holding. After the bank opens and people deposit their currency, the money sup-

"I'VE HEARD A LOT ABOUT MONEY, AND NOW I'D LIKE TO TRY SOME."

ply is the $100 of demand deposits. (There is no longer any currency outstanding, for it is all in the bank vault.) Each deposit in the bank reduces currency and raises demand deposits by exactly the same amount, leaving the money supply unchanged. Thus, *if banks hold all deposits in reserve, banks do not influence the supply of money.*

Money Creation with Fractional-Reserve Banking

Eventually, the bankers at First National Bank may start to reconsider their policy of 100-percent-reserve banking. Leaving all that money idle in their vaults seems unnecessary. Why not lend some of it out and earn a profit by charging interest on the loans? Families buying houses, firms building new factories, and students paying for college would all be happy to pay interest to borrow some of that money for a while. First National Bank has to keep some reserves so that currency is available if depositors want to make withdrawals. But if the flow of new deposits is roughly the same as the flow of withdrawals, First National needs to keep only a fraction of its deposits in reserve. Thus, First National adopts a system called **fractional-reserve banking.**

The fraction of total deposits that a bank holds as reserves is called the **reserve ratio.** This ratio is determined by a combination of government regulation and bank policy. As we discuss more fully later in the chapter, the Fed sets a minimum amount of reserves that banks must hold, called a *reserve requirement.* In addition, banks may hold reserves above the legal minimum, called *excess reserves,* so they can be more confident that they will not run short of cash. For our purpose here, we take the reserve ratio as given to examine what fractional-reserve banking means for the money supply.

Let's suppose that First National has a reserve ratio of 10 percent. This means that it keeps 10 percent of its deposits in reserve and loans out the rest. Now let's look again at the bank's T-account:

fractional-reserve banking
a banking system in which banks hold only a fraction of deposits as reserves

reserve ratio
the fraction of deposits that banks hold as reserves

FIRST NATIONAL BANK

Assets		Liabilities	
Reserves	$10.00	Deposits	$100.00
Loans	90.00		

First National still has $100 in liabilities because making the loans did not alter the bank's obligation to its depositors. But now the bank has two kinds of assets: It has $10 of reserves in its vault, and it has loans of $90. (These loans are liabilities of the people taking out the loans, but they are assets of the bank making the loans because the borrowers will later repay the bank.) In total, First National's assets still equal its liabilities.

Once again consider the supply of money in the economy. Before First National makes any loans, the money supply is the $100 of deposits in the bank. Yet when First National makes these loans, the money supply increases. The depositors still have demand deposits totaling $100, but now the borrowers hold $90 in currency. The money supply (which equals currency plus demand deposits) equals $190. Thus, *when banks hold only a fraction of deposits in reserve, banks create money.*

At first, this creation of money by fractional-reserve banking may seem too good to be true because it appears that the bank has created money out of thin air. To make this creation of money seem less miraculous, note that when First

National Bank loans out some of its reserves and creates money, it does not create any wealth. Loans from First National give the borrowers some currency and thus the ability to buy goods and services. Yet the borrowers are also taking on debts, so the loans do not make them any richer. In other words, as a bank creates the asset of money, it also creates a corresponding liability for its borrowers. At the end of this process of money creation, the economy is more liquid in the sense that there is more of the medium of exchange, but the economy is no wealthier than before.

The Money Multiplier

The creation of money does not stop with First National Bank. Suppose the borrower from First National uses the $90 to buy something from someone who then deposits the currency in Second National Bank. Here is the T-account for Second National Bank:

SECOND NATIONAL BANK

Assets		Liabilities	
Reserves	$9.00	Deposits	$90.00
Loans	81.00		

After the deposit, this bank has liabilities of $90. If Second National also has a reserve ratio of 10 percent, it keeps assets of $9 in reserve and makes $81 in loans. In this way, Second National Bank creates an additional $81 of money. If this $81 is eventually deposited in Third National Bank, which also has a reserve ratio of 10 percent, this bank keeps $8.10 in reserve and makes $72.90 in loans. Here is the T-account for Third National Bank:

THIRD NATIONAL BANK

Assets		Liabilities	
Reserves	$8.10	Deposits	$81.00
Loans	72.90		

The process goes on and on. Each time that money is deposited and a bank loan is made, more money is created.

How much money is eventually created in this economy? Let's add it up:

Original deposit	= $	100.00
First National lending	= $	90.00 [= .9 × $100.00]
Second National lending	= $	81.00 [= .9 × $90.00]
Third National lending	= $	72.90 [= .9 × $81.00]
•		•
•		•
•		•
Total money supply	= $1,000.00	

It turns out that even though this process of money creation can continue forever, it does not create an infinite amount of money. If you laboriously add the infinite sequence of numbers in the foregoing example, you find the $100 of reserves generates $1,000 of money. The amount of money the banking system generates with each dollar of reserves is called the **money multiplier.** In this imaginary economy, where the $100 of reserves generates $1,000 of money, the money multiplier is 10.

What determines the size of the money multiplier? It turns out that the answer is simple: *The money multiplier is the reciprocal of the reserve ratio.* If R is the reserve ratio for all banks in the economy, then each dollar of reserves generates $1/R$ dollars of money. In our example, $R = 1/10$, so the money multiplier is 10.

This reciprocal formula for the money multiplier makes sense. If a bank holds $1,000 in deposits, then a reserve ratio of $1/10$ (10 percent) means that the bank must hold $100 in reserves. The money multiplier just turns this idea around: If the banking system as a whole holds a total of $100 in reserves, it can have only $1,000 in deposits. In other words, if R is the ratio of reserves to deposits at each bank (that is, the reserve ratio), then the ratio of deposits to reserves in the banking system (that is, the money multiplier) must be $1/R$.

This formula shows how the amount of money banks create depends on the reserve ratio. If the reserve ratio were only $1/20$ (5 percent), then the banking system would have 20 times as much in deposits as in reserves, implying a money multiplier of 20. Each dollar of reserves would generate $20 of money. Similarly, if the reserve ratio were $1/5$ (20 percent), deposits would be 5 times reserves, the money multiplier would be 5, and each dollar of reserves would generate $5 of money. *Thus, the higher the reserve ratio, the less of each deposit banks loan out, and the smaller the money multiplier.* In the special case of 100-percent-reserve banking, the reserve ratio is 1, the money multiplier is 1, and banks do not make loans or create money.

> **money multiplier**
> the amount of money the banking system generates with each dollar of reserves

The Fed's Tools of Monetary Control

As we have already discussed, the Federal Reserve is responsible for controlling the supply of money in the economy. Now that we understand how fractional-reserve banking works, we are in a better position to understand how the Fed carries out this job. Because banks create money in a system of fractional-reserve banking, the Fed's control of the money supply is indirect. When the Fed decides to change the money supply, it must consider how its actions will work through the banking system.

The Fed has three tools in its monetary toolbox: open-market operations, reserve requirements, and the discount rate. Let's discuss how the Fed uses each of these tools.

Open-Market Operations
As we noted earlier, the Fed conducts **open-market operations** when it buys or sells government bonds. To increase the money supply, the Fed instructs its bond traders at the New York Fed to buy bonds from the public in the nation's bond markets. The dollars the Fed pays for the bonds increase the number of dollars in the economy. Some of these new dollars are held as currency, and some are deposited in banks. Each new dollar held as currency increases the money supply by exactly $1. Each new dollar deposited in a bank increases the money supply to an even greater extent because it increases reserves and, thereby, the amount of money that the banking system can create.

> **open-market operations**
> the purchase and sale of U.S. government bonds by the Fed

To reduce the money supply, the Fed does just the opposite: It sells government bonds to the public in the nation's bond markets. The public pays for these bonds with its holdings of currency and bank deposits, directly reducing the amount of money in circulation. In addition, as people make withdrawals from banks, banks find themselves with a smaller quantity of reserves. In response, banks reduce the amount of lending, and the process of money creation reverses itself.

Open-market operations are easy to conduct. In fact, the Fed's purchases and sales of government bonds in the nation's bond markets are similar to the transactions that any individual might undertake for his own portfolio. (Of course, when an individual buys or sells a bond, money changes hands, but the amount of money in circulation remains the same.) In addition, the Fed can use open-market operations to change the money supply by a small or large amount on any day without major changes in laws or bank regulations. Therefore, open-market operations are the tool of monetary policy that the Fed uses most often.

reserve requirements
regulations on the minimum amount of reserves that banks must hold against deposits

Reserve Requirements The Fed also influences the money supply with **reserve requirements,** which are regulations on the minimum amount of reserves that banks must hold against deposits. Reserve requirements influence how much money the banking system can create with each dollar of reserves. An increase in reserve requirements means that banks must hold more reserves and, therefore, can loan out less of each dollar that is deposited; as a result, it raises the reserve ratio, lowers the money multiplier, and decreases the money supply. Conversely, a decrease in reserve requirements lowers the reserve ratio, raises the money multiplier, and increases the money supply.

The Fed uses changes in reserve requirements only rarely because frequent changes would disrupt the business of banking. When the Fed increases reserve requirements, for instance, some banks find themselves short of reserves, even though they have seen no change in deposits. As a result, they have to curtail lending until they build their level of reserves to the new required level.

discount rate
the interest rate on the loans that the Fed makes to banks

The Discount Rate The third tool in the Fed's toolbox is the **discount rate,** the interest rate on the loans that the Fed makes to banks. A bank borrows from the Fed when it has too few reserves to meet its reserve requirements. This might occur because the bank made too many loans or because it has experienced unexpectedly high withdrawals. When the Fed makes such a loan to a bank, the banking system has more reserves than it otherwise would, and these additional reserves allow the banking system to create more money.

The Fed can alter the money supply by changing the discount rate. A higher discount rate discourages banks from borrowing reserves from the Fed. Thus, an increase in the discount rate reduces the quantity of reserves in the banking system, which in turn reduces the money supply. Conversely, a lower discount rate encourages banks to borrow from the Fed, increases the quantity of reserves, and increases the money supply.

The Fed uses discount lending not only to control the money supply but also to help financial institutions when they are in trouble. For example, in 1984, rumors circulated that Continental Illinois National Bank had made a large number of bad loans, and these rumors induced many depositors to withdraw their deposits. As part of an effort to save the bank, the Fed acted as a lender of last resort and loaned Continental Illinois more than $5 billion. Similarly, when the stock market crashed on October 19, 1987, many Wall Street brokerage firms found themselves temporarily in need of funds to finance the high volume of stock trading. The next morning, before the stock market opened, Fed Chairman

Alan Greenspan announced the Fed's "readiness to serve as a source of liquidity to support the economic and financial system." Many economists believe that Greenspan's reaction to the stock crash was an important reason it had so few repercussions.

Problems in Controlling the Money Supply

The Fed's three tools—open-market operations, reserve requirements, and the discount rate—have powerful effects on the money supply. Yet the Fed's control of the money supply is not precise. The Fed must wrestle with two problems, each of which arises because much of the money supply is created by our system of fractional-reserve banking.

The first problem is that the Fed does not control the amount of money that households choose to hold as deposits in banks. The more money households deposit, the more reserves banks have, and the more money the banking system can create. And the less money households deposit, the less reserves banks have, and the less money the banking system can create. To see why this is a problem, suppose that one day people begin to lose confidence in the banking system and, therefore, decide to withdraw deposits and hold more currency. When this happens, the banking system loses reserves and creates less money. The money supply falls, even without any Fed action.

The second problem of monetary control is that the Fed does not control the amount that bankers choose to lend. When money is deposited in a bank, it creates more money only when the bank loans it out. Because banks can choose to hold excess reserves instead, the Fed cannot be sure how much money the banking system will create. For instance, suppose that one day bankers become more cautious about economic conditions and decide to make fewer loans and hold greater reserves. In this case, the banking system creates less money than it otherwise would. Because of the bankers' decision, the money supply falls.

Hence, in a system of fractional-reserve banking, the amount of money in the economy depends in part on the behavior of depositors and bankers. Because the Fed cannot control or perfectly predict this behavior, it cannot perfectly control the money supply. Yet if the Fed is vigilant, these problems need not be large. The Fed collects data on deposits and reserves from banks every week, so it is quickly aware of any changes in depositor or banker behavior. It can, therefore, respond to these changes and keep the money supply close to whatever level it chooses.

CASE STUDY | BANK RUNS AND THE MONEY SUPPLY

Although you have probably never witnessed a bank run in real life, you may have seen one depicted in movies such as *Mary Poppins* or *It's a Wonderful Life*. A bank run occurs when depositors suspect that a bank may go bankrupt and, therefore, "run" to the bank to withdraw their deposits.

Bank runs are a problem for banks under fractional-reserve banking. Because a bank holds only a fraction of its deposits in reserve, it cannot satisfy withdrawal requests from all depositors. Even if the bank is in fact *solvent* (meaning that its assets exceed its liabilities), it will not have enough cash on hand to allow all depositors immediate access to all of their money. When a run occurs,

THE KOBAL COLLECTION

A NOT-SO-WONDERFUL BANK RUN

FYI

The Federal Funds Rate

If you read about U.S. monetary policy in the newspaper, you will find much discussion of the *federal funds rate.* This raises several questions:

Q: What is the federal funds rate?

A: The federal funds rate is the short-term interest rate that banks charge one another for loans. If one bank finds itself short of reserves while another bank has excess reserves, the second bank can lend some reserves to the first. The loans are temporary—typically overnight. The price of the loan is the federal funds rate.

Q: Does the federal funds rate matter only for banks?

A: Not at all. While only banks borrow directly in the federal funds market, the economic impact of this market is much broader. Because different parts of the financial system are highly interconnected, interest rates on different kinds of loans are strongly correlated with one another. So when the federal funds rate rises or falls, other interest rates often move in the same direction.

Q: What does the Federal Reserve have to do with the federal funds rate?

A: In recent years, the Federal Reserve has set a target goal for the federal funds rate. When the Federal Open Market Committee meets approximately every six weeks, it decides whether to raise or lower that target.

Q: How can the Fed make the federal funds rate hit the target it sets?

A: Although the actual federal funds rate is set by supply and demand in the market for loans among banks, the Fed can use open-market operations to influence that market. For example, when the Fed buys bonds in open-market operations, it injects reserves into the banking system. With more reserves in the system, fewer banks find themselves in need of borrowing reserves to meet reserve requirements. The fall in demand for borrowing reserves decreases the price of such borrowing, which is the federal funds rate. Conversely, when the Fed sells bonds and withdraws reserves from the banking system, more banks find themselves short of reserves, and they bid up the price of borrowing reserves. Thus, open-market purchases lower the federal funds rate, and open-market sales raise the federal funds rate.

Q: But don't these open-market operations affect the money supply?

A: Yes, absolutely. When the Fed announces a change in the federal funds rate, it is committing itself to the open-market operations necessary to make change happen, and these open-market operations will change the supply of money. Decisions by the FOMC to change the target for the federal funds rate are also decisions to change the money supply. They are two sides of the same coin. Other things equal, a decrease in the target for the federal funds rate means an expansion in the money supply, and an increase in the target for the federal funds rate means a contraction in the money supply.

the bank is forced to close its doors until some bank loans are repaid or until some lender of last resort (such as the Fed) provides it with the currency it needs to satisfy depositors.

Bank runs complicate the control of the money supply. An important example of this problem occurred during the Great Depression in the early 1930s. After a wave of bank runs and bank closings, households and bankers became more cautious. Households withdrew their deposits from banks, preferring to hold their money in the form of currency. This decision reversed the process of money creation, as bankers responded to falling reserves by reducing bank loans. At the same time, bankers increased their reserve ratios so that they would have enough cash on hand to meet their depositors' demands in any future bank runs. The higher reserve ratio reduced the money multiplier, which also reduced the money supply. From 1929 to 1933, the money supply fell by 28 percent, even without the Federal Reserve taking any deliberate contractionary action. Many economists point to this massive fall in the money supply to explain the high unemployment and falling prices that prevailed during this period. (In future chapters, we examine the mechanisms by which changes in the money supply affect unemployment and prices.)

Today, bank runs are not a major problem for the U.S. banking system or the Fed. The federal government now guarantees the safety of deposits at most banks, primarily through the Federal Deposit Insurance Corporation (FDIC). Depositors do not run on their banks because they are confident that, even if their bank goes bankrupt, the FDIC will make good on the deposits. The policy of government deposit insurance has costs: Bankers whose deposits are guaranteed may have too little incentive to avoid bad risks when making loans. But one benefit of deposit insurance is a more stable banking system. As a result, most people see bank runs only in the movies.   •

Quick Quiz   Describe how banks create money.   •   If the Fed wanted to use all three of its policy tools to decrease the money supply, what would it do?

CONCLUSION

Some years ago, a book made the best-seller list with the title *Secrets of the Temple: How the Federal Reserve Runs the Country.* Although no doubt an exaggeration, this title did highlight the important role of the monetary system in our daily lives. Whenever we buy or sell anything, we are relying on the extraordinarily useful social convention called "money." Now that we know what money is and what determines its supply, we can discuss how changes in the quantity of money affect the economy. We begin to address that topic in the next chapter.

SUMMARY

- The term *money* refers to assets that people regularly use to buy goods and services.
- Money serves three functions. As a medium of exchange, it provides the item used to make transactions. As a unit of account, it provides the way in which prices and other economic values are recorded. As a store of value, it provides a way of transferring purchasing power from the present to the future.
- Commodity money, such as gold, is money that has intrinsic value: It would be valued even if it were not used as money. Fiat money, such as paper dollars, is money without intrinsic value: It would be worthless if it were not used as money.

- In the U.S. economy, money takes the form of currency and various types of bank deposits, such as checking accounts.
- The Federal Reserve, the central bank of the United States, is responsible for regulating the U.S. monetary system. The Fed chairman is appointed by the president and confirmed by Congress every 4 years. The chairman is the lead member of the Federal Open Market Committee, which meets about every 6 weeks to consider changes in monetary policy.
- The Fed controls the money supply primarily through open-market operations: The purchase of government bonds increases the money supply,

and the sale of government bonds decreases the money supply. The Fed can also expand the money supply by lowering reserve requirements or decreasing the discount rate, and it can contract the money supply by raising reserve requirements or increasing the discount rate.

- When banks loan out some of their deposits, they increase the quantity of money in the economy. Because of this role of banks in determining the money supply, the Fed's control of the money supply is imperfect.

KEY CONCEPTS

money, p. 338
medium of exchange, p. 339
unit of account, p. 339
store of value, p. 339
liquidity, p. 339
commodity money, p. 339
fiat money, p. 340

currency, p. 341
demand deposits, p. 342
Federal Reserve (Fed), p. 344
central bank, p. 344
money supply, p. 345
monetary policy, p. 345
reserves, p. 346

fractional-reserve banking, p. 347
reserve ratio, p. 347
money multiplier, p. 349
open-market operations, p. 349
reserve requirements, p. 350
discount rate, p. 350

QUESTIONS FOR REVIEW

1. What distinguishes money from other assets in the economy?

2. What is commodity money? What is fiat money? Which kind do we use?

3. What are demand deposits and why should they be included in the stock of money?

4. Who is responsible for setting monetary policy in the United States? How is this group chosen?

5. If the Fed wants to increase the money supply with open-market operations, what does it do?

6. Why don't banks hold 100 percent reserves? How is the amount of reserves banks hold related to the amount of money the banking system creates?

7. What is the discount rate? What happens to the money supply when the Fed raises the discount rate?

8. What are reserve requirements? What happens to the money supply when the Fed raises reserve requirements?

9. Why can't the Fed control the money supply perfectly?

PROBLEMS AND APPLICATIONS

1. Which of the following are money in the U.S. economy? Which are not? Explain your answers by discussing each of the three functions of money.
   a. a U.S. penny
   b. a Mexican peso
   c. a Picasso painting
   d. a plastic credit card

2. What characteristics of an asset make it useful as a medium of exchange? As a store of value?

3. Go to the website of the Federal Reserve Bank of St. Louis (http://www.stlouisfed.org) to find some information about the Fed. Find a map of the Federal Reserve districts. If you live in the United States, find what district you live in. Where is the Federal Reserve Bank for your dis-

trict located? (Extra credit: What state has two Federal Reserve Banks?)

4. Your uncle repays a $100 loan from Tenth National Bank (TNB) by writing a $100 check from his TNB checking account. Use T-accounts to show the effect of this transaction on your uncle and on TNB. Has your uncle's wealth changed? Explain.

5. Beleaguered State Bank (BSB) holds $250 million in deposits and maintains a reserve ratio of 10 percent.
   a. Show a T-account for BSB.
   b. Now suppose that BSB's largest depositor withdraws $10 million in cash from her account. If BSB decides to restore its reserve ratio by reducing the amount of loans outstanding, show its new T-account.
   c. Explain what effect BSB's action will have on other banks.
   d. Why might it be difficult for BSB to take the action described in part (b)? Discuss another way for BSB to return to its original reserve ratio.

6. You take $100 you had kept under your pillow and deposit it in your bank account. If this $100 stays in the banking system as reserves and if banks hold reserves equal to 10 percent of deposits, by how much does the total amount of deposits in the banking system increase? By how much does the money supply increase?

7. The Federal Reserve conducts a $10 million open-market purchase of government bonds. If the required reserve ratio is 10 percent, what is the largest possible increase in the money supply that could result? Explain. What is the smallest possible increase? Explain.

8. Suppose that the T-account for First National Bank is as follows:

Assets		Liabilities	
Reserves	$100,000	Deposits	$500,000
Loans	400,000		

   a. If the Fed requires banks to hold 5 percent of deposits as reserves, how much in excess reserves does First National now hold?

   b. Assume that all other banks hold only the required amount of reserves. If First National decides to reduce its reserves to only the required amount, by how much would the economy's money supply increase?

9. Suppose that the reserve requirement for checking deposits is 10 percent and that banks do not hold any excess reserves.
   a. If the Fed sells $1 million of government bonds, what is the effect on the economy's reserves and money supply?
   b. Now suppose the Fed lowers the reserve requirement to 5 percent, but banks choose to hold another 5 percent of deposits as excess reserves. Why might banks do so? What is the overall change in the money multiplier and the money supply as a result of these actions?

10. Assume that the banking system has total reserves of $100 billion. Assume also that required reserves are 10 percent of checking deposits and that banks hold no excess reserves and households hold no currency.
   a. What is the money multiplier? What is the money supply?
   b. If the Fed now raises required reserves to 20 percent of deposits, what is the change in reserves and the change in the money supply?

11. The economy of Elmendyn contains 2,000 $1 bills.
   a. If people hold all money as currency, what is the quantity of money?
   b. If people hold all money as demand deposits and banks maintain 100 percent reserves, what is the quantity of money?
   c. If people hold equal amounts of currency and demand deposits and banks maintain 100 percent reserves, what is the quantity of money?
   d. If people hold all money as demand deposits and banks maintain a reserve ratio of 10 percent, what is the quantity of money?
   e. If people hold equal amounts of currency and demand deposits and banks maintain a reserve ratio of 10 percent, what is the quantity of money?

 For further information on topics in this chapter, additional problems, examples, applications, online quizzes, and more, please visit our website at http://mankiw.swlearning.com.

Money Growth and Inflation

Although today you need a couple of dollars to buy yourself an ice-cream cone, life was very different 70 years ago. In one Trenton, New Jersey, candy store (run, incidentally, by my grandmother in the 1930s), ice-cream cones came in two sizes. A cone with a small scoop of ice cream cost three cents. Hungry customers could buy a large scoop for a nickel.

You are probably not surprised at the increase in the price of ice cream. In our economy, most prices tend to rise over time. This increase in the overall level of prices is called *inflation*. Earlier in the book, we examined how economists measure the inflation rate as the percentage change in the consumer price index (CPI), the GDP deflator, or some other index of the overall price level. These price indexes show that, over the past 70 years, prices have risen on average about 4 percent per year. Accumulated over so many years, a 4 percent annual inflation rate leads to a 16-fold increase in the price level.

Inflation may seem natural and inevitable to a person who grew up in the United States during the second half of the 20th century, but in fact, it is not inevitable at all. There were long periods in the 19th century during which most prices fell—a phenomenon called *deflation*. The average level of prices in the U.S. economy was 23 percent lower in 1896 than in 1880, and this deflation was a major issue in the presidential election of 1896. Farmers, who had accumulated large debts, were suffering when the fall in crop prices reduced their incomes and thus their ability to pay off their debts. They advocated government policies to reverse the deflation.

Although inflation has been the norm in more recent history, there has been substantial variation in the rate at which prices rise. During the 1990s, prices rose at an average rate of about 2 percent per year. By contrast, in the 1970s, prices rose by 7 percent per year, which meant a doubling of the price level over the decade. The public often views such high rates of inflation as a major economic problem. In fact, when President Jimmy Carter ran for reelection in 1980, challenger Ronald Reagan pointed to high inflation as one of the failures of Carter's economic policy.

International data show an even broader range of inflation experiences. In 2005, while the U.S. inflation rate was about 3 percent, inflation was 12 percent in Russia and 15 percent in Venezuela. And even these higher inflation rates are moderate by historical standards. In Germany after World War I, the price of a newspaper rose from 0.3 marks in January 1921 to 70,000,000 marks less than two years later, with other prices rising by similar amounts. An extraordinarily high rate of inflation such as this is called *hyperinflation*.

What determines whether an economy experiences inflation and, if so, how much? This chapter answers this question by developing the *quantity theory of money.* Chapter 1 summarized this theory as one of the *Ten Principles of Economics:* Prices rise when the government prints too much money. This insight has a long and venerable tradition among economists. The quantity theory was discussed by the famous 18th-century philosopher and economist David Hume and has been advocated more recently by the prominent economist Milton Friedman. This theory of inflation can explain both moderate inflations, such as those we have experienced in the United States, and hyperinflations, such as those experienced in interwar Germany and, more recently, in some Latin American countries.

After developing a theory of inflation, we turn to a related question: Why is inflation a problem? At first glance, the answer to this question may seem obvious: Inflation is a problem because people don't like it. In the 1970s, when the United States experienced a relatively high rate of inflation, opinion polls placed inflation as the most important issue facing the nation. President Ford echoed this sentiment in 1974 when he called inflation "public enemy number one." Ford wore a "WIN" button on his lapel—for Whip Inflation Now.

But what, exactly, are the costs that inflation imposes on a society? The answer may surprise you. Identifying the various costs of inflation is not as straightforward as it first appears. As a result, although all economists decry hyperinflation, some economists argue that the costs of moderate inflation are not nearly as large as the general public believes.

THE CLASSICAL THEORY OF INFLATION

We begin our study of inflation by developing the quantity theory of money. This theory is often called "classical" because it was developed by some of the earliest thinkers about economic issues. Most economists today rely on this theory to explain the long-run determinants of the price level and the inflation rate.

The Level of Prices and the Value of Money

Suppose we observe over some period of time the price of an ice-cream cone rising from a nickel to a dollar. What conclusion should we draw from the fact that people are willing to give up so much more money in exchange for a cone? It is possible that people have come to enjoy ice cream more (perhaps because some chemist has developed a miraculous new flavor). Yet that is probably not the case. It is more likely that people's enjoyment of ice cream has stayed roughly the same and that, over time, the money used to buy ice cream has become less valuable. Indeed, the first insight about inflation is that it is more about the value of money than about the value of goods.

This insight helps point the way toward a theory of inflation. When the consumer price index and other measures of the price level rise, commentators are often tempted to look at the many individual prices that make up these price indexes: "The CPI rose by 3 percent last month, led by a 20 percent rise in the price of coffee and a 30 percent rise in the price of heating oil." Although this approach does contain some interesting information about what's happening in the economy, it also misses a key point: Inflation is an economy-wide phenomenon that concerns, first and foremost, the value of the economy's medium of exchange.

"SO WHAT'S IT GOING TO BE? THE SAME SIZE AS LAST YEAR OR THE SAME PRICE AS LAST YEAR?"

The economy's overall price level can be viewed in two ways. So far, we have viewed the price level as the price of a basket of goods and services. When the price level rises, people have to pay more for the goods and services they buy. Alternatively, we can view the price level as a measure of the value of money. A rise in the price level means a lower value of money because each dollar in your wallet now buys a smaller quantity of goods and services.

It may help to express these ideas mathematically. Suppose P is the price level as measured, for instance, by the consumer price index or the GDP deflator. Then P measures the number of dollars needed to buy a basket of goods and services. Now turn this idea around: The quantity of goods and services that can be bought with \$1 equals $1/P$. In other words, if P is the price of goods and services measured in terms of money, $1/P$ is the value of money measured in terms of goods and services. Thus, when the overall price level rises, the value of money falls.

Money Supply, Money Demand, and Monetary Equilibrium

What determines the value of money? The answer to this question, like many in economics, is supply and demand. Just as the supply and demand for bananas determines the price of bananas, the supply and demand for money determines the value of money. Thus, our next step in developing the quantity theory of money is to consider the determinants of money supply and money demand.

First consider money supply. In the preceding chapter, we discussed how the Federal Reserve, together with the banking system, determines the supply of money. When the Fed sells bonds in open-market operations, it receives dollars in exchange and contracts the money supply. When the Fed buys government bonds, it pays out dollars and expands the money supply. In addition, if any of these dollars are deposited in banks which then hold them as reserves, the money multiplier swings into action, and these open-market operations can have an even greater effect on the money supply. For our purposes in this chapter, we ignore the complications introduced by the banking system and simply take the quantity of money supplied as a policy variable that the Fed controls.

Now consider money demand. Most fundamentally, the demand for money reflects how much wealth people want to hold in liquid form. Many factors influence the quantity of money demanded. The amount of currency that people hold in their wallets, for instance, depends on how much they rely on credit cards and on whether an automatic teller machine is easy to find. And as we will emphasize in Chapter 21, the quantity of money demanded depends on the interest rate that a person could earn by using the money to buy an interest-bearing bond rather than leaving it in a wallet or low-interest checking account.

Although many variables affect the demand for money, one variable stands out in importance: the average level of prices in the economy. People hold money because it is the medium of exchange. Unlike other assets, such as bonds or stocks, people can use money to buy the goods and services on their shopping lists. How much money they choose to hold for this purpose depends on the prices of those goods and services. The higher prices are, the more money the typical transaction requires, and the more money people will choose to hold in their wallets and checking accounts. That is, a higher price level (a lower value of money) increases the quantity of money demanded.

What ensures that the quantity of money the Fed supplies balances the quantity of money people demand? The answer, it turns out, depends on the time horizon being considered. Later in this book, we will examine the short-run answer, and we will see that interest rates play a key role. In the long run, however, the answer is different and much simpler. *In the long run, the overall level of prices adjusts to the level at which the demand for money equals the supply.* If the price level is above the equilibrium level, people will want to hold more money than the Fed has created, so the price level must fall to balance supply and demand. If the price level is below the equilibrium level, people will want to hold less money than the Fed has created, and the price level must rise to balance supply and demand. At the equilibrium price level, the quantity of money that people want to hold exactly balances the quantity of money supplied by the Fed.

Figure 1 illustrates these ideas. The horizontal axis of this graph shows the quantity of money. The left vertical axis shows the value of money $1/P$, and the right vertical axis shows the price level P. Notice that the price-level axis on the right is inverted: A low price level is shown near the top of this axis, and a high price level is shown near the bottom. This inverted axis illustrates that when the value of money is high (as shown near the top of the left axis), the price level is low (as shown near the top of the right axis).

The two curves in this figure are the supply and demand curves for money. The supply curve is vertical because the Fed has fixed the quantity of money available. The demand curve for money is downward sloping, indicating that when the value of money is low (and the price level is high), people demand a larger quantity of it to buy goods and services. At the equilibrium, shown in the figure as point A, the quantity of money demanded balances the quantity of money supplied. This equilibrium of money supply and money demand determines the value of money and the price level.

The Effects of a Monetary Injection

Let's now consider the effects of a change in monetary policy. To do so, imagine that the economy is in equilibrium and then, suddenly, the Fed doubles the supply of money by printing some dollar bills and dropping them around the country from helicopters. (Or less dramatically and more realistically, the Fed could inject money into the economy by buying some government bonds from the public in open-market operations.) What happens after such a monetary injection? How does the new equilibrium compare to the old one?

The horizontal axis shows the quantity of money. The left vertical axis shows the value of money, and the right vertical axis shows the price level. The supply curve for money is vertical because the quantity of money supplied is fixed by the Fed. The demand curve for money is downward sloping because people want to hold a larger quantity of money when each dollar buys less. At the equilibrium, point A, the value of money (on the left axis) and the price level (on the right axis) have adjusted to bring the quantity of money supplied and the quantity of money demanded into balance.

FIGURE 1

How the Supply and Demand for Money Determine the Equilibrium Price Level

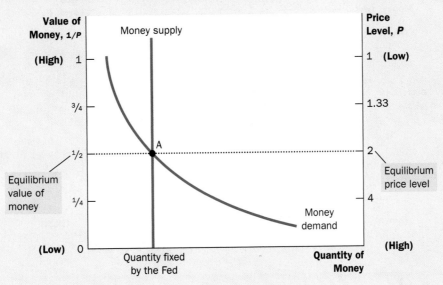

Figure 2 shows what happens. The monetary injection shifts the supply curve to the right from MS_1 to MS_2, and the equilibrium moves from point A to point B. As a result, the value of money (shown on the left axis) decreases from $1/2$ to $1/4$, and the equilibrium price level (shown on the right axis) increases from 2 to 4. In other words, when an increase in the money supply makes dollars more plentiful, the result is an increase in the price level that makes each dollar less valuable.

This explanation of how the price level is determined and why it might change over time is called the **quantity theory of money.** According to the quantity theory, the quantity of money available in the economy determines the value of money, and growth in the quantity of money is the primary cause of inflation. As economist Milton Friedman once put it, "Inflation is always and everywhere a monetary phenomenon."

quantity theory of money
a theory asserting that the quantity of money available determines the price level and that the growth rate in the quantity of money available determines the inflation rate

A Brief Look at the Adjustment Process

So far, we have compared the old equilibrium and the new equilibrium after an injection of money. How does the economy get from the old to the new equilibrium? A complete answer to this question requires an understanding of short-

2 FIGURE

An Increase in the Money Supply

When the Fed increases the supply of money, the money supply curve shifts from MS_1 to MS_2. The value of money (on the left axis) and the price level (on the right axis) adjust to bring supply and demand back into balance. The equilibrium moves from point A to point B. Thus, when an increase in the money supply makes dollars more plentiful, the price level increases, making each dollar less valuable.

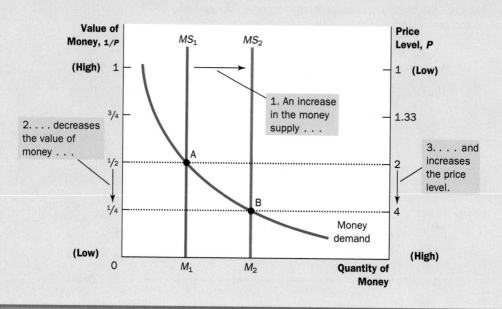

run fluctuations in the economy, which we examine later in this book. Yet even now, it is instructive to consider briefly the adjustment process that occurs after a change in money supply.

The immediate effect of a monetary injection is to create an excess supply of money. Before the injection, the economy was in equilibrium (point A in Figure 2). At the prevailing price level, people had exactly as much money as they wanted. But after the helicopters drop the new money and people pick it up off the streets, people have more dollars in their wallets than they want. At the prevailing price level, the quantity of money supplied now exceeds the quantity demanded.

People try to get rid of this excess supply of money in various ways. They might use it buy goods and services. Or they might use this excess money to make loans to others by buying bonds or by depositing the money in a bank savings account. These loans allow other people to buy goods and services. In either case, the injection of money increases the demand for goods and services.

The economy's ability to supply goods and services, however, has not changed. As we saw in the chapter on production and growth, the economy's output of goods and services is determined by the available labor, physical capital, human capital, natural resources, and technological knowledge. None of these is altered by the injection of money.

Thus, the greater demand for goods and services causes the prices of goods and services to increase. The increase in the price level, in turn, increases the quantity of money demanded because people are using more dollars for every transaction. Eventually, the economy reaches a new equilibrium (point B in Figure 2) at which the quantity of money demanded again equals the quantity of money supplied. In this way, the overall price level for goods and services adjusts to bring money supply and money demand into balance.

The Classical Dichotomy and Monetary Neutrality

We have seen how changes in the money supply lead to changes in the average level of prices of goods and services. How do monetary changes affect other economic variables, such as production, employment, real wages, and real interest rates? This question has long intrigued economists, including David Hume in the 18th century.

Hume and his contemporaries suggested that economic variables should be divided into two groups. The first group consists of **nominal variables**—variables measured in monetary units. The second group consists of **real variables**—variables measured in physical units. For example, the income of corn farmers is a nominal variable because it is measured in dollars, whereas the quantity of corn they produce is a real variable because it is measured in bushels. Nominal GDP is a nominal variable because it measures the dollar value of the economy's output of goods and services; real GDP is a real variable because it measures the total quantity of goods and services produced and is not influenced by the current prices of those goods and services. The separation of real and nominal variables is now called the **classical dichotomy.** (A *dichotomy* is a division into two groups, and *classical* refers to the earlier economic thinkers.)

Application of the classical dichotomy is tricky when we turn to prices. Most prices are quoted in units of money and, therefore, are nominal variables. When we say that the price of corn is $2 a bushel or that the price of wheat is $1 a bushel, both prices are nominal variables. But what about a *relative* price—the price of one thing compared to another? In our example, we could say that the price of a bushel of corn is 2 bushels of wheat. This relative price is not measured in terms of money. When comparing the prices of any two goods, the dollar signs cancel, and the resulting number is measured in physical units. Thus, while dollar prices are nominal variables, relative prices are real variables.

This lesson has many applications. For instance, the real wage (the dollar wage adjusted for inflation) is a real variable because it measures the rate at which people exchange goods and services for a unit of labor. Similarly, the real interest rate (the nominal interest rate adjusted for inflation) is a real variable because it measures the rate at which people exchange goods and services today for goods and services in the future.

Why separate variables into these groups? The classical dichotomy is useful because different forces influence real and nominal variables. According to classical analysis, nominal variables are influenced by developments in the economy's monetary system, whereas money is largely irrelevant for explaining real variables.

This idea was implicit in our discussion of the real economy in the long run. In previous chapters, we examined how real GDP, saving, investment, real interest rates, and unemployment are determined without mentioning the existence

nominal variables
variables measured in monetary units

real variables
variables measured in physical units

classical dichotomy
the theoretical separation of nominal and real variables

of money. In that analysis, the economy's production of goods and services depends on productivity and factor supplies, the real interest rate balances the supply and demand for loanable funds, the real wage balances the supply and demand for labor, and unemployment results when the real wage is for some reason kept above its equilibrium level. These conclusions have nothing to do with the quantity of money supplied.

Changes in the supply of money, according to classical analysis, affect nominal variables but not real variables. When the central bank doubles the money supply, the price level doubles, the dollar wage doubles, and all other dollar values double. Real variables, such as production, employment, real wages, and real interest rates, are unchanged. The irrelevance of monetary changes for real variables is called **monetary neutrality.**

An analogy helps explain monetary neutrality. As the unit of account, money is the yardstick we use to measure economic transactions. When a central bank doubles the money supply, all prices double, and the value of the unit of account falls by half. A similar change would occur if the government were to reduce the length of the yard from 36 to 18 inches: With the new unit of measurement, all *measured* distances (nominal variables) would double, but the *actual* distances (real variables) would remain the same. The dollar, like the yard, is merely a unit of measurement, so a change in its value should not have real effects.

Is monetary neutrality realistic? Not completely. A change in the length of the yard from 36 to 18 inches would not matter in the long run, but in the short run, it would lead to confusion and mistakes. Similarly, most economists today believe that over short periods of time—within the span of a year or two—monetary changes affect real variables. Hume himself also doubted that monetary neutrality would apply in the short run. (We will study short-run nonneutrality later in the book, and this topic will help explain why the Fed changes the money supply over time.)

Yet classical analysis is right about the economy in the long run. Over the course of a decade, monetary changes have significant effects on nominal variables (such as the price level) but only negligible effects on real variables (such as real GDP). When studying long-run changes in the economy, the neutrality of money offers a good description of how the world works.

Velocity and the Quantity Equation

We can obtain another perspective on the quantity theory of money by considering the following question: How many times per year is the typical dollar bill used to pay for a newly produced good or service? The answer to this question is given by a variable called the **velocity of money.** In physics, the term *velocity* refers to the speed at which an object travels. In economics, the velocity of money refers to the speed at which the typical dollar bill travels around the economy from wallet to wallet.

To calculate the velocity of money, we divide the nominal value of output (nominal GDP) by the quantity of money. If P is the price level (the GDP deflator), Y the quantity of output (real GDP), and M the quantity of money, then velocity is

$$V = (P \times Y)/M.$$

To see why this makes sense, imagine a simple economy that produces only pizza. Suppose that the economy produces 100 pizzas in a year, that a pizza sells

monetary neutrality
the proposition that changes in the money supply do not affect real variables

velocity of money
the rate at which money changes hands

for $10, and that the quantity of money in the economy is $50. Then the velocity of money is

$$V = (\$10 \times 100)/\$50$$
$$= 20.$$

In this economy, people spend a total of $1,000 per year on pizza. For this $1,000 of spending to take place with only $50 of money, each dollar bill must change hands on average 20 times per year.

With slight algebraic rearrangement, this equation can be rewritten as

$$M \times V = P \times Y.$$

This equation states that the quantity of money (M) times the velocity of money (V) equals the price of output (P) times the amount of output (Y). It is called the **quantity equation** because it relates the quantity of money (M) to the nominal value of output ($P \times Y$). The quantity equation shows that an increase in the quantity of money in an economy must be reflected in one of the other three variables: The price level must rise, the quantity of output must rise, or the velocity of money must fall.

In many cases, it turns out that the velocity of money is relatively stable. For example, Figure 3 shows nominal GDP, the quantity of money (as measured by M2), and the velocity of money for the U.S. economy since 1960. During the

quantity equation
the equation $M \times V = P \times Y$, which relates the quantity of money, the velocity of money, and the dollar value of the economy's output of goods and services

---

This figure shows the nominal value of output as measured by nominal GDP, the quantity of money as measured by M2, and the velocity of money as measured by their ratio. For comparability, all three series have been scaled to equal 100 in 1960. Notice that nominal GDP and the quantity of money have grown dramatically over this period, while velocity has been relatively stable.

FIGURE 3

Nominal GDP, the Quantity of Money, and the Velocity of Money

Source: U.S. Department of Commerce; Federal Reserve Board.

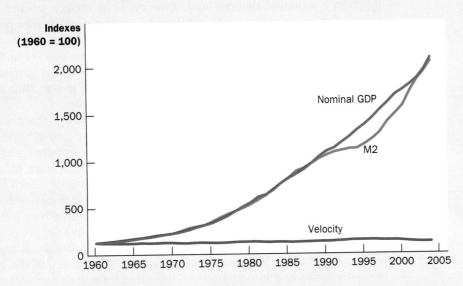

period, the money supply and nominal GDP both increased about 20-fold. By contrast, the velocity of money, although not exactly constant, has not changed dramatically. Thus, for some purposes, the assumption of constant velocity may be a good approximation.

We now have all the elements necessary to explain the equilibrium price level and inflation rate. Here they are:

1. The velocity of money is relatively stable over time.
2. Because velocity is stable, when the central bank changes the quantity of money (M), it causes proportionate changes in the nominal value of output (P × Y).
3. The economy's output of goods and services (Y) is primarily determined by factor supplies (labor, physical capital, human capital, and natural resources) and the available production technology. In particular, because money is neutral, money does not affect output.
4. With output (Y) determined by factor supplies and technology, when the central bank alters the money supply (M) and induces proportional changes in the nominal value of output (P × Y), these changes are reflected in changes in the price level (P).
5. Therefore, when the central bank increases the money supply rapidly, the result is a high rate of inflation.

These five steps are the essence of the quantity theory of money.

CASE STUDY | MONEY AND PRICES DURING FOUR HYPERINFLATIONS

Although earthquakes can wreak havoc on a society, they have the beneficial by-product of providing much useful data for seismologists. These data can shed light on alternative theories and, thereby, help society predict and deal with future threats. Similarly, hyperinflations offer monetary economists a natural experiment they can use to study the effects of money on the economy.

Hyperinflations are interesting in part because the changes in the money supply and price level are so large. Indeed, hyperinflation is generally defined as inflation that exceeds 50 percent *per month*. This means that the price level increases more than 100-fold over the course of a year.

The data on hyperinflation show a clear link between the quantity of money and the price level. Figure 4 graphs data from four classic hyperinflations that occurred during the 1920s in Austria, Hungary, Germany, and Poland. Each graph shows the quantity of money in the economy and an index of the price level. The slope of the money line represents the rate at which the quantity of money was growing, and the slope of the price line represents the inflation rate. The steeper the lines, the higher the rates of money growth or inflation.

Notice that in each graph the quantity of money and the price level are almost parallel. In each instance, growth in the quantity of money is moderate at first and so is inflation. But over time, the quantity of money in the economy starts growing faster and faster. At about the same time, inflation also takes off. Then

This figure shows the quantity of money and the price level during four hyperinflations. (Note that these variables are graphed on *logarithmic* scales. This means that equal vertical distances on the graph represent equal *percentage* changes in the variable.) In each case, the quantity of money and the price level move closely together. The strong association between these two variables is consistent with the quantity theory of money, which states that growth in the money supply is the primary cause of inflation.

FIGURE 4

Money and Prices during Four Hyperinflations

Source: Adapted from Thomas J. Sargent, "The End of Four Big Inflations," in Robert Hall, ed., *Inflation* (Chicago: University of Chicago Press, 1983), pp. 41–93.

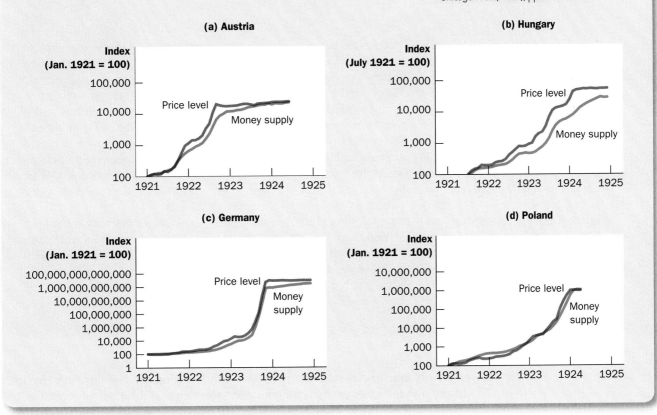

when the quantity of money stabilizes, the price level stabilizes as well. These episodes illustrate well one of the *Ten Principles of Economics:* Prices rise when the government prints too much money. •

The Inflation Tax

If inflation is so easy to explain, why do countries experience hyperinflation? That is, why do the central banks of these countries choose to print so much money that its value is certain to fall rapidly over time?

The answer is that the governments of these countries are using money creation as a way to pay for their spending. When the government wants to build roads, pay salaries to police officers, or give transfer payments to the poor or

In The News

The German Hyperinflation

The German experience between the two world wars remains one of history's most vivid examples of hyperinflation and its horrific consequences.

Loads of Money

"For these ten marks I sold my virtue," were the words a Berliner noticed written on a banknote in 1923. He was buying a box of matches, all the note was worth by then. That was in the early days. By November 5th, a loaf of bread cost 140 billion marks. Workers were paid twice a day, and given half-hour breaks to rush to the shops with their satchels, suitcases or wheelbarrow, to buy something, anything, before their paper money halved in value yet again. By mid-November, when a new currency was issued, prices had added twelve zeros since the first world war began in 1914.

Currencies have collapsed, and inflation turned hyper-, in other places: in Shanghai awaiting Maoist takeover in 1949, in Argentina in 1989, when, in July alone, prices rose 197%. But Germany's was the most spectacular bout of inflation ever to hit an advanced economy; and none has had more awful results. It was not the main reason for Hitler's rise, but it was as the leader of a failed mini-coup during the crisis that most Germans first heard of him. And the anger of those who had lost their all fed Nazism's growth.

The origins of the hyperinflation lay in the war, and the readiness of Germany's legislature to let the authorities suspend the individual's right to convert banknotes into gold. The central bank was also authorized to use government and commercial paper as part of the reserves it was required to hold against newly issued notes. This freed the government to finance the war by running the printing presses, with the usual effect: prices rose. By the end of 1918 the mark had fallen more than 50% against the dollar.

The government continued to run a huge deficit. From 1919 to 1923, taxes never exceeded 35% of expenditure. The gap was covered by heroic money-printing. The public finances, bad enough anyway, were worsened by the Allies'

---

inflation tax
the revenue the government raises by creating money

elderly, it first has to raise the necessary funds. Normally, the government does this by levying taxes, such as income and sales taxes, and by borrowing from the public by selling government bonds. Yet the government can also pay for spending simply by printing the money it needs.

When the government raises revenue by printing money, it is said to levy an **inflation tax.** The inflation tax is not exactly like other taxes, however, because no one receives a bill from the government for this tax. Instead, the inflation tax is subtler. When the government prints money, the price level rises, and the dollars in your wallet are less valuable. Thus, *the inflation tax is like a tax on everyone who holds money.*

The importance of the inflation tax varies from country to country and over time. In the United States in recent years, the inflation tax has been a trivial source of revenue: It has accounted for less than 3 percent of government revenue. During the 1770s, however, the Continental Congress of the fledgling United States relied heavily on the inflation tax to pay for military spending. Because the new government had a limited ability to raise funds through regular taxes or borrowing, printing dollars was the easiest way to pay the American demands for reparations, enough not just to compensate for damage done but to pay the pensions of Allied combatants. Even ignoring the part due to be paid in some bonds of dubious worth, the total was $12.5 billion—a huge amount for the time, about half Britain's GDP. How could it be found? The Allies did not want to see German exports boom, nor were they united in encouraging payment in labor to rebuild Europe. So—roll the presses. Notes in circulation increased from 29.2 billion marks in November 1918 to 497 quintillion (497 plus 18 zeros) five years later.

As early as 1919, when the peace treaty was signed, Keynes had warned that the settlement imposed on Germany would ruin it. By early 1922, even the *Times,* much given to berating Germany for allegedly failing to meet its promises to disarm, was warning that the Allied demands would lead to "further production of paper marks on a massive scale. In the present state of German finances, that would mean a big

step on the way to Moscow." To Auschwitz, in the event, but the analysis of money-printing was sound enough. In vain: the victorious powers shut their ears.

Later that year, the German government defaulted on its reparations payments. In response, in January 1923 French and Belgian troops occupied the Ruhr, Germany's industrial heartland. The direct economic cost was huge; the Ruhr provided 85% of Germany's coal. But, besides that, the government backed a campaign of passive resistance—in effect, a general strike. To pay the 2 million workers involved, it printed more money. This was enough to tip the economy over the edge.

Prices roared up. So did unemployment, modest as 1923 began. As October ended, 19% of metal-workers were officially out of work, and half of those left were on short time. Feeble attempts had been made to stabilize prices. Some German states had issued their own would-be stable currency: Baden's was

secured on the revenue of state forests, Hanover's convertible into a given quantity of rye. The central authorities issued what became known as "gold loan" notes, payable in 1935. Then, on November 15th, came the Rentenmark, worth 1,000 billion paper marks, or just under 24 American cents, like the gold mark of 1914.

Prices quite soon stabilized, but the damage was done. Millions had seen their life savings evaporate, and were ready later to believe that Germany had been stabbed in the back by a conspiracy of Jews, international financiers and local appeasers. Elias Canetti, a German writer, likened the Nazis' treatment of Jews to the great inflation: depreciation to the point where they could be "destroyed with impunity by the million." He strained the analogy. But he was right that a debauched currency was one reason why a whole country could lose its virtue.

soldiers. As the quantity theory predicts, the result was a high rate of inflation: Prices measured in terms of the continental dollar rose more than 100-fold over a few years.

Almost all hyperinflations follow the same pattern as the hyperinflation during the American Revolution. The government has high spending, inadequate tax revenue, and limited ability to borrow. As a result, it turns to the printing press to pay for its spending. The massive increases in the quantity of money lead to massive inflation. The inflation ends when the government institutes fiscal reforms—such as cuts in government spending—that eliminate the need for the inflation tax.

The Fisher Effect

According to the principle of monetary neutrality, an increase in the rate of money growth raises the rate of inflation but does not affect any real variable. An important application of this principle concerns the effect of money on interest rates. Interest rates are important variables for macroeconomists to understand because they link the economy of the present and the economy of the future through their effects on saving and investment.

To understand the relationship between money, inflation, and interest rates, recall the distinction between the nominal interest rate and the real interest rate. The *nominal interest rate* is the interest rate you hear about at your bank. If you have a savings account, for instance, the nominal interest rate tells you how fast the number of dollars in your account will rise over time. The *real interest rate* corrects the nominal interest rate for the effect of inflation to tell you how fast the purchasing power of your savings account will rise over time. The real interest rate is the nominal interest rate minus the inflation rate:

$$\text{Real interest rate} = \text{Nominal interest rate} - \text{Inflation rate}.$$

For example, if the bank posts a nominal interest rate of 7 percent per year and the inflation rate is 3 percent per year, then the real value of the deposits grows by 4 percent per year.

We can rewrite this equation to show that the nominal interest rate is the sum of the real interest rate and the inflation rate:

$$\text{Nominal interest rate} = \text{Real interest rate} + \text{Inflation rate}.$$

This way of looking at the nominal interest rate is useful because different economic forces determine each of the two terms on the right side of this equation. As we discussed earlier in the book, the supply and demand for loanable funds determine the real interest rate. And according to the quantity theory of money, growth in the money supply determines the inflation rate.

Let's now consider how the growth in the money supply affects interest rates. In the long run over which money is neutral, a change in money growth should not affect the real interest rate. The real interest rate is, after all, a real variable. For the real interest rate not to be affected, the nominal interest rate must adjust one-for-one to changes in the inflation rate. Thus, *when the Fed increases the rate of money growth, the long-run result is both a higher inflation rate and a higher nominal interest rate.* This adjustment of the nominal interest rate to the inflation rate is called the **Fisher effect,** after economist Irving Fisher (1867–1947), who first studied it.

Fisher effect
the one-for-one adjustment of the nominal interest rate to the inflation rate

Keep in mind that our analysis of the Fisher effect has maintained a long-run perspective. The Fisher effect does not hold in the short run to the extent that inflation is unanticipated. A nominal interest rate is a payment on a loan, and it is typically set when the loan is first made. If inflation catches the borrower and lender by surprise, the nominal interest rate they set will fail to reflect the rise in prices. To be precise, the Fisher effect states that the nominal interest rate adjusts to expected inflation. Expected inflation moves with actual inflation in the long run but not necessarily in the short run.

The Fisher effect is crucial for understanding changes over time in the nominal interest rate. Figure 5 shows the nominal interest rate and the inflation rate in the U.S. economy since 1960. The close association between these two variables is clear. The nominal interest rate rose from the early 1960s through the 1970s because inflation was also rising during this time. Similarly, the nominal interest rate fell from the early 1980s through the 1990s because the Fed got inflation under control.

This figure uses annual data since 1960 to show the nominal interest rate on 3-month Treasury bills and the inflation rate as measured by the consumer price index. The close association between these two variables is evidence for the Fisher effect: When the inflation rate rises, so does the nominal interest rate.

FIGURE **5**

The Nominal Interest Rate and the Inflation Rate

Source: U.S. Department of Treasury; U.S. Department of Labor.

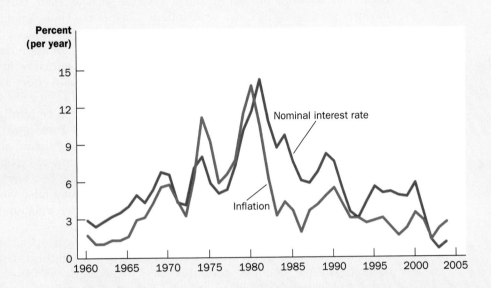

Quick Quiz   The government of a country increases the growth rate of the money supply from 5 percent per year to 50 percent per year. What happens to prices? What happens to nominal interest rates? Why might the government be doing this?

THE COSTS OF INFLATION

In the late 1970s, when the U.S. inflation rate reached about 10 percent per year, inflation dominated debates over economic policy. And even though inflation has been low over the past decade, it remains a closely watched macroeconomic variable. One study found that *inflation* is the economic term mentioned most often in U.S. newspapers (far ahead of second-place finisher *unemployment* and third-place finisher *productivity*).

Inflation is closely watched and widely discussed because it is thought to be a serious economic problem. But is that true? And if so, why?

A Fall in Purchasing Power? The Inflation Fallacy

If you ask the typical person why inflation is bad, he will tell you that the answer is obvious: Inflation robs him of the purchasing power of his hard-earned dollars. When prices rise, each dollar of income buys fewer goods and services. Thus, it might seem that inflation directly lowers living standards.

Yet further thought reveals a fallacy in this answer. When prices rise, buyers of goods and services pay more for what they buy. At the same time, however, sellers of goods and services get more for what they sell. Because most people earn their incomes by selling their services, such as their labor, inflation in incomes goes hand in hand with inflation in prices. Thus, *inflation does not in itself reduce people's real purchasing power.*

People believe the inflation fallacy because they do not appreciate the principle of monetary neutrality. A worker who receives an annual raise of 10 percent tends to view that raise as a reward for her own talent and effort. When an inflation rate of 6 percent reduces the real value of that raise to only 4 percent, the worker might feel that she has been cheated of what is rightfully her due. In fact, as we discussed in the chapter on production and growth, real incomes are determined by real variables, such as physical capital, human capital, natural resources, and the available production technology. Nominal incomes are determined by those factors and the overall price level. If the Fed were to lower the inflation rate from 6 percent to zero, our worker's annual raise would fall from 10 percent to 4 percent. She might feel less robbed by inflation, but her real income would not rise more quickly.

If nominal incomes tend to keep pace with rising prices, why then is inflation a problem? It turns out that there is no single answer to this question. Instead, economists have identified several costs of inflation. Each of these costs shows some way in which persistent growth in the money supply does, in fact, have some effect on real variables.

Shoeleather Costs

As we have discussed, inflation is like a tax on the holders of money. The tax itself is not a cost to society: It is only a transfer of resources from households to the government. Yet most taxes give people an incentive to alter their behavior to avoid paying the tax, and this distortion of incentives causes deadweight losses for society as a whole. Like other taxes, the inflation tax also causes deadweight losses because people waste scarce resources trying to avoid it.

How can a person avoid paying the inflation tax? Because inflation erodes the real value of the money in your wallet, you can avoid the inflation tax by holding less money. One way to do this is to go to the bank more often. For example, rather than withdrawing $200 every four weeks, you might withdraw $50 once a week. By making more frequent trips to the bank, you can keep more of your wealth in your interest-bearing savings account and less in your wallet, where inflation erodes its value.

shoeleather costs
the resources wasted when inflation encourages people to reduce their money holdings

The cost of reducing your money holdings is called the **shoeleather cost** of inflation because making more frequent trips to the bank causes your shoes to wear out more quickly. Of course, this term is not to be taken literally: The actual cost of reducing your money holdings is not the wear and tear on your shoes but the time and convenience you must sacrifice to keep less money on hand than you would if there were no inflation.

The shoeleather costs of inflation may seem trivial. And in fact, they are in the U.S. economy, which has had only moderate inflation in recent years. But this cost is magnified in countries experiencing hyperinflation. Here is a description of one person's experience in Bolivia during its hyperinflation (as reported in the August 13, 1985, issue of *The Wall Street Journal*):

> When Edgar Miranda gets his monthly teacher's pay of 25 million pesos, he hasn't a moment to lose. Every hour, pesos drop in value. So, while his wife rushes to market to lay in a month's supply of rice and noodles, he is off with the rest of the pesos to change them into black-market dollars.
>
> Mr. Miranda is practicing the First Rule of Survival amid the most out-of-control inflation in the world today. Bolivia is a case study of how runaway inflation undermines a society. Price increases are so huge that the figures build up almost beyond comprehension. In one six-month period, for example, prices soared at an annual rate of 38,000 percent. By official count, however, last year's inflation reached 2,000 percent, and this year's is expected to hit 8,000 percent—though other estimates range many times higher. In any event, Bolivia's rate dwarfs Israel's 370 percent and Argentina's 1,100 percent—two other cases of severe inflation.
>
> It is easier to comprehend what happens to the thirty-eight-year-old Mr. Miranda's pay if he doesn't quickly change it into dollars. The day he was paid 25 million pesos, a dollar cost 500,000 pesos. So he received $50. Just days later, with the rate at 900,000 pesos, he would have received $27.

As this story shows, the shoeleather costs of inflation can be substantial. With the high inflation rate, Mr. Miranda does not have the luxury of holding the local money as a store of value. Instead, he is forced to convert his pesos quickly into goods or into U.S. dollars, which offer a more stable store of value. The time and effort that Mr. Miranda expends to reduce his money holdings are a waste of resources. If the monetary authority pursued a low-inflation policy, Mr. Miranda would be happy to hold pesos, and he could put his time and effort to more productive use. In fact, shortly after this article was written, the Bolivian inflation rate was reduced substantially with more restrictive monetary policy.

Menu Costs

Most firms do not change the prices of their products every day. Instead, firms often announce prices and leave them unchanged for weeks, months, or even years. One survey found that the typical U.S. firm changes its prices about once a year.

Firms change prices infrequently because there are costs of changing prices. Costs of price adjustment are called **menu costs,** a term derived from a restaurant's cost of printing a new menu. Menu costs include the cost of deciding on new prices, the cost of printing new price lists and catalogs, the cost of sending these new price lists and catalogs to dealers and customers, the cost of advertising the new prices, and even the cost of dealing with customer annoyance over price changes.

menu costs
the costs of changing prices

Inflation increases the menu costs that firms must bear. In the current U.S. economy, with its low inflation rate, annual price adjustment is an appropriate business strategy for many firms. But when high inflation makes firms' costs rise rapidly, annual price adjustment is impractical. During hyperinflations, for example, firms must change their prices daily or even more often just to keep up with all the other prices in the economy.

Relative-Price Variability and the Misallocation of Resources

Suppose that the Eatabit Eatery prints a new menu with new prices every January and then leaves its prices unchanged for the rest of the year. If there is no inflation, Eatabit's relative prices—the prices of its meals compared to other prices in the economy—would be constant over the course of the year. By contrast, if the inflation rate is 12 percent per year, Eatabit's relative prices will automatically fall by 1 percent each month. The restaurant's relative prices will be high in the early months of the year, just after it has printed a new menu, and low in the later months. And the higher the inflation rate, the greater is this automatic variability. Thus, because prices change only once in a while, inflation causes relative prices to vary more than they otherwise would.

Why does this matter? The reason is that market economies rely on relative prices to allocate scarce resources. Consumers decide what to buy by comparing the quality and prices of various goods and services. Through these decisions, they determine how the scarce factors of production are allocated among industries and firms. When inflation distorts relative prices, consumer decisions are distorted, and markets are less able to allocate resources to their best use.

Inflation-Induced Tax Distortions

Almost all taxes distort incentives, cause people to alter their behavior, and lead to a less efficient allocation of the economy's resources. Many taxes, however, become even more problematic in the presence of inflation. The reason is that lawmakers often fail to take inflation into account when writing the tax laws. Economists who have studied the tax code conclude that inflation tends to raise the tax burden on income earned from savings.

One example of how inflation discourages saving is the tax treatment of *capital gains*—the profits made by selling an asset for more than its purchase price. Suppose that in 1980 you used some of your savings to buy stock in Microsoft Corporation for $10 and that in 2005 you sold the stock for $50. According to the tax law, you have earned a capital gain of $40, which you must include in your income when computing how much income tax you owe. But suppose the overall price level doubled from 1980 to 2005. In this case, the $10 you invested in 1980 is equivalent (in terms of purchasing power) to $20 in 2005. When you sell your stock for $50, you have a real gain (an increase in purchasing power) of only $30. The tax code, however, does not take account of inflation and assesses you a tax on a gain of $40. Thus, inflation exaggerates the size of capital gains and inadvertently increases the tax burden on this type of income.

Another example is the tax treatment of interest income. The income tax treats the *nominal* interest earned on savings as income, even though part of the nominal interest rate merely compensates for inflation. To see the effects of this policy,

T A B L E   1

How Inflation Raises the
Tax Burden on Saving

In the presence of zero inflation, a 25 percent tax on interest income reduces the real interest rate from 4 percent to 3 percent. In the presence of 8 percent inflation, the same tax reduces the real interest rate from 4 percent to 1 percent.

	Economy A (price stability)	Economy B (inflation)
Real interest rate	4%	4%
Inflation rate	0	8
Nominal interest rate (real interest rate + inflation rate)	4	12
Reduced interest due to 25 percent tax (.25 × nominal interest rate)	1	3
After-tax nominal interest rate (.75 × nominal interest rate)	3	9
After-tax real interest rate (after-tax nominal interest rate − inflation rate)	3	1

consider the numerical example in Table 1. The table compares two economies, both of which tax interest income at a rate of 25 percent. In Economy A, inflation is zero, and the nominal and real interest rates are both 4 percent. In this case, the 25 percent tax on interest income reduces the real interest rate from 4 percent to 3 percent. In Economy B, the real interest rate is again 4 percent, but the inflation rate is 8 percent. As a result of the Fisher effect, the nominal interest rate is 12 percent. Because the income tax treats this entire 12 percent interest as income, the government takes 25 percent of it, leaving an after-tax nominal interest rate of only 9 percent and an after-tax real interest rate of only 1 percent. In this case, the 25 percent tax on interest income reduces the real interest rate from 4 percent to 1 percent. Because the after-tax real interest rate provides the incentive to save, saving is much less attractive in the economy with inflation (Economy B) than in the economy with stable prices (Economy A).

The taxes on nominal capital gains and on nominal interest income are two examples of how the tax code interacts with inflation. There are many others. Because of these inflation-induced tax changes, higher inflation tends to discourage people from saving. Recall that the economy's saving provides the resources for investment, which in turn is a key ingredient to long-run economic growth. Thus, when inflation raises the tax burden on saving, it tends to depress the economy's long-run growth rate. There is, however, no consensus among economists about the size of this effect.

One solution to this problem, other than eliminating inflation, is to index the tax system. That is, the tax laws could be rewritten to take account of the effects of inflation. In the case of capital gains, for example, the tax code could adjust the purchase price using a price index and assess the tax only on the real gain. In the case of interest income, the government could tax only real interest income by excluding that portion of the interest income that merely compensates for inflation. To some extent, the tax laws have moved in the direction of indexation. For example, the income levels at which income tax rates change are adjusted automatically each year based on changes in the consumer price index. Yet many other aspects of the tax laws—such as the tax treatment of capital gains and interest income—are not indexed.

In an ideal world, the tax laws would be written so that inflation would not alter anyone's real tax liability. In the world in which we live, however, tax laws are far from perfect. More complete indexation would probably be desirable, but it would further complicate a tax code that many people already consider too complex.

Confusion and Inconvenience

Imagine that we took a poll and asked people the following question: "This year the yard is 36 inches. How long do you think it should be next year?" Assuming we could get people to take us seriously, they would tell us that the yard should stay the same length—36 inches. Anything else would just complicate life needlessly.

What does this finding have to do with inflation? Recall that money, as the economy's unit of account, is what we use to quote prices and record debts. In other words, money is the yardstick with which we measure economic transactions. The job of the Federal Reserve is a bit like the job of the Bureau of Standards—to ensure the reliability of a commonly used unit of measurement. When the Fed increases the money supply and creates inflation, it erodes the real value of the unit of account.

It is difficult to judge the costs of the confusion and inconvenience that arise from inflation. Earlier, we discussed how the tax code incorrectly measures real incomes in the presence of inflation. Similarly, accountants incorrectly measure firms' earnings when prices are rising over time. Because inflation causes dollars at different times to have different real values, computing a firm's profit—the difference between its revenue and costs—is more complicated in an economy with inflation. Therefore, to some extent, inflation makes investors less able to sort out successful from unsuccessful firms, which in turn impedes financial markets in their role of allocating the economy's saving to alternative types of investment.

A Special Cost of Unexpected Inflation: Arbitrary Redistributions of Wealth

So far, the costs of inflation we have discussed occur even if inflation is steady and predictable. Inflation has an additional cost, however, when it comes as a surprise. Unexpected inflation redistributes wealth among the population in a way that has nothing to do with either merit or need. These redistributions occur because many loans in the economy are specified in terms of the unit of account—money.

Consider an example. Suppose that Sam Student takes out a $20,000 loan at a 7 percent interest rate from Bigbank to attend college. In 10 years, the loan will come due. After his debt has compounded for 10 years at 7 percent, Sam will owe Bigbank $40,000. The real value of this debt will depend on inflation over the decade. If Sam is lucky, the economy will have a hyperinflation. In this case, wages and prices will rise so high that Sam will be able to pay the $40,000 debt out of pocket change. By contrast, if the economy goes through a major deflation, then wages and prices will fall, and Sam will find the $40,000 debt a greater burden than he anticipated.

This example shows that unexpected changes in prices redistribute wealth among debtors and creditors. A hyperinflation enriches Sam at the expense of Bigbank because it diminishes the real value of the debt; Sam can repay the loan in less valuable dollars than he anticipated. Deflation enriches Bigbank at Sam's expense because it increases the real value of the debt; in this case, Sam has to repay the loan in more valuable dollars than he anticipated. If inflation were predictable, then Bigbank and Sam could take inflation into account when setting the nominal interest rate. (Recall the Fisher effect.) But if inflation is hard to predict, it imposes risk on Sam and Bigbank that both would prefer to avoid.

This cost of unexpected inflation is important to consider together with another fact: Inflation is especially volatile and uncertain when the average rate of inflation is high. This is seen most simply by examining the experience of different countries. Countries with low average inflation, such as Germany in the late 20th century, tend to have stable inflation. Countries with high average inflation, such as many countries in Latin America, tend to have unstable inflation. There are no known examples of economies with high, stable inflation. This relationship between the level and volatility of inflation points to another cost of inflation. If a country pursues a high-inflation monetary policy, it will have to bear not only the costs of high expected inflation but also the arbitrary redistributions of wealth associated with unexpected inflation.

CASE STUDY | *THE WIZARD OF OZ* AND THE FREE-SILVER DEBATE

As a child, you probably saw the movie *The Wizard of Oz*, based on a children's book written in 1900. The movie and book tell the story of a young girl, Dorothy, who finds herself lost in a strange land far from home. You probably did not know, however, that the story is actually an allegory about U.S. monetary policy in the late 19th century.

From 1880 to 1896, the price level in the U.S. economy fell by 23 percent. Because this event was unanticipated, it led to a major redistribution of wealth. Most farmers in the western part of the country were debtors. Their creditors were the bankers in the east. When the price level fell, it caused the real value of these debts to rise, which enriched the banks at the expense of the farmers.

According to Populist politicians of the time, the solution to the farmers' problem was the free coinage of silver. During this period, the United States was operating with a gold standard. The quantity of gold determined the money supply and, thereby, the price level. The free-silver advocates wanted silver, as well as gold, to be used as money. If adopted, this proposal would have

In The News

How to Protect Your Savings from Inflation

As we have seen, unexpected changes in the price level redistribute wealth among debtors and creditors. This would no longer be true if debt contracts were written in real, rather than nominal, terms. In 1997, the U.S. Treasury started issuing bonds with a return indexed to the price level. In the following article, written a few months before the policy was implemented, two prominent economists discuss the merits of this policy.

Inflation Fighters for the Long Term

By John Y. Campbell and Robert J. Shiller

Treasury Secretary Robert Rubin announced on Thursday that the government plans to issue inflation-indexed bonds—that is, bonds whose interest and principal payments are adjusted upward for inflation, guaranteeing their real purchasing power in the future.

This is a historic moment. Economists have been advocating such bonds for many long and frustrating years.

Index bonds were first called for in 1822 by the economist Joseph Lowe. In the 1870s, they were championed by the British economist William Stanley Jevons. In the early part of this century, the legendary Irving Fisher made a career of advocating them.

In recent decades, economists of every political stripe—from Milton Friedman to James Tobin, Alan Blinder to Alan Greenspan—have supported them. Yet, because there was little public clamor for such an investment, the government never issued indexed bonds.

Let's hope this lack of interest does not continue now that they will become available. The success of the indexed bonds depends on whether the public understands them—and buys them. Until now, inflation has made government bonds a risky investment. In 1966, when the inflation rate was only 3 percent, if someone had bought a 30-year government bond yielding 5 percent, he would have expected that by now his investment would be worth 180 percent of its original value. However, after years of higher-than-expected inflation, the in-

AN EARLY DEBATE OVER MONETARY POLICY

© MGM/THE KOBAL COLLECTION

increased the money supply, pushed up the price level, and reduced the real burden of the farmers' debts.

The debate over silver was heated, and it was central to the politics of the 1890s. A common election slogan of the Populists was "We Are Mortgaged. All but Our Votes." One prominent advocate of free silver was William Jennings Bryan, the Democratic nominee for president in 1896. He is remembered in part for a speech at the Democratic party's nominating convention in which he said, "You shall not press down upon the brow of labor this crown of thorns. You shall not crucify mankind upon a cross of gold." Rarely since then have politicians waxed so poetic about alternative approaches to monetary policy. Nonetheless, Bryan lost the election to Republican William McKinley, and the United States remained on the gold standard.

L. Frank Baum, author of the book *The Wonderful Wizard of Oz*, was a midwestern journalist. When he sat down to write a story for children, he made the characters represent protagonists in the major political battle of his time.

vestment is worth only 85 percent of its original value.

Because inflation has been modest in recent years, many people today are not worried about how it will affect their savings. This complacency is dangerous: Even a low rate of inflation can seriously erode savings over long periods of time.

Imagine that you retire today with a pension invested in Treasury bonds that pay a fixed $10,000 each year, regardless of inflation. If there is no inflation, in 20 years the pension will have the same purchasing power that it does today. But if there is an inflation rate of only 3 percent per year, in 20 years your pension will be worth only $5,540 in today's dollars. Five percent inflation over 20 years will cut your purchasing power to $3,770, and 10 percent will reduce it to a pitiful $1,390. Which of these scenarios is likely? No one knows. Inflation ultimately depends on the people who are elected and appointed as guardians of our money supply.

At a time when Americans are living longer and planning for several decades of retirement, the insidious effects of inflation should be of serious concern. For this reason alone, the creation of inflation-indexed bonds, with their guarantee of a safe return over long periods of time, is a welcome development.

No other investment offers this kind of safety. Conventional government bonds make payments that are fixed in dollar terms; but investors should be concerned about purchasing power, not about the number of dollars they receive. Money market funds make dollar payments that increase with inflation to some degree, since short-term interest rates tend to rise with inflation. But many other factors also influence interest rates, so the real income from a money market fund is not secure.

The stock market offers a high rate of return on average, but it can fall as well as rise. Investors should remember the bear market of the 1970s as well as the bull market of the 1980s and 1990s.

Inflation-indexed government bonds have been issued in Britain for 15 years, in Canada for 5 years, and in many other countries, including Australia, New Zealand, and Sweden. In Britain, which has the world's largest indexed-bond market, the bonds have offered a yield 3 to 4 percent higher than the rate of inflation. In the United States, a safe long-term return of this sort should make indexed bonds an important part of retirement savings.

We expect that financial institutions will take advantage of the new inflation-indexed bonds and offer innovative new products. Indexed-bond funds will probably appear first, but indexed annuities and even indexed mortgages—monthly payments would be adjusted for inflation—should also become available. [*Author's note:* Since this article was written, some of these indexed products have been introduced, but their use is not yet widespread.]

Although the Clinton administration may not get much credit for it today, the decision to issue inflation-indexed bonds is an accomplishment that historians decades hence will single out for special recognition.

Although modern commentators on the story differ somewhat in the interpretation they assign to each character, there is no doubt that the story highlights the debate over monetary policy. Here is how economic historian Hugh Rockoff, writing in the *Journal of Political Economy* in 1990, interprets the story:

DOROTHY:	Traditional American values
TOTO:	Prohibitionist party, also called the Teetotalers
SCARECROW:	Farmers
TIN WOODSMAN:	Industrial workers
COWARDLY LION:	William Jennings Bryan
MUNCHKINS:	Citizens of the East
WICKED WITCH OF THE EAST:	Grover Cleveland
WICKED WITCH OF THE WEST:	William McKinley

WIZARD: Marcus Alonzo Hanna, chairman of the Republican party

Oz: Abbreviation for ounce of gold

YELLOW BRICK ROAD: Gold standard

In the end of Baum's story, Dorothy does find her way home, but it is not by just following the yellow brick road. After a long and perilous journey, she learns that the wizard is incapable of helping her or her friends. Instead, Dorothy finally discovers the magical power of her *silver* slippers. (When the book was made into a movie in 1939, Dorothy's slippers were changed from silver to ruby. The Hollywood filmmakers were more interested in showing off the new technology of Technicolor than telling a story about 19th-century monetary policy.)

Although the Populists lost the debate over the free coinage of silver, they did eventually get the monetary expansion and inflation that they wanted. In 1898, prospectors discovered gold near the Klondike River in the Canadian Yukon. Increased supplies of gold also arrived from the mines of South Africa. As a result, the money supply and the price level started to rise in the United States and other countries operating on the gold standard. Within 15 years, prices in the United States were back to the levels that had prevailed in the 1880s, and farmers were better able to handle their debts.   •

Quick Quiz   List and describe six costs of inflation.

CONCLUSION

This chapter discussed the causes and costs of inflation. The primary cause of inflation is simply growth in the quantity of money. When the central bank creates money in large quantities, the value of money falls quickly. To maintain stable prices, the central bank must maintain strict control over the money supply.

The costs of inflation are subtler. They include shoeleather costs, menu costs, increased variability of relative prices, unintended changes in tax liabilities, confusion and inconvenience, and arbitrary redistributions of wealth. Are these costs, in total, large or small? All economists agree that they become huge during hyperinflation. But their size for moderate inflation—when prices rise by less than 10 percent per year—is more open to debate.

Although this chapter presented many of the most important lessons about inflation, the discussion is incomplete. When the central bank reduces the rate of money growth, prices rise less rapidly, as the quantity theory suggests. Yet as the economy makes the transition to this lower inflation rate, the change in monetary policy will have disruptive effects on production and employment. That is, even though monetary policy is neutral in the long run, it has profound effects on real variables in the short run. Later in this book we will examine the reasons for short-run monetary nonneutrality to enhance our understanding of the causes and costs of inflation.

SUMMARY

- The overall level of prices in an economy adjusts to bring money supply and money demand into balance. When the central bank increases the supply of money, it causes the price level to rise. Persistent growth in the quantity of money supplied leads to continuing inflation.

- The principle of monetary neutrality asserts that changes in the quantity of money influence nominal variables but not real variables. Most economists believe that monetary neutrality approximately describes the behavior of the economy in the long run.

- A government can pay for some of its spending simply by printing money. When countries rely heavily on this "inflation tax," the result is hyperinflation.

- One application of the principle of monetary neutrality is the Fisher effect. According to the Fisher effect, when the inflation rate rises, the nominal interest rate rises by the same amount so that the real interest rate remains the same.

- Many people think that inflation makes them poorer because it raises the cost of what they buy. This view is a fallacy, however, because inflation also raises nominal incomes.

- Economists have identified six costs of inflation: shoeleather costs associated with reduced money holdings, menu costs associated with more frequent adjustment of prices, increased variability of relative prices, unintended changes in tax liabilities due to nonindexation of the tax code, confusion and inconvenience resulting from a changing unit of account, and arbitrary redistributions of wealth between debtors and creditors. Many of these costs are large during hyperinflation, but the size of these costs for moderate inflation is less clear.

KEY CONCEPTS

quantity theory of money, p. 361
nominal variables, p. 363
real variables, p. 363
classical dichotomy, p. 363

monetary neutrality, p. 364
velocity of money, p. 364
quantity equation, p. 365
inflation tax, p. 368

Fisher effect, p. 370
shoeleather costs, p. 372
menu costs, p. 373

QUESTIONS FOR REVIEW

1. Explain how an increase in the price level affects the real value of money.

2. According to the quantity theory of money, what is the effect of an increase in the quantity of money?

3. Explain the difference between nominal and real variables and give two examples of each. According to the principle of monetary neutrality, which variables are affected by changes in the quantity of money?

4. In what sense is inflation like a tax? How does thinking about inflation as a tax help explain hyperinflation?

5. According to the Fisher effect, how does an increase in the inflation rate affect the real interest rate and the nominal interest rate?

6. What are the costs of inflation? Which of these costs do you think are most important for the U.S. economy?

7. If inflation is less than expected, who benefits— debtors or creditors? Explain.

PROBLEMS AND APPLICATIONS

1. Suppose that this year's money supply is $500 billion, nominal GDP is $10 trillion, and real GDP is $5 trillion.
   a. What is the price level? What is the velocity of money?
   b. Suppose that velocity is constant and the economy's output of goods and services rises by 5 percent each year. What will happen to nominal GDP and the price level next year if the Fed keeps the money supply constant?
   c. What money supply should the Fed set next year if it wants to keep the price level stable?
   d. What money supply should the Fed set next year if it wants inflation of 10 percent?

2. Suppose that changes in bank regulations expand the availability of credit cards so that people need to hold less cash.
   a. How does this event affect the demand for money?
   b. If the Fed does not respond to this event, what will happen to the price level?
   c. If the Fed wants to keep the price level stable, what should it do?

3. It is often suggested that the Federal Reserve try to achieve zero inflation. If we assume that velocity is constant, does this zero-inflation goal require that the rate of money growth equal zero? If yes, explain why. If no, explain what the rate of money growth should equal.

4. Suppose that a country's inflation rate increases sharply. What happens to the inflation tax on the holders of money? Why is wealth that is held in savings accounts *not* subject to a change in the inflation tax? Can you think of any way holders of savings accounts are hurt by the increase in the inflation rate?

5. Hyperinflations are extremely rare in countries whose central banks are independent of the rest of the government. Why might this be so?

6. Let's consider the effects of inflation in an economy composed only of two people: Bob, a bean farmer, and Rita, a rice farmer. Bob and Rita both always consume equal amounts of rice and beans. In 2005, the price of beans was $1, and the price of rice was $3.
   a. Suppose that in 2006 the price of beans was $2 and the price of rice was $6. What was inflation? Was Bob better off, worse off, or unaffected by the changes in prices? What about Rita?
   b. Now suppose that in 2006 the price of beans was $2 and the price of rice was $4. What was inflation? Was Bob better off, worse off, or unaffected by the changes in prices? What about Rita?
   c. Finally, suppose that in 2006 the price of beans was $2 and the price of rice was $1.50. What was inflation? Was Bob better off, worse off, or unaffected by the changes in prices? What about Rita?
   d. What matters more to Bob and Rita—the overall inflation rate or the relative price of rice and beans?

7. If the tax rate is 40 percent, compute the before-tax real interest rate and the after-tax real interest rate in each of the following cases.

a. The nominal interest rate is 10 percent and the inflation rate is 5 percent.

b. The nominal interest rate is 6 percent and the inflation rate is 2 percent.

c. The nominal interest rate is 4 percent and the inflation rate is 1 percent.

8. What are your shoeleather costs of going to the bank? How might you measure these costs in dollars? How do you think the shoeleather costs of your college president differ from your own?

9. Recall that money serves three functions in the economy. What are those functions? How does inflation affect the ability of money to serve each of these functions?

10. Suppose that people expect inflation to equal 3 percent, but in fact, prices rise by 5 percent. Describe how this unexpectedly high inflation rate would help or hurt the following:

a. the government

b. a homeowner with a fixed-rate mortgage

c. a union worker in the second year of a labor contract

d. a college that has invested some of its endowment in government bonds

11. Explain one harm associated with unexpected inflation that is *not* associated with expected inflation. Then explain one harm associated with both expected and unexpected inflation.

12. Explain whether the following statements are true, false, or uncertain.

a. "Inflation hurts borrowers and helps lenders, because borrowers must pay a higher rate of interest."

b. "If prices change in a way that leaves the overall price level unchanged, then no one is made better or worse off."

c. "Inflation does not reduce the purchasing power of most workers."

 For further information on topics in this chapter, additional problems, examples, applications, online quizzes, and more, please visit our website at http://mankiw.swlearning.com.

The Influence of Monetary and Fiscal Policy on Aggregate Demand

Imagine that you are a member of the Federal Open Market Committee, the group at the Federal Reserve that sets monetary policy. You observe that the president and Congress have agreed to cut government spending. How should the Fed respond to this change in fiscal policy? Should it expand the money supply, contract the money supply, or leave the money supply the same?

To answer this question, you need to consider the impact of monetary and fiscal policy on the economy. In the preceding chapter, we used the model of aggregate demand and aggregate supply to explain short-run economic fluctuations. We saw that shifts in the aggregate-demand curve or the aggregate-supply curve cause fluctuations in the economy's overall output of goods and services and its overall level of prices. As we noted in the previous chapter, monetary and fiscal policy can each influence aggregate demand. Thus, a change in one of these policies can lead to short-run fluctuations in output and prices. Policymakers will want to anticipate this effect and, perhaps, adjust the other policy in response.

In this chapter, we examine in more detail how the government's policy tools influence the position of the aggregate-demand curve. These tools include monetary policy (the supply of money set by the central bank) and fiscal policy (the levels of government spending and taxation set by the president and Congress).

We have previously discussed the long-run effects of these policies. In Chapters 12 and 13, we saw how fiscal policy affects saving, investment, and long-run economic growth. In Chapters 16 and 17, we saw how the Fed controls the money supply and how the money supply affects the price level in the long run. We now see how these policy tools can shift the aggregate-demand curve and, in doing so, affect macroeconomic variables in the short run.

As we have already learned, many factors influence aggregate demand besides monetary and fiscal policy. In particular, desired spending by households and firms determines the overall demand for goods and services. When desired spending changes, aggregate demand shifts. If policymakers do not respond, such shifts in aggregate demand cause short-run fluctuations in output and employment. As a result, monetary and fiscal policymakers sometimes use the policy levers at their disposal to try to offset these shifts in aggregate demand and thereby stabilize the economy. Here we discuss the theory behind these policy actions and some of the difficulties that arise in using this theory in practice.

HOW MONETARY POLICY INFLUENCES AGGREGATE DEMAND

The aggregate-demand curve shows the total quantity of goods and services demanded in the economy for any price level. The preceding chapter discussed three reasons the aggregate-demand curve slopes downward:

- *The wealth effect:* A lower price level raises the real value of households' money holdings, which are part of their wealth. Higher real wealth stimulates consumer spending and thus increases the quantity of goods and services demanded.
- *The interest-rate effect:* A lower price level reduces the amount of money people want to hold. As people try to lend out their excess money holdings, the interest rate falls. The lower interest rate stimulates investment spending and thus increases the quantity of goods and services demanded.
- *The exchange-rate effect:* When a lower price level reduces the interest rate, investors move some of their funds overseas in search of higher returns. This movement of funds causes the real value of the domestic currency to fall in the market for foreign-currency exchange. Domestic goods become less expensive relative to foreign goods. This change in the real exchange rate stimulates spending on net exports and thus increases the quantity of goods and services demanded.

These three effects occur simultaneously to increase the quantity of goods and services demanded when the price level falls and to decrease it when the price level rises.

Although all three effects work together to explain the downward slope of the aggregate-demand curve, they are not of equal importance. Because money holdings are a small part of household wealth, the wealth effect is the least important of the three. In addition, because exports and imports represent only a small fraction of U.S. GDP, the exchange-rate effect is not large for the U.S. economy. (This effect is more important for smaller countries, which typically export and import a higher fraction of their GDP.) *For the U.S. economy, the most important reason for the downward slope of the aggregate-demand curve is the interest-rate effect.*

To better understand aggregate demand, we now examine the short-run determination of interest rates in more detail. Here we develop the **theory of liquidity preference.** This theory of interest-rate determination will help explain the downward slope of the aggregate-demand curve, as well as how monetary and fiscal policy can shift this curve. By shedding new light on aggregate demand, the theory of liquidity preference expands our understanding of what causes short-run economic fluctuations and what policymakers can potentially do about them.

theory of liquidity preference
Keynes's theory that the interest rate adjusts to bring money supply and money demand into balance

The Theory of Liquidity Preference

In his classic book *The General Theory of Employment, Interest, and Money,* John Maynard Keynes proposed the theory of liquidity preference to explain what factors determine an economy's interest rate. The theory is, in essence, just an application of supply and demand. According to Keynes, the interest rate adjusts to balance the supply and demand for money.

You may recall that economists distinguish between two interest rates: The *nominal interest rate* is the interest rate as usually reported, and the *real interest rate* is the interest rate corrected for the effects of inflation. When there is no inflation, the two rates are the same. But when borrowers and lenders expect prices to rise over the course of the loan, they agree to a nominal interest rate that exceeds the real interest rate by the expected rate of inflation. The higher nominal interest rate compensates for the fact that they expect the loan to be repaid in less valuable dollars.

Which interest rate are we now trying to explain with the theory of liquidity preference? The answer is both. In the analysis that follows, we hold constant the expected rate of inflation. This assumption is reasonable for studying the economy in the short run, as we are now doing. Thus, when the nominal interest rate rises or falls, the real interest rate that people expect to earn rises or falls as well. For the rest of this chapter, when we refer to changes in the interest rate, you should envision the real and nominal interest rates moving in the same direction.

Let's now develop the theory of liquidity preference by considering the supply and demand for money and how each depends on the interest rate.

Money Supply   The first piece of the theory of liquidity preference is the supply of money. As we first discussed in Chapter 16, the money supply in the U.S. economy is controlled by the Federal Reserve. The Fed alters the money supply primarily by changing the quantity of reserves in the banking system through the purchase and sale of government bonds in open-market operations. When the Fed buys government bonds, the dollars it pays for the bonds are typically deposited in banks, and these dollars are added to bank reserves. When the Fed sells government bonds, the dollars it receives for the bonds are withdrawn from the banking system, and bank reserves fall. These changes in bank reserves, in turn, lead to changes in banks' ability to make loans and create money. In addition to these open-market operations, the Fed can alter the money supply by changing reserve requirements (the amount of reserves banks must hold against deposits) or the discount rate (the interest rate at which banks can borrow reserves from the Fed).

These details of monetary control are important for the implementation of Fed policy, but they are not crucial in this chapter. Our goal here is to examine how changes in the money supply affect the aggregate demand for goods and services. For this purpose, we can ignore the details of how Fed policy is implemented and simply assume that the Fed controls the money supply directly. In other words, the quantity of money supplied in the economy is fixed at whatever level the Fed decides to set it.

Because the quantity of money supplied is fixed by Fed policy, it does not depend on other economic variables. In particular, it does not depend on the interest rate. Once the Fed has made its policy decision, the quantity of money supplied is the same, regardless of the prevailing interest rate. We represent a fixed money supply with a vertical supply curve, as in Figure 1.

Money Demand   The second piece of the theory of liquidity preference is the demand for money. As a starting point for understanding money demand, recall that any asset's *liquidity* refers to the ease with which that asset is converted into the economy's medium of exchange. Money is the economy's medium of exchange, so it is by definition the most liquid asset available. The liquidity of money explains the demand for it: People choose to hold money instead of other assets that offer higher rates of return because money can be used to buy goods and services.

1 **FIGURE**

Equilibrium in the Money Market

According to the theory of liquidity preference, the interest rate adjusts to bring the quantity of money supplied and the quantity of money demanded into balance. If the interest rate is above the equilibrium level (such as at r_1), the quantity of money people want to hold (M_1^d) is less than the quantity the Fed has created, and this surplus of money puts downward pressure on the interest rate. Conversely, if the interest rate is below the equilibrium level (such as at r_2), the quantity of money people want to hold (M_2^d) is greater than the quantity the Fed has created, and this shortage of money puts upward pressure on the interest rate. Thus, the forces of supply and demand in the market for money push the interest rate toward the equilibrium interest rate, at which people are content holding the quantity of money the Fed has created.

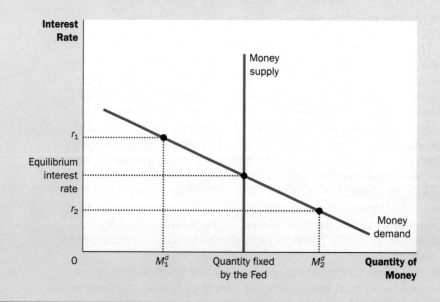

Although many factors determine the quantity of money demanded, the one emphasized by the theory of liquidity preference is the interest rate. The reason is that the interest rate is the opportunity cost of holding money. That is, when you hold wealth as cash in your wallet, instead of as an interest-bearing bond, you lose the interest you could have earned. An increase in the interest rate raises the cost of holding money and, as a result, reduces the quantity of money demanded. A decrease in the interest rate reduces the cost of holding money and raises the quantity demanded. Thus, as shown in Figure 1, the money-demand curve slopes downward.

Equilibrium in the Money Market According to the theory of liquidity preference, the interest rate adjusts to balance the supply and demand for money. There is one interest rate, called the *equilibrium interest rate*, at which the quantity of money demanded exactly balances the quantity of money supplied. If the interest rate is at any other level, people will try to adjust their portfolios of assets and, as a result, drive the interest rate toward the equilibrium.

For example, suppose that the interest rate is above the equilibrium level, such as r_1 in Figure 1. In this case, the quantity of money that people want to hold, M_1^d, is less than the quantity of money that the Fed has supplied. Those people who are holding the surplus of money will try to get rid of it by buying interest-bearing bonds or by depositing it in an interest-bearing bank account. Because bond issuers and banks prefer to pay lower interest rates, they respond to this surplus of money by lowering the interest rates they offer. As the interest rate falls, people become more willing to hold money until, at the equilibrium interest rate, people are happy to hold exactly the amount of money the Fed has supplied.

Conversely, at interest rates below the equilibrium level, such as r_2 in Figure 1, the quantity of money that people want to hold, M_2^d, is greater than the quantity of money that the Fed has supplied. As a result, people try to increase their holdings of money by reducing their holdings of bonds and other interest-bearing assets. As people cut back on their holdings of bonds, bond issuers find that they have to offer higher interest rates to attract buyers. Thus, the interest rate rises and approaches the equilibrium level.

The Downward Slope of the Aggregate-Demand Curve

Having seen how the theory of liquidity preference explains the economy's equilibrium interest rate, we now consider its implications for the aggregate demand for goods and services. As a warm-up exercise, let's begin by using the theory to reexamine a topic we already understand—the interest-rate effect and the downward slope of the aggregate-demand curve. In particular, suppose that the overall level of prices in the economy rises. What happens to the interest rate that balances the supply and demand for money, and how does that change affect the quantity of goods and services demanded?

As we discussed in Chapter 17, the price level is one determinant of the quantity of money demanded. At higher prices, more money is exchanged every time a good or service is sold. As a result, people will choose to hold a larger quantity of money. That is, a higher price level increases the quantity of money demanded for any given interest rate. Thus, an increase in the price level from P_1 to P_2 shifts the money-demand curve to the right from MD_1 to MD_2, as shown in panel (a) of Figure 2.

FYI

Interest Rates in the Long Run and the Short Run

At this point, we should pause and reflect on a seemingly awkward embarrassment of riches. It might appear as if we now have two theories for how interest rates are determined. In an earlier chapter, we said that the interest rate adjusts to balance the supply and demand for loanable funds (that is, national saving and desired investment). By contrast, we just established here that the interest rate adjusts to balance the supply and demand for money. How can we reconcile these two theories?

To answer this question, we must again consider the differences between the long-run and short-run behavior of the economy. Three macroeconomic variables are of central importance: the economy's output of goods and services, the interest rate, and the price level. According to the classical macroeconomic theory we developed earlier in the book, these variables are determined as follows:

1. *Output* is determined by the supplies of capital and labor and the available production technology for turning capital and labor into output. (We call this the natural rate of output.)
2. For any given level of output, the *interest rate* adjusts to balance the supply and demand for loanable funds.
3. Given output and the interest rate, the *price level* adjusts to balance the supply and demand for money. Changes in the supply of money lead to proportionate changes in the price level.

These are three of the essential propositions of classical economic theory. Most economists believe that these propositions do a good job of describing how the economy works *in the long run*.

Yet these propositions do not hold in the short run. As we discussed in the preceding chapter, many prices are slow to adjust to changes in the money supply; this is reflected in a short-run aggregate-supply curve that is upward sloping rather than vertical. As a result, the overall price level cannot, by itself, move to balance the supply and demand for money in the short run. This stickiness of the price level forces the interest rate to move to bring the money market into equilibrium. These changes in the interest rate, in turn, affect the aggregate demand for goods and services. As aggregate demand fluctuates, the economy's output of goods and services moves away from the level determined by factor supplies and technology.

For issues concerning the short run, then, it is best to think about the economy as follows:

1. The *price level* is stuck at some level (based on previously formed expectations) and, in the short run, is relatively unresponsive to changing economic conditions.
2. For any given price level, the *interest rate* adjusts to balance the supply and demand for money.
3. The interest rate that balances the money market influences the quantity of goods and services demanded and thus the level of *output*.

Notice that this precisely reverses the order of analysis used to study the economy in the long run.

The different theories of the interest rate are useful for different purposes. When thinking about the long-run determinants of interest rates, it is best to keep in mind the loanable-funds theory. This approach highlights the importance of an economy's saving propensities and investment opportunities. By contrast, when thinking about the short-run determinants of interest rates, it is best to keep in mind the liquidity-preference theory. This theory highlights the importance of monetary policy.

Notice how this shift in money demand affects the equilibrium in the money market. For a fixed money supply, the interest rate must rise to balance money supply and money demand. The higher price level has increased the amount of money people want to hold and has shifted the money demand curve to the

An increase in the price level from P_1 to P_2 shifts the money-demand curve to the right, as in panel (a). This increase in money demand causes the interest rate to rise from r_1 to r_2. Because the interest rate is the cost of borrowing, the increase in the interest rate reduces the quantity of goods and services demanded from Y_1 to Y_2. This negative relationship between the price level and quantity demanded is represented with a downward-sloping aggregate-demand curve, as in panel (b).

FIGURE 2

The Money Market and the Slope of the Aggregate-Demand Curve

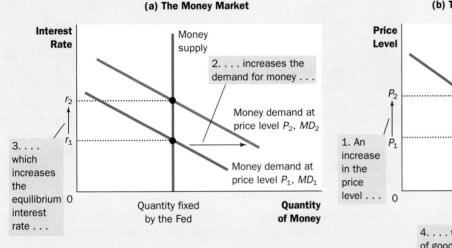

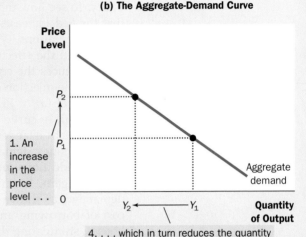

right. Yet the quantity of money supplied is unchanged, so the interest rate must rise from r_1 to r_2 to discourage the additional demand.

This increase in the interest rate has ramifications not only for the money market but also for the quantity of goods and services demanded, as shown in panel (b). At a higher interest rate, the cost of borrowing and the return to saving are greater. Fewer households choose to borrow to buy a new house, and those who do buy smaller houses, so the demand for residential investment falls. Fewer firms choose to borrow to build new factories and buy new equipment, so business investment falls. Thus, when the price level rises from P_1 to P_2, increasing money demand from MD_1 to MD_2 and raising the interest rate from r_1 to r_2, the quantity of goods and services demanded falls from Y_1 to Y_2.

This analysis of the interest-rate effect can be summarized in three steps: (1) A higher price level raises money demand. (2) Higher money demand leads to a higher interest rate. (3) A higher interest rate reduces the quantity of goods and services demanded. Of course, the same logic works in reverse as well: A lower price level reduces money demand, which leads to a lower interest rate, and this in turn increases the quantity of goods and services demanded. The end result of this analysis is a negative relationship between the price level and the quantity of goods and services demanded, as illustrated by a downward-sloping aggregate-demand curve.

Changes in the Money Supply

So far, we have used the theory of liquidity preference to explain more fully how the total quantity demanded of goods and services in the economy changes as the price level changes. That is, we have examined movements along the downward-sloping aggregate-demand curve. The theory also sheds light, however, on some of the other events that alter the quantity of goods and services demanded. Whenever the quantity of goods and services demanded changes *for a given price level*, the aggregate-demand curve shifts.

One important variable that shifts the aggregate-demand curve is monetary policy. To see how monetary policy affects the economy in the short run, suppose that the Fed increases the money supply by buying government bonds in open-market operations. (Why the Fed might do this will become clear later, after we understand the effects of such a move.) Let's consider how this monetary injection influences the equilibrium interest rate for a given price level. This will tell us what the injection does to the position of the aggregate-demand curve.

As panel (a) of Figure 3 shows, an increase in the money supply shifts the money-supply curve to the right from MS_1 to MS_2. Because the money-demand curve has not changed, the interest rate falls from r_1 to r_2 to balance money supply and money demand. That is, the interest rate must fall to induce people to hold the additional money the Fed has created.

Once again, the interest rate influences the quantity of goods and services demanded, as shown in panel (b) of Figure 3. The lower interest rate reduces the cost of borrowing and the return to saving. Households buy more and larger houses, stimulating the demand for residential investment. Firms spend more on

3 FIGURE

A Monetary Injection

In panel (a), an increase in the money supply from MS_1 to MS_2 reduces the equilibrium interest rate from r_1 to r_2. Because the interest rate is the cost of borrowing, the fall in the interest rate raises the quantity of goods and services demanded at a given price level from Y_1 to Y_2. Thus, in panel (b), the aggregate-demand curve shifts to the right from AD_1 to AD_2.

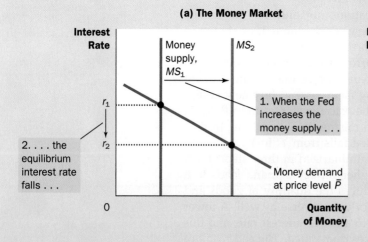

(a) The Money Market

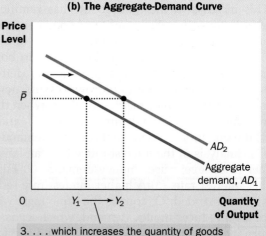

(b) The Aggregate-Demand Curve

new factories and new equipment, stimulating business investment. As a result, the quantity of goods and services demanded at a given price level, $\bar{P}$, rises from Y_1 to Y_2. Of course, there is nothing special about $\bar{P}$: The monetary injection raises the quantity of goods and services demanded at every price level. Thus, the entire aggregate-demand curve shifts to the right.

To sum up: *When the Fed increases the money supply, it lowers the interest rate and increases the quantity of goods and services demanded for any given price level, shifting the aggregate-demand curve to the right. Conversely, when the Fed contracts the money supply, it raises the interest rate and reduces the quantity of goods and services demanded for any given price level, shifting the aggregate-demand curve to the left.*

The Role of Interest-Rate Targets in Fed Policy

How does the Federal Reserve affect the economy? Our discussion here and earlier in the book has treated the money supply as the Fed's policy instrument. When the Fed buys government bonds in open-market operations, it increases the money supply and expands aggregate demand. When the Fed sells government bonds in open-market operations, it decreases the money supply and contracts aggregate demand.

Discussions of Fed policy often treat the interest rate, rather than the money supply, as the Fed's policy instrument. Indeed, in recent years, the Federal Reserve has conducted policy by setting a target for the *federal funds rate*—the interest rate that banks charge one another for short-term loans. This target is reevaluated every six weeks at meetings of the Federal Open Market Committee (FOMC). The FOMC has chosen to set a target for the federal funds rate (rather than for the money supply, as it has done at times in the past) in part because the money supply is hard to measure with sufficient precision.

The Fed's decision to target an interest rate does not fundamentally alter our analysis of monetary policy. The theory of liquidity preference illustrates an important principle: *Monetary policy can be described either in terms of the money supply or in terms of the interest rate.* When the FOMC sets a target for the federal funds rate of, say, 6 percent, the Fed's bond traders are told: "Conduct whatever open-market operations are necessary to ensure that the equilibrium interest rate equals 6 percent." In other words, when the Fed sets a target for the interest rate, it commits itself to adjusting the money supply to make the equilibrium in the money market hit that target.

As a result, changes in monetary policy can be viewed either in terms of changing the interest rate target or in terms of changing the money supply. When you read in the newspaper that "the Fed has lowered the federal funds rate from 6 to 5 percent," you should understand that this occurs only because the Fed's bond traders are doing what it takes to make it happen. To lower the federal funds rate, the Fed's bond traders buy government bonds, and this purchase increases the money supply and lowers the equilibrium interest rate (just as in Figure 3). Similarly, when the FOMC raises the target for the federal funds rate, the bond traders sell government bonds, and this sale decreases the money supply and raises the equilibrium interest rate.

The lessons from this analysis are simple: Changes in monetary policy aimed at expanding aggregate demand can be described either as increasing the money supply or as lowering the interest rate. Changes in monetary policy aimed at contracting aggregate demand can be described either as decreasing the money supply or as raising the interest rate.

| C A S E | WHY THE FED WATCHES THE STOCK MARKET |
| STUDY | (AND VICE VERSA) |

"Irrational exuberance." That was how Federal Reserve Chairman Alan Greenspan once described the booming stock market of the late 1990s. He was right that the market was exuberant: Average stock prices increased about four-fold during this decade. And perhaps it was even irrational: In the first few years of the following decade, the stock market took back some of these large gains, as stock prices experienced a pronounced decline, falling by about 40 per-cent from 2000 to 2003.

Regardless of how we view the booming market, it does raise an important question: How should the Fed respond to stock-market fluctuations? The Fed has no reason to care about stock prices in themselves, but it does have the job of monitoring and responding to developments in the overall economy, and the stock market is a piece of that puzzle. When the stock market booms, house-holds become wealthier, and this increased wealth stimulates consumer spend-ing. In addition, a rise in stock prices makes it more attractive for firms to sell new shares of stock, and this stimulates investment spending. For both reasons, a booming stock market expands the aggregate demand for goods and services.

As we discuss more fully later in the chapter, one of the Fed's goals is to stabi-lize aggregate demand, for greater stability in aggregate demand means greater stability in output and the price level. To do this, the Fed might respond to a stock-market boom by keeping the money supply lower and interest rates higher than it otherwise would. The contractionary effects of higher interest rates would offset the expansionary effects of higher stock prices. In fact, this analysis does describe Fed behavior: Real interest rates were kept high by historical standards during the "irrationally exuberant" stock-market boom of the late 1990s.

The opposite occurs when the stock market falls. Spending on consumption and investment declines, depressing aggregate demand and pushing the econ-omy toward recession. To stabilize aggregate demand, the Fed needs to increase the money supply and lower interest rates. And indeed, that is what it typically does. For example, on October 19, 1987, the stock market fell by 22.6 percent—its biggest one-day drop in history. The Fed responded to the market crash by increasing the money supply and lowering interest rates. The federal funds rate fell from 7.7 percent at the beginning of October to 6.6 percent at the end of the month. In part because of the Fed's quick action, the economy avoided a reces-sion. Similarly, as we discussed in a case study in the preceding chapter, the Fed also reduced interest rates during the stock market declines of 2001 and 2002, although this time monetary policy was not quick enough to avert a recession.

While the Fed keeps an eye on the stock market, stock-market participants also keep an eye on the Fed. Because the Fed can influence interest rates and economic activity, it can alter the value of stocks. For example, when the Fed raises interest rates by reducing the money supply, it makes owning stocks less attractive for two reasons. First, a higher interest rate means that bonds, the alternative to stocks, are earning a higher return. Second, the Fed's tightening of monetary policy reduces the demand for goods and services, which reduces profits. As a result, stock prices often fall when the Fed raises interest rates. •

Quick Quiz   Use the theory of liquidity preference to explain how a decrease in the money supply affects the equilibrium interest rate. How does this change in mone-tary policy affect the aggregate-demand curve?

HOW FISCAL POLICY INFLUENCES AGGREGATE DEMAND

The government can influence the behavior of the economy not only with monetary policy but also with fiscal policy. **Fiscal policy** refers to the government's choices regarding the overall level of government purchases or taxes. Earlier in the book, we examined how fiscal policy influences saving, investment, and growth in the long run. In the short run, however, the primary effect of fiscal policy is on the aggregate demand for goods and services.

fiscal policy
the setting of the level of government spending and taxation by government policymakers.

Changes in Government Purchases

When policymakers change the money supply or the level of taxes, they shift the aggregate-demand curve indirectly by influencing the spending decisions of firms or households. By contrast, when the government alters its own purchases of goods and services, it shifts the aggregate-demand curve directly.

Suppose, for instance, that the U.S. Department of Defense places a $20 billion order for new fighter planes with Boeing, the large aircraft manufacturer. This order raises the demand for the output produced by Boeing, which induces the company to hire more workers and increase production. Because Boeing is part of the economy, the increase in the demand for Boeing planes means an increase in the total quantity of goods and services demanded at each price level. As a result, the aggregate-demand curve shifts to the right.

By how much does this $20 billion order from the government shift the aggregate-demand curve? At first, one might guess that the aggregate-demand curve shifts to the right by exactly $20 billion. It turns out, however, that this is not the case. There are two macroeconomic effects that make the size of the shift in aggregate demand differ from the change in government purchases. The first—the multiplier effect—suggests that the shift in aggregate demand could be *larger* than $20 billion. The second—the crowding-out effect—suggests that the shift in aggregate demand could be *smaller* than $20 billion. We now discuss each of these effects in turn.

The Multiplier Effect

When the government buys $20 billion of goods from Boeing, that purchase has repercussions. The immediate impact of the higher demand from the government is to raise employment and profits at Boeing. Then, as the workers see higher earnings and the firm owners see higher profits, they respond to this increase in income by raising their own spending on consumer goods. As a result, the government purchase from Boeing raises the demand for the products of many other firms in the economy. Because each dollar spent by the government can raise the aggregate demand for goods and services by more than a dollar, government purchases are said to have a **multiplier effect** on aggregate demand.

This multiplier effect continues even after this first round. When consumer spending rises, the firms that produce these consumer goods hire more people and experience higher profits. Higher earnings and profits stimulate consumer spending once again and so on. Thus, there is positive feedback as higher demand leads to higher income, which in turn leads to even higher demand. Once all these effects are added together, the total impact on the quantity of goods and services demanded can be much larger than the initial impulse from higher government spending.

multiplier effect
the additional shifts in aggregate demand that result when expansionary fiscal policy increases income and thereby increases consumer spending

Figure 4 illustrates the multiplier effect. The increase in government purchases of $20 billion initially shifts the aggregate-demand curve to the right from AD_1 to AD_2 by exactly $20 billion. But when consumers respond by increasing their spending, the aggregate-demand curve shifts still further to AD_3.

This multiplier effect arising from the response of consumer spending can be strengthened by the response of investment to higher levels of demand. For instance, Boeing might respond to the higher demand for planes by deciding to buy more equipment or build another plant. In this case, higher government demand spurs higher demand for investment goods. This positive feedback from demand to investment is sometimes called the *investment accelerator.*

A Formula for the Spending Multiplier

A little high school algebra permits us to derive a formula for the size of the multiplier effect that arises when an increase in government purchases induces increases in consumer spending. An important number in this formula is the *marginal propensity to consume* (MPC)—the fraction of extra income that a household consumes rather than saves. For example, suppose that the marginal propensity to consume is $3/4$. This means that for every extra dollar that a household earns, the household spends $0.75 ($3/4$ of the dollar) and saves $0.25. With an MPC of $3/4$, when the workers and owners of Boeing earn $20 billion from the government contract, they increase their consumer spending by $3/4 \times$ $20 billion, or $15 billion.

To gauge the impact on aggregate demand of a change in government purchases, we follow the effects step by step. The process begins when the government spends $20 billion, which implies that national income (earnings and profits) also rises by this amount. This increase in income in turn raises consumer

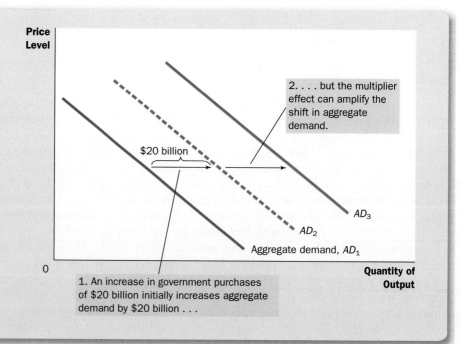

4 **FIGURE**

The Multiplier Effect
An increase in government purchases of $20 billion can shift the aggregate-demand curve to the right by more than $20 billion. This multiplier effect arises because increases in aggregate income stimulate additional spending by consumers.

spending by $MPC \times \$20$ billion, which in turn raises the income for the workers and owners of the firms that produce the consumption goods. This second increase in income again raises consumer spending, this time by $MPC \times (MPC \times \$20$ billion). These feedback effects go on and on.

To find the total impact on the demand for goods and services, we add up all these effects:

Change in government purchases	=	$\$20$ billion
First change in consumption	=	$MPC \times \$20$ billion
Second change in consumption	=	$MPC^2 \times \$20$ billion
Third change in consumption	=	$MPC^3 \times \$20$ billion
•		•
•		•
•		•

Total change in demand =
$(1 + MPC + MPC^2 + MPC^3 + \ldots) \times \$20$ billion.

Here "..." represents an infinite number of similar terms. Thus, we can write the multiplier as follows:

$$\text{Multiplier} = 1 + MPC + MPC^2 + MPC^3 + \ldots.$$

This multiplier tells us the demand for goods and services that each dollar of government purchases generates.

To simplify this equation for the multiplier, recall from math class that this expression is an infinite geometric series. For x between -1 and $+1$,

$$1 + x + x^2 + x^3 + \ldots = 1 / (1 - x).$$

In our case, $x = MPC$. Thus,

$$\text{Multiplier} = 1 / (1 - MPC).$$

For example, if MPC is $3/4$, the multiplier is $1 / (1 - 3/4)$, which is 4. In this case, the $\$20$ billion of government spending generates $\$80$ billion of demand for goods and services.

This formula for the multiplier shows an important conclusion: The size of the multiplier depends on the marginal propensity to consume. While an MPC of $3/4$ leads to a multiplier of 4, an MPC of $1/2$ leads to a multiplier of only 2. Thus, a larger MPC means a larger multiplier. To see why this is true, remember that the multiplier arises because higher income induces greater spending on consumption. The larger the MPC is, the greater is this induced effect on consumption, and the larger is the multiplier.

Other Applications of the Multiplier Effect

Because of the multiplier effect, a dollar of government purchases can generate more than a dollar of aggregate demand. The logic of the multiplier effect, however, is not restricted to changes in government purchases. Instead, it applies to any event that alters spending on any component of GDP—consumption, investment, government purchases, or net exports.

For example, suppose that a recession overseas reduces the demand for U.S. net exports by $10 billion. This reduced spending on U.S. goods and services depresses U.S. national income, which reduces spending by U.S. consumers. If the marginal propensity to consume is $3/4$ and the multiplier is 4, then the $10 billion fall in net exports means a $40 billion contraction in aggregate demand.

As another example, suppose that a stock-market boom increases households' wealth and stimulates their spending on goods and services by $20 billion. This extra consumer spending increases national income, which in turn generates even more consumer spending. If the marginal propensity to consume is $3/4$ and the multiplier is 4, then the initial impulse of $20 billion in consumer spending translates into an $80 billion increase in aggregate demand.

The multiplier is an important concept in macroeconomics because it shows how the economy can amplify the impact of changes in spending. A small initial change in consumption, investment, government purchases, or net exports can end up having a large effect on aggregate demand and, therefore, the economy's production of goods and services.

The Crowding-Out Effect

The multiplier effect seems to suggest that when the government buys $20 billion of planes from Boeing, the resulting expansion in aggregate demand is necessarily larger than $20 billion. Yet another effect is working in the opposite direction. While an increase in government purchases stimulates the aggregate demand for goods and services, it also causes the interest rate to rise, and a higher interest rate reduces investment spending and puts downward pressure on aggregate demand. The reduction in aggregate demand that results when a fiscal expansion raises the interest rate is called the **crowding-out effect.**

crowding-out effect
the offset in aggregate demand that results when expansionary fiscal policy raises the interest rate and thereby reduces investment spending

To see why crowding out occurs, let's consider what happens in the money market when the government buys planes from Boeing. As we have discussed, this increase in demand raises the incomes of the workers and owners of this firm (and because of the multiplier effect, of other firms as well). As incomes rise, households plan to buy more goods and services and, as a result, choose to hold more of their wealth in liquid form. That is, the increase in income caused by the fiscal expansion raises the demand for money.

The effect of the increase in money demand is shown in panel (a) of Figure 5. Because the Fed has not changed the money supply, the vertical supply curve remains the same. When the higher level of income shifts the money-demand curve to the right from MD_1 to MD_2, the interest rate must rise from r_1 to r_2 to keep supply and demand in balance.

The increase in the interest rate, in turn, reduces the quantity of goods and services demanded. In particular, because borrowing is more expensive, the demand for residential and business investment goods declines. That is, as the increase in government purchases increases the demand for goods and services, it may also crowd out investment. This crowding-out effect partially offsets the impact of government purchases on aggregate demand, as illustrated in panel (b) of Figure 5. The increase in government purchases initially shifts the aggregate-demand curve from AD_1 to AD_2, but once crowding out takes place, the aggregate-demand curve drops back to AD_3.

To sum up: *When the government increases its purchases by $20 billion, the aggregate demand for goods and services could rise by more or less than $20 billion depending on whether the multiplier effect or the crowding-out effect is larger.*

Panel (a) shows the money market. When the government increases its purchases of goods and services, the resulting increase in income raises the demand for money from MD_1 to MD_2, and this causes the equilibrium interest rate to rise from r_1 to r_2. Panel (b) shows the effects on aggregate demand. The initial impact of the increase in government purchases shifts the aggregate-demand curve from AD_1 to AD_2. Yet because the interest rate is the cost of borrowing, the increase in the interest rate tends to reduce the quantity of goods and services demanded, particularly for investment goods. This crowding out of investment partially offsets the impact of the fiscal expansion on aggregate demand. In the end, the aggregate-demand curve shifts only to AD_3.

F I G U R E   5

The Crowding-Out Effect

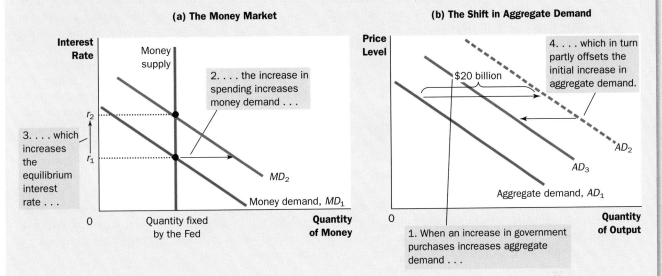

Changes in Taxes
================

Changes in Taxes

The other important instrument of fiscal policy, besides the level of government purchases, is the level of taxation. When the government cuts personal income taxes, for instance, it increases households' take-home pay. Households will save some of this additional income, but they will also spend some of it on consumer goods. Because it increases consumer spending, the tax cut shifts the aggregate-demand curve to the right. Similarly, a tax increase depresses consumer spending and shifts the aggregate-demand curve to the left.

   The size of the shift in aggregate demand resulting from a tax change is also affected by the multiplier and crowding-out effects. When the government cuts taxes and stimulates consumer spending, earnings and profits rise, which further stimulates consumer spending. This is the multiplier effect. At the same time, higher income leads to higher money demand, which tends to raise interest rates. Higher interest rates make borrowing more costly, which reduces investment spending. This is the crowding-out effect. Depending on the size of the multiplier and crowding-out effects, the shift in aggregate demand could be larger or smaller than the tax change that causes it.

FYI

How Fiscal Policy Might Affect Aggregate Supply

So far, our discussion of fiscal policy has stressed how changes in government purchases and changes in taxes influence the quantity of goods and services demanded. Most economists believe that the short-run macroeconomic effects of fiscal policy work primarily through aggregate demand. Yet fiscal policy can potentially also influence the quantity of goods and services supplied.

For instance, consider the effects of tax changes on aggregate supply. One of the *Ten Principles of Economics* in Chapter 1 is that people respond to incentives. When government policymakers cut tax rates, workers get to keep more of each dollar they earn, so they have a greater incentive to work and produce goods and services. If they respond to this incentive, the quantity of goods and services supplied will be greater at each price level, and the aggregate-supply curve will shift to the right.

Some economists, called *supply-siders,* have argued that the influence of tax cuts on aggregate supply is large. According to some supply-siders, the influence is so large that a cut in tax rates will stimulate enough additional production and income that tax revenue will actually increase. This is certainly a theoretical possibility, but most economists do not consider it the normal case. While the supply-side effects of taxes are important to consider, they are usually not large enough to cause tax revenue to rise when tax rates fall.

Like changes in taxes, changes in government purchases can also potentially affect aggregate supply. Suppose, for instance, that the government increases expenditure on a form of government-provided capital, such as roads. Roads are used by private businesses to make deliveries to their customers; an increase in the quantity of roads increases these businesses' productivity. Hence, when the government spends more on roads, it increases the quantity of goods and services supplied at any given price level and, thus, shifts the aggregate-supply curve to the right. This effect on aggregate supply is probably more important in the long run than in the short run, however, because it would take some time for the government to build the new roads and put them into use.

In addition to the multiplier and crowding-out effects, there is another important determinant of the size of the shift in aggregate demand that results from a tax change: households' perceptions about whether the tax change is permanent or temporary. For example, suppose that the government announces a tax cut of $1,000 per household. In deciding how much of this $1,000 to spend, households must ask themselves how long this extra income will last. If households expect the tax cut to be permanent, they will view it as adding substantially to their financial resources and, therefore, increase their spending by a large amount. In this case, the tax cut will have a large impact on aggregate demand. By contrast, if households expect the tax change to be temporary, they will view it as adding only slightly to their financial resources and, therefore, will increase their spending by only a small amount. In this case, the tax cut will have a small impact on aggregate demand.

An extreme example of a temporary tax cut was the one announced in 1992. In that year, President George H. W. Bush faced a lingering recession and an upcoming reelection campaign. He responded to these circumstances by announcing a reduction in the amount of income tax that the federal government was withholding from workers' paychecks. Because legislated income tax rates did not change, however, every dollar of reduced withholding in 1992 meant an extra dollar of taxes due on April 15, 1993, when income tax returns for 1992 were to be filed. Thus, this "tax cut" actually represented only a short-term loan from the government. Not surprisingly, the impact of the policy on consumer spending and aggregate demand was relatively small.

Quick Quiz   Suppose that the government reduces spending on highway construction by $10 billion. Which way does the aggregate-demand curve shift? Explain why the shift might be larger than $10 billion. Explain why the shift might be smaller than $10 billion.

USING POLICY TO STABILIZE THE ECONOMY

We have seen how monetary and fiscal policy can affect the economy's aggregate demand for goods and services. These theoretical insights raise some important policy questions: Should policymakers use these instruments to control aggregate demand and stabilize the economy? If so, when? If not, why not?

The Case for Active Stabilization Policy

Let's return to the question that began this chapter: When the president and Congress cut government spending, how should the Federal Reserve respond? As we have seen, government spending is one determinant of the position of the aggregate-demand curve. When the government cuts spending, aggregate demand will fall, which will depress production and employment in the short run. If the Federal Reserve wants to prevent this adverse effect of the fiscal policy, it can act to expand aggregate demand by increasing the money supply. A monetary expansion would reduce interest rates, stimulate investment spending, and expand aggregate demand. If monetary policy responds appropriately, the combined changes in monetary and fiscal policy could leave the aggregate demand for goods and services unaffected.

This analysis is exactly the sort followed by members of the Federal Open Market Committee. They know that monetary policy is an important determinant of aggregate demand. They also know that there are other important determinants as well, including fiscal policy set by the president and Congress. As a result, the Fed's Open Market Committee watches the debates over fiscal policy with a keen eye.

This response of monetary policy to the change in fiscal policy is an example of a more general phenomenon: the use of policy instruments to stabilize aggregate demand and, as a result, production and employment. Economic stabilization has been an explicit goal of U.S. policy since the Employment Act of 1946. This act states that "it is the continuing policy and responsibility of the federal government to ... promote full employment and production." In essence, the government has chosen to hold itself accountable for short-run macroeconomic performance.

The Employment Act has two implications. The first, more modest, implication is that the government should avoid being a cause of economic fluctuations. Thus, most economists advise against large and sudden changes in monetary and fiscal policy, for such changes are likely to cause fluctuations in aggregate demand. Moreover, when large changes do occur, it is important that monetary and fiscal policymakers be aware of and respond to the other's actions.

The second, more ambitious, implication of the Employment Act is that the government should respond to changes in the private economy to stabilize aggregate demand. The act was passed not long after the publication of Keynes's *The General Theory of Employment, Interest, and Money,* which has been one of the most influential books ever written about economics. In it, Keynes emphasized the key role of aggregate demand in explaining short-run economic fluctuations. Keynes claimed that the government should actively stimulate aggregate demand when aggregate demand appeared insufficient to maintain production at its full-employment level.

Keynes (and his many followers) argued that aggregate demand fluctuates because of largely irrational waves of pessimism and optimism. He used the term "animal spirits" to refer to these arbitrary changes in attitude. When pessimism reigns, households reduce consumption spending, and firms reduce investment spending. The result is reduced aggregate demand, lower production, and higher unemployment. Conversely, when optimism reigns, households and firms increase spending. The result is higher aggregate demand, higher production, and inflationary pressure. Notice that these changes in attitude are, to some extent, self-fulfilling.

In principle, the government can adjust its monetary and fiscal policy in response to these waves of optimism and pessimism and, thereby, stabilize the economy. For example, when people are excessively pessimistic, the Fed can expand the money supply to lower interest rates and expand aggregate demand. When they are excessively optimistic, it can contract the money supply to raise interest rates and dampen aggregate demand. Former Fed chairman William McChesney Martin described this view of monetary policy very simply: "The Federal Reserve's job is to take away the punch bowl just as the party gets going."

CASE STUDY | KEYNESIANS IN THE WHITE HOUSE

When a reporter in 1961 asked President John F. Kennedy why he advocated a tax cut, Kennedy replied, "To stimulate the economy. Don't you remember your Economics 101?" Kennedy's policy was, in fact, based on the analysis of fiscal policy we have developed in this chapter. His goal was to enact a tax cut, which would raise consumer spending, expand aggregate demand, and increase the economy's production and employment.

In choosing this policy, Kennedy was relying on his team of economic advisers. This team included such prominent economists as James Tobin and Robert Solow, who later would win Nobel prizes for their contributions to economics. As students in the 1940s, these economists had closely studied John Maynard Keynes's *General Theory,* which then was only a few years old. When the Kennedy advisers proposed cutting taxes, they were putting Keynes's ideas into action.

Although tax changes can have a potent influence on aggregate demand, they have other effects as well. In particular, by changing the incentives that people face, taxes can alter the aggregate supply of goods and services. Part of the Kennedy proposal was an investment tax credit, which gives a tax break to firms that invest in new capital. Higher investment would not only stimulate aggregate demand immediately but would also increase the economy's productive capacity over time. Thus, the short-run goal of increasing production through higher aggregate demand was coupled with a long-run goal of increasing production through higher aggregate supply. And indeed, when the tax cut Kennedy proposed was finally enacted in 1964, it helped usher in a period of robust economic growth.

Since the 1964 tax cut, policymakers have from time to time used fiscal policy as a tool for controlling aggregate demand. For example, when President George W. Bush moved into the Oval Office in 2001, he faced an economy that was heading into recession. One of his first policy initiatives was a substantial and permanent tax cut. Bush explained, "The best way to increase demand for goods and services is to let people keep more of their own money. And when somebody meets that demand by additional production, somebody is more likely to find a job." •

The Case against Active Stabilization Policy

Some economists argue that the government should avoid active use of monetary and fiscal policy to try to stabilize the economy. They claim that these policy instruments should be set to achieve long-run goals, such as rapid economic growth and low inflation, and that the economy should be left to deal with short-run fluctuations on its own. Although these economists may admit that monetary and fiscal policy can stabilize the economy in theory, they doubt whether it can do so in practice.

The primary argument against active monetary and fiscal policy is that these policies affect the economy with a long lag. As we have seen, monetary policy works by changing interest rates, which in turn influence investment spending. But many firms make investment plans far in advance. Thus, most economists believe that it takes at least six months for changes in monetary policy to have much effect on output and employment. Moreover, once these effects occur, they can last for several years. Critics of stabilization policy argue that because of this lag, the Fed should not try to fine-tune the economy. They claim that the Fed often reacts too late to changing economic conditions and, as a result, ends up being a cause of rather than a cure for economic fluctuations. These critics advocate a passive monetary policy, such as slow and steady growth in the money supply.

Fiscal policy also works with a lag, but unlike the lag in monetary policy, the lag in fiscal policy is largely attributable to the political process. In the United States, most changes in government spending and taxes must go through congressional committees in both the House and the Senate, be passed by both legislative bodies, and then be signed by the president. Completing this process can take months and, in some cases, years. By the time the change in fiscal policy is passed and ready to implement, the condition of the economy may well have changed.

These lags in monetary and fiscal policy are a problem in part because economic forecasting is so imprecise. If forecasters could accurately predict the condition of the economy a year in advance, then monetary and fiscal policymakers could look ahead when making policy decisions. In this case, policymakers could stabilize the economy despite the lags they face. In practice, however, major recessions and depressions arrive without much advance warning. The best policymakers can do at any time is to respond to economic changes as they occur.

Automatic Stabilizers

automatic stabilizers
changes in fiscal policy that stimulate aggregate demand when the economy goes into a recession without policymakers having to take any deliberate action

All economists—both advocates and critics of stabilization policy—agree that the lags in implementation render policy less useful as a tool for short-run stabilization. The economy would be more stable, therefore, if policymakers could find a way to avoid some of these lags. In fact, they have. **Automatic stabilizers** are changes in fiscal policy that stimulate aggregate demand when the economy goes into a recession without policymakers having to take any deliberate action.

The most important automatic stabilizer is the tax system. When the economy goes into a recession, the amount of taxes collected by the government falls automatically because almost all taxes are closely tied to economic activity. The personal income tax depends on households' incomes, the payroll tax depends on workers' earnings, and the corporate income tax depends on firms' profits. Because incomes, earnings, and profits all fall in a recession, the government's tax revenue falls as well. This automatic tax cut stimulates aggregate demand and, thereby, reduces the magnitude of economic fluctuations.

Government spending also acts as an automatic stabilizer. In particular, when the economy goes into a recession and workers are laid off, more people apply for unemployment insurance benefits, welfare benefits, and other forms of income support. This automatic increase in government spending stimulates aggregate demand at exactly the time when aggregate demand is insufficient to maintain full employment. Indeed, when the unemployment insurance system was first enacted in the 1930s, economists who advocated this policy did so in part because of its power as an automatic stabilizer.

The automatic stabilizers in the U.S. economy are not sufficiently strong to prevent recessions completely. Nonetheless, without these automatic stabilizers, output and employment would probably be more volatile than they are. For this reason, many economists oppose a constitutional amendment that would require the federal government always to run a balanced budget, as some politicians have proposed. When the economy goes into a recession, taxes fall, government spending rises, and the government's budget moves toward deficit. If the government faced a strict balanced-budget rule, it would be forced to look for ways to raise taxes or cut spending in a recession. In other words, a strict balanced-budget rule would eliminate the automatic stabilizers inherent in our current system of taxes and government spending.

Quick Quiz Suppose a wave of negative "animal spirits" overruns the economy, and people become pessimistic about the future. What happens to aggregate demand? If the Fed wants to stabilize aggregate demand, how should it alter the money supply? If it does this, what happens to the interest rate? Why might the Fed choose not to respond in this way?

CONCLUSION

Before policymakers make any change in policy, they need to consider all the effects of their decisions. Earlier in the book, we examined classical models of the economy, which describe the long-run effects of monetary and fiscal policy. There we saw how fiscal policy influences saving, investment, and long-run growth and how monetary policy influences the price level and the inflation rate.

In this chapter, we examined the short-run effects of monetary and fiscal policy. We saw how these policy instruments can change the aggregate demand for goods and services and, thereby, alter the economy's production and employment in the short run. When Congress reduces government spending to balance the budget, it needs to consider both the long-run effects on saving and growth and the short-run effects on aggregate demand and employment. When the Fed reduces the growth rate of the money supply, it must take into account the long-run effect on inflation as well as the short-run effect on production. In all parts of government, policymakers must keep in mind both long-run and short-run goals.

SUMMARY

- In developing a theory of short-run economic fluctuations, Keynes proposed the theory of liquidity preference to explain the determinants of the interest rate. According to this theory, the interest rate adjusts to balance the supply and demand for money.

- An increase in the price level raises money demand and increases the interest rate that brings the money market into equilibrium. Because the interest rate represents the cost of borrowing, a higher interest rate reduces investment and, thereby, the quantity of goods and services demanded. The downward-sloping aggregate-demand curve expresses this negative relationship between the price level and the quantity demanded.

- Policymakers can influence aggregate demand with monetary policy. An increase in the money supply reduces the equilibrium interest rate for any given price level. Because a lower interest rate stimulates investment spending, the aggregate-demand curve shifts to the right. Conversely, a decrease in the money supply raises the equilibrium interest rate for any given price level and shifts the aggregate-demand curve to the left.

- Policymakers can also influence aggregate demand with fiscal policy. An increase in government pur-

chases or a cut in taxes shifts the aggregate-demand curve to the right. A decrease in government purchases or an increase in taxes shifts the aggregate-demand curve to the left.

- When the government alters spending or taxes, the resulting shift in aggregate demand can be larger or smaller than the fiscal change. The multiplier effect tends to amplify the effects of fiscal policy on aggregate demand. The crowding-out effect tends to dampen the effects of fiscal policy on aggregate demand.

- Because monetary and fiscal policy can influence aggregate demand, the government sometimes uses these policy instruments in an attempt to stabilize the economy. Economists disagree about how active the government should be in this effort. According to advocates of active stabilization policy, changes in attitudes by households and firms shift aggregate demand; if the government does not respond, the result is undesirable and unnecessary fluctuations in output and employment. According to critics of active stabilization policy, monetary and fiscal policy work with such long lags that attempts at stabilizing the economy often end up being destabilizing.

KEY CONCEPTS

theory of liquidity preference, p. 475

fiscal policy, p. 483

multiplier effect, p. 483

crowding-out effect, p. 486

automatic stabilizers, p. 492

QUESTIONS FOR REVIEW

1. What is the theory of liquidity preference? How does it help explain the downward slope of the aggregate-demand curve?

2. Use the theory of liquidity preference to explain how a decrease in the money supply affects the aggregate-demand curve.

3. The government spends $3 billion to buy police cars. Explain why aggregate demand might increase by more than $3 billion. Explain why aggregate demand might increase by less than $3 billion.

4. Suppose that survey measures of consumer confidence indicate a wave of pessimism is sweeping the country. If policymakers do nothing, what will happen to aggregate demand? What should the Fed do if it wants to stabilize aggregate demand? If the Fed does nothing, what might Congress do to stabilize aggregate demand?

5. Give an example of a government policy that acts as an automatic stabilizer. Explain why the policy has this effect.

PROBLEMS AND APPLICATIONS

1. Explain how each of the following developments would affect the supply of money, the demand for money, and the interest rate. Illustrate your answers with diagrams.
   a. The Fed's bond traders buy bonds in open-market operations.
   b. An increase in credit-card availability reduces the cash people hold.
   c. The Federal Reserve reduces banks' reserve requirements.
   d. Households decide to hold more money to use for holiday shopping.
   e. A wave of optimism boosts business investment and expands aggregate demand.

2. The Federal Reserve expands the money supply by 5 percent.
   a. Use the theory of liquidity preference to illustrate the impact of this policy on the interest rate.
   b. Use the model of aggregate demand and aggregate supply to illustrate the impact of this change in the interest rate on output and the price level in the short run.
   c. When the economy makes the transition from its short-run equilibrium to its long-run equilibrium, what will happen to the price level?
   d. How will this change in the price level affect the demand for money and the equilibrium interest rate?
   e. Is this analysis consistent with the proposition that money has real effects in the short run but is neutral in the long run?

3. Suppose banks install automatic teller machines on every block and, by making cash readily available, reduce the amount of money people want to hold.
   a. Assume the Fed does not change the money supply. According to the theory of liquidity preference, what happens to the interest rate? What happens to aggregate demand?
   b. If the Fed wants to stabilize aggregate demand, how should it respond?

4. Consider two policies—a tax cut that will last for only 1 year and a tax cut that is expected to be permanent. Which policy will stimulate greater spending by consumers? Which policy will have the greater impact on aggregate demand? Explain.

5. The economy is in a recession with high unemployment and low output.
   a. Draw a graph of aggregate demand and aggregate supply to illustrate the current situation. Be sure to include the aggregate-demand curve, the short-run aggregate-supply curve, and the long-run aggregate-supply curve.
   b. Identify an open-market operation that would restore the economy to its natural rate.
   c. Draw a graph of the money market to illustrate the effect of this open-market operation. Show the resulting change in the interest rate.
   d. Draw a graph similar to the one in part (a) to show the effect of the open-market operation

on output and the price level. Explain in words why the policy has the effect that you have shown in the graph.

6. In the early 1980s, new legislation allowed banks to pay interest on checking deposits, which they could not do previously.
   a. If we define money to include checking deposits, what effect did this legislation have on money demand? Explain.
   b. If the Federal Reserve had maintained a constant money supply in the face of this change, what would have happened to the interest rate? What would have happened to aggregate demand and aggregate output?
   c. If the Federal Reserve had maintained a constant market interest rate (the interest rate on nonmonetary assets) in the face of this change, what change in the money supply would have been necessary? What would have happened to aggregate demand and aggregate output?

7. Suppose economists observe that an increase in government spending of $10 billion raises the total demand for goods and services by $30 billion.
   a. If these economists ignore the possibility of crowding out, what would they estimate the marginal propensity to consume (*MPC*) to be?
   b. Now suppose the economists allow for crowding out. Would their new estimate of the *MPC* be larger or smaller than their initial one?

8. Suppose the government reduces taxes by $20 billion, that there is no crowding out, and that the marginal propensity to consume is ³/₄.
   a. What is the initial effect of the tax reduction on aggregate demand?
   b. What additional effects follow this initial effect? What is the total effect of the tax cut on aggregate demand?
   c. How does the total effect of this $20 billion tax cut compare to the total effect of a $20 billion increase in government purchases? Why?

9. Suppose government spending increases. Would the effect on aggregate demand be larger if the Federal Reserve took no action in response or if the Fed were committed to maintaining a fixed interest rate? Explain.

10. In which of the following circumstances is expansionary fiscal policy more likely to lead to a short-run increase in investment? Explain.
    a. When the investment accelerator is large or when it is small?
    b. When the interest sensitivity of investment is large or when it is small?

11. For various reasons, fiscal policy changes automatically when output and employment fluctuate.
    a. Explain why tax revenue changes when the economy goes into a recession.
    b. Explain why government spending changes when the economy goes into a recession.
    c. If the government were to operate under a strict balanced-budget rule, what would it have to do in a recession? Would that make the recession more or less severe?

12. Some members of Congress have proposed a law that would make price stability the sole goal of monetary policy. Suppose such a law were passed.
    a. How would the Fed respond to an event that contracted aggregate demand?
    b. How would the Fed respond to an event that caused an adverse shift in short-run aggregate supply?

    In each case, is there another monetary policy that would lead to greater stability in output?

13. Go to the website of the Federal Reserve, http://www.federalreserve.gov, to learn more about monetary policy. Find a recent report, speech, or testimony by the Fed chairman or another Fed governor. What does it say about the state of the economy and recent decisions about monetary policy?

 For further information on topics in this chapter, additional problems, examples, applications, online quizzes, and more, please visit our website at http://mankiw.swlearning.com.

Macroeconomics
Principles and Policy

Tenth Edition

William J. Baumol
New York University and Princeton University

Alan S. Blinder
Princeton University

THOMSON

SOUTH-WESTERN

Australia · Canada · Mexico · Singapore · Spain · United Kingdom · United States

6

THE GOALS OF MACROECONOMIC POLICY

When men are employed, they are best contented.

BENJAMIN FRANKLIN

Inflation is repudiation.

CALVIN COOLIDGE

Someone once quipped that you could turn a parrot into an economist by teaching him just two words: supply and demand. And now that you have been through Chapter 5, you see what he meant. Sure enough, economists think of the process of *economic growth* as having two essential ingredients:

Inputs are the labor, machinery, buildings, and other resources used to produce outputs.

Outputs are the goods and services that the economy produces.

- The first ingredient is *aggregate supply.* Given the available supplies of **inputs** like labor and capital, and the technology at its disposal, an economy is able to produce a certain volume of **outputs,** measured by GDP. This *capacity to produce* normally increases from one year to the next as the supplies of inputs grow and the technology improves. The theory of aggregate supply will be our focus in Chapters 7 and 10.
- The second ingredient is *aggregate demand.* How much of the capacity to produce is actually *utilized* depends on how many of these goods and services people and businesses want to *buy.* We begin building a theory of aggregate demand in Chapters 8 and 9.

CONTENTS

Corresponding to these two ingredients, economists visualize a dual task for those who make macroeconomic policy. First, *policy should create an environment in which the economy can expand its productive capacity rapidly*, because that is the ultimate source of higher living standards. This first task is the realm of **growth policy,** and it is taken up in the next chapter. Second, *policy makers should manage aggregate demand so that it grows in line with the economy's capacity to produce*, avoiding as much as possible the cycles of boom and bust that we saw in the last chapter. This is the realm of *stabilization policy*. As we noted in the last chapter, inadequate growth of aggregate demand can lead to high *unemployment*, while excessive growth of aggregate demand can lead to high *inflation*. Both are to be avoided.

Growth policy refers to government policies intended to make the economy grow faster in the long run.

Thus, the goals of macroeconomic policy can be summarized succinctly as *achieving rapid but relatively smooth growth with low unemployment and low inflation*. Unfortunately, that turns out to be a tall order. In chapters to come, we will explain why these goals cannot be attained with machine-like precision, and why improvement on one front often spells deterioration on another. Along the way, we will pay a great deal of attention to both the *causes* of and *cures* for sluggish growth, high unemployment, and high inflation.

But before getting involved in such weighty issues of theory and policy, we pause in this chapter to take a close look at the three goals themselves. How fast can—or should—the economy grow? Why does a rise in unemployment cause such social distress? Why is inflation so loudly deplored? The answers to some of these questions may seem obvious at first. But, as you will see, there is more to them than meets the eye.

The chapter is divided into three main parts, corresponding to the three goals. An appendix explains how inflation is measured.

PART 1: THE GOAL OF ECONOMIC GROWTH

To residents of a prosperous society like ours, economic growth—the notion that standards of living rise from one year to the next—seems like part of the natural order of things. But it is not. Historians tell us that living standards barely changed from the Roman Empire to the dawn of the Industrial Revolution—a period of some sixteen centuries! Closer in time, per capita incomes have tragically declined in most of the former Soviet Union and some of the poorest countries of Africa in recent decades. Economic growth is *not* automatic.

Growth is also a very slow, and therefore barely noticeable, process. The typical American will consume about 3 percent more goods and services in 2005 than he or she did in 2004. Can you perceive a difference that small? Perhaps not, but such tiny changes, when compounded for decades or even centuries, transform societies. During the twentieth century, for example, living standards in the United States increased by a factor of more than seven—which means that your ancestors in the year 1900 consumed roughly 14 percent as much food, clothing, shelter, and other amenities as you do today. Try to imagine how your family would fare on one seventh of its current income.

PRODUCTIVITY GROWTH: FROM LITTLE ACORNS . . .

Small differences in growth rates make an enormous difference—*eventually*. To illustrate this point, think about the relative positions of three major nations—the United States, the United Kingdom, and Japan—at two points in history: 1870 and 1979. In 1870, the United States was a young, upstart nation. Although already among the most prosperous countries on earth, the United States was in no sense yet a major power. The United Kingdom, by contrast, was the preeminent economic and military power of the world. The Victorian era was at its height, and the sun never set on the

The Wonders of Compound Interest

Growth rates, like interest rates, *compound* so that, for example, ten years of growth at 3 percent per year leaves the economy *more than* 30 percent larger. How much more? The answer is 34.4 percent. To see how we get this figure, start with the fact that $100 left in a bank account for one year at 3 percent interest grows to $103, which is 1.03 × $100. If left for a second year, that $103 will grow another 3 percent—to 1.03 × $103 = $106.09, which is already more than $106. Compounding has begun.

SOURCE: © Corbis

Notice that 1.03 × $103 is $(1.03)^2 \times \$100$. Similarly, after three years the original $100 will grow to $(1.03)^3 \times \$100 = \$109.27$. As you can see, each additional year adds another 1.03 growth factor to the multiplication. Now returning to answer our original question, after ten years of compounding, the depositor will have $(1.03)^{10} \times \$100 = \$134.39$ in the bank. Thus her balance will have grown by 34.4 percent. By identical logic, an economy growing at 3 percent per year for ten years will expand 34.4 percent in total.

You may not be impressed by the difference between 30 percent and 34.4 percent. If so, follow the logic for longer periods. After 20 years of 3 percent growth, the economy will be 80.6 percent bigger (because $(1.03)^{20} = 1.806$), not just 60 percent bigger. After 50 years, cumulative growth will be 338 percent, not 150 percent. And after a century, it will be 1,822 percent, not just 300 percent. Now we are talking about large discrepancies! No wonder Einstein once said, presumably in jest, that compounding was the most powerful force in the universe.

The arithmetic of growth leads to a convenient "doubling rule" that you can do in your head. If something (the money in a bank account, the GDP of a country, and so on) grows at an annual rate of g percent, how long will it take to double? The approximate answer is $70/g$, so the rule is often called "the Rule of 70." For example, at a 2 percent growth rate, something doubles in about $70/2 = 35$ years. At a 3 percent growth rate, doubling takes roughly $70/3 = 23.33$ years. Yes, small differences in growth rates can make a large difference.

British Empire. Meanwhile, somewhere across the Pacific was an inconsequential island nation called Japan. In 1870, Japan had only recently opened up to the West and was economically backward.

Now fast-forward more than a century. By 1979, the United States had become the world's preeminent economic power, Japan had emerged as the clear number two, and the United Kingdom had retreated into the second rank of nations. Obviously, the Japanese economy grew faster than the U.S. economy during this century, while the British economy grew more slowly, or else this stunning transformation of relative positions would not have occurred. But the magnitudes of the differences in growth rates may astound you.

Over the 109-year period, GDP per capita in the United States grew at a 2.3 percent compound annual rate while the United Kingdom's growth rate was 1.8 percent—a difference of merely 0.5 percent per annum, but compounded for more than a century. And what of Japan? What growth rate propelled it from obscurity into the front rank of nations? The answer is just 3.0 percent, a mere 0.7 percent per year faster than the United States. These numbers show vividly what a huge difference a 0.5 or 0.7 percentage point change in the growth rate makes, *if sustained for a long time.*

Economists define the *productivity* of a country's labor force (or **"labor productivity"**) as the amount of output a typical worker turns out in an hour of work. For example, if output is measured by GDP, productivity would be measured by GDP divided by the total number of hours of work. It is the growth rate of productivity that determines whether living standards will rise rapidly or slowly.

Labor productivity is the amount of output a worker turns out in an hour (or a week, or a year) of labor. If output is measured by GDP, it is GDP per hour of work.

PRODUCTIVITY GROWTH IS (ALMOST) EVERYTHING IN THE LONG RUN As we pointed out in our list of *Ideas for Beyond the Final Exam*, only rising productivity can raise standards of living in the long run. Over long periods of time, small differences in rates of productivity growth compound like interest in a bank account and can make an enormous difference to a society's prosperity. Nothing contributes more to material well-being, to the reduction of poverty, to increases in leisure time, and to a country's ability to finance education, public health, environmental improvement, and the arts than its productivity growth rate.

IDEAS FOR
BEYOND THE
FINAL EXAM

ISSUE: *Is Faster Growth Always Better?*

How fast should the U.S. economy, or any economy, grow? At first, the question may seem silly. Isn't it obvious that we should grow as fast as possible? After all, that will make us all richer. For the most part, economists agree; faster growth is generally preferred to slower growth. But as we shall see in a few pages, further thought suggests that the apparently naive question is not quite as silly as it sounds. Growth comes at a cost. So more may not always be better.

THE CAPACITY TO PRODUCE: POTENTIAL GDP AND THE PRODUCTION FUNCTION

Potential GDP is the real GDP that the economy would produce if its labor and other resources were fully employed.

The **labor force** is the number of people holding or seeking jobs.

Questions like how fast our economy can or should grow require quantitative answers. Economists have invented the concept of **potential GDP** to measure the economy's normal capacity to produce goods and services. Specifically, potential GDP is the real gross domestic product (GDP) an economy *could* produce if its **labor force** were fully employed.

Note the use of the word *normal* in describing capacity. Just as it is possible to push a factory beyond its normal operating rate (by, for example, adding a night shift), it is possible to push an economy beyond its normal full-employment level by working it very hard. For example, we observed in the last chapter that the unemployment rate dropped as low as 1.2 percent under abnormal conditions during World War II. So when we talk about employing the labor force fully, we do not mean a measured unemployment rate of zero.

Conceptually, we estimate potential GDP in two steps. First, we count up the available supplies of labor, capital, and other productive resources. Then we estimate how much *output* these *inputs* could produce if they were all fully utilized. This second step—the transformation of inputs into outputs—involves an assessment of the economy's *technology*. The more technologically advanced an economy, the more output it will be able to produce from any given bundle of inputs—as we emphasized in Chapter 3's discussion of the production possibilities frontier.

The economy's **production function** shows the volume of output that can be produced from given inputs (such as labor and capital), given the available technology.

To help us understand how technology affects the relationship between inputs and outputs, it is useful to introduce a tool called the **production function**—which is simply a mathematical or graphical depiction of the relationship between inputs and outputs. We will use a graph in our discussion.

For a given level of technology, Figure 1 shows how output (measured by real GDP on the vertical axis) depends on labor input (measured by hours of work on the horizontal axis). To read these graphs, and to relate them to the concept of potential GDP,

FIGURE 1

The Economy's
Production Function

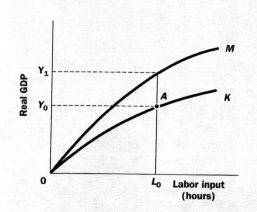

(a) Effect of better technology

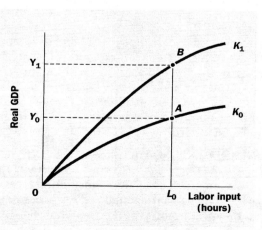

(b) Effect of more capital

SOURCE: Bureau of Labor Statistics. Data pertain to the nonfarm business sector.

begin with the black curve *OK* in Panel (a), which shows how GDP depends on labor input, *holding both capital and technology constant.* Naturally, output rises as labor inputs increase as we move outward along the curve *OK*, just as you would expect. If the country's labor force can supply L_0 hours of work when it is fully employed, then *potential GDP* is Y_0 (see point *A*). If the technology improves, the production function will shift upward—say, to the blue curve labeled *OM*—meaning that the *same* amount of labor input will now produce *more* output. The graph shows that potential GDP increases to Y_1.

Now what about capital? Panel (b) shows two production functions. The black curve OK_0 applies when the economy has some lower capital stock, K_0. The higher, blue curve OK_1 applies when the capital stock is some higher number, K_1. Thus, the production function tells us that potential GDP will be Y_0 if the capital stock is K_0 (see point *A*) but Y_1 if the capital stock is K_1 instead (see point *B*). Once again, this relationship is just what you expect: The economy can produce *more* output with the *same* amount of labor if workers have more capital to work with.

You can hardly avoid noticing the similarities between the two panels of Figure 1: Better technology, as in Panel (a), or more capital, as in Panel (b), affects the production function in more or less the same way. In general:

Either more capital or better technology will shift the production function upward and therefore raise potential GDP.

■ THE GROWTH RATE OF POTENTIAL GDP

With this new tool, it is but a short jump to potential growth rates. If the *size* of potential GDP depends on the size of the economy's labor force, the amount of capital and other resources it has, and its technology, it follows that the *growth rate* of potential GDP must depend on:

- The growth rate of the labor force
- The growth rate of the nation's capital stock
- The rate of technical progress

To sharpen the point, observe that real GDP is, by definition, the product of the total hours of work in the economy times the amount of output produced per hour—what we have just called *labor productivity:*

GDP = Hours of work × Output per hour = Hours of work × Labor productivity.

For example, in the United States today, using very rough numbers, GDP is about $12 trillion and total hours of work per year are about 240 billion. Thus labor productivity is roughly $12 trillion/240 billion hours = $50 per hour.

How fast can the economy increase its productive capacity? By transforming the preceding equation into growth rates, we have our answer: The growth rate of potential GDP is the *sum* of the growth rates of labor input (hours of work) and labor productivity:[1]

Growth rate of potential GDP = Growth rate of labor input + Growth rate of labor productivity

In the United States in recent decades, labor input has been increasing at a rate of about 1 percent per year. But labor productivity growth, which was very slow until the mid-1990s, has leaped upward since then—averaging about 3 percent per annum from 1995 to 2004 . Together, these two figures imply an estimated growth rate of potential GDP in the 4 percent range.

---

[1] You may be wondering about what happened to capital. The answer, as we have just seen in our discussion of the production function, is that one of the main determinants of potential GDP, and thus of labor productivity, is the amount of capital that each worker has to work with. Accordingly, the role of capital is incorporated into the productivity number.

TABLE 1
Recent Growth Rates of Real GDP in the United States

Years	Growth Rate per Year
1994–1996	3.1%
1996–1998	4.3
1998–2000	4.1
2000–2002	1.3
2002–2004	3.7
1994–2004	**3.3**

Do the growth rates of potential GDP and actual GDP match up? The answer is an important one to which we will return often in this book:

Over long periods of time, the growth rates of actual and potential GDP are normally quite similar. But the two often diverge sharply over short periods owing to cyclical fluctuations.

Table 1 illustrates this point with some recent U.S. data. Since 1994, GDP growth rates over two-year periods have ranged from as low as 1.3 percent per annum to as high as 4.3 percent. Over the entire ten-year period, GDP growth averaged 3.3 percent, which is probably a bit below current estimates of the growth rate of potential GDP.

The next chapter is devoted to studying the *determinants* of economic growth and some *policies* that might speed it up. But we already know from the production function that there are two basic ways to boost a nation's growth rate—other than faster population growth and simply working harder. One is accumulating more capital. Other things being equal, a nation that builds more capital for its future will grow faster. The other way is by improving technology. When technological breakthroughs are coming at a fast and furious pace, an economy will grow more rapidly. We will discuss both of these factors in detail in the next chapter. First, however, we need to address the more basic question posed earlier in this chapter.

? ISSUE REVISITED: *Is Faster Growth Always Better?*

It might seem that the answer to this question is obviously yes. After all, faster growth of either labor productivity or GDP per person is the route to higher living standards. But exceptions have been noted.

For openers, some social critics have questioned the desirability of faster economic growth as an end in itself, at least in the rich countries. Faster growth brings more wealth, and to most people the desirability of wealth is beyond question. "I've been rich and I've been poor. Believe me, honey, rich is better," singer Sophie Tucker once told an interviewer. And most people seem to share her sentiment. To those who hold this belief, a healthy economy is one that produces vast quantities of jeans, pizzas, cars, and computers.

Yet the desirability of further economic growth for a society that is already quite wealthy has been questioned on several grounds. Environmentalists worry that the sheer increase in the volume of goods imposes enormous costs on society in the form of pollution, crowding, and proliferation of wastes that need disposal. It has, they argue, dotted our roadsides with junkyards, filled our air with pollution, and poisoned our food with dangerous chemicals.

Some psychologists and social critics argue that the never-ending drive for more and better goods has failed to make people happier. Instead, industrial progress has transformed the satisfying and creative tasks of the artisan into the mechanical and dehumanizing routine of the assembly-line worker. In the United States, it seems to be driving people to work longer and longer hours. The question is whether the vast outpouring of material goods is worth all the stress and environmental damage. In fact, surveys of self-reported happiness show that residents of richer countries are no happier, on average, than residents of poorer countries.

But despite this, most economists continue to believe that more growth is better than less. For one thing, slower growth would make it extremely difficult to finance programs that improve the quality of life—including efforts to protect the environment. Such programs are costly, and economic growth makes the additional resources available. Second, it would be difficult to prevent further economic growth even if we were so inclined. Mandatory controls are abhorrent to most Americans; we cannot order people to stop being inventive and hard working. Third, slower economic growth would seriously hamper efforts to eliminate poverty—both within our own country and throughout the world. Much of the earth's population still lives in a state of extreme want. These unfortunate people are far less interested in clean air and fulfillment in the workplace than they are in more food, better clothing, and sturdier shelters.

All that said, economists concede that faster growth is not *always* better. One important reason will occupy our attention later in Parts VI and VII: An economy that grows too fast may generate inflation. Why? You were introduced to the answer at the end of the last chapter: Inflation rises when *aggregate demand* races ahead of *aggregate supply*. In plain English, an economy will become inflationary when people's demands for goods and services expand faster than its capacity to produce them. So we probably do not want to grow faster than the growth rate of potential GDP, at least not for long.

Should society then seek the maximum possible growth rate of *potential* GDP? Well, maybe not. After all, more rapid growth does not come for free. We have noted that building more capital is one good way to speed the growth of potential GDP. But the resources used to manufacture jet engines and computer servers could be used to make home air conditioners and video games instead. Building more capital imposes an obvious cost on a society: The citizens must consume less today. This point does not constitute a brief against investing for the future. Indeed, most economists believe we need to do more of that. But we must realize that faster growth through capital formation comes at a cost—an *opportunity cost*. Here, as elsewhere, you don't get something for nothing.

PART 2: THE GOAL OF LOW UNEMPLOYMENT

We noted earlier that actual GDP growth can differ sharply from potential GDP growth over periods as long as several years. These *macroeconomic fluctuations* have major implications for employment and unemployment. In particular:

> When the economy grows more *slowly* than its potential, it fails to generate enough new jobs for its ever-growing labor force. Hence, *the* unemployment rate *rises.* Conversely, GDP growth *faster* than the economy's potential leads to a *falling unemployment rate.*

The **unemployment rate** is the number of unemployed people, expressed as a percentage of the labor force.

High unemployment is socially wasteful. When the economy does not create enough jobs to employ everyone who is willing to work, a valuable resource is lost. Potential goods and services that might have been produced and enjoyed by consumers are lost forever. This lost output is the central economic cost of high unemployment, and we can measure it by comparing actual and potential GDP.

That cost is considerable. Table 2 summarizes the idleness of workers and machines, and the resulting loss of national output, for some of the years of lowest economic activity in recent decades. The second column lists the civilian unemployment rate, and thus measures unused labor resources. The third lists the percentage of industrial capacity that U.S. manufacturers were actually using, which indicates the extent to which plant and equipment went unused. The fourth column estimates the shortfall between potential and actual real GDP. We see that unemployment has cost the people of the United States as much as an 8.1 percent reduction in their real incomes.

Although Table 2 shows extreme examples, our inability to utilize all of the nation's available resources was a persistent economic problem for decades. The red line in Figure 2 shows actual real GDP in the United States from 1954 to 2004, while the black line shows potential GDP. The graph makes it clear that actual GDP has fallen short of potential GDP more often than it has exceeded it, especially during the 1973–1993 period. In fact:

> A conservative estimate of the cumulative gap between actual and potential GDP over the years 1974 to 1993 (all evaluated in 2000 prices) is roughly $1,750 billion. At 2005 levels, this loss in output as a result of unemployment would be over two months worth of production. And there is no way to redeem those losses. The labor wasted in 1992 cannot be utilized in 2005.

TABLE 2

The Economic Costs of High Unemployment

Year	Civilian Unemployment Rate	Capacity Utilization Rate	Real GDP Lost Due to Idle Resources
1958	6.8%	75.0%	4.8%
1961	6.7	77.3	4.1
1975	8.5	73.4	5.4
1982	9.7	71.3	8.1
1992	7.5	79.4	2.6
2003	6.0	73.4	2.2

SOURCES: Bureau of Labor Statistics, Federal Reserve System, and Congressional Budget Office.

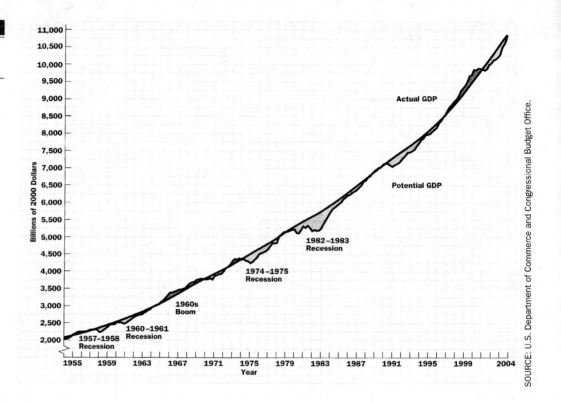

FIGURE 2

Actual and Potential GDP in the United States since 1954

SOURCE: U.S. Department of Commerce and Congressional Budget Office.

THE HUMAN COSTS OF HIGH UNEMPLOYMENT

If these numbers seem a bit dry and abstract, think about the human costs of being unemployed. Years ago, job loss meant not only enforced idleness and a catastrophic drop in income, it often led to hunger, cold, ill health, even death. Here is how one unemployed worker during the Great Depression described his family's plight in a mournful letter to the governor of Pennsylvania:

> I have been out of work for over a year and a half. Am back almost thirteen months and the landlord says if I don't pay up before the 1 of 1932 out I must go, and where am I to go in the cold winter with my children? If you can help me please for God's sake and the children's sakes and like please do what you can and send me some help, will you, I cannot find any work. . . . Thanksgiving dinner was black coffee and bread and was very glad to get it. My wife is in the hospital now. We have no shoes to were [sic]; no clothes hardly. Oh what will I do I sure will thank you.[2]

Nowadays, unemployment does not hold quite such terrors for most families, although its consequences remain dire enough. Our system of unemployment insurance (discussed later in this chapter) has taken part of the sting out of unemployment, as have other social welfare programs that support the incomes of the poor. Yet most families that still suffer painful losses of income and, often, severe noneconomic consequences when a breadwinner becomes unemployed.

Even families that are well protected by unemployment compensation suffer when joblessness strikes. Ours is a work-oriented society. A man's place has always been in the office or shop, and lately this has become true for women as well. A worker forced into idleness by a recession endures a psychological cost that is no less real for our inability to measure it. Martin Luther King Jr. put it graphically: "In our society, it is

---

[2] From *Brother, Can You Spare a Dime? The Great Depression 1929–1933*, by Milton Meltzer, p. 103. Copyright 1969 by Milton Meltzer. Reprinted by permission of Alfred A. Knopf, Inc.

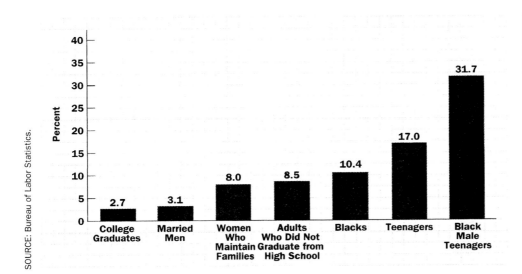

SOURCE: Bureau of Labor Statistics.

FIGURE 3

Unemployment Rates
for Selected Groups,
2004

murder, psychologically, to deprive a man of a job. . . . You are in substance saying to that man that he has no right to exist."[3] High unemployment has been linked to psychological and physical disorders, divorces, suicides, and crime.

It is important to realize that these costs, whether large or small in total, are distributed most unevenly across the population. In 2004, for example, the unemployment rate among all workers averaged 5.5 percent. But, as Figure 3 shows, 10.4 percent of black workers were unemployed, as were 8 percent of women who maintained families. For teenagers, the situation was worse still, with unemployment at 17 percent, and that of black male teenagers 31.7 percent. College graduates had the lowest rate—2.7 percent. Overall unemployment varies from year to year, but these relationships are typical:

> In good times and bad, married men suffer the least unemployment and teenagers suffer the most; nonwhites are unemployed much more often than whites; blue-collar workers have above-average rates of unemployment; well-educated people have below-average unemployment rates.[4]

It is worth noting that unemployment in the United States has been much lower than in most other industrialized countries in recent years. For example, during 2003, when the U.S. unemployment rate averaged 6.0 percent, the comparable figures were 6.9 percent in Canada, 9.3 percent in France, 8.8 percent in Italy, and 9.7 percent in Germany.[5]

■ COUNTING THE UNEMPLOYED: THE OFFICIAL STATISTICS

We have been using unemployment figures without considering where they come from or how accurate they are. The basic data come from a monthly survey of about 60,000 households conducted for the U.S. Bureau of Labor Statistics. The census taker asks several questions about the employment status of each member of the household and, on the basis of the answers, classifies each person as *employed, unemployed,* or *not in the labor force.*

The Employed   The first category is the simplest to define. It includes everyone currently at work, including part-time workers. Although some part-timers work less

[3] Quoted in Coretta Scott King (ed.), *The Words of Martin Luther King* (New York: Newmarket Press; 1983), p. 45.

[4] Unemployment rates for men and women are about equal.

[5] The numbers for foreign countries are based (approximately) on U.S. unemployment concepts.

than a full week by choice, others do so only because they cannot find suitable full-time jobs. Nevertheless, these workers are counted as employed, even though many would consider them "underemployed."

The Unemployed   The second category is a bit trickier. For persons not currently working, the survey first determines whether they are temporarily laid off from a job to which they expect to return. If so, they are counted as unemployed. The remaining workers are asked whether they actively sought work during the previous four weeks. If they did, they are also counted as unemployed.

Out of the Labor Force   But if they failed to look for a job, they are classified as *out of the labor force* rather than unemployed. This seems a reasonable way to draw the distinction—after all, not *everyone* wants to work. Yet there is a problem: Research shows that many unemployed workers give up looking for jobs after a while. These so-called **discouraged workers** are victims of poor job prospects, just like the officially unemployed. But when they give up hope, the measured unemployment rate—which is the ratio of the number of unemployed people to the total labor force—actually declines.

Involuntary part-time work, loss of overtime or shortened work hours, and discouraged workers are all examples of "hidden" or "disguised" unemployment. People concerned about such phenomena argue that we should include them in the official unemployment rate because, if we do not, the magnitude of the problem will be underestimated. Others, however, argue that measured unemployment overestimates the problem because, to count as unemployed, potential workers need only *claim* to be looking for jobs, even if they are not really interested in finding them.

Sticking with the official data, Figure 4 displays an interesting recent development. After climbing for about twenty-five years, the percentage of the American population at work has declined sharply since 2000. The reasons include both rising unemployment and more discouraged workers. Figure 4 goes a long way toward explaining why Americans were so unhappy with the state of the job market in 2003 and 2004.

> A **discouraged worker** is an unemployed person who gives up looking for work and is therefore no longer counted as part of the labor force.

■ TYPES OF UNEMPLOYMENT

Providing jobs for those willing to work is one principal goal of macroeconomic policy. How are we to define this goal?

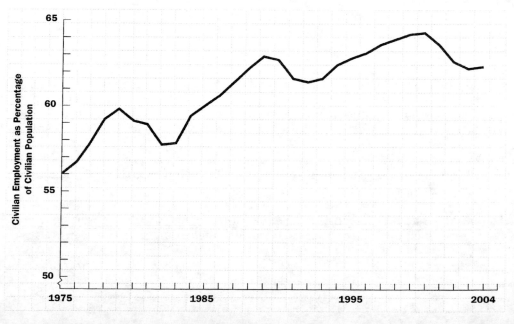

FIGURE 4

Civilian Employment as a Percentage of Civilian Population, 1975–2004.

SOURCE: Bureau of Labor Statistics

POLICY DEBATE

Does the Minimum Wage Cause Unemployment?

ementary economic reasoning— ummarized in the simple supply-de- and diagram to the right—suggests hat setting a minimum wage (*W* in he graph) above the free-market age (*w* in the graph) must cause nemployment. In the graph, unem- loyment is the horizontal gap be- ween the quantity of labor supplied oint *B*) and the quantity demanded oint *A*) at the minimum wage. ndeed, the conclusion seems so lementary that generations of conomists took it for granted. The rgument seems compelling. Indeed, arlier editions of this book, for ex- mple, confidently told students that higher minimum wage must lead o higher unemployment.

But some surprising economic re- earch published in the 1990s cast serious doubt on this conven- ional wisdom.* For example, economists David Card and Alan rueger compared employment changes at fast-food restaurants in Jew Jersey and nearby Pennsylvania after New Jersey, but not ennsylvania, raised its minimum wage in 1992. To their surprise, he New Jersey stores did *more* net hiring than their Pennsylvania ounterparts. Similar results were found for fast-food stores in exas after the federal minimum wage was raised in 1991, and in

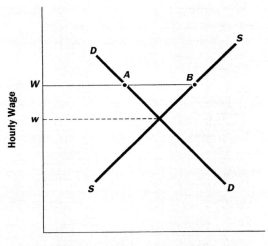

Number of Workers

California after the statewide mini- mum wage was increased in 1988. In none of these cases did a higher minimum wage seem to reduce em- ployment—in contrast to the impli- cations of simple economic theory.

The research of Card and Krueger, and of others who reached similar conclusions, was controversial from the start, and remains so. Thus, a policy question that had been deemed closed now seems to be open: Does the minimum wage re- ally cause unemployment?

Resolution of this debate is of more than academic interest. In 1996, President Clinton recom- mended and Congress passed an in- crease in the federal minimum wage—justifying its action, in part, by the new research suggesting that unemployment would not rise as a result. In the 2004 presidential campaign, Senator Kerry advo- cated another increase in the minimum wage, a policy that Presi- dent Bush opposed. Research can have consequences.

*See David Card and Alan Krueger, *Myth and Measurement: The New Economics of the Minimum Wage* (Princeton, N.J.: Princeton University Press; 1995).

We have already noted that a zero measured unemployment rate would clearly be an *incorrect* answer. Ours is a dynamic, highly mobile economy. Households move from one state to another. Individuals quit jobs to seek better positions or retool for more attractive occupations. These and other decisions produce some minimal amount of unemployment—people who are literally between jobs. Economists call this **frictional unemployment**, and it is unavoidable in our market economy. The critical distinguishing feature of frictional unemployment is that it is short-lived. A frictionally unemployed person has every reason to expect to find a new job soon.

A second type of unemployment can be difficult to distinguish from frictional un- employment but has very different implications. **Structural unemployment** arises when jobs are eliminated by changes in the economy, such as automation or perma- nent changes in demand. The crucial difference between frictional and structural un- employment is that, unlike frictionally unemployed workers, structurally unemployed workers cannot realistically be considered "between jobs." Instead, their skills and ex- perience may be unmarketable in the changing economy in which they live. They are thus faced with either prolonged periods of unemployment or the necessity of mak- ing major changes in their skills or occupations.

The remaining type of unemployment, **cyclical unemployment,** will occupy most of our attention. Cyclical unemployment rises when the level of economic activity de- clines, as it does in a recession. Thus, when macroeconomists speak of maintaining "full employment," they mean limiting unemployment to its frictional and structural components—which means, roughly, producing at potential GDP. A key question, therefore, is: How much measured unemployment constitutes full employment?

Frictional unemploy- ment is unemployment that is due to normal turnover in the labor market. It includes people who are temporarily between jobs because they are moving or changing oc- cupations, or are unem- ployed for similar reasons.

Structural unemploy- ment refers to workers who have lost their jobs because they have been displaced by automation, because their skills are no longer in de- mand, or because of similar reasons.

Cyclical unemployment is the portion of unemploy- ment that is attributable to a decline in the economy's total production. Cyclical unemployment rises during recessions and falls as pros- perity is restored.

■ HOW MUCH EMPLOYMENT IS "FULL EMPLOYMENT"?

Full employment is a situation in which everyone who is willing and able to work can find a job. At full employment, the measured unemployment rate is still positive.

President John F. Kennedy was the first to commit the federal government to a specific numerical goal for unemployment. He picked a 4 percent target, but that goal was subsequently rejected as being unrealistically ambitious. When the government abandoned the 4 percent unemployment target in the 1970s, no new number was put in its place. Instead, we have experienced a long-running national debate over exactly how much measured unemployment corresponds to **full employment**—a debate that continues to this day.

In the early 1990s, many economists believed that full employment came at a measured unemployment rate as high as 6 percent. But others disputed that estimate as unduly pessimistic. As it happened, real-world events decisively rejected the notion that the full-employment unemployment rate was 6 percent. The boom of the late 1990s pushed the unemployment rate below 5 percent by the summer of 1997, and it remained there every month until September 2001—even falling as low as 3.9 percent in 2000. All this left economists guessing where full employment might be. Official government reports issued early in 2005 estimated the full-employment unemployment rate to be slightly above 5 percent, but no one was totally confident in such estimates.

■ UNEMPLOYMENT INSURANCE: THE INVALUABLE CUSHION

Unemployment insurance is a government program that replaces some of the wages lost by eligible workers who lose their jobs.

One major reason why America's unemployed workers no longer experience the complete loss of income that devastated so many during the 1930s is our system of **unemployment insurance**—one of the most valuable institutional innovations to emerge from the trauma of the Great Depression.

Each of the fifty states administers an unemployment insurance program under federal guidelines. Although the precise amounts vary, the average weekly benefit check in 2004 was about $262, which amounted to approximately 50 percent of average earnings. Although a 50 percent drop in earnings still poses serious problems, the importance of this 50 percent income cushion can scarcely be exaggerated, especially because it may be supplemented by funds from other welfare programs. Families that are covered by unemployment insurance rarely go hungry or are dispossessed from their homes when they lose their jobs.

Eligibility for benefits varies by state, but some criteria apply quite generally. Only experienced workers qualify, so persons just joining the labor force (such as recent college graduates) or reentering after prolonged absences (such as women returning to the job market after years of child rearing) cannot collect benefits. Neither can those who quit their jobs, except under unusual circumstances. Also, benefits end after a stipulated period of time, normally six months. For all of these reasons, only some 37 percent of the roughly 8.1 million people who were unemployed in an average week in 2004 actually received benefits.

The importance of unemployment insurance to the unemployed is obvious. But significant benefits also accrue to citizens who never become unemployed. During recessions, billions of dollars are paid out in unemployment benefits. And because recipients probably spend most of their benefits, unemployment insurance limits the severity of recessions by providing additional purchasing power when and where it is most needed.

The unemployment insurance system is one of several cushions built into our economy since 1933 to prevent another Great Depression. By giving money to those who become unemployed, the system helps prop up aggregate demand during recessions.

Although the U.S. economy is now probably "depression-proof," this should not be a cause for too much rejoicing, for the many recessions we have had since the 1950s—most recently in 2001—amply demonstrate that we are far from "recession-proof."

The fact that unemployment insurance and other social welfare programs replace a significant fraction of lost income has led some skeptics to claim that unemployment is no longer a serious problem. But the fact is that unemployment insurance is just what the name says—an *insurance* program. And insurance can never prevent a catastrophe from occurring; it simply spreads the costs among many people instead of letting all of the costs fall on the shoulders of a few unfortunate souls. As we noted earlier, unemployment robs the economy of output it could have produced, and no insurance policy can insure society against such losses.

Our system of payroll taxes and unemployment benefits spreads the costs of unemployment over the entire population. But it does not eliminate the basic economic cost.

In that case, you might ask, why not cushion the blow even more by making unemployment insurance much more generous, as many European countries have done? The answer is that there is also a downside to unemployment insurance. When unemployment benefits are very generous, people who lose their jobs may be less than eager to look for new jobs. The right level of unemployment insurance strikes an appropriate balance between the benefit of supporting the incomes of unemployed people and the cost of raising the unemployment rate a bit.

▦ PART 3: THE GOAL OF LOW INFLATION

Both the human and economic costs of inflation are less obvious than the costs of unemployment. But this does not make them any less real, for if one thing is crystal clear about inflation, it is that people do not like it.

With inflation very low for years now, inflation barely registers as a problem in national public opinion polls. But when inflation was high, it often headed the list—generally even ahead of unemployment. Surveys also show that inflation, like unemployment, makes people unhappy. Finally, studies of elections suggest that voters penalize the party that occupies the White House when inflation is high. The fact is beyond dispute: People dislike inflation. The question is, why?

The **purchasing power** of a given sum of money is the volume of goods and services that it will buy.

■ INFLATION: THE MYTH AND THE REALITY

At first, the question may seem ridiculous. During inflationary times, people pay higher prices for the same quantities of goods and services they had before. So more and more income is needed just to maintain the same standard of living. Is it not obvious that this erosion of **purchasing power**—that is, the decline in what money will buy—makes everyone worse off?

▦ Inflation and Real Wages

This would indeed be the case were it not for one very significant fact. The wages that people earn are also prices—prices for labor services. During a period of inflation, wages also rise. In fact, the average wage typically rises more or less in step with prices. Thus, contrary to popular myth, workers as a group are not usually victimized by inflation.

The purchasing power of wages—what is called the real wage rate—is not systematically eroded by inflation. Sometimes wages rise faster than prices, and sometimes prices rise faster than wages. In the long run, wages tend to outstrip prices as new capital equipment and innovation increase output per worker.

Figure 5 illustrates this simple fact. The blue line shows the rate of increase of prices in the United States for each year since 1948, and the black line shows the rate of increase of wages. The difference between the two, shaded in red in the diagram, indicates the rate of growth of *real* wages. Generally, wages rise faster than prices,

SOURCE: The *Wall Street Journal*—Permission, Cartoon Features Syndicate.

"Sure, you're raising my allowance. But am I actually gaining any purchasing power?"

The **real wage rate** is the wage rate adjusted for inflation. Specifically, it is the nominal wage divided by the price index. The real wage thus indicates the volume of goods and services that the nominal wages will buy.

Calculating the Real Wage: A Real Example

The *real* wage shows not how many dollars a worker is paid for an hour of work (that is called the *nominal* wage), but rather the *purchasing power* of that money. It indicates what an hour's worth of work can buy. As noted in the definition of the real wage in the margin, we calculate the real wage by *dividing* the nominal wage by the price level. The rule is:

$$\text{Real wage} = \frac{\text{Nominal wage}}{\text{Price level}}$$

Here's a concrete example. Between 1998 and 2003, the average hourly wage in the United States rose from $13 to $15.35, an increase of 18 percent over five years. Sounds pretty good for American workers. But over those same five years, the Consumer Price Index (CPI), the most commonly-used index of the price level, rose by almost 13 percent, from 163 to 184. This means that the real wages in the two years were:

$$\text{Real wage in 1998} = \frac{\$13.00}{163} = .0798$$

$$\text{Real wage in 1998} = \frac{\$15.35}{184} = .0834$$

for an increase of just 4.5 percent over the five years, which is much less than 13 percent.[6]

FIGURE 5

Rates of Change of Wages and Prices in the United States since 1948

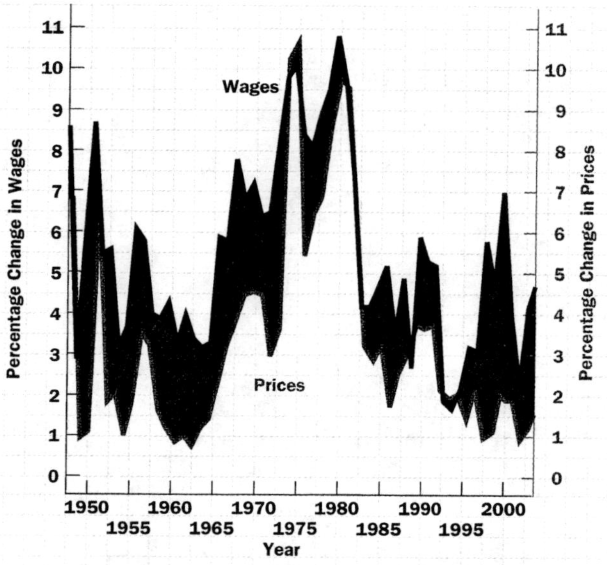

SOURCE: Bureau of Labor Statistics. Data pertain to nonfarm business sector.

reflecting the steady advance of labor productivity; therefore, real wages rise. But this is not always the case; the graph shows several instances in which inflation outstripped wage increases.

The feature of Figure 5 that virtually jumps off the page is the way the two lines dance together. Wages normally rise rapidly when prices rise rapidly, and they rise slowly when prices rise slowly. But you should not draw any hasty conclusions from this association. It does not, for example, imply that rising prices *cause* rising wages or that rising wages *cause* rising prices. Remember the warnings given in Chapter 1 about trying to infer causation just by looking at data. But analyzing cause and effect is not our purpose right now. We merely want to dispel the myth that inflation inevitably erodes real wages.

Why is this myth so widespread? Imagine a world without inflation in which wages are rising 2 percent per year because of the increasing productivity of labor. Now imagine that, all of a sudden, inflation sets in and prices start rising 3 percent per year but nothing else changes. Figure 5 suggests that, with perhaps a small delay, wage increases will accelerate to 2 + 3 = 5 percent per year.

Will workers view this change with equanimity? Probably not. To each worker, the 5 percent wage increase will be seen as something he earned by the sweat of his brow. In his view, he *deserves* every penny of his 5 percent raise. In a sense, he is right because "the sweat of his brow" earned him a 2 percent increment in real wages that, when the inflation rate is 3 percent, can be achieved only by increasing his money wages by 5 percent. An economist would divide the wage increase in the following way:

Reason for Wages to Increase	Amount
Higher productivity	2%
Compensation for higher prices	3%
Total	5%

---

[6] As explained in the appendix, it is conventional to multiply index numbers by 100, which would make the two real wage numbers 7.98 and 8.34, respectively. That does not alter the percentage change.

But the worker will probably keep score differently. Feeling that he earned the entire 5 percent raise by his own merits, he will view inflation as having "robbed" him of three fifths of his just deserts. The higher the rate of inflation, the more of his raise the worker will feel has been stolen from him.

Of course, nothing could be farther from the truth. Basically, the economic system rewards the worker with *the same 2 percent real wage increment for higher productivity, regardless of the rate of inflation.* The "evils of inflation" are often exaggerated because people fail to understand this point.

The Importance of Relative Prices

A related misperception results from failure to distinguish between a *rise in the general price level* and a change in **relative prices,** which is a rise in one price relative to another. To see the distinction most clearly, imagine first a *pure inflation* in which *every* price rises by 10 percent during the year, so that relative prices do not change. Table 3 gives an example in which the price of movie tickets increases from $6.00 to $6.60, the price of candy bars from 50 cents to 55 cents, and the price of automobiles from $9,000 to $9,900. After the inflation, just as before, it will still take 12 candy bars to buy a movie ticket, 1,500 movie tickets to buy a car, and so on. A person who manufactures candy bars in order to purchase movie tickets is neither helped nor harmed by the inflation. Neither is a car dealer with a sweet tooth.

> An item's **relative price** is its price in terms of some other item rather than in terms of dollars.

But real inflations are not like this. When there is 10 percent general inflation—meaning that the "average price" rises by 10 percent—some prices may jump 20 percent or more while others actually fall.[7] Suppose that, instead of the price increases shown in Table 3, prices rise as shown in Table 4. Movie prices go up by 25 percent, but candy prices do not change. Surely, candy manufacturers who love movies will be disgruntled because it now costs 15 candy bars instead of 12 to get into the theater. They will blame inflation for raising the price of movie tickets, even though their real problem stems from the *increase in the price of movies relative to candy.* (They would have been hurt as much if movie tickets had remained at $6 while the price of candy fell to 40 cents.)

Because car prices have risen by only 5 percent, theater owners in need of new cars will be delighted by the fact that an auto now costs only 1,260 movie admissions—just as they would have cheered if car prices had fallen to $7,560 while movie tickets remained at $6. However, they are unlikely to attribute their good fortune to inflation. Indeed, they should not. What has actually happened is that *cars became cheaper relative to movies.*

Because real-world inflations proceed at uneven rates, relative prices are always changing. There are gainers and losers, just as some would gain and others lose if relative prices were to change without any general inflation. Inflation, however, gets a bad name because losers often blame inflation for their misfortune, whereas gainers rarely credit inflation for their good luck.

TABLE 3			
Pure Inflation			
Item	Last Year's Price	This Year's Price	Increase
Candy bar	$0.50	$0.55	10%
Movie ticket	6.00	6.60	10
Automobile	9,000	9,900	10

TABLE 4			
Real-World Inflation			
Item	Last Year's Price	This Year's Price	Increase
Candy bar	$0.50	$0.50	0%
Movie ticket	6.00	7.50	25
Automobile	9,000	9,450	5

Inflation is not usually to blame when some goods become more expensive relative to others.

These two kinds of misconceptions help explain why respondents to public opinion polls often cite inflation as a major national issue, why higher inflation rates depress consumers, and why voters express their ire at the polls when inflation is high. But not all of the costs of inflation are mythical. Let us now turn to some of the real costs.

---

[7] How statisticians figure out "average" price increases is discussed in the appendix to this chapter.

INFLATION AS A REDISTRIBUTOR OF INCOME AND WEALTH

We have just seen that the *average* person is neither helped nor harmed by inflation. But almost no one is exactly average! Some people gain from inflation and others lose. For example, senior citizens trying to scrape by on pensions or other fixed incomes suffer badly from inflation. Because they earn no wages, it is little solace to them that wages keep pace with prices. Their pension incomes do not.[8]

This example illustrates a general problem. Think of pensioners as people who "lend" money to an organization (the pension fund) when they are young, expecting to be paid back with interest when they are old. Because of the rise in the price level during the intervening years, the unfortunate pensioners get back dollars that are worth less in purchasing power than those they originally loaned. In general:

Those who lend money are often victimized by inflation.

Although lenders may lose heavily, borrowers may do quite well. For example, homeowners who borrowed money from banks in the form of mortgages back in the 1950s, when interest rates were 3 or 4 percent, gained enormously from the surprisingly virulent inflation of the 1970s. They paid back dollars of much lower purchasing power than those that they borrowed. The same is true of other borrowers.

Borrowers often gain from inflation.

Because the redistribution caused by inflation generally benefits borrowers at the expense of lenders,[9] and because both lenders and borrowers can be found at every income level, we conclude that:

Inflation does not systematically steal from the rich to aid the poor, nor does it always do the reverse.

Why, then, is the redistribution caused by inflation so widely condemned? Because its victims are selected capriciously. No one legislates the redistribution. No one enters into it voluntarily. The gainers do not earn their spoils, and the losers do not deserve their fate. Moreover, inflation robs particular classes of people of purchasing power year after year—people living on private pensions, families who save money and "lend" it to banks, and workers whose wages and salaries do not adjust to higher prices. Even if the average person suffers no damage from inflation, that fact offers little consolation to those who are its victims. This is one fundamental indictment of inflation.

Inflation redistributes income in an arbitrary way. Society's income distribution should reflect the interplay of the operation of free markets and the purposeful efforts of government to alter that distribution. Inflation interferes with and distorts this process.

REAL VERSUS NOMINAL INTEREST RATES

But wait. Must inflation always rob lenders to bestow gifts upon borrowers? If both parties see inflation coming, won't lenders demand that borrowers pay a higher interest rate as compensation for the coming inflation? Indeed they will. For this reason, economists draw a sharp distinction between *expected* inflation and *unexpected* inflation.

What happens when inflation is fully expected by both parties? Suppose Diamond Jim wants to borrow $1,000 from Scrooge for one year, and both agree that, in the absence of inflation, a fair rate of interest would be 3 percent. This means that Diamond Jim would pay back $1,030 at the end of the year for the privilege of having $1,000 now.

If both men expect prices to increase by 6 percent, Scrooge may reason as follows: "If Diamond Jim pays me back $1,030 one year from today, that money will buy less

[8] The same is not true of Social Security benefits, which are automatically increased to compensate recipients for changes in the price level.
[9] By the same token, *deflation* generally benefits lenders at the expense of borrowers, because the borrowers must pay back money of greater purchasing power.

than what $1,000 buys today. Thus, I'll really be *paying him* to borrow from me! I'm no philanthropist. Why don't I charge him 9 percent instead? Then he'll pay back $1,090 at the end of the year. With prices 6 percent higher, this will buy roughly what $1,030 is worth today. So I'll get the same 3 percent increase in purchasing power that we would have agreed on in the absence of inflation and won't be any worse off. That's the least I'll accept."

Diamond Jim may follow a similar chain of logic. "With no inflation, I was willing to pay $1,030 one year from now for the privilege of having $1,000 today, and Scrooge was willing to lend it. He'd be crazy to do the same with 6 percent inflation. He'll want to charge me more. How much should I pay? If I offer him $1,090 one year from now, that will have roughly the same purchasing power as $1,030 today, so I won't be any worse off. That's the most I'll pay."

This kind of thinking may lead Scrooge and Diamond Jim to write a contract with a 9 percent interest rate—3 percent as the increase in purchasing power that Diamond Jim pays to Scrooge and 6 percent as compensation for expected inflation. Then, if the expected 6 percent inflation actually materializes, neither party will be made better or worse off by inflation.

This example illustrates a general principle. The 3 percent increase in purchasing power that Diamond Jim agrees to turn over to Scrooge is called the **real rate of interest.** The 9 percent contractual interest charge that Diamond Jim and Scrooge write into the loan agreement is called the **nominal rate of interest.** The nominal rate of interest is calculated by adding the *expected rate of inflation* to the real rate of interest. The general relationship is:

> **Nominal interest rate = Real interest rate + Expected inflation rate**

Expected inflation is added to compensate the lender for the loss of purchasing power that the lender expects to suffer as a result of inflation. Because of this:

> Inflation that is accurately predicted need not redistribute income between borrowers and lenders. If the *expected* rate of inflation that is embodied in the nominal interest rate matches the *actual* rate of inflation, no one gains and no one loses. However, to the extent that expectations prove incorrect, inflation will still redistribute income.[10]

It need hardly be pointed out that errors in predicting the rate of inflation are the norm, not the exception. Published forecasts bear witness to the fact that economists have great difficulty in predicting the rate of inflation. The task is no easier for businesses, consumers, and banks. This is another reason why inflation is so widely condemned as unfair and undesirable. It sets up a guessing game that no one likes.

> The **real rate of interest** is the percentage increase in purchasing power that the borrower pays to the lender for the privilege of borrowing. It indicates the increased ability to purchase goods and services that the lender earns.

> The **nominal rate of interest** is the percentage by which the money the borrower pays back exceeds the money that she borrowed, making no adjustment for any decline in the purchasing power of this money that results from inflation.

■ INFLATION DISTORTS MEASUREMENTS

So inflation imposes costs on society because it is difficult to predict. But other costs arise even when inflation is predicted accurately. Many such costs stem from the fact that people are simply unaccustomed to thinking in inflation-adjusted terms and so make errors in thinking and calculation. Many laws and regulations that were designed for an inflation-free economy malfunction when inflation is high. Here are some important examples.

▨ Confusing Real and Nominal Interest Rates

People frequently confuse *real* and *nominal* interest rates. For example, most Americans viewed the 12 percent mortgage interest rates that banks charged in 1980 as scandalously high but saw the 6 percent mortgage rates of 2004 as great bargains. In truth, with inflation around 2 percent in 2004 and 10 percent in 1980, the real interest rate in 2004 (about 4 percent) was above the bargain-basement real rates in 1980 (about 2 percent).

---

[10] *Exercise:* Who gains and who loses if the inflation turns out to be only 4 percent instead of the 6 percent that Scrooge and Diamond Jim expected? What if the inflation rate is 8 percent?

The Malfunctioning Tax System

The tax system is probably the most important example of inflation illusion at work. The law does not recognize the distinction between nominal and real interest rates; it simply taxes *nominal* interest regardless of how much real interest it represents. Similarly, **capital gains**—the difference between the price at which an investor sells an asset and the price that she paid for it—are taxed in nominal, not real, terms. As a result, our tax system can do strange things when inflation is high. An example will show why.

A **capital gain** is the difference between the price at which an asset is sold and the price at which it was bought.

Between 1981 and 2003, the price level roughly doubled. Consider some stock that was purchased for $20,000 in 1981 and sold for $35,000 in 2003. The investor actually *lost* purchasing power while holding the stock because $20,000 of 1981 money could buy roughly what $40,000 could buy in 2003. Yet because the law levies taxes on nominal capital gains, with no correction for inflation, the investor would have been taxed on the $15,000 *nominal* capital gain—even though she suffered a *real* capital loss of $5,000.

Many economists have proposed that this (presumably unintended) feature of the law be changed by taxing only real capital gains, that is, capital gains in excess of inflation. To date, Congress has not agreed. This little example illustrates a pervasive and serious problem:

> Because it fails to recognize the distinction between nominal and real capital gains, or between nominal and real interest rates, our tax system levies high, and presumably unintended, tax rates on capital income when there is high inflation. Thus the laws that govern our financial system can become counterproductive in an inflationary environment, causing problems that were never intended by legislators. Some economists feel that the high tax rates caused by inflation discourage saving, lending, and investing—and therefore retard economic growth.

Thus, failure to understand that high *nominal* interest rates can still be low *real* interest rates has been known to make the tax code misfire, to impoverish savers, and to inhibit borrowing and lending. And it is important to note that *these costs of inflation are not purely redistributive.* Society as a whole loses when mutually beneficial transactions are prohibited by dysfunctional legislation.

Why, then, do such harmful laws stay on the books? The main reason appears to be a lack of understanding of the difference between real and nominal interest rates. People fail to understand that it is normally the *real* rate of interest that matters in an economic transaction because only that rate reveals how much borrowers pay and lenders receive *in terms of the goods and services that money can buy.* They focus on the high *nominal* interest rates caused by inflation, even when these rates correspond to low real interest rates.

> The difference between real and nominal interest rates, and the fact that the real rate matters economically whereas the nominal rate is often politically significant, are matters that are of the utmost importance and yet are understood by very few people—including many who make public policy decisions.

OTHER COSTS OF INFLATION

Another cost of inflation is that rapidly changing prices make it risky to enter into long-term contracts. In an extremely severe inflation, the "long term" may be only a few days from now. But even moderate inflations can have remarkable effects on long-term loans. Suppose a corporation wants to borrow $1 million to finance the purchase of some new equipment and needs the loan for 20 years. If inflation averages 2 percent over this period, the $1 million it repays at the end of 20 years will be worth $672,971 in today's purchasing power. But if inflation averages 5 percent instead, it will be worth only $376,889.

Lending or borrowing for this long a period is obviously a big gamble. With the stakes so high, the outcome may be that neither lenders nor borrowers want to get involved in long-term contracts. But without long-term loans, business investment may become impossible. The economy may stagnate.

Inflation also makes life difficult for the shopper. You probably have a group of stores that you habitually patronize because they carry the items you want to buy at (roughly) the prices you want to pay. This knowledge saves you a great deal of time and energy. But when prices are changing rapidly, your list quickly becomes obsolete. You return to your favorite clothing store to find that the price of jeans has risen drastically. Should you buy? Should you shop around at other stores? Will they have also raised their prices? Business firms have precisely the same problem with their suppliers. Rising prices force them to shop around more, which imposes costs on the firms and, more generally, reduces the efficiency of the entire economy.

■ THE COSTS OF LOW VERSUS HIGH INFLATION

The preceding litany of the costs of inflation alerts us to one very important fact: *Predictable inflation is far less burdensome than unpredictable inflation.* When is inflation most predictable? When it proceeds year after year at a modest and more or less steady rate. Thus, the *variability of the inflation rate* is a crucial factor. Inflation of 3 percent per year for three consecutive years will exact lower social costs than inflation that is 2 percent in the first year, zero in the second year, and 7 percent in the third year. In general:

> Steady inflation is more predictable than variable inflation and therefore has smaller social and economic costs.

But the *average level of inflation* also matters. Partly because of the inflation illusions mentioned earlier and partly because of the more rapid breakdown in normal customer relationships that we have just mentioned, steady inflation at 6 percent per year is more damaging than steady inflation at 3 percent per year.

Economists distinguish between *low inflation*, which is a modest economic problem, and *high inflation*, which can be a devastating one, partly on the basis of the average level of inflation and partly on its variability. If inflation remains steady and low, prices may rise for a long time, but at a moderate and fairly constant pace, allowing people to adapt. For example, inflation in the United States has been remarkably steady since 1991, never dropping below 1.6 percent nor rising above 3.4 percent.

Very high inflations typically last for short periods of time and are often marked by highly variable inflation rates from month to month or year to year. In recent decades, for example, countries ranging from Argentina to Israel to Russia have experienced bouts of inflation exceeding 100 percent or even 1,000 percent per year. (See "Hyperinflation and the Piggy Bank" on the next page.) Each of these episodes severely disrupted the affected country's economy.

The German hyperinflation after World War I is perhaps the most famous episode of runaway inflation. Between December 1922 and November 1923, when a hard-nosed reform program finally broke the spiral, wholesale prices in Germany increased by almost 100 million percent! But even this experience was dwarfed by the great Hungarian inflation of 1945–1946, the greatest inflation of them all. For a period of one year, the *monthly* rate of inflation averaged about 20,000 percent. In the final month, the price level skyrocketed 42 quadrillion percent!

If you review the costs of inflation that have been discussed in this chapter, you will see why the distinction between low and high inflation is so fundamental. Many economists think we can live rather nicely in an environment of steady, low inflation. No one believes we can survive very well under extremely high inflation.

When inflation is steady and low, the rate at which prices rise is relatively easy to predict. It can therefore be taken into account in setting interest rates. Under high

Hyperinflation and the Piggy Bank

Whereas mild inflations are barely notice-able in everyday life, hyperinflation makes all sorts of normal economic activities more difficult and transforms a society in strange and unexpected ways. This article, excerpted from the *New York Times,* illustrates some of the problems that hyperinflation created for Nicaraguans in 1989.

For generations, Nicaraguans have guarded their savings in piggy banks. . . . But no longer. In a country where inflation re-cently reached 161 percent for a 2-week period, a penny saved is a penny spent. "No one wants a bank now," said a pot-ter who has given over his kilns to making beer mugs. "We've given up even making them."

The demise of the piggy bank is only the least of the complica-tions that have vexed the public as inflation and government ef-forts to combat it have sent the value of the Nicaraguan córdoba fluctuating wildly . . .

SOURCE: © The Image Bank/Getty Images

That kind of uncertainty has left the banking system in shambles, despite savings accounts that offer up to 70 percent interest a month. . . . And it has left a legacy of quirks that now extends throughout the country's daily life. . . .

In many parts of the country, enterprising mechanics have converted the nation's once-precious stock of coins into something more valuable: metal washers to fit the nuts and bolts of rapidly deteriorating machinery. . . .

In Managua, it is still necessary to deposit a copper-colored 1-córdoba coin to make a pay phone call. But . . . not everybody even remem-bers what a 1-córdoba coin looks like, and fewer still actually own one. That is probably just as well for the phone system, because if anyone bothered to carry the coins, they could make about 26,250 phone calls for a dollar. . . .

SOURCE: Mark A. Uhlig, "Is Nicaraguan Bank an Endangered Species?" *New York Times,* June 22, 1989, p.2. Copyright © 1989 by the New York Times Company. Reprinted by permission.

inflation, especially if prices are rising at ever-increasing or highly variable rates, this is extremely difficult, and perhaps impossible, to do. The potential redistributions be-come monumental, and lending and borrowing may cease entirely.

Any inflation makes it difficult to write long-term contracts. Under low, creeping inflation, the "long term" may be twenty years, or ten years, or five years. By contrast, under high, galloping inflation, the "long term" may be measured in days or weeks. Restaurant prices may change daily. Airfares may go up while you are in flight. When it is impossible to enter into contracts of any duration longer than a few days, eco-nomic activity becomes paralyzed. We conclude that:

The horrors of hyperinflation are very real. But they are either absent in low, steady infla-tions or present in such muted forms that they can scarcely be considered horrors.

SOURCE: © Camera Press/Globe Photos, Inc.

These children in Germany during the hyperinflation of the 1920s are building a pyramid with cash, worth no more than the sand or sticks used by children elsewhere.

■ LOW INFLATION DOES NOT NECESSARILY LEAD TO HIGH INFLATION

We noted earlier that inflation is surrounded by a mythology that bears precious little relation to reality. It seems appropriate to conclude this chapter by disposing of one particularly persistent myth: that low inflation is a slippery slope that invariably leads to high inflation.

There is neither statistical evidence nor theoretical support for the belief that low inflation inevitably leads to high inflation. To be sure, inflations sometimes speed up. At other times, however, they slow down.

Although creeping inflations have many causes, runaway inflations have occurred only when the government has printed incredible amounts of money, usually to finance wartime expenditures. In the German inflation of 1923, the government finally found that its printing presses could not produce enough paper money to keep pace with the exploding prices. Not that it did not try—by the end of the inflation, the *daily* output of currency exceeded 400 quadrillion marks! The Hungarian authorities in 1945–1946 tried even harder: The average growth rate of the money supply was more than 12,000 percent *per month*. Needless to say, these are not the kind of inflation problems that are likely to face industrialized countries in the foreseeable future.

But that does not mean there is nothing wrong with low inflation. We have spent several pages analyzing the very real costs of even modest inflation. A case against moderate inflation can indeed be built, but it does not help this case to shout slogans like "Creeping inflation always leads to galloping inflation." Fortunately, it is simply not true.

SUMMARY

1. Macroeconomic policy strives to achieve rapid and reasonably stable growth while keeping both unemployment and inflation low.

2. Only rising productivity can raise standards of living in the long run. And seemingly small differences in productivity growth rates can compound to enormous differences in living standards. This is one of our *Ideas for Beyond the Final Exam*.

3. The **production function** tells us how much output the economy can produce from the available supplies of labor and capital, given the state of technology.

4. The growth rate of **potential GDP** is the sum of the growth rate of the **labor force** plus the growth rate of **labor productivity**. The latter depends on, among other things, technological change and investment in new capital.

5. Over long periods of time, the growth rates of actual and potential GDP match up quite well. But, owing to macroeconomic fluctuations, the two can diverge sharply over short periods.

6. Although some psychologists, environmentalists, and social critics question the merits of faster economic growth, economists generally assume that faster growth of potential GDP is socially beneficial.

7. When GDP is below its potential, unemployment is above **"full employment."** High unemployment exacts heavy financial and psychological costs from those who are its victims, costs that are borne quite unevenly by different groups in the population.

8. **Frictional unemployment** arises when people are between jobs for normal reasons. Thus, most frictional unemployment is desirable.

9. **Structural unemployment** is due to shifts in the pattern of demand or to technological change that makes certain skills obsolete.

10. **Cyclical unemployment** is the portion of unemployment that rises when real GDP grows more slowly than potential GDP and falls when the opposite is true.

11. Today, after years of extremely low unemployment, economists are unsure where full employment lies. Some think it may be at a measured unemployment rate near 5 percent.

12. **Unemployment insurance** replaces about one half of the lost income of unemployed persons who are insured. But fewer than half of the unemployed actually collect benefits, and no insurance program can bring back the lost output that could have been produced had these people been working.

13. People have many misconceptions about inflation. For example, many believe that inflation systematically erodes **real wages** and blame inflation for any unfavorable changes in relative prices. Both of these ideas are myths.

14. Other costs of inflation are real, however. For example, inflation often redistributes income from lenders to borrowers.

15. This redistribution is ameliorated by adding the expected rate of inflation to the interest rate. But such expectations often prove to be inaccurate.

16. The **real rate of interest** is the **nominal rate of interest** minus the **expected rate of inflation**.

17. Because the real rate of interest indicates the command over real resources that the borrower surrenders to the lender, it is of primary economic importance. But public attention often is riveted on nominal rates of interest, and this confusion can lead to costly policy mistakes.

18. Because nominal—not real—**capital gains** and interest are taxed, our tax system levies heavy taxes on income from capital when inflation is high.

19. Low inflation that proceeds at moderate and fairly predictable rates year after year carries far lower social costs than does high or variable inflation. But even low, steady inflations entail costs.

20. The notion that low inflation inevitably accelerates into high inflation is a myth with no foundation in economic theory and no basis in historical fact.

KEY TERMS

TEST YOURSELF

1. Two countries start with equal GDPs. The economy of Country A grows at an annual rate of 2 percent while the economy of Country B grows at an annual rate of 3 percent. After 25 years, how much larger is Country B's economy than Country A's economy? Why is the answer *not* 25 percent?

2. If output rises by 35 percent while hours of work increase by 40 percent, has productivity increased or decreased? By how much?

3. Most economists believe that from 1994 to 2000, actual GDP in the United States grew faster than potential GDP. What, then, should have happened to the unemployment rate over those six years? Then, from 2000 to 2003, actual GDP likely grew slower than potential GDP. What should have happened to the unemployment rate over those three years. (Check the data on the inside back cover of this book to see what actually happened.)

4. Country A and Country B have identical population growth rates of 1.1 percent per annum, and everyone in each country always works 40 hours per week. Labor productivity grows at a rate of 2 percent in Country A and a rate of 2.5 percent in Country B. What are the growth rates of potential GDP in the two countries?

5. What is the *real interest rate* paid on a credit-card loan bearing 14 percent nominal interest per year, if the rate of inflation is

   a. zero?

   b. 3 percent?

   c. 6 percent?

   d. 12 percent?

   e. 16 percent?

6. Suppose you agree to lend money to your friend on the day you both enter college at what you both expect to be a zero *real* rate of interest. Payment is to be made at graduation, with interest at a fixed *nominal* rate. If inflation proves to be *lower* during your college years than what you both had expected, who will gain and who will lose?

DISCUSSION QUESTIONS

1. If an earthquake destroys some of the factories in Poorland, what happens to Poorland's potential GDP? What happens to Poorland's potential GDP if it acquires some new advanced technology from Richland, and starts using it?

2. Why is it not as terrible to become unemployed nowadays as it was during the Great Depression?

3. "Unemployment is no longer a social problem because unemployed workers receive unemployment benefits and other benefits that make up for most of their lost wages." Comment.

4. Why is it so difficult to define *full employment?* What unemployment rate should the government be shooting for today?

5. Show why each of the following complaints is based on a misunderstanding about inflation:

   a. "Inflation must be stopped because it robs workers of their purchasing power."

   b. "Inflation makes it impossible for working people to afford many of the things they were hoping to buy."

   c. "Inflation must be stopped today, for if we do not stop it, it will surely accelerate to ruinously high rates and lead to disaster."

APPENDIX *How Statisticians Measure Inflation*

■ INDEX NUMBERS FOR INFLATION

Inflation is generally measured by the change in some index of the general price level. For example, between 1974 and 2004 the Consumer Price Index (CPI), the most widely used measure of the price level, rose from 49.3 to 188.9—an increase of 283 percent. The meaning of the *change* is clear enough. But what are the meanings of the 49.3 figure for the price level of 1974 and the 188.9 figure for 2004? Both are **index numbers.**

An **index number** expresses the cost of a market basket of goods relative to its cost in some "base" period, which is simply the year used as a basis of comparison.

Because the CPI currently uses 1982–1984 as its base period, the CPI of 188.9 for 2004 means that it cost $188.90 in 2004 to purchase the same basket of several hundred goods and services that cost $100 in 1982–1984.

Now in fact, the particular list of consumer goods and services under scrutiny did not actually cost $100 in 1982–1984. When constructing index numbers, by convention the index is set at 100 in the base period. This conventional figure is then used to obtain index numbers for other years in a very simple way. Suppose that the budget needed to buy the roughly 350 items included in the CPI was $2,000 per month in 1982–1984 and $3,778 per month in 2004. Then the index is defined by the following rule:

$$\frac{\text{CPI in 2004}}{\text{CPI in 1982–1984}}$$
$$= \frac{\text{Cost of market basket in 2004}}{\text{Cost of the market basket in 1982–1984}}$$

Because the CPI in 1982–1984 is set at 100:

$$\frac{\text{CPI in 2004}}{100} = \frac{\$3,778}{\$2,000} = 1.889$$

or

$$\text{CPI in 2004} = 188.9$$

Exactly the same sort of equation enables us to calculate the CPI in any other year. We have the following rule:

$$\text{CPI in given year} = \frac{\text{Cost of market basket in given year}}{\text{Cost of market basket in base year}} \times 100$$

Of course, not every combination of consumer goods that cost $2,000 in 1982–1984 rose to $3,778 by 2004. For example, a color TV set that cost $400 in 1983 might still have cost $400 in 2004, but a $400 hospital bill in 1983 might have ballooned to $2,000. The index number

problem refers to the fact that there is no perfect cost-of-living index because no two families buy precisely the same bundle of goods and services, and hence no two families suffer precisely the same increase in prices. Economists call this **the index number problem:**

When relative prices are changing, there is no such thing as a "perfect price index" that is correct for every consumer. Any statistical index will understate the increase in the cost of living for some families and overstate it for others. At best, the index can represent the situation of an "average" family.

■ THE CONSUMER PRICE INDEX

The **Consumer Price Index (CPI),** which is calculated and announced each month by the Bureau of Labor Statistics (BLS), is surely the most closely watched price index. When you read in the newspaper or see on television that the "cost of living rose by 0.2 percent last month," chances are the reporter is referring to the CPI.

The **Consumer Price Index (CPI)** is measured by pricing the items on a list representative of a typical urban household budget.

To know which items to include and in what amounts, the BLS conducts an extensive survey of spending habits roughly once every decade. As a consequence, the *same* bundle of goods and services is used as a standard for ten years or so, whether or not spending habits change.[11] Of course, spending habits do change, and this variation introduces a small error into the CPI's measurement of inflation.

A simple example will help us understand how the CPI is constructed. Imagine that college students purchase only three items—hamburgers, jeans, and movie tickets—and that we want to devise a cost-of-living index (call it SPI, or "Student Price Index") for them. First, we would conduct a survey of spending habits in the base year. (Suppose it is 1983.) Table 5 represents the hypothetical results. You will note that the frugal students of that day spent only $100 per month: $56 on hamburgers, $24 on jeans, and $20 on movies.

Table 6 presents hypothetical prices of these same three items in 2004. Each price has risen by a different amount, ranging from 25 percent for jeans up to 50 percent for hamburgers. By how much has the SPI risen?

---

[11] Economists call this a *base-period weight index* because the relative importance it attaches to the price of each item depends on how much money consumers actually chose to spend on the item during the base period.

TABLE 5			
Results of Student Expenditure Survey, 1983			
Item	Average Price	Average Quantity Purchased per Month	Average Expenditure per Month
Hamburger	$ 0.80	70	$56
Jeans	24.00	1	24
Movie ticket	5.00	4	20
Total			$100

TABLE 6		
Prices in 2004		
Item	Price	Increase over 1983
Hamburger	$1.20	50%
Jeans	30.00	25
Movie ticket	7.00	40

TABLE 7	
Cost of 1983 Student Budget in 2004 Prices	
70 Hamburgers at $1.20	$84
1 pair of jeans at $30	30
4 movie tickets at $7	28
Total	$142

Pricing the 1983 student budget at 2004 prices, we find that what once cost $100 now costs $142, as the calculation in Table 7 shows. Thus, the SPI, based on 1983 = 100, is

$$\text{SPI} = \frac{\text{Cost of budget in 2004}}{\text{Cost of budget in 1983}} \times 100 = \frac{\$142}{\$100} \times 100 = 142$$

So, the SPI in 2004 stands at 142, meaning that students' cost of living has increased 42 percent over the 21 years.

■ USING A PRICE INDEX TO "DEFLATE" MONETARY FIGURES

One of the most common uses of price indexes is in the comparison of monetary figures relating to two different points in time. The problem is that, if there has been inflation, the dollar is not a good measuring rod because it can buy less now than it did in the past.

Here is a simple example. Suppose the average student spent $100 per month in 1983 but $140 per month in 2004. If there was an outcry that students had become spendthrifts, how would you answer the charge?

The obvious answer is that a dollar in 2004 does not buy what it did in 1983. Specifically, our SPI shows us

that it takes $1.42 in 2004 to purchase what $1 would purchase in 1983. To compare the spending habits of students in the two years, we must divide the 2004 spending figure by 1.42. Specifically, *real* spending per student in 2004 (where "real" is defined by 1983 dollars) is:

$$\text{Real spending in 2004} = \frac{\text{Nominal spending in 2004}}{\text{Price index of 2004}} \times 100$$

Thus:

$$\text{Real spending in 2004} = \frac{\$140}{142} \times 100 = \$98.59$$

This calculation shows that, despite appearances to the contrary, the change in nominal spending from $100 to $140 actually represented a small *decrease* in real spending.

This procedure of dividing by the price index is called **deflating**, and it serves to translate noncomparable monetary figures into more directly comparable real figures.

> **Deflating** is the process of finding the real value of some monetary magnitude by dividing by some appropriate price index.

A good practical illustration is the real wage, a concept we have discussed in this chapter. As we saw in the boxed insert on page 110, we obtain the real wage by dividing the nominal wage by the price level.

■ USING A PRICE INDEX TO MEASURE INFLATION

In addition to deflating nominal magnitudes, price indexes are commonly used to measure *inflation*, that is, the *rate of increase* of the price level. The procedure is straightforward. The data on the inside back cover (column 13) show that the CPI was 49.3 in 1974 and 44.4 in 1973. The ratio of these two numbers, 49.3/44.4, is 1.11, which means that the 1974 price level was 11 percent greater than the 1973 price level. Thus, the *inflation rate* between 1973 and 1974 was 11 percent. The same procedure holds for any two adjacent years. Most recently, the CPI rose from 184 in 2003 to 188.9 in 2004. The ratio of these two numbers is 188.9/184 = 1.027, meaning that the inflation rate from 2003 to 2004 was 2.7 percent.

■ THE GDP DEFLATOR

In macroeconomics, one of the most important of the monetary magnitudes that we have to deflate is the nominal gross domestic product (GDP).

> The price index used to deflate nominal GDP is called the **GDP deflator**. It is a broad measure of economy-wide inflation; it includes the prices of all goods and services in the economy.

Our general principle for deflating a nominal magnitude tells us how to go from nominal GDP to real GDP:

$$\text{Real GDP} = \frac{\text{Nominal GDP}}{\text{GDP deflator}} \times 100$$

As with the CPI, the 100 simply serves to establish the base of the index as 100, rather than 1.00.

Some economists consider the GDP deflator to be a better measure of overall inflation than the Consumer Price Index. The main reason is that the GDP deflator is based on a broader market basket. As mentioned earlier, the CPI is based on the budget of a typical urban family. By contrast, the GDP deflator is constructed from a market basket that includes *every* item in the GDP—that is, every final good and service produced by the economy. Thus, in addition to prices of consumer goods, the GDP deflator includes the prices of airplanes, lathes, and other goods purchased by businesses—especially computers, which fall in price every year. It also includes government services.

For this reason, the two indexes rarely give the same measure of inflation. Usually the discrepancy is minor. But sometimes it can be noticeable, as in 2000 when the CPI recorded a 3.4 percent inflation rate over 1999 while the GDP deflator recorded an inflation rate of only 2.2 percent.

SUMMARY

1. Inflation is measured by the percentage increase in an **index number** of prices, which shows how the cost of some basket of goods has changed over a period of time.

2. Because relative prices are always changing, and because different families purchase different items, no price index can represent precisely the experience of every family.

3. The **Consumer Price Index (CPI)** tries to measure the cost of living for an average urban household by pricing a typical market basket every month.

4. Price indexes such as the CPI can be used to **deflate** nominal figures to make them more comparable. Deflation amounts to dividing the nominal magnitude by the appropriate price index.

5. The inflation rate between two adjacent years is computed as the percentage change in the price index between the first year and the second year.

6. The **GDP deflator** is a broader measure of economy-wide inflation than the CPI because it includes the prices of all goods and services in the economy.

KEY TERMS

Index number 119	Consumer Price Index 119	GDP deflator 120
Index number problem 119	Deflating 120	

TEST YOURSELF

1. Below you will find the yearly average values of the Dow Jones Industrial Average, the most popular index of stock market prices, for four different years. The Consumer Price Index for each year (on a base of 1982-1984 = 100) can be found on the inside back cover of this book. Use these numbers to deflate all five stock market values. Do real stock prices always rise every decade?

Year	Dow Jones Industrial Average
1970	753
1980	891
1990	2,679
2000	10,735

2. Below you will find nominal GDP and the GDP deflator (based on 2000=100) for the years 1984, 1994, and 2004.

   a. Compute real GDP for each year.

   b. Compute the percentage change in nominal and real GDP from 1984 to 1994, and from 1994 to 2004.

   c. Compute the percentage change in the GDP deflator over these two periods.

GDP Statistics	1984	1994	2004
Nominal GDP (Billions of dollars)	3,933	7,072	11,735
GDP deflator	67.6	90.3	108.3

3. Fill in the blanks in the following table of GDP statistics:

	2002	2003	2004
Nominal GDP	10,481		11,735
Real GDP	10,083	10,398	
GDP deflator		105.7	108.2

4. Use the following data to compute the College Price Index for 2004 using the base 1982 = 100.

Item	Price in 1982	Quantity per Month in 1982	Price in 2004
Button-down shirts	$10	1	$25
Loafers	25	1	55
Sneakers	10	3	35
Textbooks	12	12	40
Jeans	12	3	30
Restaurant meals	5	11	14

5. Average hourly earnings in the U.S. economy during several past years were as follows:

1970	1980	1990	2000
$3.23	$6.66	$10.01	$13.75

Use the CPI numbers provided on the inside back cover of this book to calculate the real wage (in 1982–1984 dollars) for each of these years. Which decade had the fastest growth of money wages? Which had the fastest growth of real wages?

6. The example in the appendix showed that the Student Price Index (SPI) rose by 42 percent from 1983 to 2004. You can understand the meaning of this better if you do the following:

a. Use Table 5 to compute the fraction of total spending accounted for by each of the three items in 1983. Call these values the "expenditure weights."

b. Compute the weighted average of the percentage increases of the three prices shown in Table 6, using the expenditure weights you just computed.

You should get 42 percent as your answer. This shows that "inflation," as measured by the SPI, is a weighted average of the percentage price increases of all the items that are included in the index.

THE DEBATE OVER MONETARY AND FISCAL POLICY

The love of money is the root of all evil.

THE NEW TESTAMENT

Lack of money is the root of all evil.

GEORGE BERNARD SHAW

U p to now, our discussion of stabilization policy has been almost entirely objective and technical. In seeking to understand how the national economy works and how government policies affect it, we have mostly ignored the intense economic and political controversies that surround the actual conduct of monetary and fiscal policy. Chapters 14 through 16 cover precisely these issues.

We begin this chapter by introducing an alternative theory of how monetary policy affects the economy, known as *monetarism*. Although the monetarist and Keynesian *theories* seem to contradict one another, we will see that the conflict is more apparent than real. However, important differences *do* arise among economists over the appropriate design and execution of monetary *policy*. These differences are the central concern of the chapter. We will learn about the continuing debates over the nature of aggregate supply, over the relative virtues of monetary versus fiscal policy, and over whether the Federal Reserve should try to control the money stock or interest rates. As we will see, the resolution of these issues is crucial to the proper conduct of stabilization policy and, indeed, to the decision of whether the government should try to stabilize the economy at all.

CONTENTS

? **ISSUE:** *Should We Forsake Stabilization Policy?*

We have suggested several times in this book that well-timed changes in fiscal or monetary policy can mitigate fluctuations in inflation and unemployment. For example, when the U.S. economy sagged after the terrorist attacks in September 2001, *both* fiscal policy *and* monetary policy turned more expansionary. These actions might be called "textbook responses," reflecting the lessons you have learned in Chapters 11 and 13.

But some economists argue that these lessons are best forgotten. In practice, they claim, attempts at macroeconomic stabilization are likely to do more harm than good. Policy makers are therefore best advised to follow fixed *rules* rather than use their best judgment on a case-by-case basis.

Nothing we have said so far leads to this conclusion. But we have not yet told the whole story. By the end of the chapter you will have encountered several arguments in favor of rules, and so you will be in a better position to make up your own mind on this important issue.

■ VELOCITY AND THE QUANTITY THEORY OF MONEY

Velocity indicates the number of times per year that an "average dollar" is spent on goods and services. It is the ratio of nominal gross domestic product (GDP) to the number of dollars in the money stock. That is:

$$Velocity = \frac{Nominal\ GDP}{Money\ stock}$$

In the previous chapter, we studied the *Keynesian* view of how monetary policy influences real output and the price level. But another, older model provides a different way to look at these matters. This model, known as the *quantity theory of money*, is easy to understand once we introduce one new concept: **velocity.**

In Chapter 12, we learned that because barter is so cumbersome, virtually all economic transactions in advanced economies use money. Thus, if there are $10 trillion worth of transactions in an economy during a particular year, and there is an average money stock of $2 trillion during that year, then each dollar of money must have been used an average of five times during the year.

The number 5 in this example is called the *velocity of circulation*, or *velocity* for short, because it indicates the *speed* at which money circulates. For example, a particular dollar bill might be used to buy a haircut in January; the barber might use it to purchase a sweater in March; the storekeeper might then use it to pay for gasoline in May; the gas station owner could pay it out to a house painter in October; and the painter might spend it on a Christmas present in December. In this way, the same dollar is used five times during the year. If it were used only four times during the year, its velocity would be 4, and so on.

No one has data on every transaction in the economy. To make velocity an operational concept, economists need a workable measure of the dollar volume of all transactions. As mentioned in the previous chapter, the most popular choice is nominal gross domestic product (GDP), even though it ignores many transactions that use money, such as the huge volume of activity in financial markets. If we accept nominal GDP as our measure of the money value of transactions, we are led to a concrete definition of velocity as the ratio of nominal GDP to the number of dollars in the money stock. Because nominal GDP is the product of real GDP (Y) times the price level (P), we can write this definition in symbols as follows:

$$\textbf{Velocity} = \frac{\textbf{Value of transactions}}{\textbf{Money stock}} = \frac{\textbf{Nominal GDP}}{M} = \frac{P \times Y}{M}$$

The **equation of exchange** states that the money value of GDP transactions must be equal to the product of the average stock of money times velocity. That is:

$$M \times V = P \times Y$$

By multiplying both sides of the equation by M, we arrive at an identity called the **equation of exchange,** which relates the money supply and nominal GDP:

$$\textbf{Money supply} \times \textbf{Velocity} = \textbf{Nominal GDP}$$

Alternatively, stated in symbols, we have:

$$M \times V = P \times Y$$

Here we have an obvious link between the stock of money, M, and the nominal value of the nation's output. This connection is merely a matter of arithmetic, however—not of economics. For example, it does not imply that the Fed can raise nominal GDP by increasing M. Why not? Because V might simultaneously fall enough to prevent the product $M \times V$ from rising. In other words, if more dollar bills circulated than before, but each bill changed hands more slowly, total spending might not rise. Thus, we need an auxiliary assumption to change the arithmetic identity into an economic theory:

> The **quantity theory of money** transforms the equation of exchange from an arithmetic identity into an economic model by assuming that changes in velocity are so minor that velocity can be taken to be virtually constant.

The **quantity theory of money** assumes that velocity is (approximately) constant. In that case, nominal GDP is proportional to the money stock.

You can see that if V never changed, the equation of exchange would be a marvelously simple model of the determination of nominal GDP—far simpler than the Keynesian model that took us several chapters to develop. To see this, it is convenient to rewrite the equation of exchange in growth-rate form:

$$\%\Delta M + \%\Delta V = \%\Delta P + \%\Delta Y$$

If V was constant (making its percentage change zero), this equation would say, for example, that if the Federal Reserve wanted to make nominal GDP grow by 4.7 percent per year, it need merely raise the money supply by 4.7 percent per year. In such a simple world, economists could use the equation of exchange to *predict* nominal GDP growth by predicting the growth rate of money. And policy makers could *control* nominal GDP growth by controlling growth of the money supply.

In the real world, things are not so simple because velocity is not a fixed number. But variable velocity does not necessarily destroy the usefulness of the quantity theory. As we explained in Chapter 1, all economic models make assumptions that are at least mildly unrealistic. Without such assumptions, they would not be models at all, just tedious descriptions of reality. The question is really whether the assumption of constant velocity is a useful abstraction from annoying detail or a gross distortion of the facts.

Figure 1 sheds some light on this question by showing the behavior of velocity since 1929. Note that the figure includes two different measures of velocity, labeled V_1 and V_2. Why? Recall from Chapter 12 that we can measure money in several ways, the most popular of which are M1 and M2. Because velocity (V) is simply nominal GDP divided by the money stock (M), we get a *different* measure of V for *each* measure of M. Figure 1 shows the velocities of both M1 and M2.

FIGURE 1

Velocity of Circulation, 1929–2004

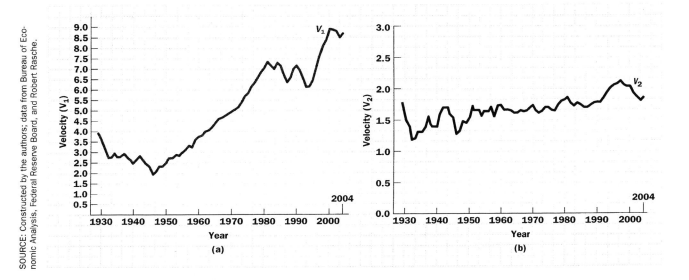

(a)   (b)

You will undoubtedly notice the stark difference in the behavior of V_1 versus V_2. V_1 is nowhere near constant; it displays a clear downward trend from 1929 until 1946, a pronounced upward trend until about 1981, and quite erratic behavior since then. V_2 is much closer to constant, but it has risen noticeably since the 1980s. Furthermore, closer examination of monthly or quarterly data reveals rather substantial fluctuations in velocity, by either measure. Because velocity is not constant in the short run, predictions of nominal GDP growth based on assuming constant velocity have not fared well, regardless of how M is measured. In a word, the strict quantity theory of money is not an adequate model of aggregate demand.

Some Determinants of Velocity

Because it is abundantly clear that velocity is a variable, not a constant, the equation of exchange is useful as a model of GDP determination only if we can explain movements in velocity. What factors decide whether a dollar will be used to buy goods and services four or five or six times per year? While numerous factors are relevant, two are important enough to merit discussion here.

Efficiency of the Payments System   Money is convenient for conducting transactions, which is why people hold it. But money has one important *dis*advantage: Cash pays no interest, and ordinary checking accounts pay very little. Thus, if it were possible to convert interest-bearing assets into money on short notice and at low cost, a rational individual might prefer to use, say, credit cards for most purchases, making periodic transfers to her checking account as necessary. That way, the same volume of transactions could be accomplished with lower money balances. By definition, velocity would rise.

The incentive to limit cash holdings thus depends on the ease and speed with which it is possible to exchange money for other assets—which is what we mean by the "efficiency of the payments system." As computerization has speeded up banks' bookkeeping procedures, as financial innovations have made it possible to transfer funds rapidly between checking accounts and other assets, and as credit cards have come to be used instead of cash, the need to hold money balances has declined and velocity has risen.

In practice, improvements in the payments system pose severe practical problems for analysts interested in predicting velocity. A host of financial innovations, beginning in the 1970s and continuing to the present day (some of which were mentioned in Chapter 12's discussion of the definitions of money), have transformed forecasting velocity into a hazardous occupation. In fact, many economists believe the task is impossible and should not even be attempted.

Interest Rates   A second key determinant of velocity is the rate of interest. The reason is implicit in what we have already said: The higher the rate of interest, the greater the *opportunity cost* of holding money. Therefore, as interest rates rise, people want to hold smaller cash balances. So the existing stock of money circulates faster, and velocity rises.

It is this factor that most directly undercuts the usefulness of the quantity theory of money as a guide for monetary policy. In the previous chapter, we learned that expansionary monetary policy, which increases bank reserves and the money supply, also decreases the interest rate. But if interest rates fall, other things being equal, velocity (*V*) also falls. Thus, *when the Fed raises the money supply (M), the product M × V may increase by a smaller percentage than does M itself.*

Thus, we conclude that:

Velocity is not a strict constant but depends on such things as the efficiency of the financial system and the rate of interest. Only by studying these determinants of velocity can we hope to predict the growth rate of nominal GDP from knowledge of the growth rate of the money supply.

Monetarism: The Quantity Theory Modernized

Adherents to a school of thought called **monetarism** try to do precisely that. Monetarists realize that velocity changes, but they claim that such changes are fairly *predictable*—certainly in the long run and perhaps even in the short run. As a result, they conclude that the best way to study economic activity is to start with the equation of exchange in growth-rate form:

Monetarism is a mode of analysis that uses the equation of exchange to organize and analyze macroeconomic data.

$$\%\Delta M + \%\Delta V = \%\Delta P + \%\Delta Y$$

From here, careful study of the determinants of money growth (which we provided in the previous two chapters) and of changes in velocity (which we just sketched) can be used to *predict* the growth rate of nominal GDP. Similarly, given an understanding of movements in V, controlling M can give the Fed excellent control over nominal GDP. These ideas are the central tenets of monetarism.

The monetarist and Keynesian approaches can be thought of as alternative theories of aggregate demand. Keynesians divide economic knowledge into four neat compartments marked C, I, G, and $(X - IM)$ and unite them all with the equilibrium condition that $Y = C + I + G + (X - IM)$. In Keynesian analysis, money affects the economy by first affecting interest rates. Monetarists, by contrast, organize their knowledge into two alternative boxes labeled M and V, and then use the identity $M \times V = P \times Y$ to predict aggregate demand. In the monetarist model, the role of money is not necessarily limited to working through interest rates.

The bit of arithmetic that multiplies M and V to get $P \times Y$ is neither more nor less profound than the one that adds up C, I, G and $(X - IM)$ to get Y, and certainly both are correct. The real question is which framework is more *useful* in practice. That is, which approach works better as a model of aggregate demand?

Although there is no generally correct answer for all economies in all periods of time, a glance back at Figure 1 (page 267) will show you why most economists had abandoned monetarism by the early 1990s. During the 1960s and 1970s, velocity (at least V_2) was fairly stable, which helped monetarism win many converts—in the United States and around the world. Since then, however, velocity has behaved so erratically here and in many other countries that there are few real monetarists left.

Nonetheless, as we will see later in this chapter, some faint echoes of the debate between Keynesians and monetarists can still be heard. Furthermore, few economists doubt that there is a strong *long-run* relationship between M and P. They just question whether this relationship is useful in the short run. (See the box "Does Money Growth Always Cause Inflation?" on the next page.)

■ FISCAL POLICY, INTEREST RATES, AND VELOCITY

As we learned in the previous chapter, Keynesian economics provides a powerful and important role for *monetary* policy: An increase in bank reserves and the money supply reduces interest rates, which, in turn, stimulates the demand for investment. But *fiscal* policy also exerts a powerful influence on interest rates.

To see how, think about what happens to real output and the price level following, say, a rise in government spending. We learned in Chapter 11 that both real GDP (Y) and the price level (P) rise, so nominal GDP certainly rises. But Chapter 13's analysis of the market for bank reserves taught us that rising prices and/or rising output—by increasing the volume of transactions—push the demand curve for bank deposits, and therefore for reserves, outward to the right. With no change in the supply of reserves, the rate of interest must rise. *So expansionary fiscal policy raises interest rates.*

POLICY DEBATE

Does Money Growth Always Cause Inflation?

Monetarists have long claimed that, in the famous words of Milton Friedman, "inflation is always and everywhere a monetary phenomenon." By this statement, Friedman means that changes in the growth rate of the money supply (%ΔM) are far and away the principal cause of changes in the inflation rate (%ΔP)—in all places and at all times.

Few economists question the dominant role of rapid money growth in accounting for extremely high rates of inflation. During the German hyperinflation of the 1920s, for example, money was being printed so fast that the printing presses had a difficult time keeping up the pace! But most economists question the words "always and everywhere" in Friedman's dictum. Aren't many cases of moderate inflation driven by factors other than the growth rate of the money supply?

The answer appears to be "yes." The accompanying charts use recent U.S. history as an illustration. In the scatter diagram on the left, each point records both the growth rate of the M2 money supply and the inflation rate (as measured by the Consumer Price Index) for a particular year between 1979 and 2004. Because of the years 1979–1981, there seems to be a weak positive relationship between the two variables. But no relationship at all appears for the years 1982–2004.

Monetarists often argue that this comparison is unfair because the effect of money supply growth on inflation operates with a lag of perhaps two years. So the right hand scatter diagram compares inflation with money supply growth *two years earlier.* It tells a pretty similar story. More sophisticated versions of scatter plots like these have led most economists to reject the monetarist claim that inflation and money supply growth are tightly linked.

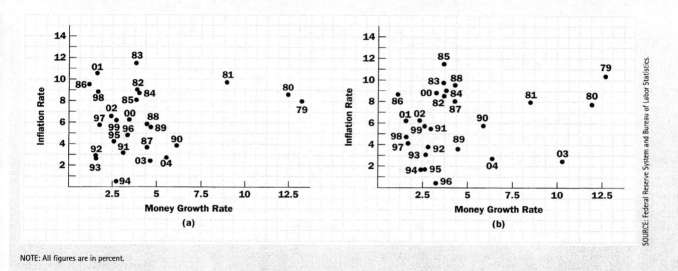

SOURCE: Federal Reserve System and Bureau of Labor Statistics.

NOTE: All figures are in percent.

If the government uses its spending and taxing weapons in the opposite direction, the same process works in reverse. Falling output and (possibly) falling prices shift the demand curve for reserves inward to the left. With a fixed supply curve, equilibrium in the market for reserves leads to a lower interest rate. Thus:

Monetary policy is not the only type of policy that affects interest rates. Fiscal policy does, too. Specifically, increases in government spending or tax cuts normally push interest rates up, whereas restrictive fiscal policies normally pull interest rates down.

The apparently banal fact that changes in fiscal policy move interest rates up and down has several important consequences. Here are two.

▒ Application: The Multiplier Formula Revisited

We have just noted that expansionary fiscal policy raises interest rates. We also know that higher interest rates deter private investment spending. So when the government raises the G component of $C + I + G + (X - IM)$, one side effect will probably be a reduction in the I component. Consequently, total spending will rise by *less* than simple multiplier analysis might suggest. The fact that a surge in government demand (G) discourages some private demand (I) provides another reason why the oversimplified multiplier formula of earlier chapters, $1/(1 - MPC)$, exaggerates the size of the multiplier:

> Because a rise in G (or, for that matter, an autonomous rise in any component of total expenditure) pushes interest rates higher, and hence deters some investment spending, the increase in the sum $C + I + G + (X - IM)$ is smaller than what the oversimplified multiplier formula predicts.

Combining this observation with our previous analysis of the multiplier, we now have the following complete list of

REASONS WHY THE OVERSIMPLIFIED FORMULA OVERSTATES THE MULTIPLIER

1. It ignores variable imports, which reduce the size of the multiplier.
2. It ignores price-level changes, which reduce the size of the multiplier.
3. It ignores the income tax, which reduces the size of the multiplier.
4. It ignores the rising interest rates that accompany any autonomous increase in spending, which also reduce the size of the multiplier.

With so many reasons, it is no wonder that the actual multiplier, which is estimated to be less than two for the U.S. economy, is so much less than the oversimplified formula suggests.

Application: The Government Budget and Investment

One major argument for reducing the government's budget deficit is that lower deficits should lead to higher levels of private investment spending. We can now see why. The government reduces its deficit by engaging in *contractionary* fiscal policies—lower spending or higher taxes. As we have just seen, any such measure should *reduce* real interest rates. These lower real interest rates should spur investment spending. This simple insight will play a major role in the next chapter.

■ DEBATE: SHOULD WE RELY ON FISCAL OR MONETARY POLICY?

The Keynesian and monetarist approaches are like two different languages. But it is well known that language influences attitudes in many subtle ways. For example, the Keynesian language biases things toward thinking first about fiscal policy simply because G is a part of $C + I + G + (X - IM)$. By contrast, the monetarist approach, working through the equation of exchange, $M \times V = P \times Y$, puts the spotlight on M. In fact, years ago economists engaged in a spirited debate in which extreme monetarists claimed that fiscal policy was futile, whereas extreme Keynesians argued that monetary policy was useless. Today, such arguments are rarely heard.

Instead of arguing over which type of policy is more *powerful*, economists nowadays debate which type of medicine—fiscal or monetary—cures the patient more *quickly*. Until now, we have ignored questions of timing and pretended that the authorities noticed the need for stabilization policy instantly, decided on a course of action right away, and administered the appropriate medicine at once. In reality, each of these steps takes time.

First, delays in data collection mean that the most recent data describe the state of the economy a few months ago. Second, one of the prices of democracy is that the government often takes a distressingly long time to decide what should be done, to muster the necessary political support, and to put its decisions into effect. Finally, our $12 trillion economy is a bit like a sleeping elephant that reacts rather sluggishly to moderate fiscal and monetary prods. As it turns out, these *lags in stabilization policy*, as they are called, play a pivotal role in the choice between fiscal and monetary policy. Here's why.

The main policy tool for manipulating consumer spending (C) is the personal income tax, and Chapter 8 documented why the fiscal policy planner can feel fairly confident that each \$1 of tax reduction will lead to about 90 to 95 cents of additional spending *eventually*. But not all of this extra spending happens at once.

First, consumers must learn about the tax change. Then they may need to be convinced that the change is permanent. Finally, there is simple force of habit: Households need time to adjust their spending habits when circumstances change. For all these reasons, consumers may increase their spending by only 30 to 50 cents for each \$1 of additional income within the first few months after a tax cut. Only gradually will they raise their spending up to about 90 to 95 cents for each additional dollar of income.

Lags are much longer for investment (I), which provides the main vehicle by which monetary policy affects aggregate demand. Planning for capacity expansion in a large corporation is a long, drawn-out process. Ideas must be submitted and approved, plans must be drawn up, funding acquired, orders for machinery or contracts for new construction placed. And most of this activity occurs *before* any appreciable amount of money is spent. Economists have found that much of the response of investment to changes in either interest rates or tax provisions takes several *years* to develop.

The fact that C responds more quickly than I has important implications for the choice among alternative stabilization policies. The reason is that the most common varieties of fiscal policy either affect aggregate demand directly—G is a component of $C + I + G + (X - IM)$—or work through consumption with a relatively short lag, whereas monetary policy primarily affects investment. Therefore:

> Conventional types of fiscal policy actions, such as changes in G or in personal taxes, probably affect aggregate demand much more promptly than do monetary policy actions.

So is fiscal policy a superior stabilization tool? Not quite. The lags we have just described, which are beyond policy makers' control, are not the only ones affecting the timing of stabilization policy. Additional lags stem from the behavior of the policy makers themselves! We refer here to the delays that occur while policy makers study the state of the economy, contemplate which steps they should take, and put their decisions into effect.

Here monetary policy has a huge advantage. The Federal Open Market Committee (FOMC) meets eight times each year, and more often if necessary. So monetary policy decisions are made frequently. And once the Fed decides on a course of action, it can execute its plan immediately by buying or selling Treasury bills in the open market.

In contrast, federal budgeting procedures operate on an annual budget cycle. Except in unusual cases, major fiscal policy initiatives can occur only at the time of the annual budget. In principle, tax laws can be changed at any time, but the wheels of Congress grind slowly and are often gummed up by partisan politics. For these reasons, it may take many months for Congress to change fiscal policy. President George W. Bush's tax cut proposal in 2001 was in some sense the proverbial exception that proves the rule. Congress passed it in record time—but that still took about four months. In sum, only in rare circumstances can the government take important fiscal policy actions on short notice. Thus:

> Policy lags are normally much shorter for monetary policy than for fiscal policy.

So where does the combined effect of expenditure lags and policy lags leave us? With nothing very conclusive, we are afraid. In practice, most students of stabilization policy have come to believe that the unwieldy and often partisan nature of our political system make active use of fiscal policy for stabilization purposes difficult, if not impossible. Monetary policy, they claim, is the only realistic game in town, and therefore must bear the entire burden of stabilization policy.

■ DEBATE: SHOULD THE FED CONTROL THE MONEY SUPPLY OR INTEREST RATES?

Another major controversy that raged for decades focused on how the Federal Reserve should conduct monetary policy. Most economists argued that the Fed should use its open-market operations to control the rate of interest (r), which is how we have portrayed monetary policy up to now. But others, especially monetarists, insisted that the Fed should concentrate on controlling bank reserves or some measure of the money supply (M) instead. This debate echoes even today in Europe, where the European Central Bank (ECB), unlike the Fed, claims to pay considerable attention to the growth of the money supply.

To understand the nature of this debate, we must first understand why the Fed cannot control both M and r at the same time. Figure 2 will help us see why. It looks just like Figure 8 of the previous chapter (see page 262), except that the horizontal axis now measures the *money supply* instead of *bank reserves*. The switch from reserves to money is justified by something we learned in Chapters 12 and 13: that the money supply is "built up" from the Fed's supply of bank reserves via the process of multiple expansion.[1] As you will recall, this leads to an approximate proportional relationship between the two—meaning that if bank reserves go up by X percent then the money supply rises by approximately X percent.[2] Because M is basically proportional to bank reserves, anything we can analyze in the market for reserves can be analyzed in just the same way in the market for *money*—which is the market depicted in Figure 2.

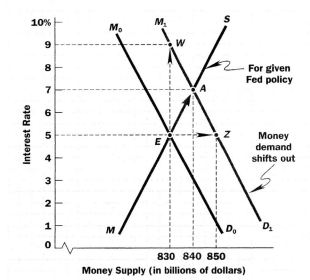

For given Fed policy

Money demand shifts out

Money Supply (in billions of dollars)

FIGURE 2

The Federal Reserve's Policy Dilemma

The diagram shows an initial equilibrium in the money market at point E, where money demand curve M_0D_0 crosses money supply curve MS. Here the interest rate is $r = 5$ percent and the money stock is $M = \$830$ billion. We assume that these are the Fed's targets: It wants to keep the money supply and interest rates just where they are.

If the demand curve for money holds still, everything works out fine. But suppose the demand for money is not so obliging. Suppose, instead, that the demand curve shifts outward to the position indicated by the blue line M_1D_1 in Figure 2. We learned in the previous chapter that such a shift might occur because output increases or because prices rise, thereby increasing the volume of transactions. Or it might happen simply because people decide to hold more bank deposits. But whatever the reason, the Fed can no longer achieve *both* of its previous targets.

If the Fed does nothing, the outward shift of the demand curve will push up both the quantity of money (M) and the rate of interest (r). Figure 2 shows these changes graphically as the move from point E to point A. If the demand curve for money shifts outward from M_0D_0 to M_1D_1, and monetary policy does not change (so the supply schedule does not move), the money stock rises to $\$840$ billion and the interest rate rises to 7 percent.

Now suppose the Fed is targeting the money supply and is unwilling to let M rise. In that case, it must use *contractionary* open-market operations to prevent M from rising. But in so doing, it will push r up even higher, as point W in Figure 2 shows. After the demand curve for money shifts outward, point E is no longer attainable. The Fed must instead choose from among the points on the blue line M_1D_1, and point W is the point on this line that keeps the money supply at $\$830$ billion. The Fed can hold M at $\$830$ billion by reducing bank reserves just enough to push the money supply curve *inward* so that it passes through point W. (Pencil this shift in for yourself on the diagram.) But the interest rate will skyrocket to 9 percent.

Alternatively, if the Federal Reserve is pursuing an interest rate target, it might decide that the rise in r must be avoided. In this case, the Fed would be forced to engage in *expansionary* open-market operations to prevent the outward shift of the demand

---

[1] If you need to review this process, turn back to Chapter 12, especially pages 240–246.
[2] For further details on this proportionality relationship, including some numerical examples, see Test Yourself Question 5 at the end of this chapter.

curve for money from pushing *r* up. In terms of Figure 2, the interest rate can be held at 5 percent by adding just enough bank reserves to shift the money supply curve *outward* so that it passes through point Z. But doing this will push the money supply up to $850 billion. (Again, try penciling in the requisite shift of the money supply schedule.) To summarize this discussion:

> When the demand curve for money shifts outward, the Fed must tolerate a rise in interest rates, a rise in the money stock, or both. It cannot control *both* the supply of money *and* the interest rate. If it tries to keep *M* steady, then *r* will rise even more. Conversely, if it tries to stabilize *r*, then *M* will rise even more.

Two Imperfect Alternatives

For years, economists debated how a central bank should deal with its inability to control both the money supply and the rate of interest. Should it adhere rigidly to a target growth path for bank reserves and the money supply, regardless of the consequences for interest rates—which is the monetarist policy? Should it hold interest rates steady, even if that requires sharp gyrations in reserves and the money stock—which is roughly what the Fed does now? Or is some middle ground more appropriate? Let us first explore the issues and then consider what has actually been done.

The main problem with imposing rigid targets on the *supply* of money is that the *demand* for money does not cooperate by growing smoothly and predictably from month to month; instead it dances around quite a bit in the short run. This variability presents the recommendation to control the money supply with two problems:

1. It is almost impossible to achieve. Because the volume of money in existence depends on *both* the demand *and* the supply curves, keeping *M* on target in the face of significant fluctuations in the demand for money would require exceptional dexterity.
2. For reasons just explained, rigid adherence to money-stock targets might lead to wide fluctuations in interest rates, which could create an unsettled atmosphere for business decisions.

But powerful objections can also be raised against exclusive concentration on interest rate movements. Because increases in output and prices shift the demand schedule for money outward (as shown in Figure 2), a central bank determined to keep interest rates from rising would have to expand the money supply in response. Conversely, when GDP sagged, it would have to contract the money supply to keep rates from falling. Thus, interest rate pegging would make the money supply expand in boom times and contract in recessions, with potentially grave consequences for the stability of the economy. Ironically, this is precisely the sort of monetary behavior the Federal Reserve System was designed to prevent. Hence, if the Fed is to control interest rates, it had better formulate flexible targets, not fixed ones.

What Has the Fed Actually Done?

For most of U.S. post–World War II history, the predominant view held that the interest rate was much more important of the two targets. The rationale was that gyrating interest rates would cause abrupt and unsettling changes in investment spending, which in turn would make the entire economy fluctuate. Stabilizing interest rates was therefore believed to be the best way to stabilize GDP. If doing so required fluctuations in the money supply, so be it. Consequently, the Fed focused on interest rates and paid little attention to the money supply. That is more or less the Fed's view today as well.

During the 1960s, this prevailing view came under attack by Milton Friedman and other monetarists. These economists argued that the Fed's obsession with stabilizing interest rates actually *destabilized* the economy by making the money supply fluctuate too much. For this reason, they urged the Fed to stop worrying about fluctuations in interest rates and make the money supply grow at a constant rate from month to month and year to year.

Monetarism made important inroads at the Fed during the inflationary 1970s, especially in October 1979 when then-Chairman Paul Volcker announced a major change in the conduct of monetary policy. Henceforth, he asserted, the Fed would stick more closely to its target for money-stock growth regardless of the implications for interest rates. Interest rates would go wherever the law of supply and demand took them.

According to our analysis, this change in policy should have led to wider fluctuations in interest rates—and it certainly did. Unfortunately, the Fed ran into some bad luck. The ensuing three years were marked by unusually severe gyrations in the demand for money, so the ups and downs of interest rates were far more extreme than anyone had expected. Figure 3 shows just how volatile interest rates were between late 1979 and late 1982. As you might imagine, this erratic performance provoked some heavy criticism of the Fed.

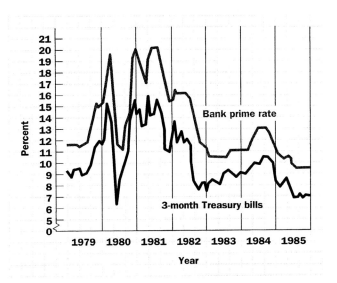

FIGURE 3

The Behavior of Interest Rates, 1979–1985

Then, in October 1982, Chairman Volcker announced that the Fed was temporarily abandoning its attempts to stick to a target growth path for the money supply. Although he did not say so, his announcement presumably meant that the Fed went back to paying more attention to interest rates. As you can see in Figure 3, interest rates did become much more stable after the change in policy. Most observers think this greater stability was no coincidence.

After 1982, the Fed gradually distanced itself from the position that the money supply should grow at a constant rate. Finally, in 1993, Chairman Alan Greenspan officially confirmed what many people already knew: that the Fed was no longer using the various *M*s to guide policy. He strongly hinted that the Fed was targeting interest rates, especially *real* interest rates, instead—a hint that has been repeated many times since then. In truth, the Fed had little choice. The demand curve for money behaved so erratically and so unpredictably in the 1980s and 1990s that stabilizing the money stock was probably impossible and certainly undesirable. And at least so far, the Fed has shown little interest in returning to the *M*s.

■ DEBATE: THE SHAPE OF THE AGGREGATE SUPPLY CURVE

Another lively debate over stabilization policy revolves around the shape of the economy's aggregate supply curve. Many economists think of the aggregate supply curve as quite flat, as in Figure 4(a) on the next page, so that large increases in output can be achieved with little inflation. But other economists envision the supply curve as steep, as shown in Figure 4(b), so that prices respond strongly to changes in output. The differences for public policy are substantial.

If the aggregate supply curve is flat, expansionary fiscal or monetary policy that raises the aggregate demand curve can buy large gains in real GDP at low cost in terms of inflation. In Figure 5(a) on the next page, stimulation of demand pushes the aggregate demand curve outward from D_0D_0 to D_1D_1, thereby moving the economy's equilibrium from point E to point A. The substantial rise in output ($400 billion in the diagram) is accompanied by only a pinch of inflation (1 percent). So the antirecession policy is quite successful.

Conversely, when the supply curve is flat, a restrictive stabilization policy is not a very effective way to bring inflation down. Instead, it serves mainly to reduce real output, as Figure 5(b) shows. Here a leftward shift of the aggregate demand curve from D_0D_0 to D_2D_2 moves equilibrium from point E to point B, lowering real GDP by $400 billion but cutting the price level by merely 1 percent. Fighting inflation by

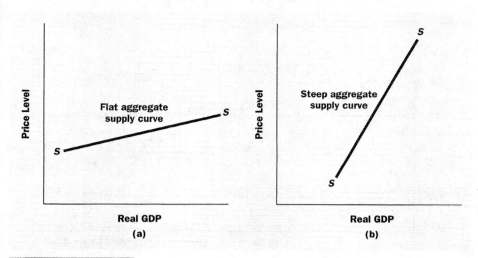

FIGURE 4

Alternative Views of the
Aggregate Supply Curve

contracting aggregate demand is obviously quite costly in this example.

Things are just the reverse if the aggregate supply curve is steep. In that case, expansionary fiscal or monetary policies will cause a good deal of inflation without boosting real GDP much. This situation is depicted in Figure 6(a) on the next page, in which expansionary policies shift the aggregate demand curve outward from $D_0 D_0$ to $D_1 D_1$, thereby moving the economy's equilibrium from E to A. Output rises by only $100 billion but prices shoot up 10 percent.

Similarly, contractionary policy is an effective way to bring down the price level without much sacrifice of output, as shown by the shift from E to B in Figure 6(b). Here it takes only a $100 billion loss of output (from $6,000 billion to $5,900 billion) to "buy" 10 percent less inflation.

As we can see, deciding whether the aggregate supply curve is steep or flat is clearly of fundamental importance to the proper conduct of stabilization policy. If the supply curve is flat, stabilization policy is much more effective at combating recession than inflation. If the supply curve is steep, precisely the reverse is true.

But why does the argument persist? Why can't economists just determine the shape of the aggregate supply curve and stop arguing? The answer is that supply conditions in the real world are far more complicated than our simple diagrams suggest. Some industries may have flat supply curves, whereas others have steep ones. For reasons explained in Chapter 10, supply curves shift over time. And, unlike laboratory scientists, economists cannot perform controlled experiments that would reveal the shape of the aggregate supply curve directly. Instead, they must use statistical inference to make educated guesses.

FIGURE 5

Stabilization Policy
with a Flat Aggregate
Supply Curve

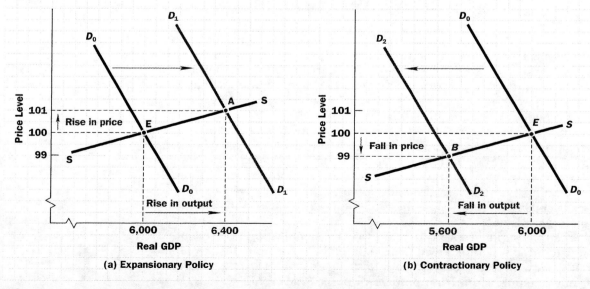

(a) Expansionary Policy

(b) Contractionary Policy

NOTE: Real GDP in billions of dollars per year.

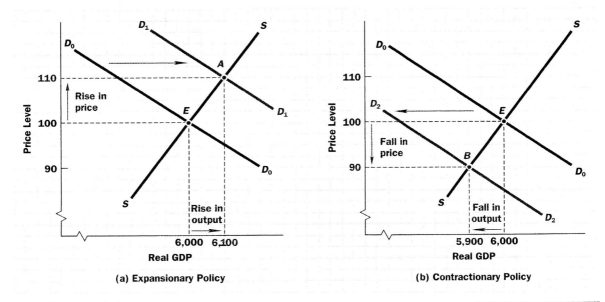

(a) Expansionary Policy

(b) Contractionary Policy

NOTE: Real GDP in billions of dollars per year.

FIGURE 6

Stabilization Policy with a Steep Aggregate Supply Curve

Although empirical research continues, our understanding of aggregate supply remains less settled than our understanding of aggregate demand. Nevertheless, many economists believe that the outline of a consensus view has emerged. This view holds that *the steepness of the aggregate supply schedule depends on the time period under consideration.*

In the very short run, the aggregate supply curve is quite flat, making Figure 5 the more relevant picture of reality. Over short time periods, therefore, fluctuations in aggregate demand have large effects on output but only minor effects on prices. In the long run, however, the aggregate supply curve becomes quite steep, perhaps even vertical. In that case, Figure 6 is a better representation of reality, so that changes in demand affect mainly prices, not output.[3] The implication is that:

Any change in aggregate demand will have most of its effect on *output* in the short run but on *prices* in the long run.

■ DEBATE: SHOULD THE GOVERNMENT INTERVENE?

We have yet to consider what may be the most fundamental and controversial debate of all—the issue posed at the beginning of the chapter. Is it likely that government policy can successfully stabilize the economy? Or are even well-intentioned efforts likely to do more harm than good?

This controversy has raged for several decades, with no end in sight. The debate is partly political or philosophical. Liberal economists tend to be more intervention-minded and hence more favorably disposed toward an activist stabilization policy. Conservative economists are more inclined to keep the government's hands off the economy and hence advise adhering to fixed rules. Such political differences are not surprising. But more than ideology propels the debate. We need to understand the economics.

Critics of stabilization policy point to the lags and uncertainties that surround the operation of both fiscal and monetary policies—lags and uncertainties that we have stressed repeatedly in this and earlier chapters. Will the Fed's actions have the desired effects on the money supply? What will these actions do to interest rates and spending? Can fiscal policy actions be taken promptly? How large is the expenditure multiplier? The list could go on and on.

---

[3] The reasoning behind the view that the aggregate supply curve is flat in the short run but steep in the long run will be developed in Chapter 16.

The Fed Fights Recession

The great American economic boom of the 1990s ended about midway through 2000, and the U.S. growth rate plummeted. By January 2001, the Federal Open Market Committee was alarmed enough to start cutting interest rates in an attempt to give the economy a boost. By late summer, the Fed had shaved three full percentage points off the Federal funds rate, and several members of the FOMC were beginning to think they had done enough to stimulate growth.

Then came the horrific terrorist attacks of September 11, which changed everything. The Fed quickly concluded that the shock of the attacks would not just disrupt economy activity but also damage consumer and business confidence. Six days later, at a hastily arranged telephonic meeting, it reduced the Federal funds rate by one half percentage point; and it continued to cut the rate for the rest of the year, bringing it all the way down to 1.75 percent—the lowest since 1961. But when the economy did not snap back, the Fed started cutting rates again, lowering the Federal funds rate to an astonishing 1 percent in June 2003—and then holding it at that extraordinarily low level for a year. Only in June 2004 did the Fed conclude that the economy was sufficiently healthy that the FOMC could safely begin to restore interest rates to more normal levels.

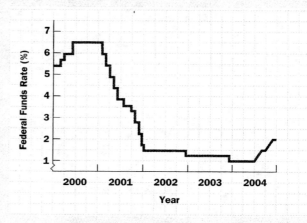

Federal Funds Rate, 2000–2004

SOURCE: Federal Reserve

These skeptics look at this formidable catalog of difficulties, add a dash of skepticism about our ability to forecast the future state of the economy, and worry that stabilization policy may fail. They therefore advise both the fiscal and monetary authorities to pursue a passive policy rather than an active one—adhering to fixed rules that, although incapable of ironing out every bump in the economy's growth path, will at least keep it roughly on track in the long run.

Advocates of active stabilization policies admit that perfection is unattainable. But they are much more optimistic about the prospects for success, and they are much *less* optimistic about how smoothly the economy would function in the absence of demand management. They therefore advocate discretionary increases in government spending (or decreases in taxes) and lower interest rates when the economy has a recessionary gap—and the reverse when the economy has an inflationary gap. Such policies, they believe, will help keep the economy closer to its full-employment growth path.

Each side can point to evidence that buttresses its own view. Activists look back with pride at the tax cut of 1964 and the sustained period of economic growth that it helped to introduce. They also point to the tax cut of 1975 (which was quickly enacted at just about the trough of a severe recession), the Federal Reserve's switch to "easy money" in 1982, the Fed's expert steering of the economy between 1992 and 2000, and its quick response to the threat to the economy after September 11, 2001. Advocates of rules remind us of the government's refusal to curb what was obviously a situation of runaway demand during the 1966–1968 Vietnam buildup, its overexpansion of the economy in 1972, the monetary overkill that helped bring on the sharp recession of 1981–1982, and the inadequate antirecession policies of the early 1990s.

The historical record of fiscal and monetary policy is far from glorious. Although the authorities have sometimes taken appropriate and timely actions to stabilize the economy, at other times they clearly either took inappropriate steps or did nothing at all. The question of whether the government should adopt passive rules or attempt an activist stabilization policy therefore merits a closer look. As we shall see, the *lags* in the effects of policy discussed earlier in this chapter play a pivotal role in the debate.

Lags and the Rules-versus-Discretion Debate

Lags lead to a fundamental difficulty for stabilization policy—a difficulty so formidable that it has prompted some economists to conclude that attempts to stabilize economic activity are likely to do more harm than good. To see why, refer to Figure 7, which charts the behavior of both actual and potential GDP over the course of a business cycle in a hypothetical economy with no stabilization policy. At point A, the economy begins to slip into a recession and does not recover to full employment until point D. Then, between points D and E, it overshoots potential GDP and enters an inflationary boom.

The argument in favor of stabilization policy runs something like this: Policy makers recognize that the recession is a serious problem at point B, and they take appropriate actions. These actions have their major effects around point C and therefore limit both the depth and the length of the recession.

But suppose the lags are really longer and less predictable than those just described. Suppose, for example, that actions do not come until point C and that stimulative policies do not have their major effects until after point D. Then policy will be of little help during the recession and will actually do harm by overstimulating the economy during the ensuing boom. Thus:

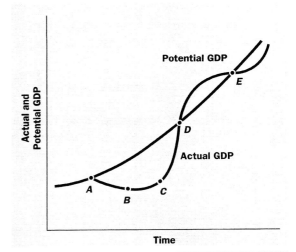

FIGURE 7

A Typical Business Cycle

In the presence of long lags, attempts at stabilizing the economy may actually succeed in destabilizing it.

For this reason, some economists argue that we are better off leaving the economy alone and relying on its natural self-corrective forces to cure recessions and inflations. Instead of embarking on periodic programs of monetary and fiscal stimulus or restraint, they advise policy makers to stick to fixed rules that ignore current economic events.

For monetary policy, we have already mentioned the monetarist policy rule: The Fed should keep the money supply growing at a constant rate. For fiscal policy, proponents of rules often recommend that the government resist the temptation to manage aggregate demand actively and rely instead on the economy's automatic stabilizers, which we discussed in Chapter 11 (see page 212).

■ DIMENSIONS OF THE RULES-VERSUS-DISCRETION DEBATE

Are the critics right? Should we forget about discretionary policy and put the economy on autopilot—relying on automatic stabilizers and the economy's natural, self-correcting mechanisms? As usual, the answer depends on many factors.

How Fast Does the Economy's Self-Correcting Mechanism Work?

In Chapter 10, we emphasized that the economy has a self-correcting mechanism. If recessions and inflations will disappear quickly by themselves, the case for intervention is weak. That is, if such problems typically last only a short time, then lags in discretionary stabilization policy mean that the medicine will often have its major effects only after the disease has run its course. In fact, a distinct minority of economists used precisely this reasoning to argue against a fiscal stimulus after the September 11, 2001, terrorist attacks. In terms of Figure 7, this is a case in which point D comes very close to point A.

Although extreme advocates of rules argue that this is indeed what happens, most economists agree that the economy's self-correcting mechanism is slow and not terribly reliable, even when supplemented by the automatic stabilizers. On this count, then, a point is scored for discretionary policy.

How Long Are the Lags in Stabilization Policy?

We just explained why long and unpredictable lags in monetary and fiscal policy make it hard for stabilization policy to do much good. Short, reliable lags point in just the opposite direction. Thus advocates of fixed rules emphasize the length of lags while proponents of discretion tend to discount them.

Who is right depends on the circumstances. Sometimes policy makers take action promptly, and the economy receives at least some stimulus from expansionary policy within a year after slipping into a recession. The tax cut of 2001 and the Fed's sharp monetary stimulus in the fall of 2001 are the most recent examples. Although far from perfect, the effects of such timely actions are felt soon enough to do some good. But, as we have seen, very slow policy responses may actually prove destabilizing. Because history offers examples of each type, we can draw no general conclusion.

How Accurate Are Economic Forecasts?

One way to compress the policy-making lag dramatically is to forecast economic events accurately. If we could see a recession coming a full year ahead of time (which we certainly *cannot* do), even a rather sluggish policy response would still be timely. In terms of Figure 7, this would be a case in which the recession is predicted well before point *A*.

Over the years, economists in universities, government agencies, and private businesses have developed a number of techniques to assist them in predicting what the economy will do. Unfortunately, none of these methods is terribly accurate. To give a rough idea of magnitudes, forecasts of either the inflation rate or the real GDP growth rate for the year ahead typically err by $\pm\,^{3}/_{4}$ to 1 percentage point. But, in a bad year for forecasters, errors of 2 or 3 percentage points are common.

Is this record good enough? That depends on how the forecasts are used. It is certainly not good enough to support *fine tuning*—that is, attempts to keep the economy always within a hair's breadth of full employment. But it probably is good enough for policy makers interested in using discretionary stabilization policy to close persistent and sizable gaps between actual and potential GDP.

The Size of Government

One bogus argument that is nonetheless sometimes heard is that active fiscal policy must inevitably lead to a growing public sector. Because proponents of fixed rules tend also to oppose big government, they view this growth as undesirable. Of course, others think that a larger public sector is just what society needs.

This argument, however, is completely beside the point because, as we pointed out in Chapter 11: *One's opinion about the proper size of government should have nothing to do with one's view on stabilization policy.* For example, President George W. Bush is as conservative as they come and, at least rhetorically, devoted to shrinking the size of the public sector.[4] But his tax-cutting initiatives in 2001–2003 constituted an extremely activist fiscal policy to spur the economy. Furthermore, most stabilization policy these days consists of monetary policy, which neither increases nor decreases the size of government.

Uncertainties Caused by Government Policy

Advocates of rules are on stronger ground when they argue that frequent changes in tax laws, government spending programs, or monetary conditions make it difficult for

---

[4] In fact, the size of the federal government has expanded rapidly during his presidency, in part because of national security concerns.

firms and consumers to formulate and carry out rational plans. They argue that the authorities can provide a more stable environment for the private sector by adhering to fixed rules, so that businesses and consumers will know exactly what to expect.

No one disputes that a more stable environment is better for private planning. Even so, supporters of discretionary policy emphasize that *stability in the economy* is more important than *stability in the government budget* (or in Federal Reserve operations). The whole idea of stabilization policy is to *prevent* gyrations in the pace of economic activity by *causing* timely gyrations in the government budget (or in monetary policy). Which atmosphere is better for business, they ask: one in which fiscal and monetary rules keep things peaceful on Capitol Hill and at the Federal Reserve while recessions and inflations wrack the economy, or one in which government changes its policy abruptly on occasion but the economy grows more steadily? They think the answer is self-evident. The question, of course, is whether stabilization policy can succeed in practice.

A Political Business Cycle?

A final argument put forth by advocates of rules is political rather than economic. Fiscal policy decisions are made by elected politicians: the president and members of Congress. When elections are on the horizon (and for members of the House of Representatives, they *always* are), these politicians may be as concerned with keeping their jobs as with doing what is right for the economy. This situation leaves fiscal policy subject to "political manipulation"—lawmakers may take inappropriate actions to attain short-run political goals. A system of purely automatic stabilization, its proponents argue, would eliminate this peril.

It is certainly *possible* that politicians could deliberately *cause* economic instability to help their own reelection. Indeed, some observers of these "political business cycles"

Between Rules and Discretion

In recent years, a number of economists and policy makers have sought a middle ground between saddling monetary policy makers with rigid rules and giving them complete discretion, as the Federal Reserve has in the United States.

One such approach is called "inflation targeting." As practiced in the United Kingdom, inflation targeting starts when an elected official (the Chancellor of the Exchequer, who is roughly equivalent to the U.S. Secretary of the Treasury) chooses a numerical target for the inflation rate—currently, this target is 2 percent for consumer prices. The United Kingdom's central bank, the Bank of England, is then bound by law to try to reach this target. In that sense, the system functions somewhat like a *rule*. However, monetary policy makers are given complete *discretion* as to how they go about trying to achieve this goal. Neither the Chancellor nor Parliament interferes with day-to-day monetary policy decisions.

Another approach is called the "Taylor rule," after Professor John Taylor of Stanford, who is currently serving as President Bush's Undersecretary of the Treasury for International Affairs. Almost a decade ago, Taylor noticed that the Fed's interest rate decisions during the Greenspan era could be described by a simple algebraic equation. This equation, now called the Taylor rule, starts with a 2 percent *real* interest rate, and then instructs the Fed to *lower* the rate of interest in proportion to any recessionary gap, and to *raise* the interest rate in proportion to any excess of inflation above

2 percent (which is the Fed's presumed inflation goal). No central bank uses the Taylor rule as a mechanical rule; nor did Taylor intend it to be used as such. But many central banks around the world, including the Fed, find the Taylor rule useful as a benchmark to guide their decision making.

The Bank of England's Monetary Policy Committee

"Daddy's not mad at you, dear—Daddy's mad at the Fed."

have claimed that several American presidents have taken full advantage of the opportunity. Furthermore, even without any insidious intent, politicians may take the wrong actions for perfectly honorable reasons. Decisions in the political arena are never clear-cut, and it certainly is easy to find examples of grievous errors in the history of U.S. fiscal policy.

Taken as a whole, then, the political argument against discretionary fiscal policy seems to have a great deal of merit. But what are we to do about it? It is unrealistic to believe that fiscal decisions could or should be made by a group of objective and nonpartisan technicians. Tax and budget policies require inherently *political* decisions that, in a democracy, should be made by elected officials.

This fact may seem worrisome in view of the possibilities for political chicanery. But it should not bother us any more (or any less) than similar maneuvering in other areas of policy making. After all, the same problem besets international relations, national defense, formulation and enforcement of the law, and so on. Politicians make all these decisions, subject only to sporadic accountability at elections. Is there really any reason why fiscal decisions should be different?

But monetary policy *is* different. Because Congress was concerned that elected officials focused on the short run would pursue inflationary monetary policies, it long ago gave day-to-day decisionmaking authority over monetary policy to the unelected technocrats at the Federal Reserve. Politics influences monetary policy only indirectly: The Fed must report to Congress, and the president has the power to appoint Federal Reserve governors to his liking.

? ISSUE REVISITED: *What Should Be Done?*

So where do we come out on the question posed at the start of this chapter? On balance, is it better to pursue the best discretionary policy we can, knowing full well that we will never achieve perfection? Or is it wiser to rely on fixed rules and the automatic stabilizers?

In weighing the pros and cons, your basic view of the economy is crucial. Some economists believe that the economy, if left unmanaged, would generate a series of ups and downs that would be difficult to predict, but that it would correct each of them by itself in a relatively short time. They conclude that, because of long lags and poor forecasts, our ability to anticipate whether the economy will need stimulus or restraint by the time policy actions have their effects is quite limited. Consequently, they advocate fixed rules.

Other economists liken the economy to a giant glacier with a great deal of inertia. Under this view, if we observe an inflationary or recessionary gap today, it will likely still be there a year or two from now because the self-correcting mechanism works slowly. In such a world, accurate forecasting is not imperative, even if policy lags are long. If we base policy on a forecast of a 4 percent gap between actual and potential GDP a year from now, and the gap turns out to be only 2 percent, we still will have done the right thing despite the inaccurate forecast. So holders of this view of the economy tend to support discretionary policy.

There is certainly no consensus on this issue, either among economists or politicians. After all, the question touches on political ideology as well as economics, and liberals often look to government to solve social problems, whereas conservatives consistently point out that many efforts of government fail despite the best intentions. A prudent view of the matter might be that:

The case for active discretionary policy is strong when the economy has a serious deficiency or excess of aggregate demand. However, advocates of fixed rules are right that it is unwise to try to iron out every little wiggle in the growth path of GDP.

But one thing seems certain: The rules-versus-discretion debate is likely to go on for quite some time.

A Nobel Prize for the Rules-versus-Discretion Debate

In 2004, the economists Finn Kydland of Carnegie-Mellon University and Edward Prescott of Arizona State University were awarded the Nobel Prize for a fascinating contribution to the rules-versus-discretion debate. They called attention to a general problem that they labeled "time inconsistency," and their analysis of this problem led them to conclude that the Fed should follow a rule.

A close-to-home example will bring out the basic time inconsistency problem. Your instructor announces in September that a final exam will be given in December. The main purpose of the exam is to ensure that students study and learn the course materials, and the exam itself represents work for the faculty and stress for the students. So, when December rolls around, it may appear "optimal" to call off the exam

SOURCE: © AFP/Getty Images

at the last moment. Of course, if that started happening regularly, students would soon stop studying for exams. So actually giving the exam is the better long-run policy. One way to solve this time inconsistency problem is to adopt a simple *rule* stating that announced exams will always be given, rather than allowing individual faculty members to cancel exams at their *discretion*.

Kydland and Prescott argued that monetary policy makers face a similar time inconsistency problem. They first announce a stern anti-inflation policy (giving an exam). But then, when the moment of truth (December) arrives, they may relent because they don't want to cause unemployment (all that work and stress). Their suggested solution: The Fed and other central banks should adopt *rules* that remove period-by-period *discretion*.

SUMMARY

1. **Velocity** (V) is the ratio of nominal GDP to the stock of money (M). It indicates how quickly money circulates.

2. One important determinant of velocity is the rate of interest (r). At higher interest rates, people find it less attractive to hold money because money pays zero or little interest. Thus, when r rises, money circulates faster, and V rises.

3. **Monetarism** is a type of analysis that focuses attention on velocity and the money supply (M). Although monetarists realize that V is not constant, they believe that it is predictable enough to make it a useful tool for policy analysis and forecasting.

4. Because it increases the volume of transactions, and hence increases the demands for bank deposits and therefore bank reserves, expansionary fiscal policy pushes interest rates higher. Higher interest rates reduce the multiplier by deterring some types of spending, especially investment.

5. Because fiscal policy actions affect aggregate demand either directly through G or indirectly through C, the expenditure lags between fiscal actions and their effects on aggregate demand are probably fairly short. By contrast, monetary policy operates mainly on investment, I, which responds slowly to changes in interest rates.

6. However, the policy-making lag normally is much longer for fiscal policy than for monetary policy. Hence, when the two lags are combined, it is not clear which type of policy acts more quickly.

7. Because it cannot control the demand curve for money, the Federal Reserve cannot control both M and r. If the demand for money changes, the Fed must decide whether it wants to hold M steady, hold r steady, or adopt some compromise position.

8. Monetarists emphasize the importance of stabilizing the growth path of the money supply, whereas the predominant Keynesian view puts more emphasis on keeping interest rates on target.

9. In practice, the Fed has changed its views on this issue several times. For decades, it attached primary importance to interest rates. Between 1979 and 1982, it stressed its commitment to stable growth of the money supply. But, since then, the focus has clearly returned to interest rates.

10. When the aggregate supply curve is very flat, changes in aggregate demand will have large effects on the nation's real output but small effects on the price level. Under those circumstances, stabilization policy works well as an antirecession device, but it has little power to combat inflation.

11. When the aggregate supply curve is steep, changes in aggregate demand have small effects on real output but large effects on the price level. In such a case, stabilization policy can do much to fight inflation but is not a very effective way to cure unemployment.

12. The aggregate supply curve is likely to be relatively flat in the short run but relatively steep in the long run. Hence, stabilization policy affects mainly output in the short run but mainly prices in the long run.

13. When the lags in the operation of fiscal and monetary policy are long and unpredictable, attempts to stabilize economic activity may actually destabilize it.

14. Some economists believe that our imperfect knowledge of the channels through which stabilization policy works, the long lags involved, and the inaccuracy of forecasts make it unlikely that discretionary stabilization policy can succeed.

15. Other economists recognize these difficulties but do not believe they are quite as serious. They also place much less faith in the economy's ability to cure recessions and inflations on its own. They therefore think that discretionary policy is not only advisable, but essential.

16. Stabilizing the economy by fiscal policy need not imply a tendency toward "big government."

KEY TERMS

Velocity   266

Equation of exchange   266

Quantity theory of money   267

Effect of interest rate on velocity   268

Monetarism   269

Effect of fiscal policy on interest rates   269

Lags in stabilization policy   271

Controlling M versus controlling r 272

Rules versus discretionary policy   279

TEST YOURSELF

1. How much money by the M1 definition (cash plus checking account balances) do you typically have at any particular moment? Divide this amount into your total income over the past twelve months to obtain your own personal velocity. Are you typical of the nation as a whole?

2. The following table provides data on nominal gross domestic product and the money supply (M1 definition) in recent selected years. Compute velocity in each year. Can you see any trend? How does it compare with the trend that prevailed from 1975 to 2000?

Year	End-of-Year Money Supply (M1)	Nominal GDP
2000	$1,088	$9,817
2001	1,179	10,128
2002	1,217	10,487
2003	1,293	11,004

NOTE: Amounts are in billions.

3. Use a supply and demand diagram similar to Figure 2 to show the choices open to the Fed following an unexpected *decline* in the demand for money. If the Fed is following a monetarist policy, what will happen to the rate of interest?

4. Which of the following events would strengthen the argument for the use of discretionary policy, and which would strengthen the argument for rules?

a. Structural changes make the economy's self-correcting mechanism work more quickly and reliably than before.

b. New statistical methods are found that improve the accuracy of economic forecasts.

c. A Democratic president is elected when there is an overwhelmingly Republican Congress. Congress and the president differ sharply on what should be done about the national economy.

5. (More difficult) The money supply (M) is the sum of bank deposits (D) plus currency in the hands of the public (call that C). Suppose the required reserve ratio is 20 percent and the Fed provides $50 billion in bank reserves (R = $50 billion).

a. First assume that people hold no currency (C = 0). How large will the money supply (M) be? If the Fed increases bank reserves to R = $60 billion, how large will M be then?

b. Next, assume that people hold 20 cents worth of currency for each dollar of bank deposits, that is, C = $0.2D$. If the Fed creates R = $50 billion worth of reserves, how large will M be now? (Hint: First figure out what D must be, then add the appropriate amount of currency to get M. Remember that M = D + C.) If the Fed once again increases bank reserves to R = $60 billion, how large will M be then?

c. What do you notice about the relationship between M and R?

DISCUSSION QUESTIONS

1. Use the concept of opportunity cost to explain why velocity is higher at higher interest rates.

2. How does monetarism differ from the quantity theory of money?

3. Given the behavior of velocity shown in Figure 1, would it make more sense for the Federal Reserve to formulate targets for M1 or M2?

4. Distinguish between the expenditure lag and the policy lag in stabilization policy. Does monetary or fiscal policy have the shorter expenditure lag? What about the policy lag?

5. Explain why their contrasting views on the shape of the aggregate supply curve lead some economists to argue much more strongly for stabilization policies to fight unemploy-

ment and other economists to argue much more strongly for stabilization policies to fight inflation.

6. Explain why lags make it possible that policy actions intended to stabilize the economy will actually destabilize it.

7. Many observers think that the Federal Reserve succeeded in using deft applications of monetary policy to "fine-tune" the U.S. economy into the full-employment zone in the 1990s without worsening inflation. Use the data on money supply, interest rates, real GDP, unemployment, and the price level given on the inside back cover of this book to evaluate this claim.

8. After 2000, U.S. economic performance deteriorated. (See the data on the inside back cover of this book.) Can this decline be blamed on inferior monetary or fiscal policy? (You may want to ask your instructor about this question.)

16

THE TRADE-OFF BETWEEN INFLATION AND UNEMPLOYMENT

We must seek to reduce inflation at a lower cost in lost output and unemployment.

JIMMY CARTER

As early as our list of *Ideas for Beyond the Final Exam* in Chapter 1, we noted that there is a bothersome *trade-off between inflation and unemployment*: High-growth policies that reduce unemployment tend to raise inflation, and slow-growth policies that reduce inflation tend to raise unemployment. We also observed, in Chapter 14, that the trade-off looks rather different in the short run than in the long run because the aggregate supply curve is fairly flat in the short run but quite steep (perhaps even vertical) in the long run. A statistical relationship called the *Phillips curve* seeks to summarize the quantitative dimensions of the trade-off between inflation and unemployment in both the short and long runs. This chapter is about the Phillips curve.

CONTENTS

? **ISSUE:** *Is the Trade-Off between Inflation and Unemployment a Relic of the Past?*

In the late 1990s, unemployment in the United States fell to extremely low levels—the lowest in 30 years. Yet, in stark contrast to prior experience, inflation did not rise. In fact, it fell slightly. This pleasant conjunction of events, which was nearly unprecedented in U.S. history, set many people talking about a glorious "New Economy" in which there was no longer any trade-off between inflation and unemployment. The soaring stock market, especially for technology stocks, added to the euphoria.

Is the long-feared trade-off really just a memory now? Can the modern economy speed along without fear of rising inflation? Or does faster growth eventually have inflationary consequences? These are the central questions for this chapter. Our answers, in brief, are: no, no, and yes. And we devote most of this chapter to explaining them.

DEMAND-SIDE INFLATION VERSUS SUPPLY-SIDE INFLATION: A REVIEW

We begin by reviewing some of what we learned about inflation in earlier chapters. One major cause of inflation, although certainly not the only one, is *excessive growth of aggregate demand.* We know that any autonomous increase in spending—whether by consumers, investors, the government, or foreigners—will have a multiplier effect on aggregate demand. So each additional \$1 of C or I or G or $(X - IM)$ will lead to more than \$1 of additional demand. We also know that firms normally find it profitable to supply additional output only at higher prices. Hence, a stimulus to aggregate demand will normally pull up both real output and prices.

Figure 1, which is familiar from earlier chapters, reviews this conclusion. Initially, the economy is at point A, where aggregate demand curve D_0D_0 intersects aggregate supply curve SS. Then something happens to increase spending, and the aggregate demand curve shifts horizontally to D_1D_1. The new equilibrium is at point B, where both prices and output are higher than they were at A. Thus, the economy experiences both inflation and increased output. The slope of the aggregate supply curve measures the amount of inflation that accompanies any specified rise in output and therefore encapsulates the trade-off between inflation and economic growth.

But we also have learned in this book (especially in Chapter 10) that inflation does not always originate from the demand side. Anything that retards the growth of aggregate supply—for example, an increase in the price of foreign oil—can shift the economy's aggregate supply curve inward. This sort of inflation is illustrated in Figure 2, where the aggregate supply curve shifts inward from S_0S_0 to S_1S_1, and the economy's equilibrium consequently moves from point A to point B. Prices rise as output falls. We have *stagflation.*

Thus, although inflation can emanate from either the demand side or the supply side of the economy, a crucial difference arises between the two sources. **Demand-side inflation** is normally accompanied by rapid growth of real GDP (as in Figure 1), whereas **supply-side inflation** is normally accompanied by stagnant or even falling GDP (as in Figure 2). This distinction has major practical importance, as we shall see in this chapter.

FIGURE 1

Inflation from the Demand Side

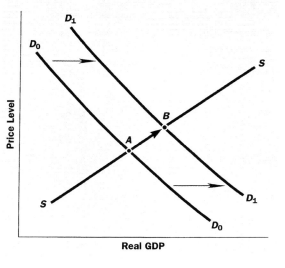

Real GDP

Demand-side inflation is a rise in the price level caused by rapid growth of aggregate demand.

Supply-side inflation is a rise in the price level caused by slow growth (or decline) of aggregate supply.

◼ ORIGINS OF THE PHILLIPS CURVE

Let us begin by supposing that most economic fluctuations are driven by gyrations in *aggregate demand*. In that case, we have just seen that GDP growth and inflation should rise and fall together. Is this what the data show?

We will see shortly, but first let us translate the prediction into a corresponding statement about the relationship between inflation and unemployment. Faster growth of real output naturally means faster growth in the number of jobs and, hence, lower unemployment. Conversely, slower growth of real output means slower growth in the number of jobs and, hence, higher unemployment. So we conclude that, if business fluctuations emanate from the demand side, unemployment and inflation should move in opposite directions: Unemployment should be low when inflation is high, and inflation should be low when unemployment is high.

Figure 3 illustrates the idea. The unemployment rate in the United States in 2004 averaged 5.4 percent (which we round to 5 percent in the figure), and the inflation rate was about 2 percent. Point B in Figure 3 records these two numbers. Had aggregate demand grown faster, inflation would have been higher and unemployment would have been lower. For the sake of concreteness, we suppose that unemployment would have been 4 percent and inflation would have been 3 percent—as shown by point A in Figure 3. By contrast, had aggregate demand grown more slowly than it actually did, unemployment would have been higher and inflation lower. In Figure 3, we suppose that unemployment would have been 6 percent and inflation would have been just 1 percent (point C). This figure displays the principal empirical implication of our theoretical model:

> If fluctuations in economic activity are primarily caused by variations in the rate at which the aggregate demand curve shifts outward from year to year, then the data should show an inverse relationship between unemployment and inflation.

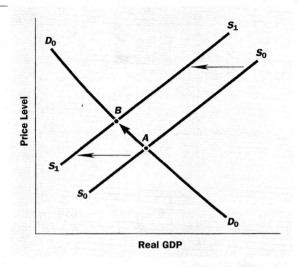

FIGURE 2

Inflation from the Supply Side

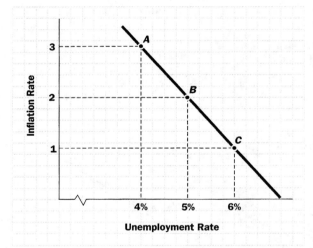

FIGURE 3

Origins of the Phillips Curve

Now we are ready to look at real data. Do we actually observe such an inverse relationship between inflation and unemployment? More than 40 years ago, the economist A. W. Phillips plotted data on unemployment and the rate of change of money *wages* (not prices) for several extended periods of British history on a series of scatter diagrams, one of which is reproduced on the next page as Figure 4. He then sketched in a curve that seemed to "fit" the data well. This type of curve, which we now call a **Phillips curve,** shows that wage inflation normally is high when unemployment is low and is low when unemployment is high. So far, so good. These data illustrate the short run trade-off between inflation and unemployment, one of our *Ideas for Beyond the Final Exam.*

Phillips curves are more commonly constructed for price inflation; Figure 5 shows a Phillips-type diagram for the post–World War II United States. The curve appears to fit the data well. As viewed through the eyes of our theory, these facts suggest that economic

A **Phillips curve** is a graph depicting the rate of unemployment on the horizontal axis and either the rate of inflation or the rate of change of money wages on the vertical axis. Phillips curves are normally downward sloping, indicating that higher inflation rates are associated with lower unemployment rates.

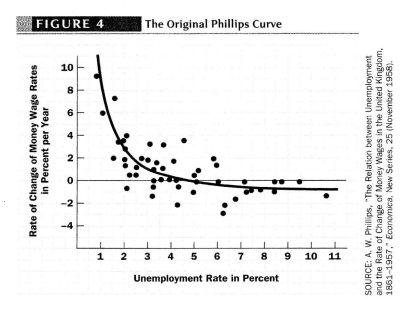

FIGURE 4   The Original Phillips Curve

SOURCE: A. W. Phillips, "The Relation between Unemployment and the Rate of Change of Money Wages in the United Kingdom, 1861–1957," *Economica*, New Series, 25 (November 1958).

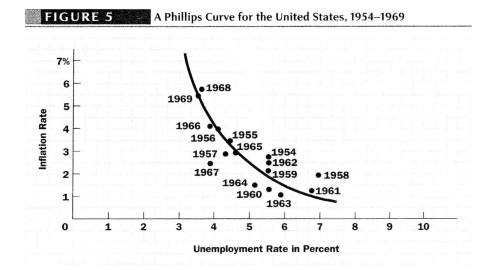

FIGURE 5   A Phillips Curve for the United States, 1954–1969

fluctuations in Great Britain between 1861 and 1913 and in the United States between 1954 and 1969 probably arose primarily from changes in the growth of aggregate demand. The simple model of demand-side inflation really does seem to describe what happened.

During the 1960s and early 1970s, economists often thought of the Phillips curve as a "menu" of choices available to policy makers. In this view, policy makers could opt for low unemployment and high inflation—as in 1969, or for high unemployment coupled with low inflation—as in 1961. The Phillips curve, it was thought, described the quantitative trade-off between inflation and unemployment. And for a number of years it seemed to work.

Then something happened. The economy in the 1970s and early 1980s behaved far worse than the Phillips curve had led economists to expect. In particular, given the unemployment rates in each of those years, inflation was astonishingly high by historical standards. This fact is shown clearly by Figure 6, which simply adds to Figure 5 the points for 1970 to 1984. So something went wrong with the old view of the Phillips curve as a menu for policy choices. But what?

SUPPLY-SIDE INFLATION AND THE COLLAPSE OF THE PHILLIPS CURVE

There are two major answers to this question, and a full explanation contains elements of each. We begin with the simpler answer, which is that much of the inflation in the years from 1972 to 1982 did not emanate from the demand side. Instead, the 1970s and early 1980s were full of adverse "supply shocks"—events such as the crop failures of 1972–1973 and the oil price increases of 1973–1974 and 1979–1980. These events pushed the economy's aggregate supply curve inward to the left, as was shown in Figure 2 (page 307). What kind of "Phillips curve" will be generated when economic fluctuations come from the supply side?

Figure 2 reminds us that output will decline (or at least grow more slowly) and prices will rise when the economy is hit by an adverse supply shock. Now, in a growing population with more people looking for jobs each year, a stagnant economy that does not generate enough new jobs will suffer a rise in unemployment. Thus, inflation and unemployment will increase at the same time:

> If fluctuations in economic activity emanate from the supply side, higher rates of inflation will be associated with higher rates of unemployment, and lower rates of inflation will be associated with lower rates of unemployment.

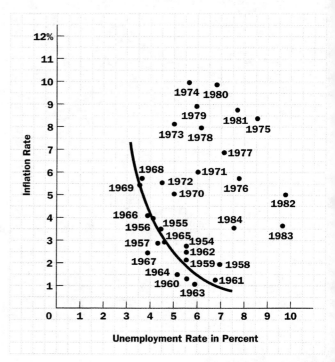

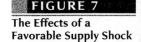

FIGURE 6

A Phillips Curve for the United States?

The major supply shocks of the 1970s stand out clearly in Figure 6. (Remember—these are real data, not textbook examples.) Food prices soared from 1972 to 1974, and again in 1978. Energy prices skyrocketed in 1973–1974, and again in 1979–1980. Clearly, the inflation and unemployment data generated by the U.S. economy in 1972–1974 and in 1978–1980 are consistent with our model of supply-side inflation. Many economists believe that supply shocks, rather than abrupt changes in aggregate demand, made the Phillips curve shift.

FIGURE 7

The Effects of a Favorable Supply Shock

Explaining the Fabulous 1990s

Now let's stand this analysis of supply shocks on its head. Suppose the economy experiences a *favorable* supply shock, rather than an adverse one, so that the aggregate supply curve shifts *outward* at an unusually rapid rate. Any number of factors—such as a drop in oil prices, bountiful harvests, or exceptionally rapid technological advance—can have this effect.

Whatever the cause, Figure 7—which duplicates Figure 14 of Chapter 10—depicts the consequences. The aggregate demand curve shifts outward as usual, but the aggregate supply curve shifts out more than it would in a "normal" year. So the economy's equilibrium winds up at point *B* rather than

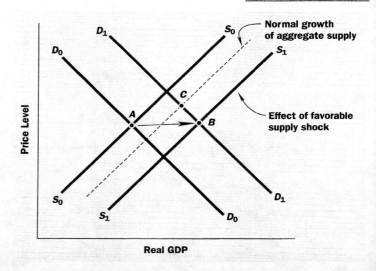

at point C, meaning that economic growth is *faster* (B is to the right of C) and inflation is *lower* (B is below C). Thus, inflation falls while rapid growth reduces unemployment.

Figure 7 more or less characterizes the experience of the U.S. economy from 1996 to 1998. Oil prices plummeted, lowering costs to American businesses and households. Stunning advances in technology made computer prices drop even more rapidly than usual. And the rising value of the U.S. dollar made imported goods cheaper to Americans.[1] Thus, we benefited from a series of favorable supply shocks, and the effects were just as depicted in Figure 7. The U.S. economy grew rapidly, and both inflation and unemployment fell at the same time.

?   **ISSUE RESOLVED:** *Why Inflation and Unemployment Both Declined*

We now have the answer to the question posed at the start of this chapter. We need nothing particularly new or mysterious to explain the marvelous economic performance of the second half of the 1990s. According to the basic macroeconomic theory taught in this book, favorable supply shocks should produce rapid economic growth with falling inflation. The U.S. economy did so well, in part, because we were so fortunate.

WHAT THE PHILLIPS CURVE IS NOT

So one view is that adverse supply shocks caused the stagflation of the 1970s and 1980s. But there is another view of what went wrong with the Phillips curve. It holds that policy makers misinterpreted the Phillips curve and tried to pick combinations of inflation and unemployment that were simply unsustainable.

Specifically, we have learned that the Phillips curve is a *statistical relationship* between inflation and unemployment that we expect to emerge *if business cycle fluctuations arise mainly from changes in the growth of aggregate demand*. But in the 1970s and 1980s, the curve was widely misinterpreted as depicting a number of *alternative equilibrium points* that the economy could achieve and from which policy makers could choose.

To understand the flaw in this reasoning, let us quickly review an earlier lesson. We know from Chapter 10 that the economy *self-correcting mechanism* that will cure both inflations and recessions *eventually*, even if the government does nothing. This idea is important in this context because it tells us that many combinations of output and prices cannot be maintained indefinitely. Some will self-destruct. Specifically, if the economy finds itself far from the normal full-employment level of unemployment, forces will be set in motion that tend to erode the inflationary or recessionary gap.

Figure 8 depicts the case of a recessionary gap where aggregate supply curve S_0S_0 intersects aggregate demand curve DD at point A. With equilibrium output well below potential GDP, the economy has unused industrial capacity and unsold output, so inflation will be tame. At the same time, the availability of unemployed workers eager for jobs limits the rate at which labor can push up wage rates. But wages are the main component of business costs, so when they decline (relative to what they would have been without a recession) so do costs. The lower costs, in turn, stimulate greater production. Figure 8 illustrates this process by an outward shift of the aggregate supply curve—from S_0S_0 to the blue curve S_1S_1.

As the figure shows, the outward shift of the aggre-

FIGURE 8

e Elimination of a
cessionary Gap

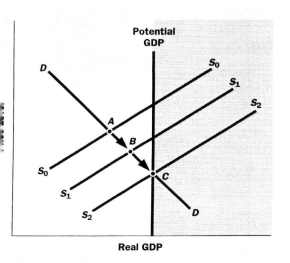

Potential GDP

S_0

S_1

S_2

D

A

B

C

S_0

S_1

S_2

D

Real GDP

---
[1] The dollar and imports will be discussed in detail in Chapter 19.

gate supply curve brought on by the recession pushes equilibrium output up as the economy moves from point *A* to point *B*. Thus, the size of the recessionary gap begins to shrink. This process continues until the aggregate supply curve reaches the position indicated by the red curve S_2S_2 in Figure 8. Here wages have fallen enough to eliminate the recessionary gap, and the economy has reached a full-employment equilibrium at point *C*.[2]

We can relate this sequence of events to our discussion of the origins of the Phillips curve with the help of Figure 9, which is a hypothetical Phillips curve. Point *a* in Figure 9 corresponds to point *A* in Figure 8: It shows the initial recessionary gap with unemployment (assumed to be 6.5 percent) above full employment, which we assume to occur at 5 percent.

But we have just seen that point *A* in Figure 8—and therefore also point *a* in Figure 9—is not sustainable. The economy tends to rid itself of the recessionary gap through the disinflation process we have just described. The adjustment path from *A* to *C* depicted in Figure 8 would appear on our Phillips curve diagram as a movement toward less inflation and less unemployment—something like the red arrow from point *a* to point *c* in Figure 9.

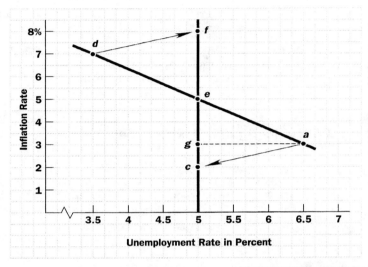

Similarly, points representing inflationary gaps—such as point *d* in Figure 9—are also not sustainable. They, too, are gradually eliminated by the self-correcting mechanism that we studied in Chapter 10. Wages are forced up by the abnormally low unemployment, which in turn pushes prices higher. Higher prices deter investment spending by forcing up interest rates, and they deter consumer spending by lowering the purchasing power of consumer wealth. The inflationary process continues until the amount people want to spend is brought into balance with the amount firms want to supply at normal full employment. During such an adjustment period, unemployment and inflation both rise—as indicated by the red arrow from point *d* to point *f* in Figure 9. Putting these two conclusions together, we see that:

> On a Phillips curve diagram such as Figure 9, neither points corresponding to an inflationary gap (like point *d*) nor points corresponding to a recessionary gap (like point *a*) can be maintained indefinitely. Inflationary gaps lead to rising unemployment and rising inflation. Recessionary gaps lead to falling inflation and falling unemployment.

All the points that are sustainable in the long run (such as *c*, *e*, and *f*) correspond to the same rate of unemployment, which is therefore called the **natural rate of unemployment.** The natural rate corresponds to what we have so far been calling the "full-employment" unemployment rate.

Thus, the Phillips curve connecting points *d*, *e*, and *a* is not a menu of policy choices at all. Although we can move from a point such as *e* to a point such as *d* by stimulating aggregate demand sufficiently, the economy will not be able to remain at point *d*. We cannot keep unemployment at such a low level indefinitely. Instead, policy makers must choose from among points such as *c*, *e*, and *f*, all of which correspond to the same "natural" rate of unemployment. For obvious reasons, the line connecting these points has been dubbed the **vertical long-run Phillips curve.** It is

FIGURE 9

The Vertical Long-Run Phillips Curve

The economy's self-correcting mechanism always tends to push the unemployment rate back toward a specific rate of unemployment that we call the **natural rate of unemployment.**

The **vertical (long-run) Phillips curve** shows the menu of inflation/unemployment choices available to society in the long run. It is a vertical straight line at the natural rate of unemployment.

---

[2] This simple analysis assumes that the aggregate demand curve does not move during the adjustment period. If it is shifting to the right, the recessionary gap will disappear even faster, but inflation will not slow down as much. (*Exercise:* Construct the diagram for this case by adding a shift of the aggregate demand curve to Figure 8.)

this vertical Phillips curve, connecting points such as *e* and *f*, that represents the true long-run menu of policy choices. We thus conclude:

IDEAS FOR BEYOND THE FINAL EXAM

THE TRADE-OFF BETWEEN INFLATION AND UNEMPLOYMENT In the short run, it is possible to "ride up the Phillips curve" toward lower levels of unemployment by stimulating aggregate demand. (See, for example, point *d* in Figure 9.) Conversely, by restricting the growth of demand, it is possible to "ride down the Phillips curve" toward lower rates of inflation (such as point *a* in Figure 9). Thus, there is a *trade-off between unemployment and inflation in the short run*. Stimulating demand will improve the unemployment picture but worsen inflation; restricting demand will lower inflation but aggravate the unemployment problem.

However, there is no such trade-off in the long run. The economy's self-correcting mechanism ensures that unemployment will eventually return to the natural rate no matter what happens to aggregate demand. In the long run, faster growth of demand leads only to higher inflation, not to lower unemployment; and slower growth of demand leads only to lower inflation, not to higher unemployment.

■ FIGHTING UNEMPLOYMENT WITH FISCAL AND MONETARY POLICY

Now let us apply this analysis to a concrete policy problem—one that has troubled many policy makers in the United States and in other countries. Should the government's ability to manage aggregate demand through fiscal and monetary policy be used to combat unemployment? If so, how? To focus the discussion, we will deal with a recent, real-world example.

The unemployment rate in the United States bottomed out at 3.8 percent in April 2000, a rate that most economists thought was well below the natural rate of unemployment (something like point *d* in Figure 9). It then began to creep up gradually, and by August 2001 stood at 4.9 percent—which may be close to the natural rate (see point *e* in the figure). Then the terrorist attacks of September 11, 2001 occurred, and within a few months unemployment had risen to 5.7 percent. By December, the economy was in a position resembling point *a* in Figure 9, with a recessionary gap.

Even if fiscal and monetary policy makers did nothing, the economy's self-correcting mechanism would have gradually eroded the recessionary gap. Both unemployment and inflation would have declined gradually as the economy moved along the red arrow from point *a* to point *c* in Figure 9. Eventually, as the diagram shows, the economy would have returned to its natural rate of unemployment (assumed here to be 5 percent) and inflation would have fallen—in the example, from 3 percent to 2 percent.

This eventual outcome is quite satisfactory: Both unemployment and inflation are lower at the end of the adjustment period (point *c*) than at the beginning (point *a*). But it may take an agonizingly long time to get there. And American policy makers in 2001 did not view patience as a virtue. The Federal Reserve moved almost immediately after the terrorist attacks, cutting interest rates several times by year end. Fiscal policy reacted as well. Spending on defense and security was increased immediately after the attacks, the first phase of the 2001 tax cut kicked in, and Congress passed a small fiscal stimulus package.

According to the theory we have learned, such a large dose of expansionary fiscal and monetary policy should have pushed the economy up the short-run Phillips curve from a point like *a* toward a point like *e* in Figure 9. Compared to simply relying on the self-correcting mechanism, then, the strong stabilization policy response presumably led to a faster recovery from the 2001 recession. That was certainly the intent of the president, Congress, and the Fed. But Figure 9 points out that it also probably left us with a higher inflation rate (5 percent in the figure, about 2 percent in reality).

This example illustrates the range of choices open to policy makers: They can wait patiently while the economy's self-correcting mechanism pulls unemployment down to the natural rate—leading to a long-run equilibrium like point *c* in Figure 9. Alternatively, they can rush the process along with expansionary monetary and fiscal policy—and wind up with the same unemployment rate but higher inflation (point *e*). In what sense, then, do policy makers face a *trade-off* between inflation and unemployment? The answer illustrated by this diagram is:

The cost of reducing unemployment more rapidly by expansionary fiscal and monetary policies is a permanently higher inflation rate.

■ WHAT SHOULD BE DONE?

Should the government pay the inflationary costs of fighting unemployment? When the transitory benefit (lower unemployment for a while) is balanced against the permanent cost (higher inflation), have we made a good bargain?

We have noted that the U.S. government opted for a strong policy response in 2001. Thus two forces were at work simultaneously: The self-correcting mechanism was pulling the economy toward point *c* in Figure 9, even as the expansionary monetary and fiscal policies were pushing it toward point *e*. The net result was an intermediate path—something like the dotted line leading to point *g* in Figure 9. As this book went to press in 2005, the economy was growing nicely and unemployment was between 5 and 5½ percent.

How do policy makers make decisions like this? Our analysis highlights three critical issues on which the answer depends.

▩ The Costs of Inflation and Unemployment

In Chapter 6, we examined the social costs of inflation and unemployment. Most of the benefits of lower unemployment, we concluded, translate easily into dollars and cents. Basically, we need only estimate the higher real GDP each year. However, the costs of the permanently higher inflation rate are more difficult to measure. So there is considerable controversy over the costs and benefits of using demand management to fight unemployment.

Economists and political leaders who believe that inflation is extremely costly may deem it unwise to accept the inflationary consequences of reducing unemployment faster. And indeed, a few dissenters in 2001 were worried about future inflation. Most U.S. policy makers apparently disagreed with that view, however. They decided that reducing unemployment was more important. But things do not always work out that way. In recent decades, many European governments have avoided expansionary stabilization policies rather than accept higher inflation.

▩ The Slope of the Short-Run Phillips Curve

The shape of the short-run Phillips curve is also critical. Look back at Figure 9, and imagine that the Phillips curve connecting points *a*, *e*, and *d* was much steeper. In that case, the inflationary costs of using expansionary policy to reduce unemployment would be more substantial. By contrast, if the short-run Phillips curve was much flatter than the one shown in Figure 9, unemployment could be reduced with less inflationary cost.

▩ The Efficiency of the Economy's Self-Correcting Mechanism

We have emphasized that, once a recessionary gap opens, the economy's natural self-correcting mechanism will eventually close it—even in the absence of any policy response. The obvious question is: How long must we wait? If the self-correcting mechanism—which works through reductions in wage inflation—is fast and reliable, high unemployment will not last very long. So the costs of waiting will be small. But if wage inflation responds only slowly to unemployment, the costs of waiting may be enormous. That has evidently been true in much of Europe, where unemployment has remained persistently high for years.

Inflation Targeting and the Philips Curve

In Chapter 31, we mentioned *inflation targeting* as a new approach to monetary policy that is gaining adherents in many countries. In practice, inflation targeting requires monetary policy makers to rely heavily on the Phillips curve. Why? Because a central bank with, say, a 2 percent inflation target is obligated to pursue a monetary policy that it believes will drive the inflation rate to 2 percent after, say, a year or two. But how does the central bank know which policy will accomplish this goal?

Knowing the proper policy with certainty is, of course, out of the question. But a central bank can use a model similar to the aggregate supply/demand model taught in this book to *estimate* how its policy choices will affect the unemployment rate, say, this year and next. Then it can use a Phillips curve to *estimate* how that unemployment path will affect inflation. In fact, that is more or less what inflation-targeting central banks from New Zealand to Sweden do.

The efficacy of the self-correcting mechanism is also surrounded by controversy. Most economists believe that the weight of the evidence points to extremely sluggish wage behavior: Wage inflation appears to respond slowly to economic slack. In terms of Figure 9, this lag means that the economy will traverse the path from *a* to *c* at an agonizingly slow pace, so that a long period of weak economic activity will be necessary to bring down inflation.

But a significant minority opinion finds this assessment far too pessimistic. Economists in this group argue that the costs of reducing inflation are not nearly so severe and that the key to a successful anti-inflation policy is how it affects people's *expectations* of inflation. To understand this argument, we must first understand why expectations are relevant to the Phillips curve.

INFLATIONARY EXPECTATIONS AND THE PHILLIPS CURVE

Recall from Chapter 10 that the main reason why the economy's aggregate supply curve slopes upward—that is, why output increases as the price level rises—is that businesses typically purchase labor and other inputs under long-term contracts that fix input costs in money terms. (The money wage rate is the clearest example.) As long as such contracts are in force, *real* wages fall as the prices of goods rise. Labor therefore becomes cheaper in real terms, which persuades businesses to expand employment and output. Buying low and selling high is, after all, the recipe for higher profits.

Table 1 illustrates this general idea in a concrete example. We suppose that workers and firms agree today that the money wage to be paid a year from now will be $10 per hour. The table then shows the real wage corresponding to each alternative inflation rate. For example, if inflation is 4 percent, the real wage a year from now will be $10.00/1.04 = $9.62. Clearly, the higher the inflation rate, the higher the price level at the end of the year and the lower the real wage.

Lower real wages provide an incentive for firms to increase output, as we have just noted. But lower real wages also impose losses of purchasing power on workers. Thus, workers are, in some sense, "cheated" by inflation if they sign a contract specifying a fixed money wage in an inflationary environment.

Many economists doubt that workers will sign such contracts *if they can see inflation coming*. Would it not be wiser, these economists ask, to insist on being compensated for the coming inflation? After all, firms should be willing to offer higher money wages if they

	TABLE 1		
Money and Real Wages under Unexpected Inflation			
Inflation Rate	Price Level 1 Year from Now	Wage per Hour 1 Year from Now	Real Wage per Hour 1 Year from Now
0%	100	$10.00	$10.00
2	102	10.00	9.80
4	104	10.00	9.62
6	106	10.00	9.43

OTE: Each real wage figure is obtained by dividing the $10 nominal wage by the corresponding price level a year later and multiplying by 100. Thus, for example, when the inflation rate 4 percent, the real wage at the end of the year is ($10.00/104) × 100 = $9.62.

expect inflation, because they realize that higher money wages need not imply higher *real* wages.

Table 2 illustrates the mechanics of such a deal. For example, if people expect 4 percent inflation, the contract could stipulate that the wage rate be increased to $10.40 (which is 4 percent more than $10) at the end of the year. That would keep the real wage at $10 (because $10.40/1.04 = $10.00), the same as it would be under zero inflation. The other money wage figures in Table 2 are derived similarly.

If workers and firms behave this way, and if they forecast inflation accurately, then the real wage will not decline as the price level rises. Instead, prices and wages will go up together, leaving the real wage unchanged. Workers will not lose from inflation, and firms will not gain. (Notice that, in Table 2, the expected future real wage is $10 per hour regardless of the expected inflation rate.) But then there would be no reason for firms to raise production when the price level rises. In a word, the aggregate supply curve would become vertical. In general:

> If workers can see inflation coming, and if they receive compensation for it, inflation does not erode *real* wages. But if real wages do not fall, firms have no incentives to increase production. In such a case, the economy's aggregate supply curve will not slope upward but, rather, will be a vertical line at the level of output corresponding to potential GDP.

Such a curve is shown in Panel (a) of Figure 10. Because a vertical aggregate supply curve leads to a vertical Phillips curve, it follows that even the *short-run* Phillips curve would be vertical under these circumstances, as in Panel (b) of Figure 10.[3]

If this analysis is correct, it has profound implications for the costs and benefits of fighting inflation. To see this, refer once again to Figure 9 (page 311), but now use the graph to depict the strategy of fighting inflation by causing a recession. Suppose we start at point *e*, with 5 percent inflation. To move to point *c* (representing 2 percent inflation), the economy must take a long and unpleasant detour through point *a*. Specifically, contractionary policies must push the economy down the Phillips curve toward point *a* before the self-correcting mechanism takes over and moves the economy from *a* to *c*. In words, we must endure a recession to reduce inflation.

But what if even the *short-run* Phillips curve were *vertical* rather than downward sloping? In this case, the unpleasant recessionary detour would not be necessary. It

TABLE 2

Money and Real Wages under Expected Inflation

Expected Inflation Rate	Expected Price Level 1 Year from Now	Wage per Hour 1 Year from Now	Expected Real Wage per Hour 1 Year from Now
0%	100	$10.00	$10.00
2	102	10.20	10.00
4	104	10.40	10.00
6	106	10.60	10.00

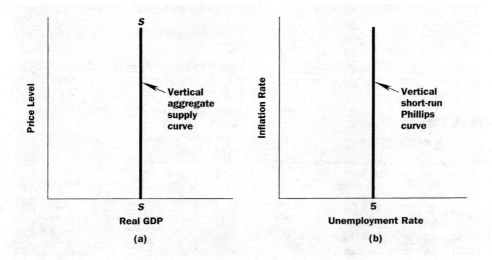

FIGURE 10

A Vertical Aggregate Supply Curve and the Corresponding Vertical Phillips Curve

(a)

(b)

---

[3] Test Yourself Question 1 at the end of the chapter asks you to demonstrate that a vertical aggregate supply curve leads to a vertical Phillips curve.

would be possible for inflation to fall without unemployment rising. The economy could move vertically downward from point *e* to point *c*.

Does this optimistic analysis describe the real world? Can we really slay the inflationary dragon so painlessly? Not necessarily, for our discussion of expectations so far has made at least one unrealistic assumption: that businesses and workers can predict inflation accurately. Under this assumption, as Table 2 shows, real wages are unaffected by inflation—leaving the aggregate supply curve vertical, even in the short run.

But forecasts of inflation are often inaccurate. Suppose workers underestimate inflation. For example, suppose they expect 4 percent inflation but actually get 6 percent. Then real wages will decline by 2 percent. More generally, real wages will fall if workers underestimate inflation at all. The effects of inflation on real wages will be somewhere in between those shown in Tables 1 and 2.[4] So firms will retain some incentive to raise production as the price level rises. The aggregate supply curve will retain its upward slope. We thus conclude that:

The short-run aggregate supply curve is *vertical* when inflation is predicted accurately but *upward sloping* when inflation is underestimated. Thus, only *unexpectedly* high inflation will raise output, because only unexpected inflation reduces real wages.[5] Similarly, only an *unexpected* decline in inflation will lead to a recession.

Because people often fail to anticipate changes in inflation correctly, this analysis seems to leave our earlier discussion of the Phillips curve almost intact for practical purposes. Indeed, most economists nowadays believe that the Phillips curve slopes downward in the short run but is vertical in the long run.

■ THE THEORY OF RATIONAL EXPECTATIONS

Rational expectations are forecasts that, while not necessarily correct, are the best that can be made given the available data. Rational expectations, therefore, cannot err systematically. If expectations are rational, forecasting errors are pure random numbers.

However, a vocal minority of economists disagrees. This group, believers in the hypothesis of **rational expectations,** insists that the Phillips curve is vertical even in the short run. To understand their point of view, we must first explain what rational expectations are. Then we will see why rational expectations have such radical implications for the trade-off between inflation and unemployment.

▒ What Are Rational Expectations?

In many economic contexts, people must formulate expectations about what the future will bring. For example, those who invest in the stock market need to forecast the future prices of the stocks they buy and sell. Likewise, as we have just discussed, workers and businesses may want to forecast future prices before agreeing on a money wage. Rational expectations is a controversial hypothesis about how such forecasts are made.

As used by economists, a forecast (an "expectation") of a future variable is considered rational if the forecaster makes *optimal* use of all relevant information that is *available* at the time of the forecast. Let us elaborate on the two italicized words in this definition, using as an example a hypothetical stock market investor who has rational expectations.

First, proponents of rational expectations recognize that *information is limited*. An investor interested in Google stock would like to know how much profit the company will make in the coming years. Armed with such information, she could predict the future price of Google stock more accurately. But that information is simply not available. The investor's forecast of the future price of Google shares is not "irrational" just because she cannot foresee the future. On the other hand, if Google stock normally goes down on Fridays and up on Mondays, she should be aware of this fact.

Next, we have the word *optimal*. As used by economists, it means using proper statistical inference to process all the relevant information that is available before

---

[4] To make sure you understand why, construct a version of Table 2 based on the assumption that workers expect 4 percent inflation (and hence set next year's wage at $10.40 per hour), regardless of what the actual rate of inflation is. If you create this table correctly, it will show that higher inflation leads to lower real wages, as in Table 1.

[5] To see this point, compare Tables 1 and 2.

making a forecast. In brief, to have rational expectations, your forecasts do not have to be correct, but they cannot have systematic errors that you could avoid by applying better statistical methods. This requirement, although exacting, is not quite as outlandish as it may seem. A good billiards player makes expert use of the laws of physics even without understanding the theory. Similarly, an experienced stock market investor may make good use of information even without formal training in statistics.

Rational Expectations and the Trade-Off

Let us now see how some economists have used the hypothesis of rational expectations to deny any trade-off between inflation and unemployment—even in the short run.

Although they recognize that inflation cannot always be predicted accurately, proponents of rational expectations insist that workers will not make *systematic* errors. Remember that our argument leading to a sloping short-run Phillips curve tacitly assumed that workers are slow to recognize changes. They thus *underestimate* inflation when it is rising and *overestimate* inflation when it is falling. Many observers see such errors as a realistic description of human behavior. But advocates of rational expectations disagree, claiming that it is fundamentally illogical. Workers, they argue, will always make the best possible forecast of inflation, using all the latest data and the best available economic models. Such forecasts will sometimes be too high and sometimes too low, but they will not err systematically in one direction or the other. Consequently:

If expectations are rational, the difference between the *actual* rate of inflation and the *expected* rate of inflation (the forecasting error) must be a pure random number, that is:

Inflation = Expected inflation + a random number

Now recall that the argument in the previous section concluded that employment is affected by inflation only to the extent that inflation *differs* from what was expected. But, under rational expectations, no *predictable* change in inflation can make the *expected* rate of inflation deviate from the *actual* rate of inflation. The difference between the two is simply a random number. Hence, according to the rational expectations hypothesis, unemployment will always remain at the natural rate—except for random, and therefore totally unpredictable, gyrations due to forecasting errors. Thus:

If expectations are rational, inflation can be reduced without a period of high unemployment because the short-run Phillips curve, like the long-run Phillips curve, will be vertical.

According to the rational expectations view, the government's ability to manipulate aggregate demand gives it no ability to influence real output and unemployment because the aggregate supply curve is vertical—even in the short run. (To see why, experiment by moving an aggregate demand curve when the aggregate supply curve is vertical, as in Panel (a) of Figure 10 on page 315.) The government's manipulations of aggregate demand are planned ahead and are therefore predictable, and any *predictable* change in aggregate demand will change the *expected* rate of inflation. It will therefore leave real wages unaffected.

The government can influence output only by making *unexpected* changes in aggregate demand. But unexpected changes are not easy to engineer if expectations are rational, because people will understand what policy makers are up to. For example, if the authorities typically react to high inflation by reducing aggregate demand, people will soon come to anticipate this reaction. And *anticipated* reductions in aggregate demand do not cause *unexpected* changes in inflation.

An Evaluation

Believers in rational expectations are optimistic that we can reduce inflation without losing any output, even in the short run. Are they right?

As a piece of pure logic, the rational expectations argument is impeccable. But as is common in world of economic policy, controversy arises over how well the theoretical idea applies in practice. Although the theory has attracted many adherents, the evidence to date leads most economists to reject the extreme rational expectationist position in favor of the view that a trade-off between inflation and unemployment does exist in the short run. Here are some of the reasons.

Contracts May Embody Outdated Expectations   Many contracts for labor and other raw materials cover such long periods of time that the expectations on which they were based, although rational at the time, may appear "irrational" from today's point of view. For example, some three-year labor contracts were drawn up in 1996, when inflation had been running near 3 percent for years. It might have been rational then to expect the 1999 price level to be about 9 percent higher than the 1996 price level, and to have set wages for 1999 accordingly. By 1997, however, inflation had fallen to below 2 percent, and such an expectation would have been plainly irrational. But it might already have been written into contracts. If so, real wages wound up higher than intended, giving firms an incentive to reduce output and therefore employment—even though no one behaved irrationally.

Expectations May Adjust Slowly   Many people believe that inflationary expectations do not adapt as quickly to changes in the economic environment as the rational expectations theory assumes. If, for example, the government embarks on an anti-inflation policy, workers may continue to expect high inflation for a while. Thus, they may continue to insist on rapid money wage increases. Then, if inflation actually slows down, real wages will rise faster than anyone expected, and unemployment will result. Such behavior may not be strictly rational, but it may be realistic.

When Do Workers Receive Compensation for Inflation?   Some observers question whether wage agreements typically compensate workers for expected inflation in advance, as assumed by the rational expectations theory. More typically, they argue, wages catch up to actual inflation after the fact. If so, real wages will be eroded by inflation, as in the conventional view.

What the Facts Show   The facts have not been kind to the rational expectations hypothesis. The theory suggests that unemployment should hover around the natural rate most of the time, with random gyrations in one direction or the other. Yet this is not what the data show. The theory also predicts that preannounced (and thus expected) anti-inflation programs should be relatively painless. Yet, in practice, fighting inflation has proved very costly in virtually every country. Finally, many direct tests of the rationality of expectations have cast doubt on the hypothesis. For example, survey data on people's expectations rarely meet the exacting requirements of rationality.

But all these problems with rational expectations should not obscure a basic truth. In the long run, the rational expectations view should be more or less correct because people will not cling to incorrect expectations indefinitely. As Abraham Lincoln pointed out with characteristic wisdom, you cannot fool all the people all the time.

WHY ECONOMISTS (AND POLITICIANS) DISAGREE

This chapter has now taught us some of the reasons why economists may disagree about the proper conduct of stabilization policy. It also helps us understand some of the related political debates.

Should the government take strong actions to prevent or reduce inflation? You will say *yes* if you believe that (1) inflation is more costly than unemployment, (2) the short-run Phillips curve is steep, (3) expectations react quickly, and (4) the economy's self-correcting mechanism works smoothly and rapidly. These views on the economy tend to be held by monetarists and rational expectationists.

But you will say *no* if you believe that (1) unemployment is more costly than inflation, (2) the short-run Phillips curve is flat, (3) expectations react sluggishly, and (4) the self-correcting mechanism is slow and unreliable. These views are held by many Keynesian economists, so it is not surprising that they often oppose using recession to fight inflation.

The tables turn, however, when the question becomes whether to use demand management to bring a recession to a rapid end. The Keynesian view of the world—that unemployment is costly, that the short-run Phillips curve is flat, that expectations adjust slowly, and that the self-correcting mechanism is unreliable—leads to the conclusion that the benefits of fighting unemployment are high and the costs are low. Keynesians are therefore eager to fight recessions. The monetarist and rational expectationist positions on these four issues are precisely the reverse, and so are the policy conclusions.

■ THE DILEMMA OF DEMAND MANAGEMENT

We have seen that the makers of monetary and fiscal policy face an unavoidable trade-off. If they stimulate aggregate demand to reduce unemployment, they will aggravate inflation. If they restrict aggregate demand to fight inflation, they will cause higher unemployment.

But wait. Early in the chapter we learned that when inflation comes from the supply side, inflation and unemployment are *positively* correlated: They go up or down together. Does this mean that monetary and fiscal policy makers can escape the trade-off between inflation and unemployment? Unfortunately not.

IDEAS FOR BEYOND THE FINAL EXAM

Shifts of the aggregate supply curve can cause inflation and unemployment to rise or fall together, and thus can destroy the statistical Phillips curve relationship. Nevertheless, anything that monetary and fiscal policy can do will make unemployment and inflation move in *opposite* directions because monetary and fiscal policies influence only the *aggregate demand* curve, not the *aggregate supply* curve.

Thus, no matter what the source of inflation, and no matter what happens to the Phillips curve, the monetary and fiscal policy authorities still face the disagreeable trade-off between inflation and unemployment. Many policy makers have failed to understand this principle, and it is one of the *Ideas* that we hope you will remember well *Beyond the Final Exam*.

Naturally, the unpleasant nature of this trade-off has led both economists and public officials to search for a way out of the dilemma. We conclude this chapter by considering some of these ideas—none of which is a panacea.

■ ATTEMPTS TO REDUCE THE NATURAL RATE OF UNEMPLOYMENT

One highly desirable approach—if only we knew how to do it—would be to reduce the natural rate of unemployment. Then we could enjoy lower unemployment without higher inflation. The question is: How?

The most promising approaches have to do with education, training, and job placement. The data clearly show that more educated workers are unemployed less frequently than less educated ones are. Vocational training and retraining programs, if successful, help unemployed workers with obsolete skills acquire abilities that are currently in demand. By so doing, they both raise employment and help alleviate upward pressures on wages in jobs where qualified workers are in short supply.

Government and private job placement and counseling services play a similar role. Such programs try to match workers to jobs better by funneling information from prospective employers to prospective employees.

These ideas sound sensible and promising, but two big problems arise in implementation. First, training and placement programs often look better on paper than they do in practice, where they achieve only modest successes. Too often, people are trained for jobs that do not exist by the time they finish their training—if, indeed, the jobs ever existed.

Second, the high cost of these programs restricts the number of workers who can be accommodated, even in successful programs. For this reason, publicly-supported job training is done on a very small scale in the United States—much less than in

Why Did the Natural Rate of Unemployment Fall?

In 1995, most economists believed that the natural rate of unemployment in the United States was approximately 6 percent—and certainly not lower than 5.5 percent. If unemployment fell below that critical rate, they said, inflation would start to rise. Experience in the late 1990s belied that view. The unemployment rate dipped below 5.5 percent in the summer of 1996—and kept falling. By the end of 1998, it was below 4.5 percent. For a few months in 2001, it dipped below 4 percent. And there were still no signs of rising inflation.

One reason for such amazing macroeconomic performance was discussed in this chapter: A series of favorable supply shocks pushed the aggregate supply curve outward at an unusually rapid pace. But it also appears that the natural rate of unemployment fell in the 1990s. Why?

Economists do not have a complete answer to this question, but a few pieces of the puzzle are understood. For one thing, the U.S. working population aged—and mature workers are normally unemployed less often than are young workers. The rise of temporary-help agencies and Internet job searching capabilities helped match workers to jobs better. Ironically, record-high levels of incarceration probably reduced unemployment, because many of those in jail would otherwise probably have been unemployed. It is also believed (though difficult to prove) that the weak labor markets of the early 1990s left labor more docile, thereby driving down the unemployment rate consistent with constant inflation.

Whatever the reasons, it does appear that the United States can now sustain a lower unemployment than it could a decade ago.

---

most European countries. Small expenditures can hardly be expected to make a large dent in the natural rate of unemployment.

But many observers believe the natural rate of unemployment has fallen in the United States despite these problems. Why? One reason is that *work experience* has much in common with formal training—workers become more productive by learning on the job. As the American workforce has aged, the average level of work experience has increased, which, according to many economists, has lowered the natural rate of unemployment. (For some other possible reasons, see "Why Did the Natural Rate of Unemployment Fall?")

INDEXING

Indexing refers to provisions in a law or contract whereby monetary payments are automatically adjusted whenever a specified price index changes. Wage rates, pensions, interest payments on bonds, income taxes, and many other things can be indexed in this way, and have been. Sometimes such contractual provisions are called *escalator clauses*.

Indexing—which refers to provisions in a law or contract that automatically adjust monetary payments whenever a specific price index changes—presents a very different approach to the inflation-unemployment dilemma. Instead of trying to improve the terms of the trade-off, *indexing seeks to reduce the social costs of inflation.*

The most familiar example of indexing is an escalator clause in a wage agreement. Escalator clauses provide for automatic increases in money wages—without the need for new contract negotiations—whenever the price level rises by more than a specified amount. Such agreements thus act to protect workers partly from inflation. Nowadays, with inflation so low and stable, relatively few workers are covered by escalator clauses. But they used to be more common.

Interest payments on bonds or bank accounts can also be indexed, and the U.S. government began doing so with a small fraction of its bonds in 1997. The most extensive indexing to be found in the United States today, however, appears in government transfer payments. Social Security benefits, for instance, are indexed so that retirees are not victimized by inflation.

Some economists believe that the United States should follow the example of several foreign countries and adopt a more widespread indexing system. Why? Because, they argue, it would take most of the sting out of inflation. To see how, let us review some of the social costs of inflation that we enumerated in Chapter 6.

One important cost is the capricious redistribution of income caused by unexpected inflation. We saw that borrowers and lenders normally incorporate an *inflation premium* equal to the *expected rate of inflation* into the nominal interest rate. Then, if inflation turns out to be higher than expected, the borrower has to pay the lender only the agreed-on nominal interest rate, including the premium for *expected* inflation; he does not have to compensate the lender for the (higher) *actual* inflation. Thus, the borrower enjoys a windfall gain and the lender loses out. The opposite happens if inflation turns out to be lower than expected.

But if interest rates on loans were indexed, none of this would occur. Borrowers and lenders would agree on a fixed *real* rate of interest, and the borrower would compensate the lender for whatever actual inflation occurred. No one would have to guess what the inflation rate would be.[6]

A second social cost mentioned in Chapter 6 stems from the fact that our tax system levies taxes on nominal interest and nominal capital gains. As we learned, this flaw in the tax system leads to extremely high effective tax rates in an inflationary environment. But indexing can cure this problem. We need only rewrite the tax code so that only *real* interest payments and *real* capital gains are taxed.

In the face of all these benefits, why does our economy not employ more indexing? One obvious reason is that inflation has been low for years. Indexing received much more attention in the 1970s and early 1980s, when inflation was high. A second reason is that some economists fear that indexing will erode society's resistance to inflation. With the costs of inflation so markedly reduced, they ask, what will stop governments from inflating more and more? They fear that the answer is: Nothing. Voters who stand to lose nothing from inflation are unlikely to pressure their legislators into stopping it. Opponents of indexing worry that a mild inflationary disease could turn into a ravaging epidemic in a highly indexed economy.

SUMMARY

1. Inflation can be caused either by rapid growth of aggregate demand or by sluggish growth of aggregate supply.

2. When fluctuations in economic activity emanate from the **demand side,** prices will rise rapidly when real output grows rapidly. Because rapid growth means more jobs, unemployment and inflation will be inversely related.

3. This inverse relationship between unemployment and inflation is called the **Phillips curve.** U.S. data for the 1950s and 1960s display a clear Phillips-curve relation, but data for the 1970s and 1980s do not.

4. The Phillips curve is not a menu of long-run policy choices for the economy, because the self-correcting mechanism guarantees that neither an inflationary gap nor a recessionary gap can last indefinitely.

5. Because of the self-correcting mechanism, the economy's true long-run choices lie along a **vertical long-run Phillips curve,** which shows that the so-called **natural rate of unemployment** is the only unemployment rate that can persist indefinitely.

6. In the short run, the economy can move up or down along its short-run Phillips curve. Temporary reductions in unemployment can be achieved at the cost of higher inflation, and temporary increases in unemployment can be used to fight inflation. This **short-run trade-off between inflation and unemployment** is one of our *Ideas for Beyond the Final Exam.*

7. Whether it is advisable to use unemployment to fight inflation depends on four principal factors: the relative social costs of inflation versus unemployment, the efficiency of the economy's self-correcting mechanism, the shape of the short-run Phillips curve, and the speed at which inflationary expectations are adjusted.

8. If workers expect inflation to occur, and if they demand (and receive) compensation for inflation, output will be independent of the price level. Both the aggregate supply curve and the short-run Phillips curve are vertical in this case.

9. Errors in predicting inflation will change real wages and therefore the quantity of output that firms wish to supply. Thus, unpredicted movements in the price level will lead to a normal, upward-sloping aggregate supply curve.

10. According to the **rational expectations** hypothesis, errors in predicting inflation are purely random. As a consequence, except for some random gyrations, the aggregate supply curve is vertical even in the short run.

11. Many economists reject the rational expectations view. Some deny that expectations are "rational" and believe instead that people tend, for example, to underpredict inflation when it is rising. Others point out that contracts signed years ago may not embody expectations that are "rational" in terms of what we know today.

12. When fluctuations in economic activity are caused by shifts of the aggregate supply curve, output will grow slowly (causing unemployment to rise) when inflation rises. Hence, the rates of unemployment and inflation will be positively correlated. Many observers feel that this sort of stagflation is why the Phillips curve collapsed in the 1970s. Similarly, a series of favorable supply shocks help explain the 1990s combination of low inflation and strong economic growth.

---

[6] For example, an indexed loan with a 2 percent real interest rate would require a 5 percent nominal interest payment if inflation were 3 percent, a 7 percent nominal interest payment if inflation were 5 percent, and so on.

13. Even if inflation is initiated by supply-side problems, so that inflation and unemployment rise together, the monetary and fiscal authorities still face this trade-off: Anything they do to improve unemployment is likely to worsen inflation, and anything they do to reduce inflation is likely to aggravate unemployment. (This is part of one of our *Ideas for Beyond the Final Exam*.) The reason behind it is that monetary and fiscal policy mainly influence the aggregate demand curve, not the aggregate supply curve.

14. Policies that improve the functioning of the labor market—including retraining programs and employment services—can, in principle, lower the natural rate of unemployment. To date, however, the U.S. government has enjoyed only modest success with these measures.

15. **Indexing** is another way to approach the trade-off problem. Instead of trying to improve the trade-off, it concentrates on reducing the social costs of inflation. Opponents of indexing worry, however, that the economy's resistance to inflation may be lowered by indexing.

KEY TERMS

Demand–side inflation 306

Supply-side inflation 306

Phillips curve 307

Stagflation caused by supply shocks 309

Self-correcting mechanism 310

Natural rate of unemployment 311

Vertical (long-run) Phillips curve 311

Trade-off between unemployment and inflation in the short run and in the long run 312

Rational expectations 316

Indexing (escalator clauses) 320

Real versus nominal interest rates 321

TEST YOURSELF

1. Show that, if the economy's aggregate supply curve is vertical, fluctuations in the growth of aggregate demand produce only fluctuations in inflation with no effect on output.

2. Long-term government bonds now pay approximately 5 percent nominal interest. Would you prefer to trade yours in for an indexed bond that paid a 3 percent real rate of interest? What if the real interest rate offered were 2 percent? What if it were 1 percent? What do your answers to these questions reveal about your personal attitudes toward inflation?

DISCUSSION QUESTIONS

1. When inflation and unemployment fell together in the 1990s, some observers claimed that policy makers no longer faced a trade-off between inflation and unemployment. Were they correct?

2. "There is no sense in trying to shorten recessions through fiscal and monetary policy because the effects of these policies on the unemployment rate are sure to be temporary." Comment on both the truth of this statement and its relevance for policy formulation.

3. Why is it said that decisions on fiscal and monetary policy are, at least in part, political decisions that cannot be made on "objective" economic criteria?

4. What is a Phillips curve? Why did it seem to work so much better in the period from 1954 to 1969 than it did in the 1970s?

5. Explain why expectations of inflation affect the wages that result from labor-management bargaining.

6. What is meant by "rational" expectations? Why does the hypothesis of rational expectations have such stunning implications for economic policy? Would believers in rational expectations want to shorten a recession by expanding aggregate demand? Would they want to fight inflation by reducing aggregate demand? Relate this analysis to your answer to Test Yourself Question 1.

7. It is often said that the Federal Reserve Board typically cares more about inflation and less about unemployment than the administration. If this is true, why might President Bush be worried about what the Fed might do to interest rates this year?

8. The year 2004 closed with the unemployment rate around 5 1/2 percent, real GDP rising approximately at the growth rate of potential GDP, inflation around 2 percent, and the federal budget showing a massive deficit.

   a. Give one or more arguments for engaging in expansionary monetary or fiscal policies under these circumstances.

   b. Give one or more arguments for engaging in contractionary monetary or fiscal policies under these circumstances.

   c. Which arguments do you find more persuasive?

THE INTERNATIONAL MONETARY SYSTEM: ORDER OR DISORDER?

Cecily, you will read your Political Economy in my absence. The chapter on the Fall of the Rupee you may omit.
It is somewhat too sensational.

MISS PRISM IN OSCAR WILDE'S *THE IMPORTANCE OF BEING EARNEST*

Miss Prism, the Victorian tutor, may have had a better point than she knew. In the summer of 1997, the Indonesian rupiah (not the Indian rupee) fell and economic disaster quickly followed. The International Monetary Fund rushed to the rescue with billions of dollars and pages of advice. But its plan failed, and some say it may even have helped precipitate the bloody riots that led to the fall of the Indonesian government.

This chapter does not concentrate on such sensational political upheavals. Rather, it focuses on a seemingly mundane topic: how the market determines rates of exchange among different national currencies. Nevertheless, events in Southeast Asia in 1997–1998, in Brazil and Russia in 1998–1999, and in Turkey and Argentina in 2001–2002 have amply demonstrated that dramatic exchange rate movements can have severe human as well as financial consequences. This chapter and the next will help us understand why.

CONTENTS

PUZZLE: *Why Has the Dollar Been Sagging?*

Many observers speak of "American exceptionalism." One way in which America differs from other countries is that its media and citizens pay little attention to the international value of its currency. So you may have missed the fact that the U.S. dollar, which was worth almost 1.2 euros as recently as February 2002 fell to a low of around 0.73 euro in December 2004. (As this book goes to press, the dollar is worth 0.78 euro.) In most countries, a 40 percent decline in the exchange rate in less than two years would have been headline news—almost daily. But in the United States, it rarely got off the financial pages.

But it happened nonetheless. A 40 percent decline is a large drop. What caused the dollar to fall so far? Does the decline signal some deep-seated problem with the U.S. economy? We will learn some of the answers to these and related questions in this chapter. But to do that, we first need to understand what determines exchange rates.

WHAT ARE EXCHANGE RATES?

We noted in the previous chapter that international trade is more complicated than domestic trade. There are no national borders to be crossed when, say, California lettuce is shipped to Massachusetts. The consumer in Boston pays with *dollars*, just the currency that the farmer in Modesto wants. If that same farmer ships her lettuce to Japan, however, consumers there will have only Japanese yen with which to pay, rather than the dollars the farmer in California wants. Thus, for international trade to take place, there must be some way to convert one currency into another. The rates at which such conversions are made are called **exchange rates.**

he **exchange rate** states he price, in terms of one urrency, at which another urrency can be bought.

There is an exchange rate between every pair of currencies. For example, one British pound is currently the equivalent of about $1.90. The exchange rate between the pound and the dollar, then, may be expressed as roughly "$1.90 to the pound" (meaning that it costs $1.90 to buy a pound) or about "53 pence to the dollar" (meaning that it costs 0.53 of a British pound to buy a dollar).

Exchange rates vis-à-vis the United States dollar have changed dramatically over time. In a nutshell, the dollar soared in the period from mid-1980 to early 1985, fell relative to most major currencies from early 1985 until early 1988, and then fluctuated with no clear trend until the spring of 1995. From then until early 2002, the dollar was mostly on the rise. Then, from February 2002 through December 2004, the dollar reversed course and fell steadily. (Since December 2004, the dollar has regained some of its lost ground. But most economist expect it to fall further.) This chapter seeks to explain such currency movements.

nation's currency is said appreciate when ex-hange rates change so that unit of its currency can uy more units of foreign urrency.

Under our present system, currency rates change frequently. When other currencies become more expensive in terms of dollars, we say that they have **appreciated** relative to the dollar. Alternatively, we can look at this same event as the dollar buying less foreign currency, meaning that the dollar has **depreciated** relative to another currency.

What is a depreciation to one country must be an appreciation to the other.

nation's currency is said depreciate when ex-hange rates change so that unit of its currency can uy fewer units of foreign urrency.

For example, if the cost of a pound *rises* from $1.50 to $1.90, the cost of a U.S. dollar in terms of pounds simultaneously *falls* from 67 pence to 53 pence. The United Kingdom has experienced a currency *appreciation* while the United States has experienced a currency *depreciation*. In fact, the two mean more or less the same thing. As you may have noticed, these two ways of viewing the exchange rate are reciprocals of one another, that is, $1/1.5 = 0.67$ and $1/1.9 = 0.53$. And of course, when a number goes up, its reciprocal goes down.

When many currencies are changing in value at the same time, the dollar may be appreciating with respect to one currency but depreciating with respect to another. Table 1 offers a selection of exchange rates prevailing in July 1980, February 1985, June 1995, April 2002, and April 2005, showing how many dollars or cents it cost at

			TABLE 1				
			Exchange Rates with the U.S. Dollar				
			Cost in Dollars				
Country	Currency	Symbol	July 1980	Feb. 1985	June 1995	April 2002	April 2005
Australia	dollar	$	$1.16	$0.74	$0.72	$0.53	$0.77
Canada	dollar	$	0.87	0.74	0.73	0.63	$0.82
France	franc	FF	0.25	0.10	0.20	*	*
Germany	mark	DM	0.57	0.30	0.71	*	*
Italy	lira	L	0.0012	0.00049	0.0061	*	*
Japan	yen	¥	0.0045	0.0038	0.0118	0.0076	0.0092
Mexico	new peso	$	44.0†	5.0†	0.16	0.11	0.09
Sweden	krona	Kr	0.24	0.11	0.14	0.10	0.14
Switzerland	franc	S.Fr.	0.62	0.36	0.86	0.60	0.83
United Kingdom	pound	£	2.37	1.10	1.59	1.44	1.88
—	euro	€	—	—	—	0.88	1.29

NOTE: Exchange rates are in U.S. dollars per unit of foreign currency.

*These exchange rates were locked together at the start of the euro in January 1999.

†On January 1, 1993, the peso was redefined so that 1,000 old pesos were equal to one new peso. Hence, the numbers 44 and 5 listed for July 1980 and February 1985 were actually 0.044 and 0.005 on the old basis.

each of those times to buy each unit of foreign currency. Between February 1985 and April 2002, the dollar *depreciated* sharply relative to the Japanese yen and most European currencies. For example, the British pound rose from $1.10 to $1.44. During that same period, however, the dollar *appreciated* dramatically relative to the Mexican peso; it bought about 0.2 pesos in 1985 but more than 9 in 2002.[1]

Although the terms "appreciation" and "depreciation" are used to describe movements of exchange rates in free markets, a different set of terms is employed to describe decreases and increases in currency values that are set by government decree. When an officially set exchange rate is altered so that a unit of a nation's currency can buy fewer units of foreign currency, we say that a **devaluation** of that currency has occurred. When the exchange rate is altered so that the currency can buy more units of foreign currency, we say that a **revaluation** has taken place. We will say more about devaluation and revaluation shortly, but first let's look at how the free market determines exchange rates.

A **devaluation** is a reduction in the official value of a currency.

A **revaluation** is an increase in the official value of a currency.

■ EXCHANGE RATE DETERMINATION IN A FREE MARKET

In 1999, eleven European countries adopted a new common currency, the euro. But why does a euro now cost about $1.30 and not $1 or $1.60? In a world of **floating exchange rates,** with no government interferences, the answer would be straightforward. Exchange rates would be determined by the forces of supply and demand, just like the prices of apples, computers, and haircuts.

In a leap of abstraction, imagine that the dollar and the euro are the only currencies on earth, so the market need determine only one exchange rate. Figure 1 on the next page depicts the determination of this exchange rate at the point (denoted *E* in the figure) where demand curve *DD* crosses supply curve *SS*. At this price ($1.30 per euro), the number of euros demanded is equal to the number of euros supplied.

Floating exchange rates are rates determined in free markets by the law of supply and demand.

In a free market, exchange rates are determined by supply and demand. At a rate below the equilibrium level, the number of euros demanded would exceed the number supplied, and the price of a euro would be bid up. At a rate above the equilibrium level, quantity supplied would exceed quantity demanded, and the price of a euro would fall. Only at the equilibrium exchange rate is there no tendency for the exchange rate to change.

---

[1] In fact, the dollar bought about 200 pesos in February 1985, but that is because the old peso was replaced by a new peso in January 1993, which moved the decimal point three places.

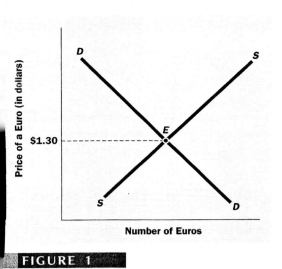

FIGURE 1

Determination of
Exchange Rates in a
Free Market

As usual, supply and demand determine price. But in this case, we must ask: Where do the supply and demand come from? Why does anyone demand a euro? The answer comes in three parts:

- *International trade in goods and services.* This factor was the subject of the previous chapter. If, for example, Jane Doe, an American, wants to buy a new BMW, she will first have to buy euros with which to pay the car dealer in Munich.[2] Thus Jane's demand for a European car leads to a demand for European currency. In general, *demand for a country's exports leads to demand for its currency.*[3]
- *Purchases of physical assets such as factories and machinery overseas.* If IBM wants to buy a small French computer manufacturer, the owners will no doubt want to receive euros. So IBM will first have to acquire European currency. In general, *direct foreign investment leads to demand for a country's currency.*
- *International trade in financial instruments such as stocks and bonds.* If American investors want to purchase Italian stocks, they will first have to acquire the euros that the sellers will insist on for payment. In this way, demand for European financial assets leads to demand for European currency. Thus, *demand for a country's financial assets leads to demand for its currency.* In fact, nowadays the volume of international trade in financial assets among the major countries of the world is so large that it swamps the other two sources of demand.

Now, where does the supply come from? To answer this question, just turn all of these transactions around. Europeans who want to buy U.S. goods and services, make direct investments in the United States, or purchase U.S. financial assets will have to offer their euros for sale in the foreign-exchange market (which is mainly run through banks) to acquire the needed dollars. To summarize:

> The *demand* for a country's currency is derived from the demands of foreigners for its export goods and services and for its assets—including financial assets, such as stocks and bonds, and real assets, such as factories and machinery. The *supply* of a country's currency arises from its imports, and from foreign investment by its own citizens.

To illustrate the usefulness of even this simple supply and demand analysis, think about how the exchange rate between the dollar and the euro should change if Europeans become attracted by the prospects of large gains on the U.S. stock markets. To purchase U.S. stocks, foreigners will first have to purchase U.S. dollars—which means selling some of their euros. In terms of the supply-demand diagram in Figure 2, the increased desire of Europeans to acquire U.S. stocks would shift the supply curve for euros out from S_1S_1 (the black line in the figure) to S_2S_2 (the blue line). Equilibrium would shift from point E to point A, and the exchange rate would fall from $1.30 per euro to $1.00 per euro. Thus the increased supply of euros by European citizens would cause the euro to *depreciate* relative to the dollar. (This is precisely what happened during the U.S. stock market boom of the late 1990s.)

EXERCISE Test your understanding of the supply and demand analysis of exchange rates by showing why each of the following events would lead to an appreciation of the euro (a depreciation of the dollar) in a free market:

1. American investors are attracted by prospects for profit on the German stock market.

---

[2] Actually, she will not do so because banks generally handle foreign exchange transactions for consumers. An American bank probably will buy the euros for her. Even so, the effect is exactly the same as if Jane had done it herself.

[3] See Discussion Question 2 at the end of this chapter.

2. A recession in Italy cuts Italian purchases of American goods.
3. Interest rates on government bonds rise in France but are stable in the United States. (*Hint:* Which country's citizens will be attracted to invest by high interest rates in the other country?)

To say that supply and demand determine exchange rates in a free market is at once to say everything and to say nothing. If we are to understand the reasons why some currencies appreciate whereas others depreciate, we must look into the factors that move the supply and demand curves. Economists believe that the principal determinants of exchange rate movements differ significantly in the short, medium, and long runs. So in the next three sections, we turn to the analysis of exchange rate movements over these three "runs," beginning with the short run.

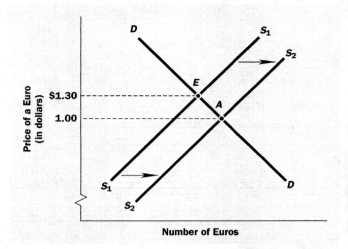

FIGURE 2

The Effect of a Foreign Stock Market Boom on the Exchange Rate

Interest Rates and Exchange Rates: The Short Run

Most experts in international finance agree that interest rates and financial flows are the major determinants of exchange rates—certainly in the short run, and probably in the medium run as well. Specifically, one variable that often seems to call the tune in the short run is *interest rate differentials*. A multitrillion-dollar pool of so-called *hot money*—owned by banks, investment funds, multinational corporations, and wealthy individuals of all nations—travels rapidly around the globe in search of the highest interest rates.

As an example, suppose British government bonds pay a 5 percent rate of interest when yields on equally safe American government securities rise to 7 percent. British investors will be attracted by the higher interest rates in the United States and will offer pounds for sale in order to buy dollars, planning to use those dollars to buy American securities. At the same time, American investors will find it more attractive to keep their money at home, so fewer pounds will be demanded by Americans.

When the demand schedule for pounds shifts inward and the supply curve shifts outward, the effect on price is predictable: The pound will depreciate, as Figure 3 shows. In the figure, the supply curve of pounds shifts outward from S_1S_1 to S_2S_2 when British investors seek to sell pounds in order to purchase more U.S. securities. At the same time,

FIGURE 3

The Effect of a Rise in U.S. Interest Rates

American investors wish to buy fewer pounds because they no longer desire to invest as much in British securities. Thus, the demand curve shifts inward from D_1D_1 to D_2D_2. The result, in our example, is a depreciation of the pound from $1.90 to $1.60. In general:

Other things equal, countries that offer investors higher rates of return attract more capital than countries that offer lower rates. Thus, a rise in interest rates often will lead to an appreciation of the currency, and a drop in interest rates will lead to a depreciation.

Think of interest rate differentials, in this context, as standing in for the relative returns on all sorts of financial assets in the two countries. In the late 1990s and the early part of this decade, prospective returns on American assets rose well

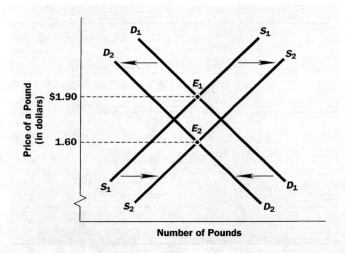

above comparable returns in most other countries—especially those in Europe and Japan. In consequence, foreign capital was attracted here, American capital stayed at home, and the dollar soared. Similarly, if a nation suffers from capital flight, as Argentina did in 2001, it must offer extremely high interest rates to attract foreign capital.

Economic Activity and Exchange Rates: The Medium Run

The medium run is where the theory of exchange rate determination is most unsettled. Economists once reasoned as follows: Because consumer spending increases when income rises and decreases when income falls, the same thing is likely to happen to spending on imported goods. So *a country's imports will rise quickly when its economy booms and rise only slowly when its economy stagnates.*

For the reasons illustrated in Figure 4, then, a boom in the United States should shift the *demand* curve for euros *outward* as Americans seek to acquire more euros to buy more European goods. And that, in turn, should lead to an appreciation of the euro (depreciation of the dollar). In the figure, the euro rises in value from $1.30 to $1.40.

However, if Europe was booming at the same time, Europeans would be buying more American exports, which would shift the *supply* curve of euros outward. (Europeans must offer more euros for sale to get the dollars they want.) On balance, the value of the dollar might rise or fall. It appears that what matters is whether exports are growing faster than imports.

FIGURE 4

The Effect of an Economic Boom Abroad on the Exchange Rate

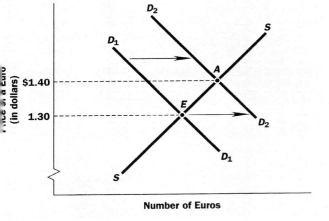

Number of Euros

A country whose aggregate demand grows faster than the rest of the world's normally finds its imports growing faster than its exports. Thus, its demand curve for foreign currency shifts outward more rapidly than its supply curve. *Other things equal,* that will make its currency depreciate.

This reasoning is sound—so far as it goes. And it leads to the conclusion that a "strong economy" might produce a "weak currency." But the three most important words in the preceding paragraph are "other things equal." Usually, they are not. Specifically, a booming economy will normally offer more attractive prospects to investors than a stagnating one—higher interest rates, rising stock market values, and so on. This difference in prospective investment returns, as we noted earlier, should attract capital and boost its currency value.

So there appears to be a kind of tug of war. Thinking about trade in goods and services leads to the conclusion that faster growth should *weaken* the currency. But thinking about trade in financial assets (such as stocks and bonds) leads to precisely the opposite conclusion: Faster growth should *strengthen* the currency. Which side wins this tug of war?

As we have suggested, it is usually no contest—at least among the major currencies of the world. In the modern world, the evidence seems to say that trade in financial assets is the dominant factor. For example, rapid growth in the United States in the second half of the 1990s was accompanied by a sharply *appreciating* dollar even though U.S. imports soared, as investors from all over the world brought funds to America. We conclude that:

Stronger economic performance often leads to currency *appreciation* because it improves prospects for investing in the country.

The Purchasing-Power Parity Theory: The Long Run

We come at last to the long run, where an apparently simple principle ought to govern exchange rates. As long as goods can move freely across national borders, exchange rates should eventually adjust so that the same product costs the same amount of money, whether measured in dollars in the United States, euros in Germany, or yen in Japan—except for differences in transportation costs and the like. This simple statement forms the basis of the major theory of exchange rate determination in the long run:

The *purchasing-power parity theory of exchange rate determination* holds that the exchange rate between any two national currencies adjusts to reflect differences in the price levels in the two countries.

An example will illustrate the basic truth in this theory and also suggest some of its limitations. Suppose German and American steel is identical and that these two nations are the only producers of steel for the world market. Suppose further that steel is the only tradable good that either country produces.

Question: If American steel costs $180 per ton and German steel costs 144 euros per ton, what must be the exchange rate between the dollar and the euro?

Answer: Because 144 euros and $180 each buy a ton of steel, the two sums of money must be of equal value. Hence, each euro must be worth $1.25. Why? Any higher price for a euro, such as $1.50, would mean that steel would cost $216 per ton (144 euros at $1.50 each) in Germany but only $180 per ton in the United States. In that case, all foreign customers would shop for their steel in the United States—which would increase the demand for dollars and decrease the demand for euros. Similarly, any exchange rate below $1.25 per euro would send all the steel business to Germany, driving the value of the euro up toward its purchasing-power parity level.

EXERCISE Show why an exchange rate of $1 per euro is too low to lead to an equilibrium in the international steel market.

The purchasing-power parity theory is used to make long-run predictions about the effects of inflation on exchange rates. To continue our example, suppose that steel (and other) prices in the United States rise while prices in Europe remain constant. The purchasing-power parity theory predicts that the euro will appreciate relative to the dollar. It also predicts the amount of the appreciation. After the U.S. inflation, suppose that the price of American steel is $216 per ton, while German steel still costs 144 euros per ton. For these two prices to be equivalent, 144 euros must be worth $216, or one euro must be worth $1.50. The euro, therefore, must have risen from $1.25 to $1.50.

According to the purchasing-power parity theory, differences in domestic inflation rates are a major cause of exchange rate movements. If one country has higher inflation than another, its exchange rate should be depreciating.

For many years, this theory seemed to work tolerably well. Although precise numerical predictions based on purchasing-power parity calculations were never very accurate (see "Purchasing Power Parity and the Big Mac" on the following page), nations with higher inflation did at least experience depreciating currencies. But in the 1980s and 1990s, even this rule broke down. For example, although the U.S. inflation rate was consistently higher than both Germany's and Japan's, the dollar nonetheless rose sharply relative to both the German mark and the Japanese yen from 1980 to 1985. The same thing happened again between 1995 and 2002. Clearly, the theory is missing something. What?

Many things. But perhaps the principal failing of the purchasing-power parity theory is, once again, that it focuses too much on trade in goods and services. Financial assets such as stocks and bonds are also traded actively across national borders—and in vastly greater dollar volumes than goods and services. In fact, the astounding *daily* volume of foreign exchange transactions exceeds $1.5 trillion, which is more than an entire *month's* worth of world trade in goods and services. The vast majority of these transactions are financial. If investors decide that, say, U.S. assets are a better bet than Japanese assets, the dollar will rise, even if our inflation rate is well above Japan's. For this and other reasons:

Purchasing-Power Parity and the Big Mac

Since 1986, *The Economist* magazine has been using a well-known international commodity—the Big Mac—to assess the purchasing-power parity theory of exchange rates, or as the magazine once put it, "to make exchange-rate theory more digestible."

Here's how it works. In theory, the local price of a Big Mac, when translated into U.S. dollars by the exchange rate, should be the same everywhere in the world. The following numbers show that the theory does not work terribly well.

For example, although a Big Mac costs an average of $3 in the United States, it sold for about 10.3 yuan in China. Using the official exchange rate of about 8.2 yuan to the dollar, that amounted to just $1.26. Thus, according to the hamburger parity theory, the yuan was grossly undervalued.

By how much? The price in China was just 42 percent of the price in the United States ($1.26/$3.00). So the yuan was 58 percent below its Big Mac parity—and therefore should appreciate. The other numbers in the table have similar interpretations.

SOURCE: © 2002 Don Couch Photography

True Big Mac aficionados may find these data helpful when planning international travel. But can deviations from Big Mac parity predict exchange rate movements? Surprisingly, they can.

When the economist Robert Cumby studied Big Mac prices and exchange rates in 14 countries over a ten-year period, he found that deviations from hamburger parity were transitory. Their "half-life" was just a year, meaning that 50 percent of the deviation tended to disappear within a year. Thus the undervalued currencies in the accompanying table would be predicted to appreciate during 2005, whereas the overvalued currencies would be expected to depreciate.

Deviations from Big Mac Purchasing Power Parity, December 2004

Country	Big Mac Prices (converted to dollars)	Percent Over (+) or Under (−) Valuation Against Dollar
United States	**$3.00**	—
Switzerland	5.46	+82%
Euro area	3.75	+25
Great Britain	3.61	+20
Canada	2.60	−13
Japan	2.50	−17
Mexico	2.12	−29
Brazil	1.99	−34
Russia	1.49	−50
China	1.26	−58

Most economists believe that other factors are much more important than relative price levels for exchange rate determination in the short run. But in the long run, purchasing-power parity plays an important role.

Market Determination of Exchange Rates: Summary

You have probably noticed a theme here: International trade in financial assets certainly dominates short-run exchange rate changes, may dominate medium-run changes, and also influences long-run changes. We can summarize this discussion of exchange rate determination in free markets as follows:

1. We expect to find *appreciating* currencies in countries that offer investors *higher rates of return* because these countries will attract capital from all over the world.

2. To some extent, these are the countries that are *growing faster* than average because strong growth tends to produce attractive investment prospects. However, such fast-growing countries will also be importing relatively more than other countries, which tends to pull their currencies *down*.

3. Currency values generally will appreciate in countries with *lower inflation rates* than the rest of the world's, because buyers in foreign countries will demand their goods and thus drive up their currencies.

Reversing each of these arguments, we expect to find *depreciating* currencies in countries with relatively high inflation rates, low interest rates, and poor growth prospects.

■ WHEN GOVERNMENTS FIX EXCHANGE RATES: THE BALANCE OF PAYMENTS

Some exchange rates today are truly floating, determined by the forces of supply and demand without government interference. Many others are not. Furthermore, some people claim that exchange rate fluctuations are so troublesome that the world would be better off with fixed exchange rates. For these reasons, we turn next to a system of **fixed exchange rates,** or rates that are set by governments.

Naturally, under such a system the exchange rate, being fixed, is not closely watched. Instead, international financial specialists focus on a country's *balance of payments*—a term we must now define—to gauge movements in the supply of and demand for a currency.

To understand what the balance of payments is, look at Figure 5, which depicts a situation that might represent, say, Argentina in the winter of 2001–2002—an overvalued currency. Although the supply and demand curves for pesos indicate an equilibrium exchange rate of $0.50 to the peso (point E), the Argentine government is holding the rate at $1.00. Notice that, at $1 per peso, more people supply pesos than demand them. In the example, suppliers offer to sell 8 billion pesos per year, but purchasers want to buy only 4 billion.

> **Fixed exchange rates** are rates set by government decisions and maintained by government actions.

This gap between the 8 billion pesos that some people wish to sell and the 4 billion pesos that others wish to buy is what we mean by Argentina's **balance of payments deficit**—4 billion pesos (or $4 billion) per year in this hypothetical case. It appears as the horizontal distance between points A and B in Figure 5.

How can governments flout market forces in this way? Because sales and purchases on any market must be equal, the excess of quantity supplied over quantity demanded—or 4 billion pesos per year in this example—must be bought by the Argentine government. To purchase these pesos, it must give up some of the foreign currency that it holds as reserves. Thus, the Bank of Argentina would be losing about $4 billion in reserves per year as the cost of keeping the peso at $1.

FIGURE 5

A Balance of Payments Deficit

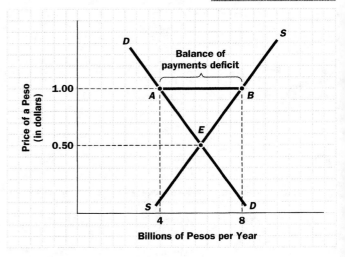

Naturally, this situation cannot persist forever, as the reserves eventually will run out. This is the fatal flaw of a fixed exchange rate system. Once speculators become convinced that the exchange rate can be held for only a short while longer, they will sell the currency in massive amounts rather than hold on to money whose value they expect to fall. That is precisely what began to happen to Argentina in 2001. Lacking sufficient reserves, the Argentine government succumbed to market forces and let the peso float in early 2002. It promptly depreciated.

For an example of the reverse case, a severely undervalued currency, we can look at contemporary China. Figure 6 on the next page depicts demand and supply curves for Chinese yuan that intersect at an equilibrium price of 15 cents per yuan (point E in the diagram). Yet, in the example, we suppose that the Chinese authorities are holding the rate at 12 cents. At this rate, the quantity of yuan demanded (1,000 billion) greatly exceeds the quantity supplied (600 billion). The difference is China's **balance of payments surplus,** shown by the horizontal distance AB.

China can keep the rate at 12 cents only by selling all the additional yuan that foreigners want to buy—400 billion yuan per year in this example. In return, the country must buy the equivalent amount of U.S. dollars ($48 billion). All of this activity serves to increase China's reserves of U.S. dollars. But notice one important difference between this case and the overvalued peso:

> The **balance of payments deficit** is the amount by which the quantity supplied of a country's currency (per year) exceeds the quantity demanded. Balance of payments deficits arise whenever the exchange rate is pegged at an artificially high level.
>
> The **balance of payments surplus** is the amount by which the quantity demanded of a country's currency (per year) exceeds the quantity supplied. Balance of payments surpluses arise whenever the exchange rate is pegged at an artificially low level.

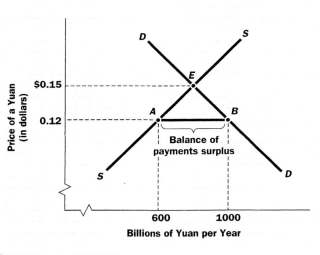

FIGURE 6

Balance of Payments
urplus

The accumulation of reserves rarely will force a central bank to revalue in the way that losses of reserves can force a devaluation.

This asymmetry is a clear weakness in a fixed exchange rate system. In principle, an exchange rate disequilibrium can be cured either by a *devaluation* by the country with a balance of payments deficit or by an upward *revaluation* by the country with a balance of payments surplus. In practice, though, only deficit countries are forced to act.

Why do surplus countries refuse to revalue? One reason is often a stubborn refusal to recognize some basic economic realities. They tend to view the disequilibrium as a problem only for the deficit countries and, therefore, believe that the deficit countries should take the corrective steps. This view, of course, is nonsense in a worldwide system of fixed exchange rates. Some currencies are overvalued *because* some other currencies are undervalued. In fact, the two statements mean exactly the same thing.

The other reason why surplus countries resist upward revaluations is that such actions would make their products more expensive to foreigners and thus cut into their export sales. This, in fact, is presumed to be the main reason why China maintains an undervalued currency despite the protestations of many other nations. China's leaders believe that vibrant export industries are the key to growth and development.

The balance of payments comes in two main parts. The **current account** totes up exports and imports of goods and services, cross-border payments of interest and dividends, and cross-border gifts. It is close, both conceptually and numerically, to what we have called net exports ($X - IM$) in previous chapters. The United States has been running large current account deficits for years.

But that represents only one part of our balance of payments, for it leaves out all purchases and sales of assets. Purchases of U.S. assets by foreigners bring foreign currency to the United States, and purchases of foreign assets cost us foreign currency. Netting the capital flows in each direction gives us our surplus or deficit on **capital account**. In recent years, this part of our balance of payments has registered persistently large *surpluses* as foreigners have acquired massive amounts of U.S. assets.

In what sense, then, does the overall balance of payments balance? There are two possibilities. If the exchange rate is *floating*, all private transactions—current account plus capital account—must add up to zero because dollars purchased = dollars sold. But if, instead, the exchange rate is *fixed*, as shown in Figures 5 and 6, the two accounts need not balance one another. Government purchases or sales of foreign currency make up the surplus or deficit in the overall balance of payments.

e **current account** bal-
ce includes international
rchases and sales of
ods and services, cross-
rder interest and dividend
yments, and cross-border
ts to and from both pri-
te individuals and govern-
ents. It is approximately
e same as net exports.

e **capital account** bal-
ce includes purchases and
es of financial assets to
d from citizens and com-
nies of other countries.

A BIT OF HISTORY: THE GOLD STANDARD AND THE BRETTON WOODS SYSTEM

It is difficult to find examples of strictly fixed exchange rates in the historical record. About the only time exchange rates were truly fixed was under the old gold standard, at least when it was practiced in its ideal form.[4]

The Classical Gold Standard

gold standard is a
y to fix exchange rates by
ining each participating
rency in terms of gold
allowing holders of
h participating currency
onvert that currency
gold.

Under the **gold standard,** governments maintained fixed exchange rates by an automatic equilibrating mechanism that went something like this: All currencies were de-

---

[4] As a matter of fact, although the gold standard lasted (on and off) for hundreds of years, it was rarely practiced in its ideal form. Except for a brief period of fixed exchange rates in the late nineteenth and early twentieth centuries, governments periodically adjusted exchange rates even under the gold standard.

fined in terms of gold; indeed, some were actually made of gold. When a nation ran a balance of payments *deficit*, it had to *sell gold* to finance the deficit. Because the domestic money supply was based on gold, losing gold to foreigners meant that the money supply fell *automatically*, which raised interest rates. The higher interest rates attracted foreign capital. At the same time, this restrictive "monetary policy" pulled down output and prices, which discouraged imports and encouraged exports. The balance of payments problem quickly rectified itself.

This automatic adjustment process meant, however, that under the gold standard no nation had control of its domestic monetary policy. An analogous problem arises in any system of fixed exchange rates, regardless of whether it makes use of gold:

Under fixed exchange rates, monetary policy must be dedicated to pegging the exchange rate. It cannot, therefore, be used to manage aggregate demand.

The gold standard posed one other serious difficulty: The world's commerce was at the mercy of gold discoveries. Major gold finds would mean higher prices and booming economic conditions, through the standard monetary-policy mechanisms that we studied in earlier chapters. When the supply of gold failed to keep pace with growth of the world economy, prices had to fall in the long run and employment had to fall in the short run.

The Bretton Woods System

The gold standard collapsed for good amid the financial chaos of the Great Depression of the 1930s and World War II. Without it, the world struggled through a serious breakdown in international trade.

As the war drew to a close, representatives of the industrial nations, including John Maynard Keynes of Great Britain, met at a hotel in Bretton Woods, New Hampshire, to devise a stable monetary environment that would restore world trade. Because the United States held the lion's share of the world's reserves at the time, these officials naturally turned to the dollar as the basis for the new international economic order.

The Bretton Woods agreements reestablished fixed exchange rates based on the free convertibility of the U.S. dollar into gold. The United States agreed to buy or sell gold to maintain the $35 per ounce price that President Franklin Roosevelt had established in 1933. The other signatory nations, which had almost no gold in any case, agreed to buy and sell *dollars* to maintain their exchange rates at agreed-upon levels.

The Bretton Woods system succeeded in refixing exchange rates and restoring world trade—two notable achievements. But it also displayed the flaws of any fixed exchange rate system. Changes in exchange rates were permitted only as a last resort—which, in practice came to mean that the country had a chronic *deficit* in the balance of payments of sizable proportions. Such nations were allowed to *devalue* their currencies relative to the dollar. So the system was not really one of fixed exchange rates but, rather, one in which rates were "fixed until further notice." Because devaluations came only after a long run of balance of payments deficits had depleted the country's reserves, these devaluations often could be clearly foreseen and normally had to be large. Speculators therefore saw glowing opportunities for profit and would "attack" weak currencies with waves of selling.

A second problem arose from the asymmetry mentioned earlier: Deficit nations could be forced to devalue while surplus nations could resist upward revaluations. Because the value of the U.S. dollar was fixed in terms of gold, the United States was the one nation in the world that had no way to devalue its currency. The only way the dollar could fall was if the surplus nations would revalue their currencies upward. But they did not adjust frequently enough, so the United States developed an overvalued currency and chronic balance of payments deficits.

The overvalued dollar finally destroyed the Bretton Woods system in 1971, when President Richard Nixon unilaterally ended the game by announcing that the United States would no longer buy or sell gold at $35 per ounce.

ADJUSTMENT MECHANISMS UNDER FIXED EXCHANGE RATES

Under the Bretton Woods system, devaluation was viewed as a last resort, to be used only after other methods of adjusting to payments imbalances had failed. What were these other methods?

We encountered most of them in our earlier discussion of exchange rate determination in free markets. Any factor that *increases the demand* for, say, Argentine pesos or that *reduces the supply* will push the value of the peso upward—if it is free to adjust. But if the exchange rate is pegged, the balance of payments deficit will shrink instead. (Try this for yourself using Figure 5 on page 355.)

Recalling our earlier discussion of the factors that underlie the demand and supply curves, we see that one way a nation can shrink its balance of payments deficit is to *reduce its aggregate demand*, thereby discouraging imports and cutting down its demand for foreign currency. Another is to *lower its rate of inflation*, thereby encouraging exports and discouraging imports. Finally, it can *raise its interest rates* to attract more foreign capital.

In other words, deficit nations are expected to follow restrictive monetary and fiscal policies *voluntarily*, just as they would have done *automatically* under the classical gold standard. However, just as under the gold standard, this medicine is often unpalatable.

A surplus nation could, of course, take the opposite measures: pursuing *expansionary* monetary and fiscal policies to increase economic growth and *lower* interest rates. By increasing the supply of the country's currency and reducing the demand for it, such actions would reduce that nation's balance of payments surplus. But surplus countries often do not relish the inflation that accompanies expansionary policies, and so, once again, they leave the burden of adjustment to the deficit nations. The general point about fixed exchange rates is that:

> Under a system of fixed exchange rates, a country's government loses some control over its domestic economy. Sometimes balance of payments considerations may force it to contract its economy in order to cut down its demand for foreign currency, even though domestic needs call for expansion. At other times, the domestic economy may need to be reined in, but balance of payments considerations suggest expansion.

That was certainly the case in Argentina in 2002, when interest rates soared to attract foreign capital, and the government pursued contractionary fiscal policies to curb the country's appetite for imports. Both contributed to a long and deep recession. Argentina took the bitter medicine needed to defend its fixed exchange rate for quite a while. But high unemployment eventually led to riots in the streets, toppled the government, and persuaded the Argentine authorities to abandon the fixed exchange rate.

WHY TRY TO FIX EXCHANGE RATES?

hen it's agreed. Until the ollar firms up, we let the amshell float."

In view of these and other problems with fixed exchange rates, why did the international financial community work so hard to maintain them for so many years? And why do some nations today still fix their exchange rates? The answer is that floating exchange rates also pose problems.

Chief among these worries is the possibility that freely floating rates might prove to be highly variable rates, thereby adding an unwanted element of risk to foreign trade. For example, if the exchange rate is $1.25 to the euro, then a Parisian dress priced at 200 euros will cost $250. But should the euro appreciate to $1.40, that same dress would cost $280. An American department store thinking of buying the dress may need to place its order far in advance and will want to know the cost *in dollars*. It may be worried about the possibility that the value of the euro will rise, making the dress cost more than $250. And such worries might inhibit trade.

There are two responses to this concern. First, freely floating rates might prove to be fairly stable in practice. Prices of most ordinary goods and services, for example, are determined by supply and demand in free markets and do not fluctuate unduly. Unfortunately, experience since 1973 has dashed this hope. Exchange rates have proved to be extremely volatile, which is why some observers now favor greater fixity in exchange rates.

A second possibility is that speculators might relieve business firms of exchange rate risks—for a fee, of course. Consider the department store example. If each euro costs $1.25 today, the department store manager can assure herself of paying exactly $250 for the dress several months from now by arranging for a speculator to deliver 200 euros to her at $1.25 per euro on the day she needs them. If the euro appreciates in the interim, the speculator, not the department store, will take the financial beating. Of course, if the euro depreciates, the speculator will pocket the profits. Thus, speculators play an important role in a system of floating exchange rates.

The widespread fears that speculative activity in free markets will lead to wild gyrations in prices, although occasionally valid, are often unfounded. The reason is simple.

> To make profits, international currency speculators must *buy* a currency when its value is low (thus helping to support the currency by pushing up its demand curve) and *sell* it when its value is high (thus holding down the price by adding to the supply curve). This means that successful speculators must come into the market as *buyers* when demand is weak (or when supply is strong) and come in as *sellers* when demand is strong (or supply is scant). In doing so, they help limit price fluctuations. Looked at the other way around, speculators can *destabilize* prices only if they are systematically willing to lose money.[5]

Notice the stark—and ironic—contrast to the system of fixed exchange rates in which speculation often leads to wild "runs" on currencies that are on the verge of devaluation—as happened in Mexico in 1995, several Southeast Asian countries in 1997–1998, Brazil in 1999, and Argentina in 2001. Speculative activity, which may well be *destabilizing* under fixed rates, is more likely to be *stabilizing* under floating rates.[6]

We do not mean to imply that speculation makes floating rates trouble-free. At the very least, speculators will demand a fee for their services—a fee that adds to the costs of trading across national borders. In addition, speculators will not assume *all* exchange rate risks. For example, few contracts on foreign currencies last more than, say, a year or two. Thus, a business cannot easily protect itself from exchange rate changes over periods of many years. Finally, speculative markets can and do get carried away from time to time, moving currency rates in ways that are difficult to understand, that frustrate the intentions of governments, and that devastate some people—as happened in Mexico in 1995 and in Southeast Asia in 1997.

Despite all of these problems, international trade has flourished under floating exchange rates. So perhaps exchange rate risk is not as burdensome as some people think.

■ THE CURRENT "NONSYSTEM"

The international financial system today is an eclectic blend of fixed and floating exchange rates, with no grand organizing principle. Indeed, it is so diverse that it is often called a "nonsystem."

Some currencies are still pegged in the old Bretton Woods manner. One prominent example is China, which maintains a fixed value for its currency by standing ready to buy or sell U.S. dollars as necessary. (In recent years, it has been buying steadily.) A few small countries, such as Panama and Ecuador, have taken the more extreme step of actually adopting the U.S. dollar as their domestic currencies. Other nations tie their currencies to a hypothetical "basket" of several currencies, rather than to a single currency.

More nations, however, let their exchange rates float, although not always freely. Such floating rates change slightly on a day-to-day basis, and market forces determine the basic trends, up or down. But governments do not hesitate to intervene to moderate

---

[5] See Test Yourself Question 4 at the end of the chapter.

[6] After their respective currency crises in 1995 and 1999, both Mexico and Brazil floated their currencies. Each weathered the subsequent international financial storms rather nicely. But Argentina, with its fixed exchange rate, struggled.

exchange movements whenever they feel such actions are appropriate. Typically, interventions are aimed at ironing out what are deemed to be transitory fluctuations. But sometimes central banks oppose basic exchange rate trends. For example, the Federal Reserve and other central banks sold dollars aggressively in 1985 to push the dollar *down,* and then bought dollars in 1994 and 1995 to push the dollar *up.* As we will discuss in the next chapter, the Japanese have acquired hundreds of billions of dollars in recent years trying to prevent the yen from floating up too much. The terms *dirty float* or *managed float* have been coined to describe this mongrel system.

The Role of the IMF

The International Monetary Fund (IMF), which was established at Bretton Woods in 1944, examines the economies of all its member nations on a regular basis. When a country runs into serious financial difficulties, it may turn to the Fund for help. The IMF typically provides loans, but with many strings attached. For example, if the country has a large current account deficit—as is normally the case when countries come to the IMF—the Fund will typically insist on contractionary fiscal and monetary policies to curb the country's appetite for imports. Often, this mandate spells recession.

During the 1990s, the IMF found itself at the epicenter of a series of very visible economic crises: in Mexico in 1995, in Southeast Asia in 1997, in Russia in 1998, and in Brazil in 1999. In 2001, Turkey and Argentina ran into trouble and appealed to the IMF for help. Although each case was different, they shared some common elements.

Most of these crises were precipitated by the collapse of a fixed exchange rate pegged to the U.S. dollar. In each case, the currency plummeted, with ruinous consequences. Questions were raised about the country's ability to pay its bills. In each case, the IMF arrived on the scene with both money and lots of advice, determined to stave off default. In the end, each country suffered through a severe recession—or worse.

The IMF's increased visibility naturally brought it increased criticism. Some critics complained that the Fund set excessively strict conditions on its client states, requiring them, for example, to cut their government budgets and raise interest rates during recessions—which made bad economic situations even worse.

Other critics worried that the Fund was serving as a bill collector for banks and other financial institutions from the United States and other rich countries. Because the banks loaned money irresponsibly, these critics argued, they deserved to lose some of it. By bailing them out of their losses, the IMF simply encouraged more reckless behavior in the future.

Suggestions for reform are everywhere (see the box "Does the International Monetary System Need Reform?"), and some minor changes have been made in the IMF's procedures. But the debate rages on.

The Volatile Dollar

As mentioned earlier, floating exchange rates have not proved to be stable exchange rates. No currency illustrates this point better than the U.S. dollar. (See Figure 7.) As Table 1 showed, in July 1980 a U.S. dollar bought less than 2 German marks, about 4 French francs, and about 830 Italian lire. Then it started rising like a rocket (see Figure 7). By the time it peaked in February 1985, the mighty dollar could buy more than 3 German

FIGURE 7

The Ups and Downs of the Dollar

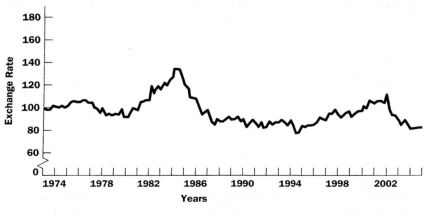

NOTE: Exchange rate relative to major currencies, March 1973 = 100.

POLICY DEBATE

Does the International Monetary System Need Reform?

Robert Rubin, America's former Treasury secretary, wants to "modernize the architecture of the international financial markets." Eisuke Sakakibara, Japan's top international finance official, is thinking of a "Bretton Woods II." Alan Greenspan, chairman of the Federal Reserve, wants to review the "patchwork of arrangements" governing international finance. After East Asia's crisis, activism is in the air. . . .

It is easy to see why. . . . Policymakers worry that today's financial architecture, designed at Bretton Woods in 1944 for a world of limited capital mobility, may not be capable of dealing with an ever more global capital market. For international finance has been revolutionised. Formerly closed economies have cast off controls and embraced foreign funds. Better technology and financial innovation have made it easy to move money instantaneously.

The benefits are obvious: the expansion of private flows to developing countries. . . . But vast inflows can quickly become huge outflows. And financial crises can spread overnight between apparently unconnected markets. The five worst-affected Asian economies (South Korea, Indonesia, Thailand, Malaysia, and the Philippines) received $93 billion of private capital flows in 1996. In 1997 they saw an outflow of $12 billion.

[One] reform to reinforce capital markets is better regulation. . . . Countless banking crises—in rich and poor countries alike—have shown that the combination of free capital flows and badly regulated banks is disastrous. . . . Others go much further, arguing that a global capital market needs global financial regulation, not a hotch-potch of national supervisors of varying quality. . . .

For many conservatives, particularly in America's Congress, the answer is to curb, or even eliminate, the IMF. It is the prospect of bail-outs, they argue, that encourages governments to profligacy and investors to recklessness. . . .

SOURCE: © Cvinai Dithajohn/EPA/Landov

For those who see East Asia's crisis primarily as one of panic, . . . far more urgent is the need to control the capital flows themselves. . . . For those who are uneasy with the speed with which funds flow around the globe, the perennial idea of a tax on currency transactions has surfaced again. . . .

With such an array of possible reforms, it is hardly surprising that international officials are confused and uncertain [whereas] their political masters demand quick action.

SOURCE: "The Perils of Global Capital," from *The Economist*, April 11, 1998. Copyright © 1998 The Economist Newspaper Ltd. All rights reserved. Reprinted with permission. Further reproduction prohibited. http://www.economist.com

Authors' note: Politicians may have wanted "quick action" in 1998, but few of the items on this list have actually happened. The debate goes on.

---

marks, about 10 French francs, and more than 2,000 Italian lire. Such major currency changes affect world trade dramatically.

The rising dollar was a blessing to Americans who traveled abroad or who bought foreign goods—because foreign prices, when translated to dollars by the exchange rate, looked cheap to Americans.[7] But the arithmetic worked just the other way around for U.S. firms seeking to sell their goods abroad; foreign buyers found everything American very expensive.[8] It was no surprise, therefore, that as the dollar climbed our exports fell, our imports rose, and many of our leading manufacturing industries were decimated by foreign competition. An expensive currency, Americans came to learn, is a mixed blessing.

From early 1985 until early 1988, the value of the dollar fell even faster than it had risen. The cheaper dollar curbed American appetites for imports and alleviated the plight of our export industries, many of which boomed. However, rising prices for imported goods and foreign vacations were a source of consternation to many American consumers.

Over the following seven years, the overall value of the dollar did not change very much—although there was a small downward drift. Then, in the spring of 1995, the dollar began another sizable ascent which lasted until early 2002. Since then, the dollar has mostly been falling, as we noted at the start of this chapter, and it is now close

---

[7] *Exercise:* How much does a 100-euro hotel room in Paris cost in dollars when the euro is worth $1.25? $1? 80 cents?
[8] *Exercise*: How much does a $55 American camera cost a German consumer when the euro is worth $1.20? $1? 80 cents?

to its 1995 low. All in all, the behavior of the dollar has been anything but boring. Fortunes have been made and lost speculating on what it will do next.

The Birth of the Euro

As noted earlier, floating exchange rates are no panacea. One particular problem confronted the members of the European Union (EU). As part of their long-range goal to create a unified market like that of the United States, they perceived a need to establish a single currency for all member countries—a monetary union.

The process of convergence to a single currency took place in steps, more or less as prescribed by the Treaty of Maastricht (1992), over a period of years. Member nations encountered a number of obstacles along the way. But to the surprise of many skeptics, all such obstacles were overcome, and the euro became a reality on schedule. Electronic and checking transactions in 11 of the 15 EU nations were denominated in euros rather than in national currencies in 1999, the number of participating countries rose to 12 when Greece joined the monetary union,[9] and euro coins and paper money were introduced successfully in 2002. Each of these transformations went remarkably smoothly.

The establishment of the euro was a great economic experiment that marked a giant step beyond merely fixing exchange rates. A government can end a fixed exchange rate regime at any time. And, as we have seen, speculators sometimes break fixed exchange rates even when governments want to maintain them. But the single European currency was created by an international treaty and is more or less invulnerable to speculative attack because it *abolished* exchange rates among the participating nations. Just as there has long been no exchange rate between New York and New Jersey, now there is no exchange rate between Germany and France. Monetary unions may create other problems, but exchange rate instability should not be one of them.

PUZZLE RESOLVED: *Why the Dollar Rose and then Fell*

What we have learned in this chapter helps us understand what has brought the dollar down since 2002. The story actually begins well before that.

During the Great Boom of the late 1990s, the United States was *the* place to invest. Funds poured in from all over the world to purchase American stocks, American bonds, and even American companies—especially in the information technology field. Yahoo! was indeed a fitting name for the age. As we have learned in this chapter, the rising demand for U.S. assets should have bid up the price of U.S. currency—and it did (see Figure 7 again).

"His mood is pegged to the dollar"

But the soaring dollar sowed the seeds of its own destruction. Two of its major effects were (a) to make U.S. goods and services look much more expensive to potential buyers abroad and (b) to make foreign goods look much cheaper to Americans. So our imports grew much faster than our exports. In brief, we developed a huge *current account deficit* (which is roughly exports *minus* imports) to match our large *capital account surplus*.

The Internet bubble, of course, started to burst in 2000, pulling the stock market down with it. Then the September 11, 2001, terrorist attacks raised doubts about the strength of the U.S. economy. For these and other reasons, foreign investors apparently began to question the wisdom of holding so many American assets. With the U.S. current account still deeply in the red, and the foreign demand for U.S. capital sagging, there was only way for the (freely floating) dollar to go: down. And so it has. Most economists think the dollar will continue to decline until our current account deficit shrinks substantially.

---

[9] As of this writing, three EU members (Sweden, Denmark, and the United Kingdom) have chosen not to join the monetary union.

SUMMARY

1. **Exchange rates** state the value of one currency in terms of other currencies, and thus translate one country's prices into the currencies of other nations. Exchange rates therefore influence patterns of world trade.

2. If governments do not interfere by buying or selling their currencies, exchange rates will be determined in free markets by the usual laws of supply and demand. Such a system is said to be based on **floating exchange rates.**

3. Demand for a nation's currency is derived from foreigners' desires to purchase that country's goods and services or to invest in its assets. Under floating rates, anything that increases the demand for a nation's currency will cause its exchange rate to **appreciate.**

4. Supply of a nation's currency is derived from the desire of that country's citizens to purchase foreign goods and services or to invest in foreign assets. Under floating rates, anything that increases the supply of a nation's currency will cause its exchange rate to **depreciate.**

5. Purchasing-power parity plays a major role in very-long-run exchange rate movements. The **purchasing-power parity theory** states that relative price levels in any two countries determine the exchange rate between their currencies. Therefore, countries with relatively low inflation rates normally will have appreciating currencies.

6. Over shorter periods, however, purchasing-power parity has little influence over exchange rate movements. The pace of economic activity and, especially, the level of interest rates exert greater influences.

7. Capital movements are typically the dominant factor in exchange rate determination in the short and medium runs. A nation that offers international investors higher interest rates, or better prospective returns on investments, will typically see its currency appreciate.

8. An exchange rate can be fixed at a nonequilibrium level if the government is willing and able to mop up any excess of quantity supplied over quantity demanded, or provide any excess of quantity demanded over quantity supplied. In the

first case, the country is suffering from a **balance of payments deficit** because of its overvalued currency. In th second case, an undervalued currency has given it a **balance of payments surplus.**

9. The **gold standard** was a system of **fixed exchang rates** in which the value of every nation's currency w fixed in terms of gold. This system created problems b cause nations could not control their own money sup plies and because the world could not control its tot supply of gold.

10. After World War II, the gold standard was replaced by th **Bretton Woods system,** in which exchange rates we fixed in terms of U.S. dollars, and the dollar was in tur tied to gold. This system broke up in 1971, when the do lar became chronically overvalued.

11. Since 1971, the world has moved toward a system of rel: tively free exchange rates, but with plenty of exception We now have a thoroughly mixed system of "dirty" ("managed" floating, which continues to evolve and adapt.

12. Floating rates are not without their problems. For exan ple, importers and exporters justifiably worry about fluctuations in exchange rates.

13. Under floating exchange rates, investors who speculate o international currency values provide a valuable service b assuming the risks of those who do not wish to speculat Normally, speculators stabilize rather than destabilize e: change rates, because that is how they make profits.

14. The U.S. dollar rose dramatically in value from 1980 t 1985, making our imports cheaper and our exports mo expensive. From 1985 to 1988, the dollar tumbled, whic had precisely the reverse effects. Then the dollar climbe again between 1995 and 2002, leading once again to a larg trade imbalance. Since 2002, the dollar has mostly bee falling.

15. The European Union has established a single currency, th euro, for most of its member nations.

KEY TERMS

Exchange rate 348

Appreciation 348

Depreciation 348

Devaluation 349

Revaluation 349

Floating exchange rates 349

Purchasing-power parity theory 353

Fixed exchange rates 355

Balance of payments deficit and surplus 355

Current account 356

Capital account 356

Gold standard 356

Bretton Woods system 357

International Monetary Fund (IMF) 360

"Dirty" or "managed" float 360

TEST YOURSELF

1. Use supply and demand diagrams to analyze the effect of the following actions on the exchange rate between the dollar and the yen:

   a. Japan opens its domestic markets to more foreign competition.

   b. Investors come to believe that values on the Tokyo stock market will fall.

   c. The Federal Reserve cuts interest rates in the United States.

   d. The U.S. government, to help settle the problems of the Middle East, gives huge amounts of foreign aid to Israel and her Arab neighbors.

   e. The United States has a recession while Japan booms.

   f. Inflation in the United States exceeds that in Japan.

2. For each of the following transactions, indicate how it would affect the U.S. balance of payments if exchange rates were fixed:

   a. You spent the summer traveling in Europe.

   b. Your uncle in Canada sent you $20 as a birthday present.

   c. You bought a new Honda, made in Japan.

   d. You bought a new Honda, made in Ohio.

   e. You sold some stock you own on the Tokyo Stock Exchange.

3. Suppose each of the transactions listed in Test Yourself Question 2 was done by many Americans. Indicate how each would affect the international value of the dollar if exchange rates were floating.

4. We learned in this chapter that successful speculators buy a currency when demand is weak and sell it when demand is strong. Use supply and demand diagrams for two different periods (one with weak demand, the other with strong demand) to show why this activity will limit price fluctuations.

DISCUSSION QUESTIONS

1. What items do you own or routinely consume that are produced abroad? From what countries do these items come? Suppose Americans decided to buy fewer of these things. How would that affect the exchange rates between the dollar and these currencies?

2. If the dollar appreciates relative to the euro, will the German camera you have wanted become more or less expensive? What effect do you imagine this change will have on American demand for German cameras? Does the American demand curve for euros, therefore, slope upward or downward? Explain.

3. During the first half of the 1980s, inflation in (West) Germany was consistently lower than that in the United States. What, then, does the purchasing-power parity theory predict should have happened to the exchange rate between the mark and the dollar between 1980 and 1985? (Look at Table 1 to see what actually happened.)

4. How are the problems of a country faced with a balance of payments deficit similar to those posed by a government regulation that holds the price of milk above the equilibrium level? (*Hint:* Think of each in terms of a supply-demand diagram.)

5. Under the old gold standard, what do you think happened to world prices when a huge gold strike occurred in California in 1849? What do you think happened when the world went without any important new gold strikes for 20 years or so?

6. Explain why the members of the Bretton Woods conference in 1944 wanted to establish a system of fixed exchange rates. What flaw led to the ultimate breakdown of the system in 1971?

7. Suppose you want to reserve a hotel room in London for the coming summer but are worried that the value of the pound may rise between now and then, making the room too expensive for your budget. Explain how a speculator could relieve you of this worry. (Don't actually try it. Speculators deal only in very large sums!)

8. In 2003 and 2004, market forces raised the international value of the Japanese yen. Why do you think the government of Japan was unhappy about this currency appreciation? (*Hint:* Japan was trying to emerge from a recession at the time.) If they wanted to stop the yen's appreciation, what actions could the Bank of Japan (Japan's central bank) and the Federal Reserve have taken? Why might the central banks have failed in this attempt?